New in This Edition!!

"Windows 95 Common Controls"

- Progress Bar
- Trackbar
- Up-down (Spin)
- Image lists
- List View
- Tree View
- Rich Edit

"Property Pages and Sheets and Wizards"

- Adding a property page to an application
- Building your own Wizard to guide a user through a process

"Sockets, MAPI, and the Internet"

- Winsock support
- MAPI and the Windows 95 logo program
- ISAPI extensions and filters

"Help"

- Adding topics to the Help menu
- Handling context-sensitive help
- Adding topics to the table of contents

"Building an ActiveX control"

- ActiveX controls and what they do
- Step-by-step instructions to build a rolling die

"Building an Internet Application with the WinInet Classes"

- Using the FTP, Gopher, HTTP, Finger, and Whois protocols
- Query application reveals a site's full Internet presence

"ActiveX Controls for the Internet"

- Embedding an ActiveX control into a Web page for Internet Explorer
- Embedding an ActiveX control into a Web page for Netscape Navigator
- Design considerations for Internet controls
- Optimizations in OLE Control Wizard
- Asynchronous and URL monikers
- Adding a cached property to a control

"Multitasking with Windows Threads"

- Semaphores
- Critical sections
- Threading models

Special Edition Using Visual C++ has been the industry leader in providing comprehensive coverage of the Visual C++ and MFC features for software developers. In this edition, we have added the latest information on advancements in Windows software development—including Windows 95, Windows NT and the Internet—to the already extensive Visual C++ and MFC coverage. The preceding directory guides you to these latest additions.

Hope you enjoy the book.

Kate Gregory

Special Edition

USING
VISUAL C++™
4.2

Special Edition

Using
Visual C++™
4.2

Written by Kate Gregory, Clayton Walnum, and Paul Kimmel

Special Edition Using Visual C++ 4.2

Library of Congress Catalog No.: 96-69950

ISBN: 0-7897-0893-0

98 97   6 5 4 3

Interpretation of the printing code: the rightmost double-digit number is the year of the book's printing; the rightmost single-digit number, the number of the book's printing. For example, a printing code of 96-1 shows that the first printing of the book occurred in 1996.

Screen reproductions in this book were created using Collage Plus from Inner Media, Inc., Hollis, NH.

Credits

PRESIDENT
Roland Elgey

PUBLISHER
Joseph B. Wikert

PUBLISHING MANAGER
Fred Slone

DIRECTOR OF MARKETING
Lynn E. Zingraf

EDITORIAL SERVICES DIRECTOR
Elizabeth Keaffaber

MANAGING EDITOR
Sandy Doell

TITLE MANAGER
Bryan Gambrel

PROJECT DIRECTOR
Angela Kozlowski

PRODUCTION EDITOR
Matthew B. Cox

EDITORS
Kelli Brooks
Sean Dixon
Bill McManus
Jeani Smith

PRODUCT MARKETING MANAGER
Kim Margolius

ASSISTANT PRODUCT MARKETING MANAGER
Christy M. Miller

TECHNICAL EDITORS
David Medinets
Bob Reselman
Daniel Berkowitz
Marc Gusmano

TECHNICAL SPECIALIST
Nadeem Muhammed

ACQUISITIONS COORDINATOR
Carmen Krikorian

OPERATIONS COORDINATOR
Patricia J. Brooks

EDITORIAL ASSISTANT
Andrea Duvall

BOOK DESIGNER
Ruth Harvey

COVER DESIGNER
Dan Armstrong

PRODUCTION TEAM
Stephen Adams
Debra Bolhuis
Marcia Brizendine
Kevin Cliburn
Jason Hand
Daniel Harris
Bob LaRoche
Angela Perry
Casey Price
Kaylene Riemen
Laura Robbins
Bobbi Satterfield
Staci Somers
Donna Wright

INDEXER
Chris Wilcox

Composed in *Century Old Style* and *ITC Franklin Gothic* by Que Corporation.

"To my family: Brian, Beth, and Kevin, you are all I truly need" -KMG

About the Authors

Kate Gregory is a founding partner of Gregory Consulting Limited (**www.gregcons.com**) and longtime C++ programmer. Her experience with C++ stretches back to before Visual C++ existed, at which point she enthusiastically converted. Gregory Consulting develops software and Internet sites, and specializes in combining software development with Web site development to create active sites. Kate teaches on a variety of related topics including C++, Object-Oriented techniques, using the Internet, HTML, and Java. Her books for Que include "*Using UseNet Newsgroups*" and "*Building Internet Applications with Visual C++*," and she has contributed to the "*VBPJ Guide to Visual Basic*," "*Designing Windows 95 Help Systems*," and a previous "*Special Edition Using Visual C++*" before undertaking this edition. She welcomes mail at **kate@gregcons.com** and provides updates for this book at the **gregcons** Web site.

Paul Kimmel is the author of *Building Delphi 2 Database Applications* and *Using Borland C++ 5* also from Que. He is the president of the Okemos, Michigan-based Software Conceptions, Inc. which offers software developer training and custom application development around the world. In the mid-Michigan area, we offer training at our partners-in-training location, Automation Resource Corporation founded by Janice Szur. Software Conceptions can be reached at **softcon@sojourn.com** or CompuServe at **70353,2711**. Paul is the father of three boys: Trevor, Douglas, Noah, and a girl, Alex, and loving husband to Lori.

Clayton Walnum, who has a degree in Computer Science, has been writing about computers for almost 15 years and has published hundreds of articles in major computer publications. He is also the author of over 25 books, which cover such diverse topics as programming, computer gaming, and application programs. His most recent book is *Windows 95 Game SDK Strategy Guide*, also published by Que. His other titles include the award-winning *Building Windows 95 Applications with Visual Basic* (Que); *3-D Graphics Programming with OpenGL* (Que); *Borland C++ 4.x Tips, Tricks, and Traps* (Que); *Turbo C++ for Rookies* (Que); *Dungeons of Discovery* (Que); *PC Picasso: A Child's Computer Drawing Kit* (Sams); *Powermonger: The Official Strategy Guide* (Prima); *DataMania: A Child's Computer Organizer* (Alpha Kids); *Adventures in Artificial Life* (Que); and *C-manship Complete* (Taylor Ridge Books). Mr. Walnum lives in Connecticut with his wife Lynn and their four children: Christopher, Justin, Stephen, and Caitlynn.

Acknowledgments

Kate Gregory: To my husband, Brian, and my wonderful children, Beth and Kevin, my heart-felt thanks once again for all the understanding and support. My neglected family and friends have also earned my gratitude, by not complaining too loudly about my absences from their lives. Writing a book takes a team effort and this one is no exception. My coauthors, technical editors, and illustrators all deserve to share the credit for the good things you see here. The mistakes and omissions I have to claim as mine alone. To Fred Slone, Angela Kozlowski, Matthew Cox, and the other terrific Que people who made this happen, thank you for doing such a great job. Special thanks go out to those readers of my earlier books who took the time to send me email with questions, corrections, and suggestions: you have helped this book to exist, because without readers, writers cannot write. Keep up the good work!

We'd Like to Hear from You!

As part of our continuing effort to produce books of the highest possible quality, Que would like to hear your comments. To stay competitive, we *really* want you, as a computer book reader and user, to let us know what you like or dislike most about this book or other Que products.

You can mail comments, ideas, or suggestions for improving future editions to the address below, or send us a fax at (317) 581-4663. Our staff and authors are available for questions and comments through our Internet site, at **http://www.mcp.com/que**, and Macmillan Computer Publishing also has a forum on CompuServe (type **GO QUEBOOKS** at any prompt).

In addition to exploring our forum, please feel free to contact me personally to discuss your opinions of this book: I'm **akozlowski@que.mcp.com** on the Internet.

Thanks in advance—your comments will help us to continue publishing the best books available on new computer technologies in today's market.

Angela Kozlowski
Product Director
Que Corporation
201 W. 103rd Street
Indianapolis, Indiana 46290
USA

Contents at a Glance

Introduction   1

I Using Developer Studio

1   Working with Developer Studio   7
2   Developer Studio Commands   29
3   AppWizard and ClassWizard   75

II The MFC Library

4   Overview: What's in an Application?   99
5   Messages and Commands   113
6   The Document/View Paradigm   129
7   Dialog and Controls   149
8   Win95 Common Controls   173
9   Property Pages and Sheets and Wizards   209
10   Utility and Collection Classes   229
11   Drawing on the Screen   255
12   Persistence and File I/O   277
13   Sockets, MAPI, and the Internet   295
14   Database Access   311
15   MFC Macros and Globals   341

III Building a Simple MFC Application

16   Choosing an Application Type and Building an Empty Shell   355
17   Building Menus and Dialogs   371
18   Interface Issues   395
19   Printing and Print Preview   415
20   Debugging   433
21   Help   469

IV ActiveX Applications and ActiveX Custom Controls

22   ActiveX Concepts   495
23   Building an ActiveX Container Application   507
24   Building an ActiveX Server Application   545
25   ActiveX Automation   575
26   Building an ActiveX Control   595

V Advanced Topics

27 Internet Programming with the WinInet Classes 627

28 Building an Internet ActiveX Control 649

29 Power-User Features in Developer Studio 671

30 Power-User C++ Features 685

31 Multitasking with Windows Threads 715

32 Additional Advanced Topics 739

Index 757

Contents

Introduction   1

    Who Should Read This Book?   2

    Before You Start Reading   2

    Conventions Used in This Book   2

    Time to Get Started   4

I | Using Developer Studio

1 Working with Developer Studio   7

    Developer Studio: An Integrated Development Environment   8

    Choosing a View   8

    Looking at Documentation   10

    Looking at Interface Elements   13

        Accelerators   13

        Dialog Boxes   13

        Icons   14

        Menus   15

        The String Table   17

        Toolbars   17

        Version Information   18

    Looking at Your Code, Arranged by Class   19

    Looking at Your Code, Arranged by File   22

    Output and Error Messages   23

    Editing Your Code   23

        Basic Typing and Editing   24

        Working with Blocks of Text   24

        Syntax Coloring   25

        Shortcut Menu   25

        Source File Toolbar   26

    From Here...   27

2 Developer Studio Commands 29

Learning the Menu System: Slow and Steady   30
Using File Menu   30
Edit   39
Using the View Menu   48
Insert   52
Build   54
Tools   60
Window   63
Help   67

Toolbars: One Click   70

From Here...   74

3 AppWizard and ClassWizard 75

Creating a Windows Application   76
Deciding How Many Documents the Application Supports   76
Databases   78
OLE Support   79
Appearance and Other Options   80
Other Options   83
File and Class Names   84
Creating the Application   84

Creating DLLs, Console Applications, and More   85
MFC AppWizard (DLL)   86
OLE Control Wizard   87
Application   89
Dynamic Link Library   89
Console Application   89
Static Library   89
Makefile   89
Custom AppWizard   89
ISAPI Extension Wizard   90

Changing Your AppWizard Decisions   90

Making Menus Work with ClassWizard   90

Making Dialog Boxes Work with ClassWizard   92

Dealing with Messages from the Wizard Bar   93

From Here...   94

II | The MFC Library

4 Overview: What's in an Application?   99

Programming for Windows   100

A C-Style Windows Class   100

Window Creation   101

Programming in C++   104

Encapsulating the Windows API   105

Inside *CWnd*   105

What Are All These Classes, Anyway?   107

CObject   107

CCmdTarget   108

CWnd   108

All Those Other Classes   109

From Here...   111

5 Messages and Commands   113

Message Routing   114

Message Loops   114

Message Maps   116

Using ClassWizard to Catch Messages   120

List of Messages   121

Commands   123

Command Updates   124

Using ClassWizard to Catch Commands and Command Updates   126

From Here...   127

6 The Document/View Paradigm   129

Understanding the Document Class   130

Understanding the View Class   131

Creating the Rectangles Application   133

Running the Rectangles Application   139

Exploring the Rectangles Application   139

Declaring Storage for Document Data   140

Initializing Document Data   140

Serializing Document Data   141

Displaying Document Data   142

Modifying Document Data   143

Other View Classes   144

Document Templates, Views, and Frame Windows   147

From Here...   148

7 **Dialog and Controls   149**

Understanding Dialog Boxes   150

Creating a Dialog-Box Resource   151

Defining Dialog-Box and Control IDs   152

A Dialog Box's Resources   152

Introducing the Dialog Application   153

Exploring the Dialog Application   154

Displaying a Simple Dialog Box   154

Writing a Dialog-Box Class   155

Using the Dialog-Box Class   159

Programming Controls   162

Introducing the Control1 Application   163

Exploring the Control1 Application   164

Declaring a Friend Function   164

Associating MFC Classes with Controls   165

Initializing the Dialog Box's Controls   166

Responding to the OK Button   168

Handling the Dialog Box in the Window Class   170

From Here...   171

8 **Win95 Common Controls   173**

The Win95 Controls Application   174

The Progress Bar Control   174

Creating the Progress Bar   174

Initializing the Progress Bar   176

Manipulating the Progress Bar   176

The Trackbar Control   177

Creating the Trackbar   177

Initializing the Trackbar   178

Manipulating the Trackbar   180

The Up-Down Control   180

Creating the Up-Down Control   181

The Image List Control   182

Creating the Image List   183

Initializing the Image List   184

The List View Control   185

Creating the List View   187

Initializing the List View   189

Associating the List View with Its Image Lists   189

Creating the List View's Columns   189

Creating the List View's Items   191

Manipulating the List View   193

The Tree View Control   195

Creating the Tree View   196

Initializing the Tree View   197

Creating the Tree View's Items   197

Manipulating the Tree View   200

The Rich Edit Control   201

Creating the Rich Edit Control   202

Initializing the Rich Edit Control   203

Manipulating the Rich Edit Control   205

From Here...   208

9 Property Pages and Sheets and Wizards   209

Introducing Property Sheets   210

Creating the Property Sheet Demo Application   211

Running the Property Sheet Demo Application   220

Understanding the Property Sheet Demo Application   221

Changing Property Sheets to Wizards   222

Running the Wizard Demo Application   222

Creating Wizard Pages   224

Setting the Wizard's Buttons   224

Responding to the Wizard's Buttons   225

Displaying a Wizard   226

From Here...   227

10 Utility and Collection Classes 229

The Array Classes 230
Introducing the Array Demo Application 231
Declaring and Initializing the Array 233
Adding Elements to the Array 233
Reading Through the Array 234
Removing Elements from the Array 235

The List Classes 236
Introducing the List Demo Application 237
Declaring and Initializing the List 239
Adding a Node to the List 240
Deleting a Node from the List 241
Iterating Over the List 242
Cleaning Up the List 243

The Map Classes 244
Introducing the Map Demo Application 244
Creating and Initializing the Map 245
Retrieving a Value from the Map 246
Iterating Over the Map 247

The String Class 248

The Time Classes 249
Using a *CTime* Object 250
Using a *CTimeSpan* Object 252

Collection Class Templates 253

From Here... 254

11 Drawing on the Screen 255

Understanding Device Contexts 256

Introducing the Paint1 Application 257

Exploring the Paint1 Application 258
Painting in an MFC Program 259
Using Fonts 261
Using Pens 264
Using Brushes 265
Switching the Display 267
Sizing and Positioning the Window 268

Scrolling Windows 269

Running the Scroll Application 270

Initializing the Scroll Bars 271

Updating the Scroll Bars 272

From Here... 275

12 Persistence and File I/O 277

Objects and Persistence 278

The File Demo Application 278

A Review of Document Classes 279

A Quick Look at File Demo's Source Code 280

Creating a Persistent Class 282

The File Demo 2 Application 283

Looking at the *CMessages* Class 284

Using the *CMessages* Class in the Program 286

Reading and Writing Files Directly 288

The File Demo 3 Application 288

The *CFile* Class 289

Exploring the File Demo 3 Application 290

Creating Your Own *CArchive* Objects 293

From Here... 293

13 Sockets, MAPI, and the Internet 295

Using Windows Sockets 296

Winsock in MFC 297

Messaging API (MAPI) 300

What Is MAPI? 300

Win95 Logo Requirements 302

Advanced Use of MAPI 303

Using New Internet Classes in Visual C++ 4.2 305

Using Internet Server API (ISAPI) Classes 307

From Here... 310

14 Database Access 311

Understanding Database Concepts 312

Using the Flat Database Model 312

Using the Relational Database Model   312

Accessing a Database   314

The Visual C++ ODBC Classes   314

Creating an ODBC Database Program   315

Registering the Database   315

Creating the Basic Employee Application   317

Creating the Database Display   320

Adding and Deleting Records   324

Examining the *OnRecordAdd()* Function   328

Examining the *OnMove()* Function   329

Examining the *OnRecordDelete()* Function   330

Sorting and Filtering   331

Examining the *OnSortDept()* Function   335

Examining the *DoFilter()* Function   336

Using ODBC versus DAO   337

From Here...   339

15 **MFC Macros and Globals   341**

Ten Categories of Macros and Globals   342

Application Information and Management Functions   342

ClassWizard Comment Delimiters   343

Collection Class Helpers   344

CString Formatting and Message-Box Display   344

Data Types   345

Using Diagnostic Services   346

Exception Processing   347

Using Message-Map Macros   348

Run-Time Object Model Services   349

Standard Command and Window IDs   350

From Here...   350

III **Building a Simple MFC Application**

16 **Choosing an Application Type and Building an Empty Shell   355**

A Dialog-Based Application   356

A Single Document Interface Application   361
  Other Files   365

A Multiple Document Interface Application   365

AppWizard Decisions and This Book   367

From Here...   369

17 Building Menus and Dialogs   371

Building an Application That Displays a String   372
  Creating an Empty Shell with AppWizard   372
  Displaying a String   372

Building the ShowString Menus   375

Building the ShowString Dialogs   379
  ShowString's About Box   379
  ShowString's Options Dialog   381

Making the Menu Work   382
  The Dialog Class   382
  Catching the Message   384

Making the Dialog Work   386

Adding Appearance Options to the Options Dialog   387
  Changing the Options Dialog   388
  Adding Member Variables to the Dialog Class   389
  Adding Member Variables to the Document   390
  Changing *OnToolsOptions()*   391
  Changing *OnDraw()*   392

From Here...   394

18 Interface Issues   395

Working with Toolbars   396
  Deleting Toolbar Buttons   396
  Adding Buttons to a Toolbar   398
  The *CToolBar* Class's Member Functions   401

Working with Status Bars   402
  Creating a New Command ID   404
  Creating the Default String   405
  Adding the ID to the Indicators Array   406
  Creating the Pane's Command-Update Handler   407
  Setting the Status Bar's Appearance   408

The Registry   409

How the Registry Is Set Up   410

The Predefined Keys   410

Using the Registry in an MFC Application   411

The Status Bar Demo Application Revisited   412

From Here...   413

19   Printing and Print Preview   415

Understanding Basic Printing and Print Preview with MFC   416

Scaling   418

Printing Multiple Pages   420

Setting the Origin   426

MFC and Printing   428

From Here...   431

20   Debugging   433

Using the Developer Studio Basic Debugging Features   434

Debugging Menus, Hotkeys, and Toolbars   434

Stepping Through a Project in the Developer Studio   439

Development vs. Delivery Constraints   444

Employing *ASSERT* and *TRACE*   445

Understanding *ASSERT* and *TRACE*   446

Using *ASSERT* Constructively   448

Applying Code Tracing Techniques   450

Exploring MFC Debugging Features and Classes   451

Using MFC Tracer   452

Defining a *Dump* Member Function   452

MFC Run-Time Type Identification   456

Advanced Data Watching Tips   458

What Are AutoExpand and AutoDowncast?   458

Using Data Tips, Watch Windows, and QuickWatch   459

Techniques for Sealing Memory Leaks   461

Using the MFC *CMemoryState* Class   462

Using *DEBUG_NEW*   464

Blocking Memory Leaks During an Exception   465

From Here...   467

21 Help 469

Different Kinds of Help   470

Getting Help   470

Presenting Help   471

Using Help   471

Programming Help   472

Components of the Help System   473

Help Support from AppWizard   474

Planning Your Help Approach   475

Programming for Command Help   477

Programming for Context Help   478

Writing Help Text   481

Changing Placeholder Strings   482

Adding Topics   485

Changing the "How to Modify Text" Topic   488

Adjustments to the Contents   488

From Here…   491

IV | ActiveX Applications and ActiveX Custom Controls

22 ActiveX Concepts   495

The Purpose of ActiveX   496

Object Linking   498

Object Embedding   499

Containers and Servers   501

Toward a More Intuitive User Interface   502

The Component Object Model   503

ActiveX Automation   504

ActiveX Controls   505

From Here…   506

23 Building an ActiveX Container Application   507

Changing ShowString   508

AppWizard Generated ActiveX Container Code   508

Returning the ShowString Functionality   523

Moving, Resizing, and Tracking   524

Handling Multiple Objects and Object Selection   528
   Hit Testing   528
   Drawing Multiple Items   529
   Handling Single Clicks   530
   Handling Double-Clicks   532

Implementing Drag and Drop   533
   Implementing a Drag Source   533
   Implementing a Drop Target   534
   Registering the View as a Drop Target   534
   Setting Up Function Skeletons and Adding Member
   Variables   535
   OnDragEnter   536
   OnDragOver   538
   OnDragLeave   540
   OnDragDrop   541
   Testing the Drag Target   542

Deleting an Object   542

From Here...   543

24   Building an ActiveX Server Application   545

Adding Server Capabilities to ShowString   546
   AppWizard's Server Boilerplate   546
   Showing a String Again   560

Applications That Are Both Container and Server   566
   Building Another Version of ShowString   566
   Nesting and Recursion Issues   566

ActiveX Documents   568
   What ActiveX Documents Do   568
   Making ShowString an ActiveX Document Server   570

From Here...   573

25   ActiveX Automation   575

Designing ShowString Again   576
   AppWizard's Automation Boilerplate   576
   Properties to Expose   579
   The *OnDraw()* Function   584
   Showing the Window   586

DispTest 588

Type Libraries and ActiveX Internals 591

From Here… 593

26 Building an ActiveX Control 595

A Rolling-Die Control 596
Building the Control Shell 596
AppWizard's Code 598
Designing the Control 601

Displaying the Current Value 601
Adding a property 601
Writing the Drawing Code 603

Reacting to a Mouse Click and Rolling the Die 605
Notifying the Container 606
Rolling the Die 607

A Better User Interface 608
A Bitmap Icon 609
Displaying Dots 609

Property Sheets 613
Digits Versus Dots 613
User-Selected Colors 617

Future Improvements 623
Enable and Disable Rolling 623
Dice with Unusual Numbers of Sides 623
Arrays of Dice 624

From Here… 624

V | Advanced Topics

27 Internet Programming with the WinInet Classes 627

Designing the Internet Query Application 628

Building the Query Dialog Box 629

Querying HTTP Sites 632

Querying FTP Sites 637

Querying Gopher Sites 639

Using Gopher to Send a Finger Query 641

Using Gopher to Send a Whois Query   644

Future Work   646

From Here...   647

28   Building an Internet ActiveX Control   649

Embedding an ActiveX Control into a Microsoft Explorer Web Page   650

Embedding an ActiveX Control into a Netscape Navigator Web Page   653

Choosing between ActiveX and Java   654

Using AppWizard to Create Faster ActiveX Controls   655

Speeding Control Loads with Asynchronous Properties   659
    Properties   660
    Using BLOBs   661
    Changing Dieroll   662
    Testing and Debugging Dieroll   668

The Base Control Framework and the ActiveX Template Library (ATL)   669

From Here...   670

29   Power-User Features in Developer Studio   671

Using Component Gallery   672

Introducing Custom AppWizards   675

Integrating External Tools   678

Using Editor Emulation   680

Using Optimization   682

From Here...   683

30   Power-User C++ Features   685

Understanding Exceptions   686
    Simple Exception Handling   686
    Exception Objects   687
    Placing the *catch* Block   688
    Handling Multiple Types of Exceptions   690

Exploring Templates   692
   Introducing Templates   692
   Creating Function Templates   692
   Creating Class Templates   695

Using Run-Time Type Information   699
   Introducing RTTI   699
   Performing Safe Downcasts   700
   Getting Object Information   701
   Preparing to Use RTTI   702
   A Common Use for RTTI   704

Namespaces   709
   Defining a Namespace   710
   Namespace Scope Resolution   711
   Unnamed Namespaces   712
   Namespace Aliases   712

From Here...   713

31   Multitasking with Windows Threads   715
Understanding Simple Threads   716

Understanding Thread Communication   719
   Communicating with Global Variables   720
   Communicating with User-Defined Messages   721
   Communicating with Event Objects   723

Using Thread Synchronization   726
   Using Critical Sections   726
   Using Mutexes   731
   Using Semaphores   733

From Here...   737

32   Additional Advanced Topics   739
Creating Console Applications   740
   Creating a Console Executable   740
   Scaffolding Discrete Algorithms   741

Creating and Using a 32-bit Dynamic Link Library   744
   Making a 32-bit DLL   747
   Using 32-bit DLLs   751

Sending Messages and Commands   752

Considering International Software Development Issues   754

From Here   756

Index   757

Introduction

Visual C++ is a powerful and complex tool for building 32-bit applications for Window 95 and Windows NT. These applications are far larger and more complex than their predecessors for 16-bit Windows, or older programs that did not use a graphical user interface. Yet as program size and complexity have grown, programmer effort has actually decreased, at least for programmers who are using the right tools.

Visual C++ is one of the right tools. With its code-generating Wizards it can produce the shell of a working Windows application in seconds. The class library included with Visual C++, the Microsoft Foundation Classes, has become the industry standard for Windows software development in a variety of C++ compilers. The visual editing tools make layout of menus and dialogs a snap. The time you invest in learning to use this product will pay itself back on your first Windows programming project. ■

Who Should Read This Book?

This book will teach you how to use Visual C++ to build 32-bit Windows applications, including database applications, Internet applications, and applications that tap the power of the ActiveX technology. That's a tall order, and to fit all that in less than a thousand pages, some things had to go. This book will **not** teach you:

- **The C++ programming language:** You should already be familiar with C++.
- **How to use Windows applications:** You should be a proficient Windows user, able to resize and move Windows, double-click, and recognize familiar toolbar buttons, for example.
- **How to use Visual C++ as a C compiler:** If you already work in C, you can use Visual C++ as your compiler, but new developers should take the plunge to C++.
- **Windows programming without MFC:** This too is OK for those who know it, but not something to learn now that MFC exists.
- **The internals of ActiveX programming:** This is covered in other books, referred to in the ActiveX chapters, but this book tells you only what you need to know to make it work.

Before You Start Reading

You will need a copy of Visual C++ 4.2, and need to have it installed. The installation process is simple and easy to follow, so it's not covered in this book.

Before you buy Visual C++ 4.2, you'll need a 32-bit Windows operating system: Either Windows 95 or Windows NT Server or Workstation. That means your machine will have to be reasonably powerful and modern: Let's say a 486 or better for your processor, at least 16 MB of RAM and 500 MB of disk space, and a screen that can do 800 × 600 pixel displays, or even finer resolutions. The illustrations in this book were all prepared at a resolution of 800 × 600, and as you'll see, there are times when things get a little crowded.

Finally, you need to make a resolution: That you will follow along as you go, clicking and typing and trying things out. You don't need to type all the code if you don't want to: It's all on the CD-ROM for you to look at. But you should be ready to open the files and look at the code as you go.

Conventions Used in This Book

One thing this book has plenty of is code. Sometimes, we just need to show you a line or two, so we mix it in with the text like this:

```
int SomeFunction( int x, int y);
{
        return x+y;
}
```

You can tell the difference between code and regular text by the fonts we use for each of them. Sometimes, we need to discuss a piece of code that is too large to mix in with the text: you'll find an example in Listing 1.

Listing I.1

```
CHostDialog dialog(m_pMainWnd);
    if (dialog.DoModal() == IDOK)
    {
      AppSocket = new CSocket();
      if (AppSocket->Connect(dialog.m_hostname,119))
      {
              while (AppSocket->GetStatus() == CONNECTING)
              {
                      YieldControl();
              }
              if (AppSocket->GetStatus() == CONNECTED)
              {
                      CString response = AppSocket->GetLine();
                      SocketAvailable = TRUE;
              }
      }
    }
      if (!SocketAvailable)
      {
              AfxMessageBox("Can't connect to server. Please
              ➥quit.",MB_OK¦MB_ICONSTOP);
      }
```

The character on the second last line (➥) is called the code continuation character. It shows a place where we had to break a line of code to fit it on the page, but the line is not broken there in reality. If you're typing code in from the book, don't break the line there, just keep going. If you're reading along in the code from the CD-ROM, don't get confused when the line doesn't break there.

Remember, the code is in the book so that you can understand what is going on, not for you to type in. All the code is on the CD-ROM as well. Sometimes, we'll work our way through the development of an application and show several versions of a block of code as we go—the final version is on the CD-ROM.

 TIP This is a Tip: A shortcut or interesting feature you might want to know about.

N O T E This is a Note: It covers a subtle but important point. Don't skip notes even if you're the kind who skips tips. ▪

CAUTION

This is a caution, and it's serious. It warns you of horrible consequences if you make a false step, so be sure to read all of these that you come across.

TROUBLESHOOTING

Everyone runs into problems now and then while programming. We've anticipated some of them—and we discuss how to get out of whatever trouble you're in.

When a word is in *italic*, like the word italic just was, it's usually being defined. (Sometimes we're just emphasizing it.) The names of variables, functions, C++ classes, and things you should type are all in `monospaced` font. Internet URLs are in **bold** type. Remember, a URL never ends with punctuation, so ignore any comma or period after the URL.

Time to Get Started

That just about wraps things up for the introduction. We've told you what you need to get started, and given you some advanced warning about the notations we use throughout the book—now it's your turn. Jump right in, learn all about writing Windows applications with MFC, and then get started on some development of your own! Good luck and have fun. ●

Using Developer Studio

1   Working with Developer Studio   7

2   Developer Studio Commands   29

3   AppWizard and ClassWizard   75

Working with Developer Studio

When you buy Microsoft Visual C++, you actually get Microsoft Developer Studio with the Visual C++ component activated. Developer Studio is far more than just a compiler, and you have far more to learn than you may think. The interface is very visual, which means that there are many possibilities greeting you when you first run Visual C++. ■

The components of Developer Studio

Developer Studio is more than just a compiler.

The project workspace window

This tabbed window lists the project contents in one of three ways, or the contents of Books Online.

The Info view

This changeable table of contents for Books Online makes navigation much faster.

The Resource view

Your menus, dialog boxes, bitmaps, and resources are together.

The Class view

Shows all the classes, and all the variables and functions they contain. See if a variable is public or private, or double-click a function to jump to its source code.

The File view

When you want to open a file rather than look at part of a class, this makes opening one simple.

The output window and status bar

At the bottom of the screen inform and provide you with results.

The code editor

Type in code, fix mistakes, and watch your application take shape.

Developer Studio: An Integrated Development Environment

Microsoft Visual C++ is one component of the Microsoft Developer Studio. The capabilities of this one piece of software are astonishing. It is called an integrated development environment because within a single tool, you can:

- Read documentation and Books Online
- Generate starter applications without writing code
- View a project several different ways
- Edit source and include files
- Build the visual interface (menus and dialog boxes) of your application
- Compile and link
- Debug an application while it runs

Visual C++ is, technically speaking, just one component of Developer Studio. You can buy, for example, Microsoft's FORTRAN compiler, and use it in Developer Studio as well. Looking at it another way, Visual C++ is more than just Developer Studio, since the Microsoft Foundation Classes (MFC) that are becoming the standard for C++ Windows programming are a class library and not related to the development environment. In fact, the major C++ compilers all use MFC now. However, for most people, Visual C++ and Developer Studio mean the same thing, and in this book the names are used interchangeably.

Choosing a View

With Visual C++, you work on a single application as a *project*. A project is a collection of files: source, headers, resources, settings, and configuration information. Developer Studio is designed to enable work on all aspects of a single project at once. You create a new application by creating a new project. When you want to work on your application, you open the project (a file with the extension .mdp) rather than open each code file independently. The interface of Developer Studio, shown in Figures 1.1 and 1.2, is designed to work with a project and is divided into several zones. The zones that make up the Developer Studio interface are:

- Across the top: menus and toolbars. These are discussed in Chapter 2, "Developer Studio Commands."
- On the left: the Project Workspace window.
- On the right: your main working area where you edit files or read documentation.
- Across the bottom: the output window and status bar.

 TIP   Open Developer Studio and try to resize the panes and follow along as functions are described in this chapter.

FIG. 1.1
The Developer Studio interface presents a lot of information. The Project Workspace window is on the left.

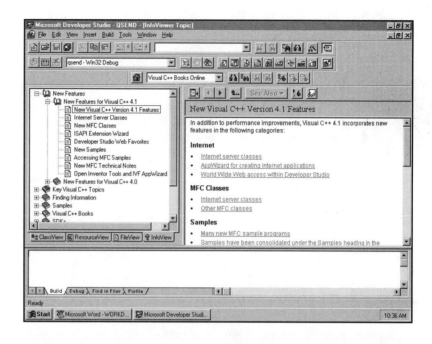

FIG. 1.2
When the Project Workspace window is narrowed, the words on the tabs are replaced with icons.

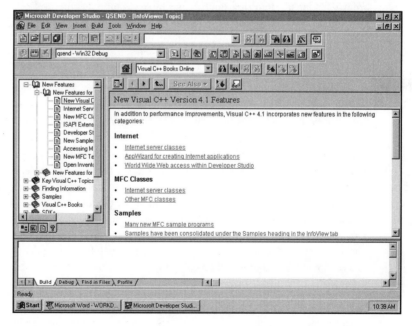

The Project Workspace window determines which way you look at your project, and what is in the main working area: documentation, code files, or resources (menus, icons, and dialog boxes). Each of these views is discussed in detail in a separate section in this chapter:

- The Info View is discussed in the "Looking at Documentation" section
- The Resource View is discussed in the "Looking at Interface Elements" section
- The Class View is discussed in the "Looking at Your Code, Arranged by Class" section
- The File View is discussed in the "Looking at Your Code, Arranged by File" section

Developer Studio actually uses two different files to keep track of all the information about your project. The *make file*, with a .mak extension, contains the names of all the files in the project, what directories they are in, compiler and linker options, and other information required by everyone who may work on the project. The project workspace file, with a .mdp extension, contains the name and location of the make file and all your personal settings for Developer Studio—colors, fonts, toolbars, which files are open and how their MDI windows are sized and located, breakpoints from your most recent debugging session, and so on. If someone else is going to work on your project, you give that person a copy of the make file but not the project workspace file. To open the project, open the project workspace file. The make file is opened automatically.

Looking at Documentation

When you first start Developer Studio and no project is open, the only tab in the Project Workspace window is the InfoView tab. When a project is open there are other tabs to choose from. Clicking the InfoView tab brings a table of contents into the Project Workspace window and an InfoViewer topic window into the main working area, as shown in Figures 1.1 and 1.2. The table of contents is an outline that can be expanded or collapsed. Double-clicking an entry in the table of contents displays that entry in the InfoViewer topic window.

TIP If your Project Workspace window is too narrow for reading the topic headings in the table of contents, you can scroll the window with the horizontal scroll bar. You can also pause the mouse cursor over any topic heading, and a small box like a Tool Tip appears showing the full heading for the topic.

Within the InfoViewer topic window, documentation is displayed as *hypertext*. Words and phrases that are highlighted act as *links*; clicking a link displays different information. There are two kinds of links: *popups* and *jumps*. Clicking a popup link, displayed in gray by default, pops up a small window, which typically contains a definition. Clicking a jump link, displayed in underlined green by default, closes the topic you are viewing and opens a related topic. To change the colors of the links, choose Tools, Options to bring up the Options dialog box. As shown in Figure 1.3, select the Format tab and choose InfoViewer Topic window from the list box on the left. Be cautious when changing these colors; they were chosen for a reason.

By default, the InfoViewer window is maximized to fill the entire working area, and the title bar of Developer Studio has InfoViewer Topic added to it. By clicking the Restore button under the main Restore button for all of Developer Studio, you can arrange the InfoViewer MDI window within the main working area. This allows you to compare two help topics or a help topic and a piece of code. Figure 1.4 shows the InfoViewer window restored; notice how the toolbar stays with the window. There is an InfoViewer toolbar as well—it is the lowest toolbar in these figures, and is discussed in Chapter 2, "Developer Studio Commands." If you want, the topic window can also be minimized.

FIG. 1.3

The Format tab of the Options dialog box (reached from the Tools menu) is used to set link colors.

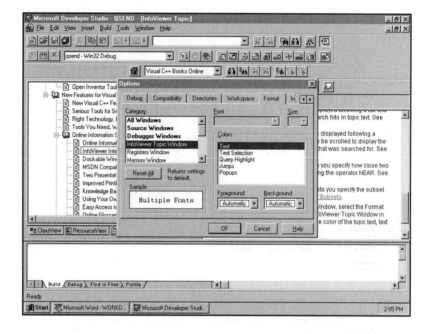

FIG. 1.4

The InfoViewer topic window does not have to be maximized.

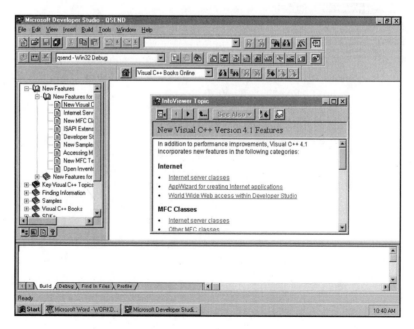

The toolbar across the top of the InfoViewer topic window has the following seven buttons:

- *Sync Contents*—When you follow jump links, the table of contents in the project workspace window does not change. This button redraws the table of contents to match the location of the topic you are now viewing.

  Keyboard shortcut: Ctrl+S

- *Previous in Contents*—This button jumps you to the previous section according to the table of contents. You may not have viewed that topic yet.

  Keyboard shortcut: Ctrl+Shift+P

- *Next in Contents*—This buttons jumps you to the next section according to the table of contents. You may not have viewed that topic yet.

  Keyboard shortcut: Ctrl+Shift+N

- *Go Back*—This button jumps you to the topic you were viewing when you clicked a link that led to this topic, or used the table of contents to navigate to a new topic.

  Keyboard shortcut: Ctrl+B

- *See Also*—This button, when available, brings up a list of related topics. Not all topics have related topics available.

  Keyboard shortcut: Ctrl+Shift+S

- *Add Bookmark*—This button adds a bookmark, saved with your Developer Studio settings, to this topic. After you have added a bookmark, the last three buttons on the InfoViewer toolbar are enabled to let you move around your list of bookmarks.

  Keyboard shortcut: Ctrl+Shift+B

- *Add/Edit Annotation*—An annotation is an added note by the user, typically you. The piece of paper on this button is yellow when there is an annotation for the topic, white when there is not. Click it to add a new annotation or change an old one. For a list of annotations, choose Edit, Go To and then highlight InfoViewer Annotations from the list box on the left. Drop down the box on the right and choose the annotation you want to see. To close the annotation pane, click the button again.

  Keyboard shortcut: Ctrl+Shift+A

If you are short on screen space you can get rid of this toolbar and use the keyboard shortcuts instead. Right-click in the topic window and uncheck Show Toolbar. If you forget the keyboard shortcuts, all these commands are available from the right-click menu, shown in Figure 1.5.

FIG. 1.5
The InfoViewer topic window has a number of shortcuts available on the right-click menu.

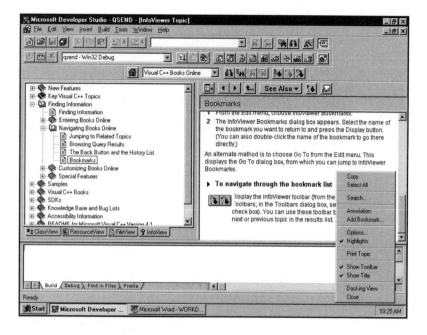

Looking at Interface Elements

Clicking the Resource View tab in the project workspace window brings up an expandable and collapsible outline of the visual elements of your program: accelerators, dialog boxes, icons, menus, the string table, toolbars, and version information. These resources define the way users interact with your program. Chapter 17, "Building Menus and Dialogs," covers the work involved in creating and editing these resources. The next few sections cover the way in which you can look at completed resources.

 Open one of the projects on the CD that comes with this book, or a sample project from Visual C++, and follow along as functions are described in this section.

Accelerators

Accelerators associate key combinations with menu items. Figure 1.6 shows an accelerator resource created by AppWizard. All these accelerator combinations are made for you when you create a new application. You can add hot keys for specific menu items if necessary.

Dialog Boxes

Dialog boxes are the way your application gets information from users. When a dialog resource is being displayed in the main working area, as in Figure 1.7, a control palette floats over the working area. Each small icon on the palette represents a control (edit box, list box, button, and so on) that can be inserted onto your dialog box. By choosing Edit, Properties, the

Properties box shown in Figure 1.7 is displayed. Here the behavior of a control or of the whole dialog box can be controlled.

FIG. 1.6

Accelerators associate key combinations with menu items.

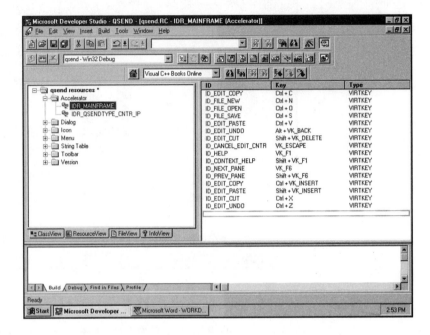

 T I P Click the pushpin at the top left of the Properties box to keep it displayed even when a different item is highlighted. The box displays the properties of each item you click.

This method of editing dialog boxes is one of the reasons for the name Visual C++. In this product, if you want a button to be a little lower on a dialog box, you click it with the mouse, drag it to the new position, and release the mouse button. Similarly, if you want the dialog box larger or smaller, grab a corner or edge and drag it to the new size just like any other sizable window. Before Visual C++ was released, the process would have involved coding and pixel counting, and taken many minutes rather than just a few seconds. This visual approach to dialog box building made Windows programming accessible to many more programmers.

Icons

Icons are small bitmaps that represent your program or its documents. For example, when a program is minimized an icon is used to represent it. A larger version of that icon is used to represent both the program and its documents within an Explorer window. And when an MDI window is minimized within your application, the minimized window is represented by an icon. Figure 1.8 shows the default icon provided by AppWizard for minimized MDI windows. One of your first tasks is to replace this with an icon that more clearly represents the work your program performs.

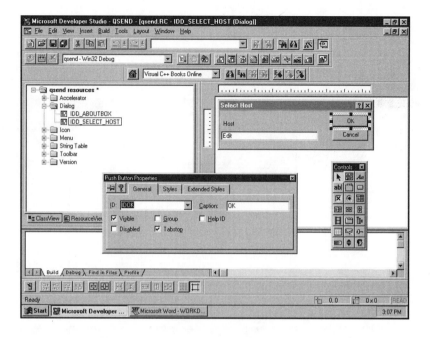

FIG. 1.7
Dialog boxes get
information from the
user.

An icon is a 32×32 pixel bitmap that can be edited with any number of drawing tools, including the simple bitmap editor included in Developer Studio. The interface is very similar to Microsoft Paint or Microsoft Paintbrush in Zoom mode. You can draw one pixel at a time by clicking, or freehand lines by clicking and dragging. You can work on the small or zoomed versions of the icon and see the effects at once in both places.

Menus

Menus are the way that users tell your program what to do. Keyboard shortcuts (accelerators) are linked to menu items, as are toolbar buttons. AppWizard creates the standard menus for a new application, and you edit those and create new ones in this view. Later, you'll use ClassWizard to connect menu items to functions within your code. Figure 1.9 shows a menu displayed in the resource view. Choose Edit, Properties to display the properties box for the menu item. Every menu item has the following three components:

■ *Resource ID*—This uniquely identifies this menu item. Accelerators and toolbar buttons are linked to resource IDs. The convention is to build the ID from the menu choices that lead to the item. In Figure 1.9, the resource ID is ID_FILE_OPEN.

■ *Caption*—This is the text that appears for a menu choice. In Figure 1.9, the caption is &Open...\tCtrl+O. The & means that the O will appear underlined, and the menu item can be selected by typing O when the menu is displayed. The \t is a tab, and the Ctrl+O is the accelerator for this menu item, as defined in Figure 1.6.

■ *Prompt*—A prompt appears in the status bar when the highlight is on the menu item or the cursor is over the associated toolbar button. In Figure 1.9, the prompt is Open an existing document\nOpen. Only the portion before the newline (\n) is displayed in the status bar. The second part of the prompt, Open, is the text for the tool tip that appears if the user pauses the mouse over a toolbar button with this resource ID. All of this functionality is provided for you automatically by the framework of Visual C++ and MFC.

FIG. 1.8

Icons represent your application and its documents.

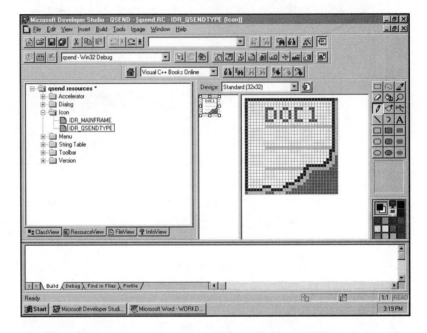

FIG. 1.9

Menus are the way your application receives commands.

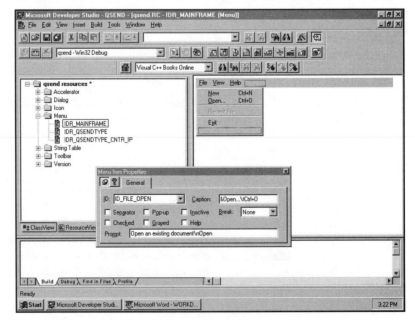

The String Table

The string table is a list of strings within your application. Many strings, such as the static text on dialog boxes or the prompts for menu items, can be accessed in far simpler ways than through the string table, but some are reached only through it. For example, a default name or value can be kept in the string table, and changed without recompiling any code, though the resources will have to be compiled and the project linked. Each of these could be hard coded into the program, but then changes would require a full recompile. Figure 1.10 shows the string table for a sample application. To change a string, bring up the Properties dialog box and change the caption. Strings cannot be changed within the main working area.

FIG. 1.10
The string table stores all the prompts and text in your application.

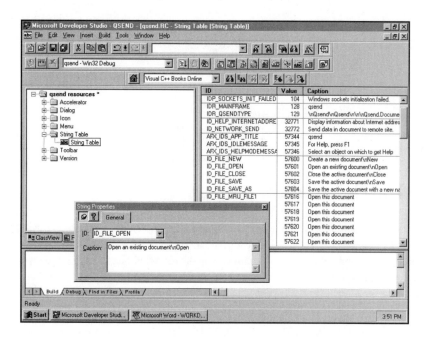

Toolbars

Toolbars are the lines of small buttons typically located directly underneath the menus of an application. Each button is linked to a menu item, and its appearance depends on the state of the menu item. If a menu item is grayed, the corresponding toolbar button is grayed as well. If a menu item is checked, the corresponding toolbar button is typically drawn as a pushed-in button. In this way, toolbar buttons serve as indicators as well as mechanisms for giving commands to the application.

A toolbar button has two parts: a bitmap of the button and a resource ID. When a user clicks the button, it is just as though the menu item with the same resource ID was chosen. Figure 1.11 shows a typical toolbar and the properties of the File, Open button on that toolbar. In this view you can change the resource ID of any button, and edit the bitmap with the same tools used to edit icons.

rIG. 1.11
Toolbar buttons are
associated with menu
items through a
resource ID.

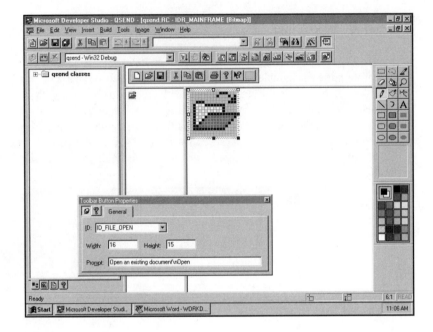

Version Information

One of the goodies that comes with Visual C++ is an installation program called Install Shield.
This utility is discussed in more detail in Chapter 32, "Additional Advanced Topics." It uses
the version information resource when installing your application on a user's machine. For
example, if a user is installing an application that has already been installed, the installation
program may not have to copy as many files. It may alert the user if an old version is being
installed over a new version, and so on.

When you create an application with AppWizard, version information like that in Figure 1.12 is
generated for you automatically. Before attempting to change any of it, make sure you understand how installation programs use it.

FIG. 1.12
Version information is used by install programs.

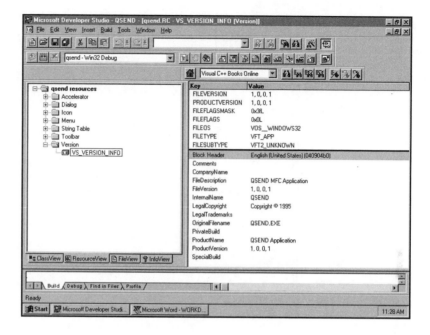

Part

I

Ch

1

Looking at Your Code, Arranged by Class

The Class view shows the classes in your application. Under each class, the member variables and functions are shown, as demonstrated in Figure 1.13. Member functions are shown first with a purple icon next to them, followed by member variables with a turquoise icon. Protected members have a key next to the icon, while private members have a padlock.

Double-clicking a function name brings up the source for that function in the main working area, as shown in Figure 1.13. Double-clicking a variable name brings up the header file in which the variable is declared, as shown in Figure 1.14.

Right-clicking the name of a member function brings up a substantial shortcut menu, with the following menu items:

- *Go To Definition*—Opens the source (.cpp) file at the code for this function.
- *Go To Declaration*—Opens the header (.h) file at the declaration of this function.
- *Set Breakpoint*—Sets a breakpoint. Breakpoints are discussed in Chapter 20, "Debugging."
- *References*—Brings up a list of the places where the function is called within your application.
- *Calls*—Displays a collapsible and expandable outline of all the functions that this function calls. Figure 1.15 shows a sample Call Graph window, discussed more fully in Chapter 2, "Developer Studio Commands."
- *Called by*—Displays a Callers Graph listing the functions this function is called by.

FIG. 1.13
The Class view shows the functions and variables in each class in your application.

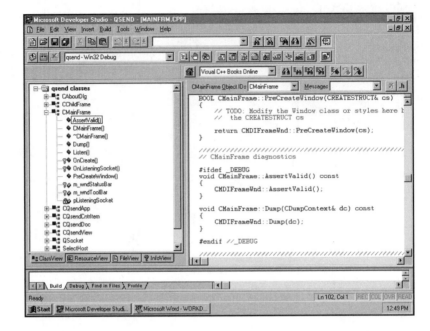

FIG. 1.14
The Class view makes it easy to view source or header code.

- *Group by Access*—Rearranges the order of the list. By default, functions are listed in alphabetical order, followed by data members in alphabetical order. With this option toggled on, functions come first (public, then protected, then private functions, alphabetically in each section) followed by data members (again public, then protected, then private data members, alphabetically in each section).
- *Title Tips*—Displays tool tip-like overlays for function or variable names that are too short to fit in the project workspace window.
- *Docking View*—Keeps the project workspace window docked at the side of the main working area.
- *Hide*—Hides the project workspace window. To redisplay it choose View, Project Workspace.
- *Properties*—Displays the properties of the function (name, return type, parameters).

Right-clicking the name of a member variable brings up a shortcut menu with less menu items. The items are as follows:

- *Go To Definition*—Opens the header (.h) file at the declaration of this variable.
- *References*—Brings up a list of the places where the variable is used within your application.
- *Group by Access*—Rearranges the order of the list. By default, functions are listed in alphabetical order, followed by data members in alphabetical order. With this option toggled on, functions come first (public, then protected, then private functions, alphabetically in each section) followed by data members (again public, then protected, then private data members, alphabetically in each section).
- *Title Tips*—Displays tool tip-like overlays for function or variable names that are too short to fit in the project workspace window.
- *Docking View*—Keeps the project workspace window docked at the side of the main working area.
- *Hide*—Hides the project workspace window. To redisplay it choose View, Project Workspace.
- *Properties*—Displays the properties of the variable (name and type).

When the main working area is displaying a source or header file, you can edit your code as described in the later section "Editing Your Code."

FIG. 1.15

The Call Graph window lists all the functions that your function calls, and all the functions they call, and so on.

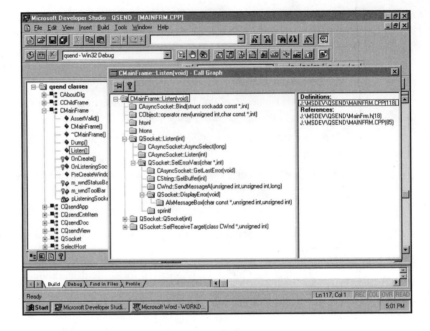

Looking at Your Code, Arranged by File

The File view is much like the Class view in that you can display and edit source and header files. However, it gives you access to parts of your file that are outside of class definitions, and makes it easy to open noncode files like resources and plain text. The project workspace window contains a tree view of the source files in your project. All the header files are grouped together under Dependencies, as shown in Figure 1.16.

Double-clicking a filename displays that file in the main working area. You can then edit the file (even if it is not a source or header file) as described in the later section "Editing Your Code."

FIG. 1.16
The File view displays
source and header files.

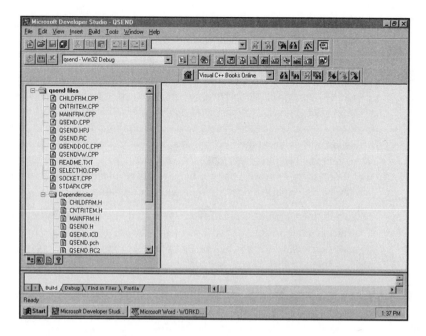

Output and Error Messages

Across the bottom of the Developer Studio screen is the Output view. This is a tabbed view that shows output and error messages from a variety of Developer Studio functions.

 T I P If there is no Output view on your screen, choose View, Output from the menu to restore the view.

The four tabs in the Output View are the following:

- *Build*—Displays the results of compiling and linking.
- *Debug*—Used when debugging, as discussed in Chapter 20, "Debugging."
- *Find in Files*—Displays the results of the Find In Files search, discussed in Chapter 2, "Developer Studio Commands."
- *Profile*—Displays profiler output, as discussed in Chapter 29, "Power-User Features in Developer Studio."

Editing Your Code

For most people, editing code is the most important thing you do in a development environment. If you've used any other editor or word processor before, you can handle the basics of the Developer Studio editor right away. You should be able to type in code, fix your mistakes, and move around in source or header files just by using the basic Windows techniques you would expect to be able to use. But since this is a programmer's editor, there are some nice features you should know about.

Basic Typing and Editing

To add text into a file, click where you want the text to go and start typing. By default, the editor is in *Insert mode*, which means your new text pushes the old text over. To switch to *Overstrike mode*, press the Ins key. Now your text types over the text that is already there. The OVR indicator on the status bar reminds you that you are in Overstrike mode. Pressing Ins again puts you back in Insert mode. Move around in the file by clicking with the mouse or use the cursor keys. To move a page or more at a time, use the PageUp and PageDown keys or the scrollbar at the right hand side of the main working area.

By default, the window for the file you are editing is maximized within the main working area. You can click the Restore button at the top right, just under the Restore button for all of Developer Studio, to show the file in a smaller window. If you have several files open at once you can arrange them so that you can see them side-by-side, as shown in Figure 1.17.

FIG. 1.17
Your files are in MDI windows so you can edit several at once, side-by-side.

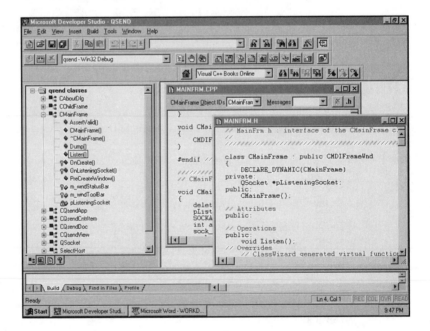

Working with Blocks of Text

Much of the time, you will want to perform an action on a block of text within the editor. First, you select the block by clicking at one end of it and, holding the mouse button down, moving the mouse to the other end of the block, then releasing the mouse button. This should be familiar from so many other Windows applications. Not surprisingly, at this point you can copy or cut the block to the Clipboard, replace it with text you type, or with the current contents of the Clipboard, or delete it.

 T I P To select columns of text, as shown in Figure 1.18, hold down the Alt key as you select the block.

FIG. 1.18

Selecting columns makes fixing indents much simpler. Hold down the Alt key as you select the block.

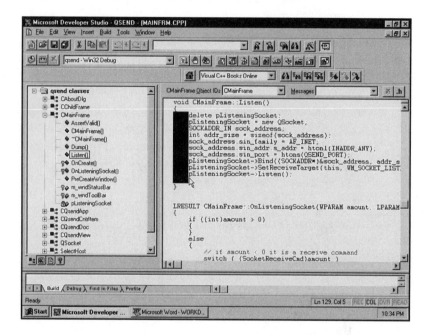

Syntax Coloring

One thing you may have noticed is the color scheme used to present your code. Developer Studio highlights the elements of your code with *syntax coloring*. By default, your code is black, with comments in green and keywords (reserved words in C++ like public, private, new, or int) in blue. You can also arrange for special colors for strings, numbers, or operators (like + and -) if you want, using the Format tab of the Options dialog box, reached by choosing Tools, Options. This is discussed in more detail in Chapter 2, "Developer Studio Commands."

Syntax coloring can really help you spot silly mistakes. If you forget to close a C-style comment, the huge swath of green in your file points out the problem right away. If you type inr where you meant to type int, the inr isn't blue, and that alerts you to a mistyped keyword. This means you can prevent most compiler errors before you even compile.

Shortcut Menu

Many of the actions you are likely to perform are available on the shortcut menu. The items on that menu are as follows:

- *Cut*—Cuts the selected text to the Clipboard
- *Copy*—Copies the selected text to the Clipboard
- *Paste*—Replaces the selected text with the Clipboard contents, or if no text is selected, inserts the Clipboard contents at the cursor
- *Insert/Remove Breakpoint*—Inserts a breakpoint at the cursor, or removes one that is already there
- *Enable Breakpoint*—Enables a disabled breakpoint (breakpoints are discussed in Chapter 20, "Debugging")
- *Insert File Into Project*—Adds the file you are editing to the project you have open
- *Open*—Opens the file whose name is under the cursor
- *Go To Definition*—Opens the file where the item under the cursor is defined (header for a variable, source for a function) and positions the cursor at the definition of the item
- *Go To Reference*—Positions the cursor at the next reference to the variable or function whose name is under the cursor
- *ClassWizard*—Brings up ClassWizard
- *Toolbar*—Toggles the toolbar on this source window
- *Properties*—Brings up the Property sheet

Not all the items are enabled at once—for example, Cut and Copy are only enabled when there is a selection. Insert File Into Project is only enabled when the file you are editing is not in the project you have open. All of these actions have menu and toolbar equivalents and are discussed more fully in Chapter 2, "Developer Studio Commands."

Source File Toolbar

The editing window for source (.cpp) files has a toolbar that the windows for header (.h) and other files do not. (You can see it in Figures 1.13, 1.17, and 1.18.) This toolbar is commonly called the WizardBar and is a shortcut to the actions you would most likely perform with ClassWizard. (Using ClassWizard is covered in detail in Chapter 3, "AppWizard and ClassWizard.") The following four elements are on the bar:

- *Object IDs drop-down box*—Choose an Object ID here just as you would in ClassWizard
- *Messages drop-down box*—Choose a message here (messages this object catches are bold; if you choose a message this object doesn't catch, ClassWizard offers to add a message handler to this object)
- *Delete function button*—Click here to stop catching this message and delete the function
- *Header file button*—Click here to open the header (.h) file that goes with this source file

If you are a newcomer to Visual C++ and ClassWizard, the WizardBar is probably a little terse for you right now. After you are more familiar with using ClassWizard to connect Windows messages to your code, you will appreciate the convenience this feature offers.

From Here...

The user interface of Developer Studio is very visual, encouraging you to move from view to view of your project: looking at your resources, classes, and files, or checking the online documentation. The main screen is divided into panes which you can resize to suit your own needs, and there are many shortcut menus, reached by right-clicking in different places on the screen, to simplify common tasks. This chapter has covered about half of the interface of Visual C++. To learn more, check these chapters and parts:

- The next chapter, "Developer Studio Commands," covers the other half of the user interface: telling Developer Studio to do things and using menus and toolbar buttons.

- Chapter 3, "AppWizard and ClassWizard," introduces you to the tools that Microsoft has developed to make coding faster and easier.

- Part II, "The MFC Library," covers (in twelve chapters) the enormous body of code available for you to draw on and use in your own programs.

- Part III, "Building a Simple MFC Application," devotes six chapters to the how-tos of MFC programming in this development environment.

- Part IV, "ActiveX Applications and ActiveX Custom Controls," brings you up-to-date on the biggest trend in Windows programming right now, ActiveX. It's a must for anyone who wants that Windows 95 logo on their software.

- Finally Part V, "Advanced Topics," covers material not every programmer needs, but that can save you a great deal of time if you do need it.

Developer Studio Commands

In the previous chapter, you met the Developer Studio interface and saw what information it presents you. In this chapter, the focus is how you tell Developer Studio what to do—with menus, toolbars, and keyboard shortcuts. This chapter offers a thorough overview of the Developer Studio and how to customize it to suit your development style. ■

Developer Studio menus

Contains descriptions and advantageous uses of menu elements.

Developer Studio toolbars

Describes the many powerful shortcuts on the toolbars that facilitate rapid application and development.

Docking windows and toolbars

Windows developers need many aspects of their program during development and testing. The Microsoft Developer Studio enables you to create a modular view and dock windows in a tiled fashion.

Customizing the Developer Studio

Demonstrates how to complete the fit and finish of the Developer Studio to suit your preferred work habits.

Learning the Menu System: Slow and Steady

Developer Studio has many menus. Some commands are three or four levels deep under the menu structure. In most cases, there are far quicker ways to accomplish the same thing, but for a new user, the menus are an easier way to learn because you can rely on reading the menu items as opposed to memorizing shortcuts. The following lists the menus across the top of Developer Studio and what they do:

- *File*—For actions related to entire files, like opening, closing, and printing
- *Edit*—For copying, cutting, pasting, as well as displaying and changing properties
- *View*—For changing the appearance of Developer Studio, including toolbars and subwindows like the Project Workspace window
- *Insert*—For adding files or components to your project
- *Build*—For compiling, linking, and debugging
- *Tools*—For customizing the Developer Studio and accessing stand-alone utilities.
- *Window*—To change which window is maximized or has focus
- *Help*—To use the InfoViewer system (not the usual online help)

The following section presents each Developer Studio menu in turn and mentions keyboard shortcuts and toolbar buttons where they exist.

Using File Menu

The File menu, shown in Figure 2.1, collects most of the commands that affect entire files or the entire project.

FIG. 2.1

The File menu has actions for files like Open, Close, and Print.

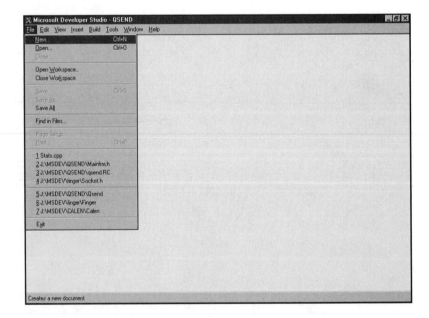

The following are the commands located under the File menu:

- New
- Open
- Close
- Open Workspace
- Close Workspace
- Save
- Save As
- Save All
- Find In Files
- Page Setup
- Print
- Up to 4 recent files (1,2,3,4)
- Up to 4 recent workspaces (5,6,7,8)
- Exit

File New (Ctrl+N) Choosing this menu item brings up the New dialog box, shown in Figure 2.2. You can create one of eight different new items from this dialog box.

FIG. 2.2
The New dialog box is used to create new files or workspaces.

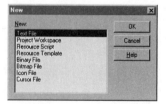

Some of the items in the New dialog box have equivalent menu items. Placing the mouse cursor over a button will display a DataTip, which tells you the buttons function. The following are the eight different new items found in this dialog box:

- *Text File*—An ordinary source, header, or plain text file. This file is named Text1 (the naming convention is Text and a numerical prefix starting with 1 for the first file and so on) and can be renamed with File, Save As. (New Source File is on the Standard toolbar.)

- *Project Workspace*—An entire new project. Choosing this item brings up AppWizard, discussed in Chapter 3, "AppWizard and ClassWizard."

- *Resource Script*—A file with an .rc extension that describes all the resources for your project. Generally your resource scripts are generated by AppWizard.

- *Resource Template*—A list of the resources you want included in a new script.

- *Binary File*—Any binary file. You edit it with the rudimentary hexadecimal editor provided by Developer Studio.

- *Bitmap File*—A bitmap image, 48×48 pixels by default.

- *Icon File*—A bitmap that will be used as an icon, 32×32 pixels with no ability to change the size.

- *Cursor File*—A bitmap, 32×32 pixels, with a *hot spot* that defines the location of a click with that cursor. (For example, the standard arrow cursor has its hot spot at the tip of the arrow.)

Though you can create resources like bitmaps and icons with the File, New menu item and then add those resources into the project, most people go to the Resource View and choose Insert Resource instead. The first two items, Accelerator and Bitmap, are the ones most people choose from this dialog box.

File Open (Ctrl+O) Choosing this item brings up the Open dialog box, as shown in Figure 2.3. (It's the standard Windows File Open dialog box, so it should be pretty familiar.) The file type defaults to Common Files with .c, .cpp, .cxx, .h, or .rc extensions. By clicking the drop-down box you can open almost any kind of file, including executables and workspaces.

FIG. 2.3
The familiar File Open dialog box is used to open a variety of file types.

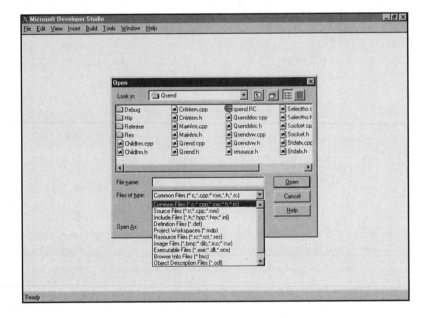

 TIP Don't forget the list of recently opened files further down the File menu. That can save a lot of typing or clicking.

File Close Choosing the File, Close item closes the file that has current focus; if no file has focus, the item is grayed. You can also close a file by clicking the cancel button, depicted by an X, in the top-right corner. You may also close the focus window by double-clicking the icon in the upper right-hand corner. (The icon used to be the system menu, denoted by a minus on a button.)

N O T E As a sidebar, it is important to remember the various ways in which Windows programs may be closed by users. The previous paragraph mentioned three of them. It will be beneficial to remember this when you are writing applications, so you write programs where any close activity converges on the same code and thus the same activity. ■

File Open Workspace Use this item to open a workspace. (You can use File, Open and change the file type to Project Workspace, but using File, Open Workspace is quicker.) The standard Windows 95 and Windows NT open file dialogs enable you to select from almost any file type related to C++ development. The Open Workspace dialog defers to files that are related to projects, like makefiles and project files (refer to fig. 2.4).

FIG. 2.4
The Open Workspace dialog box is slightly different from the usual Open dialog box; there are less file types and a different starting directory.

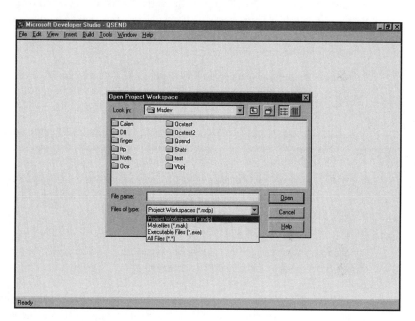

File Close Workspace Software development is project centric. There are too many files, and it would be aggravating to manually keep track of all of the files of which even a single executable or DLL were comprised. Selecting File, Close Workspace closes all of the views associated with the current project.

File Save (Ctrl+S) Use this item to save the file that has focus at the moment; if no file has focus the item is grayed. There is a Save button on the Standard toolbar as well.

File Save As Use this item to save a file and change its name at the same time. It saves the file that has focus at the moment; if no file has focus, the item is grayed.

File Save All This item saves all the files that are currently open. All files are saved just before a compile and when the application is closed, but if you aren't compiling very often and are making a lot of changes, it's a good idea to save all your files every 15 minutes or so. (You can do it less often if the idea of losing that amount of work doesn't bother you.) (The Save All button is on the Standard toolbar.)

Saving Files   You will be creating many kinds of files during the course of developing a single project. You may use the File, Save, File, Save As, and File, Save All options during project development. I would suggest saving frequently. If you haven't developed a consistent habit, consider saving at the end of every logical transition—perhaps the completion of a function or a particularly challenging stretch of code.

N O T E   Like almost all other Windows programs, selecting File, Save defaults to File, Save As if you are saving the file for the first time. ■

Further, you may discover that using just these file saving items is not completely satisfactory. Windows is still capable of losing chains and clusters, which means even if you save frequently the data in your files could become disassociated with the file names. I would suggest acquiring a habit of saving to a diskette every half hour to hour, or based on the importance and complexity of the code under construction.

Combining frequent project saving, backups, and a version control system is going to alleviate at least one problem of software development, that of lost work in progress.

File Find In Files   There was a utility developed on UNIX, called grep. Later grep.com for DOS based systems was developed and is still distributed with some developers tools. Grep— some of you may remember—enables you to perform searches across many files.

N O T E   I mentioned grep because it is still a viable tool for find text in program source files. And, you may not always want to load the Developer Studio to find some text in files. A down and dirty grep-like tool can be contrived from a DOS command

for %%f in (*.cpp *.h *.c) do find *some code* %%f

It is often many times cheaper to scrounge for existing code than it is to write new code. You will need as many tools as possible to assist in this endeavor. ■

File, Find In Files is like an integrated grep-tool. This useful command searches for a word or phrase within a large number of files at once. In its simplest form, shown in Figure 2.5, you enter a word or phrase into the Find What edit box, restrict the search to certain types of files in the In Files of Type box, and choose the folder to conduct the search within in the In Folder edit box. The following checkboxes in the bottom half of the dialog box set the options for the search:

- ■ *Look in subfolders*—Work through all the subfolders of the chosen folder if this is checked.
- ■ *Regular expression*—The Find What box is treated as a regular expression (see the following sidebar "Regular Expressions") if this box is checked.
- ■ *Match case*—If this is checked, Chapter in the Find What box matches only Chapter, not chapter or CHAPTER. Upper- and lowercase must match.
- ■ *Match whole word only*—If this is checked, table in the Find What box matches only table, not suitable or tables.

FIG. 2.5

The simplest Find In Files approach searches for a string within a folder and its subfolders.

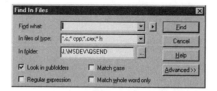

Using Regular Expressions with Find In Files Many of the Find and Replace operations within Developer Studio can use regular expressions to create a more powerful tool. For example, if you want to search for a string only at the end of a line, or one of several similar strings, you can do so by constructing an appropriate regular expression, entering it in the search dialog box, and instructing Developer Studio to use regular expressions for the search.

When regular expressions are being used, some characters give up their usual meaning and instead stand in for one or more other characters. Regular expressions in Developer Studio are built from ordinary characters mixed in with these special entries. See Table 2.1 for expressions.

Part
I

Ch
2

Table 2.1   Regular Expressions That Can Be Used with Find In Files

Entry	Matches
^	Start of the line.
$	End of the line.
.	Any single character.
[]	Any one of the characters within the brackets (use - for a range, ^ for "except").
\~	Anything except the character that follows next.
*	Zero or more of the next character.
+	One or more of the next character.
\(\)	Doesn't match specially, but saves part of the match string to be used in the replacement string. Up to nine portions can be tagged like this.
\{\}	Either of the characters within the {}.
{\}	Just like [].
\:a	A single letter or number.
\:b	Whitespace (tabs or spaces).
\:c	A single letter.
\:d	A single numerical digit.
\:n	An unsigned number.

continues

Table 2.1	Continued
Entry	**Matches**
\:z	An unsigned integer
\:h	A hexadecimal number
\:i	A string of characters that meets the rules for C++ identifiers (starts with a letter, number, or underscore)
\:w	A string of letters only
\:q	A quoted string surrounded by double or single quotes
\	Removes the special meaning from the character that follows

You don't have to type these in if you have trouble remembering them. Next to the Find What box is an arrowhead pointing to the right. Click there to bring up a shortcut menu of all these fields, and click any one of them to insert it into the Find What box. (You need to be able to read these symbols to understand what expression you are building, and there's no arrowhead on the toolbar Find box.) Remember to check the Regular Expressions box so that these regular expressions are evaluated properly.

The bulleted list below exemplifies some of the many possible variations of text and code you can use with Find In Files:

- ^test$ matches only test alone on a line.
- doc[1234] matches doc1, doc2, doc3, or doc4 but not doc5.
- doc[1-4] matches the same strings as above but requires less typing.
- doc[^56] matches doca, doc1, and anything else that starts with doc and is not doc5 or doc6.
- If the Find What box contains (\Good\) morning and the replace box is \1 afternoon, then Good morning is changed to Good afternoon.
- H\~ello matches Hillo and Hxllo (and lots more) but not Hello.
- \{x\!y\}z matches xz and yz.
- New *York matches New York but also NewYork and New   York.
- New +York matches New York and New   York but not NewYork.
- New.*k matches Newk, Newark, and New York, plus lots more.
- \:n matches 0.123, 234, and 23.45 (among others) but not -12.
- World$ matches World at the end of a line but World\$ matches only World$ anywhere on a line.

It is also possible to use the regular expressions you may have learned for two other popular editors: Brief and Epsilon. This is discussed under "Tools Options" later in this chapter.

Using Advanced Text Finding Features   At the bottom right of the Find in Files dialog box is the Advanced button. Clicking it expands the dialog box to that shown in Figure 2.6 and allows you to search several different folders at once.

T I P   If you highlight a block of text before selecting Find In Files, that text is put into the Find What box for you. If no text is highlighted, the word or identifier under the cursor is put into the Find What box.

FIG. 2.6

Advanced Find in Files searches for a string within several folders and their subfolders.

The results of the Find in Files command appear in the Find in Files tab of the output window; the output window will be visible after this operation if it was not already. You can resize this window like any other window, by holding the mouse over the border until it becomes a sizing cursor, and you can scroll around within the window in the usual way. Double-clicking a filename in the output list opens that file, with the cursor on the line where the match was found.

File Page Setup   This item brings up the Page Setup dialog box, shown in Figure 2.7. Here you specify the header, footer, and margins—left, right, top, and bottom. The header and footer can contain any text including one or more special fields, which you add by clicking the arrow next to the edit box or entering the codes yourself.

The File, Page Setup dialog is enabled when a text view has the focus. The Page Setup enables you to format the printed code page output. The options are as follows:

- ■ *Filename*—The name of the file being printed (&f)
- ■ *Page Number*—The current page number (&p)
- ■ *Current Time*—The time the page was printed (&t)
- ■ *Current Date*—The date the page was printed (&d)
- ■ *Left Align*—Align this portion to the left (&l)
- ■ *Right Align*—Align this portion to the right (&r)
- ■ *Center*—Center this portion (this is the default alignment) (&c)

Part
I

Ch
2

Headers are placed a quarter of an inch from the top of the page and footers are one-half inch from the bottom.

FIG. 2.7
The Page Setup dialog box lays out your printed pages the way you want.

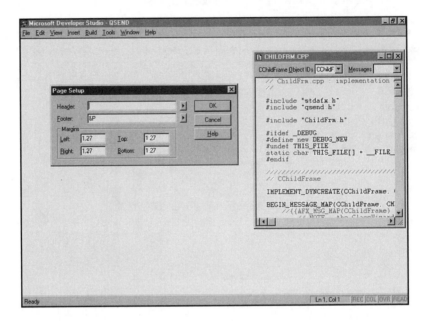

File Print (Ctrl+P)   Choosing this item prints the file with focus according to your Page Setup settings. (The item is grayed if no file has focus.) The Print dialog box, shown in Figure 2.8, has you confirm the printer you want to print on. If you have some text highlighted, the Selection radio button is enabled. Choosing it lets you print just the selected text; otherwise only the All radio button is enabled, which prints the entire file. If you forget to set the headers, footers, and margins before choosing File, Print, the Setup button brings up the Page Setup dialog box discussed in the previous section. There is no way to print only certain pages, or to cancel printing once it has started.

Recent Files and Workspaces   The recent files and workspaces groups of items are between Print and Exit. The items are the names of files and workspaces which have been opened most recently, up to the last four of each. The menu entries are real timesavers if you work on several projects at once. Developer Studio adds the names of up to four files and four projects onto the menu as you open them. Whenever you want to open a file, before you click that toolbar button and prepare to point and click your way to the file, think first if it might be on the File menu. Menus aren't always the slower way to go!

File Exit   Probably the most familiar Windows menu item of all, this closes Developer Studio. You can also click the X in the top-right corner, or double-click what used to be the system menu in the top left. If you have made changes without saving, you get a chance to save each file on your way out.

FIG. 2.8
The Print dialog box confirms your choice to print a file.

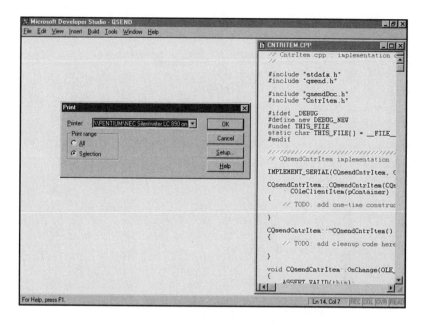

Edit

The Edit menu, shown in Figure 2.9, collects actions related to changing text in a source file.

FIG. 2.9
The Edit menu holds items that change the text in a file.

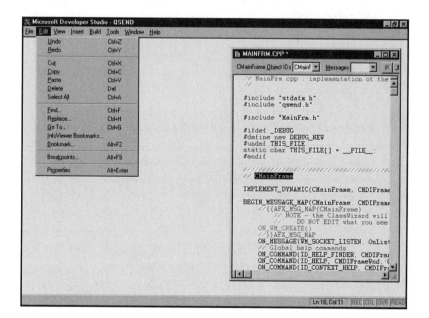

The following items are on this menu:

- Undo
- Redo
- Cut
- Copy
- Paste
- Delete
- Select All
- Find
- Replace
- Go To
- InfoViewer Bookmarks
- Bookmark
- Breakpoints
- Properties

Edit Undo (Ctrl+Z)   The Undo items is the oops menu item. Selecting Edit, Undo has saved me from having to re-open a saved file a few dozen times. If you are saving often, then you have a backup plan if you are unable to undo. Most operations, like text edits and deleting text, can be undone. There are some things that can not be undone however, making frequent saves a good contingency plan. When Undo is disabled, it is an indication that nothing needs to be undone or that you can not undo the last operation.

There is an Undo button on the Standard toolbar. Clicking the button displays a stack (reverse order list from most recent to least recent) of operations that can be undone. You must select a contiguous range of undo items including the first, second, and so on. You can not pick and choose.

Edit Redo (Ctrl+Y)   As you undo actions, the name given to the operations moves from the Undo to the Redo list (Redo is next to Undo on the toolbar). If you undo a little too much, choose Edit, Redo to un-undo them (if that makes sense.) Selecting Undo or Redo from the menu works backwards performing the operation from the most recent to the least recent operations that can be undone or redone. Using the toolbar combobox enables you to perform several of each in one step.

Edit Cut (Ctrl+X)   This item cuts the currently highlighted text to the Clipboard. That means a copy of it goes to the Clipboard and the text itself is deleted from your file. The Cut (represented as shears) button is on the Standard toolbar.

Edit Copy (Ctrl+C)   Editing buttons on the toolbar are grouped next to the scissors (Cut). Edit, Copy copies the currently selected text or item to the Windows Clipboard.

Edit Paste (Ctrl+V)   Choosing this item copies the Clipboard contents at the cursor, or replaces the highlighted text with the Clipboard contents if any text is highlighted. The Paste item and button are disabled if there are no datum in the Clipboard in a format appropriate for pasting to the focus window. In addition to text, you can copy and paste menu items, dialog box items, and other resources. The Paste button is on the Standard toolbar.

 TIP Did you know that you can use the Cut and Paste steps and the clipboard to grab icons and text from any Windows program to another? (Something Jonathan Wild would appreciate.)

Edit Delete (Del)   Edit, Del clears the selected text or item. If what you deleted is undeletable, then the Undo button will be enabled and the last operation added to the Undo button combobox. Deleted material does not go to the Clipboard and cannot be retrieved except by Undo-ing the delete.

Edit Select All (Ctrl+A)   Euphemistically the snatch and grab button, selecting Edit, Select All highlights everything in the file with focus that can be selected. For example, if a text file has focus, the entire file is selected. If a dialog box has focus, every control on it is selected.

To select many items on a dialog box, click the first item and then Ctrl+click each of the remaining items. It is often faster to use Edit Select All to select everything, and then Ctrl+click to unselect the few items you do not want highlighted.

Edit Find (Ctrl+F)   The Find dialog box shown in Figure 2.10 enables you to search for text within the file that currently has the focus. Enter a word or phrase into the Find What edit box. The following checkboxes set the options for the search:

- ■ *Regular expression*—The Find What box is treated as a regular expression (see previous sidebar "Regular Expressions") if this box is checked.
- ■ *Match case*—If this is checked, `Chapter` in the Find What box matches only `Chapter`, not `chapter` or `CHAPTER`. Upper- and lowercase must match.
- ■ *Match whole word only*—If this is checked, `table` in the Find What box matches only `table`, not `suitable` or `tables`.
- ■ *Direction*—Choose the Up radio button to search backwards, and the Down radio button to search forwards through the file.

 TIP If you highlight a block of text before selecting Edit Find, that text is put into the Find What box for you. If no text is highlighted, the word or identifier under the cursor is put into the Find What box.

A typical use for the Find dialog is to enter some text and in conjunction use the Find Next button until you find the precise occurrence of the text for which you are searching. But you may want to combine the Find feature with bookmarks (discussed a little later in this section), and put a bookmark on each line that has an occurrence of the string. Click the Mark All button in the Find dialog box to add temporary, unnamed bookmarks on match lines; they are indicated with a blue oval in the margin.

FIG. 2.10

The Find dialog box is used to find a string within the file that has focus.

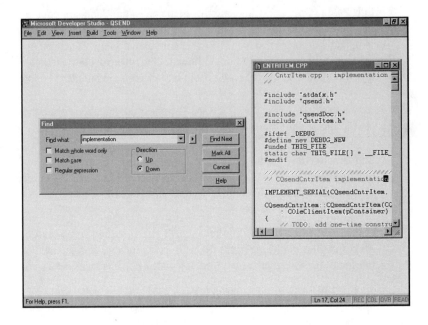

There is a Find edit box on the Standard toolbar. Enter the text you want to search for in the box and press Enter to search forward. Regular expressions are used if you have turned them on using the Find dialog box. To repeat a search, click the Find Next or Find Previous—icons with binoculars with clockwise and counter-clockwise arrows, respectively—buttons on the Standard toolbar.

Edit Replace (Ctrl+H)   This item brings up the Replace dialog box, shown in Figure 2.11. It is very similar to the Find dialog box but is used to replace the found text with new text. Enter one string into the Find What edit box and the replacement string into the Replace With edit box. The three checkboxes, Regular Expression, Match Case, and Match Whole Word Only, have the same meaning as on the Find dialog box (discussed in the previous section). The Replace In radio buttons allow you to restrict the search-and-replace operation to a block of highlighted text, if you prefer.

To see the next match before you agree to replace it, click Find Next. To replace the next match, or the match you have just found, click Replace. If you are confident that there won't be any false matches, you can click Replace All to do the rest of the file all at once. (If you realize after you click Replace All that you were wrong, there is always Edit, Undo.)

Edit Go To (Ctrl+G)   The Edit, Go To item (see fig. 2.12) is a central navigation point. It enables you to go to a particular line number (the default), address, reference, or bookmark, among other things. To use the Go To dialog, select what it is you are going to from the list (shown in fig. 2.12) and enter the value: if the Line is selected, enter a line number; if a bookmark is selected, pick the particular bookmark from the combobox, and so on.

FIG. 2.11

The Replace dialog box is used to replace one string with another.

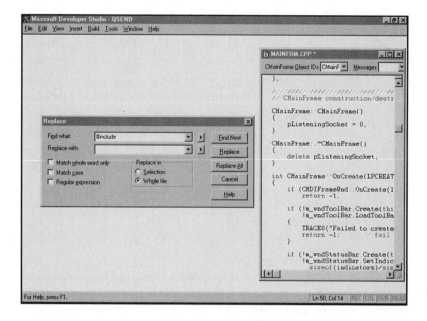

FIG. 2.12

The Go To dialog box moves you around within your project.

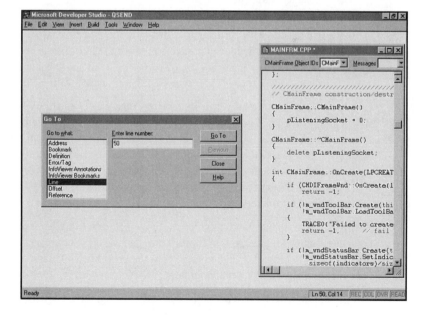

Part

I

Ch

2

The following are examples of bookmarks, line numbers, or addresses in the file to which you can move the cursor:

- *Address*—In the Memory or Disassembly windows, as explained in Chapter 20, "Debugging," you can go to an address given by a debugger expression.

- *Bookmark*—In a text file you can go to a bookmark, though you are more likely to use Edit, Bookmarks or the bookmark-related buttons on the Edit toolbar.

- *Definition*—If the cursor is over the name of a function, this opens the source (.cpp) file at its definition. If the cursor is over a variable, it opens the include (.h) file.

- *Error/Tag*—After a compile you can move from error to error by double-clicking them within the output window by using this dialog box, or (most likely) by pressing F4.

- *InfoViewer Annotation*—If you have added many of your own notes to InfoViewer topics, you can review them through this selection.

- *InfoViewer Bookmark*—This is one way to cycle through your InfoViewer bookmarks, but most of the time the InfoViewer toolbar or Edit, Infoviewer Bookmarks is a better way.

- *Line*—This is the default selection. The line number that is filled in for you is your current line.

- *Offset*—Offset refers to an Offset address. In a segmented architecture absolute addresses were contrived by adding the segment and offset address. Referring to memory by its offset is a throwback to segmented addressing; you may enter the offset address as a hexadecimal or decimal number.

- *Reference*—Enter a name, like a function or object name, and the cursor will be placed on the line of code where the name is defined. The Reference Go To even works if it is a name you did not define. (For example, given the line of code `cout << "Greetings from mars!" << endl;`, entering `operator<<` will focus the cursor in the `ostream.h` file on an overloaded `operator<<` line of code. A very useful item indeed.)

Edit InfoViewer Bookmarks   This item brings up a list of your InfoViewer bookmarks, as shown in Figure 2.13. When you first bring up the dialog box, the Name box is filled in with the name of the InfoViewer topic you most recently displayed. Clicking Add adds a bookmark to that topic; Close closes the dialog box; Delete deletes the bookmark; Display shows a list of the topics in InfoViewer; and, Help gives you regular help (not InfoViewer) about the dialog box. When the Book button heading is down, the bookmarks are sorted by book; click the Name button heading to sort them by name instead.

The InfoViewer toolbar (not the toolbar at the top of each InfoViewer topic window) has a number of buttons related to InfoViewer bookmarks. Help Bookmark List brings up the dialog box; Previous Bookmark in List goes back to the previous bookmark; and Next Bookmark in List moves forward to the next bookmark.

Edit Bookmark (Alt+F2)   This item is used to manage the bookmarks within your text files, which are completely independent of any InfoViewer bookmarks you may have set.

The bookmark list is shown in Figure 2.14. Note that temporary bookmarks set by the Find command are not included on this list.

FIG. 2.13

The InfoViewer Bookmarks dialog box manages the bookmarks you have set in the online help system.

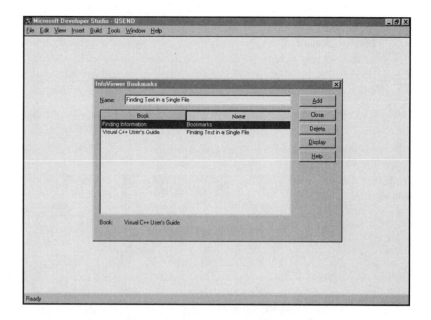

FIG. 2.14

The Bookmarks dialog box manages the bookmarks you have set in text files.

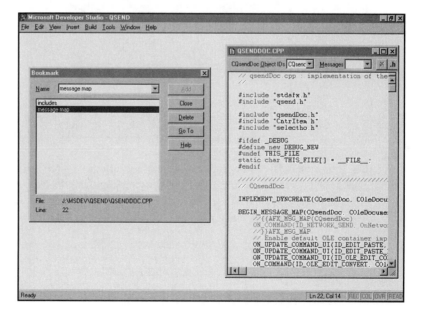

To add a named bookmark for the line you are on and have it saved with the file, type a name in the Name box and click Add. To go to a named bookmark, choose it from the list box and click Go To. There are buttons on the Edit toolbar to add or delete a bookmark at the cursor, move to the next or previous bookmark, and clear all bookmarks in the file.

Edit Breakpoints (Alt+F9)   A breakpoint pauses program execution. (A break is sometimes more colorfully referred to as soft-ice.) At the lowest level (the ROM BIOS) there is support for breakpoints, the interrupt 3 function. In fact, adding an int 0x03, assembler instruction still works. Luckily we have more powerful ways to break program execution.

The Edit, Breakpoints item displays the Breakpoints dialog box, shown in Figure 2.15 and discussed in Chapter 20, "Debugging." It enables you to set simple as well as conditional breakpoint, based on iterations over a line of code and logical conditional tests.

FIG. 2.15

The Breakpoints dialog box is used in debugging your application.

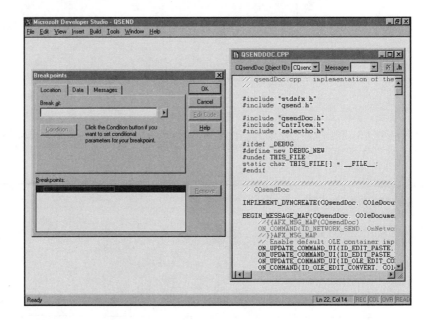

Edit Properties (Alt+Enter)   Choosing this item brings up a property sheet. The property sheets for different items vary widely, as shown in Figures 2.16, 2.17, and 2.18, which illustrate the property sheet for an entire source file, an accelerator table selected in the project workspace window, and one key in that accelerator table, respectively.

FIG. 2.16
The property sheet for a source file reminds you of the name and size, and lets you set the language (used for syntax coloring) and tab size.

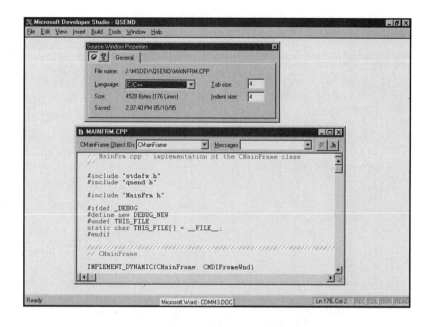

FIG. 2.17
The property sheet for an accelerator table is where you set the language, enabling you to include multiple tables in one application.

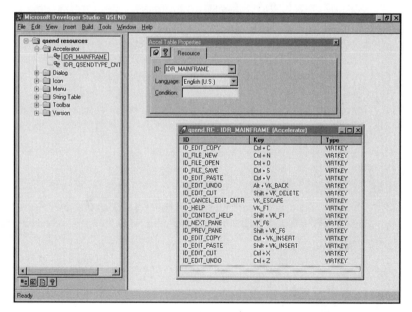

FIG. 2.18

The property sheet for an entry in an accelerator table gives you full control over the keystrokes associated with the resource ID.

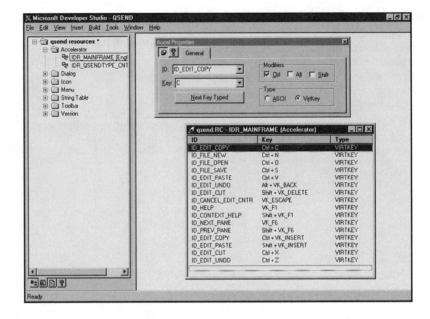

Property sheets are a powerful way of editing non-source file entities such as resources. For functions and variables, however, it's usually easier to make the changes in the source file. Some rather obscure effects can only be achieved through property sheets. For example, to turn off syntax coloring for a file, use the property sheet to set the language to None. (The effect will be observed after the window is repainted by Windows.)

TIP The property normally disappears as soon as you click something else. If you click the pushpin button in the top-left corner, it stays "pinned" to the screen as you work, displaying the properties of all the entities you are working with.

Using the View Menu

The View menu, shown in Figure 2.19, collects actions that are related to the appearance of Developer Studio—which windows are open, what toolbars are visible, and so on.

- ClassWizard
- Resource Symbols
- Resource Includes
- Full Screen
- Toolbars
- Info Viewer Query Results
- Info Viewer History List
- Project Workspace

FIG. 2.19

The View menu controls the appearance of Developer Studio.

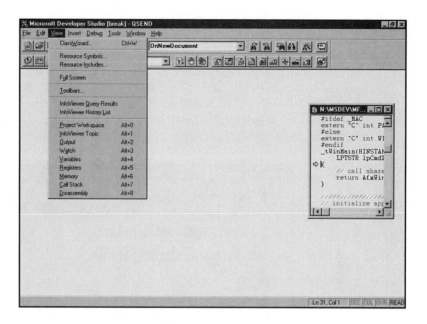

- Info Viewer Topic
- Output
- Watch
- Variables
- Registers
- Memory
- Call Stack
- Disassembly

View ClassWizard (Ctrl+W)   ClassWizard is probably the most-used tool in the Developer Studio. Whenever you add a resource (menu, dialog box, control, and so on), you connect it to your code with ClassWizard. When you are working with OLE, you use ClassWizard to set up properties, methods, and events. If you use custom messages, you use ClassWizard to arrange for them to be caught. Some of the functionality of ClassWizard has been captured in the WizardBar on the top of source (.cpp) file windows, but much more is reached through this menu item or the ClassWizard button on the Standard toolbar.

ClassWizard and the Wizard bar are discussed in Chapter 3, "AppWizard and ClassWizard."

CAUTION

All changed files are saved when you bring up ClassWizard, just as they are saved before a compile. If you've been making changes that you may not want saved, don't bring up ClassWizard.

View Resource Symbols This item brings up the Resource Symbols dialog box, shown in Figure 2.20. It displays the resource IDs, such as ID_EDIT_COPY, used in your application. The large list box at the top of the dialog box lists resource IDs, and the smaller box below it reminds you where this resource is used—on a menu, in an accelerator, in the string table, and so on. The buttons along the right side are used to make changes. Click New to create a new resource ID; Delete to delete this resource ID (if it is not in use); Change to change the ID (if it is in use by only one resource); and View Use to open the resource (menu, string table, and so on) that is highlighted in the lower list.

FIG. 2.20

The Resource Symbols dialog box displays resource IDs.

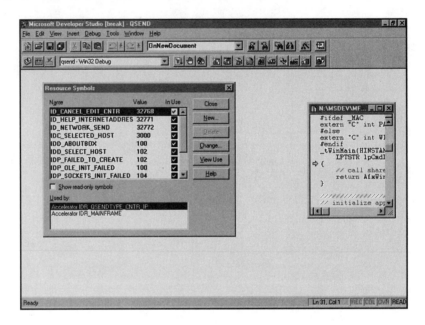

There is a Resource Symbols button on the Resource toolbar that brings up the same dialog box.

View Resource Includes Choosing this item brings up the Resource Includes dialog box, as shown in Figure 2.21. It is unusual for you to need to change this generated material. In the rare cases where the resource.h generated for you is not quite what you need, you can add extra lines with this dialog box.

View Full Screen This item hides all the toolbars, the menus, the output window, and the project workspace window, giving you your entire screen as the main working area. One small toolbar appears whose only button is Toggle Full Screen. Click that button to restore the menus, toolbars, and windows.

View Toolbars Choosing this item brings up the Toolbar dialog box, as shown in Figure 2.22. Toolbars are discussed in a section of their own later in this chapter.

FIG. 2.21

The Resource Includes dialog box lets you insert extra directives into the file that describes the resources of your project.

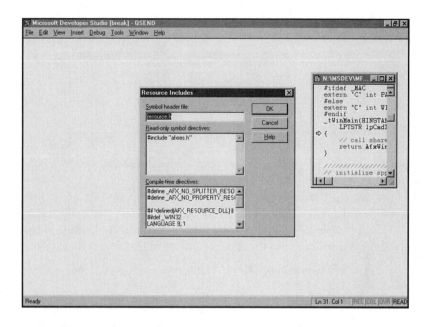

FIG. 2.22

The Toolbars dialog box is used to display or suppress any of the eight toolbars in Developer Studio.

View Info Viewer Query Results Selecting View, InfoViewer Query Results returns the results of a previous InfoViewer Query. These Query lists are generated when you choose the Query tab of the Search dialog box, reached from Help, Search, and are discussed in the "Help" menu section of this chapter.

The pushpin in the top-left corner keeps the dialog box open (even when you move focus elsewhere), and the tab along the bottom makes it easy to switch between query results and the history list.

View Info Viewer History List Choosing this item brings up a history of the InfoViewer topics you have displayed recently, like the one in Figure 2.23. Double-click any topic to display it again. Use the tab at the bottom to switch to query results, if you want. There is no InfoViewer History toolbar button, but you can use the Query Results button on the InfoViewer toolbar and then use the tabs to switch to the history list.

FIG. 2.23
The InfoViewer history list simplifies revisting Help topics.

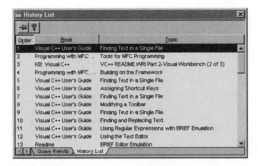

View Project Workspace (Alt+0)   Choosing this item brings up the Project Workspace window, if it is hidden. It does not take away the Project Workspace window. To hide it, right-click the window and choose Hide, or press Shift+Esc while the window has focus. There is a Project Workspace button on the Standard toolbar which hides or displays the window.

View Info Viewer Topic (Alt+1)   This item reopens your most recently viewed InfoViewer topic.

View Output (Alt+2)   This item brings up the output window, if it is hidden. To hide the output window, right-click in it and choose Hide, or press Shift+Esc while the window has focus. The output window opens automatically when you build your project or use Find in Files.

Debugging Views   The remainder of the View menu deals with windows used while debugging, which are discussed in Chapter 20, "Debugging." The remaining View menu items are the following:

- View Watch (Alt+3)
- View Variables (Alt+4)
- View Registers (Alt+5)
- View Memory (Alt+6)
- View Call Stack (Alt+7)
- View Disassembly (Alt+8)

Insert

The Insert menu is one way to add items to a project or a file. The items in the Insert are:

- File
- Resource
- Resource Copy
- Files into Project
- Project
- Component

FIG. 2.24

The Insert menu collects actions related to inserting something into your project or one of its files.

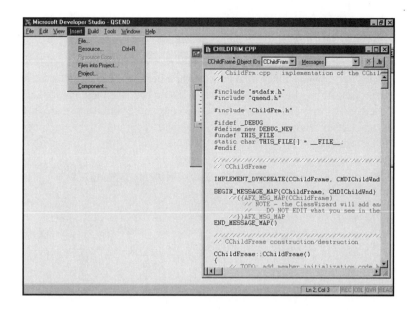

Part

I

Ch

2

Insert File   Use this item to insert, at the cursor, an entire file into the file with focus.

Insert Resource (Ctrl+R)   Use this item to add a new resource to your project. The Insert Resource dialog box, as shown in Figure 2.25, appears. Choose the type of resource to be added and click OK.

FIG. 2.25

The Insert Resource dialog box is one way to add resources to your project.

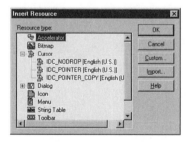

There are buttons on the Resource toolbar to add a new dialog box, menu, cursor, icon, bitmap, toolbar, accelerator, string table, or version.

Insert Resource Copy   Use this item to copy an existing resource, changing only the *language* (for example, from US English to Canadian French) or the *condition* (for example, building a debug version of a dialog box). Your project will have different language versions of the resource, allowing you to use compiler directives to determine which resource is compiled into the executable.

Insert Files into Project   When you create a new workspace with File, New, Project Workspace the resultant project will be empty. To add modules (.CPP and .H) files into your project select Insert, Files Into Project. If you use the ClassWizard or AppWizard, they will each generate several files automatically.

Insert Project While you usually have only one project in a project workspace, you can insert another. Choose this item to generate another top-level project or a subproject within this project workspace. The Insert Project dialog box, shown in Figure 2.26, looks very much like the New Project Workspace dialog box, discussed with AppWizard in Chapter 3, "AppWizard and ClassWizard." Subprojects are discussed later in this chapter, under the menu item Build Subprojects.

FIG. 2.26
The Insert Project dialog box creates new projects within this project workspace.

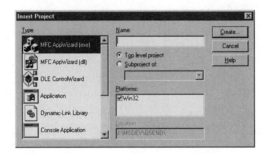

Insert Component This menu item brings up the component gallery, which allows you to use tools and controls created for another project or by a third party. The component gallery is discussed in Chapter 29, "Power-User Features in Developer Studio."

Build

The Build menu, shown in Figure 2.27, holds all the actions associated with compiling, running, and debugging your application.

- Compile
- Build
- Rebuild All
- Batch Build
- Stop Build
- Update All Dependencies
- Debug
- Execute
- Settings
- Configurations
- Subprojects
- Set Default Configuration

FIG. 2.27
The Build menu is replaced by a Debug menu after you have compiled and begin stepping through your program.

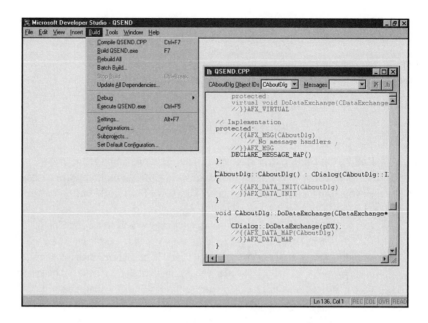

Build Compile (Ctrl+F7)   Choosing this item compiles the file with focus. This is a very useful thing to do when you are expecting to find errors or warnings, such as the first time you compile after a lot of changes. For example, if there is an error in a header file that is included in many source files, a typical build produces error messages related to that header file over and over again as each source file is compiled. If there are warnings in one of your source files, a typical build links the project, but you might prefer to stop and correct the warnings. There is a Compile button on the Project toolbar, represented by a stack of papers with an arrow pointing downward.

Build Build (F7)   This item compiles all the changed files in the project and then links them. There is a Build button on the Project toolbar.

Build Rebuild All   This item compiles all files in the project, even those that have not been changed since the last build, and then links them. There are times when a typical build misses a file that should be recompiled, and using this item corrects the problem.

Build Batch Build   Typically a project contains at least two *configurations*: Debug and Release. Usually you work with the Debug configuration, changing, building, testing, and changing again until it is ready to be released, and then build a Release version. If you ever need to build several configurations at once, use this menu item to bring up the Batch Build dialog box shown in Figure 2.28. Choose Build to compile only changed files, and Rebuild All to compile all files. If the compiles are successful, links follow.

FIG. 2.28

The Batch Build dialog box builds several configurations of your project at once.

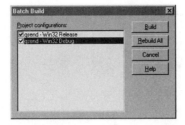

Build Stop Build (Ctrl+Break)   This item stops an ongoing build. The typical situation is when you spot an error in the output window that you know will cascade throughout the build so you stop it early to fix the error. There is a Stop Build button on the Project toolbar.

N O T E   Microsoft has done something interesting with the Build and Stop Build menu items: They both have B as a mnemonic. So many Windows programmers have learned the importance of using unique mnemonics that many don't know what happens when two items use the same letter. When you press Alt+B+B the first non-grayed item is chosen. If you are not building at the moment, Build is enabled and Stop Build is grayed, so Build is chosen. During a build, Build is grayed and Stop Build is enabled, so Stop Build is chosen. Alt+B, B is a nice convenient set of keystrokes to start or stop a build, and you don't need to remember two sets. Keep this in mind for menus you create, as long as you, too, can be sure that only one of the pair of items will ever be enabled at any time. ■

Build Update All Dependencies   Just as situations sometimes arise when only a full rebuild can clear up confusion about which files have changed recently, sometimes it is necessary to rebuild the list of dependencies. If a header file changes, all the source files that include that header file must be compiled during a build. When header files include other header files, or when files are added to a project, the list of dependencies can get messed up. This item regenerates the list and gets everything running smoothly again.

Build Debug   Debugging is a lengthy topic, discussed in Chapter 20, "Debugging."

Build Execute (Ctrl+F5)   Choosing the Build, Execute item is about the fastest way to run your program from the Developer Studio. If the executable file is up-to-date, then the program is executed immediately; otherwise, the code is compiled and linked. As a reminder, being up-to-date refers to a comparison between the date stamps of the current executable and all of the project files; if the executable date stamp is greater than or equal to that of the source files, then it is considered up-to-date.

Build Settings (Alt+F7)   This item brings up the Project Settings dialog box, which has the following eight tabs:

■ *General*—Change the static versus shared DLL decision you made when AppWizard built this project; change the directory where intermediate (source and object) or output (EXE, DLL, OCX) files are kept (see fig. 2.29).

FIG. 2.29

The General tab of the Project Settings dialog box governs where files are kept.

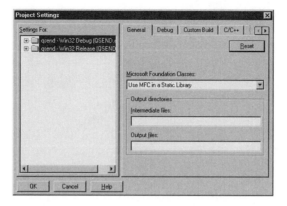

- *Debug*—These settings are discussed in Chapter 20, "Debugging."

- *Custom Build*—These settings are discussed in Chapter 29, "Power-User Features in Developer Studio."

- *C/C++*—These are your compiler settings. The Category combobox has General selected by default. To change the settings category, select a category from the combobox. Figure 2.30 shows the General category. You can change the optimization criteria (your choices are Maximize Speed, Minimize Size, Customize, or Disable if your debugging is being thrown off by the optimizer) or the warning level. The higher you set the warning level, the more warning messages you get. Most users don't change any other compiler settings.

FIG. 2.30

The C/C++ tab of the Project Settings dialog box governs compiler settings in eight categories, starting with General.

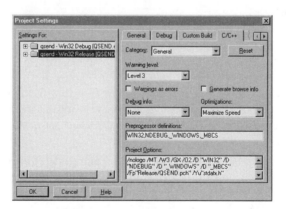

- *Link*—This tab controls linker options, which you are unlikely to need to change. The settings are divided into five categories; the General category is shown in Figure 2.31.

FIG. 2.31

The Link tab of the Project Settings dialog box governs linker settings in five categories starting with General.

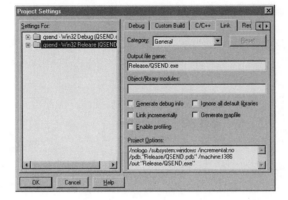

■ *Resources*—This tab, shown in Figure 2.32, is used to change the language you are working in. This changes which resources are compiled into your application and changes other resource settings.

FIG. 2.32

The Resources tab of the Project Settings dialog box governs resources settings including language.

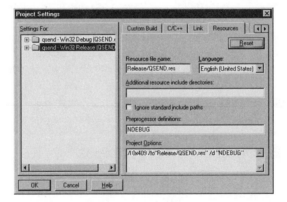

■ *OLE Types*—This tab is used by programmers who are building a type library (TLB) from a object description (ODL) file. This is discussed in Chapter 25, "ActiveX Automation."

■ *Browse Info*—This tab, shown in Figure 2.33, controls the Browse Info (.bsc) file used for the Go To Definition, Go To Declaration, and similar menu items. If you never use these, your links will be quicker if you don't generate browse information. If you want browse information, in addition to checking Build Browse info file on this tab, check Generate Browse info in the General category of the C/C++ tab.

To see the last few tabs, click the right-pointing arrow at the end of the list of tabs. You can adjust the settings for each configuration (Debug, Release, and so on) separately or all at once. Many of the panes have a Reset button that restores the settings to those you chose when you first created the project.

FIG. 2.33

The Browse Info tab of the Project Settings dialog box turns on or off the powerful browse feature.

Build Configurations   Choosing this item brings up the Configurations dialog box, shown in Figure 2.34. Here you can add or remove configurations. Use Project Settings to change the settings for the new configuration.

FIG. 2.34

The Configurations dialog box lets you add to the standard Debug and Release configurations.

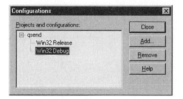

Build Subprojects   This item controls the subprojects within your project using the Subproject dialog box, shown in Figure 2.35. If you have several applications that use the same group of objects and resources, you may want to gather those objects and resources together into a subproject and then insert that subproject into each project that uses them. This transfers the responsibility for keeping those subprojects up-to-date onto Developer Studio instead of you. For example, if you add a file to the subproject, you do not need to add that file to each project that uses it.

FIG. 2.35

The Subprojects dialog box is used to manage subprojects within a project.

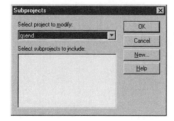

Build Set Default Configuration   The Default Project Configuration dialog box, shown in Figure 2.36, sets which of your configurations (typically Debug and Release) is the default.

The default configuration is displayed in the Project Workspace window and is the configuration built by the Build commands.

FIG. 2.36
The Default Project Configuration dialog box sets the default configuration.

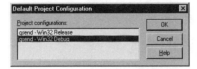

Tools

The Tools menu, shown in Figure 2.37, holds the odds-and-ends leftover commands that don't fit on any other menu.

FIG. 2.37
The Tools menu has a variety of commands that don't belong anywhere else.

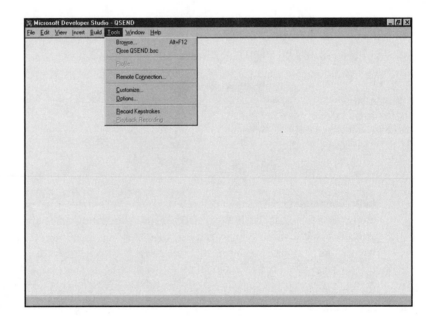

The Tools menu commands are:

- Browse
- Close Browse Info File
- Profile
- Remote Connection
- Customize
- Options
- Record Keystrokes
- Playback Recording

Tools Browse (Alt+F12)   The browser is a very powerful addition to Developer Studio; you use it whenever you go to a definition or reference, check a call graph, or otherwise explore the relationships among the classes, functions, and variables in your project. However, it's unusual to access the browser through this menu item, which brings up the Browse dialog box shown in Figure 2.38. You are more likely to use Edit, Go To, a Go To item from the right-click menu, or one of the 11 buttons on the Browse toolbar.

FIG. 2.38
The Browse dialog box is a less-common way to browse your objects, functions, and variables.

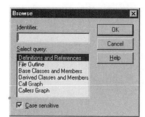

Tools Close Browse Info File   Whenever you rebuild your project, your browse file is rebuilt, too. If you rebuild your project outside Developer Studio with a tool like NMAKE, you should close the browse file first, using the menu choice, so that it can be updated.

Tools Profile   Profilers in general are tools designed to help you find the proverbial 20% of the code where 80% of the execution time is spent. Profiling in general is an exercise in timing algorithms. Those algorithms where much time is consumed by the processor are candidates for algorithm optimization. Profiling is discussed in Chapter 29, "Power-User Features in Developer Studio."

Tools Remote Connection   It is possible to run a program on one computer and debug it on another. As part of that process you use this menu item to connect the two computers. This is discussed in Chapter 20, "Debugging."

Tools Customize   Choosing this option brings up the Customize dialog box. The Toolbars pane of that dialog box is shown in Figure 2.39 with the File buttons showing. The nine buttons correspond to items on the File menu, and if you would like one of those items on any toolbar, simply drag it from the dialog box to the appropriate place on the toolbar and release it. The list box on the left side of the Toolbar tab lets you choose other menus, each with a collection of toolbar buttons you can drag to any toolbar.

The Tools tab lets you add programs to the Tools menu, and the Keyboard tab lets you change the keyboard shortcuts for commands, or add shortcuts for commands without them.

Tools Options   This item gathers up a great number of settings and options that relate to Developer Studio itself. For example, Figure 2.40 shows the Editor tab of the Options dialog box. If there is a feature of Developer Studio you don't like, you can almost certainly change it within this large dialog box.

Part

I

Ch

2

FIG. 2.39

The Toolbar pane of the Customize dialog box lets you build you own toolbars.

FIG. 2.40

The Editor tab of the Options dialog box is where you change editor settings.

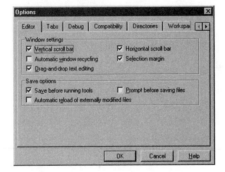

The tabs are as follows:

- *Editor*—Choose scroll bars, enable drag and drop, cover automatic saving and loading

- *Tabs*—Sets options related to tabs (inserted when you press the Tab key) and indents (inserted by the editor on new lines after language elements such as braces)

- *Debug*—Determines what information is displayed during debugging

- *Compatibility*—Lets you choose to emulate another editor (Brief or Epsilon) or just one portion of that editor's interface

- *Directories*—Sets directories in which to look for include, executable, library, and source files

- *Workspace*—Shown in Figure 2.41, sets docking windows, status bar, and project reloading

- *Format*—Sets the color scheme, including syntax coloring, for source, InfoViewer, and other windows

- *InfoViewer*—Determines the behavior and appearance of InfoViewer

FIG. 2.41

The Workspace tab of the Options dialog box sets which views dock and which float as well as reload options.

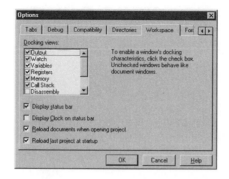

 If you are working on the same project all the time, check the Reload Last Project At Startup box on the Workspace tab of the Option dialog box. Then loading the Developer Studio and the last project is a one step process; simply loading the Developer Studio will load the last project too. If you work on a variety of different projects, uncheck this box so that Developer Studio comes up more quickly.

Tools Record Keystrokes (Ctrl+Q)   Choose this menu item to record a sequence of keystrokes you want to enter into the file with focus a number of times. A small toolbar appears with Stop and Pause buttons.

Tools Playback Recording (Ctrl+Shift+Q)   Choose this menu item to play the keystrokes recorded with Tools, Record Keystrokes. Keystrokes can only be played into the file they were recorded for.

Window

The Window menu, shown in Figure 2.42, controls the windows in the main working area of Developer Studio.

The Window, Hide menu is a personal favorite for manging the well of information presented to the developer in the Developer Studio. The Window menu items in their entirety are:

- New Window
- Split
- Hide
- Cascade
- Tile Horizontally
- Tile Vertically
- Close All
- Open Windows (1,2,3...)
- Windows

FIG. 2.42

The Window menu controls the windows in the main working area.

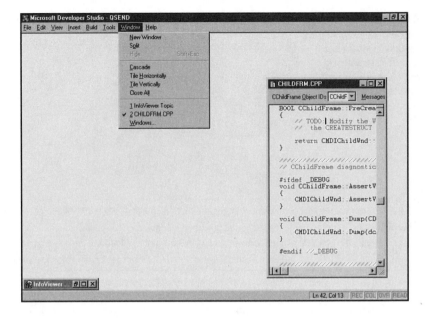

Window New Window   Choosing this item opens another window containing the same source file as the window with focus. The first window's title bar is changed, with :1 added after the file name; in the new window :2 is added after the file name. Changes made in one window are immediately reflected in the other. The windows can be scrolled, sized, and closed independently.

Window Split   Choosing this window puts crosshairs over the file with focus; when you click the mouse, the window is split into four panes along the lines of these crosshairs. You can drag these boundaries about in the usual way if they are not in the right place. Scrolling one pane scrolls its companion pane as well, so that the views stay in sync. To unsplit a window, drag a boundary right to the edge of the window and it disappears. Drag away both the horizontal and vertical boundaries and the window is no longer split.

Window Hide (Shift+Esc)   Enabled only when the Project Workspace, output, or other docked window has focus; this option hides the window.

Window Cascade   This item arranges all the windows in the main working area in the familiar cascade pattern, like the one shown in Figure 2.43. Minimized windows are not restored and cascaded.

Window Tile Horizontally   This item arranges all the windows in the main working area so that each is the full width of the working area, as shown in Figure 2.44. The file that had focus when you chose this item is at the top.

FIG. 2.43
Arranging windows in a cascade makes it easy to switch between them.

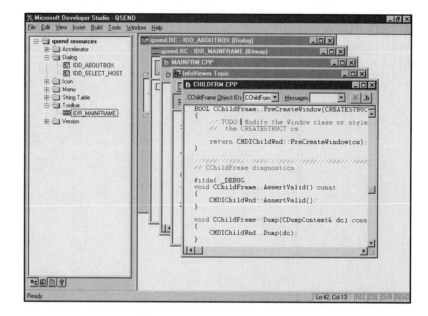

FIG. 2.44
When windows are tiled horizontally, each is the full width of the main working area.

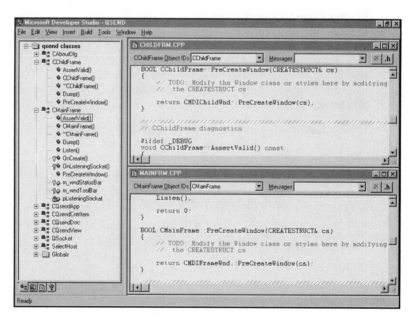

Window Tile Vertically   This item arranges all the windows in the main working area so that each is the full height of the working area, as shown in Figure 2.45. The file that had focus when you chose this item is at the left.

FIG. 2.45

When windows are tiled vertically, each is the full height of the main working area.

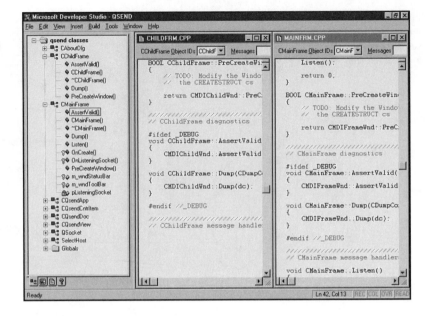

Window Close All   Choosing this item closes all the windows in the main working area. If you have any unsaved changes, you are asked whether to save them or not.

Open Windows   The bottom section of this menu lists the windows in the main working area so that you can move among them even when they are maximized. If there are more than nine open windows, only the first nine are listed. The rest can be reached by choosing <u>W</u>indow, <u>W</u>indows.

Window Windows   This item brings up the Windows dialog box, shown in Figure 2.46. From here you can close, save, or activate any window.

FIG. 2.46

The Windows dialog box allows access to any window in the main working area.

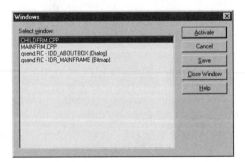

Help

There are two Help systems for Developer Studio. One is InfoViewer, the other the standard Windows Help system. Clicking Help in most dialog boxes brings up the standard Help, but choosing items on this menu activates InfoViewer. The items are as follows:

- Contents
- Search
- Keyboard
- Use Extension Help
- Define Subset
- Set Default Subsets
- Tip of the Day
- Technical Support
- Web Favorites
- About Developer Studio

Help Contents   This item opens the Project Workspace window if it is hidden, switches to the InfoViewer tab, and displays the table of contents.

Help Search   This item brings up the Search dialog box, which can be used as an index or for queries. With the Index tab, shown in Figure 2.47, you type all or part of an index term, and, as you type, the list of index terms scrolls. To open the InfoViewer topic, select a term, click List Books, then select a book from the lower list box and click Display.

FIG. 2.47

The Index tab of the Search dialog box uses the index to find InfoViewer topics.

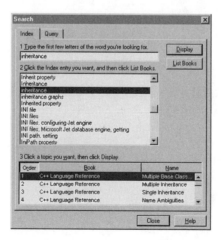

With the Query tab, shown in Figure 2.48, you enter one or more keywords, then submit the query. Results are gathered into a query results list like that shown in Figure 2.49. Double-click any topic to display it. The pushpin in the top-left corner holds this list open, or you can recall it at any time by choosing View, InfoViewer Query Results, as discussed earlier. There is a Search button on the Standard and InfoViewer toolbars.

FIG. 2.48

The Query tab of the Search dialog box is the way to submit queries that search through the entire InfoViewer text.

FIG. 2.49

The Query results list shows the topics that match your query.

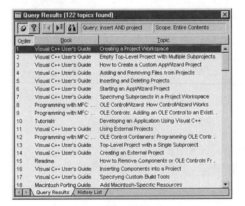

Help Keyboard   This item does not involve InfoViewer. Choosing it brings up the Help Keyboard dialog box, shown in Figure 2.50. Use the drop-down box at the top to choose the commands for which you want to see keystrokes: Bound commands (those with keystrokes assigned), All commands, or commands from the File, Edit, View, Insert, Build, Debug, Tools, Window, or Help menus. Commands related to Images and Layout are also available.

Click the title bars across the top of the table to sort the display by that column. Keystrokes cannot be changed here; choose Tools, Customize and use the Keyboard tab to change keystrokes.

Help Use Extension Help   Extension Help is when you add your own help files to Developer Studio, or use files supported by a third party. This menu item toggles its use.

FIG. 2.50

The Help Keyboard dialog box displays the keystrokes associated with commands.

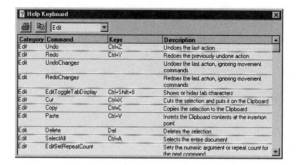

Help Define Subset   Searches through the entire InfoViewer text can be slow, and can produce too many false hits. You can restrict your use of InfoViewer to selected books within InfoViewer, called a subset. Choosing this item brings up the Define Subset dialog box, shown in Figure 2.51.

FIG. 2.51

The Define Subset dialog box is used to narrow the topics used within InfoViewer.

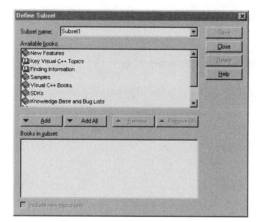

Help Set Default Subsets   Once one or more subsets of InfoViewer have been defined, choose this item to set one of them to the default used in query and index searches and the table of contents display.

Help Tip of the Day   Choosing this item brings up the Tip of the Day, like that in Figure 2.52. Some are Windows tips, others are specific to Developer Studio. If you can't wait to see a new tip each time you open Developer Studio, click Next Tip to scroll through the list. If you are annoyed by these tips on startup, uncheck the Show Tips At Startup box.

Help Technical Support   If you think you need technical support, start here. Not only do you learn how to get that support, but you may find the answer to your question.

FIG. 2.52

The Tip of the Day is a great way to learn more about Developer Studio.

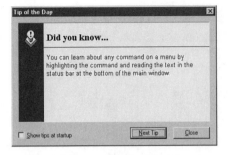

Help Web Favorites   One of the ways Microsoft supplies information about Developer Studio and other products is through the World Wide Web. Choosing this item brings up a list of Web sites as shown in Figure 2.53 (you can remove entries or add your own). When you click Go To, Internet Explorer is launched to load the site. If you do not have Internet Explorer, you can configure another Web browser after clicking Go To.

FIG. 2.53

The Web Favorites dialog box makes it easy to view World Wide Web pages relevant to Visual C++.

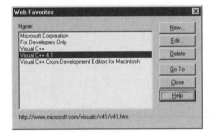

Help About Developer Studio   Choosing this item brings up the About box for Developer Studio, which includes, among other information, your Product ID.

Toolbars: One Click

After you are familiar with the sorts of actions you are likely to request of Developer Studio, the toolbars save you a lot of time. Instead of choosing File, Open, which takes two clicks and a mouse move, it is simpler to just click the Open button on the toolbar. There are, however, eight toolbars in this product, and that means a lot of little icons to learn. In this section, you will see each toolbar and which menu items the buttons correspond to.

Figure 2.54 shows all the toolbars that are available in Developer Studio and the Toolbars dialog box, which you use to set the toolbars that are displayed. You can turn ToolTips on or off here and set whether the tips include the shortcut keys for the command. Any of these toolbars can dock against any of the four edges of the working area, as shown in Figure 2.55.

FIG. 2.54
Developer Studio has eight toolbars, shown here, floating.

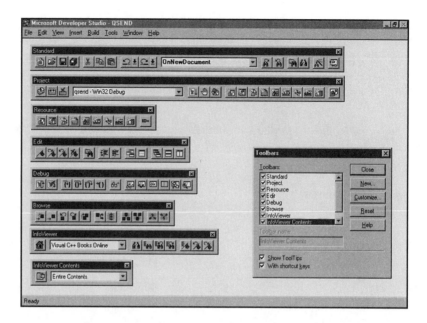

FIG. 2.55
Developer Studio toolbars can dock against any edge.

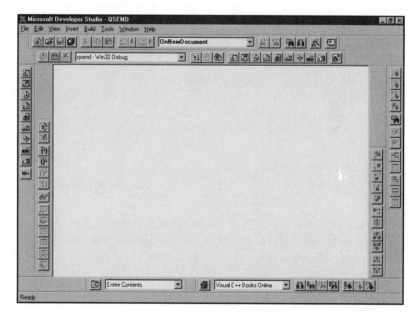

Each toolbar is discussed in turn in the sections that follow. For a full description of what each button does, refer to the section earlier in this chapter for the corresponding menu item.

Standard Toolbar   The Standard Toolbar refers to those buttons in the toolbar area on the topmost row by default. These buttons help you maintain and edit text and files in your Workspace as opposed to the Project Toolbar which contains buttons related to compiling and debugging applications. Toolbars are much easier to use since the advent of fly-by hints, or DataTips. Table 2.2 names each Standard tool button and its equivalent menu operation.

Table 2.2   Standard Toolbar Buttons and Equivalent Menu Operations from Left to Right

Button Name	Menu Equivalent
New Source File	File, New
Open	File, Open
Save	File, Save
Save All	File, Save All
Cut	Edit, Cut
Copy	Edit, Copy
Paste	Edit, Paste
Undo	Edit, Undo
Redo	Edit, Redo
Find	Edit, Find
Find Previous	Edit, Find
Find in Files	File, Find in Files
Search	Help, Search
Class Wizard	View, ClassWizard
Project Workspace	View, Project Workspace

Project Toolbar   The Project Toolbar is directly below the Standard Toolbar. The names of each of these toolbars are easily verifiable by placing the mouse cursor over the toolbar and pressing the right mouse button. The names for the Project Toolbar buttons, which are related to compiling and debugging, are defined in Table 2.3.

Table 2.3 Project Toolbar Buttons and Equivalent Menu Commands from Left to Right

Button Name	Menu Equivalent
Compile	Build, Compile
Build	Build, Build
Stop Build	Build, Stop Build
Set Default Project Configuration	Build, Set Default Project Configuration
Go	Build, Debug, Go
Insert/Remove Breakpoint	Insert/Remove Breakpoint (Speed Menu)
Remove All Breakpoints	(None)
New Dialog	Insert, Resource
New Menu	Insert, Resource
New Cursor	Insert, Resource
New Icon	Insert, Resource
New Bitmap	Insert, Resource
New Toolbar	Insert, Toolbar
New Accelerator	Insert, Resource
New String Table	Insert, Resource
New Version	Insert, Resource
Component Gallery	Insert, Component

Using Other Toolbars The default configuration displays the Standard Toolbar and the Project Toolbar. There are several other toolbars which you can open. To access these toolbars place the mouse pointer over the toolbar area and press the right mouse button.

The names of the available toolbars are Resource, Edit, Debug, Browse, InfoViewer, and InfoViewer Contents. Checked toolbar names (by default Standard and Project) indicate visible bars. Each of these toolbars is worth investigating. When you display any of the toolbars, like all toolbars there are fly-by hints which tell you the name of the action the button performs. The toolbars are each customizable and perform an action found in the menus. As an exercise experiment with the toolbars and determine for yourself how much each might facilitate your development habits.

From Here...

Chapter 2 completes our introduction to the revised Microsoft Developer Studio. Developed at Microsoft with developers in mind, this tool is highly configurable and offers a wealth of fit and finish management options.

In this chapter, you learned how to use the powerful menu features, customize toolbars, and how to find your way around the vast resources available. For more information on programming with the Microsoft Developer Studio refer to:

- Chapter 1, "Working with Developer Studio," introduces you to project flow using the Developer Studio.
- Chapter 3, "AppWizard and ClassWizard," demonstrates how Microsoft's famous wizards can move development inception along at a steady clip.
- Chapter 20, "Debugging," provides full details on debugging features and examples of how to use these tools, including sample programs.

AppWizard and ClassWizard

Visual C++ doesn't just compile code, it generates code. When you first start to build your project, AppWizard makes you a "starter app" with all the Windows boilerplates you want. Later, as you add menu items and dialog boxes, ClassWizard adds the code you need to connect those interface items to functions that handle them. Windows programming means using Windows messages, and ClassWizard makes that simple. ■

Using AppWizard to make a typical application

When most think "application" they expect an EXE file. AppWizard makes skeleton executable Windows programs in less than a minute.

Other applications AppWizard can make

Other wizards can make DLLs, ActiveX controls, console applications, libraries, makefile, Internet Server extensions and filters, and more.

If you change your mind

AppWizard can add functionality. What if you want to add functionality to an application that is built? This section shows you how.

ClassWizard and your menus

ClassWizard simplifies connecting menus to your code.

ClassWizard and your dialog boxes

Dialog boxes to gather information must also be connected to code, and ClassWizard handles most of it.

The WizardBar

Because ClassWizard is a tool you'll use often, experienced users can get to the popular parts of it without bringing up a whole dialog box.

Creating a Windows Application

AppWizard can make many different kinds of applications, but what most people want, at least at first, is an executable (.exe) program. Most people also want AppWizard to produce boiler-plate code—the classes, objects, and functions that have to be in every program. To create a program like this, Choose File, New and then choose Project Workspace from the list box in the New dialog box and click OK. This brings up the New Project Workspace dialog box shown in Figure 3.1.

FIG. 3.1
The New Project Workspace dialog box is where you choose the kind of application you want to build.

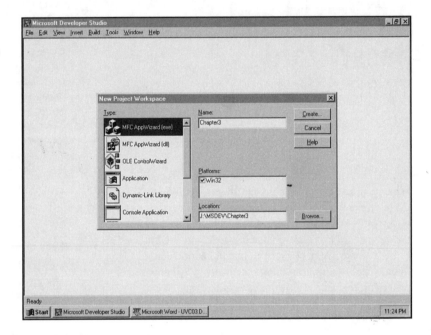

Choose MFC AppWizard (EXE) from the list box on the left, fill in a project name, and click Create. AppWizard then works through a number of steps. At each step, you make a decision about what kind of application you want, and click Next. At any time, you can click Back to return to a previous decision, Cancel to abandon the whole process, Help for more details, or Finish to skip to the end and create the application without answering any more questions (not recommended before the last step). Each step is covered in the subsections that follow.

Deciding How Many Documents the Application Supports

The first decision to communicate to AppWizard, as shown in Figure 3.2, is whether your application should be MDI, SDI, or dialog-based. AppWizard generates different code and classes for each of these application types.

FIG. 3.2

The first step in building a typical application with AppWizard is choosing the interface.

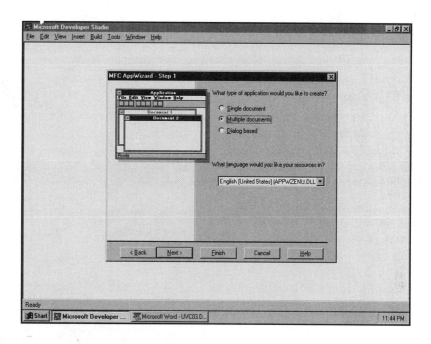

The three application types to choose among are:

- A Multiple Document Interface (MDI) application, such as Excel or Word, can open many documents (typically files) at once. There is a Window menu and a Close item on the File menu. It's a quirk of MFC that if you'd like multiple views on a single document, you must build an MDI application.

- A Single Document Interface (SDI) application, such as Notepad, has only one document open at a time. When you choose File, Open the currently open file is closed before the new one is opened.

- A dialog-based application, such as the Character Map utility that comes with Windows, does not have a document at all. There are no menus. (If you'd like to see Character Map in action, you may need to install it using Add/Remove programs under Control Panel.)

As you change the radio button selection, the picture on the left of the screen changes to remind you of what the application looks like if you choose this type of application.

N O T E Dialog-based applications are quite different from MDI or SDI applications. Many of the steps listed in the remainder of this section ask less questions or are skipped entirely for dialog-based applications, because they cannot, for example, be an OLE container or server, or access databases, because they have no menus or documents. ▧

Lower on the screen is a drop-down box to select the language for your resources. If you have set your system language to anything other than the default US English, make sure you set your resources to that language too. If you don't, you will encounter unexpected behavior from

ClassWizard later. (Of course, if your application is for users who will have their language set to US English, you might not have a choice. This is discussed in Chapter 32, "Additional Advanced Topics.") Click Next when you have made your choices.

Databases

The second step in running AppWizard to create an executable Windows program is to choose the level of database support, as shown in Figure 3.3.

FIG. 3.3

The second step of building a typical application with AppWizard is to set the database options you will use.

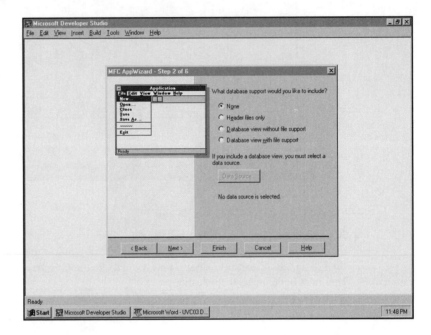

There are four choices for database support:

- If you are not writing a database application, choose None.

- If you want to have access to a database, but don't want to derive your view from CFormView or have a Record menu, choose Header Files Only.

- If you want to derive your view from CFormView and have a Record menu, but do not need to serialize a document, choose Database View Without File Support. You can update database records with Crecordset, an MFC class discussed in more detail in Chapter 14, "Database Access."

- If you want to support databases as in the previous option, but also need to serialize a document (perhaps some user options), choose Database View With File Support.

Chapter 14, "Database Access," clarifies these choices and demonstrates database programming with MFC. If you choose to have a database view, you must specify a data source now. Click the Data Source button to set this up.

As you select different radio buttons, the picture on the left changes to show you the consequences of your choice. Click Next to move to the next step.

OLE Support

The third step in running AppWizard to create an executable Windows program is to decide on the amount of OLE support you wish to include, as shown in Figure 3.4. OLE, Object Linking and Embedding, has been officially renamed ActiveX to clarify the recent technology shifts, most of which are hidden from you by MFC. The AppWizard dialog boxes still refer to it as OLE, so that is the terminology used in this chapter.

FIG. 3.4

The third step of building a typical application with AppWizard is to set the OLE options you will use.

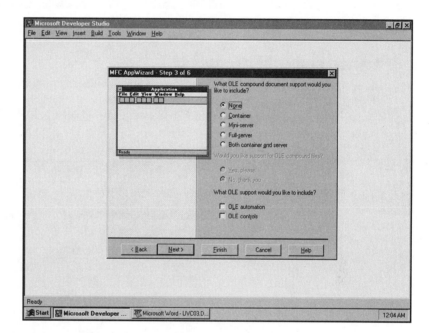

Part

I

Ch

3

There are five choices for database support:

- If you are not writing an OLE application, choose None.

- If you want your application to be able to contain embedded or linked OLE objects, such as Word documents or Excel worksheets, choose Container.

- If you want your application to serve documents that can be embedded in other applications, but do not need it to run as a stand-alone application, choose Mini Server.

- If your application will serve documents and also function as a stand-alone application, choose Full Server.

- If you want your application to be able to contain objects from other applications and also serve its objects to other applications, choose Both Container and Server.

If you choose to support OLE, you can also support compound files. Compound files contain one or more OLE objects; one of the objects can be changed without rewriting the whole file. This can save a great deal of time if you need it. Use the radio buttons in the middle of this Step 3 dialog box to say Yes, Please or No, thank you to compound files.

If you want your application to surrender control to other applications through OLE automation, check the OLE Automation checkbox. If you want your application to use OLE controls, check the OLE Controls checkbox. Click Next to move to the next step.

N O T E If you want your application to *be* an OLE control, you do not create a typical .exe application as described in this section. Creating OLE controls with OLE ControlWizard is covered in the "Creating DLLs, Console Applications, and More" section, later in this chapter. ■

Appearance and Other Options

The fourth step in running AppWizard to create an executable Windows program, as shown in Figure 3.5, is to determine some of the interface appearance options for your application. This Step 4 dialog box contains a number of independent checkboxes; check them if you want a feature, leave them unchecked if you do not.

FIG. 3.5

The fourth step of building a typical application with AppWizard is to set some interface options.

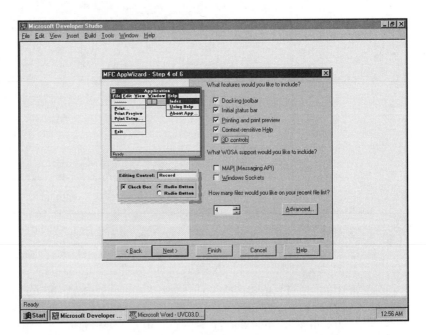

The following are the options that affect your interface appearance:

■ *Docking toolbar*—AppWizard sets up a toolbar for you. You can edit it to remove unwanted buttons, or add new ones linked to your own menu items. This is described in Chapter 18, "Interface Issues."

- *Initial status bar*—AppWizard creates a status bar to display menu prompts and messages. Later, you can write code to add indicators and other elements to this bar, as described in Chapter 18, "Interface Issues."

- *Printing and print preview*—Your application will have Print and Print Preview options on the File menu, and much of the code you need to implement printing will be generated. Chapter 19, "Printing and Print Preview," discusses the rest.

- *Context sensitive help*—Your Help menu will gain Index and Using Help options, and some of the code needed to implement Help will be provided. This decision is hard to change later. Chapter 21, "Help," describes Help implementation.

- *3D controls*—Your application will look like a typical Windows 95 application. If you do not select this option, your dialog boxes have a white background and there are no shadows around the edges of edit boxes, checkboxes, and other controls.

- *MAPI*—Your application will be able to use the Messaging API to send fax, e-mail, or other messages. Chapter 13, "Sockets, MAPI, and the Internet," discusses the Messaging API.

- *Sockets*—Your application can access the Internet directly, using protocols like ftp and http (the World Wide Web protocol). Chapter 13, "Sockets, MAPI, and the Internet," discusses Sockets. You can produce Internet programs without enabling socket support if you use the new WinInet classes, discussed in Chapter 27, "Internet Programming with the WinInet Classes."

You can also set how many files you would like to appear on the recent file list for this application. Four is the standard number; change it only if you have good reason to do so.

Clicking the Advanced button at the bottom of this Step 4 dialog box brings up the Advanced Options dialog box, which has two tabs. The Document Template Strings tab is shown in Figure 3.6. AppWizard builds many names and prompts from the name of your application, and sometimes it needs to abbreviate your application name. While it can certainly be argued that Chapter3 isn't a very good application name, if that is the name, certainly Chap3 is a better abbreviation for it than Chapte, which AppWizard suggests as the default. Until you are familiar with the names AppWizard builds, you should check them on this Document Template Strings dialog box and adjust them if necessary. You can also change the main frame caption, which appears in the title bar of your application. The file extension, if you choose one, will be incorporated into file names saved by your application and will restrict the files initially displayed when the user chooses File, Open.

The Window Styles tab is shown in Figure 3.7. Here you can change the appearance of your application quite dramatically. The first checkbox, Use Split Window, adds all the code needed to implement splitter windows like those in the code editor of Developer Studio. The remainder of the Window Styles dialog box sets the appearance of your *main frame* and, for an MDI application, of your *MDI child frames*. Frames hold windows; the system menu, title bar, minimize and maximize boxes, and window edges are all frame properties. The main frame holds your entire application. An MDI application has a number of MDI child frames, one for each document window, inside the main frame.

Part

I

Ch

3

FIG. 3.6

The Document Template Strings tab of the Advanced Options dialog box lets you adjust the way names are abbreviated.

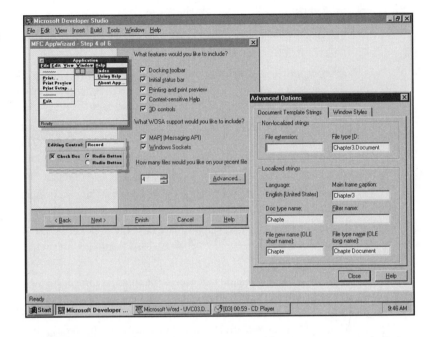

FIG. 3.7

The Window Styles tab of the Advanced Options dialog box lets you adjust the appearance of your windows.

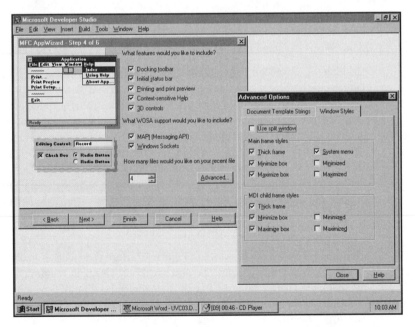

The following are the properties you can set for frames:

- *Thick frame*—The frame has a visibly thick edge, and can be resized in the usual Windows way. Uncheck this to prevent resizing.

- *Minimize box*—The frame has a Minimize box in the top-right corner.
- *Maximize box*—The frame has a Maximize box in the top-right corner.
- *System menu*—The frame has a system menu in the top-left corner.
- *Minimized*—The frame is minimized when the application starts. For SDI applications, this option will be ignored when the application is running under Windows 95.
- *Maximized*—The frame is maximized when the application starts. For SDI applications, this option will be ignored when the application is running under Windows 95.

When you made your selections, click Close to return to Step 4 and Next to move on to the next step.

Other Options

The fifth step in running AppWizard to create an executable Windows program, shown in Figure 3.8, asks the leftover questions that are not related to menus, OLE, database access, or appearance. Do you want comments inserted in your code? You certainly do. That one is easy.

Part

I

Ch

3

FIG. 3.8
The fifth step of building a typical application with AppWizard is to decide about comments and the MFC library.

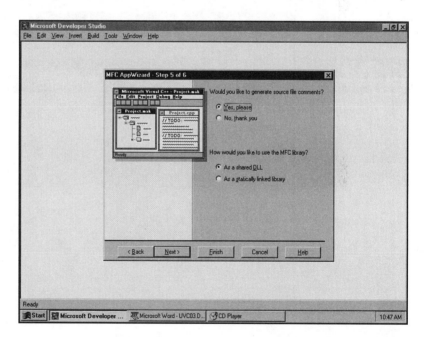

The next question is not so straightforward. Do you want the MFC library as a shared DLL, or statically linked? A DLL is a collection of functions used by many different applications. Using a DLL makes your programs smaller, but makes the installation a little more complex. Have you ever moved an executable only to find it won't run any more because it's missing DLLs? If you statically link the MFC library into your application, it is larger but it is easier to move and copy around.

If your users are likely to be developers themselves, to own at least one other application that uses the MFC DLL, or aren't intimidated by needing to install DLLs as well as the program itself, choose the shared DLL option. The smaller executable is convenient for all of you. If your users are not developers, choose the statically linked option. It reduces the technical support issues you have to face with inexperienced users. If you write a good install program, you can feel more confident about using shared DLLs.

File and Class Names

The final step in running AppWizard to create an executable Windows program is to confirm the class names and the filenames that AppWizard creates for you, as shown in Figure 3.9. You should not need to change these names unless you know your application will be used in an environment that only supports short file names. If your application includes a view class, you can change the class it inherits from; the default is CView but many developers prefer to use another view, such as CScrollView or CEditView. The eight view classes are discussed in Chapter 6, "The Document/View Paradigm." Click Finish when this Step 6 dialog box is complete.

FIG. 3.9
The final step of building a typical application with AppWizard is to confirm file names and class names.

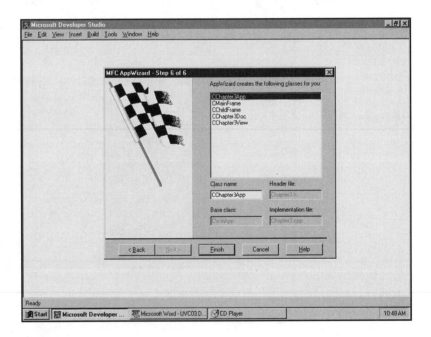

Creating the Application

After you click Finish, AppWizard shows you what is going to be created in a dialog box, like that shown in Figure 3.10. If anything here is wrong, click Cancel and then work your way back through AppWizard with the Back buttons until you reach the dialog box you need to change.

Move forward with Next, Finish, review this dialog box again, and then click OK to actually create the application. This takes a few minutes, which is hardly surprising since hundreds of lines of code, menus, dialog boxes, help text, and bitmaps are being generated for you in as many as 20 files. Let it work.

FIG. 3.10
When AppWizard is ready to build your application, you get one more chance to confirm everything.

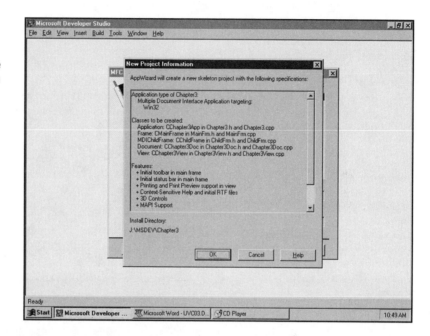

Part
I
Ch
3

If you want, you can build and run this application. Choose Build, Build and then, when it finishes, choose Build, Execute. You then have a real, working Windows application. It has an icon, it can be resized, it has menus you can bring up (and some of them even work—for example, File, Exit closes the application), it has a toolbar and a status bar—in short, it has all the things that every Windows application has. All that remains is for you to add the things that make it unique.

Creating DLLs, Console Applications, and More

Although most people use AppWizard to create an executable program, it can make many other kinds of projects. You choose File, New and then Project workspace as discussed at the start of the "Creating a Windows Application" section, but choose a different wizard from the list on the left of the New Project Workspace dialog box, shown in Figure 3.1. The following are some of the other projects AppWizard can create:

- MFC AppWizard (DLL)
- OLE Control Wizard
- Application

- Dynamic-Link Library
- Console Application
- Static Library
- Makefile
- Custom AppWizard
- ISAPI Extension Wizar

MFC AppWizard (DLL)

If you want to collect a number of functions into a DLL, and these functions use MFC classes, choose this wizard. AppWizard generates code for you to get you started. Figure 3.11 shows the only step in this process.

FIG. 3.11
AppWizard can build a DLL and generate starter code after you answer a few questions.

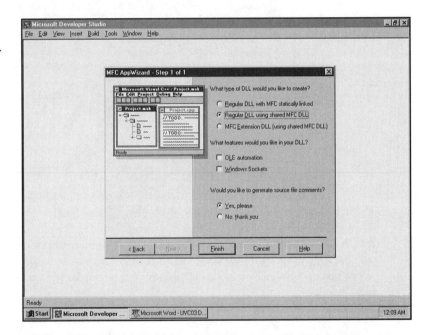

The first question you need to answer is how the MFC functions your application calls should be linked. You must select one of the three radio buttons in the top half of this Step 1 dialog box:

- Regular DLL with MFC statically linked
- Regular DLL using shared MFC DLL
- MFC Extension DLL (using shared MFC DLL)

If the applications that call your DLL are likely to be installed on systems that do not have the MFC DLL installed, you can choose to statically link the MFC DLL into yours. This makes your DLL larger, but easier to install. If you don't mind shipping multiple DLLs, or are confident the

MFC DLL is available to any application that will use your DLL, choose shared MFC DLL. If you are sure that every application that calls your DLL is an MFC application, choose MFC extension DLL for even more efficiency. C and C++ programs that do not use MFC cannot use your DLL if you choose this option.

The second question concerns extra features your DLL may use—OLE automation, discussed in Chapter 25, "ActiveX Automation," and sockets, discussed in Chapter 13, "Sockets, MAPI, and the Internet." The final question is, "Do you want comments?" Of course, you want comments to be generated for you that explain what code has been generated and what work remains to be done. Who wouldn't?

AppWizard shows you what it is going to do and then creates nine files for you to build into a DLL. Like the typical application discussed earlier in this chapter, your DLL doesn't actually do anything, but it's ready for you to build on.

OLE Control Wizard

An OLE control, commonly called an OCX, is a control you write that can be included in dialog boxes and forms. After Visual C++ 4.2 was released, Microsoft renamed the technology ActiveX, but the AppWizard dialog boxes still call them OLE controls, so that's the terminology used in this chapter. These controls are a 32-bit replacement for the VBX controls many developers have been using to achieve intuitive interfaces or to save reinventing the wheel on every project. Figure 3.12 shows the first step in creating an OCX with AppWizard, reached from the New Project Workspace dialog box by choosing OLE Control Wizard from the list on the left, filling in a project name and folder, and clicking Create.

Part

I

Ch

3

FIG. 3.12

The first step in building an OLE Control with AppWizard is to decide what files are to be incorporated.

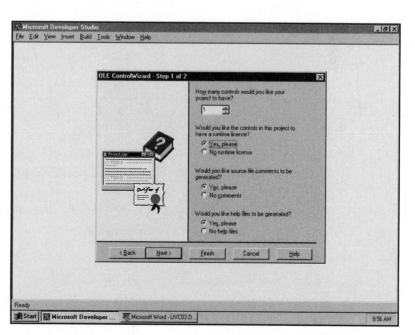

The meaning of these questions, and what you do after the starter control is built, are discussed in more detail in Chapter 26, "Building an ActiveX Control." The first question, how many controls you want, is simple: most people build their controls one to a project. Runtime licensing prevents a user who buys an application with your control in it from incorporating the control into other applications. You want comments, of course. And if your control is complex enough to need documentation, you arrange that here too. As usual, the picture on the left changes to show what you have chosen. When it's right, click Next.

Clicking Next on the Step 1 dialog box brings you to Step 2, shown in Figure 3.13. Here you set the behavior of your control.

FIG. 3.13
The second step in building a DLL is to set up the control's behavior.

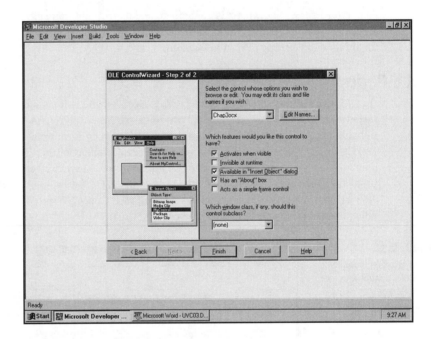

The following are the checkboxes on this Step 2 dialog box:

- *Activates when visible*:—The control asks the container to activate it after displaying it.

- *Invisible at runtime*—The control asks the container not to display it (for controls that do not need to display their data to the user).

- *Available in Insert Object dialog*—The name of the control is included in the list of objects available to users who choose Insert, Object.

- *Has an About box*—The control has an About Box that is displayed whenever its AboutBox method is called.

- *Acts as a simple frame control*—The control can contain other controls.

- *Which window class to subclass*—The control can be based on a common control such as a button or an edit box.

Click Finish and AppWizard summarizes your choices for you just as it does when creating other types of applications. Click OK and a do-nothing starter control is created for you, with roughly the same number of files as a full-blown executable application.

Application

There are times when you want to create an application in Visual C++ that does not use MFC and does not start with the boilerplate code that AppWizard produces for you. To create an Application rather than an MFC AppWizard (exe) choose Application from the left-hand list in the New Project Workspace dialog box, fill in the name and folder for your project, and click Create. You are not asked any questions; AppWizard simply creates a project file for you and opens it. You have to create all your code from scratch and insert the files into the project.

Dynamic Link Library

If you plan to build a DLL that does not use MFC and does not need any boilerplate, choose this option rather than MFC AppWizard (DLL). Again, you get an empty project created right away with no questions.

Console Application

A console application looks very much like a DOS application, though it runs in a resizable window. It has a strictly character-based interface with cursor keys rather than mouse movement. You use the Console API and character-based I/O functions like `printf()` and `scanf()` to interact with the user. As with the previous two application types, no boilerplate is generated, just an empty project.

Static Library

While most code you reuse is gathered into a DLL, you may prefer to use a static library, since that means you do not have to distribute the DLL with your application. Choose this wizard from the left-hand list in the New Project Workspace dialog box to create a project file into which you can add object files to be linked into a static library, which is then linked into your applications.

Makefile

If you want to create a project that is used with a different "make" utility than Developer Studio, choose this wizard from the left-hand list in the New Project Workspace dialog box. No code is generated. If you don't know what a make utility is, don't worry: This wizard is for those who prefer to use a stand-alone tool to replace one portion of Developer Studio.

Custom AppWizard

Perhaps you work in a large programming shop that builds a lot of applications. Although AppWizard saves a lot of time, your programmers may spend a day or two at the start of each project pasting in your own boilerplate, material that is the same in every one of your projects.

You may find it well worth your time to build a Custom AppWizard, a wizard of your very own that puts your boilerplate in as well as the standard MFC material. Once you have done this, your application type is added to the list box on the left of the New Project Workspace dialog box shown in Figure 3.1. Creating and using Custom AppWizards is discussed in Chapter 29, "Power-User Features in Developer Studio."

ISAPI Extension Wizard

ISAPI stands for Internet Server API, and refers to functions you can call to interact with a running copy of Microsoft Internet Information Server, a World Wide Web server program that serves out Web pages in response to client requests. You can use this API to write DLLs that can be used by programs that go far beyond browsing the Web to automating information retrieval. This process is discussed in Chapter 13, "Sockets, MAPI, and the Internet."

Changing Your AppWizard Decisions

Running AppWizard is a one-time thing. Assuming you are making a typical application, you choose File, New, Project Workspace, go through the six steps, create the application starter files and then never touch AppWizard again. But what if you choose, for example, not to have online Help, and then later realize you should have included it?

AppWizard, despite the name, is not really magic. It pastes in bits and pieces of code you need, and you can paste in those very same bits yourself. Here's how to find out what you need to paste in.

First, create a project with the same options you used in creating this project, and don't add any code to it. Second, in a different folder create a project with the same name, and all settings the same except the one thing you want to change (context sensitive Help in this example). Now, compare the files using WinDiff, which comes with Visual C++. Now you know what bits and pieces you need to add to your full-of-code project to implement the feature you forgot to ask AppWizard for.

Some developers, if they discover their mistake soon enough, find it quicker to create a new project with the desired features and then paste their own functions and resources from the partially-built project into the new empty one. It's only a matter of taste, but after you've gone through either process for changing your mind, I assure you that you will move a little more slowly through those AppWizard dialog boxes.

Making Menus Work with ClassWizard

Once your application is built, you are finished with AppWizard but you are likely to spend a great deal of time with ClassWizard. It handles a number of tasks that Windows programmers need to perform repeatedly, from something as simple as creating a new class to catching Windows messages or incorporating ActiveX technology into your application. In this section, you will learn more about one of the first tasks a new programmer approaches with

ClassWizard: connecting the menus in your application to code. Adding a menu item to an application is discussed, with examples, in Chapter 17, "Building Menus and Dialogs." This section gives a brief overview to help you understand what ClassWizard does.

The first step, not shown here, is to edit your menu resource to include the new menu item. Part of this process gives the menu item a name, a resource ID. It's a convention that the resource ID for a menu item is built from the name of the menu and the item. For example, when a user chooses Edit Copy, the resource ID involved is ID_EDIT_COPY. If you add a Foo menu with a Mumble item on it, the resource ID is ID_FOO_MUMBLE. As discussed in Chapter 5, "Messages and Commands," when the user chooses a menu item or clicks a toolbar button, a Windows command is sent with this resource ID as a parameter. Your next step is to arrange for your program to "catch" this command. You make those arrangements with ClassWizard.

Figure 3.14 shows the ClassWizard Message Maps tab for an application called Qsend, and its application class called CQSendApp. To see this dialog box yourself, open a project and choose View, ClassWizard then click the Message Maps tab. The details on your dialog box will be slightly different for a different application. The list box on the left lists messages and commands that this application class might catch, including ID_APP_ABOUT, the ID associated with the menu item Help About. (This resource ID is a rare exception to the naming convention discussed above.) The list box on the left lists the messages that might carry this resource ID; the COMMAND message is sent when the menu item is chosen. The list across the bottom of the dialog box lists the functions that have already been added to this class and what commands and messages they are associated with, as well as virtual functions in this derived class. OnAppAbout is highlighted because it is connected to the two highlighted choices in the upper list boxes. When a COMMAND message is sent with the resource ID ID_APP_ABOUT, the function CQSendApp::OnAppAbout() is called.

Part

I

Ch

3

FIG. 3.14

The Message Maps tab of the ClassWizard dialog box is used to connect menu items to code.

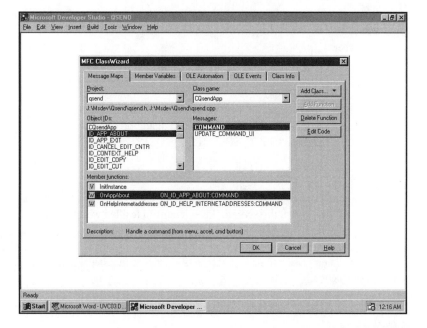

Message maps are probably the feature that sets Visual C++ and MFC apart from other approaches to Windows programming. They make it conceptually simple to arrange for one of your functions to be called when a user chooses a menu item. You will use ClassWizard over and over again as you add menu items or change the code in the functions that are connected to those menu items.

Making Dialog Boxes Work with ClassWizard

Just as ClassWizard can simplify the connection of menus to code, it can make implementing a dialog box a much simpler task as well. This procedure is covered in detail in Chapter 17, "Building Menus and Dialogs," and this section provides an illustration of the way that ClassWizard reduces your workload.

When you add a dialog box to your application, you need to do three things. First, you build the dialog box in the Resource View. Then, you build a C++ class to represent the dialog box in memory, with member variables that correspond to controls on the dialog box. Then, whenever your program wants to display the dialog box, it declares an object that is an instance of the class, sets the member variables, and displays the dialog box on-screen by calling a member function of the object.

ClassWizard makes this easier than it could be. After you build the new dialog box, you bring up ClassWizard while still looking at the dialog in Resource View, and ClassWizard offers to build a class for the dialog, as shown in Figure 3.15. Creating the class is as simple as filling in the Create New Class dialog shown in Figure 3.16.

FIG. 3.15

ClassWizard realizes you have just built a dialog, and offers to create a class to be associated with it.

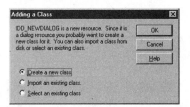

Once the class is created, you connect controls to member variables of that class with the Member Variable tab of the ClassWizard dialog box, shown in Figure 3.17. The edit control with the resource ID IDC_SELECTED_HOST is connected to the member variable m_selected_host of the class SelectHost. The two buttons on this dialog, with resource IDs ID_OK and ID_CANCEL, are not connected to member variables.

The connection between IDC_SELECTED_HOST works in two directions. Just before the dialog is shown on the screen, the edit control is filled with the value in m_selected_host. That makes it easy for you to put defaults onto a dialog box. After the user clicks OK, the value from the edit control is put into the member variable for your code to use. All of this, including creating a dialog class and using a dialog is discussed in more detail in Chapter 17, "Building Menus and Dialogs."

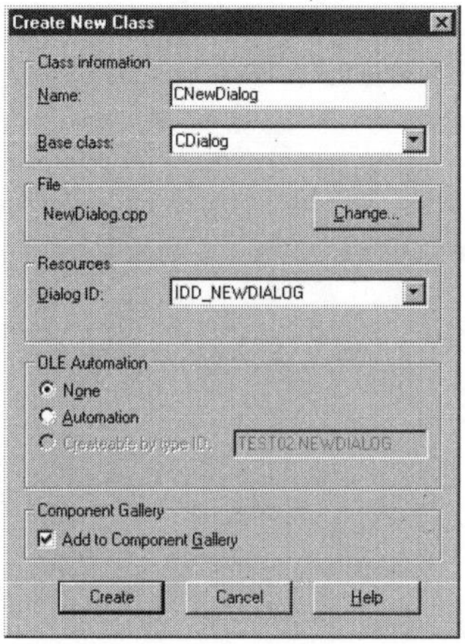

FIG. 3.16
Creating a class, with the source in one file and the header in another, inheriting from an MFC class like CDialog, is easy to arrange with ClassWizard.

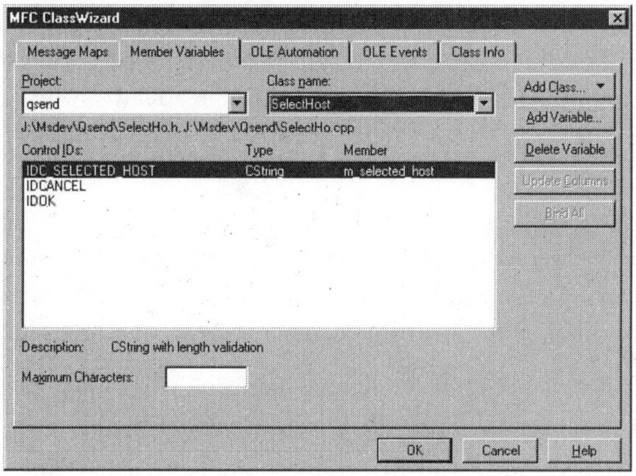

FIG. 3.17
The Member Variables tab of the ClassWizard dialog box is used to connect dialog box controls to member variables in the dialog class.

Perhaps you can imagine the structure of your application now; when the user chooses a menu item or clicks a toolbar button to tell your program to do something, one of your functions is called. That function typically initializes and displays a dialog box, then does something with the values that the user entered in the dialog box. You set up both parts of this with ClassWizard.

Dealing with Messages from the Wizard Bar

Because ClassWizard is such a useful tool, Visual C++ features a Wizard Bar for the editor window of every source file, like the one shown in Figure 3.18. The drop-down box that contains ID_APP_ABOUT is equivalent to the left list box in Figure 3.14, and the drop-down box that contains COMMAND is equivalent to the right list box in Figure 3.14. The Wizard bar scrolls the source window to CQsendApp::OnAppAbout and highlights it when this combination is selected from the drop-down boxes.

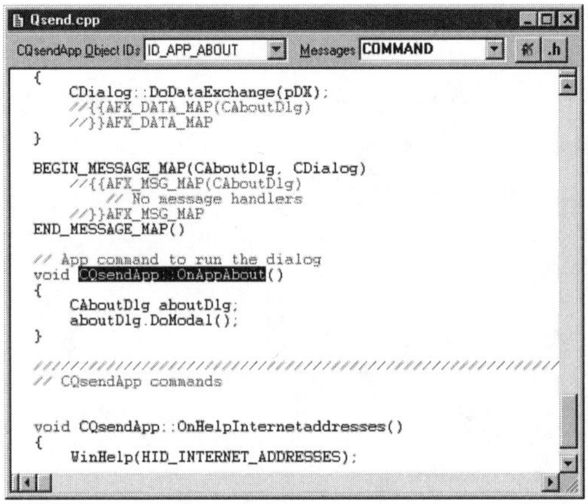

FIG. 3.18

The Wizard bar presents the same information as ClassWizard's Message Maps tab.

```
Qsend.cpp                                                    _ □ ×
CQsendApp Object IDs ID_APP_ABOUT    ▼   Messages COMMAND    ▼   ℜ .h
{
    CDialog::DoDataExchange(pDX);
    //{{AFX_DATA_MAP(CAboutDlg)
    //}}AFX_DATA_MAP
}

BEGIN_MESSAGE_MAP(CAboutDlg, CDialog)
    //{{AFX_MSG_MAP(CAboutDlg)
        // No message handlers
    //}}AFX_MSG_MAP
END_MESSAGE_MAP()

// App command to run the dialog
void CQsendApp::OnAppAbout()
{
    CAboutDlg aboutDlg;
    aboutDlg.DoModal();
}

/////////////////////////////////////////////////////////////////
// CQsendApp commands

void CQsendApp::OnHelpInternetaddresses()
{
    WinHelp(HID_INTERNET_ADDRESSES);
```

The Wizard bar is primarily used to see what function handles a message, but if you choose a message that is not handled, you are given a chance to add a function to handle it. That makes the Wizard bar a compact replacement for the Message Maps tab of ClassWizard. Most new users need a little experience with the larger dialog box before switching to the Wizard bar.

From Here...

This chapter explains the two biggest non-compiler portions of Developer Studio and Visual C++: AppWizard and ClassWizard. You will see a lot of more of these two tools and what they do throughout this book. For more information on these, check out the following chapters:

- Chapter 5, "Messages and Commands," explains Windows messages, Windows commands, and the use of the ClassWizard Message Maps tab.

- Chapter 7, "Dialog and Controls," and Chapter 8, "Win95 Common Controls," explain dialog boxes and how to create, display, and work with them.

- Chapter 9, "Property Pages and Sheets and Wizards" covers the special dialog boxes called property pages.

- Chapter 16, "Choosing an Application Type and Building an Empty Shell," presents example AppWizard sessions and discusses the code that is generated.

- Chapter 17, "Building Menus and Dialogs," works through examples of using ClassWizard for menus and dialogs.

- Part IV, "ActiveX Applications and ActiveX Custom Controls," (Chapters 22 through 26) cover the OLE Automation and OLE Events tabs of ClassWizard, used to add ActiveX (formerly called OLE) technology to your application.

- Chapter 27, "Internet Programming with the WinInet Classes," presents an example of a dialog-based application with no menus or document. It also demonstrates Internet programming without Sockets support.

- Chapter 29, "Power-User Features in Developer Studio," covers building and using a custom AppWizard.
- Chapter 32, "Additional Advanced Topics," covers building a DLL, and sending your own messages and commands.

There's one more part of Developer Studio and Visual C++ for you to meet: MFC, the Microsoft Foundation Classes. These 216 C++ classes make your life as a programmer much, much easier. You'll get to know them starting in the very next chapter.

Part

I

Ch

3

The MFC Library

4 Overview: What's in an Application? 99

5 Messages and Commands 113

6 The Document/View Paradigm 129

7 Dialog and Controls 149

8 Win95 Common Controls 173

9 Property Pages and Sheets and Wizards 209

10 Utility and Collection Classes 229

11 Drawing on the Screen 255

12 Persistence and File I/O 277

13 Sockets, MAPI, and the Internet 295

14 Database Access 311

15 MFC Macros and Globals 341

CHAPTER 4

Overview: What's in an Application?

The Microsoft Foundation Classes were written for one single purpose: To make Windows programming easier by providing classes with methods and data that handle tasks common to all Windows programs. The classes that are in MFC are designed to be useful to a Windows programmer specifically. The methods within each class perform tasks that Windows programmers often need to perform. Many of the classes have a close correspondence to structures and "windows classes" in the old Windows sense of the word class. Many of the methods correspond closely to API (Application Programming Interface) functions that are already familiar to Windows programmers. ■

Windows programming review

A brief review of Windows programming in C for those who haven't done it recently.

C++ language review

Classes, objects, member functions and variables, inheritance and encapsulation are presented quickly for those who may have forgotten their definitions.

API functions: what they are and why you should care

The useful functions provided to Windows C programmers are still used by C++ programmers, but they are wrapped up inside MFC classes that call the API functions for you.

The MFC classes arranged by category

An overview of the remainder of this part and the chapters that discuss various categories of MFC classes.

Programming for Windows

If you've programmed for Windows in C, you know that the word class was used to describe the definition of a window long before C++ programming came to Windows. A windows class is vital to any Windows C program. A standard structure holds the data that describes this windows class, and a number of standard windows classes are provided by the operating system. A programmer usually builds a new windows class for each program and registers it by calling an an API function, RegisterClass(). Windows that appear on the screen can then be created, based on that class, by calling another API function, CreateWindow().

A C-Style Windows Class

The WNDCLASS structure, which describes the windows class, is equivalent to the WNDCLASSA structure, which looks like this:

Listing 4.1 WNDCLASSA Structure from WINUSER.H

```
typedef struct tagWNDCLASSA {
    UINT        style;
    WNDPROC     lpfnWndProc;
    int         cbClsExtra;
    int         cbWndExtra;
    HINSTANCE   hInstance;
    HICON       hIcon;
    HCURSOR     hCursor;
    HBRUSH      hbrBackground;
    LPCSTR      lpszMenuName;
    LPCSTR      lpszClassName;
} WNDCLASSA, *PWNDCLASSA, NEAR *NPWNDCLASSA, FAR *LPWNDCLASSA;
```

WINUSER.H sets up two very similar windows class structures, WNDCLASSA for programs that use normal strings, and WNDCLASSW for Unicode progams. Unicode programs are covered in Chapter 32, "Additional Advanced Topics," in the "Unicode" section.

 TIP WINUSER.H is code supplied with Developer Studio. It's typically in the folder \MSDEV\include.

If you were creating a Windows program in C, you would need to fill a WNDCLASS structure. The members of the WNDCLASS structure are:

- style—A number made by combining standard styles, represented with constants like CS_GLOBALCLASS or CS_OWNDC, with the bitwise OR operator (|). A perfectly good class can be registered with a style value of 0; the other styles are for exceptions to normal procedure.

- lpfnWndProc—A pointer to a function that is the Windows Procedure (generally called the WindProc) for the class. This function is discussed in Chapter 5, "Messages and Commands."

- cbClsExtra—How many extra bytes to add to the windows class. Usually 0, but C programmers would sometimes build a windows class with extra data in it.

- cbWndExtra—How many extra bytes to add to each instance of the window. Usually 0.

- hInstance—A handle to an instance of an application, the running program that is registering this windows class. For now, just think of this as a way that the windows class can reach the application that uses it.

- hIcon—An icon to be drawn when the window is minimized. Typically this is set with a call to another API function, LoadIcon().

- hCursor—The cursor to be displayed when the mouse is over the screen window associated with this windows class. Typically this is set with a call to the API function LoadCursor().

- hbrBackground—The brush to be used for painting the background of the window. The API called GetStockObject() is the usual way to set this variable.

- lpszMenuName—A long pointer to a string that is zero terminated and contains the name of the menu for the windows class.

- lpszClassName—The name for this windows class, to be used by CreateWindow(), when a window (an instance of the windows class) is created. You would make a name up.

Window Creation

Part
II

Ch

4

If you've never written a Windows program before, you might be quite intimidated by having to fill out a structure like that. But this is the first step in Windows programming in C. However you can always find simple sample programs to copy, like this one:

```
WNDCLASS wcInit;

wcInit.style = 0;
wcInit.lpfnWndProc = (WNDPROC)MainWndProc;
wcInit.cbClsExtra = 0;
wcInit.cbWndExtra = 0;
wcInit.hInstance = hInstance;
wcInit.hIcon = LoadIcon (hInstance, MAKEINTRESOURCE(ID_ICON));
wcInit.hCursor = LoadCursor (NULL, IDC_ARROW);
wcInit.hbrBackground = GetStockObject (WHITE_BRUSH);
wcInit.lpszMenuName = "DEMO";
wcInit.lpszClassName ="NewWClass";

return (RegisterClass (&wcInit));
```

Hungarian Notation

What kind of variable name is lpszClassName? Why is it wcInit and not just Init? Because Microsoft programmers use a variable naming convention called Hungarian Notation. It is so named because it was popularized at Microsoft by a Hungarian programmer called Charles Simonyi, and probably because, at first glance, the variable names seem to be written in another language.

continues

continued

In Hungarian Notation, the variable is given a descriptive name like `Count` or `ClassName` that start with a capital letter. If it is a multi-word name, each word is capitalized. Then, before the descriptive name, letters are added to indicate the type of the variable— for example, `nCount` for an integer, or `bFlag` for a Boolean (True or False) variable. In this way the programmer should never forget a variable type, or do something foolish like passing a signed variable to a function that is expecting an unsigned value.

The style has gained widespread popularity, though some people hate it. If you long for the good old days of arguing where to put the brace brackets, or better still whether to call them brace, face, or squiggle brackets, but can't find anyone to rehash those old wars any more, you can probably find somebody to argue about Hungarian Notation instead. The arguments in favor boil down to "you catch yourself making stupid mistakes" and the arguments against to "it's ugly and hard to read." But the practical truth is that the structures used by the API and the classes defined in MFC all use Hungarian Notation, so you might as well get used to it. You'll probably find yourself doing it for your own variables too. The prefixes are:

Prefix	Variable Type	Comment
a	Array	
b	Boolean	
d	Double	
h	Handle	
i	Integer	"index into"
l	Long	
lp	Long pointer to	
lpfn	Long pointer to function	
m_	Member variable	C++ convention
n	Integer	"number of"
p	Pointer to	
s	String	
sz	Zero terminated string	
u	Unsigned integer	
C	Class	C++ convention

Many people add their own type conventions to variable names; the wc in `wcInit` stands for windows class.

Filling the `wcInit` structure and calling `RegisterClass` is fairly standard stuff, registering a class called `NewWClass` with a menu called `DEMO` and a `WindProc` called `MainWndProc`. Everything else about it is ordinary to an experienced Windows C programmer. After registering the class, when those old-time Windows programmers wanted to create a window on the screen, out popped some code like this:

```
HWND hWnd;
hInst = hInstance;
hWnd = CreateWindow (
"NewWClass",
"Demo 1",
WS_OVERLAPPEDWINDOW,
CW_USEDEFAULT,
CW_USEDEFAULT,
CW_USEDEFAULT,
CW_USEDEFAULT,
NULL,
NULL,
hInstance,
NULL);

if (! hWnd)
return (FALSE);

ShowWindow (hWnd, nCmdShow);
UpdateWindow (hWnd);
```

This code calls `CreateWindow()`, then `ShowWindow()`, and `UpdateWindow()`. The parameters to the API function `CreateWindow()` are:

- `lpClassName`—A pointer to the class name that was used in the `RegisterClass()` call.

- `lpWindowName`—The window name. You make this up.

- `dwStyle`—The window style, made by combining `#define` names with the | operator. For a primary application window like this one, `WS_OVERLAPPEDWINDOW` is standard.

- `x`—The horizontal position of the window. `CW_USEDEFAULT` lets the operating system calculate sensible defaults based on the user's screen settings.

- `y`—The vertical position of the window. `CW_USEDEFAULT` lets the operating system calculate sensible defaults based on the user's screen settings.

- `nWidth`—The width of the window. `CW_USEDEFAULT` lets the operating system calculate sensible defaults based on the user's screen settings.

- `nHeight`—The height of the window. `CW_USEDEFAULT` lets the operating system calculate sensible defaults based on the user's screen settings.

- `hWndParent`—The handle of the parent or owner window. (Some windows are created by other windows, which own them.) `NULL` means there is no parent to this window.

- `hMenu`—The handle to a menu or child-window identifier, in other words a window owned by this window. `NULL` means there are no children.

- `hInstance`—The handle of application instance that is creating this window.

- `lpParam`—A pointer to any extra parameters. None are needed in this example.

`CreateWindow()` returns a window handle—everybody calls their window handles `hWnd`—and this handle is used in the rest of the standard code. If it's `NULL`, the window creation failed. If the handle returned has any non-NULL value, the creation succeeded and the handle is passed to `ShowWindow()` and `UpdateWindow()`, which together draw the actual window on the screen.

Part
II

Ch

4

Handles

A handle is more than just a pointer. Windows programs refer to resources like windows, icons, cursors, and so on with a handle. Behind the scenes there is a handle table that tracks the address of the resource as well as information about the resource type. It's called a handle because a program uses it as a way to "get hold of" a resource. Handles are typically passed around to functions that need to use resources, and returned from functions that allocate resources.

There are a number of basic types of handles: HWND for a window handle, HICON for an icon handle and so on. No matter what kind of handle is being used, remember it's a way to reach a resource so that you can use it.

Programming in C++

This book will not teach you the C++ language, or the concepts of object-oriented programming. This section will briefly recap what you should have learned elsewhere. There are a number of important concepts to draw on, but perhaps the most important is that of *objects* and *classes*.

An object is a collection of data (variables) and functions. A C structure is simply a collection of data; in a C++ object, functions are kept with the data they use and change. One example of an object might be all of the data previously kept in the WNDCLASS structure, bundled together with all of the functions that use or return a WNDCLASS structure.

A class is the abstract idea of an object; some people say it is the definition of a class of objects. CWnd is a class, a definition of what a window is and does. An actual window on the screen is represented in memory by one CWnd object, one *instance* of the class.

The variables gathered into a class are called *member variables*, *data*, or *properties*. The functions gathered into a class are called the *member functions*, or sometimes the *methods* of the class. There are two very special functions for every class which are called not by the programmer but by the operating system. The *constructor* is called whenever an instance of the class is initialized and the *destructor* is called whenever an instance of the class goes out of scope. These functions do not return a value.

One class can be defined in terms of another: this is called *inheritance* and is a great timesaver, enabling one programmer to build on the work of others. For example, you could define a class called CSpecialWnd and use the existing definition of CWnd as a starting point, adding member variables or functions to define your new class. All objects that were instances of CSpecialWnd would have all the member variables and functions of a CWnd object as well as the extra ones you defined. The class used as a starting point (CWnd in this example) is called the *base class*, and the new class is called a *derived class*. Most of the MFC classes are designed to be used as base classes so that you can extend their features.

One final concept is that of *encapsulation*. This means hiding some of the internal details of an object from the parts of the program that use the object. For example, in a class like CWnd that describes a window, the block of code that fills a WNDCLASS structure then calls

CreateWindow(), ShowWindow(), and UpdateWindow() is gathered together into one member function. The window handle, hWnd, is a member variable, used by the member function and ignored by most of the rest of your application.

Encapsulating the Windows API

API functions create and manipulate windows on the screen, handle drawing, connect programs to Help files, facilitate threading, manage memory, and much more. When these functions are encapsulated into MFC classes, your programs can accomplish these same basic Windows tasks, with less work on your part.

There are literally thousands of API functions, and it can take six months to a year to get a good handle on the API, so this book does not attempt to present a mini-tutorial on the API. In the "Programming for Windows" section earlier in this chapter, you were reminded about two API functions, RegisterClass() and CreateWindow(). These form a good illustration of what was difficult about C Windows programming with the API, and how the MFC classes make it easier.

Inside *CWnd*

CWnd is a hugely important MFC class. Roughly a third of all the MFC classes use it as a base class—classes like CDialog, CEditView, CButton, and many more. It serves as a wrapper for the old style windows class and the API functions that create and manipulate windows classes. For example, the only public member variable is m_hWnd, the member variable that stores the window handle. This variable is set by the member function CWnd::Create() and used by almost all the other member functions when they call their associated API functions.

You might think that the call to the API function CreateWindow() would be handled automatically in the CWnd constructor, CWnd::CWnd, so that when the constructor is called to initialize a CWnd object the corresponding window on the screen is created. This would save you, the programmer, a good deal of effort, because you can't forget to call a constructor. In fact, that's not what Microsoft has chosen to do. The constructor looks like this:

```
CWnd::CWnd()
{
AFX_ZERO_INIT_OBJECT(CCmdTarget);
}
```

AFX_ZERO_INIT_OBJECT is just a macro, expanded by the C++ compiler's preprocessor, that uses the C function memset to zero out every byte of every member variable in the object, like this:

```
#define AFX_ZERO_INIT_OBJECT(base_class)
➥memset(((base_class*)this)+1, 0, sizeof(*this)
➥- sizeof(class base_class));
```

The reason why Microsoft chose not to call CreateWindow() in the constructor is that constructors cannot return a value. If something goes wrong with the window creation, there are no elegant or neat ways to deal with it. Instead, the constructor does almost nothing, a step that

Part
II

Ch

4

essentially cannot fail, and the call to CreateWindow() is done from within the member function CWnd::Create(), or the closely related CWnd::CreateEx(), which looks like this:

Listing 4.2 CWnd::CreateEx() from WINCORE.CPP

```
BOOL CWnd::CreateEx(DWORD dwExStyle, LPCTSTR lpszClassName,
 LPCTSTR lpszWindowName, DWORD dwStyle,
 int x, int y, int nWidth, int nHeight,
 HWND hWndParent, HMENU nIDorHMenu, LPVOID lpParam)
{
 // allow modification of several common create parameters
 CREATESTRUCT cs;
 cs.dwExStyle = dwExStyle;
 cs.lpszClass = lpszClassName;
 cs.lpszName = lpszWindowName;
 cs.style = dwStyle;
 cs.x = x;
 cs.y = y;
 cs.cx = nWidth;
 cs.cy = nHeight;
 cs.hwndParent = hWndParent;
 cs.hMenu = nIDorHMenu;
 cs.hInstance = AfxGetInstanceHandle();
 cs.lpCreateParams = lpParam;

 if (!PreCreateWindow(cs))
 {
 PostNcDestroy();
 return FALSE;
 }

 AfxHookWindowCreate(this);
 HWND hWnd = ::CreateWindowEx(cs.dwExStyle, cs.lpszClass,
 cs.lpszName, cs.style, cs.x, cs.y, cs.cx, cs.cy,
 cs.hwndParent, cs.hMenu, cs.hInstance, cs.lpCreateParams);

#ifdef _DEBUG
 if (hWnd == NULL)
 {
 TRACE1("Warning: Window creation failed:
 ➥GetLastError returns 0x%8.8X\n",
 GetLastError());
 }
#endif

 if (!AfxUnhookWindowCreate())
 PostNcDestroy();
 // cleanup if CreateWindowEx fails too soon

 if (hWnd == NULL)
 return FALSE;
 ASSERT(hWnd == m_hWnd); // should have been set in send msg hook
 return TRUE;
}
```

WINCORE.CPP is code supplied with Developer Studio. It's typically in the folder \MSDEV\mfc\src.

This sets up a CREATESTRUCT structure very much like a WNDCLASS, and fills it with the parameters that were passed to CreateEx(). It calls PreCreateWindow, AfxHookWindowCreate(), ::CreateWindow(), and AfxUnhookWindowCreate() before checking hWnd and returning.

 The AFX prefix on many useful MFC functions dates back to the days when Microsoft's internal name for their class library was Application Framework. The :: in the call to CreateWindow identifies it as an API function, sometimes referred to as an SDK function in this context. The other functions are member functions of CWnd that set up other background boilerplates for you.

So, on the face of it, there doesn't seem to be any savings here. You declare an instance of some CWnd object, call its Create() function, and have to pass just as many parameters as you did in the old C way of doing things. What's the point? Well, CWnd is really a class from which to inherit. Things get much simpler in the derived classes. Take CButton, for example, a class that encapsulates the concept of a button on a dialog box. A button is just a tiny little window, but its behavior is constrained—for example, the user cannot resize a button. Its Create() member function looks like this:

```
BOOL CButton::Create(LPCTSTR lpszCaption, DWORD dwStyle,
 const RECT& rect, CWnd* pParentWnd, UINT nID)
{
 CWnd* pWnd = this;
 return pWnd->Create(_T("BUTTON"), lpszCaption, dwStyle, rect, pParentWnd, nID);
}
```

That's a lot less parameters! If you want a button, you create a button, and let the class hierarchy fill in the rest.

What Are All These Classes, Anyway?

There are 216 MFC classes. Why so many? What do they do? How can any normal human keep track of them and know which one to use for what? Good questions. Questions that we'll take a pretty large piece of this book to answer. The next eight chapters tackle eight natural divisions of the MFC classes, presenting the most commonly used classes. But first, let's look at some of the more important base classes.

CObject

Figure 4.1 shows a high-level overview of the inheritance tree for the 189 classes in MFC. Only 34 MFC classes do not inherit from CObject. CObject contains the basic functionality that all the MFC classes (and most of the new classes you create) will be sure to need, like persistence support, and diagnostic output. As well, classes derived from CObject can be contained in the MFC container classes, discussed in Chapter 10, "Utility and Collection Classes."

Part

II

Ch

4

FIG. 4.1
Almost all the classes in MFC inherit from CObject.

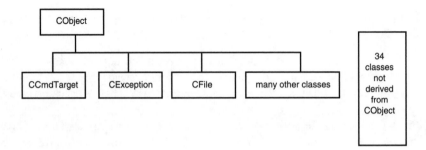

CCmdTarget

Some of the classes that inherit from CObject, like CFile and CException, and their derived classes, do not need to interact directly with the user and the operating system through messages and commands. All the classes that do need to receive messages and commands inherit from CCmdTarget. Figure 4.2 shows a bird's eye view of CCmdTarget's derived classes, generally called command targets.

FIG. 4.2
Any class that will receive a command must inherit from CCmdTarget.

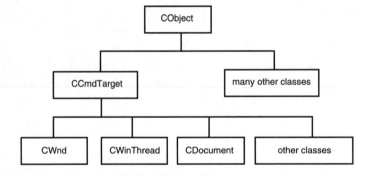

CWnd

As already mentioned, CWnd is a hugely important class. Only classes derived from CWnd can receive messages; threads and documents can receive commands but not messages.

 T I P   Chapter 5, "Messages and Commands," explores the distinction between commands and messages. Chapter 6, "The Document/View Paradigm," explains documents, and Chapter 31, "Multitasking with Windows Threads," explains threads.

CWnd provides window-oriented functionality like calls to CreateWindow and DestroyWindow, functions to handle painting the window in the screen, processing messages, talking to the Clipboard, and much more—almost 250 member functions in all. Only a handful of these will need to be overridden in derived classes. Figure 4.3 shows the classes that inherit from CWnd; there are so many control classes that to list them all would clutter up the diagram, so they are lumped together as control classes.

FIG. 4.3
Any class that will receive a message must inherit from *CWnd*, which provides lots of window-related functions.

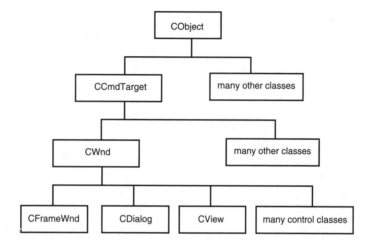

All Those Other Classes

So you've seen 10 classes so far on these three figures. What about the other 206? You'll meet them in context, some in the next eight chapters, some later than that. The following sections list a quick rundown of what's to come.

Messages and Commands   Messages form the heart of Windows programming. Whenever anything happens on a Windows machine, such as a user clicking the mouse or pressing a key, a message is triggered and sent to one or more windows, which do something about it. Visual C++ makes it easy for you to write code that catches these messages and acts on them. Chapter 5, "Messages and Commands," explains the concept of messages and how MFC and other aspects of Visual C++ lets you deal with them.

The Document/View Paradigm   A paradigm is a model, a way of looking at things. The designers of MFC chose to design the framework using the assumption that every program has something it wants to save in a file. That collection of information is referred to as the document. A view is one way of looking at a document. There are a lot of advantages to separating the view and the document, and they are explained further in Chapter 6, "The Document/View Paradigm." MFC provides classes from which to inherit your document class and your view class, so common programming tasks like implementing scroll bars are no longer your problem.

Classes for Controls and Dialogs   What Windows program doesn't have a dialog box? An edit box? A button? Dialog boxes and controls are vital to Windows user interfaces, and all of them, even the simple button or piece of static text, are windows. The common controls allow you to take advantage of the learning time users have put in on other programs, and the programming time developers have put in on the operating system, to use the same File Open dialog box as everybody else, the same hierarchical tree control, and so on. Learn more about all these controls in Chapter 7, "Dialog and Controls."

Utility and Collection Classes   Some of the most useful MFC classes don't have anything to do with windows, or drawing on the screen, or interacting with a user at all. They are just useful, the sorts of classes you would find in any C++ class library for any operating system. MFC includes a string class, a time and date class, and a number of classes for dealing with collections (arrays, linked lists, and lookup tables) of other objects. These useful classes are covered in Chapter 10, "Utility and Collection Classes."

Drawing on the Screen   No matter how smart your Windows program is, if you can't tell the user what's going on by putting some words or pictures onto the screen, no one knows what the program has done. A remarkably large amount of the work is done automatically by your view classes (one of the advantages of adopting the document/view paradigm) but there will be times you have to do the drawing yourself. You learn about device contexts, scrolling, and more in Chapter 11, "Drawing on the Screen."

Persistence and File I/O   Some good things are meant to be only temporary, like the display of a calculator or an online chat window. But most programs can save their documents to a file, and open and load that file to recreate a document that has been stored. MFC makes this remarkably easy by using archives and extending the use of the stream I/O operators >> and <<. You learn all about reading and writing to files in Chapter 12, "Persistence and File I/O."

Sockets and MAPI   Microsoft recognizes that distributed computing, in which work is shared among two or more different computers, is becoming more and more common. Programs need to talk to each other, people need to send messages across a LAN or around the world, and MFC has classes that support these kinds of communication. Sockets allow your programs to use the WinSock API as easily as the 32-bit Windows API to communicate over the Internet or other kinds of networks. MAPI concentrates on messaging, whether it's e-mail, fax, or a bulletin board system. The ISAPI extensions are used on systems that host World Wide Web pages. You see which class does what in Chapter 13, "Sockets, MAPI, and the Internet."

Database Access   Database programming just keeps getting easier. ODBC, Microsoft's Open DataBase Connectivity package, allows your code to call API functions that access a huge variety of database files—Oracle, dBASE, an Excel spreadsheet, a plain text file, old legacy mainframe systems using SQL, whatever! You call a standardly-named function and the API provided by the database vendor or a third party handles the translation. The DAO SDK, Data Access Objects Software Developers Kit, gives you access to the power of Jet, that database engine in Microsoft Access, Visual Basic, and Visual C++. If your program is using an Access database, you can use either ODBC or DAO, but will get better performance from DAO. For all other databases, use ODBC. The details are in Chapter 14, "Database Access."

From Here...

Windows programming in C was hard to learn: new programmers tended to copy a lot of sample code, sometime without understanding it all. The MFC classes are designed to hide the details from you and save your work. That's the whole purpose of a class library, after all: to keep you from reinventing the wheel. After reading the rest of the chapters in this part, you'll probably be ready to start building some applications. But if you count along as classes are introduced, you won't get to 216. That's because some are saved for after you've seen application development in action. If you can't wait to find out where the rest of the MFC classes are introduced, here's what's in store:

- Chapter 18, "Interface Issues," deals with toolbars, status bars, property sheets, print and print preview, the Registry, the command line, and the Clipboard.

- Part IV, "ActiveX Applications and ActiveX Custom Controls," covers ActiveX (formerly OLE) servers, containers, automation, and controls, and introduces the MFC classes that help you create them.

- Chapter 30, "Power-User C++ Features," covers exceptions, templates, and run-time type identification. You round out your collection of MFC classes in this chapter.

- Chapter 31, "Multitasking with Windows Threads," introduces you to threading and synchronization. There are plenty of helpful MFC classes to make writing multitasking programs almost as simple as ordinary programs.

Part

II

Ch

4

CHAPTER 5

Messages and Commands

If there is one thing that sets Windows programming apart from other kinds of programming, it is messages. Most DOS progams, for example, relied on watching (sometimes called polling) possible sources of input like the keyboard or the mouse to await input from them. A program that wasn't polling the mouse would not react to mouse input. In contrast, everything that happens in a Windows program is mediated by messages. A message is a way for the operating system to tell an application that something has happened—for example, the user has typed, clicked, or moved the mouse, or the printer has become available. A window (and every screen element is a window) can also send a message to another window, and typically most windows react to messages by passing a slightly different message along to another window. MFC has made it much easier to deal with messages, but you must understand what is going on under the surface. ▪

Message routing

Windows messages direct your program to do the things it does.

Message loops

In Windows C programming, developers wrote loops to deal with a steady stream of messages.

Message maps

MFC lightens your conceptual load by letting you catch messages without writing a message loop.

How ClassWizard helps you catch messages

Message map entries are easier to add with ClassWizard.

What messages Windows can generate

There are nearly 900 Windows messages.

Messages vs commands

A command can be routed to parts of your function that can't actually receive messages.

The command update mechanism

Some menus have items that are grayed unless conditions are met.

How Class Wizard helps you catch and update commands

Understanding command updates is tough, but arranging for them is simple with ClassWizard.

Message Routing

Messages are all referred to by their names, though the operating system uses integers to refer to them. An enormous list of #define statements connects names to numbers and lets Windows programmers talk about WM_PAINT or WM_SIZE or whatever message they need to talk about. (The WM stands for Window Message.) A message knows what window it is for, and can have up to two parameters. (Often several different values are packed into these parameters, but that's another story.)

Different messages are handled by different parts of the operating system or your application. For example, when the user moves the mouse over a window, the window gets a WM_MOUSEMOVE message, which it almost certainly passes to the operating system to deal with. The operating system redraws the mouse cursor at the new location. When the left button is clicked over a button, the button (which is a window) gets a WM_LBUTTONDOWN message and handles it, often generating another message to the window that contains the button, saying, in effect, "I was clicked."

MFC has allowed many programmers to completely ignore low-level messages like WM_MOUSEMOVE and WM_LBUTTONDOWN. They deal only with higher-level messages that mean things like "the third item in this list box has been selected" or "the Submit button has been clicked." All these kinds of messages move around in your code and the operating system code in the same way as the lower-level messages. The only difference is what piece of code "chooses" to handle them. MFC makes it much simpler to announce at the individual classes level which messages each class can handle. The old C way, which you will see in the next section, made those announcements at a higher level and interfered with the object-oriented approach to Windows programming, which involves hiding implementation details as much as possible inside objects.

Message Loops

The heart of any Windows program is the *message loop*, typically contained in a WinMain() routine. The WinMain() routine is, like the Main() in DOS or the main() in UNIX, the function called by the operating system when you run the program. You won't write any WinMain() routines; that sort of thing is now hidden away in the code that AppWizard generates for you. Still, it is happening, just as it is in Windows C programs. Listing 5.1 shows a typical WinMain().

Listing 5.1   Typical *WinMain()* Routine

```
int APIENTRY WinMain(HINSTANCE hInstance,
               HINSTANCE hPrevInstance,
               LPSTR lpCmdLine,
               int nCmdShow)
{

     MSG msg;
```

```
     if (! InitApplication (hInstance))
      return (FALSE);

     if (! InitInstance (hInstance, nCmdShow))
      return (FALSE);

     while (GetMessage (&msg, NULL, 0, 0)){
      TranslateMessage (&msg);
      DispatchMessage (&msg);
      }
      return (msg.wParam);
   }
```

In a Windows C program like this, InitApplication() typically calls RegisterWindow(), and InitInstance() typically calls CreateWindow(), as you saw in Chapter 4, "Overview: What's in an Application?" Then comes the message loop, the while loop that calls GetMessage(). The API function GetMessage() fills msg with a message destined for this application and almost always returns True, so this loop runs over and over until the program is finished. The only thing that makes GetMessage() return False is if the message it gets is WM_QUIT.

TranslateMessage() is an API function that streamlines dealing with keyboard messages. Most of the time, you don't need to know "the A key just went down," "the A key just went up," and so on. It's enough to know "the user pressed A." TranslateMessage() deals with that. It catches the WM_KEYDOWN and WM_KEYUP messages, and sends, in most cases, and WM_CHAR message in their place. Of course, with MFC, most of the time you don't care that the user pressed A. The user types into an edit box or similar control, and you can get the entire string out of it later when the user has clicked OK. So don't worry too much about TranslateMessage().

The API function DispatchMessage() calls the WindProc for the window that the message is headed for. The WindProc for a Windows C function is a huge switch statement with one case for each message the programmer planned to catch, like the one in Listing 5.2.

Part

II

Ch

5

Listing 5.2 Typical *WndProc()* Routine

```
LONG APIENTRY MainWndProc (HWND hWnd, // window handle
                    UINT message, // type of message
                    UINT wParam, // additional information
                    LONG lParam) // additional information
   {

     switch (message) {
      case WM_MOUSEMOVE:
          //handle mouse movement
      break;

      case WM_LBUTTONDOWN:
          //handle left click
      break;
```

continues

Listing 5.2   Continued

```
        case WM_RBUTTONDOWN:
            //handle right click
        break;

        case WM_PAINT:
            //repaint the window
        break;

        case WM_DESTROY: // message: window being destroyed
        PostQuitMessage (0);
        break;

        default:
        return (DefWindowProc (hWnd, message, wParam, lParam));
        }

        return (0);
    }
```

As you can surely imagine, these WindProcs get very long in a hurry. Program maintenance can be a nightmare. MFC to the rescue!

Message Maps

Message maps are part of the MFC approach to Windows programming. Instead of writing a `WinMain()` function that sends messages to your WindProc and then writing a WindProc that checks which kind of message this is and then calls another of your functions, you just write the function that will handle the message, and add a *message map* to your class that says, in effect, "I will handle this sort of message." The framework handles whatever routing is required to get that message to you.

T I P   If you've worked in Visual Basic, you should be familiar with event procedures, which handle specific events like a mouse click. The message-handling functions you will write in C++ are equivalent to event procedures. The message map is the way that events are connected to their handlers.

Message maps come in two parts: one in the `.h` file for a class and one in the corresponding `.cpp`. Typically they are generated by wizards, although in some circumstances you will add entries yourself. Listing 5.3 shows the message map from the header file of one of the classes in a simple application called ShowString, presented in Chapter 17, "Building Menus and Dialogs."

Listing 5.3   Message Map from CHAP17\showstring.h

```
//{{AFX_MSG(CShowStringApp)
afx_msg void OnAppAbout();
```

```
              // NOTE - the ClassWizard will add and remove member functions here.
              //      DO NOT EDIT what you see in these blocks of generated code!
    //}}AFX_MSG
    DECLARE_MESSAGE_MAP()
```

This declares a function called OnAppAbout(). The specially formatted comments around the declarations help ClassWizard keep track of which messages are caught by each class. DECLARE_MESSAGE_MAP() is a macro, expanded by the C++ compiler's preprocessor, that declares some variables and functions to set up some of this magic message catching.

The message map in the source file is, as shown in Listing 5.4, quite similar:

Listing 5.4 Message Map from CHAP17\showstring.cpp

```
BEGIN_MESSAGE_MAP(CShowStringApp, CWinApp)
      //{{AFX_MSG_MAP(CShowStringApp)
      ON_COMMAND(ID_APP_ABOUT, OnAppAbout)
              // NOTE - the ClassWizard will add and remove mapping macros here.
              //      DO NOT EDIT what you see in these blocks of generated code!
      //}}AFX_MSG_MAP
      // Standard file based document commands
      ON_COMMAND(ID_FILE_NEW, CWinApp::OnFileNew)
      ON_COMMAND(ID_FILE_OPEN, CWinApp::OnFileOpen)
      // Standard print setup command
      ON_COMMAND(ID_FILE_PRINT_SETUP, CWinApp::OnFilePrintSetup)
END_MESSAGE_MAP()
```

BEGIN_MESSAGE_MAP and END_MESSAGE_MAP are macros that, like DECLARE_MESSAGE_MAP in the include file, declare some member variables and functions that the framework can use to navigate the maps of all the objects in the system. There are a number of macros used in message maps, including these:

- DECLARE_MESSAGE_MAP—Used in the include file to declare that there will be a message map in the source file.

- BEGIN MESSAGE MAP—Marks the beginning of a message map in the source file.

- END MESSAGE MAP—Marks the end of a message map in the source file.

- ON_COMMAND—Used to delegate the handling of a specific command to a member function of the class.

- ON_COMMAND_RANGE—Used to delegate the handling of a group of commands, expressed as a range of command IDs, to a single member function of the class.

- ON_CONTROL—Used to delegate the handling of a specific custom-control-notification message to a member function of the class.

- ON_CONTROL_RANGE—Used to delegate the handling of a group of custom-control-notification messages, expressed as a range of control IDs, to a single member function of the class.

Part
II

Ch
5

- ON_MESSAGE—Used to delegate the handling of a user-defined message to a member function of the class.
- ON_REGISTERED_MESSAGE—Used to delegate the handling of a registered user-defined message to a member function of the class.
- ON_UPDATE_COMMAND_UI—Used to delegate the updating for a specific command to a member function of the class.
- ON_COMMAND_UPDATE_UI_RANGE—Used to delegate the updating for a group of commands, expressed as a range of command IDs, to a single member function of the class.
- ON_NOTIFY—Used to delegate the handling of a specific control-notification message with extra data to a member function of the class.
- ON_NOTIFY_RANGE—Used to delegate the handling of a group of control-notification messages with extra data, expressed as a range of child identifiers, to a single member function of the class. The controls that send these notifications are child windows of the window that catches them.
- ON_NOTIFY_EX—Used to delegate the handling of a specific control-notification message with extra data to a member function of the class that returns TRUE or FALSE to indicate if the notification should be passed on to another object for further reaction.
- ON_NOTIFY_EX_RANGE—Used to delegate the handling of a group of control-notification messages with extra data, expressed as a range of child identifiers, to a single member function of the class that returns TRUE or FALSE to indicate if the notification should be passed on to another object for further reaction. The controls that send these notifications are child windows of the window that catches them.

In addition to these, there are about 100 macros, one for each of the more common messages, that direct a single specific message to a member function. For example, ON_CREATE delegates the WM_CREATE message to a function called OnCreate(). You cannot change the function names in these macros. Typically these macros are added to your message map by ClassWizard, as demonstrated in Chapter 17, "Building Menus and Dialogs."

The message maps presented in listings 5.3 and 5.4 are for the CShowStringApp class of the ShowString application. This class handles application-level tasks like opening a new file or displaying the About box. The entry added to the header file's message map can be read as "there is a function called OnAppAbout() that takes no parameters. The entry in the source file's map means "when an ID_APP_ABOUT message arrives, call OnAppAbout()." It shouldn't be a big surprise that the OnAppAbout() member function displays the About box for the application.

But how do message maps *really work*? Every application has an object that inherits from CWinApp, and has a member function called Run(). That function calls CWinThread::Run(), which is far longer than the simple WinMain() presented earlier, but has the same message loop at its heart: call GetMessage(), call TranslateMessage(), call DispatchMessage(). Almost every window object uses the same old-style windows class, and the same WindProc, called AfxWndProc(). The WindProc, as you've already seen, knows the handle, hWnd, of the window the message is for. MFC keeps something called a handle map, a table of window handles and pointers to objects, and the framework uses this to get a pointer to the C++ object, a `CWnd*`. Next it calls `WindowProc()`, a virtual function of that object. Buttons or views might have different `WindowProc()` implementations, but through the magic of polymorphism, the right function gets called.

N O T E   Virtual functions and polymorphism are important C++ concepts for anyone working with MFC. They only arise when you are using pointers to objects, and when the class of objects to which the pointers are pointing is derived from another class. Consider as an example a class called `CDerived` that is derived from a base class called `CBase`, with a member function called `Function()` that is declared in the base class and overridden in the derived class. There are now two functions: one has the full name `CBase::Function()` and the other is `CDerived::Function()`.

If your code has a pointer to a base object, and sets that pointer equal to the address of the derived object, it can then call the function, like this:

```
CDerived derivedobject;
CBase* basepointer;
basepointer = &derivedobject;

basepointer->Function();
```

In this case, `CBase::Function()` will be called. But there are times when that is not what you want, when you have to use a `CBase` pointer but you really want `CDerived::Function()` to be called. To indicate this, in CBase, `Function()` is declared to be *virtual*. Think of it as an instruction to the compiler to override this function if there is any way to do it.

Once `Function()` is declared to be virtual in the base class, `CBase`, the code fragment above would actually call `CDerived::Function()` as desired. That's polymorphism, and that shows up again and again in using MFC classes. You use a pointer to a window, a `CWnd*`, that really points to a `CButton` or a `CView` or some other class derived from CWnd, and when a function like `WindowProc()` is called, it will be the derived function, `CButton::WindowProc()` for example, that is called. ■

`WindowProc()` calls `OnWndMsg()`, the C++ function that really handles messages. First, it checks to see if this is a message, a command, or a notification. Assuming it's a message, it looks in the message map for the class, using the member variables and functions that were set up by `DECLARE_MESSAGE_MAP`, `BEGIN_MESSAGE_MAP`, and `END_MESSAGE_MAP`. Part of what those macros arrange is to allow access to the message map entries of the base class by the functions that search the message map of the derived class. That means if a class inherits from CView, and doesn't catch a message normally caught by CView, then that message will still be caught by the same CView function as inherited by the derived class. This message map inheritance parallels the C++ inheritance but is independent of it, and saves a lot of trouble carrying virtual functions around.

Bottom line: you add a message map entry and when a message arrives, the functions called by the hidden message loop look in these tables to decide which of your objects, and which member function of the object, should handle the message. That's what's really going on behind the scenes.

The other great advantage of MFC is that the classes already catch most of the common messages and do the right thing, without any coding on your part at all. For example, you don't need to catch the message that tells you the user has chosen File, Save As—MFC classes catch it, put up the dialog box to get the new filename, handle all the behind-the-scenes work, and finally call one of your functions (which must be named `Serialize()`—App Wizard typically makes you an empty one to fill in) to actually write out the document. You only need to add message map entries for behavior that is not common to all applications.

Using ClassWizard to Catch Messages

Message maps may not be simple to read, but they are simple to create if you use ClassWizard. Figure 5.1 shows the main ClassWizard dialog box, reached by choosing View, ClassWizard or clicking the ClassWizard button on the Standard toolbar (the icon looks like a magic wand trailing stars over a class hierarchy), or by pressing Ctrl+W. ClassWizard is a tabbed dialog box, and Figure 5.1 shows the Message Map tab. At the top of the dialog box are two **drop down list** boxes, one that reminds you which project you are working on (ShowString in this case) and the other that reminds you which class owns the message map you are editing. In this case, it is the `CShowStringApp` class, whose message map you have already seen.

FIG. 5.1

ClassWizard makes catching messages simple.

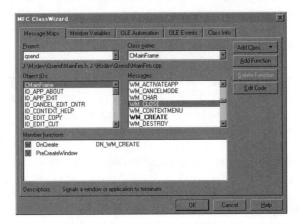

Below those single line boxes are a pair of multi-line boxes. The one on the left lists the class itself and all the commands that the user interface can generate. Commands are discussed in the "Commands" subsection of this section. With the class name highlighted, the box on the right lists all the Windows messages this class might catch. It also lists a number of virtual functions that catch common messages.

To the right of those boxes are buttons where you can add a new class to the project, add a function to the class to catch the highlighted message, remove a function that was catching a message, or open the source code for the function that catches the highlighted message. Typically, you select a class, select a message, and click Add Function to catch the message. Here's what the Add Function button sets in motion:

- Add a skeleton function to the bottom of the source file for the application
- Add an entry to the message map in the source file
- Add an entry to the message map in the include file
- Update the list of messages and member functions in the dialog box

After you add a function, clicking Edit Code makes it simple to start filling in the behavior of that function. If you prefer, double-click the function name in the Member Functions list box.

Below the Object IDs and Messages boxes is a list of the member functions of this class that are related to messages. This class has two such functions:

- OnAppAbout()—Catches the ID_APP_ABOUT command, and is labeled with a W in the list
- InitInstance()—Overrides a virtual function in CWinApp, the base class for CShowStringApp, and is labeled with a V in the list

The InitInstance function is called whenever an application first starts. You do not need to understand this function to see that ClassWizard reminds you the function has been overridden.

Finally, under the Member Functions box is a reminder of the meaning of the highlighted message. Called to implement wait cursors is a description of the DoWaitCursor virtual function.

Part

II

Ch

5

The only tricky part of message maps and message handling is deciding which class should catch the message. That's a decision you can't make until you understand all the different message and command targets that make up a typical application. The choice is usually among the following:

- The active view
- The document associated with the active view
- The frame window that holds the active view
- The application object

Views, documents, and frames are discussed in the next chapter, "The Document/View Paradigm."

List of Messages

There are almost 900 Windows messages, so you won't find a list of them all in this chapter. Usually, you arrange to catch messages with Class Wizard, and are presented with a much shorter list that is appropriate for the class you are catching messages with. Not every kind of window can receive every kind of message. For example, only classes that inherit from CListBox receive list box messages like LB_SETSEL, which directs the list box to move the highlight to a specific list item. The first component of a message name indicates the kind of window this message is destined for, or coming from. These window types are listed in Table 5.1.

Table 5.1 Windows Message Prefixes and Window Types

Prefix	Window Type
ABM, ABN	Appbar
ACM, ACN	Animation Control
BM, BN	Button
CB, CBN	Combo Box
CDM, CDN	Common Dialog
CPL	Control Panel application
DBT	Any application (device change message)
DL	Drag List Box
DM	Dialog
EM, EN	Edit box
FM, FMEVENT	File Manager
HDM, HDN	Header Control
HKM	HotKey control
IMC, IMN	IME window
LB, LBN	List Box
LVM, LVN	List View
NM	Any parent window (notification message)
PBM	Progress bar
PBT	Any application (battery power broadcast)
PSM, PSN	Property Sheet
SB	Status Bar
SBM	Scroll Bar
STM, STN	Static control
TB, TBN	Tool Bar

Prefix	Window Type
TBM	Track Bar
TCM, TCN	Tab Control
TTM, TTN	Tool Tip
TVM, TVN	Tree View
UDM	Up Down control
WM	Generic Window

What's the difference between, say, a BM message and a BN message? A BM message is a message *to* a button, such as "act as though you were just clicked." A BN message is a notification *from* a button to the window that owns it, such as "I was clicked." The same pattern holds for all the prefixes that end with M or N in the preceding table.

Sometimes the "message" prefix does not end with M; for example CB is the prefix for a message to a combo box while CBN is the prefix for a notification from a combo box to the window that owns it. For example, CB_SETCURSEL is a message to a combo box directing it to select one of its strings, while CBN_SELCHANGE is a message sent from a combo box notifying its parent that the user has changed which string is selected.

Commands

So what is a command? It is a special type of message. Windows generates a command whenever a user chooses a menu item, clicks a button, or otherwise tells the system to do something. In older versions of Windows, both menu choices and button clicks generated a WM_COMMAND message; these days you get a WM_COMMAND for a menu choice and a WM_NOTIFY for a control notification like button clicking or listbox selecting. Commands and notifications get passed around by the operating system just like any other message until they get into the top of OnWndMsg(). At that point, Windows message passing stops and MFC *command routing* starts.

Command messages all have, as their first parameter, the resource ID of the menu item that was chosen or the button that was clicked. These resource IDs are assigned according to a standard pattern—for example, the menu item File, Save has the resource ID ID_FILE_SAVE.

Command routing is the mechanism OnWndMsg() uses to send the command (or notification) to objects that can't receive messages. Only objects that inherit from CWnd can receive messages, but all objects that inherit from CCmdTarget, including CWnd and CDocument, can receive commands and notifications. (If the inheritance tree for MFC isn't uppermost in your mind, check Figure 4.2 in Chapter 4, "Overview: What's in an Application? ") That means a class that inherits from CDocument can have a message map. There won't be any entries in it for messages, only for commands and notifications, but it's still called a message map.

How on earth do the commands and notifications get to the class, though? By command routing. This gets messy, so if you don't want the inner details, skip this paragraph and the next. OnWndMsg() calls CWnd::OnCommand() or CWnd::OnNotify(). OnCommand() checks all sorts of petty stuff (like whether this menu item was grayed after the user selected it but before this piece of code started to execute) and then calls OnCmdMsg(). OnNotify() checks different conditions and then it, too, calls OnCmdMsg(). OnCmdMsg() is virtual, which means that different command targets have different implementations. The implementation for a frame window sends the command to the views and documents it contains.

That's how something that started out as a message can end up being handled by a member function of an object that is not a window, and therefore can't really catch messages.

Commands can be routed to classes that cannot catch messages.

Do you care about this? Well, a little bit. Even if you don't care how it all happens, you do care that you can arrange for the right class to handle whatever happens within your application. If the user resizes the window, a WM_SIZE message is sent, and you may have to rescale an image or do some other work inside your view. If the user chooses a menu item, a command is generated, and that means your document can handle it if that's more appropriate. You see examples of these decisions at work in the next chapter, "The Document/View Paradigm."

Command Updates

This under-the-hood tour of just how MFC connects user actions like window resizing or menu choices to your code is almost complete. All that's left is to handle the graying of menus and buttons, a process called *command updating*.

Imagine you are designing an operating system, and you know it's a good idea to have some menu items grayed to show they can't be used right now. There are two ways you can go about implementing this.

One is to have a huge table with one entry for every menu item, and a flag to indicate whether it's available or not. Whenever you have to display the menu, you can quickly check the table. Whenever the program does anything that makes the item available or unavailable, it updates the table. This is called the continuous-update approach.

The other way is not to have a table, but to check all the conditions just before your program displays the menu. This is called the update-on-demand approach and is the approach taken in Windows. In the old C way of doing things—to check whether each menu option should be grayed or not—the system sent a WM_INITMENUPOPUP message, which means "I'm about to display a menu." The giant switch in the WindProc caught that message and quickly enabled or disabled each menu item. This wasn't very object oriented, though. In an object-oriented program, different pieces of information are stored in different objects and are not generally made available to the entire program.

When it comes to updating menus, different objects "know" whether or not each item should be grayed. For example, the document knows whether or not it has been modified since it was last saved, so it can decide whether File, Save should be grayed or not; but, only the view knows whether or not some text is currently highlighted, so it can decide whether Edit, Cut and Edit, Copy should be grayed. This means that the job of updating these menus should be parceled out to various objects within the application rather than handled within the WindProc.

The MFC approach is to use a little object called a CCmdUI, a command user interface, and give this object to whomever catches a CN_UPDATE_COMMAND_UI message. You catch those messages by adding (or getting ClassWizard to add) an ON_UPDATE_COMMAND_UI macro in your message map. If you want to know what's going on behind the scenes, it's this: the operating system still sends WM_INITMENUPOPUP, then the MFC base classes like CFrameWnd take over. They make a CCmdUI, set its member variables to correspond to the first menu item, and call one of that object's own member functions, DoUpdate(). DoUpdate() in turn sends out the CN_COMMAND_UPDATE_UI message with a pointer to itself as the CCmdUI object the handlers use. Then the same CCmdUI object is reset to correspond to the second menu item, and so on, until the entire menu is ready to be displayed. The CCmdUI object is also used to gray and ungray buttons and other controls in a slightly different context. CCmdUI has these member functions:

- Enable()—Takes a True or False (defaults to True). Grays the user interface item if False; makes it available if True.
- SetCheck()—Checks or unchecks the item.
- SetRadio()—Checks or unchecks the item as part of a group of radio buttons, only one of which can be set at any time.
- SetText()—Sets the menu text or button text, if this is a button.
- DoUpdate()—Generates the message.

It's usually pretty straightforward to determine which member function you want to use. Here is a shortened version of the message map from an object called CWhoisView, a class derived from CFormView that is showing information to a user. This form view contains several edit boxes and the user may wish to paste text into one of them. The message map contains an entry to catch the update for the ID_EDIT_PASTE command, like this:

```
BEGIN_MESSAGE_MAP(CWhoisView, CFormView)
    ...
    ON_UPDATE_COMMAND_UI(ID_EDIT_PASTE, OnUpdateEditPaste)
    ...
END_MESSAGE_MAP()
```

The function that catches the update, OnUpdateEditPaste(), looks like this:

```
void CWhoisView::OnUpdateEditPaste(CCmdUI* pCmdUI)
{
 pCmdUI->Enable(::IsClipboardFormatAvailable(CF_TEXT));
}
```

This calls the API function ::IsClipboardFormatAvailable() to see if there is text in the Clipboard. Other applications may be able to paste in images or other non-text Clipboard contents, but this application cannot, and grays the menu item if there is no text available to paste.

Part
II

Ch
5

Most command update functions look just like this: they call `Enable()` with a parameter that is a call to a function that returns `True` or `False`, or perhaps a simple logical expression. Command update handlers must be fast, because 5 to 10 of them must run after the user clicks to display the menu and before the menu is actually displayed.

Using ClassWizard to Catch Commands and Command Updates

The ClassWizard dialog box shown in Figure 5.1 has the class name highlighted in the box labeled Object IDs. Below that are resource IDs of every resource (menu, toolbar, dialog box controls, and so on) that can generate a command or message when this object (view, dialog, and so on) is on the screen. If you highlight one of those, the list of messages associated with it is much smaller, as you see in Figure 5.2.

FIG. 5.2

ClassWizard allows you to catch or update commands.

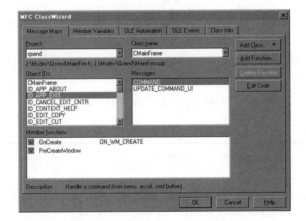

There are only two messages associated with each resource ID: COMMAND and UPDATE_COMMAND_UI. The first allows you to add a function to handle the user selecting the menu option or clicking the button—that is, to catch the command. The second allows you to add a function to set the state of the menu item, button, or other control just as the operating system is about to display it—that is, to update the command.

Clicking Add Function to add a function that catches or updates a command involves an extra step. ClassWizard gives you a chance to change the default function name, as shown in Figure 5.2. This is almost never appropriate. There is a regular pattern to the suggested names, and experienced MFC programmers come to count on function names that follow that pattern. Command handler functions, like message handlers, have names that start with On. Typically, the remainder of the function name is formed by removing the ID and the underscores from the resource ID, and capitalizing each word. Command update handlers have names that start with OnUpdate and use the same conventions for the remainder of the function name.

For example, the function that catches `ID_APP_EXIT` should be called `OnAppExit()`, and the function that updates `ID_APP_EXIT` should be called `OnUpdateAppExit()`.

FIG. 5.3
It is possible, but not wise, to change the name for your command handler or command update handler from the name suggested by ClassWizard.

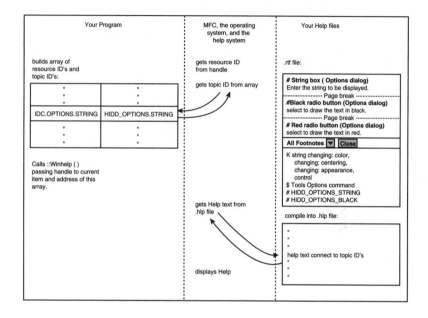

Not every command needs an update handler. The framework does some very nice work graying and ungraying for you automatically. Say you have a menu item, <u>N</u>etwork, <u>S</u>end, whose command is caught by the document. When there is no open document, this menu item is grayed by the framework, without any coding on your part. For many commands, it's enough that an object that can handle them exists, and no special updating is necessary. For others, you may want to check that something is selected or highlighted, or that no errors are present before making certain commands available. That's when you use command updating. If you'd like to see an example of command updating at work, there's one in Chapter 17, "Building Menus and Dialogs," in the "Command Updating" section.

From Here...

This chapter has provided the theory of message handling and command routing and a behind-the-scenes look at the ways MFC implements these for you. To see this theory in action, check out the following chapters:

- Chapter 6, "The Document/View Paradigm," discusses views, documents, and frames, and the way in which they interact. Issues like which class should catch certain messages are explored in more detail here.

- Chapter 11, "Drawing on the Screen," discusses what code, if any, you should write to handle messages like `WM_PAINT` and `WM_SIZE` that indicate your window needs to be redrawn.

- Chapter 12 "Persistence and File I/O," discusses the way that documents get saved and loaded in more detail, explains why you need a `Serialize()` function, and illustrates the sort of code it typically contains.

- Chapter 17, "Building Menus and Dialogs," shows how to build your own menus and dialog boxes and assign resource IDs to interface items. You see examples of ClassWizard in action, hooking interface items to code.

- Chapter 18, "Interface Issues," draws on what you have learned about menus to explain toolbars. You also see how to handle print and print preview, and use the Clipboard.

CHAPTER 6

The Document/View Paradigm

- How document objects declare their data

- How view objects access the document's data

- How to modify the document and view classes

- How to save and load a document's data

- How to edit and display a document's data

When you generate your source code with AppWizard, you get an application featuring all the bells and whistles of a commercial Windows 95 application, including a toolbar, a status bar, tool tips, menus, and even an About dialog box. However, in spite of all those features, the application really doesn't do anything useful. In order to create an application that does more than look pretty on your desktop, you've got to modify the code that AppWizard generates. This task can be easy or complex, depending upon how you want your application to look and act.

Before you can perform any modifications, however, you have to know about MFC's document/view architecture, which is a way to separate an application's data from the way the user actually views and manipulates that data. Simply, the document object is responsible for storing, loading, and saving the data, whereas the view object (which is just another type of window) enables the user to see the data on the screen and to edit that data as is appropriate to the application. In the sections that follow, you learn the basics of how MFC's document/view architecture works. ■

Understanding the Document Class

Suppose you create a basic AppWizard application named App1, after which you examine the various files generated by AppWizard. You find a class called CApp1Doc, which was derived from MFC's CDocument class. In the App1 application, CApp1Doc is the class from which the application instantiates its document object, which is responsible for holding the application's document data. It's up to you to add storage for the document by adding data members to the CApp1Doc class.

To see how this works, look at Listing 6.1, which shows the header file AppWizard creates for the CApp1Doc class.

On the CD

Listing 6.1 APP1DOC.H—The Header File for the *CApp1Doc* Class

```
// app1Doc.h : interface of the CApp1Doc class
//
/////////////////////////////////////////////////////////////////////

class CApp1Doc : public CDocument
{
protected: // create from serialization only
    CApp1Doc();
    DECLARE_DYNCREATE(CApp1Doc)

// Attributes
public:

// Operations
public:

// Overrides
    // ClassWizard generated virtual function overrides
    //{{AFX_VIRTUAL(CApp1Doc)
    public:
    virtual BOOL OnNewDocument();
    virtual void Serialize(CArchive& ar);
    //}}AFX_VIRTUAL

// Implementation
public:
    virtual ~CApp1Doc();
#ifdef _DEBUG
    virtual void AssertValid() const;
    virtual void Dump(CDumpContext& dc) const;
#endif

protected:

// Generated message map functions
protected:
```

```
    //{{AFX_MSG(CApp1Doc)
        // NOTE - the ClassWizard will add and remove member functions here.
        //    DO NOT EDIT what you see in these blocks of generated code !
    //}}AFX_MSG
    DECLARE_MESSAGE_MAP()
};

//////////////////////////////////////////////////////////////////////
```

Near the top of the listing, you can see the class declaration's Attributes section, which is followed by the `public` keyword. This is where you declare the data members that will hold your application's data. In the program that you create a little later in this chapter, the application must store an array of `CPoint` objects as the application's data. That array is declared as a member of the document class like this:

```
// Attributes
public:
    CPoint points[100];
```

Notice also in the class's header file that the `CApp1Doc` class includes two virtual member functions called `OnNewDocument()` and `Serialize()`. MFC calls the `OnNewDocument()` function whenever the user selects the File, New command (or its toolbar equivalent, if a New button exists). You can use this function to perform whatever initialization must be performed on your document's data. The `Serialize()` member function is where the document class loads and saves its data.

Understanding the View Class

As I mentioned previously, the view class is responsible for displaying and enabling the user to modify the data stored in the document object. To do this, the view object must be able to obtain a pointer to the document object. After obtaining this pointer, the view object can access the document's data members in order to display or modify them. If you look at Listing 6.2, you can see how the view class obtains a pointer to the document object.

On the CD

Listing 6.2   APP1VIEW.H—The Header File for the *CApp1View* Class

```
// app1View.h : interface of the CApp1View class
//
//////////////////////////////////////////////////////////////////////

class CApp1View : public CView
{
protected: // create from serialization only
    CApp1View();
    DECLARE_DYNCREATE(CApp1View)
```

continues

Part
II

Ch
6

Listing 6.2   Continued

```
// Attributes
public:
    CApp1Doc* GetDocument();

// Operations
public:

// Overrides
    // ClassWizard generated virtual function overrides
    //{{AFX_VIRTUAL(CApp1View)
    public:
    virtual void OnDraw(CDC* pDC);   // overridden to draw this view
    virtual BOOL PreCreateWindow(CREATESTRUCT& cs);
    protected:
    virtual BOOL OnPreparePrinting(CPrintInfo* pInfo);
    virtual void OnBeginPrinting(CDC* pDC, CPrintInfo* pInfo);
    virtual void OnEndPrinting(CDC* pDC, CPrintInfo* pInfo);
    //}}AFX_VIRTUAL

// Implementation
public:
    virtual ~CApp1View();
#ifdef _DEBUG
    virtual void AssertValid() const;
    virtual void Dump(CDumpContext& dc) const;
#endif

protected:

// Generated message map functions
protected:
    //{{AFX_MSG(CApp1View)
        // NOTE - the ClassWizard will add and remove member functions here.
        //    DO NOT EDIT what you see in these blocks of generated code !
    //}}AFX_MSG
    DECLARE_MESSAGE_MAP()
};

#ifndef _DEBUG  // debug version in app1View.cpp
inline CApp1Doc* CApp1View::GetDocument()
    { return (CApp1Doc*)m_pDocument; }
#endif
```

//

Near the top of the listing, you can see the class's public attributes, where it declares the GetDocument() function as returning a pointer to a CApp1Doc object. Anywhere in the view class that you need to access the document's data, you can call GetDocument() to obtain a pointer to the document. For example, to add a CPoint object to the aforementioned array of CPoint objects stored as the document's data, you might use the following line:

```
GetDocument()->m_points[x] = point;
```

You could, of course, do this a little differently by storing the pointer returned by GetDocument() in a local pointer variable, and then using that pointer variable to access the document's data, like this:

```
pDoc = GetDocument();
pDoc->m_points[x] = point;
```

The second version is more convenient when you need to use the document pointer in several places in the function, or if using the less clear GetDocument()->variable version makes the code hard to understand.

Notice that the view class, like the document class, also overrides a number of virtual functions from its base class. As you'll soon see, the OnDraw() function, which is the most important of these virtual functions, is where you paint your window's display. As for the other functions, MFC calls PreCreateWindow() before the window element (that is, the actual Windows window) is created and attached to the MFC window class, giving you a chance to modify the window's attributes (such as size and position). Finally, the OnPreparePrinting() function enables you to modify the Print dialog box before it's displayed to the user; the OnBeginPrinting() function gives you a chance to create GDI objects like pens and brushes that you need to handle the print job; and OnEndPrinting() is where you can destroy any objects you may have created in OnBeginPrinting().

N O T E When you first start using an application framework like MFC, it's easy to get confused about the difference between an object instantiated from an MFC class and the Windows element it represents. For example, when you create an MFC frame-window object, you're actually creating two things: The MFC object that contains functions and data, and a Windows window that you can manipulate using the functions of the MFC object. The window element is associated with the MFC class, but is also an entity unto itself. ▩

Creating the Rectangles Application

Now that you've had an introduction to documents and views, a little hands-on experience should help you better understand how these classes work. In the steps that follow, you build the Rectangles application, which demonstrates the manipulation of documents and views. Follow the first steps to create the basic Rectangles application and modify its resources:

N O T E The complete source code and executable file for the Rectangles application can be found in the CHAP06\RECS directory of this book's CD-ROM. ▩

1. Use AppWizard to create the basic files for the Rectangles program, selecting the options listed in the following table. When you're done, the New Project Information dialog box appears; it should look like Figure 6.1. Click the OK button to create the project files.

Part
II

Ch
6

FIG. 6.1

Your Project Information
dialog box should look
like this.

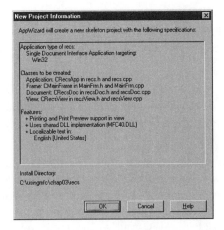

Dialog Box Name	Options to Select
New Project	Name the project recs, and set the project path to the directory into which you want to store the project's files. Leave the other options set to their defaults.
Step 1Select	Single Document.
Step 2 of 6	Leave set to defaults.
Step 3 of 6	Leave set to defaults.
Step 4 of 6	Turn off all application features except Printing and Print Preview.
Step 5 of 6	Leave set to defaults.
Step 6 of 6	Leave set to defaults.

2. Select the ResourceView tab in the project workspace window. Visual C++ displays the ResourceView window, as shown in Figure 6.2.

3. In the ResourceView window, click the plus sign next to recs resources to display the application's resources. Click the plus sign next to Menu, and then double-click the IDR_MAINFRAME menu ID. Visual C++'s menu editor appears.

4. Click the Rectangles application's Edit menu (not Visual C++'s Edit menu), and then press your keyboard's Delete key to delete the Edit menu. When you do, a dialog box asks for verification of the delete command. Click the OK button.

5. Double-click the About recs... item in the Help menu, and change it to About Rectangles. Close the menu editor.

6. Double-click the Accelerator resource in the ResourceView window. Double-click the IDR_MAINFRAME accelerator ID to bring up the accelerator editor.

7. Using your keyboard's arrow and Delete keys, delete all accelerators except ID_FILE_NEW, ID_FILE_OPEN, ID_FILE_PRINT, and ID_FILE_SAVE. Close the accelerator editor.

FIG. 6.2

The ResourceView tab displays the ResourceView window.

ResourceView tab

ResourceView window

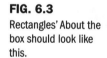

8. Double-click the Dialog resource in the ResourceView window. Double-click the `IDD_ABOUTBOX` dialog-box ID to bring up the dialog-box editor.

9. Modify the dialog box by changing the title to About Rectangles, changing the first static text string to "Rectangles, Version 1.0" and adding the static string "by Macmillan Computer Publishing," as shown in Figure 6.3. Close the dialog-box editor.

FIG. 6.3

Rectangles' About the box should look like this.

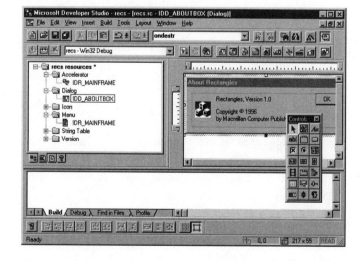

Part

II

Ch

6

10. Double-click the String Table resource in the ResourceView window. Double-click the String Table ID to bring up the string table editor.

11. Double-click the `IDR_MAINFRAME` string, and then change the first segment of the string to "Rectangles," as shown in Figure 6.4. Close the string-table editor.

FIG. 6.4

The first segment of the *IDR_MAINFRAME* string appears in your main window's title bar.

Now that you have the application's resources the way you want them, it's time to add code to the document and view classes in order to create an application that actually does something. Follow these steps to add the code that modifies the document class to handle the application's data, which is an array of CPoint objects that determine where rectangles should be drawn in the view window:

1. Click the FileView tab to display the FileView window. Then, display the project's files by clicking the plus sign next to the folder labeled "recs files," as shown in Figure 6.5.

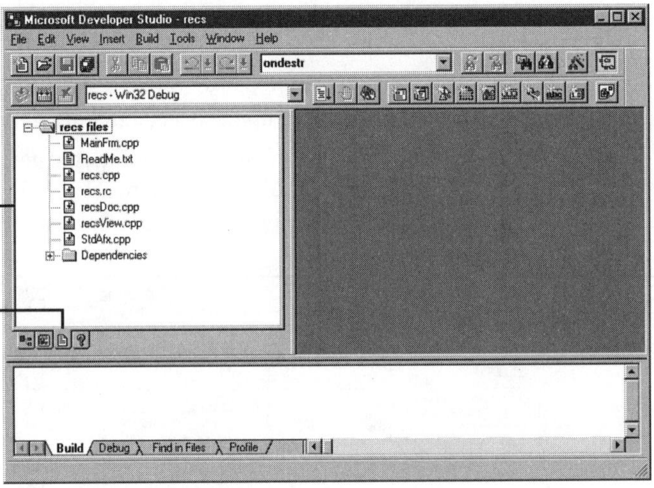

FIG. 6.5

The FileView window lists the source files that make up your project.

FileView window ⎯⎯⎯

FileView tab ⎯⎯

2. Double-click the recsDoc.cpp entry in the file list. The RECSDOC.CPP file appears in the code window. Click the Open Header button to display the class's header file.

3. Add the following lines to the CRecsDoc class's attributes section, right after the public keyword:

```
CPoint m_points[100];
UINT m_pointIndex;
```

These lines declare the document class's data members, which will store the application's data. In the case of the Rectangles application, the data in the m_points[] array represents the locations of rectangles displayed in the view window. The m_pointIndex data member holds the index of the next empty element of the array.

4. Close the RECSDOC.H file so that you can view and edit the RECSDOC.CPP file. Add the following line to the `OnNewDocument()` function, right after the (`SDI documents will reuse this document`) comment:

```
m_pointIndex = 0;
```

This line initializes the index variable each time a new document is started, ensuring that it always starts off by indexing the first element in the `m_points[]` array.

5. Add the lines shown in Listing 6.3 to the `Serialize()` function, right after the `TODO: add storing code here` comment.

Listing 6.3   LST6_3.TXT—Code for Saving the Document's Data

```
ar << m_pointIndex;

for (UINT i=0; i<m_pointIndex; ++ i)
{
    ar << m_points[i].x;
    ar << m_points[i].y;
}
```

This is the code that saves the document's data. As you can see, you have to do nothing more than use the << operator to direct the data to the archive object. You'll look at this code in more detail later in this chapter.

6. Add the lines shown in Listing 6.4 to the `Serialize()` function, right after the `TODO: add loading code here` comment.

Listing 6.4   LST6_4.TXT—Code for Loading the Document's Data

```
ar >> m_pointIndex;

for (UINT i=0; i<m_pointIndex; ++ i)
{
    ar >> m_points[i].x;
    ar >> m_points[i].y;
}

UpdateAllViews(NULL);
```

This is the code that loads the document's data. You need only use the >> operator to direct the data from the archive object into the document's data storage. You'll look at this code in more detail later in this chapter.

This finishes the modifications you must make to the document class. In the following steps, you make the appropriate changes to the view class, enabling the class to display, modify, and print the data stored in the document class:

1. Load the RECSVIEW.CPP file, and add the lines shown in Listing 6.5 to the `OnDraw()` function, right after the `TODO: add draw code for native data here` comment.

Part
II

Ch
6

Listing 6.5   LST6_5.TXT—Code for Displaying the Application's Data

```
UINT pointIndex = pDoc->m_pointIndex;

for (UINT i=0; i<pointIndex; ++i)
{
    UINT x = pDoc->m_points[i].x;
    UINT y = pDoc->m_points[i].y;
    pDC->Rectangle(x, y, x+20, y+20);
}
```

The preceding code, which iterates through the document object's m_points[] array and displays rectangles at the coordinates it finds in the array, is executed whenever the application's window needs repainting.

2. Add the following line to the very beginning of the OnPreparePrinting() function:

   pInfo->SetMaxPage(1);

   This line modifies the common Print dialog box such that the user cannot try to print more than one page.

3. Click the toolbar's ClassWizard button, or select the View, ClassWizard command from the menu bar. The ClassWizard property sheet appears.

4. Make sure that CRecsView is selected in the Class Name and Object IDs boxes. Then, double-click WM_LBUTTONDOWN in the Messages box to add the OnLButtonDown() message-response function to the class.

   The OnLButtonDown() function is now associated with Windows' WM_LBUTTONDOWN message, which means MFC will call OnLButtonDown() whenever the application receives a WM_LBUTTONDOWN message.

5. Click the Edit Code button to jump to the OnLButtonDown() function in your code. Then, add the lines shown in Listing 6.6 to the function, right after the TODO: Add your message handler code here and/or call default comment.

Listing 6.6   LST6_6.TXT—Code to Handle Left-Button Clicks

```
CRecsDoc *pDoc = GetDocument();

if (pDoc->m_pointIndex == 100)
    return;

pDoc->m_points[pDoc->m_pointIndex] = point;
++pDoc->m_pointIndex;
pDoc->SetModifiedFlag();
Invalidate();
CRecsDoc *pDoc = GetDocument();

if (pDoc->m_pointIndex == 100) // if the index is greater than the 100 rect
➥maximum leave the function
    return;
```

```
pDoc->m_points[pDoc->m_pointIndex] = point; // get the present point
 ++pDoc->m_pointIndex;   //increment the pointIndex
 pDoc->SetModifiedFlag(); //"dirty" the file, see reference below for more
➥infor about dirty files
 Invalidate(); //redraw the displayed window
```

The preceding code segment adds a point to the document's point array each time the user clicks the left mouse button over the view window. The call to Invalidate() causes MFC to call the OnDraw() function, where the window's display is redrawn with the new data.

You've now finished the complete application. Click the toolbar's Build button or select the Build, Build command from the menu bar to compile and link the application.

Running the Rectangles Application

After you have the Rectangles application compiled and linked, run it by selecting Build, Execute from the menu bar. When you do, you see the application's main window. Place your mouse pointer over the window's client area and left click. A rectangle appears. Go ahead and keep clicking. You can place up to 100 rectangles in the window (see fig. 6.6).

FIG. 6.6
You can place up to 100 rectangles in the application's window.

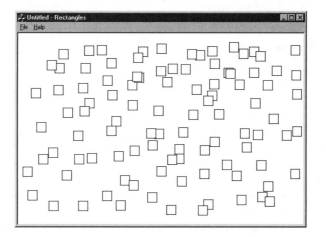

To save your work (this is work?), select the File, Save command. You can view your document in print preview by selecting the File, Print Preview command, or just go ahead and print by selecting the File, Print command. Of course, you can create a new document by selecting File, New, or load a document you previously saved by selecting File, Open. Finally, if you click Help, About Rectangles, you see the application's About dialog box.

Exploring the Rectangles Application

If you don't have much experience with AppWizard and MFC, you're probably amazed at how much you can do with a few mouse clicks and a couple of dozen lines of code. You're also

Part
II

Ch
6

probably still a little fuzzy on how the program actually works, so in the following sections, you examine the key parts of the Rectangles application.

Declaring Storage for Document Data

As you've heard already in this chapter, it is the document object in an AppWizard-generated MFC program that is responsible for maintaining the data that makes up the application's document. For a word processor, this data would be strings of text, whereas for a paint program, this data might be a bitmap. For the Rectangles application, the document's data is the coordinates of rectangles displayed in the view window.

The first step in customizing the document class, then, is to provide the storage you need for your application's data. How you do this, of course, depends on the type of data you must use. But, in every case, the variables that will hold that data should be declared as data members of the document class, as is done in the Rectangles application. Listing 6.7 shows the relevant code.

On the CD

Listing 6.7   LST6_7.TXT—Declaring the Rectangles Application's Document Data

```
// Attributes
public:

    CPoint m_points[100];
    UINT m_pointIndex;
```

In the preceding listing, the document-data variables m_points[] and m_pointIndex are declared as public members of the document class. (The m prefix indicates that the variables are members of the class, rather than global or local variables. This is a tradition that Microsoft started. You can choose to follow it or not.) The m_points[] array holds the coordinates of the rectangles displayed in the view window, and the m_pointIndex variable holds the number of the next empty element in the array. You can also think of m_pointIndex as the current rectangle count. These variables are declared as public so that the view class can access them. If you were to declare the data variables as protected or private, your compiler would whine loudly when you tried to access the variables from your view class's member functions.

The data storage for the Rectangles application is pretty trivial in nature. For a commercial-grade application, you'd almost certainly need to keep track of much more complex types of data. But the method of declaring storage for the document would be the same. You may, of course, also declare data members that you use only internally in the document class, variables that have little or nothing to do with the application's actual document data. However, you should declare such data members as protected or private.

Initializing Document Data

After you have your document's data declared, you usually need to initialize it in some way each time a new document is created. For example, in the Rectangles application, the m_pointIndex variable must be initialized to zero when a new document is started. Otherwise, m_pointIndex may contain an old value from a previous document, which could make correctly accessing the m_points[] array as tough as getting free cash from an ATM. In the Rectangles application, m_pointIndex gets initialized in the OnNewDocument() member function, as shown in Listing 6.8.

On the CD

Listing 6.8 LST6_8.TXT—The Rectangles Application's *OnNewDocument()* Function

```
BOOL CRecsDoc::OnNewDocument()
{
    if (!CDocument::OnNewDocument())
        return FALSE;

    // TODO: add reinitialization code here
    // (SDI documents will reuse this document)
    m_pointIndex = 0;

    return TRUE;
}
```

MFC calls the OnNewDocument() function whenever the user starts a new document, usually by selecting File, New. As you can see, OnNewDocument() first calls the base class's OnNewDocument(), which calls DeleteContents() and then marks the new document as clean (meaning it doesn't yet need to be saved due to changes).

What's DeleteContents()? It's another virtual member function of the CDocument class. If you want to be able to delete the contents of a document without actually destroying the document object, you can override DeleteContents() to handle this task.

Keep in mind that how you use OnNewDocument() and DeleteContents() depends on whether you're writing an SDI or MDI application. In an SDI application, the OnNewDocument() function indirectly destroys the current document by reinitializing it in preparation for new data. An SDI application, after all, can contain only a single document at a time. In an MDI application, OnNewDocument() simply creates a brand new document object, leaving the old one alone. For this reason, in an MDI application, you can perform general document initialization in the class's constructor.

Part
II

Ch
6

Serializing Document Data

If your application is going to be useful, it must be able to do more than display data; it must also be able to load and save data sets created by the user. Writing this chapter would have been a nightmare if my text disappeared every time I shut down my word processor! The act of loading and saving document data with MFC is called *serialization*. And, in spite of the complications you may have experienced with files in the past, loading and saving data with MFC is a snap, thanks to the CArchive class, an object of which is passed to the document class's Serialize() member function. Listing 6.9 shows the Rectangles application's Serialize() function.

Listing 6.9   LST6_9.TXT—The Rectangles Application's *Serialize()* Function

```
void CRecsDoc::Serialize(CArchive& ar)
{
    if (ar.IsStoring())
    {
        // TODO: add storing code here
        ar << m_pointIndex;

        for (UINT i=0; i<m_pointIndex; ++ i)
        {
            ar << m_points[i].x;
            ar << m_points[i].y;
        }
    }
    else
    {
        // TODO: add loading code here
        ar >> m_pointIndex;

        for (UINT i=0; i<m_pointIndex; ++ i)
        {
            ar >> m_points[i].x;
            ar >> m_points[i].y;
        }

        UpdateAllViews(NULL);
    }
}
```

As you can see in the listing, the Serialize() function receives a reference to a CArchive object as its single parameter. At this point, MFC has done all the file-opening work for you. All you have to do is use the CArchive object to load or save your data. How do you know which to do? MFC has already created the lines that call the CArchive object's IsStoring() member function, which returns TRUE if you need to save data and FALSE if you need to load data.

Thanks to the overloaded << and >> operators in the CArchive class, you can save and load data exactly as you're used to doing using C++ I/O objects. If you look at the Serialize() function, you may notice that about the only difference between the saving and loading of data is the operator that's used. One other difference is the call to UpdateAllViews() after loading data. UpdateAllViews() is the member function that notifies all views attached to this document that they need to redraw their data displays. When calling UpdateAllViews(), you'll almost always use NULL as the single parameter. If you should ever call UpdateAllViews() from your view class, you should send a pointer to the view as the parameter. You would only do this sort of thing, though, when using multiple views with a single document.

Displaying Document Data

Now that you've got your document class all ready to store, save, and load its data, you need to customize the view class so that it can display the document data, as well as enable the user to modify the data. In an MFC application using the document/view model, it's the view class's OnDraw() member function that is responsible for displaying data, either on the screen or the printer. Listing 6.10 shows the Rectangles application's version of OnDraw().

Listing 6.10   LST6_10.TXT—The Rectangles Application's _OnDraw()_ Function

```
void CRecsView::OnDraw(CDC* pDC)
{
    CRecsDoc* pDoc = GetDocument();
    ASSERT_VALID(pDoc);

    // TODO: add draw code for native data here
    UINT pointIndex = pDoc->m_pointIndex;

    for (UINT i=0; i<pointIndex; ++i)
    {
        UINT x = pDoc->m_points[i].x;
        UINT y = pDoc->m_points[i].y;
        pDC->Rectangle(x, y, x+20, y+20);
    }
}
```

The first thing you should notice about OnDraw() is that its single parameter is a pointer to a CDC object. A CDC object encapsulates a Windows' device context, automatically initializing the DC and providing many member functions with which you can draw your application's display. Because the OnDraw() function is responsible for updating the window's display, it's a nice convenience to have a CDC object all ready to go. (For more information on device contexts, see Chapter 11, "Drawing on the Screen.")

Also notice that, because an application that uses the document/view model stores its data in the document class, AppWizard has generously supplied the code needed to obtain a pointer to that class. In the custom code in OnDraw(), the function uses this document pointer to retrieve the value of the document's index variable (the number of rectangles currently displayed), and then uses it as a loop-control variable. The loop simply iterates through the document's m_points[] array, drawing rectangles at the coordinates contained in the CPoint objects stored in the array.

Modifying Document Data

The view object is not only responsible for displaying the application's document data; it must also (if appropriate) enable the user to edit that data. Exactly how you enable the user to edit an application's data depends a great deal upon the type of application you're building. The possibilities are endless. In the simple Rectangles application, the user can edit a document only by clicking in the view window, which adds another rectangle to the document. This happens in response to the WM_LBUTTONDOWN message, which Windows sends the application every time the user clicks the left mouse button when the mouse pointer is over the view window.

If you recall, you used ClassWizard to add the OnLButtonDown() function to the program. This is the function that MFC calls whenever the window receives a WM_LBUTTONDOWN message. It is in OnLButtonDown(), then, that the Rectangles application must modify its list of rectangles, adding the new rectangle at the window position the user clicked. Listing 6.11 shows the OnLButtonDown() function, where this data update occurs.

Listing 6.11   LST6_11.TXT—The Rectangles Application's *OnLButtonDown()* Function

```
void CRecsView::OnLButtonDown(UINT nFlags, CPoint point)
{
    // TODO: Add your message handler code here and/or call default
    CRecsDoc *pDoc = GetDocument();

    if (pDoc->m_pointIndex == 100)
        return;

    pDoc->m_points[pDoc->m_pointIndex] = point;
    ++pDoc->m_pointIndex;
    pDoc->SetModifiedFlag();
    Invalidate();

    CView::OnLButtonDown(nFlags, point);
}
```

Of the two parameters received by OnLButtonDown(), it is point that is most useful to the Rectangles application, because this CPoint object contains the coordinates at which the user just clicked. In the custom code you added to OnLButtonDown(), the function first obtains a pointer to the document object. Then, if the document object's m_pointIndex data member is equal to 100, there is no room for another rectangle. In this case, the function immediately returns, effectively ignoring the user's request to modify the document. Otherwise, the function adds the new point to the m_points[] array and increments the m_pointIndex variable.

Now that the document's data has been updated as per the user's modification, the document must be marked as "dirty" (needing saving) and the view must display the new data. A call to the document object's SetModifiedFlag() function takes care of the first task. If the user now tries to exit the program without saving the data, or tries to start a new document, MFC displays a dialog box warning the user of possible data loss. When the user saves the document's data, the document is set back to "clean." The call to Invalidate() notifies the view window that it needs repainting, which results in MFC calling the view object's OnDraw() function.

Other View Classes

Throughout this chapter, you've been using MFC's CView class for your view window. The truth is, however, that MFC offers several different view classes that are derived from CView. These additional classes provide your view window with special abilities such as scrolling and text editing. Table 6.1 lists the various view classes along with their descriptions.

Table 6.1   View Classes

Class	Description
CView	The base view class from which the specialized view classes are derived.
CScrollView	A view class that provides scrolling abilities.
CCtrlView	A base class from which view classes that implement new Windows 95 common controls (such as the ListView, TreeView, and RichEdit controls) are derived.
CEditView	A view class that provides basic text-editing features.
CRichEditView	A view class that provides more sophisticated text-editing abilities using the Windows 95 RichEdit control.
CListView	A view class that displays a Windows 95 ListView control in its window.
CTreeView	A view class that displays a Windows 95 TreeView control in its window.
CFormView	A view class that implements a form-like window using a dialog-box resource.
CRecordView	A view class that can display database records along with controls for navigating the database.
CDaoRecordView	Same as CRecordView, except used with the new DAO database classes.

To use one of these classes, you just substitute the desired class for the CView class in the application's project. When using AppWizard to generate your project, you can specify the view class you want in the wizard's Step 6 of 6 dialog box, as shown in Figure 6.7. Once you have the desired class installed as the project's view class, you can use the specific class's member functions to control the view window.

For example, when using the CScrollView class, you can call the SetScrollSizes() member function to set the view's dimensions, mapping mode, and the vertical and horizontal scroll amounts. In addition, you can retrieve the scroll position or the size of the view by calling the GetScrollPosition() or GetTotalSize() member functions, respectively. Other member functions provide additional abilities.

A CEditView object, on the other hand, gives you all the features of a Windows edit control in your view window. Using this class, you can handle various editing and printing tasks, including find-and-replace. You can retrieve or set the current printer font by calling the

Part

II

Ch

6

GetPrinterFont() or SetPrinterFont() member function or get the currently selected text by calling GetSelectedText(). Moreover, the FindText() member function locates a given text string and OnReplaceAll() replaces all occurrences of a given text string with another string.

FIG. 6.7

You can use AppWizard to select your application's base view class.

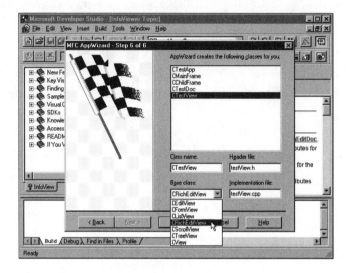

The CRichEditView class adds many features to an edit view, including paragraph formatting (such as centered, right-aligned, and bulleted text), character attributes (including underlined, bold, and italic), and the ability to set margins, fonts, and paper size. As you may have guessed, the CRichEditView class features a rich set of methods you can use to control your application's view object.

Figure 6.8 shows how the view classes fit into MFC's class hierarchy. Describing these various view classes fully is beyond the scope of this chapter. However, you can find plenty of information about them in your Visual C++ online documentation.

FIG. 6.8

The view classes all trace their ancestry back to CView.

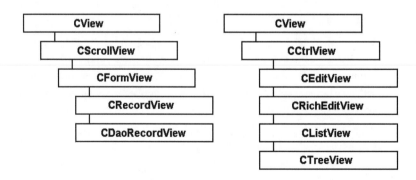

Document Templates, Views, and Frame Windows

Because you've been working with AppWizard-generated applications in this chapter, you've taken for granted a lot of what goes on in the background of an MFC document/view program. That is, much of the code that enables the frame window (your application's main window), the document, and the view window to work together is automatically generated by AppWizard and manipulated by MFC.

For example, if you look at the `InitInstance()` method of the Rectangles application's `CRecsApp` class, you'll see (among other stuff) the lines shown in Listing 6.12:

On the CD

Listing 6.12 LST6_12.TXT—Initializing an Application's Document

```
CSingleDocTemplate* pDocTemplate;
pDocTemplate = new CSingleDocTemplate(
        IDR_MAINFRAME,
        RUNTIME_CLASS(CRecsDoc),
        RUNTIME_CLASS(CMainFrame),
        RUNTIME_CLASS(CRecsView));
AddDocTemplate(pDocTemplate);
```

In Listing 6.12, you discover one of the secrets that makes the document/view system work. In that code, the program creates a document-template object. (In this case, the template is of the `CSingleDocTemplate` class.) It is the document template that links together the application's resources, document class (in this case, `CRecsDoc`), frame window (always `CMainFrame` in an AppWizard program), and the view class (in this case, `CRecsView`).

What's all that `RUNTIME_CLASS` stuff? The RUNTIME_CLASS macro enables the framework to create instances of a class at runtime, which the application object must be able to do in a program that uses the document/view architecture. In order for this macro to work, the classes that will be created dynamically must be declared and implemented as such. To do this, the class must have the `DECLARE_DYNCREATE` macro in its declaration (in the header file) and the `IMPLEMENT_DYNCREATE` macro in its implementation.

If you look at the header file for the Rectangles application's `CMainFrame` class, for example, you see the following line near the top of the class's declaration:

`DECLARE_DYNCREATE(CMainFrame)`

As you can see, the DECLARE_DYNCREATE macro requires the class's name as its single argument.

Now, if you look near the top of `CMainFrame`'s implementation file (`MAINFRM.CPP`), you see this line:

`IMPLEMENT_DYNCREATE(CMainFrame, CFrameWnd)`

The `IMPLEMENT_DYNCREATE` macro requires as arguments the name of the class and the name of the base class.

Part
II

Ch
6

If you explore the application's source code further, you'll find that the document and view classes also contain the DECLARE_DYNCREATE and IMPLEMENT_DYNCREATE macros.

After creating the document-template object, the program calls AddDocTemplate() in order to pass the object on to the application. The application then adds the document template to its list of documents. Finally, the application object uses the document template to create the document object, as well as the frame and view windows.

MFC programs support two types of document templates, one that represents SDI (single-document interface) applications, which can hold only one document at a time, and one that represents MDI (multiple-document interface) applications, which can handle multiple documents concurrently. MFC supplies two classes for these document types: CSingleDocTemplate and CMultiDocTemplate. Bet you can figure out which class goes with which document-template type!

From Here...

In this chapter, you examined how an AppWizard-generated application uses MFC to coordinate an application's document and view objects. There is, of course, a great deal more to learn about MFC before you can create your own sophisticated Windows 95 applications. If you'd like to learn more about some topics presented in this chapter, refer to the following:

- Chapter 1, "Working with Developer Studio," explains how to control your programming projects with Developer Studio.
- Chapter 3, "AppWizard and ClassWizard," shows how to use Visual C++'s wizards to create applications and classes.
- Chapter 11, "Drawing on the Screen," demonstrates how to display data in an application's window.
- Chapter 12, "Persistence and File I/O," provides the details of how to use MFC's file-handling classes.

CHAPTER 7

Dialog and Controls

When Windows and other graphically oriented user interfaces came along, programmers needed to find a new way to retrieve information from the computer user—a communication problem for the modern age. In the days of DOS, the program could simply print a prompt on-screen and direct the user to enter whatever value the program needed. With Windows, however, getting data from the user is not so simple. Because a window's client area (the area in which an application can display information) should be reserved for other purposes, a well-designed Windows application gets most user input through dialog boxes.

MFC includes several types of dialog boxes. In this chapter, you learn to use MFC to display and handle your own custom dialog boxes, which you design with Developer Studio's dialog-box editor. ■

How to create a dialog-box resource

Creating a resource is the first step toward displaying a dialog box.

How to display a dialog box

Thanks to MFC, displaying a dialog box requires a single function call.

How to write a custom dialog-box class

You can use MFC's dialog classes as the start for your custom classes.

How to extract information from a dialog box

MFC features an automatic data-transfer capability.

How to validate the contents of a dialog box's controls

Be sure the user entered the information your application is expecting.

About the different types of Windows controls

Controls enable applications to present and retrieve information.

How to associate an MFC class with a control

MFC features a special class for every type of control.

How to call control-class member functions

You can easily manipulate controls.

Understanding Dialog Boxes

As mentioned in this chapter's introduction, dialog boxes are one way a Windows application can get information from the user. Chances are that your Windows application will have several dialog boxes, each designed to retrieve a different type of information from your user. However, before you can add these dialog boxes to your program, you must create them. To make this job simpler, Developer Studio includes an excellent resource editor.

Because dialog boxes are used so extensively in Windows applications, MFC provides several classes that you can use to make dialog-box manipulation easier and more convenient. Although you can use MFC's CDialog class directly, you'll most often derive your own dialog-box class from CDialog in order to have more control over how your dialog box operates. However, MFC also provides classes for more specific types of dialog boxes, including CColorDialog, CFontDialog, and CFileDialog.

The minimum steps for adding a dialog box to your MFC application are as follows:

1. Create your dialog-box resource using Visual C++'s dialog-box editor. This process defines the appearance of the dialog box, including the types of controls it will contain.

2. Create an instance of CDialog, passing to the constructor your dialog box's resource ID and a pointer to the parent window.

3. Call the dialog-box object's DoModal() member function to display the dialog box.

Although the preceding steps are all you need to display a simple dialog box, you usually need much more control over your dialog box than these steps allow. For example, the preceding method of displaying a dialog box provides no way to retrieve data from the dialog box, which means the method is really only useful for dialog boxes that display information to the user, sort of like a glorified message box. To create a dialog box that you can control, follow this second set of steps:

1. Create your dialog-box resource using Visual C++'s dialog-box editor. This process defines the appearance of the dialog box, as well as the controls that appear in the dialog box and the types of data that the dialog box's controls will return to your program.

2. Write a dialog-box class derived from CDialog for your dialog box, including member variables for storing the dialog box's data. Initialize the member variables in the class's constructor.

3. Overload the DoDataExchange() function in your dialog-box class. In the function, call the appropriate DDX and DDV functions to perform data transfer and validation.

4. In the window class that'll display the dialog box, create member variables for the dialog-box controls whose data you want to store.

5. Create an instance of your dialog-box class.

6. Call the dialog-box object's DoModal() member function to display the dialog box.

7. When DoModal() returns, copy the dialog-box data you need to store, from the dialog-box object's member variables to the window class's matching variables.

In the rest of this chapter, you see how to perform all of the steps listed here, including how to write your dialog-box class and how to provide this class with automatic data transfer and validation. In the next section, you learn to use Developer Studio's dialog-box editor.

N O T E When you create a dialog-box class using ClassWizard, the wizard generates most of the code you need to fully control your dialog box. The following sections describe not only how to add dialog boxes to your applications without using ClassWizard, but they also describe how the code generated by ClassWizard works, should you decide to use ClassWizard. When you've finished with this chapter, you'll have a solid understanding of the dialog-box source code that AppWizard and ClassWizard generate. ■

Creating a Dialog-Box Resource

As you now know, the first step toward adding a dialog box to your MFC application is creating the dialog-box resource, which acts as a sort of template for Windows. When Windows sees the dialog-box resource in your program, it uses the commands in the resource to construct the dialog box for you. To learn how to create a dialog-box resource, just follow these steps:

1. Select the Insert, Resource command from Developer Studio's menu bar. The Insert Resource dialog box appears.

2. Double-click Dialog in the Resource Type box. The dialog-box editor appears in one of Developer Studio's panes (see fig. 7.1).

3. Select controls on the toolbox and position them on your dialog box's window, as shown in Figure 7.2.

FIG. 7.1

The dialog-box editor provides a dialog-box template and tools for modifying that template.

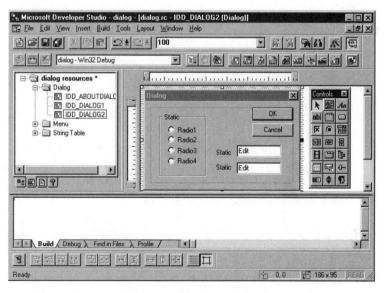

FIG. 7.2

The dialog box here shows controls placed on the dialog-box form.

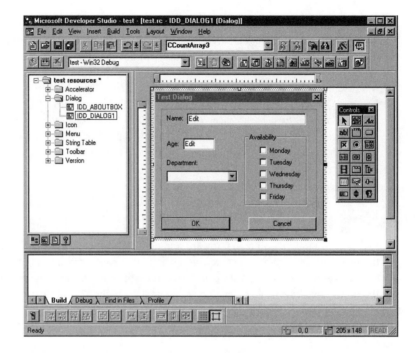

4. Double-click the controls you want to edit. The control's property sheet appears, in which you can supply your own ID, caption, and other control information.

5. Double-click the dialog box. The dialog box's property sheet, in which you can customize the dialog box's attributes, appears.

Defining Dialog-Box and Control IDs

Because dialog boxes are often unique to an application (with the exception of the common dialog boxes), you almost always create your own IDs for both the dialog box and the controls it contains. You can, if you like, accept the default IDs that the dialog-box editor creates for you. However, these IDs are generic (for example, IDD_DIALOG1, IDC_EDIT1, IDC_RADIO1, and so on), and so you may probably want to change them to something more specific. In any case, as you can tell from the default IDs, a dialog box's ID usually begins with the prefix IDD and control IDs usually begin with the prefix IDC_. You can, of course, use your own prefixes if you like, although sticking with conventions often makes your programs easier to read.

A Dialog Box's Resources

After creating a resource, Developer Studio creates or modifies at least two files that you need to add to your application. The first file is called RESOURCE.H and contains the resource IDs that you've defined. You must include RESOURCE.H in any file that refers to these IDs.

The second file Developer Studio creates or modifies has the .RC extension and is the resource script that defines all your application's resources. A resource script is like a source-code file written in a language that the resource compiler understands. The resource compiler takes the .RC file and compiles it into a .RES file, which is the binary representation of your application's resources.

When you use Developer Studio's resource editors to create your resources, you don't usually need to modify the resultant resource script directly. However, there may be times when such direct editing is convenient, so it can't hurt to learn more about how resource scripts work. Check in your favorite Windows programming manual for more information on resource scripts.

Introducing the Dialog Application

This chapter's first sample program, called Dialog, demonstrates two ways to create and display dialog boxes in your Windows applications. You can find the program, along with all its source code, in the CHAP07\DIALOG folder of this book's CD-ROM (or on your hard drive, if you installed the contents of the CD-ROM). To run the program, double-click the DIALOG.EXE file. When you do, you see the window shown in Figure 7.3.

FIG. 7.3

The Dialog application's main window displays the data collected from one of its dialog boxes.

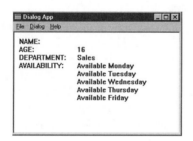

The data displayed in the window are the default values for information that can be collected by one of the program's dialog boxes. You'll take a look at that dialog box in a second, but first select the Help, About command to display the application's About dialog box. As you can see, the About dialog box only displays information to the user and does not enable the user to enter data. For this reason, the About dialog box can be created and displayed very easily in an MFC program.

To display the application's second, and much more complex, dialog box, select the Dialog, Test command. When you do this, a dialog box containing a number of controls appears. You can use these controls to enter information about an imaginary employee (see fig. 7.4). When you finish entering information, close the dialog box by clicking OK. The Dialog application's main window then displays the new information you entered into the dialog box's controls.

This second dialog box is also capable of validating its data. For example, the Name text box does not let you enter more than 30 characters. In addition, the Age text box rejects any value that doesn't fall between 16 and 100. If you enter an invalid value into the Age text box, you see a warning and are not allowed to exit the dialog box with the OK button until the value is corrected. Notice also that, if you enter new data into the dialog box and then select the Cancel button, your changes are thrown away and do not appear in the application's window.

Part

II

Ch

7

FIG. 7.4

The Test command reveals a dialog box containing several types of controls.

Exploring the Dialog Application

Now that you've had a chance to use the Dialog application, it's time to see how it works. You can find the complete listings for the Dialog application in the CHAP07 folder of this book's CD-ROM. The most pertinent source-code files for the following discussion are MAINFRM.H, MAINFRM.CPP, DLG1.H, and DLG1.CPP.

Displaying a Simple Dialog Box

Before you get too deep into learning how to create sophisticated dialog boxes, it might be nice to see how easy it can be to display simple dialog boxes that require no complex interaction with the user. A good example is the Dialog application's About dialog box, which does nothing more than display program information to the user. The hardest part of getting the About dialog box up on the screen is creating the dialog-box template with the resource editor—and that task is just a matter of positioning a few static-text controls. If you look at the `CMainFrame` class's (the frame window class's) `OnHelpAbout()` function, you see that displaying the dialog box requires only two lines of code, like this:

```
CDialog dlg(IDD_ABOUTDIALOG, this);
dlg.DoModal();
```

The first line creates a `CDialog` object that's associated with the About dialog-box template that was defined in the resource editor. The constructor's two arguments are the dialog box's resource ID and a pointer to the dialog box's parent window, which is the `CMainFrame` window. Once the dialog-box object has been constructed and associated with the template, a call to the dialog-box object's `DoModal()` member function displays the dialog box on the screen.

The `DoModal()` function handles all the user's interactions with the dialog box, which, in this case, amounts to little more than waiting for the user to click the OK button. When the user exits the dialog box, the `DoModal()` function returns and your program can continue. Because the dialog-box object is created locally on the stack, it is automatically deleted when it goes out of scope, which is when the `OnHelpAbout()` function exits. You can also create the dialog-box dynamically on the heap (that is, in the computer's unused memory), by using the `new` operator. In that case, you'd have to delete the object yourself. The following lines illustrate this technique:

```
CDialog* dlg = new CDialog(IDD_ABOUTDIALOG, this);
dlg->DoModal();
delete dlg;
```

> **N O T E** Remember that, when you need to access an object's members through a pointer to the
> object, you must use the "->" operator. On the other hand, when you want to access an
> object's members through a reference to the object, you must use the "." operator. This is exactly
> the same way you would handle a structure. In fact, a class is really nothing more than a fancy
> structure. ▨

> **N O T E** When creating your dialog box's template with the resource editor, make sure that you turn
> on the dialog box's Visible attribute, which is found in the Dialog's property sheet on the
> More Styles page. If you fail to set this style attribute, your dialog box will not appear on the screen
> properly, making the application seem to lock up. ▨

Writing a Dialog-Box Class

Displaying a simple About dialog box is all well and good. Unfortunately, most dialog boxes are much more complex, requiring that your application be able to transfer information back and forth between the program and the dialog box. Often, you may want to initialize the dialog box's controls with default values before displaying the dialog box. After the user enters information into the dialog box, you then need to extract that information so that it can be used in your program. Accomplishing this means not only creating a dialog-box template with the resource editor, but also associating that template with your own custom dialog-box class derived from MFC's `CDialog`.

The main dialog box in the Dialog application has 10 controls that the user can manipulate. These controls are the Name text box, the Age text box, the Department combo box, the five check boxes for the days of the week, and the OK and Cancel buttons. You don't have to worry about the OK and Cancel buttons, because MFC handles them for you. When you write your dialog box's class, however, you do need to provide data members for storing the information the user enters into the other controls. In the Dialog application, the `CDlg1` class, which is derived from `CDialog`, provides the needed data members as shown in Listing 7.1.

On the CD

Listing 7.1   LST7_1.TXT—Declaring Data Members for the Dialog Box's Controls

```
public:
    CString m_department;
    BOOL m_monday;
    BOOL m_tuesday;
    BOOL m_wednesday;
    BOOL m_thursday;
    BOOL m_friday;
    CString m_name;
    UINT m_age;
```

Part
II

Ch
7

Notice that these variables are declared as public data members of the class. This is important because if they were declared as private or protected, your program would not be able to access them outside of the class. (Yes, this is another case where MFC breaks the rules of strict object-oriented design, which dictates that a class's data member should never be accessed from outside the class.)

N O T E The variables you declare for your dialog box's controls must, of course, hold the appropriate type of data for the controls with which they're associated. For example, text boxes that return strings must be associated with string variables, whereas controls that return integers must be associated with integer variables. The following list shows the data types that go with each type of control: ▪

Edit box — Usually a string, but can also be other data types including `int`, `float`, and `long`

Check box — `int`

`Radio button — int`

List box — string

Combo box — string

Scroll bar — `int`

Besides the data members, your dialog-box class must supply a constructor and must override the virtual `DoDataExchange()` function, which is where the data transfer occurs. The `CDlg1` class's constructor is declared like this:

```
public:
    CDlg1(CWnd* pParent);
```

The constructor's single argument is a pointer to the dialog box's parent window. As you'll soon see, the constructor's implementation passes this pointer, as well as the dialog-box template's resource ID, on to the `CDialog` class's constructor.

The `CDlg1` class overrides the `DoDataExchange()` function like this:

```
protected:
    virtual void DoDataExchange(CDataExchange* pDX);
```

As you can see, `DoDataExchange()`'s only argument is a pointer to a `CDataExchange` object, which is responsible for handling the actual transfer of the data between the dialog box's controls and the class's data members.

With the class's header file ready to go, you can start writing the class's implementation. As always, the first step is to include the header files required to compile the code, as shown in Listing 7.2.

On the CD

Listing 7.2 LST7_2.TXT—Including the Appropriate Header Files

```
#include <afxwin.h>
#include "dialog.h"
```

```
#include "resource.h"
#include "dlg1.h"
```

The first line of Listing 7.2 includes the general header file for MFC programs. The second line brings in the Dialog class's declaration, the third is your resource IDs, and the fourth is the CDlg1 class's declaration.

The CDlg1 class's constructor is responsible for initializing the dialog-box object, as shown in Listing 7.3.

On the CD

Listing 7.3   LST7_3.TXT—Constructing a *CDlg1* Object

```
CDlg1::CDlg1(CWnd* pParent) : CDialog(IDD_TESTDIALOG, pParent)
{
    // Initialize data transfer variables.
    m_department = "Sales";
    m_monday = TRUE;
    m_tuesday = TRUE;
    m_wednesday = TRUE;
    m_thursday = TRUE;
    m_friday = TRUE;
    m_name = "";
    m_age = 16;
}
```

The CDlg1 constructor receives a single parameter, which is a pointer to the dialog box's parent window. The constructor passes this pointer, along with the dialog box's resource ID, to the base class's constructor. It is the resource ID that links the correct dialog-box template to the dialog-box class. Because you've built the ID into the class's constructor, you don't need to worry about it when you create the dialog-box object. You need only supply the pointer to the parent window.

Inside the constructor, the program initializes the data members that represent the contents of the dialog box's controls. The values stored in these variables are automatically copied to the dialog box's controls when the dialog box is displayed. When the user dismisses the dialog box, MFC copies the data from the controls into these variables, where they can be accessed by other parts of your program.

The only other function in the dialog-box class is the overridden DoDataExchange() function, which is shown in Listing 7.4.

On the CD

Listing 7.4   LST7_4.TXT—Overriding the *DoDataExchange()* Function

```
void CDlg1::DoDataExchange(CDataExchange* pDX)
{
    // Call the base class's version.
    CDialog::DoDataExchange(pDX);
```

Part
II

Ch
7

continues

Listing 7.4   Continued

```
        // Associate the data transfer variables with
        // the ID's of the controls.
        DDX_Text(pDX, IDC_NAME, m_name);
        DDV_MaxChars(pDX, m_name, 30);
        DDX_Text(pDX, IDC_AGE, m_age);
        DDV_MinMaxUInt(pDX, m_age, 16, 100);
        DDX_CBString(pDX, IDC_DEPARTMENT, m_department);
        DDX_Check(pDX, IDC_MONDAY, m_monday);
        DDX_Check(pDX, IDC_TUESDAY, m_tuesday);
        DDX_Check(pDX, IDC_WEDNESDAY, m_wednesday);
        DDX_Check(pDX, IDC_THURSDAY, m_thursday);
        DDX_Check(pDX, IDC_FRIDAY, m_friday);
}
```

It is the DoDataExchange() function that sets up MFC's capability to transfer data between the dialog-box class's data members and the dialog box's controls. The function receives a single parameter, which is a pointer to a CDataExchange object. This pointer is supplied by MFC when it calls your overridden version of the function. You don't have to do anything with this pointer except pass it on to the base class's DoDataExchange() function, as well as to various DDX and DDV functions you call to set up the dialog box's data transfer. The first line of your DoDataExchange() function should call the base class's version, passing along the pointer to the CDataExchange object.

What are DDX and DDV functions? An excellent question! MFC's DDX functions set up the link between a data member and a control. For example, in Listing 7.4, the call to DDX_Text() links the edit control whose ID is IDC_NAME to the data member m_name. This tells MFC to copy the contents of m_name to the control when the dialog box is displayed and to copy the data in the control back to m_name when the dialog box is dismissed. Notice that a DDX function's first argument is the CDataExchange pointer passed into the DoDataExchange() function. There is a DDX function for each type of control you want to include in a data transfer. These functions are listed in Table 7.1. To learn about each function's parameters, look them up in your Visual C++ online documentation.

Table 7.1   DDX Functions

Function	Description
DDX_CBIndex()	Links a combo box's index to an integer variable
DDX_CBString()	Links a combo box's string to a string variable
DDX_CBStringExact()	Links a combo box's selected string to a string variable
DDX_Check()	Links a check box with an integer variable
DDX_LBIndex()	Links a list box's index with an integer variable
DDX_LBString()	Links a list box's string to a string variable

Function	Description
DDX_LBStringExact()	Links a list box's selected string to a string variable
DDX_Radio()	Links a radio button with an integer variable
DDX_Scroll()	Links a scroll bar to an integer variable
DDX_Text()	Links a text box to a string variable

MFC's DDV functions perform data validation for controls. For example, in Listing 7.4, the call to DDV_MaxChars() tells MFC that a valid entry in the edit control linked to m_name should be no longer than 30 characters. When the text-box control reaches 30 characters, it accepts no more input from the user. On the other hand, the call to DDV_MinMaxUInt() tells MFC that the m_age variable, which is associated with the edit control whose ID is IDC_AGE, should not accept values outside the range of 16 to 100. If the user enters an invalid number in the IDC_AGE edit box, MFC displays a message, warning the user of his mistake. The user cannot exit via the dialog box's OK button until the value is corrected. Table 7.2 shows the DDV functions you can call. For more information on their parameters, please consult your Visual C++ online documentation.

Table 7.2   DDV Functions

Function	Description
DDV_MaxChars()	Limits the length of a string
DDV_MinMaxByte()	Limits a byte value to a specific range
DDV_MinMaxDouble()	Limits a double value to a specific range
DDV_MinMaxDWord()	Limits a DWORD value to a specific range
DDV_MinMaxFloat()	Limits a floating-point value to a specific range
DDV_MinMaxInt()	Limits an integer value to a specific range
DDV_MinMaxLong()	Limits a long-integer value to a specific range
DDV_MinMaxUInt()	Limits an unsigned-integer value to a specific range

N O T E   It's important that you call DDV functions immediately after the DDX function that sets up the data exchange for a control. When you do this, MFC can set the input focus to the control that contains invalid data, not only showing the user exactly where the problem is, but also enabling him to enter a new value as conveniently as possible. ■

Part

II

Ch

7

Using the Dialog-Box Class

Now that you have your dialog-box class written, you can create objects of that class within your program and display the associated dialog-box element. The first step in using your new class is to include the dialog-box class's header file in any class that will access the class. Failure to do this causes the compiler to complain that it doesn't recognize the dialog-box class. Also, when you develop the window class that will display the dialog box, you usually want to create data members that mirror the data members of the dialog-box class. This gives you a place to store information that you transfer from the dialog box. In the Dialog application, the CMainFrame class declares (in its header file) this set of member variables as shown in Listing 7.5.

On the CD

Listing 7.5   LST7_5.TXT—Declaring Storage for Dialog-Box Data

```
protected:
    CString m_name;
    UINT m_age;
    CString m_department;
    BOOL m_monday;
    BOOL m_tuesday;
    BOOL m_wednesday;
    BOOL m_thursday;
    BOOL m_friday;
```

Notice that the data members declared in Listing 7.5 have the same names as the equivalent data members in the CDlg1 class. This convention makes it easier to keep track of what the variables do. Notice also that, unlike the equivalent variables in the CDlg1 class, the CMainFrame class's variables are declared as protected, rather than as public. This is because no other class requires access to these variables in the same way that other classes require access to the dialog-box class's variables.

Just as the dialog-box class initializes its data members in its constructor, so too does the CMainFrame class, as shown in Listing 7.6.

On the CD

Listing 7.6   LST7_6.TXT—Initializing the Frame-Window's Data Members

```
m_name = "";
m_age = 16;
m_department = "Sales";
m_monday = TRUE;
m_tuesday = TRUE;
m_wednesday = TRUE;
m_thursday = TRUE;
m_friday = TRUE;
```

The constructor initializes these data members to the same values as their counterparts in the CDlg1 class. This is because, as you'll soon see, the contents of these variables will be copied into the dialog-box variables before the dialog box is displayed. Then why bother to initialize the dialog-box class's variables? To be sure that an object of the class is always created in a fully initialized state. After all, there's no guarantee that someone who uses the class will copy values into the dialog-box class before displaying the dialog box.

In the `CMainFrame` class, the program displays the dialog box in the `OnDialogTest()` function, which MFC calls when the user selects the Dialog, Test command from the application's menu bar. The `OnDialogTest()` function first creates a dialog-object of your new class, like this:

```
CDlg1 dlg(this);
```

With the dialog-box object created, the program can now access the dialog box's data members, and so initialize them to the current contents of the values stored in the `CMainFrame` class, as shown in Listing 7.7.

On the CD

Listing 7.7 LST7_7.TXT—Transferring Data to the Dialog-Box Object

```
dlg.m_name = m_name;
dlg.m_age = m_age;
dlg.m_department = m_department;
dlg.m_monday = m_monday;
dlg.m_tuesday = m_tuesday;
dlg.m_wednesday = m_wednesday;
dlg.m_thursday = m_thursday;
dlg.m_friday = m_friday;
```

You may wonder why the mainframe window class bothers to initialize the dialog box's data members before displaying the dialog box. In this program, the dialog box always appears with the last entered data in the dialog box. Because the dialog box's data disappears along with the dialog box when the dialog box is deleted (either by the object going out of scope or by being explicitly deleted with the `delete` operator). The only place the current dialog-box data is saved is in the `CMainFrame` class. If you want the dialog box to always appear with its original default values, don't bother to copy the stored values into the dialog box's data members, and instead stick with the values supplied by the dialog box's own constructor.

After the program initializes the dialog box's contents, the program calls the dialog-box object's `DoModal()` function to display the dialog box to the user, like this:

```
int result = dlg.DoModal();
```

At this point, the user has control until he dismisses the dialog box. If the user exits by pressing the OK button, `DoModal()` returns the value `IDOK` (the Cancel button causes `DoModal()` to return `IDCANCEL`). In the case of `IDOK`, the program must copy the new data from the dialog box to the `CMainFrame` class's variables, as shown in Listing 7.8.

On the CD

Listing 7.8 LST7_8.TXT—Retrieving Data from the Dialog Box

```
if (result == IDOK)
{
    // Copy the dialog's data into this class's data members.
    m_name = dlg.m_name;
    m_age = dlg.m_age;
    m_department = dlg.m_department;
    m_monday = dlg.m_monday;
```

continues

Listing 7.8 Continued

```
    m_tuesday = dlg.m_tuesday;
    m_wednesday = dlg.m_wednesday;
    m_thursday = dlg.m_thursday;
    m_friday = dlg.m_friday;

    // Force the window to show the new data.
    Invalidate();
}
```

The call to Invalidate() in Listing 7.8 forces the window's contents to be redrawn, this time using the new values retrieved from the dialog box. When the OnDialogTest() function ends, the dialog-box object goes out of scope and disappears, along with the data the user entered into it. Good thing you saved that data in the CMainFrame class!

Programming Controls

Dialog boxes are the most common object used to get information from the user in a Windows application. Of course, dialog boxes aren't much good without the many controls that can be placed in them. Edit controls, list boxes, combo boxes, radio buttons, check boxes, and other types of controls all work together to provide the application's user with convenient ways to enter data into a program. Without these controls, a dialog box is about as useful as a telephone without number buttons. In this section, you learn to program window controls in dialog boxes. You also learn new ways to extract information from a window's controls.

Until now, the programs in this chapter have featured dialog boxes containing basic controls such as edit controls and buttons. Edit controls and buttons are probably the most important types of controls at your disposal. However, often you can give your program's user easier methods of selecting the data that must be entered into the program.

There are several types of controls you can place in a dialog box, including check boxes, radio buttons, list boxes, combo boxes, and scroll bars. You should already be familiar with how these controls work, both from a user's and a programmer's point of view. If you've never programmed with Microsoft Foundation Classes, you may not be familiar with the classes with which MFC encapsulates each of the window controls. These classes include CButton, CEdit, CStatic, CListBox, and CComboBox.

Although MFC supplies classes that encapsulate the many window controls, Windows provides most of the services needed to handle these controls. A description of each window control follows:

- *Static text*—Static text is a string of characters usually used to label other controls in a dialog box or window. Although it is considered to be a window control, static text cannot be manipulated by the user. You use the CStatic class to create and manipulate static text.

■ *Edit box*—An edit control accepts text input from the user. The user can edit the text in various ways before completing the input. You use the CEdit class to create and manipulate an edit box.

■ *Pushbutton*—A button is a graphical object that triggers a command when the user clicks it. When clicked, a button's graphical image is usually animated to appear as if the button is pressed and released. You use the CButton class to create and manipulate pushbuttons.

■ *Check box*—A check box is a special type of button that toggles a checkmark when clicked. Check boxes usually represent program options that the user can select. You use the CButton class to create and manipulate check boxes.

■ *Radio button*—Radio buttons are similar to check boxes, except only one radio button in a group can be selected at any given time. Radio buttons usually represent program options that are mutually exclusive. You use the CButton class to create and manipulate radio buttons.

■ *Group box*—Often, check boxes and radio buttons are placed into group boxes, which organize the buttons into logical groups. The user cannot interact with group boxes. You use the CStatic class to create and manipulate group boxes.

■ *List box*—A list box is a rectangle containing a set of selections. These selections are usually text items but can also be bitmaps or other objects. Depending on the list box's style flags, the user can select one or several objects in the list box. You use the CListBox class to create and manipulate a list-box control.

■ *Combo box*—A combo box is similar to a list box, except it also includes an edit control in which the user can type a selection. You use the CComboBox class to create and manipulate combo boxes.

■ *Scroll bar*—A scroll bar is a graphical object containing a track that encloses a sliding box called the scroll box. By positioning the scroll box, the user can select a value from a given range. In addition to the scroll box, a scroll bar contains arrow boxes that, when clicked, move the scroll box a unit in the direction of the arrow. Although scroll bars are rarely used in dialog boxes, they can be created and manipulated by the CScrollBar class.

Introducing the Control1 Application

This chapter's second sample program is called Control1. You can find the source code and executable file for this program in the CHAP07\CONTROL1 folder on this book's CD-ROM. When you run Control1, you see the window shown in Figure 7.5. This window shows the data that the user has currently selected from the application's dialog box. At the start of the program, this data is set to default values. The EDIT CONTROL field of the display shows the current string copied from the dialog box's edit control. The RADIO BUTTON field shows which radio button in the dialog box is selected. The CHECK BOX fields show the status of each of the three check boxes. The LIST BOX field shows the string currently selected in the list box, and the COMBO BOX field shows the currently selected string in the combo box.

Part

II

Ch

7

FIG. 7.5

The Control1 application's main window displays the current settings of the main dialog box's controls.

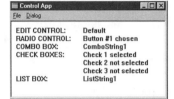

To find out where all these controls are, select the Dialog, Test command to bring up the Control Dialog dialog box shown in Figure 7.6. This dialog box contains the controls whose data is shown in the main window. You can change the controls' setting any way you want. When you exit the Control Dialog dialog box via the OK button, the main window displays the controls' new settings. Exiting the dialog box by clicking the Cancel button has no effect on the main window's display, because any changes made to the data in the dialog box are ignored.

FIG. 7.6

The Control1 application's main dialog box.

Exploring the Control1 Application

As you experiment with the Control1 application, it may seem that the program doesn't do a heck of a lot more than the dialog-box sample you created in the previous chapter. The truth is, it's not so much what the Control1 application does, but rather how it does it. Specifically, the controls in the application's dialog box are associated with MFC control classes so that the program can directly manipulate the controls. In this section, you see how this bit of MFC trickery is accomplished.

In the CHAP07\CONTROL1 folder of this book's CD-ROM, you find the complete source code for the Control1 application. The most pertinent source-code files are MAINFRM.H, MAINFRM.CPP, CNTLDLG.H, and CNTLDLG.CPP.

Declaring a Friend Function

In a previous chapter, you may recall that I mentioned two ways for a window class to get access to another class's data members. The first is to declare the class's data members as public. While this solution is easy to accomplish, it's not as elegant as it can be, because it grants access not only to the window class that must access the other class's variables, but also to any other class that might try to gain such access. I also mentioned that you can make the data members private and provide public member functions for manipulating those data members.

Another good way to limit uncontrolled access is to make the window class that needs to read information from another class a friend of the class. A class declared as a friend of another class has access to that class's public, protected, and even private data members. However, the access is limited to the friend class. No other class can access the protected and private data members.

The Control1 application uses the friend access method to share the dialog-box class's variables with the main window class. If you look at the top of the `CCntlDlg` class's header file (CNTLDLG.H), you see this line:

```
class CMainFrame;
```

This line tells the compiler that the identifier `CMainFrame` represents a class. Near the end of the `CCntlDlg` class's header file, you see why the compiler needs this information. The line

```
friend CMainFrame;
```

tells the compiler to make the `CMainFrame` class a friend of the `CCntlDlg` class, giving `CMainFrame` access to all of `CCntlDlg`'s data members. This is all the code it takes—just two lines—to limit outside access of `CCntlDlg`'s variables to the `CMainFrame` class.

Associating MFC Classes with Controls

As you know, MFC features many classes for window controls. Up until now, however, you haven't used these classes with the controls you added to your dialog boxes. This is because, in many cases, you don't need to manipulate a control at that level. You just display your dialog box and let the controls take care of themselves. There are times, though, when it's handy to be able to manipulate a control directly, which is what the many control classes, such as `CEdit`, `CButton`, and `CListBox`, enable you to do.

Each of the control classes feature member functions that do everything from initialize the contents of the control to respond to Windows messages. But to use these member functions, you must first associate the control with the appropriate class. For example, to manipulate an edit box through MFC, you must first associate that control with the `CEdit` class. Then you can use the `CEdit` class's member functions to manage the control.

To associate a control with a class, you must first get a pointer to the control. You can do this easily by calling the `GetDlgItem()` member function, which a dialog-box class inherits from `CWnd`. You call `GetDlgItem()` like this:

```
CEdit* pEditControl = (CEdit*)GetDlgItem(IDC_EDIT1);
```

The `GetDlgItem()` function returns a pointer to a `CWnd` object. (Controls are, after all, special types of windows. Every control class has `CWnd` as a base class.) Its single argument is the resource ID of the control for which you want the pointer. To gain access to the member functions of a control class, the returned `CWnd` pointer must be cast to the appropriate type of pointer. In the preceding line, you can see that `GetDlgItem()`'s return value is being cast to a `CEdit` pointer.

Part

II

Ch

7

When you have the pointer, you can access the class's member functions through that pointer. For example, to set the contents of the edit control for which the previous code line got a pointer, you use a line like this:

```
pEditControl->SetWindowText("Text for the edit control");
```

Initializing the Dialog Box's Controls

In the Control1 application, the program uses the techniques described in the previous section to create a simple data-transfer mechanism for the dialog box, without calling upon MFC's DDX functions. The dialog-box class first declares, in its header file, data members for holding the information the user entered into the dialog box, as shown in Listing 7.9.

On the CD

Listing 7.9   LST7_8.TXT—Declaring Data Members for the Dialog-Box Class

```
protected:
    CString m_edit1;
    int m_radio1;
    int m_radio2;
    int m_radio3;
    int m_check1;
    int m_check2;
    int m_check3;
    CString m_list1;
    CString m_combo1;
```

As you can see, there is one variable for each dialog-box control with which the user can interact. Notice also that these data members are declared as protected. However, in spite of their protected status, the CMainFrame class can access them, because CMainFrame is a friend class of CCntlDlg.

If you recall, the Control1 application's dialog box appears with default values already selected in its controls. For example, the edit box appears with the text "Default," and the first radio button in the radio-button group is selected. Obviously, these controls are being initialized somewhere in the program—and that somewhere is the CCntlDlg class's OnInitDialog() function. The OnInitDialog() function gets called as part of the dialog-box creation process (specifically, it responds to the WM_INITDIALOG Windows message). Because OnInitDialog() is a virtual function of the CDialog class, however, you don't need to create an entry in a message map. Just override the function in your custom dialog-box class.

In your overridden OnInitDialog(), you must first call the base class's version, like this:

```
CDialog::OnInitDialog();
```

You call the base class's version of OnInitDialog() so that the base class can perform its default initialization. Then, you can perform whatever special initialization is required by your dialog-box class. In the CCntlDlg class, that initialization is setting the various controls to their default values. First, the program sets the edit box, like this:

```
CEdit* pEdit1 = (CEdit*)GetDlgItem(IDC_EDIT1);
pEdit1->SetWindowText("Default");
```

Next, the program sets the radio-button group to its default state, which is the first button selected, like this:

```
CButton* pRadio1 = (CButton*)GetDlgItem(IDC_RADIO1);
pRadio1->SetCheck(TRUE);
```

The SetCheck() member function of the CButton class determines the check state of a button. Although the preceding example uses TRUE as the function's argument, there are actually three possible settings: 0 turns off the checkmark, 1 turns on the checkmark, and 2 sets the button control as to its "indeterminate" state. (An example of an indeterminate state might be when you highlight text that contains both underlined and normal text. Then a control that displays the state of the underlined attribute cannot be on or off, but rather must be indeterminate.) However, you can use 2 only when you've given the button the BS_3STATE or BS_AUTO3STATE style.

After setting the radio buttons, the program performs similar initialization on the first check button, like this:

```
CButton* pCheck1 = (CButton*)GetDlgItem(IDC_CHECK1);
pCheck1->SetCheck(TRUE);
```

Setting the checked state of buttons is pretty easy. Initializing a list box, however, takes a little extra work, as shown in Listing 7.10.

On the CD

Listing 7.10 LST7_10.TXT—Initializing a List Box

```
CListBox* pList1 = (CListBox*)GetDlgItem(IDC_LIST1);
pList1->AddString("ListString1");
pList1->AddString("ListString2");
pList1->AddString("ListString3");
pList1->AddString("ListString4");
pList1->AddString("ListString5");
pList1->AddString("ListString6");
pList1->SetCurSel(0);
```

The AddString() member function of the CListBox class adds a string to the contents of the list box. So, the code in Listing 7.10 adds the six selections from which the user can choose from the list box. The SetCurSel() function, also a member of the CListBox class, determines which of the entries on the list box are selected. The function's single argument is the zero-based index of the item to select. So, an index of 0 selects the first item in the list. An index of 1 initializes the list box without a selection.

A combo box is not unlike a list box when it comes to initialization, as you can see in Listing 7.11.

Part

II

Ch

7

Listing 7.11 LST7_11.TXT—Initializing a Combo Box

```
CComboBox* pCombo1 = (CComboBox*)GetDlgItem(IDC_COMBO1);
pCombo1->AddString("ComboString1");
pCombo1->AddString("ComboString2");
pCombo1->AddString("ComboString3");
pCombo1->AddString("ComboString4");
pCombo1->AddString("ComboString5");
pCombo1->AddString("ComboString6");
pCombo1->SetCurSel(0);
```

The lines in Listing 7.11 work exactly like the similar lines used to initialize the list box, adding six strings to the combo box's list, and then making the first string the default selection in the list. That is, the first string is already entered into the combo box's edit box when the dialog box appears.

N O T E If you want to create a dialog-box class that retains the most recently entered data, use OnInitDialog() to copy the contents of the appropriate class data members to the controls rather than using "hard-coded" data as is done in the Control1 application. Using this method, you enable the Windows class that creates the dialog-box object to initialize the dialog box's controls, by copying data into the dialog-box class's data members before displaying the dialog box. ▪

Responding to the OK Button

After the dialog box appears on the screen, the user can enter whatever data he likes into the dialog box's controls. The Control1 application doesn't regain control until the user exits the dialog box, by clicking either the Cancel or OK buttons. As with most dialog boxes, if the user clicks the Cancel button (indicated by a return value of IDCANCEL from DoModal()), the program simply ignores any changes that were made in the dialog box. However, if the user exits the dialog box via the OK button, the program must transfer the dialog box's data from the controls to the dialog-box class's data members. If the dialog box is allowed to close before the controls' contents are copied, the data disappears along with the dialog box.

So, to copy data from the dialog box's controls to the class's data members, a program must first know when the user has clicked the OK button. This is done by overriding the dialog-box class's OnOK() member function. In OnOK(), the program associates controls with the appropriate control classes, and then uses the class member functions to perform whatever tasks are required to process the dialog box's data before the dialog box is deleted.

N O T E If your dialog-box class needs to know, before the dialog box is removed from the screen, when the user has clicked the Cancel button, you can override the OnCancel() member function. After processing the Cancel button as required for your application, you'll usually want to call CDialog::OnCancel() to continue the cancel process. ▪

In the Control1 application, the OnOK() function first extracts the contents of the edit box, like this:

```
CEdit* pEdit1 = (CEdit*)GetDlgItem(IDC_EDIT1);
pEdit1->GetWindowText(m_edit1);
```

The first line gets a pointer to the edit control and casts it to a CEdit pointer. The program can then use the pointer to call the CEdit member function GetWindowText(), whose single argument is a string object into which the edit box's contents should be copied.

The program copies the contents of the radio buttons similarly, as shown in Listing 7.12.

On the CD

Listing 7.12 LST7_12.TXT—Storing the Status of the Radio Buttons

```
CButton* pRadio = (CButton*)GetDlgItem(IDC_RADIO1);
m_radio1 = pRadio->GetCheck();
pRadio = (CButton*)GetDlgItem(IDC_RADIO2);
m_radio2 = pRadio->GetCheck();
pRadio = (CButton*)GetDlgItem(IDC_RADIO3);
m_radio3 = pRadio->GetCheck();
```

Here, after getting a pointer to each control and casting it to the CButton class, the program calls the CButton member function GetCheck() to obtain the status of each of the radio buttons. GetCheck() returns a 0, 1, or 2, depending on whether the control is in an unchecked, checked, or indeterminate state, respectively.

The program gets the contents of the check boxes in almost exactly the same way, as shown in Listing 7.13.

On the CD

Listing 7.13 LST7_13.TXT—Storing the Status of the Check Boxes

```
CButton* pCheck = (CButton*)GetDlgItem(IDC_CHECK1);
m_check1 = pCheck->GetCheck();
pCheck = (CButton*)GetDlgItem(IDC_CHECK2);
m_check2 = pCheck->GetCheck();
pCheck = (CButton*)GetDlgItem(IDC_CHECK3);
m_check3 = pCheck->GetCheck();
```

As you can see, the CButton class handles both radio buttons and check boxes. The only difference between Listing 7.12 and 7.13 is the resource IDs used to obtain pointers to the buttons.

The following lines show how the Control1 application extracts data from the list-box control:

```
CListBox* pList1 = (CListBox*)GetDlgItem(IDC_LIST1);
int listIndex = pList1->GetCurSel();
pList1->GetText(listIndex, m_list1);
```

The first line obtains a pointer to the list-box control and associates it with the CListBox class. With the CListBox pointer in hand, the program can call the GetCurSel() member function, which returns the zero-based index of the selected item in the list box. Finally, a call to the CListBox member function GetText() copies the selected text string into the CCntlDlg class's m_list1 data member. GetText()'s two arguments are the index of the text item to get and a reference to a CString object into which to store the string. (The second argument can also be a pointer to a char array.)

As you may have guessed, the program can copy the contents of the combo box in almost exactly the same manner, like this:

```
CComboBox* pCombo1 = (CComboBox*)GetDlgItem(IDC_COMBO1);
int comboIndex = pCombo1->GetCurSel();
pCombo1->GetLBText(comboIndex, m_combo1);
```

As always, the first line gets a pointer to the control, only this time the pointer is cast to a CComboBox pointer. The second line gets the zero-based index of the selected item in the combo box, whereas the third line copies the selected text line to the CCntlDlg class's m_combo1 data member. The CComboBox class's GetLBText() member function works just like the CListBox class's GetText(), the two arguments being the index of the text item to get and a reference to a CString object into which to store the string. (Again, the second argument can also be a pointer to a char array.)

At this point in the program, all the important data has been copied from the dialog box's controls into the dialog-box class's data members, which means it's now safe to remove the dialog box from the screen. Removing the dialog box is as simple as calling the base class's OnOK() member function, like this:

```
CDialog::OnOK();
```

You can also use the OnOK() member function to perform data validation. To do this, after extracting the contents of a control, determine whether the control's data is valid. If the data is not valid, display a message box to the user describing the problem, and then return from OnOK() without calling CDialog::OnOK(). Not calling CDialog::OnOK() leaves the dialog box on the screen so the user can correct the bad entry.

Handling the Dialog Box in the Window Class

As you've seen, you can create your own data transfer and validation mechanisms by directly manipulating controls in a dialog box. Those DDX and DDV functions don't seem so mysterious now, do they? (You can, of course, do much more with your dialog box's controls than copy and validate data. In fact, after you have a pointer to a control, you can call any of the control's member functions.) The final step is to display your dialog box from within your main program, usually from a window class.

The Control1 application displays the dialog box in response to its <u>D</u>ialog, <u>T</u>est command, which is handled by the OnDialogTest() message-response function. In that function, the program first creates the dialog-box object and then calls DoModal() to display it, like this:

```
CCntlDlg dialog(this);
int result = dialog.DoModal();
```

If the user exits the dialog box by clicking the OK button, the function copies the dialog box's data into data members of the window class, and then calls Invalidate() in order to repaint the window, which displays the current data from the dialog box. The code that handles these tasks is shown in Listing 7.14.

On the CD

Listing 7.14 LST7_14.TXT—Copying the Dialog Box's Data

```
if (result == IDOK)
{
    // Save the contents of the dialog box.
    m_edit1 = dialog.m_edit1;
    m_radio1 = dialog.m_radio1;
    m_radio2 = dialog.m_radio2;
    m_radio3 = dialog.m_radio3;
    m_combo1 = dialog.m_combo1;
    m_check1 = dialog.m_check1;
    m_check2 = dialog.m_check2;
    m_check3 = dialog.m_check3;
    m_list1 = dialog.m_list1;

    // Force the window to repaint.
    Invalidate();
}
```

The dialog-box object is automatically deleted when it goes out of scope, taking all of its data with it, which is why you must copy whatever data you need from the dialog box.

From Here...

As you've learned, handling dialog boxes in an MFC program is much easier than handling them in a conventional Windows program. This is because MFC provides a powerful class, CDialog, from which you can derive custom dialog-box classes. These custom classes not only perform automatic data exchange, but also validate the contents of a dialog box's controls before the user is allowed to dismiss the dialog box.

In an MFC program, controls can be much more than just passive objects over which your program has no control. By associating a control with its MFC class, you can use the member functions of the class to handle the control any way you like. The most obvious use of the control classes is to create your own custom data transfer and validation functions. However, the creative programmer will find many ways to take advantage of the MFC control classes. If you'd like more information on these topics, check out the following chapters:

- Chapter 5, "Messages and Commands," discusses how MFC routes the messages that the various Windows controls and devices generate.
- Chapter 8, "Win95 Common Controls," provides an overview of the many special controls that you can use in Windows 95 applications.
- Chapter 9, "Property Pages and Sheets and Wizards," shows you how to program these special types of dialog boxes.
- Chapter 18, "Interface Issues," describes other ways your application can communicate with its users.

Part II

Ch 7

Win95 Common Controls

The toolbar and status bar controls are covered in Chapter 18, "Interface Issues," and property sheets and wizards are covered in Chapter 9, "Property Pages and Sheets and Wizards." ■

About Progress Bar Controls

Progress bars are an important part of providing feedback to the user about the status of a long operation.

About Trackbar Controls

Trackbar controls (also known as sliders) enable the user to select values within a given range.

About Up-Down Controls

Up-Down controls (or spinners) are another way a program can retrieve, from the user, a value from a given range.

About Image List Controls

Many Windows 95 controls require a set of images in order to function. An Image List holds those images.

About List View Controls

List View controls provide a configurable view of items in a data set.

About Tree View Controls

Tree View controls display a hierarchical view of data elements.

About Rich Edit Controls

Rich Edit controls enable you quickly to add word-processing capabilities to your application.

The Win95 Controls Application

This chapter's sample program is called Win95 Controls App. You can find the program's executable file, as well as the complete source code, in the CHAP08 folder of this book's CD-ROM. When you run the program, you see the window shown in Figure 8.1. As you can see, Win95 Controls App demonstrates six of the Windows 95 common controls: the progress bar, the trackbar, the up-down control, the list view, the tree view, and the rich edit control. In the following sections, you learn the basics of creating and using these controls in your own applications.

FIG. 8.1

The Win95 Controls App demonstrates six of Windows 95's common controls.

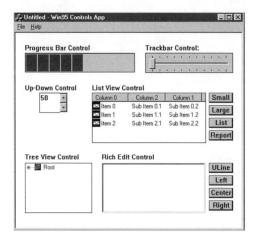

The Progress Bar Control

Probably the easiest of the new common controls to use is the progress bar, which is nothing more than a rectangle that fills in slowly with colored blocks. The more colored blocks filled in, the closer to complete a task is. When the progress bar is completely filled in, the task associated with the progress bar is also complete. You might use a progress bar to show the status of a sorting operation or to give the user visual feedback about a large file that's being loaded.

To see a progress bar in action, click anywhere in the background of Win95 Controls App's window. When you do, the progress bar starts filling with colored blocks. When the progress bar is completely filled, it starts over again. This continues until you click the window again or exit the program. Of course, in this program, the progress bar isn't tracking a real task in progress. It's simply responding to timer messages. However, the program still demonstrates how you might use a progress bar in your own applications.

Creating the Progress Bar

This may be an obvious statement, but before you can use a progress bar, you must create it. Often in an MFC program, the controls are created as part of a dialog box. However, Win95 Controls App displays its controls in the application's main window. It does this by creating all the controls in the view class's `OnCreate()` function, which responds to the `WM_CREATE` Windows message. The controls themselves are declared as data members of the view class, as shown in Listing 8.1. As you can see, the progress bar is an object of the `CProgressCtrl` class.

Listing 8.1   LST8_1.TXT—Declaring the View Class's Controls

```
protected:
    CProgressCtrl m_progressBar;
    CSliderCtrl m_trackbar;
    BOOL m_timer;
    CSpinButtonCtrl m_upDown;
    CEdit m_buddyEdit;
    CListCtrl m_listView;
    CImage list m_smallImage list;
    CImage list m_largeImage list;
    CButton m_smallButton;
    CButton m_largeButton;
    CButton m_listButton;
    CButton m_reportButton;
    CTreeCtrl m_treeView;
    CImage list m_treeImage list;
    CRichEditCtrl m_richEdit;
    CButton m_boldButton;
    CButton m_leftButton;
    CButton m_centerButton;
    CButton m_rightButton;
```

Because it takes quite a lot of code to create and initialize each of the six controls, the application relegates the details to separate functions. For example, to create the progress bar control, `OnCreate()` calls the `CreateProgressBar()` local member function, like this:

```
CreateProgressBar();
```

In `CreateProgressBar()` is where the fun begins. First, the function creates the progress bar control by calling the control's `Create()` function:

```
m_progressBar.Create(WS_CHILD | WS_VISIBLE | WS_BORDER,
    CRect(20, 40, 250, 80), this, 102);
```

This function's four arguments are the control's style flags, the control's size (as a `CRect` object), a pointer to the control's parent window, and the control's ID. (Usually, you declare a constant, such as `IDC_PROGRESSBAR`, to use as the control's ID. I used a hard-coded value to keep the code as simple as possible.) The style constants are the same constants you use for creating any type of window (a control is really nothing more than a special kind of window, after all). In this case, you need at least `WS_CHILD` (which indicates the control is a child window) and `WS_VISIBLE` (which ensures that the user can see the control). The `WS_BORDER` is a nice addition because it adds a dark border around the control, setting it off from the rest of the window.

Initializing the Progress Bar

After the progress bar control is created, it must be initialized. The CProgressCtrl class features a number of member functions that enable you to initialize and manipulate the control. Those member functions and their descriptions are listed in Table 8.1. For more information, please look the functions up in your Visual C++ online documentation.

Table 8.1   Member Functions of the *CProgressCtrl* Class

Function	Description
Create()	Creates the progress bar control
OffsetPos()	Advances the control the given number of blocks
SetPos()	Sets the control's current value
SetRange()	Sets the control's minimum and maximum values
SetStep()	Sets the value by which the control advances
StepIt()	Advances the control by one step unit

To initialize the control, you merely call the CProgressCtrl object's appropriate member functions, which Win95 Controls App does like this:

```
m_progressBar.SetRange(1, 100);
m_progressBar.SetStep(10);
m_progressBar.SetPos(50);
```

The call to SetRange() determines the values represented by the progress bar. The two arguments are the minimum and maximum values. So, after the preceding call to SetRange(), if the progress bar is set to 1, it displays no colored blocks, whereas setting the control's position to 100 fills the control with colored blocks.

Next, the CreateProgressBar() function calls SetStep(), which determines how far the progress bar advances with each increment. The larger this value, the faster the progress bar fills with colored blocks. Because the range and the step rate are related, a control with a range of 1-10 and a step rate of 1 works almost identically to a control with a range of 1-100 and a step rate of 10.

When the Win95 Controls App starts, the progress bar is already half filled with colored blocks. (This is purely for aesthetic reasons. Usually a progress bar begins its life empty.) This is because of the call to SetPos() with the value of 50, which is the midpoint of the control's range.

Manipulating the Progress Bar

In Win95 Controls App, the progress bar starts counting forward when you click in the window's background. This is because the program responds to the mouse click by starting a

timer that sends WM_TIMER messages to the program twice a second. In the view class's
OnTimer() function, the program makes the following function call:

```
m_progressBar.StepIt();
```

The StepIt() function increments the progress bar control's value by the step rate, causing
new blocks to be displayed in the control as the control's value setting counts upward. When
the control reaches its maximum, it automatically starts over.

> **N O T E** Notice that there are no CProgressCtrl member functions that control the size or
> number of blocks that will fit into the control. This attribute is controlled indirectly by the
> size of the control. ▨

The Trackbar Control

Many times in a program you may need to have the user enter a value that lies within a specific
range. For this sort of task, you use MFC's CSliderCtrl class to create a trackbar control. For
example, suppose you need the user to enter a percentage that your program needs to calculate another value. In that case, you want the user to enter only values in the range from 0 to
100. Other values would be invalid and could cause problems in your program if such invalid
values were not carefully trapped.

Using the trackbar control, you can force the user to enter a value in the specified range. Although the user can accidentally enter a wrong value (a value that doesn't accomplish what the
user wants to do), he can't enter an invalid value (one that brings your program crashing down
like a stone wall in an earthquake).

In the case of a percentage, you create a trackbar control with a minimum value of 0 and a
maximum value of 100. Moreover, to make the control easier to position, you want to place tick
marks at each setting that's a multiple of 10, giving 11 tick marks in all (including the one at 0).
Win95 Controls App creates exactly this type of trackbar.

To see the trackbar work, click the trackbar's slot. When you do, the slider moves forward or
backward and the selected value appears to the right of the control's caption. Once the trackbar
has the focus, you can also control it with your keyboard's Up and Down arrow keys, as well as
with the Page Up and Page Down keys.

Creating the Trackbar

In the Win95 Controls App application, the trackbar is created in the CreateTrackbar() local
member function, which, like CreateProgressBar(), the program calls from the view class's
(CWin95View's) OnCreate() function. In CreateTrackbar(), the program first creates the
trackbar control by calling its Create() member function, like this:

```
m_trackbar.Create(WS_CHILD | WS_VISIBLE | WS_BORDER |
    TBS_AUTOTICKS | TBS_BOTH | TBS_HORZ,
    CRect(270, 40, 450, 80), this, 101);
```

This function's four arguments are the control's style flags, the control's size (as a CRect object), a pointer to the control's parent window, and the control's ID. The style constants include the same constants you would use for creating any type of window, with the addition of special styles used with trackbars. Table 8.2 lists these special styles.

Table 8.2   Trackbar Styles

Style	Description
TBS_AUTOTICKS	Enables the trackbar to automatically draw its tick marks
TBS_BOTH	Draws tick marks on both slides of the slider
TBS_BOTTOM	Draws tick marks on the bottom of a horizontal trackbar
TBS_ENABLESELRANGE	Enables a trackbar to display a subrange of values
TBS_HORZ	Draws the trackbar horizontally
TBS_LEFT	Draws tick marks on the left side of a vertical trackbar
TBS_NOTICKS	Draws a trackbar with no tick marks
TBS_RIGHT	Draws tick marks on the right side of a vertical trackbar
TBS_TOP	Draws tick marks on the top of a horizontal trackbar
TBS_VERT	Draws a vertical trackbar

Initializing the Trackbar

After the trackbar control is created, it must be initialized. The CSliderCtrl class features many member functions that enable you to initialize and manipulate the control. Those member functions and their descriptions are listed in Table 8.3. For more information, please look up the functions in your Visual C++ online documentation.

Table 8.3   Member Functions of the *CSliderCtrl* Class

Function	Description
ClearSel()	Clears a selection from the control
ClearTics()	Clears tick marks from the control
Create()	Creates a trackbar control
GetChannelRect()	Gets the size of the control's slider
GetLineSize()	Gets the control's line size
GetNumTics()	Gets the number of tick marks
GetPageSize()	Gets the control's page size

Function	Description
GetPos()	Gets the control's position
GetRange()	Gets the control's minimum and maximum values
GetRangeMax()	Gets the control's maximum value
GetRangeMin()	Gets the control's minimum value
GetSelection()	Gets the current range selection
GetThumbRect()	Gets the size of the control's thumb
GetTic()	Gets the position of a tick mark
GetTicArray()	Gets all the control's tick positions
GetTicPos()	Gets the client coordinates of a tick mark
SetLineSize()	Sets the control's line size
SetPageSize()	Sets the control's page size
SetPos()	Sets the control's position
SetRange()	Sets the control's minimum and maximum values
SetRangeMax()	Sets the control's maximum value
SetRangeMin()	Sets the control's minimum value
SetSelection()	Sets a selected subrange in the control
SetTic()	Sets the position of a tick mark
SetTicFreq()	Sets the control's tick frequency
VerifyPos()	Determines whether the control's position is valid

Usually, when you create a trackbar control, you want to set the control's range and tick frequency. If the user is going to use the control from the keyboard, you also need to set the control's line and page size. In the Win95 Controls App application, the program initializes the trackbar as shown in Listing 8.2.

On the CD

Listing 8.2   LST8_2.TXT—Initializing the Trackbar Control

```
m_trackbar.SetRange(0, 100, TRUE);
m_trackbar.SetTicFreq(10);
m_trackbar.SetLineSize(1);
m_trackbar.SetPageSize(10);
```

The call to SetRange() sets the trackbar's minimum and maximum values to 0 and 100, respectively. The arguments are the minimum value, the maximum value, and a Boolean value indicating whether the trackbar should redraw itself after setting the range. Next, the call to

SetTicFreq() ensures that there is a tick mark at each interval of 10. (Without this function call, the trackbar would have a tick mark for each possible setting, 101 in all.) Finally, the calls to SetLineSize() and SetPageSize() determine how much the trackbar moves when the user presses his Up arrow, Down arrow, Page Up, or Page Down keys.

Manipulating the Trackbar

When you get down to it, a trackbar is really a special scrollbar control. As such, when the user moves the slider, the control generates WM_HSCROLL messages, which Win95 Controls App captures in its view class's OnHScroll() member function, shown in Listing 8.3.

On the CD

Listing 8.3   LST8_3.TXT—Responding to a Trackbar Control

```
void CWin95View::OnHScroll(UINT nSBCode, UINT nPos, CScrollBar* pScrollBar)
{
    // TODO: Add your message handler code here and/or call default

    CSliderCtrl* slider = (CSliderCtrl*)pScrollBar;
    int position = slider->GetPos();
    char s[10];
    wsprintf(s, "%d   ", position);
    CClientDC clientDC(this);
    clientDC.TextOut(390, 22, s);
    CView::OnHScroll(nSBCode, nPos, pScrollBar);
}
```

OnHScroll()'s fourth parameter is a pointer to the scroll object that generated the WM_HSCROLL message. The preceding function first casts this pointer to CSliderCtrl pointer. It then gets the current position of the trackbar's slider by calling the CSliderCtrl member function GetPos(). After the program has the slider's position, it converts the integer to a string and displays that string in the window. (If you don't understand how to display data in a window, check out Chapter 11, "Drawing on the Screen.")

The Up-Down Control

The trackbar control isn't the only way you can get a value in a predetermined range from the user. If you don't care about using the trackbar for visual feedback, you can use an up-down control, which is little more than a couple of arrows the user clicks to raise or lower the control's setting. If the trackbar control is a scroller with only a bar and a thumb, then an up-down control is the leftover arrow buttons.

In the Win95 Controls App application, you can change the setting of the up-down control by clicking either of its arrows. When you do, the value in the attached edit box changes, indicating the up-down control's current setting. After the control has the focus, you can also change its value by pressing your keyboard's Up and Down arrow keys.

Creating the Up-Down Control

In the Win95 Controls App application, the up-down control is created in the `CreateUpDownCtrl()` local member function, which the program calls from the view class's `OnCreate()` function. In `CreateUpDownCtrl()`, the program creates the up-down control by first creating the associated *buddy* control to which the up-down control communicates its current value. In this case, as is typical, the buddy control is an edit box, which is created by calling the `CEdit` class's `Create()` member function:

```
m_buddyEdit.Create(WS_CHILD | WS_VISIBLE | WS_BORDER,
    CRect(50, 120, 110, 160), this, 103);
```

This function's four arguments are the control's style flags, the control's size, a pointer to the control's parent window, and the control's ID. If you remember from the control declarations, `m_buddyEdit` is an object of the `CEdit` class.

Now that the program has created the buddy control, it can create the up-down control in much the same way, by calling the object's `Create()` member function, like this:

```
m_upDown.Create(WS_CHILD | WS_VISIBLE | WS_BORDER |
    UDS_ALIGNRIGHT | UDS_SETBUDDYINT | UDS_ARROWKEYS,
    CRect(0, 0, 0, 0), this, 104);
```

As you can guess by now, this function's four arguments are the control's style flags, the control's size, a pointer to the control's parent window, and the control's ID. As with most controls, the style constants include the same constants you use for creating any type of window. However, the `CSpinButtonCtrl` class, of which `m_upDown` is an object, defines special styles to be used with up-down controls. Table 8.4 lists these special styles.

Table 8.4   Up-Down Control Styles

Styles	Description
UDS_ALIGNLEFT	Places the up-down control on the left edge of the buddy control
UDS_ALIGNRIGHT	Places the up-down control on the right edge of the buddy control
UDS_ARROWKEYS	Enables the user to change the control's values using the keyboard's Up and Down arrow keys
UDS_AUTOBUDDY	Makes the previous window the buddy control
UDS_HORZ	Creates a horizontal up-down control
UDS_NOTHOUSANDS	Eliminates separators between each set of three digits
UDS_SETBUDDYINT	Displays the control's value in the buddy control
UDS_WRAP	Causes the control's value to wrap around to its minimum when the maximum is reached, and vice versa

After the up-down control is created, it must be initialized. The CSpinButtonCtrl class features member functions that enable you to initialize and manipulate the control. Those member functions and their descriptions are listed in Table 8.5. For more detailed information, please look up the functions in your Visual C++ online documentation.

Table 8.5 *CSpinButtonCtrl* **Member Functions**

Function	Description
Create()	Creates the up-down control
GetAccel()	Gets the control's speed
GetBase()	Gets the control's numerical base
GetBuddy()	Gets a pointer to the control's buddy control
GetPos()	Gets the control's position
GetRange()	Gets the control's minimum and maximum values
SetAccel()	Sets the control's speed
SetBase()	Sets the control's numerical base (10 for decimal, 16 for hex)
SetBuddy()	Sets the control's buddy control
SetPos()	Sets the control's position
SetRange()	Sets the control's minimum and maximum values

After creating an up-down control, you usually want to set the control's buddy, range, and position. In the Win95 Controls App application, the program initializes the control like this:

```
m_upDown.SetBuddy(&m_buddyEdit);
m_upDown.SetRange(1, 100);
m_upDown.SetPos(50);
```

Here, the up-down control's buddy is set to the edit box that was first created in CreateUpDownCtrl(). Then, the program calls SetRange() and SetPos() to give the control its starting range and position, respectively. Thanks to the UDS_SETBUDDYINT flag passed to Create() and the call to the control's SetBuddy() member function, Win95 Controls App needs to do nothing else to have the control's value appear on the screen. The control handles its buddy automatically.

The Image List Control

Often in programs you need to use a lot of images that are related in some way. For example, your application may have a toolbar with many command buttons, each of which uses a bitmap for its icon. In a case like this, it would be great to have some sort of program object that could not only hold the bitmaps, but also organize them so they can be accessed easily. That's exactly what an image list control does for you. An image list does nothing more than stores a list of related images. You can use the images any way you see fit in your program. However, several Windows 95 controls rely on image lists. These controls are:

- List view controls
- Tree view controls
- Property pages
- Toolbars

Besides the preceding controls, you will undoubtedly come up with many other uses for image lists. You might, for example, have an animation sequence that you'd like to display in a window. An image list is the perfect storage place for the frames that make up the animation, because you can easily access any frame just by using an index.

If the word *index* makes you think of arrays, you're close to understanding how an image list stores images. An image list is much like an array that holds pictures rather than integers or floating-point numbers. Just as with an array, you initialize each "element" of an image list and thereafter can access any part of the "array" using an index.

You won't, however, ever see in your running application an image list control in the same way that you can see a status bar or a progress bar control. That's because (again, like an array) an image list is nothing more than a storage structure for pictures. You can display the images stored in an image list, but you can't display the image list itself. Figure 8.2 shows how an image list is organized.

FIG. 8.2

An image list is much like an array of pictures.

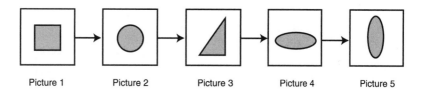

| Picture 1 | Picture 2 | Picture 3 | Picture 4 | Picture 5 |

Creating the Image List

In the Win95 Controls App application, image lists are used with the list view and tree view controls, so the image lists for the controls are created in the `CreateListView()` and `CreateTreeView()` local member functions, which the program calls from the view class's `OnCreate()` function. An image view, which is an object of the `CImageList` class, is created by its `Create()` member function, like this:

```
m_smallImageList.Create(16, 16, FALSE, 1, 0);
```

The `Create()` function's five arguments are the width of the pictures in the control, the height of the pictures, a Boolean value indicating whether the images contain a mask, the number of images initially in the list, and the number of images by which the list can dynamically grow. This last value is 0 to indicate that the list is not allowed to grow at runtime. The `Create()` function is overloaded in the `CImageList` class so that you can create image lists in various ways. You can find the other versions of `Create()` in your Visual C++ online documentation.

Initializing the Image List

After you have an image list created, you'll want to add images to it. After all, an empty image list isn't a heck of a lot of use. The easiest way to add the images is to have the images as part of your application's resource file and load them from there. For example, the following code shows how Win95 Controls App loads an icon into one of its image lists:

```
HICON hIcon = ::LoadIcon (AfxGetResourceHandle(),
    MAKEINTRESOURCE(IDI_ICON1));
m_smallImageList.Add(hIcon);
```

Here, the program first gets a handle to the icon. Then, it adds the icon to the image list by calling the image list's Add() member function. Table 8.6 lists other member functions you can use to manipulate an object of the CImageList class. As you can see, you have a lot of control over an image list if you really want to dig in.

Table 8.6 Member Functions of the *CImageList* Class

Function	Description
Add()	Adds an image to the image list
Attach()	Attaches an existing image list to an object of the CImageList class
BeginDrag()	Starts an image-dragging operation
Create()	Creates an image list control
DeleteImageList()	Deletes an image list
Detach()	Detaches an image list from an object of the CImageList class
DragEnter()	Locks a window for updates and shows the drag image
DragLeave()	Unlocks a window for updates
DragMove()	Moves the drag image
DragShowNolock()	Handles the drag image without locking the window
Draw()	Draws an image that's being dragged
EndDrag()	Ends an image-dragging operation
ExtractIcon()	Creates an icon from an image
GetBkColor()	Gets an image list's background color
GetDragImage()	Gets the image for drag operations
GetImageCount()	Gets the number of images in the control
GetImageInfo()	Gets image information
GetSafeHandle()	Gets an image list's handle

Function	Description
Read()	Gets an image list from the given archive
Remove()	Removes an image from the image list
Replace()	Replaces one image with another
SetBkColor()	Sets an image list's background color
SetDragCursorImage()	Creates an image for drag operations
SetOverlayImage()	Sets the index of an overlay mask
Write()	Writes an image list to the given archive

The List View Control

Often, computer programs need to work with lists of objects and organize those objects in such a way that the program's user can easily determine each object's attributes. An example is a group of files on a disk. Each file is a separate object that is associated with a number of attributes including the file's name, size, and the date the file was last modified. Windows shows files either as icons in a window or as a table of entries, each entry showing the attributes associated with the files. The user has full control over the way the file objects are displayed, including which attributes are shown and which are not listed. The Windows 95 common controls includes something called a list view control, which enables Windows 95 programmers to organize lists in exactly the same way Windows 95 does with files and other objects.

If you'd like to see an example of a full-fledged list view control, just open the Windows 95 Explorer (see fig. 8.3). The right side of the window shows how the list view control can organize objects in a window. (The left side of the window contains a tree view control, which you learn about later in this chapter, in the section titled "The Tree View Control.") In the figure, the list view is currently set to the report view, in which each object in the list gets its own line showing not only the object's name but also the attributes associated with that object.

As I mentioned previously in this chapter, the user can change the way objects are organized in a list view control. Figure 8.4, for example, shows the list view portion of the Explorer set to the large-icon setting, whereas Figure 8.5 shows the small-icon setting, which enables the user to see more objects (in this case, files) in the window. The list view control also provides the user with the ability to edit the names of objects in the list, as well as to sort objects based on data displayed in a particular column. (This latter function works only when the list view control is in report view.)

The Win95 Controls App application also sports a list view control, although it's not as fancy as Explorer's. To switch between the small-icon, large-icon, list, and report views, click the appropriate button to the right of the control. Figure 8.6 shows the application's list view control displaying small icons, whereas Figure 8.7 shows the large icons.

FIG. 8.3

Explorer uses a list view control to organize file information.

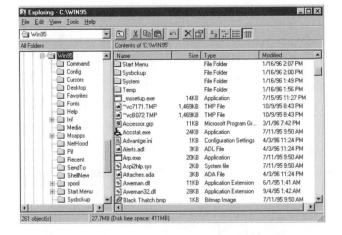

FIG. 8.4

Here's Explorer's list view control set to large icons.

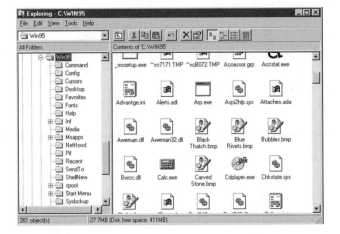

FIG. 8.5

Here's Explorer's list view control set to small icons.

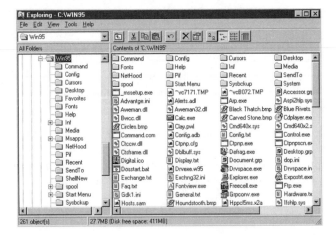

FIG. 8.6

Here's the example application's list view control set to small icons.

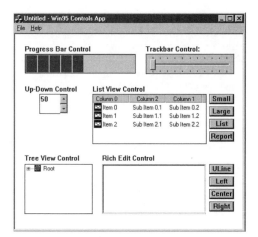

FIG. 8.7

Here's the sample application's list view control set to large icons.

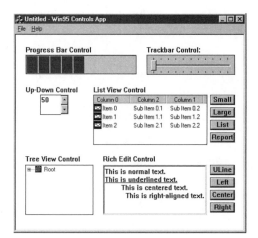

Creating the List View

In the Win95 Controls App application, the list view control is created in the CreateListView() local member function, which the program calls from the view class's OnCreate() function. In CreateListView(), the program first creates two image lists, as shown in Listing 8.4. One image list will hold the small icon for the list view, and the other will hold the large icon. In this case, the list only includes one icon.

Listing 8.4 LST8_4.TXT—Creating the List View's Image Lists

```
m_smallImageList.Create(16, 16, FALSE, 1, 0);
m_largeImageList.Create(32, 32, FALSE, 1, 0);
```

continues

Listing 8.4   Continued

```
HICON hIcon = ::LoadIcon (AfxGetResourceHandle(),
    MAKEINTRESOURCE(IDI_ICON1));
m_smallImageList.Add(hIcon);
hIcon = ::LoadIcon (AfxGetResourceHandle(),
    MAKEINTRESOURCE(IDI_ICON2));
m_largeImageList.Add(hIcon);
```

Now that the program has created the image lists, it can create the list view control, by calling the class's `Create()` member function, like this:

```
m_listView.Create(WS_VISIBLE | WS_CHILD | WS_BORDER |
    LVS_REPORT | LVS_NOSORTHEADER | LVS_EDITLABELS,
CRect(160, 120, 394, 220), this, 105);
```

Here, `Create()`'s four arguments are the control's style flags, the control's size, a pointer to the control's parent window, and the control's ID. The `CListCtrl` class, of which `m_listView` is an object, defines special styles to be used with list view controls. Table 8.7 lists these special styles and their descriptions.

Table 8.7   List View Styles

Style	Description
LVS_ALIGNLEFT	Left aligns items in the large-icon and small-icon views
LVS_ALIGNTOP	Top aligns items in the large-icon and small-icon views
LVS_AUTOARRANGE	Automatically arranges items in the large-icon and small-icon views
LVS_EDITLABELS	Enables the user to edit item labels
LVS_ICON	Sets the control to the large-icon view
LVS_LIST	Sets the control to the list view
LVS_NOCOLUMNHEADER	Shows no column headers in report view
LVS_NOITEMDATA	Stores only the state of each item
LVS_NOLABELWRAP	Disallows multiple-line item labels
LVS_NOSCROLL	Turns off scrolling
LVS_NOSORTHEADER	Turns off the button appearance of column headers
LVS_OWNERDRAWFIXED	Enables owner-drawn items in report view
LVS_REPORT	Sets the control to the report view
LVS_SHAREIMAGELISTS	Prevents the control from destroying its image lists when the control no longer needs them

Style	Description
LVS_SINGLESEL	Disallows multiple selection of items
LVS_SMALLICON	Sets the control to the small-icon view
LVS_SORTASCENDING	Sorts items in ascending order
LVS_SORTDESCENDING	Sorts items in descending order

Initializing the List View

Although not especially difficult, setting up a list view control is quite a lot more work than setting up a simpler control like a progress bar. As you already know, the list view control uses two image lists, one for its small icons and one for its large icons. A list view control also uses column headers for its report view, as well as list items and subitems. In short, to initialize a list view control, you must complete the following steps:

1. Create the list view control.
2. Associate the control with its image lists.
3. Create a column object for each column that will appear in the report view.
4. Create list items and subitems for each item that will be displayed in the list view control.

Associating the List View with Its Image Lists

You've already created your list view control, so step one is out of the way. Now, you must associate the control with its image lists (which have also already been created). The Win95 Controls App application handles the task like this:

```
m_listView.SetImageList(&m_smallImageList, LVSIL_SMALL);
m_listView.SetImageList(&m_largeImageList, LVSIL_NORMAL);
```

As you can see, the SetImageList() member function takes two parameters, which are a pointer to the image list and a flag indicating how the list is to be used. There are three constants defined for this flag: LVSIL_SMALL (which indicates that the list contains small icons), LVSIL_NORMAL (large icons), and LVSIL_STATE (state images). The SetImageList() function returns a pointer to the previously set image list, if any.

Creating the List View's Columns

The next task is to create the columns for the control's report view. You need one main column for the item itself and one column for each subitem associated with an item. For example, in Explorer's list view, the main column holds file and folder names. Each additional column holds the subitems for each item, including the file's size, type, and modification date. To create a column, you must first declare an LV_COLUMN structure. You use this structure to pass information to and from the system. The LV_COLUMN structure is defined as shown in Listing 8.5.

On the CD

Listing 8.5 LST8_5.TXT—The *LV_COLUMN* Structure

```
typedef struct _LV_COLUMN
{
    UINT mask;          // Flags indicating valid fields
    int fmt;            // Column alignment
    int cx;             // Column width
    LPSTR pszText;      // Address of string buffer
    int cchTextMax;     // Size of the buffer
    int iSubItem;       // Subitem index for this column
} LV_COLUMN;
```

The mask member of the structure must be set so that it indicates which of the other fields in the structure are valid. The flags you can use are LVCF_FMT (meaning fmt is valid), LVCF_SUBITEM (iSubItem is valid), LVCF_TEXT (pszText is valid), and LVCF_WIDTH (cx is valid). Essentially, when you give mask its value, you're telling the system which members of the structure to use and which to ignore.

The fmt member gives the column's alignment and can be LVCFMT_CENTER, LVCFMT_LEFT, or LVCFMT_RIGHT. The alignment determines how the column's label and items are positioned in the column.

N O T E The first column, which contains the main items, is always aligned to the left. The other columns in the report view can be aligned how you like. ■

The cx field specifies the width of each column, whereas pszText is the address of a string buffer. When you're using the structure to create a column (you also can use this structure to obtain information about a column), this string buffer contains the column's label. The cchTextMax member gives the size of the string buffer and is valid only when retrieving information about a column.

In Win95 Controls App's CreateListView() function, the program starts initializing the LV_COLUMN structure as shown in Listing 8.6.

On the CD

Listing 8.6 LST8_6.TXT—Initializing the *LV_COLUMN* Structure

```
LV_COLUMN lvColumn;
lvColumn.mask = LVCF_FMT ¦ LVCF_WIDTH ¦ LVCF_TEXT ¦ LVCF_SUBITEM;
lvColumn.fmt = LVCFMT_CENTER;
lvColumn.cx = 75;
```

The values being set in Listing 8.6 will be the same for every column created, so they are done first and then are not changed as the columns are created.

Next, the program creates its main column by setting the appropriate structure members and then calling the CListCtrl object's InsertColumn() member function:

```
lvColumn.iSubItem = 0;
lvColumn.pszText = "Column 0";
m_listView.InsertColumn(0, &lvColumn);
```

Setting isubItem to 0 indicates that the program is creating the first column. (Column numbers are zero-based like an array's indexes.) Finally, the program sets pszText to the column's label and calls InsertColumn() to add the column to the list view control. InsertColumn()'s two arguments are the column's index and a pointer to the LV_COLUMN structure.

The two subitem columns are created similarly, as shown in Listing 8.7.

Listing 8.7   LST8_7.TXT—Creating the SubItem Columns

```
lvColumn.iSubItem = 1;
lvColumn.pszText = "Column 1";
m_listView.InsertColumn(1, &lvColumn);
lvColumn.iSubItem = 2;
lvColumn.pszText = "Column 2";
m_listView.InsertColumn(1, &lvColumn);
```

Creating the List View's Items

With the columns created, it's time to create the items that will be listed in the columns when the control is in its report view. Creating items is not unlike creating columns. As with columns, Visual C++ defines a structure that you must initialize and pass to the function that creates the items. This structure is called LV_ITEM and is defined as shown in Listing 8.8.

Listing 8.8   LST8_8.TXT—The *LV_ITEM* Structure

```
typedef struct _LV_ITEM
{
    UINT    mask;        // Flags indicating valid fields
    int     iItem;       // Item index
    int     iSubItem;    // Sub-item index
    UINT    state;       // Item's current state
    UINT    stateMask;   // Valid item states.
    LPSTR   pszText;      // Address of string buffer
    int     cchTextMax;  // Size of string buffer
    int     iImage;      // Image index for this item
    LPARAM  lParam;      // Additional information as a 32-bit value
} LV_ITEM;
```

In the LV_ITEM structure, the mask member specifies which other members of the structure are valid. The flags you can use are LVIF_IMAGE (iImage is valid), LVIF_PARAM (lParam is valid), LVIF_STATE (state is valid), and LVIF_TEXT (meaning pszText is valid).

The iItem member is the index of the item, which you can kind of think of as the row number in report view (although the position of the items can change when they're sorted). Each item has a unique index. The iSubItem member is the index of the subitem if this structure is defining a subitem. You can think of this value as the number of the column in which the item will appear. If you're defining the main item (the first column), this value should be 0.

The `state` and `stateMask` members hold the item's current state and the item's valid states, which can be one or more of `LVIS_CUT` (the item is selected for cut and paste), `LVIS_DROPHILITED` (the item is a highlighted drop target), `LVIS_FOCUSED` (the item has the focus), and `LVIS_SELECTED` (the item is selected).

The `pszText` member is the address of a string buffer. When using the `LV_ITEM` structure to create an item, the string buffer contains the item's text. When obtaining information about the item, `pszText` is the buffer where the information will be stored, and `cchTextMax` is the size of the buffer. If `pszText` is set to `LPSTR_TEXTCALLBACK`, the item uses the callback mechanism. Finally, the `iImage` member is the index of the item's icon in the small icon and large icon image lists. If set to `I_IMAGECALLBACK`, the `iImage` member indicates that the item uses the callback mechanism.

In Win95 Controls App's `CreateListView()` function, the program starts initializing the `LV_ITEM` structure as shown in Listing 8.9.

Listing 8.9   LST8_9.TXT—Initializing the LV_ITEM Structure

```
LV_ITEM lvItem;
lvItem.mask = LVIF_TEXT ¦ LVIF_IMAGE ¦ LVIF_STATE;
lvItem.state = 0;
lvItem.stateMask = 0;
lvItem.iImage = 0;
```

The values being set in Listing 8.9 will be the same for every item created, so they are done first and then are not changed as the items are created.

Now, the program can start creating the items that will be displayed in the list view control. Listing 8.10 shows how the program creates the first item.

Listing 8.10   LST8_10.TXT—Creating a List View Item

```
lvItem.iItem = 0;
lvItem.iSubItem = 0;
lvItem.pszText = "Item 0";
m_listView.InsertItem(&lvItem);
```

In Listing 8.10, the program sets the item and subitem indexes to 0 and sets the item's text to "Item 0." The program then calls the `CListCtrl` class's `InsertItem()` member function to add the item to the list view control. This function's single argument is the address of the `LV_ITEM` structure that contains the information about the item to be created.

At this point, the list view control has three columns and one item created. However, this single item's subitems display nothing unless you initialize them. Win95 Controls App initializes the first set of subitems like this:

```
m_listView.SetItemText(0, 1, "Sub Item 0.1");
m_listView.SetItemText(0, 2, "Sub Item 0.2");
```

The SetItemText() function takes three arguments, which are the item index, the subitem index, and the text to which to set the item or subitem.

As Listing 8.11 shows, the program then creates two more items along with the items' associated subitems.

On the CD

Listing 8.11 LST8_11.TXT—Creating Additional Items and SubItems

```
lvItem.iItem = 1;
lvItem.iSubItem = 0;
lvItem.pszText = "Item 1";
m_listView.InsertItem(&lvItem);
m_listView.SetItemText(1, 1, "Sub Item 1.1");
m_listView.SetItemText(1, 2, "Sub Item 1.2");
lvItem.iItem = 2;
lvItem.iSubItem = 0;
lvItem.pszText = "Item 2";
m_listView.InsertItem(&lvItem);
m_listView.SetItemText(2, 1, "Sub Item 2.1");
m_listView.SetItemText(2, 2, "Sub Item 2.2");
```

Manipulating the List View

As I said previously, you can set a list view control to four different types of views: small icon, large icon, list, and report. In Explorer, for example, the toolbar features buttons that you can click to change the view, or you can select the view from the View menu. Although Win95 Controls App doesn't have a snazzy toolbar like Explorer, it does include four buttons that you can click to change the view. Those buttons are created in the CreateListView() function as shown in Listing 8.12.

On the CD

Listing 8.12 LST8_12.TXT—Creating the View Buttons

```
m_smallButton.Create("Small", WS_VISIBLE | WS_CHILD | WS_BORDER,
      CRect(400, 120, 450, 140), this, 106);
m_largeButton.Create("Large", WS_VISIBLE | WS_CHILD | WS_BORDER,
      CRect(400, 145, 450, 165), this, 107);
m_listButton.Create("List", WS_VISIBLE | WS_CHILD | WS_BORDER,
      CRect(400, 170, 450, 190), this, 108);
m_reportButton.Create("Report", WS_VISIBLE | WS_CHILD | WS_BORDER,
      CRect(400, 195, 450, 215), this, 109);
```

These buttons are associated with entries in the view window's message map with the message-response functions OnSmall(), OnLarge(), OnList(), and OnReport(). In other words, when the user clicks one of these buttons, its matching function gets called, where the program changes the list view control to the requested view type. For example, when the user clicks the Small button, the function shown in Listing 8.13 changes the view to the list view.

Listing 8.13   LST8_13.TXT—Changing to the List View

```
void CWin95View::OnSmall()
{
    SetWindowLong(m_listView.m_hWnd, GWL_STYLE,
        WS_VISIBLE | WS_CHILD | WS_BORDER |
        LVS_SMALLICON | LVS_EDITLABELS);
}
```

The SetWindowLong() function sets a window's attribute. Its arguments are the window's handle, a flag that specifies the value to be changed, and the new value. In this case, the GWL_STYLE flag specifies that the window's style should be changed to the style given in the third argument. Changing the list view control's style (in the preceding code, the new view style is LVS_SMALLICON) changes the type of view it displays.

Besides changing the view, there are a number of other features you can program for your list view controls. When the user does something with the control, Windows sends a WM_NOTIFY message to the parent window. By responding to these notifications, you can give your list view control its various capabilities. The most common notifications sent by a list view control are LVN_COLUMNCLICK (indicates that the user clicked a column header), LVN_BEGINLABELEDIT (indicates that the user is about to edit an item's label), and LVN_ENDLABELEDIT (indicates that the user is ending the label-editing process).

If you haven't discovered it yet, you can edit the labels of the items in Win95 Controls App's list view items. This works by the program's capturing and handling the notification messages sent by the list view control. To capture the notification messages, just override the window's OnNotify() function.

The three parameters received by OnNotify() are the message's WPARAM and LPARAM values and a pointer to a result code. In the case of a WM_NOTIFY message coming from a list view control, the WPARAM is the list view control's ID. And, if the WM_NOTIFY message is the LVN_BEGINLABELEDIT or LVN_ENDLABELEDIT notifications, the LPARAM is a pointer to a LV_DISPINFO structure, which itself contains NMHDR and LV_ITEM structures. You use the information in these structures to manipulate the item the user is trying to edit.

In OnNotify(), the program first casts the lParam parameter to a LV_DISPINFO structure, like this:

```
LV_DISPINFO* lv_dispInfo = (LV_DISPINFO*) lParam;
```

Next, the program checks whether the function is receiving a LVN_BEGINLABELEDIT notification, like this:

```
if (lv_dispInfo->hdr.code == LVN_BEGINLABELEDIT)
```

If the notification is LVN_BEGINLABELEDIT, your program can do whatever pre-editing initialization it needs to do. In the Win95 Controls App application, the function shows you how to get a pointer to the edit control being used to edit the label:

```
CEdit* pEdit = m_listView.GetEditControl();
```

The program, however, doesn't actually do anything with the control.

When handling label editing, the other notification to watch out for is LVN_ENDLABELEDIT, which this particular application does like this:

```
else if (lv_dispInfo->hdr.code == LVN_ENDLABELEDIT)
```

When the program receives this notification, the user has finished editing the label, either by typing the new label or by canceling the editing process. If the user has canceled the process, the LV_DISPINFO structure's item.pszText member will be NULL or the item.iItem member will be -1. In this case, you need do nothing more than ignore the notification. If, however, the user completed the editing process, the program must copy the new label to the item's text, which OnNotify() does like this:

```
m_listView.SetItemText(lv_dispInfo->item.iItem,
    0, lv_dispInfo->item.pszText);
```

The CListCtrl object's SetItemText() member function requires three arguments: the item index, the subitem index, and the new text. As you can see, all the information you need is stored in the LV_DISPINFO structure.

There are a lot of other things you can do with a list view control. However, there's not enough space in this chapter to get into any further detail. You can find more about these powerful controls in your Visual C++ online documentation. The ROWLIST sample program in the MSDEV\SAMPLES\MFC\GENERAL directory might be a good place to start.

The Tree View Control

In the preceding section, you learned how to use the list view control to organize the display of many items in a window. The list view control enables you to display items both as objects in a window and objects in a report organized into columns. Often, however, the data you'd like to organize for your application's user is best placed into a hierarchical view, where elements of the data are shown as they relate to each other. A good example of such a hierarchical display is the directory tree used by Windows to display directories on disk and the files they contain.

As is the case with other useful controls, Windows 95 includes the tree view control as one of its common controls. MFC provides access to this control through its CTreeCtrl class. This versatile control enables you to display data in various ways, all the while retaining the hierarchical relationship between the data objects in the view.

If you'd like to see an example of a tree view control, just open the Windows 95 Explorer (see fig. 8.8). The left side of the window shows how the tree view control organizes objects in a window. (The right side of the window contains a list view control, which you learned about in the previous section). In the figure, the tree view displays not only the storage devices on the computer, but also the directories and files stored on those devices. The tree clearly shows the hierarchical relationship between the devices, directories, and files as well as enables the user to open and close branches on the tree in order to explore it at a different level.

FIG. 8.8

A tree view control displays a hierarchical relationship between items.

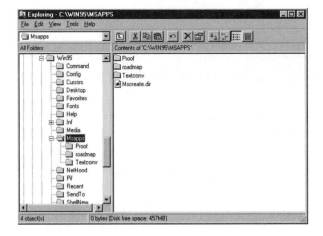

The Win95 Controls App application also contains a tree view control. You can click the tree's various nodes to expose new levels of the tree. You can even edit the labels of the items in the tree. To do this, select an item and then click it. An edit box appears into which you can type the new label.

Creating the Tree View

In the Win95 Controls App application, the tree view control is created in the `CreateTreeView()` local member function, which the program calls from the view class's `OnCreate()` function. In `CreateTreeView()`, the program first creates the image list that holds the icons used with each item in the view. Listing 8.14 shows how the program creates the image list.

On the CD

Listing 8.14 LST8_14.TXT—Creating the Tree View Control's Image List

```
m_treeImageList.Create(13, 13, FALSE, 3, 0);
HICON hIcon = ::LoadIcon(AfxGetResourceHandle(),
      MAKEINTRESOURCE(IDI_ICON3));
m_treeImageList.Add(hIcon);
hIcon = ::LoadIcon(AfxGetResourceHandle(),
      MAKEINTRESOURCE(IDI_ICON4));
m_treeImageList.Add(hIcon);
hIcon = ::LoadIcon(AfxGetResourceHandle(),
      MAKEINTRESOURCE(IDI_ICON5));
m_treeImageList.Add(hIcon);
```

Now that the program has created the image list, it can create the tree view control, by calling the class's `Create()` member function:

```
m_treeView.Create(WS_VISIBLE | WS_CHILD | WS_BORDER |
    TVS_HASLINES | TVS_LINESATROOT | TVS_HASBUTTONS |
    TVS_EDITLABELS, CRect(20, 260, 160, 360), this, 110);
```

Here, Create()'s four arguments are the control's style flags, the control's size, a pointer to the control's parent window, and the control's ID. The CTreeCtrl class, of which m_treeView is an object, defines special styles to be used with list view controls. Table 8.8 lists these special styles.

Table 8.8 Tree View Control Styles

Style	Description
TVS_DISABLEDRAGDROP	Disables drag-and-drop operations
TVS_EDITLABELS	Enables user to edit labels
TVS_HASBUTTONS	Gives each parent item a button.
TVS_HASLINES	Adds lines between items in the tree
TVS_LINESATROOT	Adds a line between the root and child items
TVS_SHOWSELALWAYS	Forces a selected item to stay selected when losing focus

Initializing the Tree View

Like the list view control, a tree view control requires some hefty set-up work. As you already know, the tree view control can use an image list for item icons. A tree view control also must contain item objects that your program creates and adds to the control. To initialize a tree view control, you must complete the following steps:

1. Create the tree view control.
2. Associate the control with its image list (optional).
3. Create the root and child items that will be displayed in the control.

The Win95 Controls App application associates the tree view control with its image list like this:

```
m_treeView.SetImageList(&m_treeImageList, TVSIL_NORMAL);
```

The creation of the tree view controls root and child items is covered in the following section.

Creating the Tree View's Items

Creating items for a tree view control is much like doing the same thing for a list view control. As with the list view, Visual C++ defines a structure that you must initialize and pass to the function that creates the items. This structure is called TV_ITEM and is defined as shown in Listing 8.15.

Listing 8.15   LST8_15.TXT—The *TV_ITEM* Structure

```
typedef struct _TV_ITEM
{
    UINT        mask;
    HTREEITEM   hItem;
    UINT        state;
    UINT        stateMask;
    LPSTR       pszText;
    int         cchTextMax;
    int         iImage;
    int         iSelectedImage;
    int         cChildren;
    LPARAM      lParam;
} TV_ITEM;
```

In the TV_ITEM structure, the mask member specifies which other members of the structure are valid. The flags you can use are TVIF_CHILDREN (cChildren is valid), TVIF_HANDLE (hItem is valid), TVIF_IMAGE (iImage is valid), TVIF_PARAM (lParam is valid), TVIF_SELECTEDIMAGE (iSelectedImage is valid), TVIF_STATE (state and stateMask are valid), and TVIF_TEXT (pszText and cchTextMax are valid).

The hItem member is the handle of the item, whereas the state and stateMask members hold the item's current state and the item's valid states, which can be one or more of TVIS_BOLD, TVIS_CUT, TVIS_DROPHILITED, TVIS_EXPANDED, TVIS_EXPANDEDONCE, TVIS_FOCUSED, TVIS_OVERLAYMASK, TVIS_SELECTED, TVIS_STATEIMAGEMASK, and TVIS_USERMASK. Please check your Visual C++ online documentation for the meanings of these flags.

The pszText member is the address of a string buffer. When using the LV_ITEM structure to create an item, the string buffer contains the item's text. When obtaining information about the item, pszText is the buffer where the information will be stored, and cchTextMax is the size of the buffer. If pszText is set to LPSTR_TEXTCALLBACK, the item uses the callback mechanism. Finally, the iImage member is the index of the item's icon in the image list. If set to I_IMAGECALLBACK, the iImage member indicates that the item uses the callback mechanism.

The iSelectedImage member is the index of the icon in the image list that represents the item when the item is selected. As with iImage, if this member is set to I_IMAGECALLBACK, the iSelectedImage member indicates that the item uses the callback mechanism. Finally, cChildren specifies whether there are child items associated with the item.

In addition to the TV_ITEM structure, you must initialize a TV_INSERTSTRUCT structure that holds information about how to insert the new structure into the tree view control. That structure is declared as shown in Listing 8.16.

Listing 8.16   LST8_16.TXT—The *TV_INSERTSTRUCT* Structure

```
typedef struct _TV_INSERTSTRUCT
{
    HTREEITEM hParent;
```

```
    HTREEITEM hInsertAfter;
      TV_ITEM    item;
} TV_INSERTSTRUCT;
```

In this structure, hParent is the handle to the parent tree-view item. A value of NULL or TVI_ROOT specifies that the item should be placed at the root of the tree. The hInsertAfter member specifies the handle of the item after which this new item should be inserted. It can also be one of the flags TVI_FIRST (beginning of the list), TVI_LAST (end of the list), or TVI_SORT (alphabetical order). Finally, the item member is the TV_ITEM structure containing information about the item to be inserted into the tree.

In Win95 Controls App's CreateTreeView() function, the program initializes the TV_ITEM structure for the root item (the first item in the tree) as shown in Listing 8.17.

On the CD

Listing 8.17   LST8_17.TXT—Creating the Root Item

```
TV_ITEM tvItem;
tvItem.mask =
       TVIF_TEXT ¦ TVIF_IMAGE ¦ TVIF_SELECTEDIMAGE;
tvItem.pszText = "Root";
tvItem.cchTextMax = 4;
tvItem.iImage = 0;
tvItem.iSelectedImage = 0;
TV_INSERTSTRUCT tvInsert;
tvInsert.hParent = TVI_ROOT;
tvInsert.hInsertAfter = TVI_FIRST;
tvInsert.item = tvItem;
HTREEITEM hRoot = m_treeView.InsertItem(&tvInsert);
```

As you can see, the CTreeCtrl member function InsertItem() actually inserts the item into the tree view control. Its single argument is the address of the TV_INSERTSTRUCT structure.

The program inserts the remaining items into the tree view control as shown in Listing 8.18.

Listing 8.18   LST8_18.TXT—Inserting the Child Items into the Tree View Control

```
// Create the first child item.
tvItem.pszText = "Child Item 1";
tvItem.cchTextMax = 12;
tvItem.iImage = 1;
tvItem.iSelectedImage = 1;
tvInsert.hParent = hRoot;
tvInsert.hInsertAfter = TVI_FIRST;
tvInsert.item = tvItem;
HTREEITEM hChildItem = m_treeView.InsertItem(&tvInsert);
// Create a child of the first child item.
tvItem.pszText = "Child Item 2";
```

continues

Listing 8.18   Continued

```
tvItem.cchTextMax = 12;
tvItem.iImage = 2;
tvItem.iSelectedImage = 2;
tvInsert.hParent = hChildItem;
tvInsert.hInsertAfter = TVI_FIRST;
tvInsert.item = tvItem;
m_treeView.InsertItem(&tvInsert);
// Create another child of the root item.
tvItem.pszText = "Child Item 3";
tvItem.cchTextMax = 12;
tvItem.iImage = 1;
tvItem.iSelectedImage = 1;
tvInsert.hParent = hRoot;
tvInsert.hInsertAfter = TVI_LAST;
tvInsert.item = tvItem;
m_treeView.InsertItem(&tvInsert);
```

Manipulating the Tree View

Just as with the list view control, you can edit the labels of the items in Win95 Controls App's tree view items. Also like the list view control, this process works by the program's capturing and handling the notification messages sent by the tree view control. In Win95 Controls App, the overridden WindowProc() function routes these WM_NOTIFY messages to the program's OnNotify() local function.

In the case of a WM_NOTIFY message coming from a tree view control, the WPARAM is the list view control's ID. And, if the WM_NOTIFY message is the TVN_BEGINLABELEDIT or TVN_ENDLABELEDIT notifications, the LPARAM is a pointer to a TV_DISPINFO structure, which itself contains NMHDR and TV_ITEM structures. You use the information in these structures to manipulate the item the user is trying to edit. As you can see in Listing 8.19, OnNotify() handles the tree-view notifications almost exactly the same way as the list-view notifications. The only difference is the names of the structures used.

Listing 8.19   LST8_19.TXT—Handling Tree-View Notifications

```
TV_DISPINFO* tv_dispInfo = (TV_DISPINFO*) lParam;
if (tv_dispInfo->hdr.code == TVN_BEGINLABELEDIT)
{
    CEdit* pEdit = m_treeView.GetEditControl();
    // Manipulate edit control here.
}
else if (tv_dispInfo->hdr.code == TVN_ENDLABELEDIT)
{
    if (tv_dispInfo->item.pszText != NULL)
    {
        m_treeView.SetItemText(tv_dispInfo->item.hItem,
        tv_dispInfo->item.pszText);
    }
}
```

The tree view control sends a number of different notification messages, including TVN_BEGINDRAG, TVN_BEGINLABELEDIT, TVN_BEGINRDRAG, TVN_DELETEITEM, TVN_ENDLABELEDIT, TVN_GETDISPINFO, TVN_ITEMEXPANDED, TVN_ITEMEXPANDING, TVN_KEYDOWN, TVN_SELCHANGED, TVN_SELCHANGING, and TVN_SETDISPINFO. Please check your Visual C++ online documentation for more information on handling the different notification messages.

The Rich Edit Control

If you took all the energy that's been expended on writing text-editing software and concentrated that energy on other, less mundane programming problems, computer science would probably be a decade ahead of where it is now. Okay, that may be an exaggeration, but it is true that, when it comes to text editors, a huge amount of effort has been dedicated to reinventing the wheel. Wouldn't it be great to have one piece of text-editing code that all programmers could use as the starting point for their own custom text editors?

With Visual C++'s CRichEditCtrl control, which gives programmers access to Windows 95's rich edit control, you can get a huge jump on any text-editing functionality that you need to install in your applications. The rich edit control is capable of handling fonts, paragraph styles, text color, and other types of tasks that are traditionally found in text editors. In fact, a rich edit control (named for the fact that it handles text in Rich Text Format, also called RTF) provides a solid starting point for any text-editing tasks that your application must handle. A rich edit control enables the user to perform the following text-editing tasks:

- Type text
- Edit text using cut-and-paste and sophisticated drag-and-drop operations
- Set text attributes such as font, point-size, and color
- Apply underline, bold, italic, strikethrough, superscript, and subscript properties to text
- Format text using various alignments and bulleted lists
- Lock text from further editing
- Save and load files

As the preceding list proves, a rich edit control is powerful. It is, in fact, almost a complete word-processor-in-a-box that you can plug into your program and use immediately. Of course, because a rich edit control offers so many features, there's a lot to learn. In this section, you get a quick introduction to how to create and manipulate the rich edit control.

To get started, try out the rich edit control included in the Win95 Controls App. First, click in the text box to give it the focus. Then, just start typing. Want to try out character attributes? Click the ULine button to add underlining to either selected text or the next text you type. To try out paragraph formatting, click either the Left, Center, or Right buttons to specify paragraph alignment. Figure 8.9 shows the rich edit control with the different character and paragraph styles used.

FIG. 8.9

A rich edit control is almost a complete word processor.

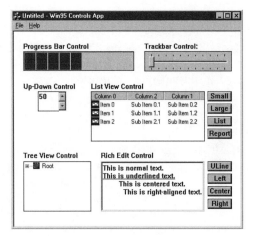

Creating the Rich Edit Control

In the Win95 Controls App application, the rich edit control is created in the `CreateRichEdit()` local member function, which the program calls from the view class's `OnCreate()` function. In `CreateRichEdit()`, the program creates the control by calling its `Create()` member function:

```
m_richEdit.Create(WS_CHILD ¦ WS_VISIBLE ¦ WS_BORDER ¦
    ES_AUTOVSCROLL ¦ ES_MULTILINE,
    CRect(180, 260, 393, 360), this, 111);
```

This function's four arguments are the control's style flags, the control's size, a pointer to the control's parent window, and the control's ID. The style constants include the same constants you would use for creating any type of window, with the addition of special styles used with rich edit controls. Table 8.9 lists these special styles.

Table 8.9 Rich Edit Styles

Style	Description
ES_AUTOHSCROLL	Automatically scrolls horizontally
ES_AUTOVSCROLL	Automatically scrolls vertically
ES_CENTER	Centers text
ES_LEFT	Left aligns text
ES_LOWERCASE	Lowercases all text.
ES_MULTILINE	Enables multiple lines
ES_NOHIDESEL	Doesn't hide selected text when losing the focus
ES_OEMCONVERT	Converts from ANSI characters to OEM characters and back to ANSI
ES_PASSWORD	Displays characters as asterisks

Style	Description
ES_READONLY	Disables editing in the control
ES_RIGHT	Right aligns text
ES_UPPERCASE	Uppercases all text
ES_WANTRETURN	Inserts return characters into text when enter is pressed

Initializing the Rich Edit Control

After the rich edit control is created, you may want to initialize it in some way. (The Win95 Controls App application doesn't perform additional initialization of the control.) The CRichEditCtrl class features a number of member functions that enable you to initialize and manipulate the control. Those member functions and their descriptions are listed in Table 8.10. For more information, please look the functions up in your Visual C++ online documentation.

Table 8.10   Member Functions of the *CRichEditCtrl* Class

Function	Description
CanPaste()	Determines whether the Clipboard's contents can be pasted into the control
CanUndo()	Determines whether the last edit can be undone
Clear()	Clears selected text
Copy()	Copies selected text to the Clipboard
Create()	Creates the control
Cut()	Cuts selected text to the Clipboard
DisplayBand()	Displays a portion of the control's text
EmptyUndoBuffer()	Resets the control's undo flag
FindText()	Finds the given text
FormatRange()	Formats text for an output target device
GetCharPos()	Gets the position of a given character
GetDefaultCharFormat()	Gets the default character format
GetEventMask()	Gets the control's event mask
GetFirstVisibleLine()	Gets the index of the first visible line
GetIRichEditOle()	Gets the IRichEditOle interface pointer for the control
GetLimitText()	Gets the maximum number of characters that can be entered

continues

Table 8.10 Continued

Function	Description
GetLine()	Gets the specified text line
GetLineCount()	Gets the number of lines in the control
GetModify()	Determines whether the control's contents have changed since the last save
GetParaFormat()	Gets the paragraph format of selected text
GetRect()	Gets the control's formatting rectangle
GetSel()	Gets the position of the currently selected text
GetSelectionCharFormat()	Gets the character format of selected text
GetSelectionType()	Gets the selected text's contents type
GetSelText()	Gets the currently selected text
GetTextLength()	Gets the length of the control's text
HideSelection()	Hides or shows selected text
LimitText()	Sets the maximum number of characters that can be entered
LineFromChar()	Gets the number of the line containing the given character
LineIndex()	Gets the character index of a given line
LineLength()	Gets the length of the given line
LineScroll()	Scrolls the text the given number of lines and characters
Paste()	Pastes the Clipboard's contents into the control
PasteSpecial()	Pastes the Clipboard's contents using the given format
ReplaceSel()	Replaces selected text with the given text
RequestResize()	Forces the control to send EN_REQUESTRESIZE notification messages
SetBackgroundColor()	Sets the control's background color
SetDefaultCharFormat()	Sets the default character format
SetEventMask()	Sets the control's event mask
SetModify()	Toggles the control's modification flag
SetOLECallback()	Sets the control's IRichEditOleCallback COM object
SetOptions()	Sets the control's options
SetParaFormat()	Sets the selection's paragraph format

Function	Description
SetReadOnly()	Disables editing in the control
SetRect()	Sets the control's formatting rectangle
SetSel()	Sets the selected text
SetSelectionCharFormat()	Sets the selected text's character format
SetTargetDevice()	Sets the control's target output device
SetWordCharFormat()	Sets the current word's character format
StreamIn()	Brings text in from an input stream
StreamOut()	Stores text in an output stream
Undo()	Undoes the last edit

Manipulating the Rich Edit Control

As you can tell from Table 8.10, you can do a lot more with a rich edit control than can possibly be described in a chapter this size. However, Win95 Controls App shows you the basics of using the rich edit control in an application, by setting character attributes and paragraph formats. When you include a rich edit control in an application, you'll probably want to give the user some control over its contents. For this reason, you usually create menu and toolbar commands for selecting the various options you want to support in the application. Win95 Controls App doesn't have an Options menu or a toolbar. However, it does create four buttons that the user can click to control the rich edit control. Listing 8.20 shows how the program creates these buttons in the CreateRichEdit() function, right after it creates the rich edit control itself.

Listing 8.20   LST8_20.TXT—Creating Editing Control Buttons

```
m_boldButton.Create("ULine", WS_VISIBLE ¦ WS_CHILD ¦ WS_BORDER,
    CRect(400, 260, 450, 280), this, 112);
m_leftButton.Create("Left", WS_VISIBLE ¦ WS_CHILD ¦ WS_BORDER,
    CRect(400, 285, 450, 305), this, 113);
m_centerButton.Create("Center", WS_VISIBLE ¦ WS_CHILD ¦ WS_BORDER,
    CRect(400, 310, 450, 330), this, 114);
m_rightButton.Create("Right", WS_VISIBLE ¦ WS_CHILD ¦ WS_BORDER,
    CRect(400, 335, 450, 355), this, 115);
```

Thanks to MFC's message mapping, these buttons are associated with the functions that respond to them. For example, when the user clicks the ULine button, MFC calls the OnULine() method, where the program toggles the underline text attribute. In OnULine(), the program first initializes a CHARFORMAT structure, like this:

```
CHARFORMAT charFormat;
charFormat.cbSize = sizeof(CHARFORMAT);
charFormat.dwMask = CFM_UNDERLINE;
```

A CHARFORMAT structure holds information about character formatting and is declared as shown in Listing 8.21.

Listing 8.21   LST8_21.TXT:—The *CHARFORMAT* Structure

```
typedef struct _charformat
{
    UINT     cbSize;
    _WPAD    _wPad1;
    DWORD    dwMask;
    DWORD    dwEffects;
    LONG     yHeight;
    LONG     yOffset;
    COLORREF crTextColor;
    BYTE     bCharSet;
    BYTE     bPitchAndFamily;
    TCHAR    szFaceName[LF_FACESIZE];
    _WPAD    _wPad2;
} CHARFORMAT;
```

In Listing 8.21, cbSize is the size of the structure; dwMask indicates which members of the structure are valid (can be a combination of CFM_BOLD, CFM_COLOR, CFM_FACE, CFM_ITALIC, CFM_OFFSET, CFM_PROTECTED, CFM_SIZE, CFM_STRIKEOUT, and CFM_UNDERLINE); dwEffects is the character effects (can be a combination of CFE_AUTOCOLOR, CFE_BOLD, CFE_ITALIC, CFE_STRIKEOUT, CFE_UNDERLINE, and CFE_PROTECTED); yHeight is the character height; yOffset is the character baseline offset (for super- and subscript characters); crTextColor is the text color; bCharSet is the character set value (see the ifCharSet member of the LOGFONT structure); bPitchAndFamily is the font pitch and family; and szFaceName is the font name.

After initializing the CHARFORMAT structure as needed to toggle underlining, the program calls the control's GetSelectionCharFormat() member function, like this:

```
m_richEdit.GetSelectionCharFormat(charFormat);
```

This function call, whose single argument is a reference to the CHARFORMAT structure, returns the current character format in the structure's dwEffects member. The program checks the result of this function to determine whether to turn underlining on or off, as shown in Listing 8.22.

Listing 8.22   LST8_22.TXT—Determining Whether to Turn Underlining On or Off

```
if (charFormat.dwEffects & CFM_UNDERLINE)
    charFormat.dwEffects = 0;
else
    charFormat.dwEffects = CFE_UNDERLINE;
m_richEdit.SetSelectionCharFormat(charFormat);
```

The call to the control's `SetSelectionCharFormat()` member function sets the character format. Its single argument is a reference to the `CHARFORMAT` structure containing information about the requested character format.

Finally, after setting the character format, the `OnULine()` function returns the focus to the rich edit control:

`m_richEdit.SetFocus();`

This is necessary because, by clicking a button, the user has removed the focus from the rich edit control. You don't want to force the user to keep switching manually back to the control every time he clicks a button, so you do it for him by calling the control's `SetFocus()` member function.

Win95 Controls App also enables the user to switch between the three types of paragraph alignment. This is accomplished similarly to toggling character formats. Listing 8.23 shows the three functions—`OnLeft()`, `OnRight()`, and `OnCenter()`—that handle the alignment commands. As you can see, the main difference is the use of the `PARAFORMAT` structure instead of `CHARFORMAT` and the call to `SetParaFormat()` instead of `SetSelectionCharFormat()`.

On the CD

Listing 8.23 LST8_23.TXT—Changing Paragraph Formats

```
void CWin95View::OnLeft()
{
    PARAFORMAT paraFormat;
    paraFormat.cbSize = sizeof(PARAFORMAT);
    paraFormat.dwMask = PFM_ALIGNMENT;
    paraFormat.wAlignment = PFA_LEFT;
    m_richEdit.SetParaFormat(paraFormat);
    m_richEdit.SetFocus();
}
void CWin95View::OnCenter()
{
    PARAFORMAT paraFormat;
    paraFormat.cbSize = sizeof(PARAFORMAT);
    paraFormat.dwMask = PFM_ALIGNMENT;
    paraFormat.wAlignment = PFA_CENTER;
    m_richEdit.SetParaFormat(paraFormat);
    m_richEdit.SetFocus();
}
void CWin95View::OnRight()
{
    PARAFORMAT paraFormat;
    paraFormat.cbSize = sizeof(PARAFORMAT);
    paraFormat.dwMask = PFM_ALIGNMENT;
    paraFormat.wAlignment = PFA_RIGHT;
    m_richEdit.SetParaFormat(paraFormat);
    m_richEdit.SetFocus();
}
```

From Here...

The Windows 95 common controls are a huge subject that could take up a book of its own. However, this chapter attempted to give you enough of an introduction that you can explore the controls further using Visual C++'s online documentation. You might also want to pick up a good book written especially for Windows 95 programming, such as *Programming the Windows 95 User Interface* by Nancy Winnick Cluts, published by Microsoft Press. For more information on related topics, try the following chapters in this book:

- Chapter 5, "Messages and Commands," discusses how MFC routes the messages that the various Windows controls and devices generate.

- Chapter 9, "Property Pages and Sheets and Wizards," shows you how to program these special types of dialog boxes.

- Chapter 11, "Drawing on the Screen," shows you how to display data and graphics in a window.

- Chapter 18, "Interface Issues," describes other ways your application can communicate with its users.

Property Pages and Sheets and Wizards

One of the newest types of graphical objects is the tabbed dialog box, also known as a *property sheet*. Windows 95 is loaded with property sheets, which organize the many options that can be modified by the user. What's a property sheet? Basically, it's a dialog box with two or more pages. You flip the pages by clicking labeled tabs located at the top of the dialog box. By using such dialog boxes to organize complex groups of options, Windows 95 enables users to find more easily the information and settings that they need. As you've probably guessed, Visual C++ 5.0 supports the Windows 95 property sheets, with the classes `CPropertySheet` and `CPropertyPage`. ■

How to create property page resources

Property sheets contain property pages, which are much like dialog boxes.

How to associate property sheets and pages with their MFC classes

MFC provides classes that enable you to easily manipulate property pages and property sheets.

How to initialize and display property sheets

Creating a property sheet is only half the battle. You also have to get the sheet up on the screen for the user.

How to convert a property sheet to a wizard

Wizards are a special type of property sheet that guides users through complex tasks.

How to respond to wizard buttons

Every wizard contains buttons that enable the user to navigate through the wizard.

Similar to property sheets are *wizards,* which use buttons to move from one page to another rather than using tabs. You've seen a lot of wizards, too. These special types of dialog boxes guide the user step-by-step through complicated processes. For example, when you use AppWizard to generate source code for a new project, the wizard guides you through the entire process. To control the wizard, you click buttons labeled Back, Next, and Finish.

Introducing Property Sheets

Finding a sample property sheet in Windows 95 is as easy as finding sand at the beach. Just click virtually any Properties command or double-click an icon in the Control Panel. For example, Figure 9.1 shows the dialog box that you see when you double-click the Control Panel's Add/Remove Programs icon. This is a property sheet that contains three pages labeled Install/Uninstall, Windows Setup, and Startup Disk, each page containing commands and options related to the page's title topic.

FIG. 9.1

The Add/Remove Programs Properties sheet contains three tabbed pages.

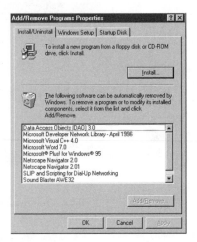

In Figure 9.1, you can see programs installed on the machine that Windows can automatically uninstall. There's also an Install button that leads to other dialog boxes that help you install new programs from floppy disk or CD-ROM. On the other hand, the Windows Setup page (Figure 9.2) helps you add or remove files from the Windows system. To get to this page, you need only click the Windows Setup tab. The Startup Disk page, of course, houses yet another set of options.

As you can see, property sheets are a great way to organize many types of related options. Gone are the days of dialog boxes so jam-packed with options that you needed a college-level course just to figure them out. In the sections that follow, you will learn to program your own tabbed property sheets using MFC's `CPropertySheet` and `CPropertyPage` classes.

FIG. 9.2

To move to the Windows Setup page, you click the Windows Setup tab.

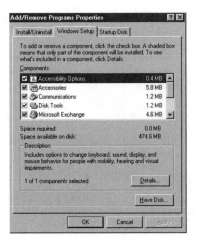

Part
II

Ch
9

Creating the Property Sheet Demo Application

Now that you've had an introduction to property sheets, it's time to learn how to build an application that uses these handy specialized dialog boxes. In the steps that come later, you'll build the Property Sheet Demo application, which demonstrates the creation and manipulation of property sheets. Follow the steps that come next to create the basic application and modify its resources.

N O T E   The complete source code and executable file for the Property Sheet application can be found in the CHAP09\PSHT directory of this book's CD-ROM. ■

1. Use AppWizard to create the basic files for the Property Sheet Demo program, selecting the options listed in the following table. When you're done, the New Project Information dialog box appears; it should look like Figure 9.3. Click the OK button to create the project files.

Dialog Box Name	Options to Select
New Project	Name the project psht and then set the project path to the directory into which you want to store the project's files. Leave the other options set to their defaults.
Step 1	Select Single Document.
Step 2 of 6	Leave set to defaults.
Step 3 of 6	Leave set to defaults.
Step 4 of 6	Turn off all application features.
Step 5 of 6	Leave set to defaults.
Step 6 of 6	Leave set to defaults.

FIG. 9.3

Your Project Information dialog box should look like this.

2. Select the ResourceView tab in the project workspace window. Visual C++ displays the ResourceView window, as shown in Figure 9.4.

FIG. 9.4

The ResourceView tab displays the ResourceView window.

ResourceView window——

ResourceView tab——

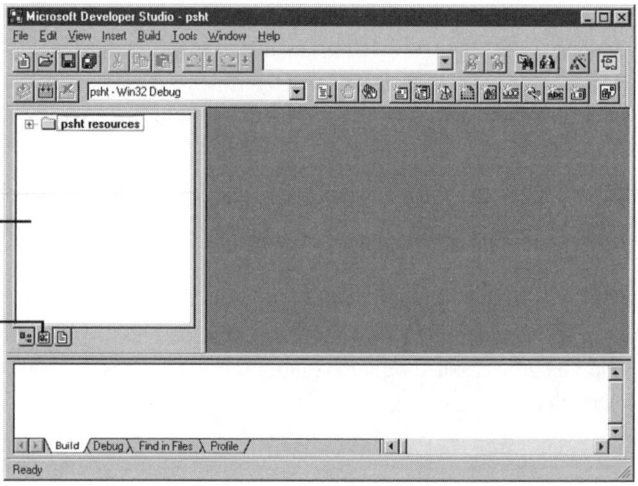

3. In the ResourceView window, click the plus sign next to psht resources to display the application's resources. Click the plus sign next to Menu and then double-click the IDR_MAINFRAME menu ID. Visual C++'s menu editor appears.

4. Click on the Property Sheet Demo application's Edit menu (not Visual C++'s Edit menu) and then press your keyboard's Delete key to delete the Edit menu. When you do, a dialog box asks for verification of the delete command. Click the OK button.

5. Double-click the About psht... item in the Help menu and change it to About Property Sheet Demo.

6. In the application's File menu, delete all menu items except Exit.

7. Add a Property Sheet item to the File menu, giving it the command ID ID_PROPSHEET, as shown in Figure 9.5. Then use your mouse to drag the new command above the Exit command, so that it's the first command in the File menu.

FIG. 9.5

Add a Property Sheet command to the File menu.

8. Double-click the Accelerator resource in the ResourceView window and highlight the IDR_MAINFRAME accelerator ID. Press your Delete key to delete all accelerators from the application.

9. Double-click the Dialog resource in the ResourceView window. Double-click the IDD_ABOUTBOX dialog box ID to bring up the dialog box editor.

10. Modify the dialog box by changing the title to "About Property Sheet Demo," changing the first static text string to "Property Sheet Demo, Version 1.0," and adding the static string "by Macmillan Computer Publishing," as shown in Figure 9.6. Close the dialog box editor.

FIG. 9.6

The About the box should look like this.

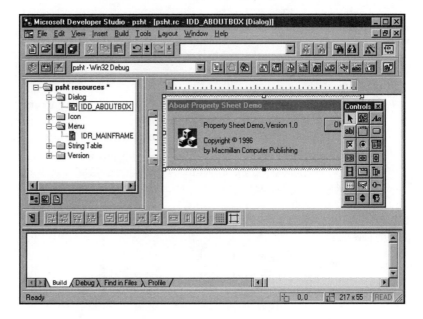

11. Double-click the String Table resource in the ResourceView window. Double-click the String Table ID to bring up the string table editor.

12. Double-click the IDR_MAINFRAME string and then change the first segment of the string to "Property Sheet Demo," as shown in Figure 9.7. Close the string table editor.

Part

II

Ch

9

FIG. 9.7

The first segment of the *IDR_MAINFRAME* string appears in your main window's title bar.

Now that you have the application's basic resources the way you want them, it's time to add the resources that define the application's property sheet. This means creating dialog box resources for each page in the property sheet. Follow the next steps to complete this task.

1. Click the New Dialog button in Developer Studio's toolbar, or press Ctrl+1 on your keyboard, to create a new dialog resource. The new dialog box appears in the dialog box editor.

    This dialog box, when properly set up, will represent the first page of the property sheet.

2. Delete the OK and Cancel buttons by selecting each with your mouse and then pressing your keyboard's Delete key.

3. Double-click the dialog box to bring up its Dialog Properties sheet. Change the ID to IDD_PAGE1DLG and the caption to Page 1, as shown in Figure 9.8.

FIG. 9.8

Double-clicking the dialog box brings up its properties.

4. Click the Styles tab. Change the Style box to Child, the Border box to Thin, and turn off the System Menu check box, as shown in Figure 9.9.

    The Child style is necessary because the property page will be a child window of the property sheet. The property sheet itself will provide the container for the property pages. (Actually, if you forget to set these styles, MFC seems to be smart enough to display the property page properly, in spite of your oversight.)

FIG. 9.9

A property page uses different styles than those in a regular dialog box.

5. Add an edit box to the property page, as shown in Figure 9.10.

FIG. 9.10

A property page can hold whatever controls you like.

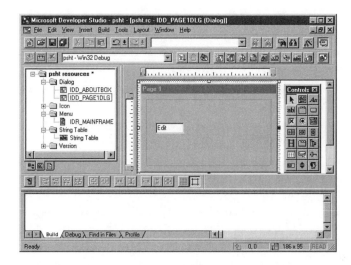

6. Create a second property page by following the previous steps 1 through 5. For this property page, use the ID IDD_PAGE2DLG, a caption of Page 2, and add a check box rather than an edit control, as shown in Figure 9.11.

FIG. 9.11

The second property page should look like this.

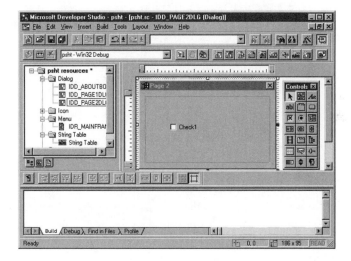

You now have all your resources created. However, you need to associate your two new property-page resources with C++ classes so that you can control them in your program. You also need a class for your property sheet, which will hold the property pages that you've created. Follow the steps given next to create the new classes.

1. Make sure that the Page 1 property page is visible in the dialog edit box and then either click the Developer Studio's ClassWizard button or select View, ClassWizard from the menu bar. The MFC ClassWizard property sheet appears, displaying the Adding A Class dialog box.

2. Select the Create New Class option and then click the OK button. The Create New Class dialog box appears.

3. In the Name box, type **CPage1**, and in the Base Class box, select CPropertyPage. Then click the Create button to create the class.

   You've now associated the property page with an object of the CPropertyPage class, which means that you can use the object to manipulate the property page as needed. The CPropertyPage class will be especially important when you learn about wizards.

4. Select the Member Variables tab of the MFC ClassWizard property sheet. With IDC_EDIT1 highlighted, click the Add Variable button. The Add Member Variable dialog box appears.

5. Name the new member variable m_edit, as shown in Figure 9.12, and then click the OK button. ClassWizard adds the member variable to the new CPage1 class.

   The member variable will hold the value of the property page's control.

FIG. 9.12

ClassWizard makes it easy to add member variables.

6. Click OK on the MFC ClassWizard Properties sheet to finalize the creation of the CPage1 class.

7. Follow steps 1 through 7 for the second property sheet. Name the class CPage2 and add a Boolean member variable called m_check for the IDC_CHECK1 control, as shown in Figure 9.13.

8. Close all the resource editor windows. Then either click the ClassWizard button or select View, ClassWizard from the menu bar. The MFC ClassWizard Properties sheet reappears.

9. Select New from the Add Class menu button. The Create New Class dialog box appears.

10. In the Name box, type **CPropSht**, select CPropertySheet in the Base Class box, and then click the Create button. ClassWizard creates the CPropSht class. Click the MFC ClassWizard Properties sheet's OK button to finalize the class.

In the finished application, you'll use the new `CPropSht` class to create and manipulate the property sheet.

FIG. 9.13

The second property page needs a Boolean member variable called *m_checkbox*.

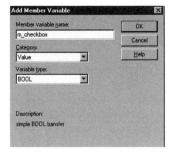

At this point, you have three new classes—`CPage1`, `CPage2`, and `CPropSht`—in your program. The first two classes are derived from MFC's `CPropertyPage` class, and the third is derived from `CPropertySheet`. Although ClassWizard has created the basic source-code files for these new classes, you still have to add code to the classes to make them work the way you want. Follow the next set of steps to complete the Property Sheet Demo application.

1. Click the FileView tab in order to display the FileView window. Then display the project's files by clicking the plus sign next to the folder labeled "psht files," as shown in Figure 9.14.

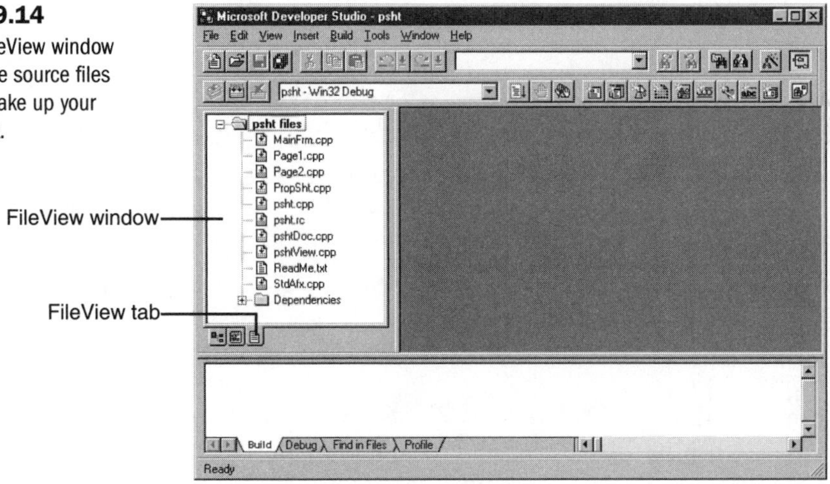

FIG. 9.14

The FileView window lists the source files that make up your project.

FileView window——

FileView tab——

2. Double-click the PropSht.cpp entry in the file list. The PROPSHT.CPP file appears in the code window. Click the Open Header button (the button with the ".h" on it) to display the class's header file.

3. Add the following lines near the top of the file, right before the beginning of the class's declaration:

```
#include "page1.h"
#include "page2.h"
```

These lines give the CPropSht class access to the CPage1 and CPage2 classes, so that the property sheet can declare member variables of these property page classes.

4. Add the following lines to the CPropSht class's attributes section, right after the public keyword:

```
CPage1 m_page1;
CPage2 m_page2;
```

These lines declare the class's data members, which are the property pages that'll be displayed in the property sheet.

5. Close the PROPSHT.H file (saving the changes) so that you can view and edit the PROPSHT.CPP file. Add the following lines to the class's second constructor:

```
AddPage(&m_page1);
AddPage(&m_page2);
```

The preceding lines add the two property pages to the property sheet when the sheet is constructed.

6. Open the PSHTVIEW.CPP file and then click the Open Header button to display the PSHTVIEW.H file. Add the following lines to the class's Attributes section, right after the line CPshtDoc* GetDocument();

```
protected:
CString m_edit;
BOOL m_check;
```

These lines declare two data members for the view class. These data members will hold the selections made in the property sheet by the user.

7. Close the PSHTVIEW.H file (saving the changes) so you can edit the PSHTVIEW.CPP file. Add the following line near the top of the file, after the #endif compiler directive:

```
#include "propsht.h"
```

This line gives the view class access to the CPropSht class, so that it can create the property sheet when requested to do so.

8. Add the following lines to the view class's constructor:

```
m_edit = "Default";
m_check = FALSE;
```

These lines initialize the class's data members so that, when the property sheet appears, these default values can be copied into the property sheet's controls. After the user changes the contents of the property sheet, these data members will always hold the last values from the property sheet, so those values can be restored to the sheet when needed.

9. Add the lines shown in Listing 9.1 to the OnDraw() function, right after the TODO: add draw code for native data here comment.

Listing 9.1 LST9_1.TXT—Code for the *OnDraw()* Function

```
pDC->TextOut(20, 20, m_edit);
if (m_check)
pDC->TextOut(20, 50, "TRUE");
else
pDC->TextOut(20, 50, "FALSE");
```

These lines display the current selections from the property sheet. At the start of the program, the default values are displayed.

10. Click the toolbar's ClassWizard button or select the View, ClassWizard command from the menu bar. The ClassWizard property sheet appears.

11. Make sure that CPshtView is selected in the Class Name and Object IDs boxes. Then add the OnPropsheet() message-response function, as shown in Figure 9.15.

The OnPropsheet() function is now associated with the Property Sheet command that you previously added to the File menu. That is, when the user selects the Property Sheet command, MFC calls OnPropsheet(), where you can respond to the command.

FIG. 9.15

Use ClassWizard to add the *OnPropsheet()* member function.

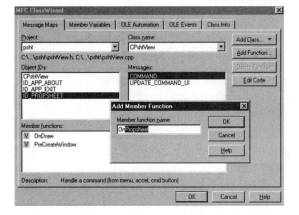

12. Click the Edit Code button to jump to the OnPropsheet() function, and then add the lines shown in Listing 9.2 right after the TODO: Add your command handler code here comment.

Listing 9.2 LST9_2.TXT—Code for the *OnPropSheet()* Function

```
CPropSht propSheet("Property Sheet", this, 0);
propSheet.m_page1.m_edit = m_edit;
propSheet.m_page2.m_check = m_check;
int result = propSheet.DoModal();
if (result == IDOK)
{
```

continues

Part

II

Ch

9

Listing 9.2   Continued

```
    m_edit = propSheet.m_page1.m_edit;
    m_check = propSheet.m_page2.m_check;
    Invalidate();
}
```

The code segment in Listing 9.2, which is discussed in more detail a little later in this chapter, creates, displays, and manages the property sheet.

You've now finished the complete application. Click the toolbar's Build button, or select the Build command from the menu bar, to compile and link the application.

Running the Property Sheet Demo Application

Once you have the program compiled, run it. When you do, you see the window shown in Figure 9.16. As you can see, the window displays two values, which are the default values for the controls in the application's property sheet. You can change these values using the property sheet. To do this, select the File menu's Property Sheet command. The property sheet appears on the screen (Figure 9.17). The property sheet contains two pages, each of which holds a single control. When you change the settings of these controls and click the property sheet's OK button, the application's window displays the new values.

FIG. 9.16

When it first starts, the Property Sheet Demo application displays default values for the property sheet's controls.

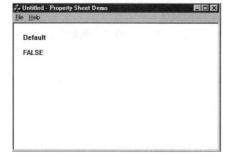

FIG. 9.17

The application's property sheet contains two pages.

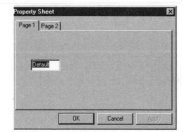

Understanding the Property Sheet Demo Application

Previously, in the section titled "Creating the Property Sheet Demo Application," you went through the process of creating Property Sheet Demo, step-by-step. During this process, you discovered that you must complete several tasks in order to add property sheets to your application. Each of those steps was explained in the step's text. However, to give you a clearer picture of what you did, the steps that are most important in the creation of a property sheet are summarized here:

1. Create a dialog box resource for each page in the property sheet. These resources should have the `Child` and `Thin` styles and should have no system menu.

2. Associate each property page resource with an object of the `CPropertyPage` class. You can do this easily with ClassWizard.

3. Create a class for the property sheet, deriving the class from MFC's `CPropertySheet` class. You can generate this class using ClassWizard.

4. In the property sheet class, add member variables for each page you'll be adding to the property sheet. These member variables must be instances of the property page classes that you created in Step 2.

5. In the property sheet's constructor, call `AddPage()` for each page in the property sheet.

6. To display the property sheet, call the property sheet's constructor and then call the property sheet's `DoModal()` member function, just as you would with a dialog box.

N O T E As you read over the steps required for creating a property sheet, be sure that you understand the difference between a property sheet and a property page. A *property sheet* is a window that contains property pages. *Property pages* are windows that hold the controls that will appear on the property sheet's pages. ▩

After you have your application written and have defined the resources and classes that represent the property sheet (or sheets; you can have more than one), you need a way to enable the user to display the property sheet when it's needed. In Property Sheet Demo, this is done by associating a menu item with a message-response function. However you handle the command to display the property sheet, though, the process of creating the property sheet is the same. First, you must call the property sheet class's constructor, which Property Sheet Demo does like this:

```
CPropSht propSheet("Property Sheet", this, 0);
```

Here, the program is creating an instance of the `CPropSht` class. This instance (or object) is called `propSheet`. The three arguments are the property sheet's title string, a pointer to the parent window (which, in this case, is the view window), and the zero-based index of the first page to display. Because the property pages are created in the property sheet's constructor, creating the property sheet also creates the property pages.

Once you have the property sheet object created, you can initialize the data members that hold the values of the property page's controls, which Property Sheet Demo does like this:

```
propSheet.m_page1.m_edit = m_edit;
propSheet.m_page2.m_check = m_check;
```

Now it's time to display the property sheet on the screen, which you do just as if it were a dialog box, by calling the property sheet's `DoModal()` member function:

```
int result = propSheet.DoModal();
```

`DoModal()` doesn't take any arguments, but it does return a value indicating which button the user clicked to exit the property sheet. In the case of a property sheet or dialog box, you'll usually want to process the information entered into the controls only if the user clicked the OK button, which is indicated by a return value of `IDOK`. Listing 9.3 shows how the Property Sheet Demo application handles the return value:

Listing 9.3   LST9_3.TXT—Handling the Property Sheet's Return Value

```
if (result == IDOK)
{
    m_edit = propSheet.m_page1.m_edit;
    m_check = propSheet.m_page2.m_check;
    Invalidate();
}
```

In Listing 9.3, the program retrieves the values of the controls from the property pages and then calls `Invalidate()` to force the window to be redrawn. If the user exits the property sheet by clicking the Cancel button, the code in the body of the `if` statement is ignored and the window is not updated.

Changing Property Sheets to Wizards

When you come right down to it, a wizard is nothing more than a property sheet that uses Back, Next, and Finish buttons instead of tabs. Because of the lack of tabs, however, the user must switch from one page to another in sequence. This forced sequence makes wizards terrific for guiding your application's users through the steps needed to complete a complex task. You've already seen how AppWizard in Visual C++ makes it easy to start a new project. You can create your own wizards that are suited to whatever application you want to build. In the following sections, you'll see how easy it is to convert a property sheet to a wizard.

Running the Wizard Demo Application

On the CD

In the CHAP09\WIZ folder of this book's CD-ROM, you'll find the Wizard Demo application. This application was built in much the same way as the Property Sheet Demo application that you created earlier in this chapter. However, as you'll soon see, there are a few differences in the Wizard Demo application that enable the user to access and use the application's wizard.

When you run the Wizard Demo application, the main window appears, including a File menu from which you can select the Wizard command. The Wizard command brings up the wizard shown in Figure 9.18.

FIG. 9.18
The Wizard Demo application displays a wizard rather than a property sheet.

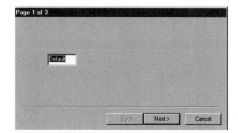

The wizard isn't too fancy, but it does demonstrate what you need to know in order to program more complex wizards. As you can see, this wizard has three pages. On the first page is an edit control and three buttons called Back, Next, and Cancel. The Back button is disabled, because there is no previous page to go back to. The Cancel button enables the user to dismiss the wizard at any time, canceling whatever process the wizard was guiding the user through. The Next button causes the next page in the wizard to be displayed.

You can change whatever is displayed in the edit control if you like. However, the magic really starts when you click the Next button, which displays Page 2 of the wizard, as shown in Figure 9.19. Page 2 contains a check box and the Back, Next, and Cancel buttons. Now, the Back button is enabled, so that you can return to Page 1 if you want to. Go ahead and click the Back button. The wizard tells you that the check box must be checked, as shown in Figure 9.20. As you'll soon see, this feature of a wizard enables you to verify the contents of a specific page before allowing the user to advance to another step.

FIG. 9.19
In Page 2 of the wizard, the Back button is enabled.

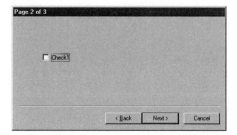

FIG. 9.20
You must select the check box before the wizard will let you leave Page 2.

After checking the check box, you can click the Back button to move back to Page 1 or click the Next button to advance to Page 3. Assuming you advance to Page 3, you see the display shown in Figure 9.21. Here, the Next button has changed to the Finish button, because you are on the wizard's last page. If you click the Finish button, the program displays a message box, after which the wizard disappears.

FIG. 9.21

This is the last page of the Wizard Demo Application's wizard.

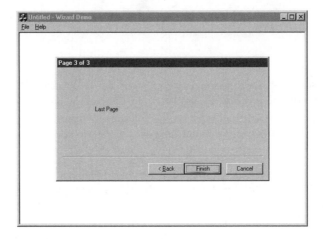

Creating Wizard Pages

As far as your application's resources go, you create wizard pages exactly as you create property sheet pages, by creating dialog boxes and changing the dialog box styles. You also need to associate each page that you create with an object of the CPropertyPage class. However, in order to take control of the pages in your wizard and keep track of what the user is doing with the wizard, there are a couple of member functions in the CPropertyPage class that you can override in your property page classes. These functions are OnSetActive(), OnWizardBack(), OnWizardNext(), and OnWizardFinish(). Read on to see how to use these functions.

Setting the Wizard's Buttons

MFC automatically calls the OnSetActive() member function immediately upon displaying a specific page of the wizard. For example, when the program displays Page 1 of the wizard, the CPage1 class's OnSetActive() function gets called. In the Wizard Demo application, the CPage1 class's version of OnSetActive() looks like Listing 9.4.

Listing 9.4   LST9_4.TXT—The *OnSetActive()* Member Function

```
BOOL CPage1::OnSetActive()
{
    // TODO: Add your specialized code here and/or call the base class
    CPropertySheet* parent = (CPropertySheet*)GetParent();
    parent->SetWizardButtons(PSWIZB_NEXT);
    return CPropertyPage::OnSetActive();
}
```

In Listing 9.4, the program first gets a pointer to the wizard's property sheet window, which is the page's parent window. Then the program calls the wizard's SetWizardButtons() function, which determines the state of the wizard's buttons. SetWizardButtons() takes a single argument, which is a set of flags indicating how the page should display its buttons. These flags are PSWIZB_BACK, PSWIZB_NEXT, PSWIZB_FINISH, and PSWIZB_DISABLEDFINISH. The button flags that you include will enable the associated button (except for the PSWIZB_DISABLEDFINISH flag, which disables the Finish button). Because the call to SetWizardButtons() in Listing 9.4 includes only the PSWIZB_NEXT flag, only the Next button in the page will be enabled.

Because the CPage2 class represents Page 2 of the wizard, its call to SetWizardButtons() enables both the Back and Next buttons, by ORing together the appropriate flags, like this:

```
parent->SetWizardButtons(PSWIZB_BACK | PSWIZB_NEXT);
```

Because Page 3 of the wizard is the last page, the CPage3 class calls SetWizardButtons(), like this:

```
parent->SetWizardButtons(PSWIZB_BACK | PSWIZB_FINISH);
```

This set of flags enables the Back button and changes the Next button to the Finish button.

Responding to the Wizard's Buttons

In the simplest case, MFC takes care of everything that needs to be done in order to flip from one wizard page to the next. That is, when the user clicks a button, MFC springs into action and performs the Back, Next, Finish, or Cancel command. However, you'll often want to perform some action of your own when the user clicks a button. For example, you may want to verify that the information that the user entered into the currently displayed page is correct. If there's a problem with the data, you can force the user to fix it before moving on.

To respond to the wizard's buttons, you can override the OnWizardBack(), OnWizardNext(), and OnWizardFinish() member functions. When the user clicks a wizard button, MFC calls the matching function in which you can do whatever is needed to process that page. An example is the way the wizard in the Wizard Demo application won't let you leave Page 2 until you've checked the check box. This is accomplished by overriding the functions shown in Listing 9.5.

Listing 9.5 LST9_5.TXT—Responding to Wizard Buttons

```
LRESULT CPage2::OnWizardBack()
{
    // TODO: Add your specialized code here and/or call the base class
    CButton *checkBox = (CButton*)GetDlgItem(IDC_CHECK1);
    if (!checkBox->GetCheck())
    {
        MessageBox("You must check the box.");
        return -1;
    }
    return CPropertyPage::OnWizardBack();
}
```

continues

Listing 9.5 LST9_5.TXT—Continued

```
LRESULT CPage2::OnWizardNext()
{
    // TODO: Add your specialized code here and/or call the base class
    CButton *checkBox = (CButton*)GetDlgItem(IDC_CHECK1);
    if (!checkBox->GetCheck())
    {
        MessageBox("You must check the box.");
        return -1;
    }
    return CPropertyPage::OnWizardNext();
}
```

In the functions in Listing 9.5, the program gets a pointer to the page's check box by calling the
GetDlgItem() function. With the pointer in hand, the program can call the check-box class's
GetCheck() function, which returns a 1 if the check box is checked. If GetCheck() returns a 0,
the program displays a message box and returns –1 from the function. Returning –1 tells MFC
to ignore the button click and not change pages.

Displaying a Wizard

As you've just learned, almost all the work involved in controlling a wizard is done in the
classes that represent the wizard's pages. The property sheet class that represents the
wizard works exactly the same as it did in the property sheet example. However, there is
one extra thing you must do when displaying a wizard, which is to call the property sheet's
SetWizardMode() member function. This function call tells MFC that it should display the
property sheet as a wizard rather than as a conventional property sheet. Listing 9.6 shows the
view class's OnWizard() member function, which is the function that responds to the File
menu's Wizard command.

Listing 9.6 LST9_6.TXT—Displaying a Property Sheet as a Wizard

```
void CWizView::OnWizard()
{
    // TODO: Add your command handler code here

    CWizSheet wizSheet("Sample Wizard", this, 0);
    wizSheet.m_page1.m_edit = m_edit;
    wizSheet.m_page2.m_check = m_check;
    wizSheet.SetWizardMode();
    int result = wizSheet.DoModal();
    if (result == ID_WIZFINISH)
    {
        m_edit = wizSheet.m_page1.m_edit;
        m_check = wizSheet.m_page2.m_check;
    }
}
```

Notice in Listing 9.6 that the program creates the wizard almost exactly the same as a property sheet, the only difference being the call to `SetWizardMode()`. The wizard is displayed exactly the same as any other dialog box, by calling the object's `DoModal()` member function. There is, however, one difference in how you respond to the result returned by `DoModal()`. Because a wizard has no OK button, `DoModal()` cannot return `IDOK`. Instead, `DoModal()` returns `ID_WIZFINISH` if the user exits via the Finish button.

From Here...

Part

II

Ch

9

Whether you're creating property sheets or wizards, Visual C++'s many classes enable you to get the job done easily. Property sheets are great for organizing many options and controls, whereas wizards (which are a special type of property sheet) are best used for guiding the user step-by-step through a complex task. To learn more about related topics, check out the following chapters:

- Chapter 1, "Working with Developer Studio," tells you what you need to know to create your own projects using Visual C++'s development tools.
- Chapter 3, "AppWizard and ClassWizard," brings you up to speed with Visual C++'s excellent automated project and code generators.
- Chapter 5, "Messages and Commands," describes MFC's message-mapping system, which enables you to respond to Windows messages.
- Chapter 7, "Dialog and Controls," gives you more background in programming dialog boxes and the controls they can contain.
- Chapter 11, "Drawing on the Screen," describes how to display information in a window.

CHAPTER 10

Utility and Collection Classes

MFC includes a lot more than classes for programming Windows graphical user interface. It also features many utility classes for handling such things as lists, arrays, times and dates, and mapped collections. By using these classes, you can gain extra power over data in your programs, as well as simplify many operations involved in using complex data structures such as lists.

For example, because MFC's array classes can change their size dynamically, you are relieved of creating oversized arrays in an attempt to ensure that the arrays are large enough for the application. In this way, you save memory. The other collection classes provide many other similar conveniences. ■

How to create array, list, and map collection objects

By using MFC's ready-to-use collection classes, you gain more power over mundane data structures.

How to add, remove, and modify collection elements

The MFC collection classes provide member functions for modifying the contents of a collection.

How to iterate over collections

When you need to search through a collection, you can use the class's iteration member functions.

How to use the time classes

Many programs need to manage the time and date. MFC's Date class is perfect for this task.

How to create your own type of collection class

You're not limited to MFC's collection classes. You can roll your own any time you need them.

The Array Classes

MFC's array classes enable you to create and manipulate one-dimensional array objects that can hold virtually any type of data. These array objects work much like the standard arrays that you're used to using in your programs, except that MFC can enlarge or shrink an array object dynamically at runtime. This means that you don't have to be concerned with dimensioning your array perfectly when it's declared. Because MFC's arrays can grow dynamically, you can forget about the memory wastage that often occurs with conventional arrays, which must be dimensioned to hold the maximum number of elements that may be needed in the program, whether or not you actually use every element.

The array classes include CByteArray, CDWordArray, CObArray, CPtrArray, CUIntArray, CWordArray, and CStringArray. As you can tell from the class names, each class is designed to hold a specific type of data. For example, the CUIntArray, which will be used in this section's examples, is an array class that can hold unsigned integers. The CPtrArray class, on the other hand, represents an array of pointers to void, and the CObArray class represents an array of objects. The array classes are all almost identical, differing only in the type of data that they store. Once you've learned to use one of the array classes, you've learned to use them all. Table 10.1 lists the member functions of the array classes and their descriptions.

Table 10.1 Member Functions of the Array Classes

Function	Description
Add()	Appends a value to the end of the array, increasing the size of the array as needed.
ElementAt()	Gets a reference to an array element's pointer.
FreeExtra()	Releases unused array memory.
GetAt()	Gets the value at the specified array index.
GetSize()	Gets the number of elements in the array.
GetUpperBound()	Gets the array's *upper bound,* which is the highest valid index at which a value can be stored.
InsertAt()	Inserts a value at the specified index, shifting existing elements upward as necessary to accommodate the insert.
RemoveAll()	Removes all the array's elements.
RemoveAt()	Removes the value at the specified index.
SetAt()	Places a value at the specified index. Because this function will not increase the size of the array, the index must be currently valid.
SetAtGrow()	Places a value at the specified index, increasing the size of the array as needed.
SetSize()	Sets the array's size, which is the number of elements the array can hold. The array can still grow dynamically beyond this size.

Introducing the Array Demo Application

To illustrate how the array classes work, this chapter includes the Array Demo application, which you can find in the CHAP10\ARRAY folder of this book's CD-ROM. When you run the program, you see the window shown in Figure 10.1. The window displays the current contents of the array. Because the application's array object (which is an instance of CUIntArray) starts off with ten elements, the values for these elements (indexed as 0 through 9) are displayed on the screen. The application enables you to change, add, or delete elements in the array and see the results.

FIG. 10.1

The Array Demo application enables you to experiment with MFC's array classes.

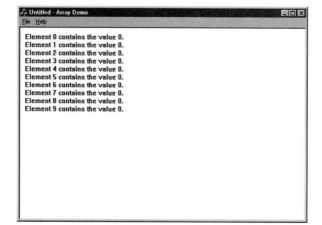

Part
II

Ch
10

You can add an element to the array in several ways. To see these choices, left-click in the application's window. The dialog box shown in Figure 10.2 appears. Type an array index in the Index box and the new value in the Value box. Then select whether you want to set, insert, or add the element. When you choose Set, the element you specify in the Index field gets changed to the value in the Value field. The insert operation creates a new array element at the location specified by the index, pushing succeeding elements forward. Finally, the Add operation just tacks the new element onto the end of the array. In this case, the program ignores the Index field of the dialog box.

Suppose, for example, that you enter 3 into the dialog box's Index field and 15 into the Value field, leaving the radio buttons set to Set. Figure 10.3 shows the result, where the program has placed the value 15 into element 3 of the array, overwriting the value that was there previously. Now you type 5 into Index, 25 into Value, and click the Insert radio button. In Figure 10.4, you can see that the program stuffs a new element 5 into the array, shoving the other elements forward. The Add radio button tells the program to add a new element to the end of the array.

An interesting thing to try—something that really shows how dynamic MFC's arrays are—is to set an array element beyond the end of the array. For example, given the program's state shown in Figure 10.4, if you type 20 in Index and 45 in Value and then choose the Set radio button, you get the results shown in Figure 10.5. Because there was no element 20, the array class created the new elements that it needed to get to 20. Try that with an old-fashioned array!

FIG. 10.2

The Add to Array dialog box enables you to add elements to the array.

FIG. 10.3

The value of 15 has been placed into array element 3.

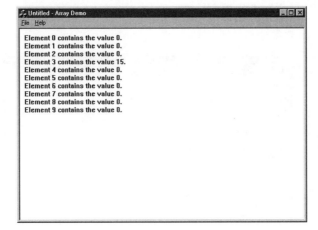

FIG. 10.4

The screen now shows the new array element 5, giving 11 elements in all.

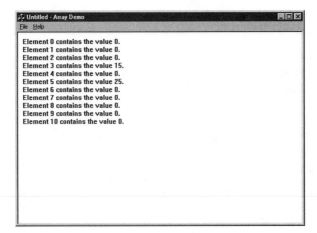

Besides adding new elements to the array, you can also delete elements in one of two ways. To do this, first right-click in the window. When you do, you see the dialog box shown in Figure 10.6. If you type an index into the Remove field and then click OK, the program deletes the selected element from the array. This is the opposite of the effect of Insert command, because the Remove command shortens the array rather than lengthening it. If you want, you can select the Remove All option in the dialog box. Then the program deletes all elements from the array, leaving it empty.

FIG. 10.5

The array class has added the elements needed in order to set element 20.

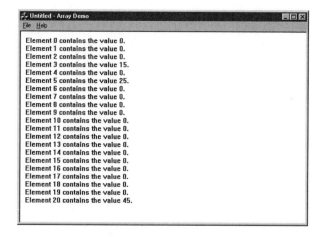

FIG. 10.6

The Remove from Array dialog box enables you to delete elements from the array.

Declaring and Initializing the Array

Now you'd probably like to see how all this array trickery works. It's really pretty simple. First, the program declares the array object as a data member of the view class, like this:

```
CUIntArray array;
```

Then, in the view class's constructor, the program initializes the array to ten elements:

```
array.SetSize(10, 5);
```

The SetSize() function takes as parameters the number of elements to give the array initially and the number of elements by which the array should grow whenever it needs to. You don't need to call SetSize() in order to use the array class. However, if you fail to do so, MFC adds elements to the array one at a time, as needed, which is a slow process (although, unless you're doing some heavy processing, you're not likely to notice any difference in speed). By giving an initial array size and the amount by which to grow, you can create much more efficient array-handling code.

Adding Elements to the Array

After setting the array size, the program waits for the user to click the left or right mouse buttons in the window. When the user does, the program springs into action, displaying the appropriate dialog box and processing the values entered into the dialog box. Listing 10.1 shows the Array Demo application's OnLButtonDown() function, which handles the left mouse button clicks.

Part II
Ch
10

Listing 10.1   LST10_1.TXT—The *OnLButtonDown()* Function

```
void CArrayView::OnLButtonDown(UINT nFlags, CPoint point)
{
    // TODO: Add your message handler code here and/or call default

    ArrayDlg dialog(this);
    dialog.m_index = 0;
    dialog.m_value = 0;
    dialog.m_radio = 0;
    int result = dialog.DoModal();
    if (result == IDOK)
    {
        if (dialog.m_radio == 0)
            array.SetAtGrow(dialog.m_index, dialog.m_value);
        else if (dialog.m_radio == 1)
            array.InsertAt(dialog.m_index, dialog.m_value, 1);
        else
            array.Add(dialog.m_value);
        Invalidate();
    }
    CView::OnLButtonDown(nFlags, point);
}
```

If the user exits the dialog box by clicking the OK button, the OnLButtonDown() function checks the value of the dialog box's m_radio data member. A value of 0 means that the first radio button (Set) is set, 1 means that the second button (Insert) is set, and 2 means that the third button (Add) is set.

If the user wants to set an array element, the program calls SetAtGrow(), giving the array index and the new value as arguments. Unlike the regular SetAt() function, which you can use only with a currently valid index number, SetAtGrow() will enlarge the array as necessary in order to set the specified array element.

When the user has selected the Insert radio button, the program calls the InsertAt() function, giving the array index and new value as arguments. This causes MFC to create a new array element at the index specified, shoving the other array elements forward. Finally, when the user has selected the Add option, the program calls the Add() function, which adds a new element to the end of the array. This function's single argument is the new value to place in the added element. The call to Invalidate() forces the window to redraw the data display with the new information.

Reading Through the Array

So that you can see what's happening as you add, change, and delete array elements, the Array Demo application's OnDraw() function reads through the array, displaying the values that it finds in each element. The code for this function is shown in Listing 10.2.

Listing 10.2   LST10_2.TXT—Array Demo's *OnDraw()* Function

```
void CArrayView::OnDraw(CDC* pDC)
{
    CArrayDoc* pDoc = GetDocument();
    ASSERT_VALID(pDoc);
    // TODO: add draw code for native data here

    // Get the current font's height.
    TEXTMETRIC textMetric;
    pDC->GetTextMetrics(&textMetric);
    int fontHeight = textMetric.tmHeight;
    // Get the size of the array.
    int count = array.GetSize();
    int displayPos = 10;
    // Display the array data.
    for (int x=0; x<count; ++x)
    {
        UINT value = array.GetAt(x);
        char s[81];
        wsprintf(s, "Element %d contains the value %u.", x, value);
        pDC->TextOut(10, displayPos, s);
        displayPos += fontHeight;
    }
}
```

Here, the program first gets the height of the current font so that it can properly space the lines of text that it displays in the window. It then gets the number of elements in the array, by calling the array object's GetSize() function. Finally, the program uses the element count to control a for loop, which calls the array object's GetAt() member function to get the value of the currently indexed array element. The program converts this value to a string for display purposes.

Removing Elements from the Array

Because it is a right button click in the window that brings up the Remove From Array dialog box, it is the program's OnRButtonDown() function that handles the element-deletion duties. That function is shown in Listing 10.3.

Listing 10.3   LST10_3.TXT—The *OnRButtonDown()* Function

```
void CArrayView::OnRButtonDown(UINT nFlags, CPoint point)
{
    // TODO: Add your message handler code here and/or call default

    ArrayDlg2 dialog(this);
    dialog.m_remove = 0;
```

continues

Listing 10.3   Continued

```
dialog.m_removeAll = FALSE;
int result = dialog.DoModal();
if (result == IDOK)
{
    if (dialog.m_removeAll)
        array.RemoveAll();
    else
        array.RemoveAt(dialog.m_remove);
    Invalidate();
}

CView::OnRButtonDown(nFlags, point);
}
```

In this function, after displaying the dialog box, the program checks the value of the dialog box's m_removeAll data member. A value of TRUE means that the user has checked this option and wants to delete all elements from the array. In this case, the program calls the array object's RemoveAll() member function. Otherwise, the program calls RemoveAt(), whose single argument specifies the index of the element to delete. The call to Invalidate() forces the window to redraw the data display with the new information.

The List Classes

Lists are like fancy arrays. Because lists (also called *linked lists*) use pointers to link their elements (called *nodes*) rather than depending upon contiguous memory locations to order values, lists are a better data structure to use when you need to be able to insert and delete items quickly. However, finding items in a list can be slower than finding items in an array, because a list often needs to be traversed sequentially in order to follow the pointers from one item to the next.

When using lists, you need to know some new vocabulary. Specifically, you need to know that the *head* of a list is the first node in the list, and the *tail* of the list is the last node in the list. You'll see these two terms used often as you explore MFC's list classes.

MFC provides three list classes that you can use to create your lists. These classes are CObList (which represents a list of objects), CPtrList (which represents a list of pointers), and CStringList (which represents a list of strings). Each of these classes has similar member functions, and the classes differ in the type of data that they can hold in their lists. Table 10.2 lists and describes the member functions of the list classes.

Table 10.2 Member Functions of the List Classes

Function	Description
AddHead()	Adds a node to the head of the list, making the node the new head.
AddTail()	Adds a node to the tail of the list, making the node the new tail.
Find()	Searches the list sequentially to find the given object pointer. Returns a POSITION value.
FindIndex()	Scans the list sequentially, stopping at the node indicated by the given index. Returns a POSITION value for the node.
GetAt()	Gets the node at the specified position.
GetCount()	Gets the number of nodes in the list.
GetHead()	Gets the list's head node.
GetHeadPosition()	Gets the head node's position.
GetNext()	When iterating over a list, gets the next node in the list.
GetPrev()	When iterating over a list, gets the previous node in the list.
GetTail()	Gets the list's tail node.
GetTailPosition()	Gets the tail node's position.
InsertAfter()	Inserts a new node after the specified position.
InsertBefore()	Inserts a new node before the specified position.
IsEmpty()	Returns TRUE if the list is empty and returns FALSE otherwise.
RemoveAll()	Removes all of a list's nodes.
RemoveAt()	Removes a single node from a list.
RemoveHead()	Removes the list's head node.
RemoveTail()	Removes the list's tail node.
SetAt()	Sets the node at the specified position.

Introducing the List Demo Application

On the CD

As you've no doubt guessed, now that you know a little about list classes and their member functions, you're going to get a chance to see lists in action. In the CHAP10\LIST folder of this book's CD-ROM, you'll find the List Demo application. When you run the application, you see the window shown in Figure 10.7. The window displays the values of the single node with which the list begins. Each node in the list can hold two different values, both of which are integers.

FIG. 10.7

A linked list has a head and a tail, with the remaining nodes in between.

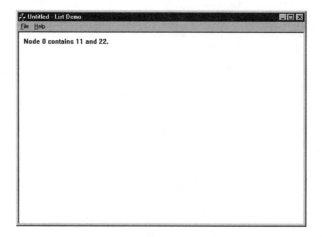

Using the List Demo application, you can experiment with adding and removing nodes from a list. To add a node, left-click in the application's window. You then see the dialog box shown in Figure 10.8. Enter the two values that you want the new node to hold and then click OK. When you do, the program adds the new node to the tail of the list and displays the new list in the window. For example, if you were to enter the values 55 and 65 into the dialog box, you'd see the display shown in Figure 10.9.

FIG. 10.8

The List Demo application starts off with one node in its list.

You can also delete nodes from the list. To do this, right-click in the window to display the Remove Node dialog box (Figure 10.10). Using this dialog box, you can choose to remove the head or tail node. If you exit the dialog box by clicking OK, the program deletes the specified node and displays the resulting list in the window.

N O T E If you try to delete nodes from an empty list, the List Demo application will display a message box, warning you of your error. If the application didn't catch this possible error, the program could crash when it tries to delete a nonexistent node. ■

FIG. 10.9

A left-click in the window brings up the Add Node dialog box.

FIG. 10.10

Each node you add to the list can hold two different values.

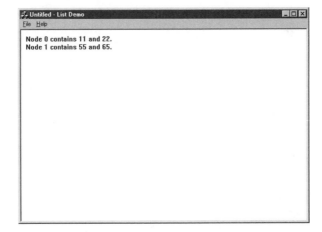

Declaring and Initializing the List

Declaring a list is as easy as declaring any other data type. Just include the name of the class you're using, followed by the name of the object. For example, the List Demo application declares its list like this:

```
CPtrList list;
```

Here, the program is declaring an object of the CPtrList class. This class holds a linked list of pointers, which means that the list can reference just about any type of information.

Although there's not much you need to do to initialize an empty list, you do need to decide what type of information will be pointed to by the pointers in the list. That is, you need to declare exactly what a node in the list will look like. The List Demo application declares a node as shown in Listing 10.4.

Listing 10.4   LST10_4.TXT—The *CNode* Structure

```
struct CNode
{
    int value1;
    int value2;
};
```

Here, a node is defined as a structure holding two integer values. However, you can create any type of data structure you like for your nodes. To add a node to a list, you use the new operator to create a node structure in memory, and then you add the returned pointer to the pointer list.

The List Demo application begins its list with a single node, which is created in the view class's constructor, as shown in Listing 10.5.

Listing 10.5 LST10_5.TXT—Creating the First Node

```
CNode* pNode = new CNode;
pNode->value1 = 11;
pNode->value2 = 22;
list.AddTail(pNode);
```

In Listing 10.5, the program first creates a new CNode structure on the heap and then sets the node's two members. After initializing the new node, a quick call to the list's AddTail() member function adds the node to the list. Because the list was empty, adding a node to the tail of the list is the same as adding the node to the head of the list. That is, the program could have also called AddHead() to add the node. In either case, the new single node is now both the head and tail of the list.

Adding a Node to the List

Although you can insert nodes into a list at any position, the easiest way to add to a list is to add a node to the head or tail, making the node the new head or tail. In the List Demo application, you left-click in the window to bring up the Add Node dialog box, so you'll want to examine the OnLButtonDown() function, which looks like Listing 10.6.

Listing 10.6 LST10_6.TXT—List Demo's *OnLButtonDown()* Function

```
void CMyListView::OnLButtonDown(UINT nFlags, CPoint point)
{
    // TODO: Add your message handler code here and/or call default

    // Create and initialize the dialog box.
    CAddDlg dialog;
    dialog.m_value1 = 0;
    dialog.m_value2 = 0;
    // Display the dialog box.
    int result = dialog.DoModal();
    // If the user clicked the OK button...
    if (result == IDOK)
    {
        // Create and initialize the new node.
        CNode* pNode = new CNode;
        pNode->value1 = dialog.m_value1;
        pNode->value2 = dialog.m_value2;
        // Add the node to the list.
        list.AddTail(pNode);
        // Repaint the window.
        Invalidate();
    }
    CView::OnLButtonDown(nFlags, point);
}
```

In Listing 10.6, after displaying the dialog box, the program checks whether the user exited the dialog with the OK button. If so, the user wants to add a new node to the list. In this case, the program creates and initializes the new node, just as it did previously for the first node that it added in the view class's constructor. The program adds the node in the same way, too, by calling the AddTail(). If you want to modify the List Demo application, one thing you could try is giving the user a choice between adding the node at the head or the tail of the list, instead of just at the tail.

Deleting a Node from the List

Deleting a node from a list can be easy or more complicated, depending on where in the list you want to delete the node. As with adding a node, dealing with nodes other than the head or tail requires that you first locate the node that you want and then get its position in the list. You'll learn about node positions in the next section, which demonstrates how to iterate over a list. To keep things simple, however, the program enables you to delete nodes only from the head or tail of the list, as shown in Listing 10.7.

Part
II

Ch

10

Listing 10.7 LST10_7.TXT—The *OnRButtonDown()* Function

```
void CMyListView::OnRButtonDown(UINT nFlags, CPoint point)
{
    // TODO: Add your message handler code here and/or call default

    // Create and initialize the dialog box.
    CRemoveDlg dialog;
    dialog.m_radio = 0;
    // Display the dialog box.
    int result = dialog.DoModal();
    // If the user clicked the OK button...
    if (result == IDOK)
    {
        CNode* pNode;
        // Make sure the list isn't empty.
        if (list.IsEmpty())
            MessageBox("No nodes to delete.");
        else
        {
            // Remove the specified node.
            if (dialog.m_radio == 0)
                pNode = (CNode*)list.RemoveHead();
            else
                pNode = (CNode*)list.RemoveTail();
            // Delete the node object and repaint the window.
            delete pNode;
            Invalidate();
        }
    }
    CView::OnRButtonDown(nFlags, point);
}
```

Here, after displaying the dialog box, the program checks whether the user exited the dialog box via the OK button. If so, the program must then check whether the user wants to delete a node from the head or tail of the list. If the Remove Head radio button was checked, the dialog box's `m_radio` data member will be 0. In this case, the program calls the list class's `RemoveHead()` member function. Otherwise, the program calls `RemoveTail()`. Both of these functions return a pointer to the object that was removed from the list. Before calling either of these member functions, however, notice how the program calls `IsEmpty()` in order to determine whether the list contains any nodes. You can't delete a node from an empty list!

N O T E Notice that, when removing a node from the list, the List Demo application calls `delete` on the pointer returned by the list. It's important to remember that, when you remove a node from a list, the node's pointer is removed from the list, but the object to which the pointer points is still in memory, where it stays until you delete it. ▪

Iterating Over the List

Often, you'll want to *iterate over* (read through) a list. You might, for example, as is the case with List Demo, want to display the values in each node of the list, starting from the head of the list and working your way to the tail. The List Demo application does exactly this in its `OnDraw()` function, as shown in Listing 10.8.

Listing 10.8   LST10_8.TXT—The List Demo Application's *OnDraw()* Function

```
void CMyListView::OnDraw(CDC* pDC)
{
    CListDoc* pDoc = GetDocument();
    ASSERT_VALID(pDoc);
    // TODO: add draw code for native data here
    // Get the current font's height.
    TEXTMETRIC textMetric;
    pDC->GetTextMetrics(&textMetric);
    int fontHeight = textM6¦ric.tmHeight;
    // Initialize values used in the loop.
    POSITION pos = list.GetHeadPosition();
    int displayPosition = 10;
    int index = 0;
    // Iterate over the list, displaying each node's values.
    while (pos != NULL)
    {
        CNode* pNode = (CNode*)list.GetNext(pos);
        char s[81];
        wsprintf(s, "Node %d contains %d and %d.",
            index, pNode->value1, pNode->value2);
        pDC->TextOut(10, displayPosition, s);
        displayPosition += fontHeight;
        ++index;
    }
}
```

In Listing 10.8, the program gets the position of the head node by calling the `GetHeadPosition()` member function. The position is a value that many of the list class's member functions use to quickly locate nodes in the list. You must have this starting position value in order to iterate over the list.

In the `while` loop, the iteration actually takes place. The program calls the list object's `GetNext()` member function, which requires as its single argument the position of the node to retrieve. The function returns a pointer to the node and sets the position to the next node in the list. When the position is `NULL`, the program has reached the end of the list. In Listing 10.8, this `NULL` value is the condition that's used to terminate the `while` loop.

Cleaning Up the List

There's one other time when you need to iterate over a list. That's when the program is about to terminate and you need to delete all the objects pointed to by the pointers in the list. The List Demo application performs this task in the view class's destructor, as shown in Listing 10.9.

Listing 10.9 LST10_9.TXT—Deleting the List's Objects

```
CMyListView::~CMyListView()
{
    // Iterate over the list, deleting each node.
    while (!list.IsEmpty())
    {
        CNode* pNode = (CNode*)list.RemoveHead();
        delete pNode;
    }
}
```

This destructor in Listing 10.9 iterates over the list in a `while` loop until the `IsEmpty()` member function returns `TRUE`. Inside the loop, the program removes the head node from the list (which makes the next node in the list the new head) and deletes the node from memory. When the list is empty, all the nodes that the program allocated have been deleted.

CAUTION

Don't forget that you're responsible for deleting every node that you create with the new operator. If you fail to delete nodes, you could leave memory allocated after your program terminates. This isn't a major problem under Windows 95, because the system cleans up memory after an application exits. However, it's always good programming practice to delete any objects you allocate in memory.

The Map Classes

You can use MFC's mapped collection classes for creating lookup tables. For example, you might want to convert digits into the words that represent the numbers. That is, you might want to use the digit 1 as a key in order to find the word *one*. A mapped collection is perfect for this sort of task. Thanks to the many MFC map classes, you can use various types of data for keys and values.

The MFC map classes are CMapPtrToPtr, CMapPtrToWord, CMapStringToOb, CMapStringToPtr, CMapStringToString, CMapWordToOb, and CMapWordToPtr. The first data type in the name is the key, and the second is the value type. So, for example, CMapStringToOb uses strings as keys and objects as values, whereas CMapStringToString, which this section uses in its examples, uses strings as both keys and values. All the map classes are similar, and so have similar member functions, which are listed and described in Table 10.3.

Table 10.3 Functions of the Map Classes

Function	Description
GetCount()	Gets the number of map elements.
GetNextAssoc()	When iterating over the map, gets the next element.
GetStartPosition()	Gets the first element's position.
IsEmpty()	Returns TRUE if the map is empty and returns FALSE otherwise.
Lookup()	Finds the value associated with a key.
RemoveAll()	Removes all the map's elements.
RemoveKey()	Removes an element from the map.
SetAt()	Adds a map element or replaces an element with a matching key.

Introducing the Map Demo Application

On the CD

This section's example program, Map Demo, displays the contents of a map and enables you to retrieve values from the map by giving the program the appropriate key. You can find the program in the CHAP10\MAP folder of this book's CD-ROM. When you run the program, you see the window shown in Figure 10.11.

The window displays the contents of the application's map object, in which digits are used as keys to access the words that represent the numbers. To retrieve a value from the map, click in the window. You then see the dialog box shown in Figure 10.12. Type the digit that you want to use for a key and then click OK. The program finds the matching value in the map and displays it in another message box. For example, if you type 8 as the key, you see the message box shown in Figure 10.13. If the key doesn't exist, the program's message box tells you so.

FIG. 10.11

The Map Demo application displays the contents of a map object.

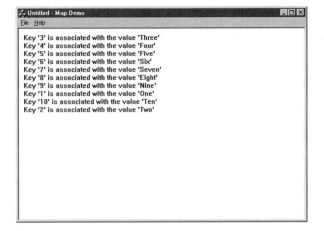

FIG. 10.12

The Get Map Value dialog box enables you to match a key with the key's value in the map.

FIG. 10.13

This message box displays the requested map value.

Creating and Initializing the Map

The Map Demo application starts off with a ten-element map. The map object is declared as a data member of the view class, like this:

```
CMapStringToString map;
```

As you can see from the declaration, this application's map is an object of the CMapStringToString class, which means that the map uses strings as keys and strings as values.

Declaring the map object doesn't, of course, fill it with values. You have to do that on your own, which the Map Demo application does in its view class's constructor, as shown in Listing 10.10.

Listing 10.10 LST10_10.TXT—Initializing the Map Object

```
map.SetAt("1", "One");
map.SetAt("2", "Two");
map.SetAt("3", "Three");
map.SetAt("4", "Four");
map.SetAt("5", "Five");
map.SetAt("6", "Six");
map.SetAt("7", "Seven");
map.SetAt("8", "Eight");
map.SetAt("9", "Nine");
map.SetAt("10", "Ten");
```

The SetAt() function takes as parameters the key and the value to associate with the key in the map. If the key already exists, the function replaces the value associated with the key with the new value given as the second argument.

Retrieving a Value from the Map

When you click in Map Demo's window, the Get Map Value dialog box appears, so you must suspect that the view class's OnLButtonDown() member function comes into play somewhere. And you'd be correct. Listing 10.11 shows this function.

**Listing 10.11 LST10_11.TXT—The Map Demo Application's
OnLButtonDown() Function**

```
void CMapView::OnLButtonDown(UINT nFlags, CPoint point)
{
    // TODO: Add your message handler code here and/or call default
    // Initialize the dialog box.
    CGetDlg dialog(this);
    dialog.m_key = "";
    // Display the dialog box.
    int result = dialog.DoModal();
    // If the user exits with the OK button...
    if (result == IDOK)
    {
        // Look for the requested value.
        CString value;
        BOOL found = map.Lookup(dialog.m_key, value);
        if (found)
            MessageBox(value);
        else
            MessageBox("No matching value.");
    }
    CView::OnLButtonDown(nFlags, point);
}
```

In OnLButtonDown(), the program displays the dialog box in the usual way, checking to see whether the user exited the dialog box by clicking the OK button. If the user did, the program calls the map object's Lookup() member function, using the key that the user entered into the dialog box as the first argument. The second argument is a reference to the string into which the function can store the value it retrieves from the map. If the key can't be found, the Lookup() function returns FALSE; otherwise, it returns TRUE. The program uses this return value in order to determine whether it should display the string value retrieved from the map or a message box indicating an error.

Iterating Over the Map

In order to display the keys and values used in the map, the program must iterate over the map, moving from one entry to the next, retrieving and displaying the information for each map element. As with the array and list examples, the Map Demo application accomplishes this in its OnDraw() function, which is shown in Listing 10.12.

Listing 10.12   LST10_12.TXT—The Map Demo Application's *OnDraw()* Function

```
void CMapView::OnDraw(CDC* pDC)
{
    CMapDoc* pDoc = GetDocument();
    ASSERT_VALID(pDoc);
    // TODO: add draw code for native data here
    TEXTMETRIC textMetric;
    pDC->GetTextMetrics(&textMetric);
    int fontHeight = textMetric.tmHeight;
    int displayPosition = 10;
    POSITION pos = map.GetStartPosition();
    CString key;
    CString value;
    while (pos != NULL)
    {
        map.GetNextAssoc(pos, key, value);
        CString str = "Key '" + key +
            "' is associated with the value '" +
            value + "'";
        pDC->TextOut(10, displayPosition, str);
        displayPosition += fontHeight;
    }
}
```

Much of this OnDraw() function is similar to other versions that you've seen in this chapter. The map iteration, however, begins when the program calls the map object's GetStartPosition() member function, which returns a position value for the first entry in the map (not necessarily the first entry that you added to the map). Inside a while loop, the program calls the map object's GetNextAssoc() member function, giving the position returned from GetStartPosition() as the single argument. GetNextAssoc() retrieves the key and value at the given position and then updates the position to the next element in the map. When the position value becomes NULL, the program has reached the end of the map.

The String Class

There are few programs that don't have to deal with text strings of one sort or another. Unfortunately, C++ is infamous for its weak string-handling capabilities, while languages like BASIC and Pascal have always enjoyed superior power when it came to these ubiquitous data types. MFC's CString class addresses C++'s string problems by providing member functions that are as handy to use as those found in other languages. Table 10.4 lists the commonly used member functions of the CString class.

Table 10.4   Commonly Used Member Functions of the *CString* Class

Function	Description
Compare()	Case-sensitive compare of two strings.
CompareNoCase()	Case-insensitive compare of two strings.
Empty()	Clears a string.
Find()	Locates a substring.
GetAt()	Gets a character at a specified position in the string.
GetBuffer()	Gets a pointer to the string's contents.
GetLength()	Gets the number of characters in the string.
IsEmpty()	Returns TRUE if the string holds no characters.
Left()	Gets the left segment of a string.
MakeLower()	Lowercases a string.
MakeReverse()	Reverses the contents of a string.
MakeUpper()	Uppercases a string.
Mid()	Gets the middle segment of a string.
Right()	Gets the right segment of a string.
SetAt()	Sets a character at a specified position in the string.
TrimLeft()	Removes leading white-space characters from a string.
TrimRight()	Removes trailing white-space characters from a string.

Besides the functions listed in the table, the CString class also defines a full set of operators for dealing with strings. Using these operators, you can do things like *concatenate* (join together) strings with the plus sign (+), assign values to a string object with the equal sign (=), access the string as a C-style string with the LPCTSTR operator, and more.

Creating a string object is quick and easy, like this:

```
CString str = "This is a test string";
```

Of course, there are lots of ways to construct your string object. The previous example is only one possibility. You can create an empty string object and assign characters to it later, you can create a string object from an existing string object, and you can even create a string from a repeating character.

Once you have the string object created, you can call its member functions and so manipulate the string in a number of ways. For example, to convert all the characters in the string to uppercase, you'd make a function call like this:

```
str.MakeUpper();
```

Or, to compare two strings, you'd make a function call something like this:

```
str.Compare("Test String");
```

You can also compare two CString objects:

```
CString testStr = "Test String";
str.Compare(testStr);
```

If you peruse your online documentation, you'll find that most of the other CString member functions are equally easy to use.

The Time Classes

If you've ever tried to manipulate time values returned from a computer, you'll be pleased to learn about MFC's CTime and CTimeSpan classes, which represent absolute times and elapsed times, respectively. The use of these classes is pretty straightforward, so there's no sample program for this section. However, the following sections will get you started with these handy classes. Before you start working with the time classes, however, look over Table 10.5, which lists the member functions of the CTime class, and Table 10.6, which lists the member functions of the CTimeSpan class.

Table 10.5 Member Functions of the *CTime* Class

Function	Description
Format()	Constructs a string representing the time object's time.
FormatGmt()	Constructs a string representing the time object's GMT (or UTC) time. This is the Greenwich mean time.
GetCurrentTime()	Creates a CTime object for the current time.
GetDay()	Gets the time object's day as an integer.
GetDayOfWeek()	Gets the time object's day of the week, starting with 1 for Sunday.
GetGmtTm()	Gets a time object's second, minute, hour, day, month, year, day of the week, and day of the year as a tm structure.
GetHour()	Gets the time object's hour as an integer.

continues

Table 10.5   Continued

Function	Description
GetLocalTm()	Gets a time object's local time, returning the second, minute, hour, day, month, year, day of the week, and day of the year in a tm structure.
GetMinute()	Gets the time object's minutes as an integer.
GetMonth()	Gets the time object's month as an integer.
GetSecond()	Gets the time object's second as an integer.
GetTime()	Gets the time object's time as a time_t value.
GetYear()	Gets the time object's year as an integer.

Table 10.6   Member Functions of the *CTimeSpan* Class

Function	Description
Format()	Constructs a string representing the time-span object's time.
GetDays()	Gets the time-span object's days.
GetHours()	Gets the time-span object's hours for the current day.
GetMinutes()	Gets the time-span object's minutes for the current hour.
GetSeconds()	Gets the time-span object's seconds for the current minute.
GetTotalHours()	Gets the time-span objects total hours.
GetTotalMinutes()	Gets the time-span object's total minutes.
GetTotalSeconds()	Gets the time-span object's total seconds.

Using a *CTime* Object

Creating a CTime object for the current time is a simple matter of calling the GetCurrentTime() function, like this:

```
CTime time = CTime::GetCurrentTime();
```

Notice that, because GetCurrentTime() is a static member function of the CTime class, you can call it without actually creating a CTime object. You do, however, have to include the class's name as part of the function call, as shown in the preceding code. As you can see, the function returns a CTime object. This object represents the current time. If you wanted to display this time, you could call upon the Format() member function, like this:

```
CString str = time.Format("DATE: %A, %B %d, %Y");
```

The `Format()` function takes as its single argument a format string that tells the function how to create the string representing the time. The previous example creates a string that looks something like this:

DATE: Saturday, April 20, 1996

The format string used with `Format()` is not unlike the format string that you use with functions like the old DOS favorite `printf()` or the Windows conversion function `wsprintf()`. That is, you specify the string's format by including literal characters along with control characters. The literal characters, such as the "DATE:" and the commas in the previous string example, are added to the string exactly as you type them, whereas the format codes are replaced with the appropriate values. For example, the `%A` in the previous code example will be replaced by the name of the day and the `%B` will be replaced by the name of the month. Although the format-string concept is the same as that used with `printf()`, the `Format()` function has its own set of format codes, which are listed in Table 10.7.

Table 10.7   Format Codes for the *Format()* Function

Code	Description
%a	Day name, abbreviated (such as Sat for Saturday).
%A	Day name, no abbreviation.
%b	Month name, abbreviated (such as Mar for March).
%B	Month name, no abbreviation.
%c	Localized date and time (for the U.S., that would be something like 03/17/96 12:15:34).
%d	Day of the month as a number (01–31).
%H	Hour in the 24-hour format (00–23).
%I	Hour in the normal 12-hour format (01–12).
%j	Day of the year as a number (001–366).
%m	Month as a number (01–12).
%M	Minute as a number (00–59).
%p	Localized a.m./p.m. indicator for 12-hour clock.
%S	Second as a number (00–59).
%U	Week of the year as a number (00–51, considering Sunday to be the first day of the week).
%w	Day of the week as a number (0–6, with Sunday being 0).
%W	Week of the year as a number (00–51, considering Monday to be the first day of the week).

continues

Table 10.7 Continued

Code	Description
%x	Localized date representation.
%X	Localized time representation.
%y	Year without the century prefix as a number (00–99).
%Y	Year with the century prefix as a decimal number (such as 1996).
%z	Name of time zone, abbreviated.
%Z	Name of time zone, no abbreviation.
%%	Percent sign.

Other CTime member functions like GetMinute(), GetYear(), and GetMonth() are obvious in their usage. However, you may like an example of using a function like GetLocalTm():

```
struct tm* timeStruct;
timeStruct = time.GetLocalTm();
```

The first line of the previous code declares a pointer to a tm structure. (The tm structure is defined by Visual C++.) The second line sets the pointer to the tm structure created by the call to GetLocalTm(). This function call essentially retrieves all of the time information at once, organized in the tm structure, which is defined in the header file TIME.H, as shown in Listing 10.13.

Listing 10.13 LST10_13.TXT—The *tm* Structure

```
struct tm {
        int tm_sec;     /* seconds after the minute - [0,59] */
        int tm_min;     /* minutes after the hour - [0,59] */
        int tm_hour;    /* hours since midnight - [0,23] */
        int tm_mday;    /* day of the month - [1,31] */
        int tm_mon;     /* months since January - [0,11] */
        int tm_year;    /* years since 1900 */
        int tm_wday;    /* days since Sunday - [0,6] */
        int tm_yday;    /* days since January 1 - [0,365] */
        int tm_isdst;   /* daylight savings time flag */
        };
```

N O T E The CTime class features a number of overloaded constructors, enabling you to create CTime objects in various ways and using various times. ■

Using a *CTimeSpan* Object

A CTimeSpan object is nothing more complex than the difference between two times. You can use CTime objects in conjunction with CTimeSpan objects to easily determine the amount of time that's elapsed between two absolute times. To do this, first create a CTime object for the current time. Then, when the time you're measuring has elapsed, create a second CTime object for the current time. Subtracting the old time object from the new one gives you a CTimeSpan object representing the amount of time that has elapsed. The example in Listing 10.14 shows how this process works.

Listing 10.14   LST10_14.TXT—Calculating a Time Span

```
CTime startTime = CTime::GetCurrentTime();
    //.
    //. Time elapses...
    //.
CTime endTime = CTime::GetCurrentTime();
CTimeSpan timeSpan = endTime - startTime;
```

Collection Class Templates

MFC includes class templates that you can use to create your own special types of collection classes. (For more information on templates, please refer to the section "Templates" in Chapter 30, "Power-User C++ Features.") Although the subject of templates can be complex, using the collection class templates is easy enough. For example, suppose that you want to create an array class that can hold structures of the type shown in Listing 10.15.

Listing 10.15   LST10_15.TXT—A Sample Structure

```
struct MyValues
{
    int value1;
    int value2;
    int value3;
};
```

The first step is to use the template to create your class, like this:

```
CArray<MyValues, MyValues&> myValueArray;
```

Here, CArray is the template that you use for creating your own array classes. The template's two arguments are the type of data to store in the array and the type of data that the new array class's member functions should use as arguments where appropriate. In this case, the type of data to store in the array is structures of the MyValues type. The second argument specifies that class member functions should expect references to MyValues structures as arguments where needed.

To build your array, you first set the array's initial size:

```
myValueArray.SetSize(10, 5);
```

Part
II

Ch
10

Then you can start adding elements to the array, like this:

```
MyValues myValues;
myValueArray.Add(myValues);
```

As you can see, once you have created your array class from the template, you use the array just as you do any of MFC's array classes, as described earlier in this chapter. Other collection class templates you can use are CList and CMap.

From Here...

MFC's collection classes provide you with a way to better organize and manipulate data in your programs. Moreover, thanks to the collection class templates, you can easily create collections of any type you need for your programs. You've probably used normal C++ arrays and maybe even linked lists in your programs before, but MFC's array and list classes boot those data structures into the 90s, giving them more power than ever. In addition, utility classes such as CTime, CTimeSpan, and CString make common programming tasks easier to implement. For information on related topics, you can refer to these chapters:

- Chapter 6, "The Document/View Paradigm," describes how MFC programs store and edit their data.
- Chapter 11, "Drawing on the Screen," shows how to display information in your application's window.
- Chapter 12, "Persistence and File I/O," demonstrates how to archive your data.
- Chapter 14, "Database Access," gives you the inside story on using database files with your applications.

Drawing on the Screen

Most applications need to display some type of data in their windows. One would think that, because Windows is a device-independent operating system, creating window displays would be easier than luring a kitten with a saucer of milk. However, it is exactly Windows' device independence that places a little extra burden on the programmer's shoulders. Because the programmer can never know in advance exactly what type of devices may be connected to a user's system, he or she can't make many assumptions about display capabilities. Functions that draw to the screen must do so indirectly through something called a *display context* (DC).

Visual C++'s MFC includes many classes that make dealing with DCs easier. These classes encapsulate such graphical objects as not only the DC itself, but also pens, brushes, fonts, and more. ■

How device contexts control your displays

You have to know how to manage device contexts before you can display anything on the screen.

How to respond to window-painting requests from Windows

When Windows knows that your application's display needs updating, it sends a message to the application.

How to create and use fonts, pens, and brushes

The basic elements that determine how your display looks are the fonts, pens, and brushes that you've created for the device context.

How to use scrolling windows

Often, your application will need to display more information than will fit in a window. Scrolling is the answer to this problem.

Understanding Device Contexts

As you know, every Windows application (in fact, every computer application) must manipulate data in some way. Most applications must also display data. Unfortunately, as we just said, because of Windows' device independence, this task is not as straightforward in Windows as it is in a nongraphical operating system like DOS.

However, although device independence forces you, the programmer, to deal with data displays indirectly, it helps you by ensuring that your programs run on all popular devices. In most cases, Windows handles devices for you through the device drivers that the user has installed on the system. These device drivers intercept the data that the application needs to display and then translates the data appropriately for the device on which it will appear, whether that is a screen, a printer, or some other output device.

To understand how all this device independence works, imagine an art teacher trying to design a course of study appropriate for all types of artists. The teacher creates a course outline that stipulates the subject of a project, the suggested colors to be used, the dimensions of the finished project, and so on. What the teacher doesn't stipulate is the surface on which the project will be painted or the materials needed to paint on that surface. In other words, the teacher stipulates only general characteristics. The details of how these characteristics are applied to the finished project are left up to each specific artist.

For example, an artist using oil paints will choose canvas as his surface and paints in the colors suggested by the instructor, as the paint. On the other hand, an artist using watercolors will select watercolor paper on which to create her work, and she will, of course, use watercolors rather than oils for paint. Finally, the charcoal artist will select the appropriate drawing surface for charcoal and will use a single color.

The instructor in the preceding scenario is much like a Windows programmer. The programmer has no idea who may eventually use the program and what kind of system that user may have. The programmer can recommend the colors in which data should be displayed and the coordinates at which the data should appear, for example, but it is the device driver—the Windows artist—that ultimately decides how the data appears.

A system with a VGA monitor may display data with fewer colors than a system with a Super VGA monitor. Likewise, a system with a monochrome monitor displays the data in only a single color. Monitors with high resolutions can display more data than lower-resolution monitors. The device drivers, much like the artists in the imaginary art school, must take the display requirements and fine-tune them to the device on which the data will actually appear. And it is a data structure called a *device context* that links the application to the device's driver.

A device context (DC) is little more than a data structure that keeps track of the attributes of a window's drawing surface. These attributes include the currently selected pen, brush, and font that will be used to draw on the screen. Unlike an artist, who can have many brushes and pens with which to work, a DC can use only a single pen, brush, or font at a time. If you want to use a pen that draws wider lines, for example, you need to create the new pen and then replace the

DC's old pen with the new one. Similarly, if you want to fill shapes with a red brush, you must create the brush and "select it into the DC," which is how Windows programmers describe replacing a tool in a DC.

A window's client area is a versatile surface that can display anything a Windows program can draw. The client area can display any type of data because everything displayed in a window, whether it be text, spreadsheet data, a bitmap, or any other type of data, is displayed graphically. MFC helps you display data by encapsulating Windows' GDI functions and objects into its DC classes.

Introducing the Paint1 Application

This chapter's first sample program, which you can find in the CHAP11\PAINT1 folder of this book's CD-ROM, shows you how to use MFC to display many types of data in an application's window. When you run the program, the main window appears, showing text drawn in various-sized fonts (Figure 11.1). When you left-click in the application's window, it switches the type of information that it displays. For example, the first time you click, the window shows a series of blue lines that get thicker as they get closer to the window's bottom (Figure 11.2). This screen is produced by creating new pens and drawing the lines with those pens. A second click brings up a display comprised of rectangles, each of which contains a different pattern. The fill patterns in the rectangles are produced by the brushes created in the program (Figure 11.3). Finally, a third click brings you back to the font display.

Part
II

Ch
11

FIG. 11.1
The font display shows how you can create different types of text output.

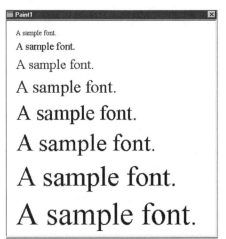

You can find the complete source-code files for the Paint1 application in the CHAP11 folder of this book's CD-ROM. In the following sections, you'll examine the techniques used in those files in order to create the program's displays. By the time you get to the end of this chapter, the words *display context* won't make you scratch your head in perplexity.

FIG. 11.2
Windows also enables you to draw with various styles of lines.

FIG. 11.3
By using different brushes, you can fill shapes with different patterns.

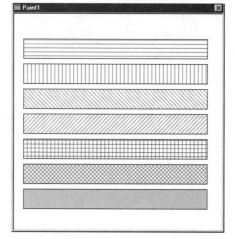

Exploring the Paint1 Application

On the CD

If you've taken the time to look over the source-code files that make up the Paint1 application, you're either now smugly confident that you know all there is to know about displaying data in a window, or you feel like you just tried to read the latest John Grisham novel in Latin. Whichever category you fall into, you'll almost certainly want to read on. You smug folks may get some surprises, while the rest of you will discover that the code isn't nearly as complex as it might appear at first glance.

Painting in an MFC Program

In Chapter 5, "Messages and Commands," you learned about message maps and how you can tell MFC which functions to call when it receives messages from Windows. One important message that every Windows program with a window must handle is WM_PAINT. Windows sends the WM_PAINT message to an application's window when the window needs to be redrawn. There are several events that cause Windows to send a WM_PAINT message. The first event occurs when the user simply runs the program. In a properly written Windows application, the application's window gets a WM_PAINT message almost immediately after being run in order to ensure that the appropriate data is displayed from the very start.

Another time a window might receive the WM_PAINT message is when the window has been resized or has recently been uncovered—either fully or partially—by another window. In either case, part of the window that wasn't visible before is now on the screen and must be updated.

Finally, a program can indirectly send itself a WM_PAINT message by invalidating its client area. Having this ability ensures that an application can change its window's contents almost any time it wishes. For example, a word processor might invalidate its window after the user pastes some text from the Clipboard.

When you studied message maps, you learned to convert a message name to a message-map macro and function name. You now know, for example, that the message-map macro for a WM_PAINT message is ON_WM_PAINT(). You also know that the matching message-map function should be called OnPaint(). This is another case where MFC has already done most of the work of matching a Windows message with its message-response function. (If all this message-map stuff doesn't sound familiar, you might want to review Chapter 5.)

So, in order to paint your window's display, you need to add an ON_WM_PAINT() entry to your message map and then write an OnPaint() function. In the OnPaint() function, you write the code that will produce your window's display. Then, whenever Windows sends your application the WM_PAINT message, MFC automatically calls OnPaint(), which draws the window's display just how you want it.

If you look near the top of the Paint1 application's MAINFRM.CPP file, which is the frame-window class's implementation file, you'll see the application's main message map, as shown in Listing 11.1.

Part II
Ch 11

Listing 11.1   LST11_1.TXT—The Application's Message Map

```
BEGIN_MESSAGE_MAP(CMainFrame, CFrameWnd)
    ON_WM_PAINT()
    ON_WM_LBUTTONDOWN()
END_MESSAGE_MAP()
```

As you can tell by the message map's entries, the application can respond to WM_PAINT and WM_LBUTTONDOWN messages. The ON_WM_PAINT() entry maps to the OnPaint() message-map function. In the first line of that function, the program creates a DC for the client area of the frame window:

```
CPaintDC* paintDC = new CPaintDC(this);
```

CPaintDC is a special class for managing *paint DCs*, which are device contexts that are used only when responding to WM_PAINT messages. In fact, if you're going to use MFC to create your OnPaint() function's paint DC, you must use the CPaintDC class. This is because an object of the CPaintDC class does more than just create a DC; it also calls the BeginPaint() Windows API function in the class's constructor and calls EndPaint() in its destructor. When a program responds to WM_PAINT messages, calls to BeginPaint() and EndPaint() are required. The CPaintDC class handles this requirement without your having to get involved in all the messy details.

As you can see, the CPaintDC constructor takes a single argument, which is a pointer to the window for which you're creating the DC. Because the preceding code line uses the new operator to create the CPaintDC object dynamically on the heap, the program must call the delete operator on the returned CPaintDC pointer when the program is finished with the DC. Otherwise, you not only leave unused objects floating around the computer's memory, but you also fail to call the CPaintDC object's destructor, which in turn never gets a chance to call EndPaint().

After creating the paint DC, the OnPaint() function uses its m_display data member to determine what type of display to draw in the window. The m_display data member can be equal to Fonts, Pens, or Brushes, three values that are defined as an enumeration in the MAINFRM.H file, like this:

```
enum {Fonts, Pens, Brushes};
```

The function checks m_display in a switch statement, calling ShowFonts(), ShowPens(), or ShowBrushes() as appropriate. It is in these three functions that the Paint1 application actually creates its displays. You'll examine these functions of your CMainFrame class in the sections to come. Notice that the pointer to the paint DC is passed as a parameter to ShowFonts(), ShowPens(), and ShowBrushes(), which must use the DC in order to draw in the application's window.

The last line in OnPaint() deletes the CPaintDC object, paintDC, freeing it from memory, as well as ensuring that its destructor gets called properly. Note that, in most programs, you may find it more convenient to create your paint DC as a local variable on the stack, as is shown in Listing 11.2. When you do this, you no longer have to be concerned with deleting the object. It's automatically deleted when it goes out of scope. In the case of the Paint1 application, it's more efficient to pass a CPaintDC pointer as an argument to other functions than it is to pass the actual object.

Listing 11.2   LST11_2.TXT—Creating the Paint DC on the Stack

```
void CMainFrame::OnPaint()
{
    CPaintDC paintDC(this);
    // Drawing code goes here.
}
```

Using Fonts

Fonts are one of the trickier GDI (Graphics Device Interface) objects to handle, so you might as well get them out of the way first. In order to select and use fonts, you must be familiar with the LOGFONT structure, which contains a wealth of information about a font, and you must know how to create new fonts when they're needed. Moreover, there are more typefaces and font types than galaxies in the universe (okay, maybe not quite that many), which means that you can never be sure exactly how your user's system is set up.

As we said, a Windows font is described in the LOGFONT structure, which is outlined in Table 11.1. The LOGFONT description in Table 11.1, however, gives only an overview of the structure. Before experimenting with custom fonts, you may want to look up this structure in your Visual C++ online help, where you'll find a more complete description of each of its fields, including the many constants that are already defined for use with the structure.

Table 11.1   *LOGFONT* Fields and Their Descriptions

Field	Description
lfHeight	Height of font in logical units.
lfWidth	Width of font in logical units.
lfEscapement	Angle at which to draw the text.
lfOrientation	Character tilt in tenths of a degree.
lfWeight	Used to select normal (400) or boldface (700) text.
lfItalic	A nonzero value indicates italics.
lfUnderline	A nonzero value indicates an underlined font.
lfStrikeOut	A nonzero value indicates a strikethrough font.
lfCharSet	Font character set.
lfOutPrecision	How to match requested font to actual font.
lfClipPrecision	How to clip characters that run over clip area.
lfQuality	Print quality of the font.
lfPitchAndFamily	Pitch and font family.
lfFaceName	Typeface name.

The LOGFONT structure holds a complete description of the font. This structure contains 14 fields, although many of the fields can be set to 0 or the default values, depending on the program's needs. In the ShowFonts() function, the Paint1 application creates its LOGFONT as shown in Listing 11.3.

Listing 11.3   LST11_3.TXT—Initializing a *LOGFONT* Structure

```
LOGFONT logFont;
logFont.lfHeight = 8;
logFont.lfWidth = 0;
logFont.lfEscapement = 0;
logFont.lfOrientation = 0;
logFont.lfWeight = FW_NORMAL;
logFont.lfItalic = 0;
logFont.lfUnderline = 0;
logFont.lfStrikeOut = 0;
logFont.lfCharSet = ANSI_CHARSET;
logFont.lfOutPrecision = OUT_DEFAULT_PRECIS;
logFont.lfClipPrecision = CLIP_DEFAULT_PRECIS;
logFont.lfQuality = PROOF_QUALITY;
logFont.lfPitchAndFamily = VARIABLE_PITCH | FF_ROMAN;
strcpy(logFont.lfFaceName, "Times New Roman");
```

In the lines in Listing 11.3, the font is set to be eight pixels high, as determined by the value of the lfHeight field. Note that, in most cases, you should set the width to 0, as determined by lfWidth, which allows Windows to select a width that best matches the height. You can, however, create compressed or expanded fonts by experimenting with the lfWidth field.

The font's italic, underline, and strikeout attributes can be turned on by supplying a nonzero value for the lfItalic, lfUnderline, and lfStrikeOut fields. For example, the window shown in Figure 11.4 shows how the Paint1 application's font display would look if you set the lfItalic and lfUnderline members of the LOGFONT structure to 1.

FIG. 11.4

You can create all types of fonts by manipulating values in the *LOGFONT* structure.

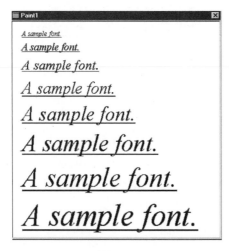

In order to show the many fonts that are displayed in its window, the Paint1 application creates its fonts in a `for` loop, modifying the value of the `LOGFONT` structure's `lfHeight` member each time through the loop, using the loop variable, `x`, to calculate the new font height, like this:

```
logFont.lfHeight = 16 + (x * 8);
```

Because `x` starts at 0, the first font created in the loop will be 16 pixels in height. Each time through the loop, the new font will be eight pixels higher than the previous one.

After setting the font's height, the program creates a `CFont` object:

```
CFont* font = new CFont();
```

In case it's not obvious, `CFont` is MFC's font class. Using the `CFont` class, you can create and manipulate fonts using the class's member functions. One of the most important member functions is `CreateFontIndirect()`, which `DisplayFonts()` calls like this:

```
font->CreateFontIndirect(&logFont);
```

`CreateFontIndirect()` takes a single argument, which is the address of the `LOGFONT` structure that contains the font's attributes. When Windows receives the information stored in the `LOGFONT` structure, it will do its best to create the requested font. The font created isn't always exactly the font requested, so Windows fills in the `LOGFONT` structure with a description of the font that it managed to create.

After the program calls `CreateFontIndirect()`, the `CFont` object has been associated with a Windows font. At this point, you can select the font into the DC, like this:

```
CFont* oldFont = paintDC->SelectObject(font);
```

Remember that, in order to use a new graphical object with a DC, you must first select that object into the DC. The preceding call to the paint DC's `SelectObject()` member function replaces the current font in the DC with the new one. `SelectObject()`'s single parameter is the address of the new font. `SelectObject()` returns a pointer to the old font object that was deselected from the DC. You'll soon see why you must save this pointer.

After selecting the new font into the DC, you can use the font to draw text on the screen. In the `ShowFonts()` function, the first step in displaying text is to determine where in the window to draw the text:

```
position += logFont.lfHeight;
```

The local variable `position` holds the vertical position in the window at which the next line of text should be printed. This position depends upon the height of the current font. After all, if there's not enough space between the lines, the larger fonts will overlap the smaller ones. When Windows created the new font, it stored the font's height (which is most likely the height that you requested, but, then again, maybe not) in the `LOGFONT` structure's `lfHeight` member. By adding the value stored in `lfHeight`, the program can determine the next position at which to display the line of text, using the DC object's `TextOut()` member function:

```
paintDC->TextOut(20, position, "A sample font.");
```

Part
II

Ch
11

Here, TextOut()'s first two arguments are the X,Y coordinates in the window at which to print the text. The third argument is the text to print. TextOut() actually has a fourth argument, which is the number of characters to print. If you leave this last parameter off, MFC just assumes that you want to display the entire string given as the second argument.

Now you get to see why the program saved the pointer of the old font that was deselected from the DC when the program selected the new font. You must never delete a GDI object such as a font from a DC while it's still selected into the DC. That means you must first deselect the new font from the DC before deleting it in preparation for creating the next font. Unfortunately, if you search through your Windows programming manuals, you'll discover that there is no DeselectObject() function. This actually makes sense when you think about it. If you were allowed to deselect GDI objects without selecting new ones, you could leave the DC without a pen, brush, or other important object. So the only way to deselect an object is to select a new object into the DC. Therefore, to deselect the new font, the Paint1 application selects the old font back into the DC, like this:

```
paintDC->SelectObject(oldFont);
```

This time, the program doesn't bother to save the pointer returned from SelectObject() because that pointer is for the new font that the program created. The program already has that pointer stored in font. A quick call to delete gets rid of the font object, so the program can create the next font it needs for the display:

```
delete font;
```

Using Pens

You'll be pleased to know that pens are much easier to deal with than fonts, mostly because you don't have to fool around with complicated data structures like LOGFONT. In fact, to create a pen, you need only supply the pen's line style, thickness, and color. The Paint1 application's ShowPens() function displays in its window lines drawn using different pens created within a for loop. Within the loop, the program first creates a custom pen, like this:

```
CPen* pen = new CPen(PS_SOLID, x*2+1, RGB(0, 0, 255));
```

The first argument shown in the preceding line of code is the line's style, which can be one of the styles listed in Table 11.2. Note that only solid lines can be drawn with different thicknesses. Patterned lines always have a thickness of 1. The second argument in the preceding code is the line thickness, which, in the ShowPens() function, is calculated using the loop variable x as a multiplier.

Finally, the third argument is the line's color. The RGB macro takes three values for the red, green, and blue color components and converts them into a valid Windows color reference. The values for the red, green, and blue color components can be anything from 0 to 255—the higher the value, the brighter that color component. The previous code line creates a bright red pen. If all the color values were 0, the pen would be black; if the color values were all 255, the pen would be white.

Table 11.2 Pen Styles

Style	Description
PS_DASH	Specifies a pen that draws dashed lines
PS_DASHDOT	Specifies a pen that draws dash-dot patterned lines
PS_DASHDOTDOT	Specifies a pen that draws dash-dot-dot patterned lines
PS_DOT	Specifies a pen that draws dotted lines
PS_INSIDEFRAME	Specifies a pen that's used with shapes, where the line's thickness must not extend outside of the shape's frame
PS_NULL	Specifies a pen that draws invisible lines
PS_SOLID	Specifies a pen that draws solid lines

After creating the new pen, the program selects it into the DC, saving the pointer to the old pen, like this:

```
CPen* oldPen = paintDC->SelectObject(pen);
```

Once the pen is selected into the DC, the program can draw a line with the pen. To do this, the program first calculates a vertical position for the new line and then calls the paint DC's MoveTo() and LineTo() member functions, like this:

```
position +=  x * 2 + 10;
paintDC->MoveTo(20, position);
paintDC->LineTo(400, position);
```

The MoveTo() function positions the starting point of the line, whereas the LineTo() function draws a line—using the pen currently selected into the DC—from the point set with MoveTo() to the coordinates given as the function's two arguments.

Finally, the last step is to restore the DC by reselecting the old pen and deleting the new pen, which is no longer selected into the DC:

```
paintDC->SelectObject(oldPen);
delete pen;
```

N O T E If you want to control the style of a line's end points or want to create your own custom patterns for pens, you can use the alternate CPen constructor, which requires a few more arguments than the CPen constructor described in this section. To learn how to use this alternate constructor, look up CPen in your Visual C++ on-line documentation. ▪

Using Brushes

Creating and using brushes in an MFC program is not unlike using pens. In fact, just as with pens, you can create both solid and patterned brushes. You can even create brushes from bitmaps that contain your own custom fill patterns. As you've seen, the Paint1 application displays rectangles that have been filled by both patterned and solid rectangles. These rectangles are produced in the ShowBrushes() function, which, like the font and pen functions you've already examined, creates its graphical objects within a for loop. In the first line of the loop's body, the program defines a pointer to a CBrush object:

```
CBrush* brush;
```

Then, depending on the value of the loop variable x, the program creates either a solid or a patterned brush, as shown in Listing 11.4:

Listing 11.4 LST11_4.TXT—Creating Brush Objects

```
if (x == 6)
    brush = new CBrush(RGB(0,255,0));
else
    brush = new CBrush(x, RGB(0,160,0));
```

In the code lines in Listing 11.4, if x equals 6, the program calls the version of the CBrush constructor that creates a solid brush. The constructor's single argument is a COLORREF value, which is easily produced using the RGB macro that you were introduced to in the section on pens. For any other value of x, the program creates a patterned brush, using x as the pattern index. The second CBrush constructor takes the pattern index and the brush color as its two arguments. Although not used in the code segment in Listing 11.4, Windows defines several constants for the brush patterns (or *hatch styles,* as they're often called). Those constants are HS_BDIAGONAL, HS_CROSS, HS_DIAGCROSS, HS_FDIAGONAL, HS_HORIZONTAL, and HS_VERTICAL.

Once the program has created the new brush, a call to the paint DC's SelectObject() member function selects the brush into the DC and returns a pointer to the old brush:

```
CBrush* oldBrush = paintDC->SelectObject(brush);
```

Now the program calculates a new drawing position, and then it draws a rectangle with the new brush:

```
position += 50;
paintDC->Rectangle(20, position, 400, position + 40);
```

Rectangle() is just one of the shape-drawing functions that you can call. Rectangle() takes as arguments the coordinates of the rectangle's upper-left and lower-right corners. When you run the Paint1 application and look at the brush window, you'll see that each rectangle is bordered by a thin black line. This line was drawn by the DC's default black pen. If you had selected a different pen into the DC, Windows would have used that pen to draw the rectangle's border. For example, in Figure 11.5, the Paint1 program shows rectangles drawn with a red, six-pixel-thick pen.

After drawing a rectangle, the program deselects the new brush from the DC and deletes it:

```
paintDC->SelectObject(oldBrush);
delete brush;
```

FIG. 11.5
Shape-drawing
functions frequently
draw borders with the
currently selected pen.

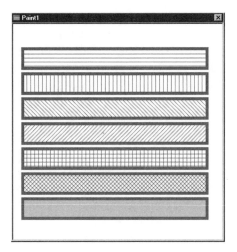

Switching the Display

As you know, when you click in the Paint1 application's window, the window's display changes. This seemingly magical feat is actually easy to accomplish. The program routes WM_LBUTTONDOWN messages to the OnLButtonDown() message-response function, which sets the m_display flag as appropriate. At the program startup, the CMainFrame class's constructor initializes its data member m_display to Fonts, so that the window initially appears with the fonts displayed. When the user clicks in the window, the OnLButtonDown() function changes the value of m_display, as shown in Listing 11.5.

Listing 11.5   LST11_5.TXT—Changing the Value of m_display

```
if (m_display == Fonts)
    m_display = Pens;
else if (m_display == Pens)
    m_display = Brushes;
else
    m_display = Fonts;
```

As you can see, depending on its current value, m_display is set to the next display type in the series. Of course, just changing the value of m_display doesn't accomplish much. The program still needs to redraw the contents of its window. Because OnPaint() determines which display to paint based on the value of m_display, all the program needs to do is to get OnPaint() to execute. This task is accomplished by calling the CMainFrame class's Invalidate() function:

```
Invalidate();
```

A call to Invalidate() tells Windows that all of the window needs to be repainted. This causes Windows to generate a WM_PAINT message for the window. Thanks to MFC's message mapping, the WM_PAINT message gets routed to OnPaint(). Although it's not used in the example in Listing 11.5, Invalidate() actually has one argument, which MFC gives the default value of TRUE. This Boolean argument tells Windows whether to erase the window's background. If you use FALSE for this argument, Windows leaves the background alone. In Figure 11.6, you can see what happens to the Paint1 application if Invalidate() gets called with an argument of FALSE.

FIG. 11.6

Without the program's erasing the background, the Paint1 application's windows get a bit messy.

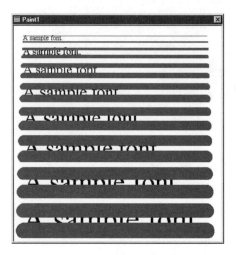

Sizing and Positioning the Window

Although Windows is perfectly happy to choose a position and size for your application's window, often you may want to have control over these attributes. In an MFC program, you can size and position a window by overriding the window class's PreCreateWindow() function. This method of positioning a window is especially useful in an AppWizard-generated program, because you don't usually call Create() directly in such applications. Although the Paint1 application wasn't created by AppWizard, it does override the' window class's PreCreateWindow() function to position the window, as shown in Listing 11.6.

Listing 11.6   LST11_6.TXT—Overriding the *PreCreateWindow()*
Member Function

```
BOOL CMainFrame::PreCreateWindow(CREATESTRUCT& cs)
{
    // Set size of the main window.
    cs.cx = 440;
    cs.cy = 460;
    // Call the base class's version.
    BOOL returnCode = CFrameWnd::PreCreateWindow(cs);
    return returnCode;
}
```

The `PreCreateWindow()` function, which MFC calls right before the window element that'll be associated with the class is created, receives one parameter, a reference to a CREATESTRUCT structure. The CREATESTRUCT structure contains essential information about the window that's about to be created and is declared by Windows, as shown in Listing 11.7.

Listing 11.7   LST11_7.TXT—The *CREATESTRUCT* Structure

```
typedef struct tagCREATESTRUCT {
    LPVOID     lpCreateParams;
    HANDLE     hInstance;
    HMENU      hMenu;
    HWND       hwndParent;
    int        cy;
    int        cx;
    int        y;
    int        x;
    LONG       style;
    LPCSTR     lpszName;
    LPCSTR     lpszClass;
    DWORD      dwExStyle;
} CREATESTRUCT;
```

If you've programmed Windows without application frameworks like MFC, you'll recognize the information stored in the CREATESTRUCT structure. You supply much of this information when calling the Windows API function `CreateWindow()` to create your application's window. Of special interest to MFC programmers are the cx, cy, x, and y members of this structure. By changing cx and cy, you can set the width and height, respectively, of the window. Similarly, modifying x and y changes the window's position. By overriding `PreCreateWindow()`, you get a chance to fiddle with the CREATESTRUCT structure before Windows uses it to create the window.

It's important that, after your own code in `PreCreateWindow()`, you call the base class's `PreCreateWindow()`. Failure to do this will leave you without a valid window, because MFC never gets a chance to pass the CREATESTRUCT structure on to Windows, and so Windows never creates your window. When overriding class member functions, you often need to call the base class's version, either before or after your own code, depending on the function. The descriptions of member functions in your Visual C++ online documentation usually indicate whether or not the base class's version must be called.

Part
II

Ch
11

Scrolling Windows

Those famous screen rectangles called *windows* were developed for two reasons. The first reason is to partition screen space between various applications and documents. The second reason is to enable the user to view portions of a document when the document is too large to completely fit into the window. The Windows operating system and MFC pretty much take care of the partitioning of screen space. However, if you want to enable the user to view portions of a large document, you must create scrolling windows.

Adding scroll bars to an application from scratch is a complicated task. Luckily for Visual C++ programmers, MFC handles many of the details involved in scrolling windows over documents. If you use the document/view architecture and derive your view window from MFC's CScrollView class, you get scrolling capabilities almost for free. I say "almost" because there are still a few details that you must handle. You'll learn those details in the following sections.

N O T E   If you create your application using AppWizard, you can specify that you want to use CScrollView as the base class for your view class. To do this, in the Step 6 Of 6 dialog box displayed by AppWizard, select your view window in the class list and then select CScrollView in the Base Class box, as shown in Figure 11.7. ■

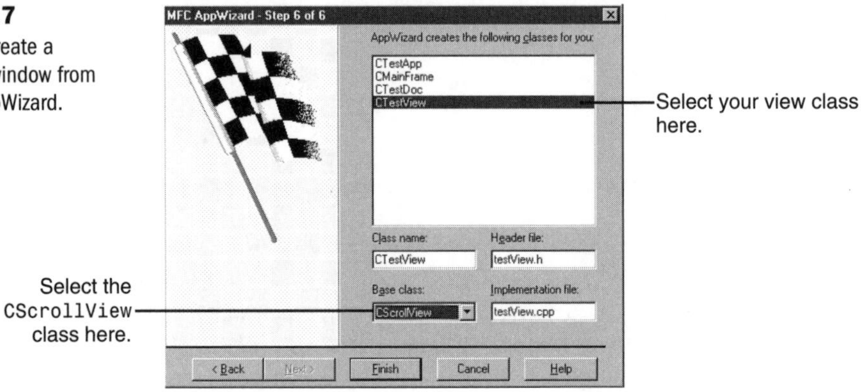

FIG. 11.7
You can create a scrolling window from within AppWizard.

Select your view class here.

Select the CScrollView class here.

Running the Scroll Application

The sample program (called Scroll) for this section enables you to experiment with a scrolling window. You can find this program, along with its complete source code, in the CHAP11 folder of this book's CD-ROM. When you run Scroll, you see the window shown in Figure 11.8. The window displays five lines of text. Each time you click in the window with your left mouse button, the application adds five lines of text to the display. When you get more lines of text than fit in the window, a vertical scroll bar appears (Figure 11.9), enabling you to scroll to the parts of the documents that you can't see.

The more lines you add to the window, the smaller the scroll thumb becomes. This is because the scroll bar represents the size of the document, and the scroll thumb represents the portion of the document that's visible. If you click in the scroll bar (not on the thumb or an arrow button), the window moves a full page forward or backward. In this case, a full page is the amount of the document that fits in the window. If you click the scroll arrows, the view moves a single line in the appropriate direction. Finally, if you right-click in the window, you can remove lines from the window, five at a time.

FIG. 11.8

The Scroll application starts off displaying five lines of text and no scroll bars.

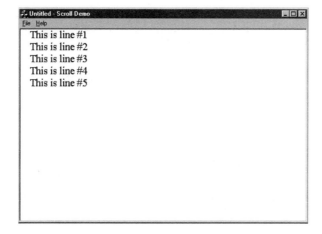

FIG. 11.9

After displaying more lines than fit in the window, the vertical scroll bar appears.

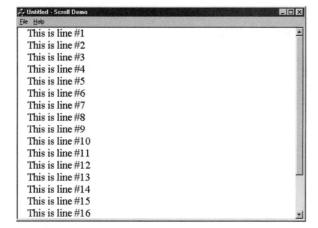

Part

II

Ch

11

Initializing the Scroll Bars

When you're using the document/view architecture, you'll usually want to initialize your scroll bars in the view window's OnInitialUpdate() member function. This is because OnInitialUpdate() gets called once early on in the window's construction. If you're using AppWizard to create your starting classes, AppWizard automatically overrides OnInitialUpdate() in your view class, and, providing that you've requested CScrollView as the base class, AppWizard also includes default scroll initialization code in the function. Listing 11.8 shows OnInitialUpdate() as it's created by AppWizard.

Listing 11.8 LST11_8.TXT—The *OnInitialUpdate()* Function

```
void CMyScrollView::OnInitialUpdate()
{
    CScrollView::OnInitialUpdate();
    CSize sizeTotal;
    // TODO: calculate the total size of this view
    sizeTotal.cx = sizeTotal.cy = 100;
    SetScrollSizes(MM_TEXT, sizeTotal);
}
```

If you examine Listing 11.8, you will see that the program constructs a CSize object called sizeTotal to hold the default width and height of the view. This CSize object is used in the call to SetScrollSizes(), which is the member function that sets up the scroll bars to the correct sizes and states for the window. This function's first argument is the mapping mode, which is usually MM_TEXT. The second argument is a reference to the CSize object that holds the size of the view.

Updating the Scroll Bars

Chances are that the default view size will not suit your application, so you'll want to change the default source code in the OnInitialUpdate() function. Even if you choose to stick with the default size, however, you'll almost certainly need to change the scroll bars as the user changes the document contained in the view window. When using strict document/view design, you'll usually make these changes in the view window's OnUpdate() member function, which you must override in your view class. OnUpdate() gets called by the document class's UpdateAllViews() member function when the user changes the document. In OnUpdate(), you must calculate the document size, page size, and line size for the document and pass those values as arguments to the SetScrollSizes() function.

Because you're not working with a real document in the Scroll application, we thought we'd simplify things by handling everything in the view class. Further, because the OnDraw() function gets called whenever the user somehow changes the view window, the view class is a good place to demonstrate how this scroll bar stuff works. In the Scroll application, OnDraw() first initializes a LOGFONT structure, as shown in Listing 11.9.

Listing 11.9 LST11_9.TXT—Initializing the Scroll Application's *LOGFONT* Structure

```
LOGFONT logFont;
logFont.lfHeight = 24;
logFont.lfWidth = 0;
logFont.lfEscapement = 0;
logFont.lfOrientation = 0;
logFont.lfWeight = FW_NORMAL;
logFont.lfItalic = 0;
logFont.lfUnderline = 0;
logFont.lfStrikeOut = 0;
```

```
logFont.lfCharSet = ANSI_CHARSET;
logFont.lfOutPrecision = OUT_DEFAULT_PRECIS;
logFont.lfClipPrecision = CLIP_DEFAULT_PRECIS;
logFont.lfQuality = PROOF_QUALITY;
logFont.lfPitchAndFamily = VARIABLE_PITCH | FF_ROMAN;
strcpy(logFont.lfFaceName, "Times New Roman");
```

Next, the program creates the font and selects it into the DC:

```
CFont* font = new CFont();
font->CreateFontIndirect(&logFont);
CFont* oldFont = pDC->SelectObject(font);
```

Now that the DC has the font, the program can display the lines of text in the window, which it does as shown in Listing 11.10.

Listing 11.10   LST11_10.TXT—Displaying the Lines of Text

```
// Initialize the position of text in the window.
UINT position = 0;
// Create and display eight example fonts.
for (int x=0; x<numLines; ++x)
{
    // Create the string to display.
    char s[25];
    wsprintf(s, "This is line #%d", x+1);
    // Print text with the new font.
    pDC->TextOut(20, position, s);
    position += logFont.lfHeight;
}
```

You should be familiar with all the code in Listing 11.10. Notice, however, that the loop that draws the text lines uses numLines as a control variable. Because numLines is the member variable that holds the number of lines to display, using it as the loop control variable ensures that the program draws the correct number of lines in the window. The numLines member variable gets initialized to 5 in the view class's constructor. From then on, it gets changed in the OnLButtonDown() and OnRButtonDown() functions, which respond to the user's mouse clicks. Calls to Invalidate() in these functions cause the window and scroll bars to be updated whenever the user changes the number of lines to display. Listing 11.11, for example, shows the code for the OnLButtonDown() function.

Listing 11.11   LST11_11.TXT—Changing the Line Count

```
void CMyScrollView::OnLButtonDown(UINT nFlags, CPoint point)
{
    // TODO: Add your message handler code here and/or call default

    // Increase number of lines to display.
    numLines += 5;
```

Part
II

Ch
11

continues

Listing 11.11 Continued

```
    // Redraw the window.
    Invalidate();
    CScrollView::OnLButtonDown(nFlags, point);
}
```

After displaying the text lines, the program is ready to adjust the size of the scrollers. In order to do this, the program must know the document, page, and line sizes. The document size is the width and height of the screen area that could hold the entire document. The program calculates the document size by using 100 for the width and using the product of numLines times the font height for the height, like this:

```
CSize docSize(100, numLines*logFont.lfHeight);
```

CSize is an MFC class that was created especially for storing the widths and heights of objects. Here, the class's constructor takes the width and height as its two arguments.

The page size is the amount that the window should scroll up and down (or left and right, when you're working with a horizontal scroll bar) when the user clicks in the scroll bar on either side of the scroll thumb. This amount is usually the size of one window. In Scroll, the program calculates the page size, like this:

```
CRect rect;
GetClientRect(&rect);
CSize pageSize(rect.right, rect.bottom+2);
```

The GetClientRect() function fills in a CRect object with the coordinates of the client window. You can use the returned rectangle to determine the size of the window, as shown in the preceding code segment.

Finally, the line size is the amount that the window should scroll when the user clicks a scroll bar's arrow buttons. With a text display, this amount is usually a full text line vertically and a single character horizontally. Scroll calculates the line size by using 0 for the horizontal amount (thus disallowing horizontal scrolling) and using the font height for the vertical amount:

```
CSize lineSize(0, logFont.lfHeight);
```

Once the program has size objects created for the document, page, and line sizes, it can set the scroll bars by calling the view class's SetScrollSizes() member function:

```
SetScrollSizes(MM_TEXT, docSize, pageSize, lineSize);
```

This function takes as arguments the mapping mode, the document size, the page size, and the line size. The first argument can be any of the mapping-mode constants defined by Windows but will usually be MM_TEXT. The other three arguments are references to CSize objects. After the program calls SetScrollSizes(), MFC will have set the scroll bars properly for the currently viewed document. MFC automatically handles the user's interaction with the scroll bars.

From Here...

You're really starting to master Visual C++ now. Take some time at this point to look over the CDC class, and the several classes derived from CDC, in your Visual C++ online documentation. You'll discover a wealth of member functions that you can use to create displays for your windows. Remember that CPaintDC is just one type of CDC-derived class, one that's used specifically in the OnPaint() message-response function. If you want to create a DC in order to paint your window in some other part of your program, you'll probably want to use the CClientDC class. To learn more about related topics, check out the following chapters:

- Chapter 1, "Working with Developer Studio," tells you what you need to know to create your own projects using Visual C++'s development tools.

- Chapter 3, "AppWizard and ClassWizard," brings you up to speed with Visual C++'s excellent automated project and code generators.

- Chapter 5, "Messages and Commands," describes MFC's message-mapping system, which enables you to respond to Windows messages.

Part
II

Ch
11

CHAPTER 12

Persistence and File I/O

One of the most important things a program must do is save a user's data after that data has been changed in some way. Without the capability to save edited data, the work the user performs with an application exists only as long as the application is running, vanishing the instant the user exits the application. Not a good way to get work done! In many cases, especially when using AppWizard to create an application, Visual C++ provides much of the code you need to save and load data. However, in some cases—most notably when you create your own object types—you have to do a little extra work to keep your user's files up-to-date. ■

How persistent objects help you keep documents up-to-date

Because persistent objects know how to save and load their own data, they're perfect for dealing with documents that contain custom data types.

How a standard Document/View application deals with persistence

When you create an application with AppWizard, you get a default version of a persistent object in the form of the document class.

How to create your own persistent class

Creating a custom persistent class requires completing several programming steps, but it's easy when you know the tricks.

How to use MFC's *CFile* class to read and write files directly

You don't need persistent objects to deal with file I/O. You can handle files the old-fashioned way, if you like.

How to create your own archive objects

Objects of the CArchive class are the heart of persistent objects. Once you understand the CFile class, you're ready to create CArchive objects, too.

Objects and Persistence

When you're writing an application, you deal with a lot of different types of objects. Some of your data objects might be simple types like integers and characters. Other objects might be instances of classes, like strings from the CString class or even objects created from your own custom classes. When using objects in applications that must create, save, and load documents, you need a way to save and load the state of those objects, so that you can re-create them exactly as the user left them at the end of the last session.

An object's capability to save and load its state is called *persistence*. Almost all of the MFC classes are persistent because they are derived either directly or indirectly from MFC's CObject class, which provides the basic functionality for saving and loading an object's state. You've already had some experience with this feature of Visual C++'s MFC. In the following section, though, you'll get a review of how MFC makes a document object persistent.

The File Demo Application

When you create a program using Visual C++'s AppWizard, you get an application that uses document and view classes to organize, edit, and display its data. As you know, the document object, which is derived from the CDocument class, is responsible for holding the application's data during a session and for saving and loading the data so that the document persists from one session to another.

In the CHAP12\FILE folder of this book's CD-ROM, you'll find the File Demo application, which demonstrates the basic techniques behind saving and loading data of an object derived from CDocument. When you run the application, you see the window shown in Figure 12.1. This window displays the contents of the current document. In this case, a document is a single string containing a short message.

FIG. 12.1

The File Demo application demonstrates basic document persistence.

When the program first begins, the message is automatically set to the string "Default Message." However, you can change this message to anything you like. To do this, select the Edit, Change Message command. You then see the dialog box shown in Figure 12.2. Type a new message in the edit box and click the OK button. The new message appears in the window.

FIG. 12.2
You can use the Change Message dialog box to edit the application's message string.

If you choose to exit the program, the document's current state is lost. The next time you run the program, you again have to change the message string. To avoid this complication, you can save the document before exiting the program. Choose the File, Save command to do this (see fig. 12.3). After saving the document, you can reload it at any time by selecting File, Open.

FIG. 12.3
Use the File menu to save and load documents.

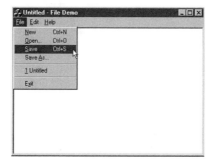

A Review of Document Classes

What you've just experienced is object persistence from the user's point of view. The programmer, of course, needs to know much more about how this persistence stuff works. Although you had some experience with document classes in Chapter 6, "The Document/View Paradigm," you'll now review the basic concepts with an eye towards extending those concepts to your own custom classes.

When working with an application created by AppWizard, there are several steps you must complete to enable your document to save and load its state. Those steps, as they apply to an SDI (Single Document Interface) application, are as follows:

1. Define the data members that will hold the document's data.
2. Initialize the data members in the document class's OnNewDocument() member function.
3. Display the current document in the view class's OnDraw() member function.
4. Provide member functions in the view class that enable the user to edit the document.

5. Add, to the document class's `Serialize()` member function, the code needed to save and load the data that comprises the document.

A Quick Look at File Demo's Source Code

In the File Demo application, the document class declares its document storage in its header file (FILEDOC.H), like this:

```
// Attributes
public:
    CString m_message;
```

In this case, the document's storage is nothing more than a single string object. Usually, your document's storage needs are much more complex. This single string, however, is enough to demonstrate the basics of a persistent document.

The document class must also initialize the document's data, which it does in the `OnNewDocument()` member function, as shown in Listing 12.1.

Listing 12.1 LST12_1.TXT—Initializing the Document's Data

```
BOOL CFileDoc::OnNewDocument()
{
    if (!CDocument::OnNewDocument())
        return FALSE;

    // TODO: add reinitialization code here
    // (SDI documents will reuse this document)

    m_message = "Default Message";

    return TRUE;
}
```

With the document class's `m_message` data member initialized, the application can display the data in the View window, which it does in the view class's `OnDraw()` function, as shown in Listing 12.2.

Listing 12.2 LST12_2.TXT—Displaying the Document's Data

```
void CFileView::OnDraw(CDC* pDC)
{
    CFileDoc* pDoc = GetDocument();
    ASSERT_VALID(pDoc);

    // TODO: add draw code for native data here

    pDC->TextOut(20, 20, pDoc->m_message);
}
```

As long as the user is happy with the contents of the document, the program doesn't need to do anything else. But, of course, an application that doesn't enable the user to edit the application's documents is mostly useless. The File Demo application displays a dialog box the user can use to edit the contents of the document, as shown in Listing 12.3.

Listing 12.3   LST12_3.TXT—Changing the Document's Data

```
void CFileView::OnEditChangemessage()
{
    // TODO: Add your command handler code here

    CChngDlg dialog(this);
    CFileDoc* pDoc = GetDocument();
    dialog.m_message = pDoc->m_message;

    int result = dialog.DoModal();

    if (result == IDOK)
    {
        pDoc->m_message = dialog.m_message;
        pDoc->SetModifiedFlag();
        Invalidate();
    }
}
```

This function, which responds to the application's Edit, Change Message command, displays the dialog box and, if the user exits the dialog box by clicking the OK button, transfers the string from the dialog box to the document's data member. The call to the document class's SetModifiedFlag() function notifies the class that its contents have been changed.

Once the user has changed the document's contents, the data must be saved before exiting the application (unless, that is, the user doesn't want to save the changes he made). The document class's Serialize() function, shown in Listing 12.4, handles the saving and loading of the document's data.

Part
II

Ch
12

Listing 12.4   LST12_4.TXT—The Document Class's *Serialize()* Function

```
void CFileDoc::Serialize(CArchive& ar)
{
    if (ar.IsStoring())
    {
        // TODO: add storing code here

        ar << m_message;
    }
    else
    {
        // TODO: add loading code here
```

continues

Listing 12.4   Continued

```
        ar >> m_message;
        UpdateAllViews(NULL);
    }
}
```

Because the CString class (of which m_message is an object) defines the >> and << operators for transferring strings to and from an archive, it's a simple task to save and load the document class's data. If the document's data contained simple data types like integers or characters, it would also be easy to save and load the data. However, what if you've created your own custom class for holding the elements of a document? How can you make an object of this class persistent? You'll find the answers to these questions in the following section.

Creating a Persistent Class

Suppose that you now want to enhance the File Demo application so that it contains its data in a custom class called CMessages. This class holds three CString objects, each of which must be saved and loaded if the application is going to work correctly. You have a couple of options. The first option is to save and load each individual string, as shown in Listing 12.5.

On the CD

Listing 12.5   LST12_5.TXT—One Way to Save the New Class's Strings

```
void CFileDoc::Serialize(CArchive& ar)
{
    if (ar.IsStoring())
    {
        // TODO: add storing code here

        ar << m_messages.m_message1;
        ar << m_messages.m_message2;
        ar << m_messages.m_message3;
    }
    else
    {
        // TODO: add loading code here

        ar >> m_messages.m_message1;
        ar >> m_messages.m_message2;
        ar >> m_messages.m_message3;
        UpdateAllViews(NULL);
    }
}
```

In the preceding example, m_messages is an object of the CMessages class. The CMessages class has three data members that make up the document's data. These data members, which are objects of the CString class, are called m_message1, m_message2, and m_message3.

Although the solution shown in Listing 12.5 is workable, it's not particularly elegant. It would be better to make the CMessages class capable of creating persistent objects. This involves completing the following steps:

1. Derive the new class from CObject.
2. Place the DECLARE_SERIAL() macro in the class's declaration.
3. Place the IMPLEMENT_SERIAL() macro in the class's implementation.
4. Override the Serialize() function in the class.
5. Provide an empty, default constructor for the class.

In the following section, you explore an application that creates persistent objects exactly as described in the preceding steps.

The File Demo 2 Application

The next sample application, File Demo 2, demonstrates the steps you take to create a class from which you can create persistent objects. You'll find this application in the CHAP12\FILE2 folder of this book's CD-ROM. When you run the application, you see the window shown in Figure 12.4. The program's window displays the three strings that make up the document's data. These three strings are contained in a custom class.

FIG. 12.4

The three strings displayed in the window are data members of a custom class.

You can edit any of the three strings, by selecting the Edit, Change Messages command. When you do, the dialog box shown in Figure 12.5 appears. Type the new string or strings that you want to display in the window, and then click the OK button. The program displays the edited strings, as well as stores the new string values in the data object.

FIG. 12.5

Use the Change Messages dialog box to edit the application's data.

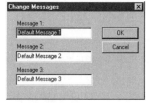

The application's File menu contains the commands you need to save or load the contents of a document. If you save the changes you make before exiting the application, you can reload the document when you restart the application. In this case, unlike the first version of the program, the document class is using a persistent object—an object that knows how to save and load its own state—as the document's data.

Looking at the *CMessages* Class

Before you can understand how the document class manages to save and load its contents successfully, you have to understand how the CMessages class, of which the document class's m_messages data member is an object, works. As you examine this class, you'll see how the aforementioned five steps for creating a persistent class have been implemented. Listing 12.6 shows the class's header file.

Listing 12.6   MESSAGES.H—The *CMessages* Class's Header File

```
// messages.h
class CMessages : public CObject
{
    DECLARE_SERIAL(CMessages)
    CMessages(){};

protected:
    CString m_message1;
    CString m_message2;
    CString m_message3;

public:
    void SetMessage(UINT msgNum, CString msg);
    CString GetMessage(UINT msgNum);
    void Serialize(CArchive& ar);
};
```

First, notice that the CMessages class is derived from MFC's CObject class. Also, notice the DECLARE_SERIAL() macro near the top of the class's declaration. This macro's single argument is the name of the class you're declaring. MFC uses this macro to create the additional function declarations needed to implement object persistence. Next, the class declares a default constructor that requires no arguments. This constructor is necessary because MFC needs to be able to create objects of the class when loading data from disk.

After the default constructor comes the class's data members, which are three objects of the CString class. The public member functions are next. SetMessage(), whose arguments are the number of the string to set and the string's new value, enables a program to change a data member. GetMessage(), on the other hand, is the complementary function, enabling a program to retrieve the current value of any of the strings. Its single argument is the number of the string to retrieve.

Finally, the class overrides the Serialize() function, where all the data saving and loading takes place. The Serialize() function is the heart of a persistent object, with each persistent class implementing it in a different way. Listing 12.7 is the class's implementation file, which defines the various member functions.

Listing 12.7   MESSAGES.CPP—The *CMessages* Class's Implementation File

```
// messages.cpp

#include "stdafx.h"
#include "messages.h"

IMPLEMENT_SERIAL(CMessages, CObject, 0)

void CMessages::SetMessage(UINT msgNum, CString msg)
{
    if (msgNum == 1)
        m_message1 = msg;
    else if (msgNum == 2)
        m_message2 = msg;
    else if (msgNum == 3)
        m_message3 = msg;
}

CString CMessages::GetMessage(UINT msgNum)
{
    if (msgNum == 1)
        return m_message1;
    else if (msgNum == 2)
        return m_message2;
    else if (msgNum == 3)
        return m_message3;
    else
        return "";
}

void CMessages::Serialize(CArchive& ar)
{
    CObject::Serialize(ar);

    if (ar.IsStoring())
    {
        ar << m_message1 << m_message2 << m_message3;
    }
    else
    {
        ar >> m_message1 >> m_message2 >> m_message3;
    }
}
```

The IMPLEMENT_SERIAL() macro is the counterpart to the DECLARE_SERIAL() macro. The IMPLEMENT_SERIAL() macro instructs MFC in how to define the functions that give the class its persistent capabilities. The macro's three arguments are the name of the class, the name of the immediate base class, and a schema number, which is like a version number. In most cases, you'll use 1 for the schema number.

There's nothing tricky about the SetMessage() and GetMessage() functions, which perform their assigned tasks straightforwardly. The Serialize() function, however, may inspire a couple of questions. First, note that the first line of the body of the function calls the base class's Serialize() function. This is a standard practice for many functions that override functions of a base class. In this case, the call to CObject::Serialize() doesn't do much, since the CObject class's Serialize() function is empty. Still, calling the base class's Serialize() function is a good habit to get into, because you may not always be working with classes derived directly from CObject.

After calling the base class's version of the function, Serialize() saves and loads its data in much the same way a document object does. Because the data members that must be serialized are CString objects, the program can use the >> and << operators to write the strings to the disk.

Using the *CMessages* Class in the Program

Now that you know how the CMessages class works, you can examine how it's used in the File Demo 2 application's document class. As you look over the document class, you see that the class uses the same steps to handle its data as the original File Demo application. The main difference is that it's now dealing with a custom class, rather than simple data types or classes defined by MFC. First, the object is declared in the document class's declaration, like this:

```
// Attributes
public:
    CMessages m_messages;
```

Next, the program initializes the data object in the document class's OnNewDocument() class, as seen in Listing 12.8.

On the CD

Listing 12.8   LST12_8.TXT—Initializing the Data Object

```
BOOL CFile2Doc::OnNewDocument()
{
    if (!CDocument::OnNewDocument())
        return FALSE;

    // TODO: add reinitialization code here
    // (SDI documents will reuse this document)

    m_messages.SetMessage(1, "Default Message 1");
    m_messages.SetMessage(2, "Default Message 2");
    m_messages.SetMessage(3, "Default Message 3");

    return TRUE;
}
```

Because the document class cannot directly access the data object's data members, it must initialize each string by calling the CMessages class's SetMessage() member function. The view class must edit the data the same way, by calling the CMessages object's member functions, as shown in Listing 12.9. The view class's `OnDraw()` function also calls the `GetMessage()` member function in order to access the `CMessages` class's strings.

On the CD

Listing 12.9 LST12_9.TXT—Editing the Data Strings

```
void CFile2View::OnEditChangemessages()
{
    // TODO: Add your command handler code here

    CFile2Doc* pDoc = GetDocument();

    CChngDlg dialog(this);
    dialog.m_message1 = pDoc->m_messages.GetMessage(1);
    dialog.m_message2 = pDoc->m_messages.GetMessage(2);
    dialog.m_message3 = pDoc->m_messages.GetMessage(3);

    int result = dialog.DoModal();

    if (result == IDOK)
    {
        pDoc->m_messages.SetMessage(1, dialog.m_message1);
        pDoc->m_messages.SetMessage(2, dialog.m_message2);
        pDoc->m_messages.SetMessage(3, dialog.m_message3);
        pDoc->SetModifiedFlag();
        Invalidate();
    }
}
```

The real action, however, happens in the document class's `Serialize()` function, where the m_messages data object is serialized out to disk. This is accomplished by calling the data object's own `Serialize()` function inside the document's `Serialize()`, as shown in Listing 12.10.

Part
II

Ch
12

On the CD

Listing 12.10 LST12_10.LST—Serializing the Data Object

```
void CFile2Doc::Serialize(CArchive& ar)
{
    m_messages.Serialize(ar);

    if (ar.IsStoring())
    {
        // TODO: add storing code here

    }
    else
    {
        // TODO: add loading code here

        UpdateAllViews(NULL);
    }
}
```

As you can see, after serializing the m_messages data object, there's not much left to do in the document class's Serialize() function, except call UpdateAllViews() if data is being loaded rather than saved. Notice that the call to m_messages.Serialize() passes the archive object as its single parameter.

Reading and Writing Files Directly

Although using MFC's built-in serialization capabilities is a handy way to save and load data, sometimes you need more control over the file-handling process. For example, you might need to deal with your files non-sequentially, something the Serialize() function and its associated CArchive object can't handle. In this case, you can handle files almost exactly as you did in your DOS programs, by creating, reading, and writing files directly. Even when you need to dig down to this level of file handling, though, MFC offers help. Specifically, you can use the CFile class to handle files directly.

The File Demo 3 Application

This book's CD-ROM contains an example program that shows how the CFile class works. You'll find this program in the CHAP12\FILE3 folder. When you run the program, you see the window shown in Figure 12.6. By selecting the Edit, Change Message command, you can edit the string that's displayed in the window (see fig. 12.7). Finally, you can save and load the displayed text string by selecting the File, Save and File, Open commands, respectively (see fig. 12.8).

FIG. 12.6

The File Demo 3 application uses the *CFile* class for direct file handling.

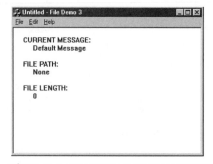

FIG. 12.7

Use the Change Message dialog box to edit the application's display string.

FIG. 12.8
The File menu enables
you to save and load the
application's display
string.

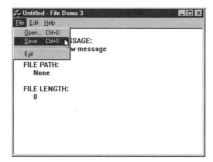

The *CFile* Class

MFC's CFile class encapsulates all the functions you need to handle any type of file. Whether you want to perform common sequential data saving and loading or want to construct a random-access file, the CFile class gets you there. Using the CFile class is a lot like handling files the old-fashioned C-style way, except the class hides some of the busy-work details from you, so that you can get the job done quickly and easily. For example, you can create a file for reading with only a single line of code. Table 12.1 shows the CFile class's member functions and their descriptions.

Table 12.1   Member Functions of the *CFile* Class

Function	Description
Abort()	Immediately closes the file with no regard for errors
Close()	Closes the file
Duplicate()	Creates a duplicate file object
Flush()	Flushes data from the stream
GetFileName()	Gets the file's filename
GetFilePath()	Gets the file's full path
GetFileTitle()	Gets the file's title (the filename without the extension)
GetLength()	Gets the file's length
GetPosition()	Gets the current position within the file
GetStatus()	Gets the file's status
LockRange()	Locks a portion of the file
Open()	Opens the file
Read()	Reads data from the file

Part
II

Ch
12

continues

Table 12.1 Continued

Function	Description
Remove()	Deletes a file
Rename()	Renames the file
Seek()	Sets the position within the file
SeekToBegin()	Sets the position to the beginning of the file
SeekToEnd()	Sets the position to the end of the file
SetFilePath()	Sets the file's path
SetLength()	Sets the file's length
SetStatus()	Sets the file's status
UnlockRange()	Unlocks a portion of the file
Write()	Writes data to the file

As you can see from the table, the CFile class offers up plenty of file-handling power. The File Demo 3 application demonstrates how to call a few of the CFile class's member functions. However, most of the other functions are just as easy to use.

Exploring the File Demo 3 Application

When the File Demo 3 application starts up, the program sets its display string to "Default Message," sets the file path to "None," and sets the file's length to 0. This is all accomplished in the view class's constructor. (For the sake of simplicity, all of the file handling is done in the view class.) When the user selects the Edit, Change Message command, the program displays the Change Message dialog box, which happens in the view class's OnEditChangemessage() member function, shown in Listing 12.11.

On the CD

Listing 12.11 LST12_11.TXT—Changing the Display String

```
void CFile3View::OnEditChangemessage()
{
    // TODO: Add your command handler code here

    CChngDlg dialog(this);
    dialog.m_message = m_message;

    int result = dialog.DoModal();

    if (result == IDOK)
    {
        m_message = dialog.m_message;
        Invalidate();
    }
}
```

In this function, the program displays the dialog box, and, if the user exits the dialog box by clicking the OK button, sets the view class's m_message data member to the string entered into the dialog box. A call to Invalidate() ensures that the new string is displayed in the window. The process of displaying dialog boxes and extracting data from them should be very familiar to you by now.

When the user selects the File, Save command, MFC calls the view class's OnFileSave() member function, which is shown in Listing 12.12.

On the CD

Listing 12.12   LST12_12.TXT—The Application's *OnFileSave()* Function

```
void CFile3View::OnFileSave()
{
    // TODO: Add your command handler code here

    // Create the file.
    CFile file("TESTFILE.TXT",
        CFile::modeCreate | CFile::modeWrite);

    // Write data to the file.
    int length = m_message.GetLength();
    file.Write((LPCTSTR)m_message, length);

    // Obtain information about the file.
    m_filePath = file.GetFilePath();
    m_fileLength = file.GetLength();

    // Close the file and repaint the window.
    file.Close();
    Invalidate();
}
```

In OnFileSave(), the program first creates the file, as well as sets the file's access mode, by calling the CFile class's constructor. The constructor takes as arguments the name of the file to create and the file access mode flags. You can use several flags at a time simply by ORing their values together, as you can see in the previous listing. These flags, which describe how to open the file and which specify the types of valid operations, are defined as part of the CFile class and are listed in Table 12.2 along with their descriptions. For more details, please refer to your Visual C++ online documentation.

Table 12.2   The File Mode Flags

Flag	Description
CFile::modeCreate	Create a new file or truncate an existing file to length 0
CFile::modeNoInherit	Disallow inheritance by a child process

continues

Part
II

Ch
12

Table 12.2 Continued

Flag	Description
CFile::modeNoTruncate	When creating the file, do not truncate the file if it already exists
CFile::modeRead	Allow read operations only
CFile::modeReadWrite	Allow both read and write operations
CFile::modeWrite	Allow write operations only
CFile::shareCompat	Allow other processes to open the file
CFile::shareDenyNone	Allow other processes read or write operations on the file
CFile::shareDenyRead	Disallow read operations by other processes
CFile::shareDenyWrite	Disallow write operations by other processes
CFile::shareExclusive	Deny all access to other processes
CFile::typeBinary	Set binary mode for the file
CFile::typeText	Set text mode for the file

After creating the file, OnFileSave() gets the length of the current message and writes it out to the file by calling the CFile object's Write() member function. This function requires, as arguments, a pointer to the buffer containing the data to write and the number of bytes to write. Notice the LPCTSTR casting operator in the call to Write(). This operator is defined by the CString class and extracts the string from the class.

Finally, the program calls the CFile object's GetFilePath() and GetLength() member functions to get the file's complete path and length, after which a call to Close() closes the file and a call to the view class's Invalidate() function causes the window to display the new information.

Reading from a file is not much different from writing to one, as you can see in Listing 12.13, which shows the view class's OnFileOpen() member function.

On the CD

Listing 12.13 LST12_13.TXT—Reading from the File

```
void CFile3View::OnFileOpen()
{
    // TODO: Add your command handler code here

    // Open the file.
    CFile file("TESTFILE.TXT", CFile::modeRead);

    // Read data from the file.
    char s[81];
```

```
    int bytesRead = file.Read(s, 80);
    s[bytesRead] = 0;
    m_message = s;

    // Get information about the file.
    m_filePath = file.GetFilePath();
    m_fileLength = file.GetLength();

    // Close the file and repaint the window.
    file.Close();
    Invalidate();
}
```

This time the file is opened using the CFile::modeRead flag, which opens the file for read operations only, after which the program creates a character buffer and calls the file object's read() member function to read data into the buffer. The read() function's two arguments are the address of the buffer and the number of bytes to read. The function returns the number of bytes actually read, which, in this case, is almost always less than the 80 requested. Using the number of bytes read, the program can add a 0 to the end of the character data, thus creating a standard C-style string that can be used to set the m_message data member. As you can see, the OnFileOpen() function calls the file object's GetFilePath(), GetLength(), and Close() member functions exactly as OnFileSave() did.

Creating Your Own *CArchive* Objects

Although you can handle files using CFile objects, you can go a step further and create your own CArchive object that you can use exactly as you use the CArchive object in the Serialize() function. To do this, you create a CFile object and pass that object to the CArchive constructor, like this:

```
CFile file("FILENAME.EXT", CFile::modeRead);
CArchive ar(&file, CArchive::store);
```

After creating the archive object, you can use it just like the archive objects that are created for you by MFC. When you're through with the archive object, you must close both the archive and the file, like this:

```
ar.Close();
file.Close();
```

From Here...

When it comes to file handling, Visual C++ and MFC give you a number of options. The easiest way to save and load (serialize) data is to take advantage of the CArchive object created for you by MFC and passed to the document class's Serialize() function. Sometimes, however, you need to create your own persistent objects, by deriving the object's class from MFC's CObject class, and then adding a default constructor, as well as the DECLARE_SERIAL() and IMPLEMENT_SERIAL() macros. You can then override the Serialize() function in your new

Part

II

Ch

12

class. If necessary, you can control file handling more directly by creating a `CFile` object and using that object's member functions to save and load data. For more information on related topics, please refer to the following chapters:

- Chapter 3, "AppWizard and ClassWizard," brings you up to speed with Visual C++'s excellent automated project and code generators, which create a document class containing the `Serialize()` function.

- Chapter 5, "Messages and Commands," describes MFC's message-mapping system, which enables you to respond to Windows messages.

- Chapter 6, "The Document/View Paradigm," discusses how data is handled in an application's document and view classes.

- Chapter 7, "Dialog and Controls," explains how to use dialog boxes in your applications.

- Chapter 14, "Database Access," describes how Visual C++ programs can interact with information stored in database files.

CHAPTER 13

Sockets, MAPI, and the Internet

There are a number of ways for your applications to communicate with other applications through a network like the Internet. This chapter introduces you to the concepts involved with these programming techniques. ■

Using Windows Sockets (Winsock)

Describes the role the Windosck.dll plays in developing communications applications.

Messaging API (MAPI)

The capability to send messages is a must to receive a Windows 95 stamp of approval from Microsoft. This section shows you how to use this powerful API.

Internet Classes New in Visual C++ 4.2

Perhaps the precursor to the information super highway. Cruise route 66 using new Internet Application development classes.

Internet Server API (ISAPI) Classes

An Application Programmer Interface is a collection of utiltiy functions collected for a similar purpose. The Internet Server API will help your applications merge onto the Information Super Highway.

Using Windows Sockets

Before the Windows operating system even existed, the Internet existed. As it grew, it became the largest TCP/IP network in the world. The early sites were UNIX machines, and a set of conventions called Berkeley sockets became the standard for TCP/IP communication between UNIX machines on the Internet. Other operating systems implemented TCP/IP communications, too, which contributed immensely to the growth of the Internet. On those operating systems, things were starting to get messy, with a wide variety of proprietary implementations of TCP/IP, when a group of over 20 vendors banded together to create the Winsock specification.

The specification defines the interface to a DLL, typically called WINSOCK.DLL or WSOCK32.DLL. Vendors write the code for the functions themselves. Applications can call the functions, confident that the name, parameter meaning, and final behavior of the function is the same no matter which DLL is installed on the machine. For example, the DLLs included with Windows 95 and Windows NT are not the same at all, but a 32-bit Winsock application can run unchanged on a Windows 95 or Windows NT machine, calling the Winsock functions in the appropriate DLL.

N O T E   Winsock is not confined to TCP/IP communication. IPX/SPX support is the second protocol supported, and there will be others. For more information, check the Winsock specification itself. The Stardust Labs Winsock Resource Page at **http://www.stardust.com/wsresource/** is a great starting point.

An important concept in sockets programming is a socket's *port*. Every site on the Internet has a numeric address called an *IP address,* typically written as four numbers separated by dots: **198.53.145.3**, for example. Programs running on that machine are all willing to talk, using sockets, to other machines. If a request arrives at **198.53.145.3**, which program should handle it?

Requests arrive at the machine carrying a *port number,* a number from 1,024 up that indicates for which program the request is intended. Some port numbers are reserved for standard use; for example, port 80 is traditionally used by Web servers to listen for Web document requests from client programs like Hotjava or Netscape Navigator.

Most socket work is *connection-based*: the two programs form a connection with a socket at each end and then send and receive data along the connection. Some applications prefer to send the data without a connection, but there is no guarantee that this data arrives. The classic example is a time server that sends out the current time to every machine near it, constantly, without waiting until it is asked. The delay in establishing a connection might make the time sent through the connection outdated, so it makes sense in this case to use a connectionless approach.

Winsock in MFC

At first, sockets programming in Visual C++ meant making API calls into the DLL. Many developers built socket classes to encapsulate these calls. Visual C++ 2.1 introduced two new classes: `CAsyncSocket` and `CSocket`, which inherits from `CAsyncSocket`. These classes handle the API calls for you, including the startup and cleanup calls that would otherwise be easy to forget.

Windows programming is *asynchronous*: there are lots of different things going on at the same time. In older versions of Windows, if one part of an application got stuck in a loop or otherwise hung up, the entire application—and sometimes the entire operating system—would stick or hang with it. This was obviously something to be avoided at all costs. Yet a socket call, perhaps a call to read some information through a TCP/IP connection to another site on the Internet, might take a long time to complete. (A function that is waiting to send or receive information on a socket is said to be *blocking*.) There are three ways around this problem:

1. Put the function that might block in a thread of its own. The thread will block, but the rest of the application will carry on.

2. Have the function return immediately after making the request, and have another function check regularly (*poll* the socket) to see if the request has completed.

3. Have the function return immediately, and send a Windows message sent when the request has completed.

Option 1 was not available until recently, and Option 2 is inefficient under Windows. So most Winsock programming adopts Option 3. The class `CAsyncSocket` implements this approach. For example, to send a string across a connected socket to another site on the Internet, you call that socket's `Send()` function. `Send()` doesn't necessarily send any data at all; it tries to, but if the socket isn't ready and waiting, `Send()` just returns. When the socket is ready, a message is sent to the socket window, which catches it and sends the data across. This is called *asynchronous Winsock programming*.

N O T E Winsock programming is not a simple topic; entire books have been written on it. One you might like to look at is Que's **Developing Internet Applications in Visual C++.** If you decide that this low-level sockets programming is the way to go, building standard programs is a good way to learn the process. ■

Part

II

Ch

13

CAsyncSocket   The CAsynchSocket class is a wrapper class for the asynchronous Winsock calls. It has a number of useful functions, which facilitate using the Winsock API. Table 13.1 lists the CASynchSocket member funtions and responsibility.

Table 13.1   CASynchSocket Member Functions

Method Name	Description
Create	`Create` is the function you call to complete the initialization when the constructor constructs a blank socket.
Accept	`Accept` is how a listening socket handles an incoming connection, filling a new socket with the address information.
AsyncSelect	`ASyncSelect` requests that a Windows message be sent when a socket is ready.
Attach	`Attach` attaches a socket handle to a `CAsyncSocket` instance, so that it can form a connection to another machine.
Bind	Bind associates an address with a socket.
Close	Closes the socket.
Connect	Connects the socket to a remote address and port.
Create	`Create` completes the initialization process begun by the constructor.
Detach	Detaches a previously attached socket handle.
FromHandle	`FromHandle` is a static function that returns a pointer to whatever `CAsyncSocket` is attached to the handle it is passed.
GetLastError	`GetlastError` returns an error code and should be called after an operation fails, to find out why.
GetPeerName	`GetPeerName` is used to find the IP address and port number of the remote socket that the calling object socket is connected to, or to fill a socket address structure with that information.
GetSockName	`GetSockName` returns the IP address and port number of this socket, or fills a socket address structure with that information.
GetSockOpt	`GetSockOpt` returns the socket options that are currently set.
IOCtl	`IOCtl` sets the mode of the socket; most commonly, to blocking or nonblocking.
Listen	`Listen` instructs a socket to watch for incoming connections.
OnAccept	`OnAccept`, a virtual function often overridden by derived classes, handles the Windows message generated when a socket has a incoming connection to accept.

Method Name	Description
OnClose	OnClose, a virtual function often overridden by derived classes, handles the Windows message generated when a socket closes.
OnConnect	OnConnect, a virtual function often overridden by derived classes, handles the Windows message generated when a socket becomes connected or has a connection attempt end in failure.
OnOutOfBandData	OnOutOfBandData, a virtual function often overridden by derived classes, handles the Windows message generated when a socket has urgent, out-of-band data ready to read.
OnReceive	onReceive, a virtual function often overridden by derived classes, handles the Windows message generated when a socket has data that could be read with Receive().
OnSend	OnSend, a virtual function often overridden by derived classes, handles the Windows message generated when a socket is ready to accept data that could be sent with Send().
Receive	Receive reads data from the remote socket to which this socket is connected.
ReceiveFrom	ReceiveFrom reads a datagram from a connectionless remote socket. (A *datagram* is one of two types of sockets, which supports a bidirectional flow of data but is potentially unsequenced and duplicated.)
Send	Send sends data to the remote socket to which this socket is connected.
SendTo	SendTo sends a datagram without a connection.
SetSockOpt	SetSocketOpt sets socket options.
ShutDown	ShutDown keeps the socket open but prevents any further send or receive calls.

If you use the CASynchSocket class, you will have to fill the socket address structures yourself, and many developers would rather delegate a lot of this work. In that case, CSocket is a better socket class.

CSocket   CSocket inherits from CAsyncSocket and so has all the functions listed for CAsyncSocket. Table 13.2 describes the new methods added in the derived Csocket class.

Table 13.2 CSocket Methods

Method Name	Description
Create	Create is the function you call to complete the initialization when the constructor constructs a blank socket.
IsBlocking	IsBlocking returns TRUE if the socket is blocking at the moment, waiting for something to happen.
CancelBlockingCall	CancelBlockingCall cancels whatever request had left the socket blocking.
OnMessagePending	OnMessagePending, a virtual function often overridden by derived classes, handles the Windows messages generated for other parts of your application while the socket is blocking.

CSocket is derived from CASynchSocket and adds the methods listed in the table.

CSocket overrides the virtual methods Attach() and FromHandle().

In the \MSDev\Samples\SDK\Win32\WSock directory, the demo program wsock.exe can be compiled and used to experiment with WINSOCK.DLL APIs directly. (You will have to open a workspace using the Makefile and build WSock.exe.) More than likely you will be interested in using the CSocket classes. There are two fun demo programs that you can use and modify to experiment with CSocket, they are Chatter and ChatSrvr. Chatter.exe can be built from the project in the \MSDev\samples\MFC\Advanced\Chatter directory and ChatSrvr.exe is located in the \MSDev\samples\MFC\Advanced\ChatSrvr directory.

Each session of Chatter emulates a user server. The ChatSrvr program is the client traffic manager. To experiment with each, run ChatSrvr using the default Channel value of 0 in the sign-on. For each session of Chatter you will need a user name, like your first name, a server name, "localhost" works fine, and the same Channel number you used for the ChatSrvr value. Each Chatter can send messages to the ChatSrvr—by typing in some text—and the ChatSrvr sends the message to everyone logged into the session. Refer to the source code in \MSDev\ samples\MFC\Advanced\Chatter\ChatDoc.Cpp to see examples of CSocket member functions in action.There are existing connectivity protocols like Microsoft mail, the World Wide Web, or FTP you will not have to implement socket connectivity from scratch.

Messaging API (MAPI)

The most popular networking feature in most offices is electronic mail. You could add code to your application to generate the right commands over a socket to transmit a mail message, but it's simpler to build on the work of others.

What Is MAPI?

MAPI is a way of pulling together applications that need to send and receive messages (*messaging applications*) with applications that know how to send and receive messages (*messaging services* and *service providers,*) in order to lower the work load of all the developers involved. Figure 13.1 shows the scope of MAPI. Note that the word *messaging* actually covers far more than just electronic mail: a MAPI service could send a fax or voice-mail message rather than an electronic-mail message. If your application uses MAPI, the messaging services such as e-mail clients that the user has installed will carry out the work of sending the messages that your application generates.

FIG. 13.1
The Messaging API covers applications that need messaging and those that provide it.

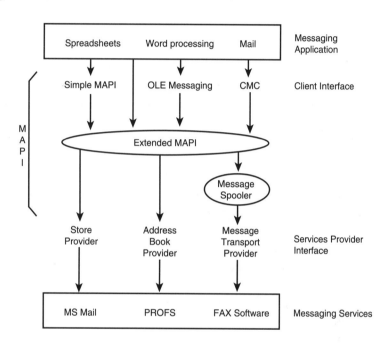

The extent to which an application uses messaging varies through a wide range:

- Some applications can send a message, but sending messages is not really what the application is about. For example, a word processor is fundamentally about entering and formatting text and then printing or saving that text. If the word processor can also send the text in a message, fine, but that's incidental. Applications like this are said to be *messaging aware* and typically use just the tip of the MAPI functionality.

- Some applications are useful without being able to send messages, but they are far more useful in an environment where messages can be sent. For example, a personal scheduler program can manage one person's To Do list whether messaging is enabled or not, but if it is enabled, a number of workgroup and client-contact features—such as sending e-mail to confirm an appointment—become available. Applications like this are said to be *messaging enabled* and use some, but not all, of the MAPI features.

- Finally, some applications are all about messaging. Without messaging, these applications are useless. They are said to be *messaging based,* and they use all of MAPI's functionality.

Win95 Logo Requirements

The number-one reason for a developer to make an application messaging aware is to meet the requirements of the Windows 95 Logo program. To qualify for the logo, an application must have a Send item on the File menu that uses MAPI to send the document. (Exceptions are granted to applications without documents.)

To add this feature to your applications, it's best to think of it before you create the empty shell with AppWizard. If you are planning ahead, here is a list of all the work you have to do to meet this part of the logo requirement:

In Step 4 of AppWizard, select the MAPI (Messaging API) check box.

That's it! The menu item is added, and message maps and functions are generated to catch the menu item and call functions that use your `Serialize()` function to send the document through MAPI. Figure 13.2 shows an application called MAPIDemo, included on the book's CD-ROM, that is just an AppWizard empty shell.

FIG. 13.2

AppWizard adds the Send item to the File menu, as well as the code that handles the item.

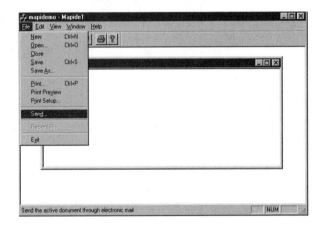

No additional code was added, beyond the code generated by the AppWizard, to this application, and the Send item is on the File menu, as you can see. If you choose this menu item, your MAPI mail client is launched to send the message. Figures 13.2 and 13.3 were captured on a machine with Microsoft Exchange installed as an Internet mail client, and so it is Microsoft Exchange that is launched, as shown in Figure 13.3.

TIP   If the Send item does not appear on your menu, make sure that you have a MAPI client installed. Microsoft Exchange is an easy-to-get MAPI client. The `OnUpdateFileSendMail()` function removes the menu item Send from the menu if no MAPI client is registered on your computer.

FIG. 13.3

Microsoft Mail is launched so the user can fill in the rest of the e-mail message around the document that is being sent.

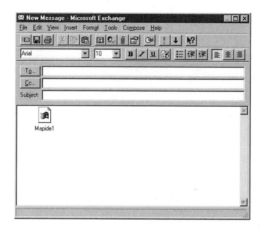

If you didn't enter Microsoft Exchange (for example) prior to executing the AppWizard, here are the steps to follow which will manually add the Send item:

1. Add the Send item to the File menu. Use a resource ID of ID_FILE_SEND_MAIL. The prompt will be supplied for you.

2. Add these two lines to the document's message map, outside the //AFX comments:

```
ON_COMMAND(ID_FILE_SEND_MAIL, OnFileSendMail)
ON_UPDATE_COMMAND_UI(ID_FILE_SEND_MAIL, OnUpdateFileSendMail)
```

Adding the mail support to your application manually is not much harder than being prepared—having a mail server configured—ahead of time so the AppWizard does it.

Advanced Use of MAPI

If you want more from MAPI than just meeting the logo requirements, things do get harder. There are actually four kinds of MAPI client interfaces:

- Simple MAPI, an older API not recommended for use in new applications
- Common Messaging Calls (CMC), a simple API for messaging-aware and messaging-enabled applications
- Extended MAPI, a full-featured API for messaging-based applications
- OLE Messaging, an API with somewhat fewer features than Extended MAPI but ideal for use with Visual C++

Common Messaging Calls   There are only ten functions in the CMC API. That makes it easy to learn, yet packs enough punch to get the job done. They are the following:

Part
II
Ch
13

- cmc_logon() connects to a mail server and identifies the user.
- cmc_logoff() disconnects from a mail server.
- cmc_send() sends a message.
- cmc_send_documents() sends one or more files.
- cmc_list() lists the messages in the user's mailbox.
- cmc_read() reads a message from the user's mailbox.
- cmc_act_on() saves or deletes a message.
- cmc_look_up() resolves names and addresses.
- cmc_query_configuration() reports what mail server is being used.
- cmc_free() frees any memory allocated by other functions.

The header file XCMC.H declares a number of structures used to hold the information that is passed to these functions. For example, recipient information is kept in this structure:

```
/*RECIPIENT*/
typedef struct {
    CMC_string              name;
    CMC_enum                name_type;
    CMC_string              address;
    CMC_enum                role;
    CMC_flags               recip_flags;
    CMC_extension FAR       *recip_extensions;
} CMC_recipient;
```

You could fill this structure with the name and address of the recipient of a mail message by using a standard dialog box or by hard-coding the entries, like this:

```
CMC_recipient recipient = {
    "Kate Gregory",
    CMC_TYPE_INDIVIDUAL,
    "SMTP:kate@gregcons.com",
    CMC_ROLE_TO,
    CMC_RECIP_LAST_ELEMENT,
    NULL };
```

The type, role, and flags use one of these predefined values:

Listing 13.1 (Excerpt from \MSDev\Include\XCMC.H) Command Definitions /* NAME TYPES */

```
#define CMC_TYPE_UNKNOWN                  ((CMC_enum) 0)
#define CMC_TYPE_INDIVIDUAL               ((CMC_enum) 1)
#define CMC_TYPE_GROUP                    ((CMC_enum) 2)

/* ROLES */
#define CMC_ROLE_TO                       ((CMC_enum) 0)
#define CMC_ROLE_CC                       ((CMC_enum) 1)
#define CMC_ROLE_BCC                      ((CMC_enum) 2)
```

```
#define CMC_ROLE_ORIGINATOR                    ((CMC_enum) 3)
#define CMC_ROLE_AUTHORIZING_USER              ((CMC_enum) 4)

/* RECIPIENT FLAGS */
#define CMC_RECIP_IGNORE                       ((CMC_flags) 1)
#define CMC_RECIP_LIST_TRUNCATED               ((CMC_flags) 2)
#define CMC_RECIP_LAST_ELEMENT                 ((CMC_flags) 0x80000000)
```

There is a message structure you could fill in the same way, or by presenting the user with a dialog to enter the message details. This structure includes a pointer to the recipient structure you have already filled. Your program then calls cmc_logon( ), cmc_send( ), and cmc_logoff( ) to complete the process.

Extended MAPI   Extended MAPI is based on COM, the OLE Component Object Model. Messages, recipients, and many other entities are defined as objects rather than as C structures. There are far more object types in Extended MAPI than there are structure types in CMC. Access to these objects is through OLE interfaces. The objects expose properties, methods, and events. These concepts are discussed in Part IV, Chapter 25, "ActiveX Automation" and Chapter 26, "Building an ActiveX Control."

OLE Messaging   If you understand OLE Automation (described in Chapter 24, "Building an ActiveX Server Application"), then you will easily understand OLE Messaging. Your application must be an OLE Automation client, however, and building such a client is beyond the scope of this chapter. Some ways to use ActiveX Messaging are in Visual Basic programming and VBA scripts for programs like Excel. Your program would set up objects and then set their exposed properties (for example, the subject line of a message object) and invoke their exposed methods (for example, the Send() method of a message object.)

The objects used in OLE Messaging include the following:

- Session
- Message
- Recipient
- Attachment

A detailed reference of these objects, as well as their properties and methods, can be found in Visual C++ Books Online (the help files) from within Developer Studio. Follow the Books Online hierarchy: SDKs, Win32 SDK, Win32 Messaging (MAPI), OLE Messaging Library.

Using New Internet Classes in Visual C++ 4.2

MFC 4.2 adds a number of new classes that eliminate the need to learn socket programming when your applications need to access standard Internet client services. Figure 13.4 shows the way these classes relate to each other. Collectively known as the WinInet classes, they are the following:

FIG. 13.4
The WinInet classes
make writing Internet
client programs easier.

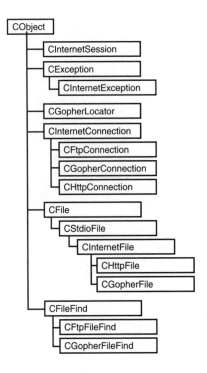

- CInternetSession
- CInternetConnection
- CInternetFile
- HttpConnection
- CHttpFile
- CGopherFile
- CFtpConnection
- CGopherConnection
- CFileFind
- CFtpFileFind
- CGopherFileFind
- CGopherLocator
- CInternetException

 T I P These classes help you write Internet **client** applications, with which users interact directly. If you want
to write **server** applications, which interact with client applications, you'll be interested in ISAPI,
discussed in the next section.

First, your program establishes a session by creating a `CInternetSession`. Then, if you have a Uniform Resource Locator (URL) to a Gopher, FTP, or Web (HTTP) resource, you can call that session's `OpenURL()` function to retrieve the resource as a read-only `CInternetFile`. Your application can read the file using `CStdioFile` functions and manipulate that data in whatever way you need.

If you do not have a URL or do not want to retrieve a read-only file, you proceed differently after establishing the session. You make a connection with a specific protocol by calling the session's `GetFtpConnection()`, `GetGopherConnection()`, or `GetHttpConnection()` functions, which return the appropriate connection object. You then call the connection's `OpenFile()` function. `CFtpConnection::OpenFile()` returns a `CInternetFile`; `CGopherConnection::OpenFile()` returns a `CGopherFile`; and `CHttpConnection::OpenFile()` returns a `CHttpFile`. The `CFileFind` class and its derived classes help you find the file you wish to open.

Chapter 27, "Internet Programming with the WinInet Classes," works through an example client program using WinInet classes to establish an Internet session and retrieve information.

N O T E Though e-mail is a standard Internet application, you'll notice that the WinInet classes do not have any e-mail functionality. That's because e-mail is handled by MAPI. There is no support for USENET news either, in the WinInet classes or elsewhere. ▪

Using Internet Server API (ISAPI) Classes

ISAPI is used to enhance and extend the capabilities of your HTTP (World Wide Web) server. ISAPI developers produce *extensions* and *filters*. Extensions are DLLs that are invoked by a user from a Web page in much the same way as CGI applications are invoked from a Web page. Filters are DLLs that run with the server and look at or change the data going to and from the server. For example, a filter might redirect requests for one file to a new location.

N O T E In order for the ISAPI extensions and filters that you write to be useful, your Web pages must be kept on a server that is running as ISAPI-compliant server like the Microsoft IIS Server. You must have permission to install DLLs onto the server, and for an ISAPI filter, you must be able to change the Registry on the server. If your Web pages are kept on a machine administered by your Internet Service Provider (ISP), you will probably not be able to use ISAPI to bring more power to your web pages. You may choose to move your pages to a dedicated server (a powerful Intel machine running Windows NT Server 4.0 and Microsoft IIS is a good combination) so that you can use ISAPI, but this will involve considerable expense. Make sure that you understand the constraints of your current Web server before embarking on a project with ISAPI.

One of the major advantages of ActiveX controls for the Internet (discussed in Chapter 28, "Building an Internet ActiveX Control") is that you do not need access to the server in order to implement them. ▪

Part
II

Ch
13

The five MFC ISAPI classes form a wrapper for the API to make it easier to use. Here they are:

- CHttpServer
- CHttpFilter
- CHttpServerContext
- CHttpFilterContext
- CHtmlStream

You application will have a server or a filter class (or both) that inherit from CHttpServer or CHttpFilter. These are rather like the classes in a normal application that inherit from CWinApp. There is only one instance of the class in each DLL, and each interaction of the server with a client is done through its own instance of the appropriate context class. (A DLL may contain both a server and a filter, but at most, one of each.) CHtmlStream is a helper class that describes a stream of HTML to be sent by a server to a client.

The ISAPI Extension Wizard is an AppWizard that simplifies creating extensions and filters. To use this wizard, choose File, New, as always, and then Project Workspace. Scroll down the list on the left and select ISAPI Extension Wizard (as shown in Figure 13.5) and then fill in the project name and folder.

FIG. 13.5

The ISAPI Extension Wizard is another kind of AppWizard.

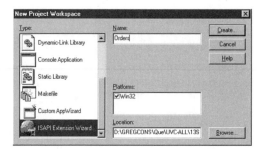

Creating a server extension is a one-step process. That step, which is also the first step for a filter, is shown in Figure 13.6. The names and descriptions for the filter and extension are based on the project name that you chose. If you use the Back button to change the project name, these names are not changed automatically. You can edit the names as you wish.

> **CAUTION**
>
> Selecting the Back button in ISAPI Extension Wizard will not change the names and descriptions; you will have to do this manually.

If you choose to create a filter, the Next button is enabled and you can move to the second step for filters, shown in Figure 13.7. This list of parameters gives you an idea of the power of an ISAPI filter. You can monitor all incoming and outgoing requests and raw data, authenticate users, log traffic, and more.

FIG. 13.6

The first step in the ISAPI Extension Wizard process is to name the components of the DLL that you are creating.

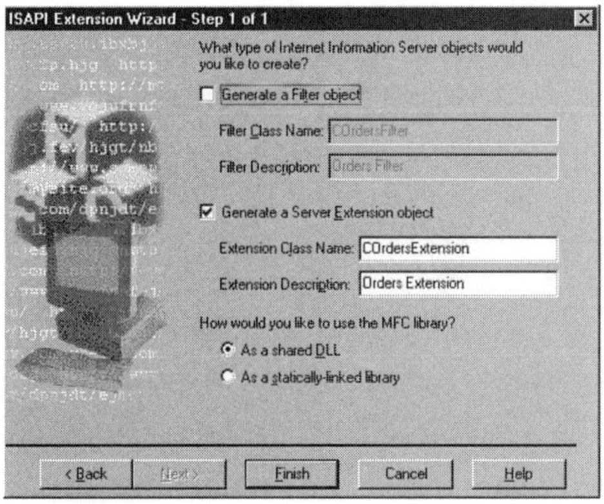

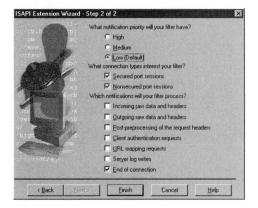

FIG. 13.7

The second step in the ISAPI Extension Wizard process is to set filter parameters.

AppWizard shows you a final confirmation screen like the one in Figure 13.8 before creating the files. When you create a server and a filter at the same time, 11 files are created for you, including source and headers for the class that inherits from CHttpServer and the class that inherits from CHttpFilter.

Writing a filter from this shell is quite simple. You have been provided with a stub function to react to each event for which notification was requested. For example, the filter class has a function called OnEndOfNetSession(), which is called when a client's session with this server is ending. You add code to this function to log, monitor, or otherwise react to this event. When the filter is complete, you edit the Registry by hand so that the server will run your DLL.

To write an extension, add one or more functions to your DLL. Each function will be passed a CHttpContext pointer, which can be used to gather information such as the user's IP address. If the function is invoked from an HTML form, additional parameters such as values of other fields on the form will also be passed to the function.

Part
II

Ch
13

FIG. 13.8

The ISAPI Extension Wizard process summarizes the files that will be created.

The details of what the function does depend on your application. If you are implementing an online ordering system, the functions involved will be lengthy and complex. Other extensions will be simpler.

When the function is complete, you place the DLL in the executable folder for the server—usually the folder where CGI programs are kept—and adjust your Web pages so that they include links to your DLL, like this:

```
Now you can <A HREF=http://www.company.com/exec/orders.dll>
place an order</A> online!
```

For more information on ISAPI programming, look for Que's new book, *SE: Using ISAPI*, due in January 1997.

From Here...

Adding the Internet to your applications is an exciting trend. It's going to make lots of work for programmers and create some powerful products that simplify the working life of anyone with an Internet connection. Just a year ago, writing Internet applications meant getting your finger-nails dirty with sockets programming, memorizing TCP/IP ports, and reading RFCs. The new WinInet and ISAPI classes, as well as improvements to the old MAPI support, mean that today you can add amazing power to your application with just a few lines of code or by selecting a box on an AppWizard dialog box.

To learn more about using the APIs introduced in this chapter and building other specific kinds of applications refer to:

- Chapter 14, "Database Access," covers the basics of database manipulation.
- Chapter 27, "Internet Programming with the WinInet Classes," lets you work through an example program built with the WinInet classes.

Database Access

Without a doubt, databases are one of the most popular computer applications. Virtually every business uses databases to keep track of everything from their customer list to the company payroll. Unfortunately, there are many different types of database applications, each of which defines its own file layouts and rules. Up until Visual C++, programming database applications was a nightmare, because it was up to the programmer to figure out all the intricacies of accessing the different types of database files.

Now, however, Visual C++ includes classes that are built upon the ODBC (Open Database Connectivity) and DAO (Data Access Objects) systems. Believe it or not, using AppWizard, you can create a simple database program without writing even a single line of C++ code. More complex tasks do require some programming, but not as much as you might think. In this chapter, then, you'll get an introduction to programming with Visual C++'s ODBC classes. You'll also learn about the similarities and differences between ODBC and DAO. Along the way, you'll create a database application that cannot only display records in a database, but also update, add, delete, sort, and filter records. ▪

About basic concepts

Regardless of what type of database you want to access, the concepts remain the same.

How the flat and relational database models differ

Flat model databases are the simplest type of databases, but relational databases are the most efficient and powerful.

About MFC's ODBC database classes

The ODBC classes enable database access without the hassles associated with programming.

How to use AppWizard to create a basic ODBC application

AppWizard is an amazing tool for creating your database.

How to implement add, delete, update, sort, and filter abilities

Although AppWizard can create a functional database program for you, you'll have to do a little programming to incorporate more sophisticated database commands.

About the differences between using MFC's ODBC and DAO classes

MFC also features a second set of database classes that is suited to creating applications that will access .mdb files.

Understanding Database Concepts

Before you can write database applications, you have to know a little about how databases work. Databases have come a long way since their invention, so there's much you can learn about them, much more than can be covered in an introductory chapter like this one. However, limited space notwithstanding, in this section, you'll get a quick introduction to basic database concepts, as well as discover the two main types of databases: flat and relational.

Using the Flat Database Model

Simply, a database is a collection of records. Each record in the database is comprised of fields. And each field contains information that's related to that specific record. For example, suppose you have an address database. In this database, you have one record for each person. Each record contains six fields: the person's name, street address, city, state, zip code, and phone number. So, a single record in your database might look like this:

```
NAME: Ronald Wilson
STREET: 16 Tolland Dr.
CITY: Hartford
STATE: CT
ZIP: 06084
PHONE: 860-555-3542
```

Your entire database will contain many records like the one shown above, each record containing information about a different person. To find a person's address or phone number, you search for their name. When you find their name, you also find all the information that's included in the record with the name. This type of database system uses the *flat database model*. For home use or for small businesses, the simple flat database model can be a powerful tool. However, for large databases that must track dozens, or even hundreds, of fields of data, the relational database model is more appropriate.

Using the Relational Database Model

A *relational database* is like several flat databases linked together. Using a relational database, you cannot only search for individual records as you can with a flat database, but you can also relate one set of records to another. This enables you to store data much more efficiently. Each set of records in a relational database is called a *table*. The database management system (DBMS) can link these tables together in various ways by comparing keys that were defined by the person who created the database.

The example relational database that you'll use in this chapter was created using Microsoft Access. The database is a simple system for tracking employees, managers, and the departments for which they work. Figures 14.1, 14.2, and 14.3 show the tables that I defined when I created the database. The Employees table contains information about each of the store's employees, the Manager's table contains information about each store department's manager, and the Departments table contains information about the departments themselves. (This database is very simple and probably not usable in the real world.)

FIG. 14.1

The Employees table contains data fields for each store employee.

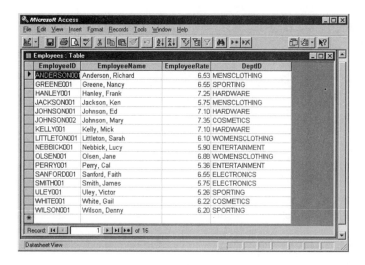

FIG. 14.2

The Managers table contains information about each store department's manager.

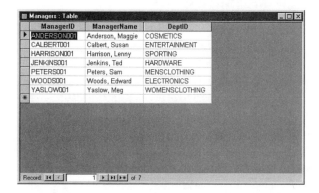

FIG. 14.3

The Departments table contains data about each store department.

Part

II

Ch

14

Accessing a Database

Relational databases are accessed using some sort of database scripting language. The most commonly used database language is SQL, which is used not only to manage databases on desktop computers, but also on the huge databases used by banks, schools, corporations, and other institutions with sophisticated database needs. Using a language like SQL, you can compare information in the various tables of a relational database and extract results that are made up of data fields from one or more tables combined.

Learning SQL, though, is a large task, one that is way beyond the scope of this book (let alone this chapter). In fact, entire college-level courses are taught on the design, implementation, and manipulation of databases. Because there isn't space in this book to cover relational databases in any useful way, you'll use the Employee table (Figure 14.1) of the Department Store database in the sample database program you'll soon develop. When you're done creating the application, you'll have learned one way you can update the tables of a relational database without learning even a word of SQL.

The Visual C++ ODBC Classes

When you create a database program with Visual C++'s AppWizard, you end up with an application that draws extensively upon the various ODBC classes that have been incorporated into MFC. The most important of these classes are CDatabase, CRecordset, and CRecordView.

AppWizard automatically generates the code needed to create an object of the CDatabase class. This object represents the connection between your application and the data source that you'll be accessing. In most cases, using the CDatabase class in an AppWizard generated program is transparent to you, the programmer. All the details are handled by the framework.

AppWizard also generates the code needed to create a CRecordset object for the application. However, how you plan to use this object depends on whether you'll need to write code that calls the object's member functions. (Unless you're doing nothing more with the database than viewing its content, you will need to call CRecordset member functions in your program.) The CRecordset object represents the actual data that's currently selected from the data source. The CRecordset object's member functions enable you to manipulate the data from the database in various ways.

Finally, the CRecordView object in your database program takes the place of the normal view window you're used to using in AppWizard-generated applications. A CRecordView window is special in that it is kind of like a dialog box that's being used as the application's display. This dialog box-type of window retains a connection to the application's CRecordset object, hustling data back and forth between the program, the window's controls, and the record set. When you first create a new database application with AppWizard, it's up to you to add edit controls to the CRecordView window. These edit controls must be bound to the database fields they represent, so the application framework knows where to display the data you want to view. In the next section, you'll see how these various database classes fit together, as you build the Employee application step-by-step.

Creating an ODBC Database Program

Although creating a simple ODBC database program is easy with Visual C++, there are a number of steps you must complete. These steps are listed below:

1. Register the database with the system.
2. Use AppWizard to create the basic database application.
3. Add code to the basic application in order to implement features not automatically supported by AppWizard.

In the following sections, you'll see how to perform the above steps as you create the Employee application, which enables you to add, delete, update, sort, and view records in the Employee's table of the sample department store database.

Registering the Database

Before you can create a database application, you must have the database that you want to access registered with the system. This process registers the selected tables in the database as data sources that you can access through the ODBC driver. Follow the steps below to accomplish this important task.

1. Create a folder called Database on your hard disk, and copy the file named DeptStore.mdb from this book's CD-ROM to the new Database folder.

   The DeptStore.mdb file is a database created with Microsoft Access. You'll be using this database as the data source for the Employee application.

2. From the Windows 95 Start menu, run Control Panel. When Control Panel appears, double-click the 32-bit ODBC icon. The Data Sources dialog box appears (Figure 14.4).

FIG. 14.4
The Data Sources dialog box.

3. Click the Add button. The Add Data Source dialog box appears. Select the Microsoft Access Driver from the list of drivers (Figure 14.5) and click the OK button.

   The Microsoft Access Driver is now the ODBC driver that will be associated with the data source you'll be creating for the Employee application.

4. When the ODBC Microsoft Access 7.0 Setup dialog box appears, enter **Department Store** into the Data Source Name text box, and enter **Department Store Database** in the Description text box (Figure 14.6).

Part
II

Ch

The data-source name is simply a way of identifying the specific data source that you're creating. The description field enables you to include more specific information about the data source.

FIG. 14.5

The Add Data Source dialog box.

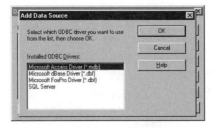

FIG. 14.6

The ODBC Microsoft Access 7.0 Setup dialog box.

5. Click the Select button. The Select Database file selector appears. Use the selector to locate and select the DeptStore.mdb file (Figure 14.7).

FIG. 14.7

The Select Database file selector.

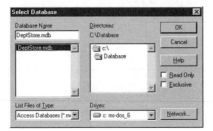

6. Click OK to finalize the database selection, and then in the ODBC Microsoft Access 7.0 Setup dialog box, click Close to finalize the data-source creation process.

Your system is now set up to access the DeptStore.mdb database file with the Microsoft Access ODBC driver.

Creating the Basic Employee Application

Now that you have your data source created and registered, it's time to create the basic Employee application. The steps that follow lead you through this process. After you've completed these steps, you'll have an application that can access and view the Employees table of the department store database.

1. Select File, New from Developer Studio's menu bar. The New dialog box appears (Figure 14.8).

FIG. 14.8
The New dialog box.

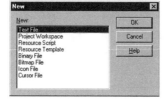

2. Select Project Workspace, and click OK. The New Project Workspace dialog box appears, as shown in Figure 14.9.

FIG. 14.9
The New Project
Workspace dialog box.

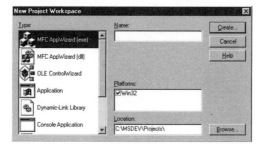

3. Make sure MFC AppWizard is selected in the Type box. Then, type **Employee** into the Name box, and click the Create button. The Step 1 dialog box appears (Figure 14.10).

FIG. 14.10
The Step 1 dialog box.

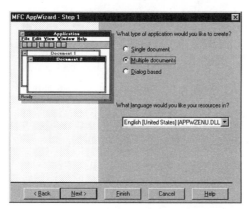

Part
II

Ch
14

4. Select Single Document, and click the Next button. The Step 2 dialog box appears, as shown in Figure 14.11.

Selecting the Single Document option ensures that the Employee application will not allow more than one window to be open at a time.

FIG. 14.11

The Step 2 dialog box.

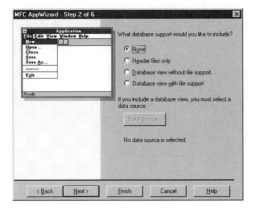

5. Select the Database View Without File Support option button, and then click the Data Source button. The Database Options dialog box appears (Figure 14.12).

By selecting the Database View Without File Support option, you're telling AppWizard to automatically generate the classes you need in order to view the contents of a database. This application will not use any supplemental files besides the database, so it doesn't need file (serializing) support.

FIG. 14.12

The Database Options dialog box.

6. In the ODBC drop-down list, select the Department Store data source. Click the OK button, and the Select Database Tables dialog box appears, as shown in Figure 14.13.

7. Select the Employees table, and click OK. The Step 2 dialog box reappears, filled in as shown in Figure 14.14.

You've now associated the Employees table of the Department Store data source with the Employee application.

FIG. 14.13

The Select Database Tables dialog box.

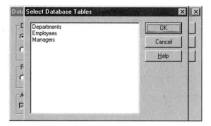

FIG. 14.14

After selecting the data source, the Step 2 dialog box should look like this.

8. Click the Next button two times. The Step 4 dialog box appears (Figure 14.15).

FIG. 14.15

The Step 4 dialog box.

9. Turn off the Printing and Print Preview option, and then click the Next button twice. Click the Finish button to finalize your selections for the Employee application. The New Project Information dialog box that appears should look like Figure 14.16.

FIG. 14.16

The New Project Information dialog box.

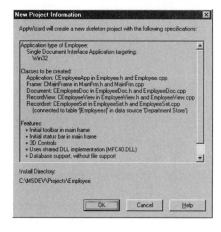

10. Click the OK button, and AppWizard creates the basic Employee application.

You've now created the basic Employee application. At this point, you can compile the application by clicking the Build button on Developer Studio's toolbar, by selecting the Build, Build command from the menu bar, or by pressing F7 on your keyboard. After the program has compiled, select the Build, Execute command from the menu bar, or press Ctrl+F5, to run the program. When you do, you see the window shown in Figure 14.17. You can use the database controls in the application's toolbar to navigate from one record in the Employee table to another. However, nothing appears in the window because you've yet to associate controls with the fields in the table that you want to view. You'll do that in the following section.

FIG. 14.17

The basic Employee application looks nice but doesn't do much.

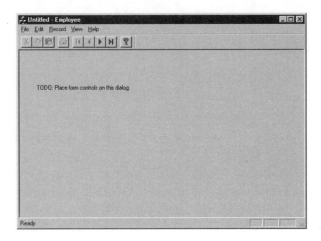

Creating the Database Display

The next step in creating the Employee database application is to modify the form that displays data in the application's window. Because this form is just a special type of dialog box, it's easy to modify with Developer Studio's resource editor, as you'll discover as you complete the following steps.

1. Select the Resource View tab to display the application's resources (Figure 14.18).

2. Open the resource tree by double-clicking the Employee Resources folder. Then, open the Dialog resource folder the same way. Double-click the IDD_EMPLOYEE_FORM dialog-box ID to open the dialog box into the resource editor (Figure 14.19).

3. Click the static string in the center of the dialog box to select it, and then press Delete on your keyboard to remove the string from the dialog box.

4. Use the dialog-box editor's tools to create the dialog box shown in Figure 14.20. When you create the edit boxes, use the following IDs: IDC_EMPLOYEE_ID, IDC_EMPLOYEE_NAME, IDC_EMPLOYEE_RATE, IDC_EMPLOYEE_DEPT. Also, set the Read-Only style (found on the Styles page of the Edit Properties property sheet) of the IDC_EMPLOYEE_ID edit box.

   Each of these edit boxes will represent a field of data in the database. The first edit box is read-only because it will hold the database's primary key, which should never be modified.

FIG. 14.18
Click the Resource View tab.

The Resource View tab

FIG. 14.19
Here, the dialog box is open in the resource editor.

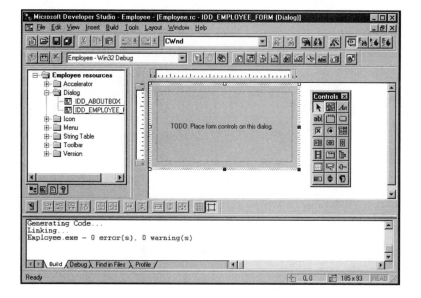

5. Click the ClassWizard button on Developer Studio's toolbar, select <u>V</u>iew, Class<u>W</u>izard from the menu bar, or press Ctrl+W on your keyboard. The MFC ClassWizard property sheet appears, as shown in Figure 14.21. (Select the Member Variables tab if necessary.)

6. With the IDC_EMPLOYEE_DEPT resource ID selected, click the <u>A</u>dd Variable button. The Add Member Variable dialog box appears.

7. Click on the arrow next to the Member Variable <u>N</u>ame drop-down list, and select m_pSet->m_DeptID, as shown in Figure 14.22.

FIG. 14.20
Your final dialog box
should look like this.

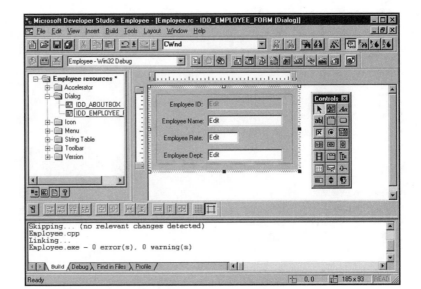

FIG. 14.21
The MFC ClassWizard
property sheet.

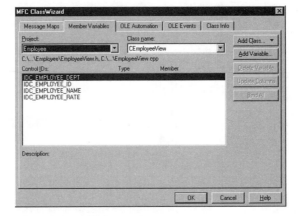

FIG. 14.22
The Add Member
Variable dialog box.

8. Associate other member variables (`m_pSet->EmployeeID`, `m_pSet->EmployeeName`, and `m_pSet->EmployeeRate`) with the edit controls in the same way. When you're done, the Member Variables page of the MFC ClassWizard property sheet should look like Figure 14.23.

By selecting member variables of the application's `CEmployeeSet` class (derived from MFC's `CRecordset` class) as member variables for the controls in the database view, you're establishing a connection through which data can flow between the controls and the data source.

FIG. 14.23

You need to define member variables for each of the edit boxes.

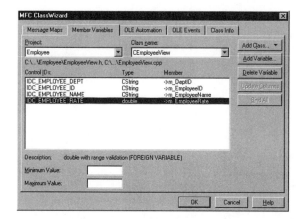

9. Click the OK button in the MFC ClassWizard property sheet in order to finalize your changes.

You've now created a data-display form for the Employee application. At this point, you can compile the application by clicking the Build button on Developer Studio's toolbar, by selecting the Build, Build command from the menu bar, or by pressing F7 on your keyboard. After the program has compiled, select the Build, Execute command from the menu bar or press Ctrl+F5 to run the program. When you do, you see the window shown in Figure 14.24. As you can see, the application now displays the contents of records in the Employee database table. Use the database controls in the application's toolbar to navigate from one record in the Employee table to another.

After you've examined the database, try updating a record. To do this, simply change one of the record's fields (except the employee ID, which is the table's primary key and can't be edited). When you move to another record, the application automatically updates the modified record. The commands in the application's Record menu also enable you to navigate through the records in the same manner as the toolbar buttons.

Notice that you've created a fairly sophisticated database-access program without writing a single line of C++ code, a pretty amazing feat. Still, the Employee application is limited. For example, it can't add or delete records. As you may have guessed, that's the next piece of the database puzzle that you'll add.

Part

II

Ch

FIG. 14.24

The Employee application now displays data in its window.

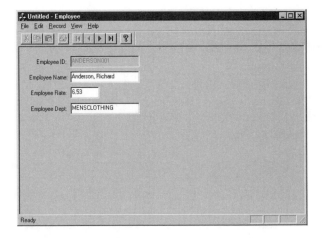

Adding and Deleting Records

Once you can add and delete records from a database table, you'll have a full-featured program for manipulating a flat (that is, not a relational) database. In this case, the "flat database" is the Employees table of the department store relational database. Adding and deleting records in a database table is an easier process than you might believe, thanks to Visual C++'s CRecordView and CRecordSet classes, which provide all the member functions you need to accomplish these common database tasks. Follow the steps below to include add and delete commands in the Employee application.

1. Select the ResourceView tab, open the Menu folder, and double-click the IDR_MAINFRAME menu ID. The menu editor appears, as shown in Figure 14.25.

FIG. 14.25

Developer Studio's menu editor is in the right-hand pane.

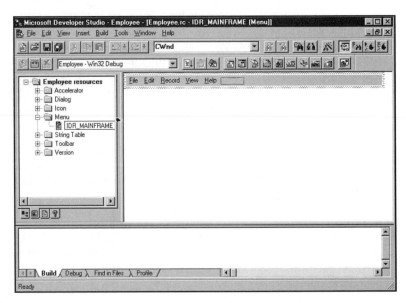

2. Open the Record menu in the editor, and double-click the blank menu item at the bottom of the menu. The Menu Item Properties property sheet appears.

3. In the ID edit box, enter **ID_RECORD_ADD**, and in the Caption box, enter **&Add Record** (Figure 14.26). When you press Enter, the menu editor adds the new command to the Record menu.

FIG. 14.26

The Menu Item Properties property sheet.

4. In the next blank menu item, add a delete command with the ID ID_RECORD_DELETE and the caption **&Delete Record**.

5. In the ResourceView pane, open the Toolbar folder, and then double-click the IDR_MAINFRAME ID. The application's toolbar appears in the resource editor.

6. Click on the blank toolbar button to select it, and then use the editor's tools to draw the icon (it's supposed to be blue) shown in Figure 14.27 on the button.

FIG. 14.27

This new button will control the Add function.

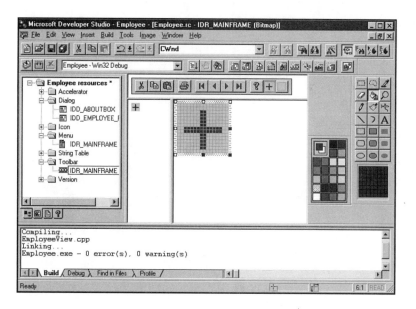

7. Double-click the new button in the toolbar. The Toolbar Button Properties property sheet appears. Select ID_RECORD_ADD in the ID box (Figure 14.28).

8. Create a new toolbar button that displays a red minus sign, giving the button the ID_RECORD_DELETE ID (Figure 14.29). Move the Add and Delete buttons to a position before the Help (question mark) button.

Part
II

Ch
14

FIG. 14.28

The Toolbar Button Properties property sheet.

FIG. 14.29

The minus-sign button will control the Delete function.

9. Click the ClassWizard button on the toolbar, select the View, ClassWizard command from the menu bar, or just press Ctrl+W on your keyboard. The MFC Class Wizard property sheet appears. (Select the Message Maps tab if necessary.)

10. Set the Class Name box to CEmployeeView, click the ID_RECORD_ADD ID in the Object IDs box, and then double-click COMMAND in the Messages box. The Add Member Function dialog box appears (Figure 14.30).

FIG. 14.30

The Add Member Function dialog box.

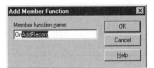

11. Click the OK button to accept the default name for the new function. The function appears in the Member Functions box, as shown in Figure 14.31.

FIG. 14.31

The new functions appear in the Member Functions box.

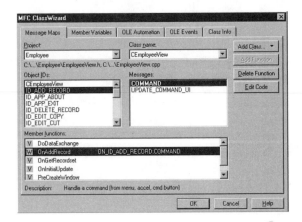

12. Add a member function for the ID_RECORD_DELETE command in the same way. Then, click the OK button on the MFC ClassWizard property sheet to finalize your changes. The ClassWizard property sheet closes.

13. Open the EmployeeView.h file, and in the Attributes section of the class's declaration, add the following lines:

```
protected:
BOOL m_bAdding;
```

14. Open the EmployeeView.cpp file, and add the following line to the class's constructor, right after the comment TODO: add construction code here:

```
m_bAdding = FALSE;
```

15. Still in EmployeeView.cpp, find the OnRecordAdd() function and add the code shown in Listing 14.1:

Listing 14.1   LST14_01.TXT:—Code for the *OnRecordAdd()* Function

```
m_pSet->AddNew();
m_bAdding = TRUE;
CEdit* pCtrl = (CEdit*)GetDlgItem(IDC_EMPLOYEE_ID);
int result = pCtrl->SetReadOnly(FALSE);
UpdateData(FALSE);
```

16. Use ClassWizard to override the OnMove() member function in the CRecordView class (Figure 14.32). Click the Edit Code button to jump to the function in the text editor.

FIG. 14.32

Override the *OnMove()* function.

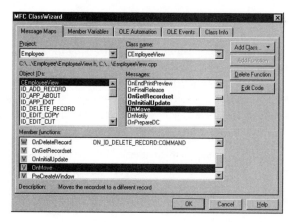

17. Replace the default code in the OnMove() function with the code shown in Listing 14.2.

Listing 14.2 LST14_02.TXT:—Code for the *OnMove()* Function

```
if (m_bAdding)
{
m_bAdding = FALSE;
UpdateData(TRUE);
if (m_pSet->CanUpdate())
m_pSet->Update();
m_pSet->Requery();
UpdateData(FALSE);
CEdit* pCtrl = (CEdit*)GetDlgItem(IDC_EMPLOYEE_ID);
pCtrl->SetReadOnly(TRUE);
return TRUE;
}
else
return CRecordView::OnMove(nIDMoveCommand);
```

18. Add the code shown in Listing 14.3 to the OnRecordDelete() function.

Listing 14.3 LST14_03.TXT:—Code for the *OnRecordDelete()* Function

```
m_pSet->Delete();
m_pSet->MoveNext();
if (m_pSet->IsEOF())
m_pSet->MoveLast();
if (m_pSet->IsBOF())
m_pSet->SetFieldNull(NULL);
UpdateData(FALSE);
```

You've now modified the Employee application so that it can add and delete, as well as update, records. After compiling the application, run it by selecting the Build, Execute command from Developer Studio's menu bar or by pressing Ctrl+F5 on your keyboard. When you do, you see the Employee application's main window, which doesn't look any different than it did in the previous section. Now, however, you can add new records by clicking the Add button on the toolbar (or by selecting the Record, Add Record command in the menu bar) and delete records by clicking the Delete button (or by clicking the Record, Delete Record command).

When you click the Add button, the application displays a blank record. Fill in the fields for the record and then, when you move to another record, the application automatically updates the database with the new record. To delete a record, just click the Delete button. The current record (the one on the screen) vanishes and is replaced by the next record in the database.

Examining the *OnRecordAdd()* Function

You now may be wondering how the C++ code you added to the application works. When you click the Add button, or select the Record, Add command, MFC routes program execution to the OnRecordAdd() command handler. In that function, the program first calls the CEmployeeSet object's AddNew() member function, like this:

```
m_pSet->AddNew();
```

The AddNew() member function sets up a blank record for the user to fill in. The new blank record doesn't appear on the screen, however, until the view window's UpdateData() function is called.

After creating the new record, the program sets the Boolean variable m_bAdding to TRUE, which indicates to the program that the user is in the process of adding a new record:

```
m_bAdding = TRUE;
```

Now, because the user is entering a new record, he needs to be able to change the contents of the Employee ID field, which is currently set to read-only. To change the read-only status of the control, the program first gets a pointer to the control and then calls the control's SetReadOnly() member function, like this:

```
CEdit* pCtrl = (CEdit*)GetDlgItem(IDC_EMPLOYEE_ID);
int result = pCtrl->SetReadOnly(FALSE);
```

The SetReadOnly() member function changes the read-only style of a control. When the function's single argument is FALSE, the control is enabled for normal editing. When the function's argument is TRUE, the control is set to its read-only state, which prevents the user from changing the value displayed in the control.

Finally, as I mentioned previously, the program must call the view window's UpdateData() member function in order to display the new blank record, like this:

```
UpdateData(FALSE);
```

When the UpdateData() function's argument is FALSE, data is transferred from the record set to the control. When the argument is TRUE, data is transferred from the control to the record set.

Examining the *OnMove()* Function

Now that the user has a blank record on the screen, he can start filling in the edit controls with the necessary data. To actually add the new record to the database, the user most move to a new record, an action that forces a call to the view window's OnMove() member function. Normally, OnMove() does nothing more than display the next record. However, because you overrode the function and added your own code, you've enabled the program to save the new record.

When OnMove() is called, the first thing the program does is check the Boolean variable m_bAdding in order to see whether the user is in the process of adding a new record:

```
if (m_bAdding)
```

If m_bAdding is FALSE, the body of the if statement is skipped and the else clause is executed. In the else clause, the program calls the base class's (CRecordView) version of OnMove(), which performs the default behavior for moving to the next record. If m_bAdding is TRUE, the body of the if statement is executed. There, the program first resets the m_bAdding flag:

```
m_bAdding = FALSE;
```

Then, the program calls `UpdateData()` to transfer data out of the view window's controls:

```
UpdateData(TRUE);
```

A call to the record set's `CanUpdate()` method determines whether it's okay to update the data source, after which a call to the record set's `Update()` member function adds the new record to the data source:

```
if (m_pSet->CanUpdate())
 m_pSet->Update();
```

In order to rebuild the record set, the program must call the record set's `Requery()` member function, like this:

```
m_pSet->Requery();
```

A call to the view window's `UpdateData()` member function transfers new data to the window's controls:

```
UpdateData(FALSE);
```

Finally, the program sets the Employee ID field back to read-only, so that the user can no longer change its contents:

```
CEdit* pCtrl = (CEdit*)GetDlgItem(IDC_EMPLOYEE_ID);
pCtrl->SetReadOnly(TRUE);
```

Examining the *OnRecordDelete()* Function

When the user clicks the Delete button (or selects the <u>D</u>elete Record command from the <u>R</u>ecord menu), the `OnRecordDelete()` function gets called. In that function, deleting the record is just a matter of calling the record set's `Delete()` function:

```
m_pSet->Delete();
```

Once the record is deleted, however, the program should display another record in its stead. That's where the call to the record set's `MoveNext()` function comes in:

```
m_pSet->MoveNext();
```

The `MoveNext()` function moves the record set forward to the next record. A problem might arise, though, when the deleted record was in the last position or when the deleted record was the only record in the record set. A call to the record set's `IsEOF()` function will determine whether the record set was at the end. If the call to `IsEOF()` returns TRUE, the record set needs to be repositioned on the last record, which it is currently beyond. The record set's `MoveLast()` function takes care of this task. The code looks like this:

```
if (m_pSet->IsEOF())
 m_pSet->MoveLast();
```

When the last record has been deleted from the record set, the record pointer will be at the beginning of the set. The program can test for this situation by calling the record set's `IsBOF()` function. If this function returns TRUE, the program sets the current record's fields to NULL, like this:

```
m_pSet->SetFieldNull(NULL);
```

Finally, the last task is to update the view window's display:

```
UpdateData(FALSE);
```

Sorting and Filtering

In many cases when you're accessing a database, you want to change the order in which the records are presented, or you may even want to search for records that fit certain criteria. MFC's ODBC database classes feature member functions that enable you to sort a set of records on any field. You can also call member functions in order to limit the records displayed to those whose fields contain given information, such as a specific name or ID. This latter operation is called *filtering*. In this section, you'll add sorting and filtering to the Employee application. Just follow the steps below.

1. Add a Sort menu to the application's menu bar, as shown in Figure 14.33. Use the IDs `ID_SORT_ID`, `ID_SORT_NAME`, `ID_SORT_RATE`, and `ID_SORT_DEPT` as the command IDs.

FIG. 14.33

The Sort menu has four commands for sorting the database.

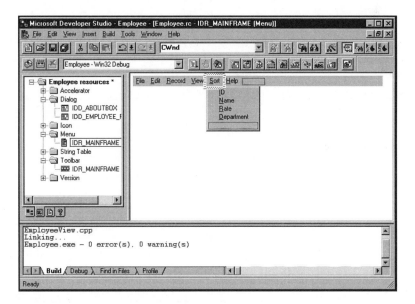

2. Use ClassWizard to add COMMAND functions for the four new sorting commands, using the function names suggested by ClassWizard. (Add the functions to the `CEmployeeView` class.) Figure 14.34 shows the resultant ClassWizard property sheet.

3. Add a Filter menu to the application's menu bar. Use the IDs `ID_FILTER_ID`, `ID_FILTER_NAME`, `ID_FILTER_RATE`, and `ID_FILTER_DEPT` as the command IDs.

4. Use ClassWizard to add COMMAND functions for the four new filtering commands, using the function names suggested by ClassWizard. (Add the functions to the `CEmployeeView` class.)

Part
II

Ch
14

5. Use Developer Studio's resource editor to create the dialog box shown in Figure 14.35. Give the edit control the ID ID_FILTERVALUE.

FIG. 14.34

After you add the four new functions, ClassWizard should look like this.

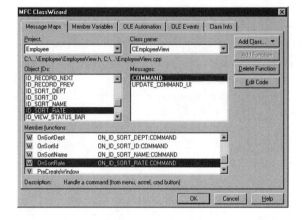

FIG. 14.35

Create this dialog box using the resource editor.

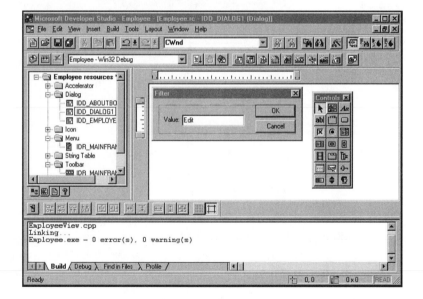

6. Start ClassWizard while the new dialog box is on the screen. The Adding a Class dialog box appears. Select the Create a New Class option.

7. Click OK, and the Create New Class dialog box appears. In the Name box, type **CFilterDlg**, as shown in Figure 14.36.

8. In the MFC ClassWizard property sheet, select the Member Variables tab. Create a variable for the IDC_FILTERVALUE control called m_filterValue, as shown in Figure 14.37. Click the OK button to dismiss ClassWizard.

FIG. 14.36
The Create New Class
dialog box.

FIG. 14.37
Create a member
variable for the edit
control.

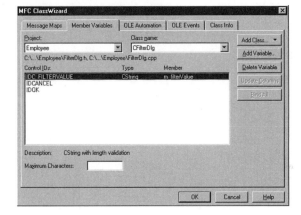

9. Add the code shown in Listing 14.4 to the OnSortDept() function.

Listing 14.4   LST14_04.TXT:—Code for the *OnSortDept()* Function

```
m_pSet->Close();
m_pSet->m_strSort = "DeptID";
m_pSet->Open();
UpdateData(FALSE);
```

---

10. Add the code shown in Listing 14.5 to the OnSortID() function.

Listing 14.5   LST14_05.TXT:—Code for the *OnSortID()* Function

```
m_pSet->Close();
m_pSet->m_strSort = "EmployeeID";
m_pSet->Open();
UpdateData(FALSE);
```

---

11. Add the code shown in Listing 14.6 to the `OnSortName()` function.

Listing 14.6   LST14_06.TXT:—Code for the *OnSortName()* Function

```
m_pSet->Close();
m_pSet->m_strSort = "EmployeeName";
m_pSet->Open();
UpdateData(FALSE);
```

12. Add the code shown in Listing 14.7 to the `OnSortRate()` function.

Listing 14.7   LST14_07.TXT:—Code for the *OnSortRate()* Function

```
m_pSet->Close();
m_pSet->m_strSort = "EmployeeRate";
m_pSet->Open();
UpdateData(FALSE);
```

13. At the top of the file, add the following line after the other `#include` directives.

```
#include "FilterDlg.h"
```

This line ensures that the `CEmployeeView` class can access the `CFilterDlg` class.

14. Add the line below to the `OnFilterDept()` function.

```
DoFilter("DeptID");
```

15. Add the line below to the `OnFilterID()` function.

```
DoFilter("EmployeeID");
```

16. Add the line below to the `OnFilterName()` function.

```
DoFilter("EmployeeName");
```

17. Add the line below to the `OnFilterRate()` function.

```
DoFilter("EmployeeRate");
```

18. Add the function shown in Listing 14.8 to the bottom of the EmployeeView.cpp file.

Listing 14.8   LST14_08.TXT:—The *DoFilter()* Function

```
void CEmployeeView::DoFilter(CString col)
{
 CFilterDlg dlg;
 int result = dlg.DoModal();

 if (result == IDOK)
 {
 CString str = col + " = '" + dlg.m_filterValue + "'";
 m_pSet->Close();
 m_pSet->m_strFilter = str;
 m_pSet->Open();
```

```
    int recCount = m_pSet->GetRecordCount();

    if (recCount == 0)
    {
    MessageBox("No matching records.");
    m_pSet->Close();
    m_pSet->m_strFilter = "";
    m_pSet->Open();
    }

    UpdateData(FALSE);
    }
}
```

19. Load the EmployeeView.h file, and add the following line to the class's Implementation section, right after the `protected` keyword.

```
    void DoFilter(CString col);
```

You've now added the ability to sort and filter records in the employee database. Go ahead and compile the application and run it. When you do, the application's main window appears, looking the same as before. Now, however, you can sort the records on any field, just by selecting a field from the Sort menu. You can also filter the records by selecting a field from the Filter menu, and then typing the filter string into the Filter dialog box that appears.

For example, if you wanted to see every employee who works in the hardware department, you'd select the Filter, Department command, and then type **HARDWARE** into the Filter dialog box. When you dismiss the dialog box, all the records that have HARDWARE for the department ID are selected. If the application can match no records to the filter string, a message box appears, after which the application reselects all the records in the Employees database table.

Examining the *OnSortDept()* Function

When the user selects the Sort, Department command, the frameworks calls the `OnSortDept()` member function, whose job it is to sort the records as directed by the user. The first thing the function must do is close the record set:

```
m_pSet->Close();
```

The record set must be closed because the program is about to create a new record set based on the criteria the user selected. Because the user requested that the database be sorted by department, the new database must perform the sort using the DeptID field. A `CRecordset` object (or any object of a class derived from `CRecordset`, such as this program's `CEmployeeSet` object) uses a special string to determine how the records should be sorted. When the record set is being created, the object checks this string, called `m_strSort`, and sorts the records accordingly. So, after closing the record set, the next thing the program does is set the sort string, like this:

```
m_pSet->m_strSort = "DeptID";
```

Part
II

Ch
14

Now that the new sort string is prepared, reopening the record set is all that's required to sort the records:

```
m_pSet->Open();
```

Although the records are now sorted, they are not yet redisplayed in the view window. As you now know, to update the display, you must call the view window's `UpdateData()` member function with an argument of `FALSE`, like this:

```
UpdateData(FALSE);
```

The other sorting functions—`OnSortName()`, `OnSortRate()`, and `OnSortID()`—all work similarly.

Examining the *DoFilter()* Function

Whenever the user selects a command from the Filter menu, the framework calls the appropriate member function, either `OnFilterDept()`, `OnFilterID()`, `OnFilterName()`, or `OnFilterRate()`. Each of these functions does nothing more than call the local member function `DoFilter()` with a string representing the field on which to filter.

Knowing the field on which to filter is only half the battle, however. The program also needs to know what value to apply to the filter. In the Employee application, this value is obtained from the user via a dialog box. So, the first thing `DoFilter()` does is display the dialog box:

```
CFilterDlg dlg;
int result = dlg.DoModal();
```

When the user closes the dialog box, `result` will contain a value representing the button used to exit. If the user clicked the OK button to exit the dialog box, `result` will be equal to `IDOK`. Therefore, the program checks for this value before doing anything else:

```
if (result == IDOK)
```

If `result` does not equal `IDOK`, the entire `if` statement gets skipped over and the `DoFilter()` function does nothing but return.

Inside the `if` statement, the function first creates the string that'll be used to filter the database. Just as you set a string to sort the database, so too do you set a string to filter the database. In this case, the string is called `m_strFilter`. The string you use to filter the database must be syntactically correct, its simplest form being

```
ColumnID = 'ColumnValue'
```

In the above statement, `ColumnID` is the name of a column in the table. In the Employee application, this is the value that the user selects from the Filter menu, being EmployeeID (listed as ID in the menu), EmployeeName (listed as Name), EmployeeRate (listed as Rate), or DeptID (listed as Department). The program constructs the filter string like this:

```
CString str = col + " = '" + dlg.m_filterValue + "'";
```

As an example, if the user were to select the Filter, Department command and then type HARDWARE into the Filter dialog box, the resultant filter string created by the above line would be

```
DeptID = 'HARDWARE'
```

With the string constructed, the program is ready to filter the database. Just as with sorting, the record set must first be closed:

```
m_pSet->Close();
```

Then, the program sets the record set's filter string, like this:

```
m_pSet->m_strFilter = str;
```

To re-create the record set based on the given filter, the program reopens the record set:

```
m_pSet->Open();
```

What happens when the given filter results in no records being selected? Good question. The DoFilter() function handles this eventuality by getting the number of records in the new record set, like this:

```
int recCount = m_pSet->GetRecordCount();
```

The program can then check to see whether the filter resulted in an empty record set:

```
if (recCount == 0)
```

If the record set is empty, the program displays a message box telling the user of the problem:

```
MessageBox("No matching records.");
```

Then, the program closes the record set, resets the filter string to an empty string, and reopens the record set:

```
m_pSet->Close();
m_pSet->m_strFilter = "";
m_pSet->Open();
```

The above code restores the record set to include all the records in the Employees table.

Finally, whether the filter resulted in a subset of records or the record set had to be restored, the program must redisplay the data, by calling UpdateData():

```
UpdateData(FALSE);
```

Using ODBC versus DAO

In the previous section, you got an introduction to Visual C++'s ODBC classes and how they're used in an AppWizard generated application. Visual C++ also features a complete set of DAO classes that you can use to create database applications. DAO is, in many ways, almost a superset of the ODBC classes, containing most of the functionality of the ODBC classes and adding a great deal of its own. Unfortunately, although DAO can read ODBC data sources for which ODBC drivers are available, it's not particularly efficient at the task. For this reason, the DAO classes are best suited for programming applications that manipulate Microsoft's .mdb database files, which are created by Microsoft Access. Other file formats that DAO can read directly are those created by Fox Pro and Excel.

The DAO classes, which use the Microsoft Jet Database Engine, are so much like the ODBC classes, you can often convert an ODBC program to DAO simply by changing the class names in the program: CDatabase becomes CDaoDatabase, CRecordset becomes CDaoRecordset, and CRecordView becomes CDaoRecordView. One big difference between ODBC and DAO, however, is the way in which the system implements the libraries. ODBC is implemented as a set of DLLs, whereas DAO is implemented as OLE objects. Using OLE objects makes DAO a bit more up to date, at least as far as architecture goes, than ODBC.

Although DAO is implemented as OLE objects, you don't have to worry about dealing with those objects directly. The MFC DAO classes handle all the details for you, providing data and function members that interact with the OLE objects. The CDaoWorkspace class provides more direct access to the DAO database-engine object through static member functions. Although MFC handles the workspace for you, you can access its member functions and data members in order to explicitly initialize the database connection.

Another difference is that the DAO classes feature a more powerful set of methods that you can use to manipulate a database. These more powerful member functions enable you to perform sophisticated database manipulations without having to write a lot of complicated C++ code or SQL statements.

In summary, ODBC and DAO similarities are listed below:

- ODBC and DAO can both manipulate ODBC data sources. However, DAO is less efficient at this task, since it is best used with .mdb database files.

- AppWizard can create a basic database application based on either the ODBC or DAO classes. Which type of application you want to create depends—at least in some part—on the type of databases with which you'll be working.

- ODBC and DAO both use objects of an MFC database class to provide a connection to the database being accessed. In ODBC, this database class is called CDatabase, whereas in DAO, the class is called CDaoDatabase. Although these classes have different names, the DAO database class contains some similar members to those found in the ODBC class.

- ODBC and DAO both use objects of a record-set class to hold the currently selected records from the database. In ODBC, this record-set class is called CRecordset, whereas in DAO, the class is called CDaoRecordset. Although these classes have different names, the DAO record-set class contains not only almost the same members as the ODBC class, but also a large set of additional member functions.

- ODBC and DAO use similar procedures for viewing the contents of a data source. That is, in both cases, the application must create a database object, create a record-set object, and then call member functions of the appropriate classes to manipulate the database.

Some differences between ODBC and DAO are listed here:

- Although both ODBC and DAO MFC classes are similar (very similar in some cases), some similar methods have different names. In addition, the DAO classes feature many member functions not included in the ODBC classes.

- ODBC uses macros and enumerations to define options that can be used when opening record sets. DAO, on the other hand, defines constants for this purpose.

- Under ODBC, snapshot record sets are the default, whereas under DAO, dynamic record sets are the default.

- The many available ODBC drivers make ODBC useful for many different database file formats, whereas DAO is best suited to applications that will need to access only .mdb files.

- ODBC is implemented as a set of DLLs, whereas DAO is implemented as OLE objects.

- Under ODBC, an object of the `CDatabase` class transacts directly with the data source. Under DAO, a `CDaoWorkspace` object sits between the `CDaoRecordset` and `CDaoDatabase` objects, thus enabling the workspace to transact with multiple database objects.

From Here...

There's no doubt that using AppWizard and MFC's database classes makes writing database applications infinitely easier than the old-fashioned, roll-up-your-sleeves method. In fact, AppWizard can generate a fully functional database browser with very little help from you. Even when you have to get your hands dirty, though, implementing additional database commands in your application is just a matter of calling a few member functions. And, although the ODBC classes are adequate for most database projects, the DAO classes are newer, more powerful, and best suited for manipulating .mdb files, such as those created by Microsoft Access.

For more information on related topics, please consult the following chapters:

- Chapter 3, "AppWizard and ClassWizard," describes the basics of using AppWizard and ClassWizard to create and modify your applications.

- Chapter 5, "Messages and Commands," shows how MFC's message-routing system works and how you can adapt that system to your own menus and commands.

- Chapter 7, "Dialog and Controls," teaches you about MFC's many control classes and how you can incorporate them into your own programs.

- Chapter 15 "MFC Macros and Globals," describes how to create resources, such as menus and dialog boxes, for your applications.

Part
II

Ch
14

MFC Macros and Globals

When you're writing programs, there are many types of data and operations that you must use again and again. Sometimes, you have to do something as simple as creating a portable integer data type. Other times, you need to do something a little more complex, like extracting a word from a long word value or storing the position of the mouse pointer. As you may know, Windows itself defines many constants and variables that you can use in your programs to help write programs faster. Using these previously defined constants and macros makes your programs more portable and more readable by other programmers. Besides the macros, global constants, and variables defined by Windows, Visual C++ adds its own set. In the following tables, you'll get a look at the most important of these globally available constants, macros, and variables. ■

Ten Categories of Macros and Globals

Because there are so many constants, macros, and globals, Visual C++ organizes its constants, macros, and globals into ten categories. Those categories are listed below. The following sections describe each of these categories and the symbols they define.

- Application information and management
- ClassWizard comment delimiters
- Collection class helpers
- CString formatting and message-box display
- Data types
- Diagnostic services
- Exception processing
- Message maps
- Run-time object model services
- Standard command and window IDs

Application Information and Management Functions

Because a typical Visual C++ application contains only one application object but many other objects created from other MFC classes, you frequently need to get information about the application in different places in a program. Visual C++ defines a set of global functions that return this information to any class in a program. These functions, which are listed in Table 15.1, can be called from anywhere within an MFC program. For example, you frequently need to get a pointer to an application's main window. The following function call accomplishes that task.

```
CWnd* pWnd = AfxGetMainWnd();
```

Table 15.1 Application Information and Management

Function	Description
AfxBeginThread()	Creates a new thread. (Please refer to Chapter 31, "Multitasking with Windows Threads," for more information on threads.)
AfxEndThread()	Terminates a thread.
AfxGetApp()	Gets the application's CWinApp pointer.
AfxGetAppName()	Gets the application's name.
AfxGetInstanceHandle()	Gets the application's instance handle.
AfxGetMainWnd()	Gets a pointer to the application's main window.

Function	Description
AfxGetResourceHandle()	Gets the application's resource handle.
AfxGetThread	Gets a pointer to a CWinThread object.
AfxRegisterClass()	Registers a window class in an MFC DLL.
AfxRegisterWndClass()	Registers a Windows window class in an MFC application.
AfxSetResourceHandle()	Sets the instance handle that determines where to load the application's default resources.
AfxSocketInit()	Initializes Windows Sockets. (Please refer to Chapter 13, "Sockets, MAPI, and the Internet," for more information.)

ClassWizard Comment Delimiters

Visual C++ defines a number of delimiters that ClassWizard uses to keep track of what it's doing, as well as to locate specific areas of source code. Although you'll rarely, if ever, use these macros yourself, you will see them embedded in your AppWizard applications, so you might like to know exactly what they do. Table 15.2 fills you in.

Table 15.2 ClassWizard Delimiters

Delimiter	Description
AFX_DATA	Starts and ends member variable declarations in header files that are associated with dialog data exchange.
AFX_DATA_INIT	In a dialog class's constructor, starts and ends dialog data exchange variable initialization.
AFX_DATA_MAP	In a dialog class's DoDataExchange() function, starts and ends dialog data exchange function calls.
AFX_DISP	Starts and ends OLE Automation declarations in header files.
AFX_DISP_MAP	Starts and ends OLE Automation mapping in implementation files.
AFX_EVENT	Starts and ends OLE event declarations in header files.
AFX_EVENT_MAP	Starts and ends OLE events in implementation files.
AFX_FIELD	Starts and ends member variable declarations in header files that are associated with database record field exchange.
AFX_FIELD_INIT	In a record set class's constructor, starts and ends record field exchange member variable initialization.

continues

Table 15.2 Continued	
Delimiter	**Description**
AFX_FIELD_MAP	In a record set class's DoFieldExchange() function, starts and ends record field exchange function calls.
AFX_MSG	Starts and ends ClassWizard entries in header files for classes that use message maps.
AFX_MSG_MAP	Starts and ends message map entries.
AFX_VIRTUAL	Starts and ends virtual function overrides in header files.

Collection Class Helpers

Because certain types of data structures are so commonly used in programming, MFC defines collection classes that enable you to get these common data structures initialized quickly and manipulated easily. MFC includes collection classes for arrays, linked lists, and mapping tables. Each of these types of collections contains elements that represent the individual pieces of data that comprise the collection. In order to make it easier to access these elements, MFC defines a set of functions (created from templates; see Chapter 30, "Power-User C++ Features," for more information on templates), shown in Table 15.3, that you can override for a particular data type.

Table 15.3 Collection Class Helper Functions	
Function	**Description**
CompareElements()	Checks elements for equality.
ConstructElements()	Constructs new elements (works similar to a class constructor).
DestructElements()	Destroys elements (works similar to a class destructor).
DumpElements()	Provides diagnostic output in text form.
HashKey()	Calculates hashing keys.
SerializeElements()	Saves or loads elements to or from an archive.

CString Formatting and Message-Box Display

If you've done much Visual C++ programming, you know that MFC features a special string class, called CString, that makes string handling under C++ less cumbersome. CString objects are used extensively throughout MFC programs. Even when dealing with strings in a resource's string table, CString objects can come in handy, as the following global functions, which replace format characters in string tables, show (see Table 15.4). There's also a global function for displaying a message box.

Table 15.4   CString Formatting and Message-Box Functions

Function	Description
AfxFormatString1()	Replaces the format characters (i.e., %1) in a string resource with a given string.
AfxFormatString2()	Replaces the format characters "%1" and "%2" in a string resource with the given strings.
AfxMessageBox()	Displays a message box.

Data Types

The most commonly used constants are those that define a portable set of data types. You've seen tons of these constants, which are named using all uppercase letters, used in Windows programs. You'll recognize many of these from the Windows SDK. Others, are included only as part of Visual C++. You use these constants exactly as you would any other data type. For example, to declare a Boolean variable, you'd write something like this:

```
BOOL flag;
```

Table 15.5 lists the most commonly used data types defined by Visual C++ for Windows 95 and NT.

Table 15.5   Commonly Used Data Types

Constant	Data Type
BOOL	Boolean value.
BSTR	32-bit pointer to character data.
BYTE	8-bit unsigned integer.
COLORREF	32-bit color value.
DWORD	32-bit unsigned integer.
LONG	32-bit signed integer.
LPARAM	32-bit window-procedure parameter.
LPCRECT	32-bit constant RECT structure pointer.
LPCSTR	32-bit string-constant pointer.
LPSTR	32-bit string pointer.
LPVOID	32-bit void pointer.
LRESULT	32-bit window-procedure return value.

continues

Table 15.5   Continued

Constant	Data Type
POSITION	The position of an element in a collection.
UINT	32-bit unsigned integer.
WNDPROC	32-bit window-procedure pointer.
WORD	16-bit unsigned integer.
WPARAM	32-bit window-procedure parameter.

Using Diagnostic Services

Once you have your program written, you're far from done. Then comes the grueling task of testing, which means rolling up your sleeves, cranking up your debugger, and weeding out all the gotchas hiding in your code. Luckily, Visual C++ provides many macros, functions, and global variables that you can use to incorporate diagnostic abilities into your projects. Using these tools, you can do everything from printing output to a debugging window to checking the integrity of memory blocks. Table 15.6 lists these valuable diagnostic macros, functions, and global variables.

Table 15.6   Diagnostic Macros, Functions, and Global Variables

Symbol	Description
AfxCheckMemory()	Verifies the integrity of allocated memory.
AfxDoForAllClasses()	Calls a given iteration function for all classes that are derived from CObject and that incorporate run-time type checking.
AfxDoForAllObjects()	Calls a given iteration function for all objects that were derived from CObject and that were allocated with the new operator.
afxDump	A global CDumpContext object that enables a program to send information to the debugger window.
AfxDump()	Dumps an object's state during a debugging session.
AfxEnableMemoryTracking()	Toggles memory tracking.
AfxIsMemoryBlock()	Checks that memory allocation was successful.
AfxIsValidAddress()	Checks that a memory address range is valid for the program.
AfxIsValidString()	Checks string pointer validity.

Symbol	Description
afxMemDF	A global variable that controls memory-allocation diagnostics. Can be set to `allocMemDF`, `DelayFreeMemDF`, or `checkAlwaysMemDF`.
AfxSetAllocHook()	Sets a user-defined hook function that is called whenever memory allocation is performed.
afxTraceEnabled	A global variable that enables or disables TRACE output.
afxTraceFlags	A global variable that enables the MFC reporting features.
ASSERT	Prints a message and exits the program if the assert expression is false.
ASSERT_VALID	Validates an object by calling the object's `AssertValid()` function.
DEBUG_NEW	Used in place of the `new` operator in order to trace memory-leak problems.
TRACE	Creates formatted strings for debugging output.
TRACE0	Same as TRACE but requires no arguments in the format string.
TRACE1	Same as TRACE but requires one argument in the format string.
TRACE2	Same as TRACE but requires two arguments in the format string.
TRACE3	Same as TRACE but requires three arguments in the format string.
VERIFY	Like ASSERT, but VERIFY evaluates the assert expression in both the Debug and Release versions of MFC. If the assertion fails, a message is printed and the program halted only in the Debug version.

Exception Processing

One of the newest elements of the C++ language is exceptions, which give a program greater control over how errors are handled. (Please refer to Chapter 30, "Power-User C++ Features," for more information on exceptions.) Visual C++ increases the value of exceptions by defining a set of macros and functions that you can use to better handle errors in your applications. These macros and functions are listed in Table 15.7.

Table 15.7   Exception Macros and Functions

Symbol	Description
AfxAbort()	Terminates an application upon a fatal error.
AfxThrowArchiveException()	Throws an archive exception.
AfxThrowDAOException()	Throws a CDaoException.
AfxThrowDBException()	Throws a CDBException.
AfxThrowFileException()	Throws a file exception.
AfxThrowMemoryException()	Throws a memory exception.
AfxThrowNotSupportedException()	Throws a not-supported exception.
AfxThrowOleDispatchException()	Throws an OLE automation exception.
AfxThrowOleException()	Throws an OLE exception.
AfxThrowResourceException()	Throws a resource-not-found exception.
AfxThrowUserException()	Throws an end-user exception.
AND_CATCH	Begins code that will catch specified exceptions not caught in the preceding TRY block.
AND_CATCH_ALL	Begins code that will catch all exceptions not caught in the preceding TRY block.
CATCH	Begins code for catching an exception.
CATCH_ALL	Begins code for catching all exceptions.
END_CATCH	Ends CATCH or AND_CATCH code blocks.
END_CATCH_ALL	Ends CATCH_ALL code blocks.
THROW	Throws a given exception.
THROW_LAST	Throws the most recent exception to the next handler.
TRY	Starts code that will accommodate exception handling.

Using Message-Map Macros

Windows is an event-driven operating system, which means that every Windows application must handle a flood of messages that flow between an application and the system. MFC does away with the clunky switch statements that early Windows programmers had to construct in order to handle messages and replaces those statements with a message map. A message map is nothing more than a table that matches a message with its message handler. (For more

information on message maps, please refer to Chapter 5, "Messages and Commands.")
In order to simplify the declaration and definition of these tables, Visual C++ defines a set of
message-map macros. Many of these macros, which are listed in Table 15.8, will already be
familiar to experienced MFC programmers.

Table 15.8   Message-Map Macros

Macro	Description
BEGIN_MESSAGE_MAP	Begins a message-map definition.
DECLARE_MESSAGE_MAP	Starts a message-map declaration.
END_MESSAGE_MAP	Ends a message-map definition.
ON_COMMAND	Begins a command-message message-map entry.
ON_COMMAND_RANGE	Begins a command-message message-map entry that maps multiple messages to a single handler.
ON_CONTROL	Begins a control-notification message-map entry.
ON_CONTROL_RANGE	Begins a control-notification message-map entry that maps multiple control IDs to a single handler.
ON_MESSAGE	Begins a user-message message-map entry.
ON_REGISTERED_MESSAGE	Begins a registered user-message message-map entry.
ON_UPDATE_COMMAND_UI	Begins a command-update message-map entry.
ON_UPDATE_COMMAND_UI_RANGE	Begins a command-update message-map entry that maps multiple command-update messages to a single handler.

Run-Time Object Model Services

Frequently in your programs, you need access to information about classes at run-time. MFC
supplies a macro for obtaining this type of information in a CRuntimeClass structure. In addition, the MFC application frameworks relies on a set of macros to declare and define run-time
abilities (such as object serialization and dynamic object creation). If you've used AppWizard at
all, you've seen these macros used in the generated source-code files. If you're an advanced
MFC programmer, you may have even used these macros yourself. Table 15.9 lists the run-
time macros and their descriptions.

Table 15.9   Run-Time Services Macros

Macro	Description
DECLARE_DYNAMIC	Used in a class declaration to enable run-time class information access.
DECLARE_DYNCREATE	Used in a class declaration to allow the class (derived from `CObject`) to be created dynamically. Also, allows run-time class information access.
DECLARE_OLECREATE	Used in a class declaration to allow object creation with OLE automation.
DECLARE_SERIAL	Used in a class declaration to allow object serialization, as well as run-time class information access.
IMPLEMENT_DYNAMIC	Used in a class implementation to enable run-time class information access.
IMPLEMENT_DYNCREATE	Used in a class implementation to allow dynamic creation of the object and run-time information access.
IMPLEMENT_OLECREATE	Used in a class implementation to enable object creation with OLE.
IMPLEMENT_SERIAL	Used in a class implementation to allow object serialization and run-time class information access.
RUNTIME_CLASS	Returns a `CRuntimeClass` structure for the given class.

Standard Command and Window IDs

There are myriad standard messages that can be generated by a user of a Windows application. For example, whenever the user selects a menu command from a standard menu like File or Edit, the program sends a message. Each of these standard commands is represented by an ID. In order to relieve the programmer of having to define the dozens of IDs that are often used in a Windows application, Visual C++ defines these symbols in a file called AFXRES.H. Some of these IDs have obvious purposes (for example, `ID_FILE_OPEN`), but many others are used internally by MFC for everything from mapping standard Windows messages to their handlers to defining string-table IDs to assigning IDs to toolbar and status-bar styles. There are far too many of these identifiers to list here. However, if you're interested in seeing them, just load the AFXRES.H file from your Visual C++ installation folder.

From Here...

Thanks to the many constants, macros, and global functions and variables defined by Visual C++, common programming tasks are easy to perform in your applications. You should take the time to look over the tables given in this chapter in order to become more familiar with the tools Visual C++ has to offer. If you look up the listed functions, constants, macros, and global variables in your Visual C++ online documentation, you can find even more information about these valuable tools.

For more information on related topics, please consult the following chapters:

- Chapter 5, "Messages and Commands," shows how MFC's message-routing system works and how to build your own message-map tables.

- Chapter 17 "Building Menus and Dialogs," describes how to create resources for your applications. These resources will undoubtedly rely upon the many resource IDs defined in AFXRES.H.

- Chapter 20 "Debugging," describes how to use macros like ASSERT and TRACE to assist you in finding programming errors.

Building a Simple MFC Application

16 Choosing an Application Type and Building an Empty
Shell 355

17 Building Menus and Dialogs 371

18 Interface Issues 395

19 Printing and Print Preview 415

20 Debugging 433

21 Help 469

Choosing an Application Type and Building an Empty Shell

AppWizard is a very effective tool. It copies in code that almost all Windows applications need. After all, you aren't the first programmer who has needed an application with resizable edges, minimize and maximize buttons, and a File menu with Open, Close, Print Setup, Print, and Exit options, are you? In this chapter you will see what code AppWizard copies in for you, and what the choices on the AppWizard dialogs really mean. ■

Inside an empty dialog-based application

A dialog-based application has no menus or document and is the simplest MFC application. See the code produced for you and what it means.

How SDI applications are built

Single Document Interface applications can have only one file open at a time. AppWizard generates different code for these applications, including code to handle command-line options.

How MDI applications differ from SDI

Multiple Document Interface applications need code to handle the multiple views and documents

Other AppWizard decisions

This section directs you to the places in this book where the consequences of AppWizard decisions like database support, ActiveX technology, and application type are explained in detail.

A Dialog-Based Application

A dialog-based application has no menus other than the system menu, and cannot save or open a file. This makes it good for simple utilities like the Windows Character Map, shown in Figure 16.1. (If you are using Windows 95, this utility may not be installed. Use Add/Remove programs under Control Panel to add it if you want to try using it.)

FIG. 16.1

Character Map is a dialog-based application.

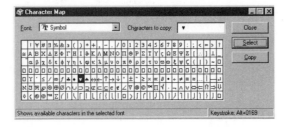

To build an empty dialog-based application, follow the steps first shown in Chapter 3, "AppWizard and ClassWizard." Choose File, New, Project Workspace to bring up the New Project Workspace of Figure 3.1. Choose MFC AppWizard (exe) from the list box on the left, enter a project name, and click Create to move to Step 1 of the AppWizard process, shown in Figure 16.2.

▶ **See** "Creating a Windows Application," **p. 76**

FIG. 16.2

To create a dialog-based application, specify your preference in Step 1 of the AppWizard process.

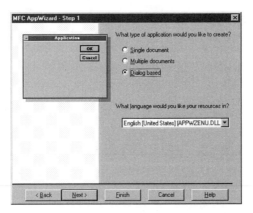

Choose Dialog Based and click Next to move to Step 2, shown in Figure 16.3.

If you would like an About item on the system menu, check the About box item. To have AppWizard lay the framework for Help, check the Context sensitive help option. The third checkbox, 3D controls, should be checked for most Windows 95 and Windows NT applications. If you want your application to surrender control to other applications through OLE Automation, check the OLE Automation checkbox. If you want your application to contain OLE controls, check the OLE Controls checkbox. If you are planning to have this application work over the Internet with sockets, check the `Windows Sockets` box. (Dialog-based apps can't use MAPI because they have no document.) Click `Next` to move to the third step, shown in Figure 16.4.

FIG. 16.3
Step 2 of the AppWizard process for a dialog-based application involves choosing Help, OLE, and Sockets settings.

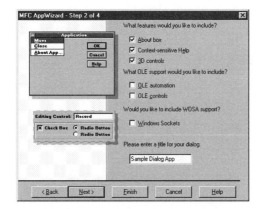

FIG. 16.4
Step 3 of the AppWizard process for a dialog-based application deals with comments and the MFC library.

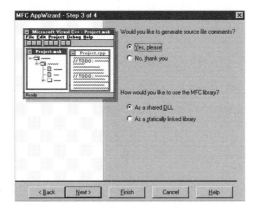

As always, you want comments in your code. The decision between static linking and a shared DLL was discussed in Chapter 3, "AppWizard and ClassWizard." If your users are likely to have the MFC DLLs already (because they are developers or because they have another product that uses the DLL), or if they won't mind installing the DLLs as well as your executable, go with the shared DLL to make a smaller executable file and a faster link. Otherwise choose `As a statically linked library`. Click `Next` to move to the final step, shown in Figure 16.5.

▶ **See** "Creating a Windows Application," **p. 76**

In this step you can change the names AppWizard chooses for files and classes. This is rarely a good idea, since it will confuse people who maintain your code if the file names can't be easily determined from the class names, and vice versa. If you realize, looking at this dialog, that you made a poor choice of project name, use `Back` to move all the way back to the New Project

Workspace dialog, change the name, click `Create`, and then use `Next` to come back to this dialog. Click `Finish` to see the summary of the files and classes to be created, like that in Figure 16.6.

FIG. 16.5

Step 4 of the AppWizard process for a dialog-based application gives you a chance to adjust file and class names.

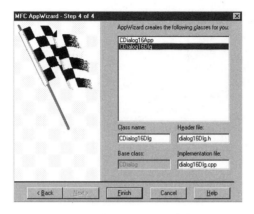

FIG. 16.6

AppWizard confirms the files and classes it will create before creating them.

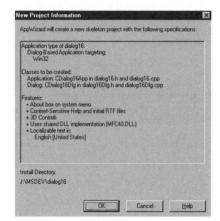

If any of the information on this dialog is not what you wanted, click `Cancel` and then use `Back` to move to the appropriate step and change your choices. When the information is right, click `OK` and watch as the application is created. Choose Build Build to compile and link the application, and then it's ready to be tested! Choose Build Execute to see it in action. Figure 16.7 shows the empty dialog-based application running, with the class view in the project workspace behind it in Developer Studio.

What did AppWizard do there? It created three classes: `CAboutDlg`, `CDialog16Dlg`, and `CDialog16App`. Dialog classes will be discussed in Chapter 17, "Building Menus and Dialogs," but you're going to look at `CDialog16App` now. The header file is shown in Listing 16.1.

FIG. 16.7

The empty application compiles the first time, and does all that a Windows application does.

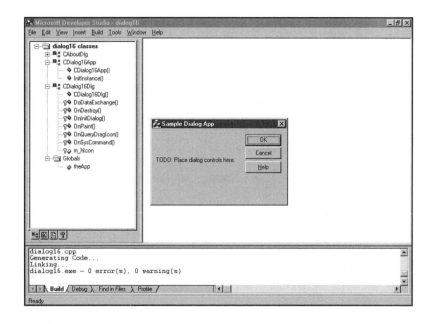

On the CD

Listing 16.1   dialog16.h—Main Header File

```
// dialog16.h : main header file for the DIALOG16 application
//

#ifndef __AFXWIN_H__
    #error include 'stdafx.h' before including this file for PCH
#endif

#include "resource.h"          // main symbols

/////////////////////////////////////////////////////////////////
// CDialog16App:
// See dialog16.cpp for the implementation of this class
//

class CDialog16App : public CWinApp
{
public:
    CDialog16App();

// Overrides
    // ClassWizard generated virtual function overrides
    //{{AFX_VIRTUAL(CDialog16App)
    public:
    virtual BOOL InitInstance();
    //}}AFX_VIRTUAL

// Implementation
```

continues

Listing 16.1   Continued

```
//{{AFX_MSG(CDialog16App)
    // NOTE - the ClassWizard will add and remove member
      ➥functions here.
    //     DO NOT EDIT what you see in these blocks of
               ➥generated code !
//}}AFX_MSG
DECLARE_MESSAGE_MAP()
};
```

CDialog16App inherits from CWinApp, which provides most of the functionality. CWinApp has a constructor and overrides the virtual function InitInstance(). Here's the constructor:

```
CDialog16App::CDialog16App()
{
    // TODO: add construction code here,
    // Place all significant initialization in InitInstance
}
```

This is a typical Microsoft constructor. Because constructors don't return values, there's no easy way to indicate that there has been a problem with the initialization. There are several different ways to deal with this; Microsoft's approach is a two-stage initialization, with a separate initializing function so that construction does no initialization. For an application, that function is called InitInstance(), shown in Listing 16.2.

Listing 16.2   CDialog16App::InitInstance()

```
BOOL CDialog16App::InitInstance()
{
    // Standard initialization
    // If you are not using these features and wish to reduce the size
    // of your final executable, you should remove from the following
    // the specific initialization routines you do not need.

#ifdef _AFXDLL
    Enable3dControls();
      // Call this when using MFC in a shared DLL
#else
    Enable3dControlsStatic();
      // Call this when linking to MFC statically
#endif

    CDialog16Dlg dlg;
    m_pMainWnd = &dlg;
    int nResponse = dlg.DoModal();
    if (nResponse == IDOK)
    {
        // TODO: Place code here to handle when the dialog is
        //   dismissed with OK
    }
    else if (nResponse == IDCANCEL)
    {
```

```
        // TODO: Place code here to handle when the dialog is
        //  dismissed with Cancel
    }

    // Since the dialog has been closed, return FALSE so that we exit the
    //  application, rather than start the application's message pump.
    return FALSE;
}
```

This enables 3D controls, since you asked for them, and then puts up the dialog box that is the entire application. Next, the function declares an instance of CDialog16Dlg, dlg, and then calls the DoModal() function of the dialog, which displays the dialog box on the screen and returns IDOK if the user clicks OK, or IDCANCEL if the user clicks Cancel. It's up to you to make that dialog box actually do something. Finally, InitInstance() returns FALSE because this is a dialog-based application and when the dialog box is closed, the application is over. As you'll see in a moment for ordinary applications, InitInstance() usually returns TRUE to mean "everything is fine, run the rest of the application," or FALSE to mean "something went wrong while initializing." But since there is no "rest of the application," dialog-based apps always return FALSE from their InitInstance().

A Single Document Interface Application

An SDI application does not bring up a dialog when it first runs, and then exit when that dialog is closed, as a dialog-based app does. Instead, it has menus that the user uses to open one document at a time and work with that document. The steps to create an empty SDI application are essentially identical to those presented for an MDI application in Chapter 3, "AppWizard and ClassWizard," in the "Creating a Windows Application" section. Rather than go through them again, this section presents the code that is generated when you choose an SDI application with no database or OLE support, with a toolbar, a status bar, Help, 3D controls, and source file comments, with the MFC library as a shared DLL.

Five classes have been created for you: if the application name was Chap16sdi the classes would be called CAboutDlg, CChap16sdiApp, CChap16sdiDoc, CChap16sdiView and Cmainframe. Dialog classes will be discussed in Chapter 17, "Building Menus and Dialogs," and the View, Doc, and Frame classes were discussed in Chapter 6, "The Document/View Paradigm." The App class header is shown in Listing 16.3.

Listing 16.3   Chap16sdi.h—Main Header File for the CHAP16SDI Application

```
// Chap16sdi.h : main header file for the CHAP16SDI application
//

#ifndef __AFXWIN_H__
    #error include 'stdafx.h' before including this file for PCH
#endif
```

continues

Listing 16.3   Continued

```
#include "resource.h"        // main symbols

//////////////////////////////////////////////////////////////////////////
// CChap16sdiApp:
// See Chap16sdi.cpp for the implementation of this class
//

class CChap16sdiApp : public CWinApp
{
public:
    CChap16sdiApp();

// Overrides
    // ClassWizard generated virtual function overrides
    //{{AFX_VIRTUAL(CChap16sdiApp)
    public:
    virtual BOOL InitInstance();
    //}}AFX_VIRTUAL

// Implementation

    //{{AFX_MSG(CChap16sdiApp)
    afx_msg void OnAppAbout();
        // NOTE - the ClassWizard will add and remove member functions here.
        //     DO NOT EDIT what you see in these blocks of generated code !
    //}}AFX_MSG
    DECLARE_MESSAGE_MAP()
};
```

So, CChap16dsiApp inherits from CWinApp, it has a constructor, it overrides InitInstance(), and there is an entry in the message map for OnAppAbout. The constructor is as simple as the earlier constructors in this chapter:

```
CChap16sdiApp::CChap16sdiApp()
{
    // TODO: add construction code here,
    // Place all significant initialization in InitInstance
}
```

InitInstance() is shown in Listing 16.4.

On the CD

Listing 16.4   CChap16sdiApp::InitInstance()

```
BOOL CChap16sdiApp::InitInstance()
{
    // Standard initialization
    // If you are not using these features and wish to reduce the size
    //  of your final executable, you should remove from the following
```

```
        // the specific initialization routines you do not need.

#ifdef _AFXDLL
      Enable3dControls();
      // Call this when using MFC in a shared DLL
#else
      Enable3dControlsStatic();
      // Call this when linking to MFC statically
#endif

      LoadStdProfileSettings();
        // Load standard INI file options (including MRU)

      // Register the application's document templates.
        // Document templates serve as the connection between
        //documents, frame windows and views.

      CSingleDocTemplate* pDocTemplate;
      pDocTemplate = new CSingleDocTemplate(
          IDR_MAINFRAME,
          RUNTIME_CLASS(CChap16sdiDoc),
          RUNTIME_CLASS(CMainFrame),
              // main SDI frame window
          RUNTIME_CLASS(CChap16sdiView));
      AddDocTemplate(pDocTemplate);

      // Parse command line for standard shell commands, DDE, file open
      CCommandLineInfo cmdInfo;
      ParseCommandLine(cmdInfo);

      // Dispatch commands specified on the command line
      if (!ProcessShellCommand(cmdInfo))
          return FALSE;

      return TRUE;
}
```

This sets up 3D controls, calls LoadStdProfileSettings() to build the list of most recently used (MRU) files, and registers the document template as discussed in Chapter 6, "The Document/View Paradigm." Next, it sets up an empty CCommandLineInfo object to hold any parameters that may have been passed to the application when it was run, and calls ParseCommandLine() to fill that. Finally it calls ProcessShellCommand() to do whatever those parameters requested. This means your application can support command line parameters to let users save time, without effort on your part. For example, if the user types at the command line Chap16sdi fooble then the application will start and will open the file called fooble. The command line parameters that ProcessShellCommand() supports are:

Parameter	Action
none	Start app and open new file.
Filename	Start app and open file.
/p filename	Start app and print file to default printer.
/pt filename printer driver port	Start app and print file to the specified printer.
/dde	Start app and await DDE command.
/Automation	Start app as an OLE automation server.
/Embedding	Start app to edit an embedded OLE item.

If you would like to implement other behavior, make a class that inherits from CCommandLineInfo to hold the parsed command line, then override CWinApp:: ParseCommandLine() and CWinApp::ProcessShellCommand() in your own App class.

T I P You may have already known that you could invoke many Windows programs from the command line; for example, typing **Notepad blah.txt** at a DOS prompt will open blah.txt in Notepad. Other command line options work too, so typing **Notepad /p blah.txt** will open blah.txt in Notepad, print it, and then close Notepad.

That's the end of InitInstance(). It returns TRUE to indicate that the rest of the application should now run.

The message map in the header file indicated that the function OnAppAbout() handles a message. Which one? Here's the message map from the source file:

```
BEGIN_MESSAGE_MAP(CChap16sdiApp, CWinApp)
    //{{AFX_MSG_MAP(CChap16sdiApp)
    ON_COMMAND(ID_APP_ABOUT, OnAppAbout)
        // NOTE - the ClassWizard will add and remove mapping macros here.
        //    DO NOT EDIT what you see in these blocks of generated code!
    //}}AFX_MSG_MAP
    // Standard file based document commands
    ON_COMMAND(ID_FILE_NEW, CWinApp::OnFileNew)
    ON_COMMAND(ID_FILE_OPEN, CWinApp::OnFileOpen)
    // Standard print setup command
    ON_COMMAND(ID_FILE_PRINT_SETUP, CWinApp::OnFilePrintSetup)
END_MESSAGE_MAP()
```

This message map catches commands from menus, as discussed in Chapter 5, "Messages and Commands." When the user chooses Help About, CChap16sdiApp::OnAppAbout() will be called. When the user chooses File New, File Open, or File Print Setup, functions from CWinApp will handle that work for you. (You would override those functions if you wanted to do something special for those menu choices.) OnAppAbout() looks like this:

```
void CChap16sdiApp::OnAppAbout()
{
    CAboutDlg aboutDlg;
    aboutDlg.DoModal();
}
```

It simply declares an object that is an instance of CAboutDlg and calls its DoModal() function to display the dialog on the screen. There's no need to handle OK or Cancel in any special way: this is just an About box.

Other Files

If you selected Context Sensitive Help, AppWizard generates.HPJ files and a number of .RTF files to give some context sensitive help. These files are discussed in Chapter 21, in the "Components of the Help System" section.

AppWizard also generates a README.TXT file that explains what all the other files are and what classes have been created. Read this file if all the similar file names start to get confusing.

A Multiple Document Interface Application

A Multiple Document Interface Application also has menus, and allows the user to have more than one document open at once. The steps to create an empty MDI application were presented in Chapter 3, "AppWizard and ClassWizard," in the "Creating a Windows Application" section. Rather than go through them again, this section presents the code that is generated when you choose an MDI application with no database or OLE support, but with a toolbar, a status bar, Help, 3D controls, source file comments, and the MFC library as a shared DLL. The focus here is on what is different from the SDI application in the previous section.

Five classes have been created for you: if the application name was Chap16mdi, the classes would be called CAboutDlg, CChap16mdiApp, CChap16mdiDoc, CChap16mdiView, CChildFrame, and CMainFrame. Dialog classes will be discussed in Chapter 17, "Building Menus and Dialogs," and the View, Doc, and Frame classes were discussed in Chapter 6, "The Document/View Paradigm." The App class header is shown in Listing 16.5.

Listing 16.5   Chap16mdi.h—Main Header File for the CHAP16MDI Application

```
// Chap16mdi.h : main header file for the CHAP16MDI application
//

#ifndef __AFXWIN_H__
    #error include 'stdafx.h' before including this file for PCH
#endif
```

continues

Listing 16.5 Continued

```
#include "resource.h"         // main symbols


/////////////////////////////////////////////////////////////////////////////
// CChap16mdiApp:
// See Chap16mdi.cpp for the implementation of this class
//

class CChap16mdiApp : public CWinApp
{
public:
     CChap16mdiApp();

// Overrides
     // ClassWizard generated virtual function overrides
     //{{AFX_VIRTUAL(CChap16mdiApp)
     public:
     virtual BOOL InitInstance();
     //}}AFX_VIRTUAL

// Implementation

     //{{AFX_MSG(CChap16mdiApp)
     afx_msg void OnAppAbout();
          // NOTE - the ClassWizard will add and remove member functions here.
          //    DO NOT EDIT what you see in these blocks of generated code !
     //}}AFX_MSG
     DECLARE_MESSAGE_MAP()
};
```

How does this differ from Chap16sdi.h? Only in the class names. The constructor is also the same as before. And OnAppAbout() is just like the SDI version. How about InitInstance()? It is in Listing 16.6.

On the CD

Listing 16.6 CChap16mdiApp::InitInstance()

```
BOOL CChap16mdiApp::InitInstance()
{
     // Standard initialization
     // If you are not using these features and wish to reduce the size
     //  of your final executable, you should remove from the following
     //  the specific initialization routines you do not need.

#ifdef _AFXDLL
     Enable3dControls();               // Call this when using MFC in a shared DLL
#else
     Enable3dControlsStatic();      // Call this when linking to MFC statically
#endif

     LoadStdProfileSettings();  // Load standard INI file options (including MRU)
```

```
    // Register the application's document templates.  Document templates
    //  serve as the connection between documents, frame windows and views.

    CMultiDocTemplate* pDocTemplate;
    pDocTemplate = new CMultiDocTemplate(
        IDR_CHAP16TYPE,
        RUNTIME_CLASS(CChap16mdiDoc),
        RUNTIME_CLASS(CChildFrame), // custom MDI child frame
        RUNTIME_CLASS(CChap16mdiView));
    AddDocTemplate(pDocTemplate);

    // create main MDI Frame window
    CMainFrame* pMainFrame = new CMainFrame;
    if (!pMainFrame->LoadFrame(IDR_MAINFRAME))
        return FALSE;
    m_pMainWnd = pMainFrame;

    // Parse command line for standard shell commands, DDE, file open
    CCommandLineInfo cmdInfo;
    ParseCommandLine(cmdInfo);

    // Dispatch commands specified on the command line
    if (!ProcessShellCommand(cmdInfo))
        return FALSE;

    // The main window has been initialized, so show and update it.
    pMainFrame->ShowWindow(m_nCmdShow);
    pMainFrame->UpdateWindow();

    return TRUE;
}
```

What's different here? Using WinDiff can help. WinDiff is a tool that comes with Visual C++ and is discussed in Chapter 32, "Additional Advanced Topics," in the "WinDiff" section. It confirms that other than the class names, the differences are:

- The MDI application includes ChildFrm.h; the SDI application does not.
- The MDI application sets up a CMultiDocTemplate and the SDI application sets up a CSingleDocTemplate, as discussed in Chapter 6, "The Document/View Paradigm."
- The MDI application sets up a mainframe window and then shows it; the SDI application does not.

This shows a major advantage of the Document/View paradigm: it allows an enormous design decision to affect only a small amount of the code in your project, and hides that decision as much as possible.

AppWizard Decisions and This Book

AppWizard asks a lot of questions, and starts you down a lot of roads at once. This chapter has explained InitInstance and shown some of the code affected by the very first AppWizard decision: whether to have AppWizard generate a Dialog-based, SDI, or MDI application. Most of the other AppWizard decisions are about topics that take an entire chapter. This table summarizes those choices and where you can learn more:

Step	Decision	Chapter	Dialog?
0	MFC DLL or non MFC DLL	32, Additional Advanced Topics	
0	OCX Control	26, Building an ActiveX Control	
0	Console Application	32, Additional Advanced Topics	
0	Custom AppWizard	29, Power-User Features in Developer Studio	
0	ISAPI Extension Wizard	13, Sockets, MAPI, and the Internet	
1	Language support	32, Additional Advanced Topics	yes
2	Database support	14, Database Access	
3	OLE Container	23, Building an ActiveX Container Application	
3	OLE Mini-server	24, Building an ActiveX Server Application	
3	OLE Full server	24, Building an ActiveX Server Application	
3	Compound files	23, Building an ActiveX Container Application	
3	OLE Automation	25, ActiveX Automation	yes
3	Using OLE Controls	26, Building an ActiveX Control	yes
4	Docking toolbar	18, Interface Issues	
4	Status bar	18, Interface Issues	
4	Printing	19, Printing and Print Preview	
4	Context sensitive help	21, Help	yes
4	3D Controls	—	yes
4	MAPI	13, Sockets, MAPI, and the Internet	
4	Windows Sockets	13, Sockets, MAPI, and the Internet	
4	Files in MRU list	—	
5	Comments in code	—	yes
5	MFC library	3, AppWizard and ClassWizard	

Step	Decision	Chapter	Dialog?
6	Base class for View	6, The Document/View Paradigm	
D2	About box	17, Building Menus and Dialogs	only

Since some of these questions are not applicable for dialog-based applications, this table has a Dialog column: "yes" indicates that this decision applies to dialog-based applications too; "only" means that this is not a decision for SDI or MDI applications, which must have a Help About menu item. An entry of — in the Chapter column means that this decision doesn't really warrant discussion. These topics get a sentence or two in passing in this chapter or Chapter 3, "AppWizard and ClassWizard."

From Here...

By now you know how to create applications that don't do much of anything. To make them do something, you need menus or dialog controls that give commands, and other dialog controls that gather more information. These are the subject of the next chapter, "Building Menus and Dialogs."

Once you have seen how to get an application to do something, you can move through the rest of Part III adding features like these:

- Toolbars, status bars, and property sheets are discussed in Chapter 18, "Interface Issues."
- Printing is covered in Chapter 19, "Printing."
- Context sensitive Help is implemented in Chapter 20, "Help."

Part
III

Ch
16

CHAPTER 17

Building Menus and Dialogs

Users tell programs to do things by choosing menu items or by clicking buttons on dialogs. They give the application details about their request by typing in edit boxes, choosing from list boxes, selecting radio buttons, checking or unchecking radio buttons, and more. This chapter builds a simple application that has menu items and dialogs, to illustrate the coding issues involved. ■

The ShowString Application

A variant on the traditional C "Hello, world!" program, ShowString displays a string, and allows the user to control the display.

Adding Menu Items

You use the ResourceView of Developer Studio to add a menu of items to an application, or to add one item to a menu.

Adding a Dialog

Building dialog boxes in Developer Studio is what earned Visual C++ its name. Drag, drop, and click your way to a custom interface.

Connecting Menus to Code

ClassWizard simplifies message handling and makes menus intuitive.

Connecting the Dialog to Code

ClassWizard handles dialog boxes almost as easily as menus.

Changing the Appearance of the View

The control over the display is added in this section. Users can set the color and centering of the text after you change the dialog box and the drawing code.

Building an Application That Displays a String

In this chapter, you will see how to develop an application very much like the traditional `"Hello, world!"` of C programming. The application simply displays a text string in the main window. The *document* (what you save in a file) contains the string and a few settings. There is a new menu item to bring up a dialog box to change the string and the settings, which control the appearance of the string. This is a deliberately simple application so that the concepts of adding menu items and adding dialogs are not obscured by trying to understand the actual brains of the application. So bring up Developer Studio and follow along.

Creating an Empty Shell with AppWizard

First, use AppWizard to create the starter application. Choose File, New and then Project Workspace. Name the project ShowString so that your class names will match those shown here. Click Create.

It doesn't matter much whether you choose SDI or MDI, but MDI will allow you to see for yourself how little effort is required to have multiple documents open at once, so choose MDI. Choose US English and then click Next.

The ShowString application needs no database support and no OLE support, so click Next on each of these steps. In AppWizard's Step 4 dialog box, set to work selecting a docking toolbar, status bar, printing and print preview, context-sensitive help, and 3-D controls, and then click Next. Choose source-file comments and shared DLL and then click Next. The class names and file names are all fine, so click Finish. Figure 17.1 shows the final confirmation dialog.

FIG. 17.1
AppWizard summarizes the design choices for ShowString.

Displaying a String

The ShowString application displays a string that will be kept in the document. You need to add a member variable to the document class, `CShowStringDoc`, and add loading and saving code to the `Serialize()` function. You can initialize the string by adding code to `OnNewDocument()` for the document and, in order to actually display it, override `OnDraw()` for the view.

Member Variable and Serialization Add a private variable to the document and a public function to get the value, by adding these lines to ShowStringDoc.h:

```
private:
    CString string;
public:
    CString GetString() {return string;}
```

The inline function will give other parts of your application a copy of the string to use whenever necessary but make it impossible for other parts to change the string.

Next, change the skeleton CShowStringDoc::Serialize() function provided by AppWizard to look like Listing 17.1. Since you used the MFC CString class, the archive has operators << and >> already defined, so this is a simple function to write. It fills the archive from the string when you are saving the document and fills the string from the archive when you are loading the document from a file.

Listing 17.1 ShowStringDoc.cpp—CShowStringDoc::Serialize()

```
void CShowStringDoc::Serialize(CArchive& ar)
{
    if (ar.IsStoring())
    {
        ar << string;
    }
    else
    {
        ar >> string;
    }
}
```

Initializing the String Whenever a new document is created, you want your application to initialize string to "Hello, world". A new document is created when the user chooses File, New. This message is caught by CShowStringApp (the message map is shown in Listing 17.2) and handled by CWinApp::OnFileNew(). Starter applications generated by AppWizard call OnFileNew() to create a blank document when they run. OnFileNew() calls the document's OnNewDocument() which actually initializes the member variables of the document.

Listing 17.2 ShowString.cpp—Message Map

```
BEGIN_MESSAGE_MAP(CShowStringApp, CWinApp)
    //{{AFX_MSG_MAP(CShowStringApp)
    ON_COMMAND(ID_APP_ABOUT, OnAppAbout)
            // NOTE - the ClassWizard will add and remove mapping macros
                here.
            //    DO NOT EDIT what you see in these blocks of generated code!
    //}}AFX_MSG_MAP
    // Standard file based document commands
    ON_COMMAND(ID_FILE_NEW, CWinApp::OnFileNew)
```

Part
III

Ch
17

continues

Listing 17.2   Continued

```
        ON_COMMAND(ID_FILE_OPEN, CWinApp::OnFileOpen)
        // Standard print setup command
        ON_COMMAND(ID_FILE_PRINT_SETUP, CWinApp::OnFilePrintSetup)
END_MESSAGE_MAP()
```

AppWizard gives you the simple OnNewDocument() shown in Listing 17.3.

Listing 17.3   ShowStringDoc.cpp—CShowStringDoc::OnNewDocument()

```
BOOL CShowStringDoc::OnNewDocument()
{
    if (!CDocument::OnNewDocument())
        return FALSE;

    // TODO: add reinitialization code here
    // (SDI documents will reuse this document)

    return TRUE;
}
```

Take away the comments and add this line in their place:

```
string = "Hello, world!";
```

(What else could it say, after all?) Leave the call to CDocument::OnNewDocument() because that will handle all the other work involved in making a new document.

Getting the String onto the Screen   Whenever your view needs to be drawn, such as when your application is first started, resized, restored, or when a window that had been covering it is taken away, the view's OnDraw() function is called to draw it. AppWizard has provided a skeleton, shown in Listing 17.4.

Listing 17.4   ShowStringView.cpp—CShowStringView::OnDraw()

```
void CShowStringView::OnDraw(CDC* pDC)
{
    CShowStringDoc* pDoc = GetDocument();
    ASSERT_VALID(pDoc);

    // TODO: add draw code for native data here
}
```

OnDraw() takes a pointer to a device context, discussed in the "Understanding Device Contexts" section of Chapter 11, "Drawing on the Screen." The device context class, CDC, has a member function called DrawText() that draws text on the screen. It is declared like this:

```
int DrawText( const CString& str, LPRECT lpRect, UINT nFormat )
```

The CString to be passed to this function is going to be the string from the document class, which can be accessed as pDoc->GetString(). The lpRect is the client rectangle of the view, returned by GetClientRect(). Finally, nFormat is the way the string should be displayed; for example, DT_CENTER means that the text should be centered from left to right within the view. DT_VCENTER means that the text should be centered up and down, but this works only for single lines of text that are identified with DT_SINGLELINE. Multiple format flags can be combined with ¦, so DT_CENTER¦DT_VCENTER¦DT_SINGLELINE is the nFormat that you want. The drawing code to be added to CShowStringView::OnDraw() looks like this:

```
CRect rect;
GetClientRect(&rect);
pDC->DrawText(pDoc->GetString(), &rect, DT_CENTER¦DT_VCENTER¦DT_SINGLELINE);
```

This sets up a CRect and passes its address to GetClientRect(), which sets the CRect to the client area of the view. DrawText() draws the document's string in the rectangle, centered vertically and horizontally.

At this point, the application should display the string properly. Build it, execute it, and you should see something like Figure 17.2. You have quite a lot of functionality: menus, toolbars, status bar, and so on, but nothing real, yet. Starting with the next section, that will change.

FIG. 17.2

ShowString starts simply, with the usual greeting.

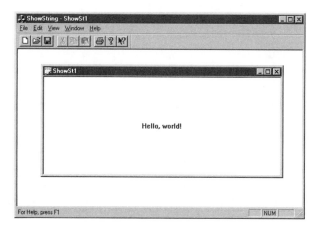

Building the ShowString Menus

AppWizard creates two menus for you, shown in the ResourceView window in Figure 17.3. IDR_MAINFRAME is the menu shown when no file is open; IDR_SHOWSTTYPE is the menu shown when a ShowString document is open. Notice that IDR_MAINFRAME has no View or Window menus and that the File menu is much shorter than the one on the IDR_SHOWSTTYPE menu, with only New, Open, Print Setup, recent files, and Exit items.

You are going to add a menu item to ShowString, so the first decision is where to add it. The user will be able to edit the string that is displayed and to set the format of the string. You could add a Value item to the Edit menu that brings up a small dialog for only the string and then

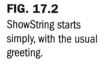

create a Format menu with one item, Appearance, that brings up the dialog to set the appearance. But the choice you are going to see here is to combine everything into one dialog and then put it on a new Tools menu, under the Options item. You may have noticed already that more and more Windows applications are standardizing on Tools, Options as the place for miscellaneous settings.

FIG. 17.3
AppWizard creates two menus for ShowString.

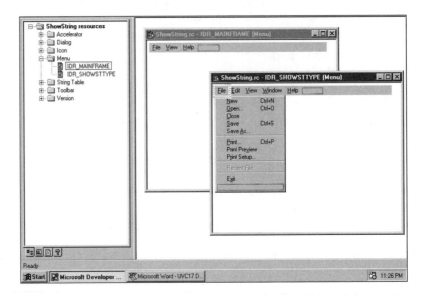

Do you need to add the item to both menus? No. When there is no document open, there is nowhere to save the changes made with this dialog. So only `IDR_SHOWSTTYPE` needs to have a menu added. Bring up the menu by double-clicking on it in the ResourceView window. At the far right of the menu, after Help, is an empty menu. Click on it and type **&Tools**. The Properties window will appear; pin it to the background by clicking the pushpin. The Caption box will contain &Tools. The menu at the end becomes the Tools menu, with an empty item underneath it; another empty menu then appears to the right of the Tools menu, as shown in Figure 17.4.

TIP The & in the Caption edit box indicates which letter should act as the key to select the menu item when it is displayed. This letter will be underlined in the menu. There is no further work required on your part.

Click the new Tools menu and drag it between the View and Window menus, corresponding to the position of Tools in products like Developer Studio and Microsoft Word. Next, click the empty subitem. The Properties box changes to show the blank properties of this item; change the caption to **&Options** and enter a sensible prompt, as shown in Figure 17.5.

FIG. 17.4

Adding the Tools menu is easy in the ResourceView window.

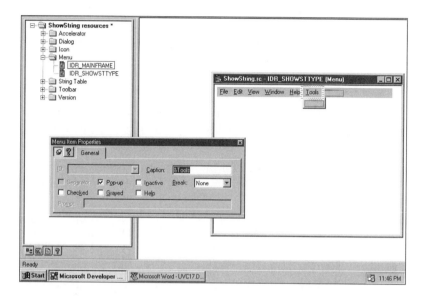

FIG. 17.5

The menu item Tools, Options will control everything that ShowString does.

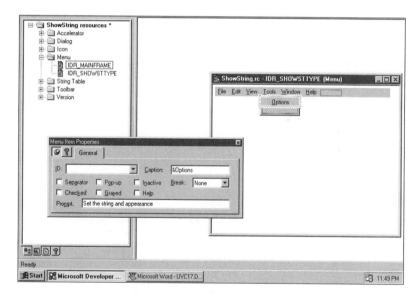

All menu items have a resource ID, and this resource ID is the way the menu items are connected to your code. Developer Studio will choose a good one for you, but it doesn't appear in the Properties box right away. Click on some other menu item and then click on Options again, and you'll see that the resource ID is ID_TOOLS_OPTIONS. Alternatively, press Enter when you are finished and the highlight will move down to the empty menu item below Options. Press the UpArrow cursor key to return the highlight to the Options item.

If you'd like to provide an accelerator, such as Ctrl+C for Edit, Copy, this is a good time to do it. Click Accelerator in the ResourceView window and then double-click IDR_MAINFRAME, the only Accelerator table in this application. At a glance, you can see what key combinations are already in use. Ctrl+O and Ctrl+P are already taken, but Ctrl+T is available. To connect Ctrl+T to Tools, Options, follow these steps:

1. Click on the empty line at the bottom of the Accelerator table. If you have closed the Properties box, bring it back by choosing Edit, Properties and then pin it in place. (Alternatively, double-click the empty line to bring up the Properties box.)

2. Click the drop-down list box labeled ID and choose ID_TOOLS_OPTIONS from the list, which is in alphabetical order. (There are a lot of entries before ID_TOOLS_OPTIONS; drag the elevator down almost to the bottom of the list or start typing the resource ID—by the time you enter ID_TO the highlight will be in the right place.)

3. Enter **T** in the Key box and make sure that the Ctrl check box is checked and that the Alt and Shift boxes are unchecked. Alternatively, click the Next Key Typed button and then type Ctrl+T, and the dialog will be filled in properly.

4. Click on another line in the Accelerator table to commit the changes.

Figure 17.6 shows the properties box for this accelerator after clicking on the newly entered line again.

FIG. 17.6

Keyboard accelerators are connected to resource IDs.

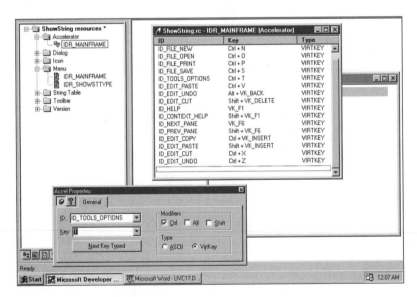

What happens when the user chooses this new menu item, Tools, Options? A dialog is displayed. So, tempting as it may be to start connecting this menu to code, it makes more sense to build the dialog first.

Building the ShowString Dialogs

As discussed in Chapter 7, "Dialog and Controls," a dialog box is a special kind of window. The controls on it are also windows. Because they are contained within the dialog box, they are *child windows*, and the dialog box is their *parent window*. There are two types of dialog boxes:

- A *modal* dialog box is on top of all the other windows in the application: the user must deal with the dialog box and then close it before going on to other work. An example of this is the dialog box that comes up when the user chooses File, Open in any Windows application.

- A *modeless* dialog box allows the user to click on the underlying application and do some other work, then return to the dialog box again. An example of this is the dialog box that comes up when the user chooses Edit, Find in many Windows applications.

The examples of modal and modeless dialog boxes are both common dialog boxes available to any Windows application. But of course many applications need dialogs that have not been conveniently provided by Microsoft, and ShowString is no exception. ShowString is actually going to have two custom dialogs: one brought up by Tools, Options, and an About box. An About box has been provided by AppWizard but needs to be changed a little, and the Options box will be built from scratch.

Part
III

Ch
17

ShowString's About Box

Figure 17.7 shows the About box that AppWizard makes for you; it will do as an About box. It contains the name of the application and the current year. To view the About box for ShowString, click on the ResourceView tab in the project workspace window. Expand the Dialogs list by clicking the + icon next to the word Dialogs, and then double click on IDD_ABOUTBOX to bring up the About dialog box resource.

You might want to add a company name to your About box. Here's how to add "Que Books," as an example. Click the line of text that reads Copyright 1996, and it will be surrounded by a selection box. Bring up the properties box, if it is not up. Edit the caption to add Que Books at the end; the changes are reflected immediately in the dialog.

 T I P If the rulers you see in Figure 17.7 don't appear when you open IDD_ABOUTBOX in Developer Studio, you can turn them on by choosing Layout, Guide Settings and selecting the Rulers and Guides radio button in the top half of the Guide Settings dialog box.

I decided to add a text string reminding users what book this application is from. Here's how to do that:

1. Size the dialog a little taller by clicking the whole dialog to select it and then clicking the sizing square in the middle of the bottom border and dragging the bottom border down a little. (This visual editing is what gave Visual C++ its name when it first came out.)

2. In the floating toolbar called Controls, click the button labeled *Aa* to get a *static control,* which means a piece of text that the user cannot change, perfect for labels like this. Click within the dialog under the other text to insert the static text there.

3. In the properties box, change the caption from Static to Using Visual C++ 5. The box automatically resizes to fit the text.

4. Holding down the Ctrl key, click on the other two static text lines in the dialog. Choose Layout, Align Controls and then Left, which aligns the edges of the three selected controls. The one you select last stays still, and the others move to align with it.

5. Choose Layout, Space Evenly, and then Down. These menu options can save you a great deal of dragging, squinting at the screen, and then dragging again.

The About box should look like Figure 17.8.

FIG. 17.7

AppWizard makes an About box for you.

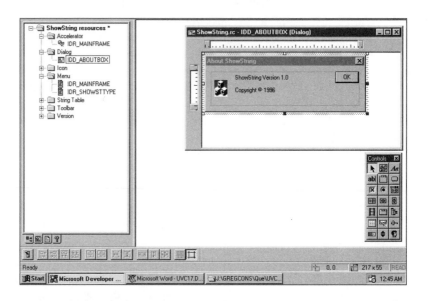

FIG. 17.8

In a matter of minutes, your About box can be customized.

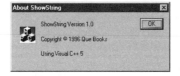

T I P   All the Layout menu items are on the Dialog toolbar.

ShowString's Options Dialog

The Options dialog is pretty simple to build. First, make a new dialog by choosing Insert, Resource and then double-clicking Dialog. An empty dialog called Dialog1 appears, with an OK and a Cancel button, as shown in Figure 17.9.

FIG. 17.9

A new dialog always has OK and Cancel buttons.

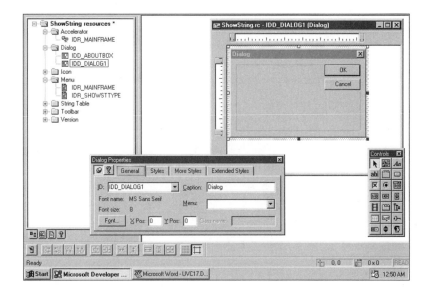

Next, follow these steps to convert the empty dialog into the Options dialog:

1. Change the ID to IDD_OPTIONS and the caption to Options.
2. In the floating toolbar called Controls, click the button labeled ab¦ to get an edit box, where the user can enter the new value for the string. Click inside the dialog to place the control and then change the ID to IDC_OPTIONS_STRING. (Control IDs should all start with "IDC" and should then mention the name of their dialog and then an identifier that is unique to that dialog.)
3. Click the sizing squares to resize the edit box as wide as possible.
4. Add a static label above the edit box and change that caption to String:.

You will revisit this dialog later, when adding the appearance abilities, but for now it's ready to be connected. It should look like Figure 17.10.

FIG. 17.10

The Options dialog is the place to change the string.

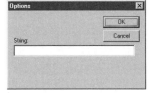

Making the Menu Work

When the user chooses Tools, Options, the Options dialog should be displayed. You use ClassWizard to arrange for one of your functions to be called when the item is chosen, and then you write the function, which will create an object of your dialog class and then display it.

The Dialog Class

ClassWizard will make the dialog class for you. While the window displaying the IDD_OPTIONS dialog has focus, choose View, ClassWizard. ClassWizard realizes there is not yet a class that corresponds to this dialog and offers to create one, as shown in Figure 17.11. Leave Create a new class selected and then click OK.

FIG. 17.11

Create a C++ class to go with the new dialog.

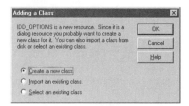

The Create New Class dialog, shown in Figure 17.12, appears. Fill it in as follows:

1. Choose a sensible name for the class, one that starts with *C* and contains the word *Dialog*; this example uses COptionsDialog.

2. The base class defaults to CDialog, which is perfect for this case.

3. At the bottom of the dialog is a check box called Add to Component Gallery. This will let you make your dialog available to other projects; the IDD_OPTIONS dialog doesn't really qualify to be shared with others, so leave it unchecked. The Component Gallery is discussed in Chapter 29, "Power-User C++ Features."

4. Click Create to create the class.

FIG. 17.12

The dialog class will inherit from *CDialog* and will not be added to the Component Gallery.

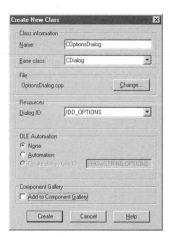

Perhaps you're curious about what code was created for you when ClassWizard made the class. The header file is shown in Listing 17.5.

Listing 17.5   OptionsDialog.h—Header File for COptionsDialog

```
// OptionsDialog.h : header file
//

/////////////////////////////////////////////////////////////////////////////
// COptionsDialog dialog

class COptionsDialog : public CDialog
{
// Construction
public:
    COptionsDialog(CWnd* pParent = NULL);   // standard constructor

// Dialog Data
    //{{AFX_DATA(COptionsDialog)
    enum { IDD = IDD_OPTIONS };
    CString     m_string;
    //}}AFX_DATA
// Overrides
    // ClassWizard generated virtual function overrides
    //{{AFX_VIRTUAL(COptionsDialog)
    protected:
    virtual void DoDataExchange(CDataExchange* pDX);   // DDX/DDV support
    //}}AFX_VIRTUAL
// Implementation
protected:
    // Generated message map functions
    //{{AFX_MSG(COptionsDialog)
        // NOTE: the ClassWizard will add member functions here
    //}}AFX_MSG
    DECLARE_MESSAGE_MAP()
};
```

There are an awful lot of comments here to help ClassWizard find its way around in the file when the time comes to add more functionality, but there is only one member variable, m_string; one constructor; and one member function, DoDataExchange(), which gets the control value into the member variable, or vice versa. The source file is not much longer; it's shown in Listing 17.6.

Listing 17.6   OptionsDialog.cpp—Implementation File for COptionsDialog

```
// OptionsDialog.cpp : implementation file
//

#include "stdafx.h"
#include "ShowString.h"
```

continues

Part

III

Ch

17

Listing 17.6   Continued

```
#include "OptionsDialog.h"

#ifdef _DEBUG
#define new DEBUG_NEW
#undef THIS_FILE
static char THIS_FILE[] = __FILE__;
#endif
//////////////////////////////////////////////////////////////////////////////
// COptionsDialog dialog
COptionsDialog::COptionsDialog(CWnd* pParent /*=NULL*/)
    : CDialog(COptionsDialog::IDD, pParent)
{
    //{{AFX_DATA_INIT(COptionsDialog)
    m_string = _T("");
    //}}AFX_DATA_INIT
}
void COptionsDialog::DoDataExchange(CDataExchange* pDX)
{
    CDialog::DoDataExchange(pDX);
    //{{AFX_DATA_MAP(COptionsDialog)
    DDX_Text(pDX, IDC_OPTIONS_STRING, m_string);
    //}}AFX_DATA_MAP
}
BEGIN_MESSAGE_MAP(COptionsDialog, CDialog)
    //{{AFX_MSG_MAP(COptionsDialog)
        // NOTE: the ClassWizard will add message map macros here
    //}}AFX_MSG_MAP
END_MESSAGE_MAP()
```

The constructor sets the string to an empty string; this code is surrounded by special ClassWizard comments that will enable it to add other variables later. The DoDataExchange() function calls DDX_Text() to transfer data from the control with the resource ID IDC_OPTIONS_STRING to the member variable m_string, or vice versa. This code, too, is surrounded by ClassWizard comments. Finally, there is an empty message map, because COptionsDialog doesn't catch any messages.

Catching the Message

There are seven classes in ShowString: CAboutDlg, CChildFrame, CMainFrame, COptionsDialog, CShowStringApp, CShowStringDoc, and CShowStringView. Which one should catch the command that is sent when the user chooses the menu item Tools, Options? The string and the options will be saved in the document and displayed in the view, so one of those two classes should handle the changing of the string. The document owns the private variable and will not let the view change the string unless you implement a public function to set the string. So it makes the most sense to have the document catch the message.

To catch the message, follow these steps:

1. Bring up ClassWizard (if it is not already up).
2. Click the Message Maps tab.

3. Select CShowStringDoc from the Class name drop-down list box.

4. Select ID_TOOLS_OPTIONS from the Object IDs list box on the left, and select COMMAND from the Messages list box on the right.

5. Click Add Function to add a function that will handle this command.

6. The Add Member Function dialog, shown in Figure 17.13, appears, giving you an opportunity to change the function name from the usual one. Do not change it; just click OK.

FIG. 17.13
ClassWizard suggests a good name for the message-catching function.

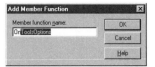

You should almost never change the names that ClassWizard suggests for message catchers. If you find that you have to, be sure to choose a name that starts with *On*.

What happened to CShowStringDoc when you arranged for the ID_TOOLS_OPTIONS message to be caught? The new message map in the header file is shown in Listing 17.7.

Listing 17.7   ShowStringDoc.h—Message Map for CShowStringDoc

```
// Generated message map functions
protected:
    //{{AFX_MSG(CShowStringDoc)
    afx_msg void OnToolsOptions();
    //}}AFX_MSG
    DECLARE_MESSAGE_MAP()
```

This is just declaring the function. In the source file, ClassWizard changed the message map as shown in Listing 17.8.

Listing 17.8   ShowStringDoc.cpp—Message Map for CShowStringDoc

```
BEGIN_MESSAGE_MAP(CShowStringDoc, CDocument)
    //{{AFX_MSG_MAP(CShowStringDoc)
    ON_COMMAND(ID_TOOLS_OPTIONS, OnToolsOptions)
    //}}AFX_MSG_MAP
END_MESSAGE_MAP()
```

This arranges for OnToolsOptions() to be called when the command ID_TOOLS_OPTIONS is sent. ClassWizard also added a skeleton for OnToolsOptions():

```
void CShowStringDoc:: OnToolsOptions()
{
    // TODO: Add your command handler code here

}
```

Part
III

Ch
17

Making the Dialog Work

OnToolsOptions() should initialize and display the dialog and then do something with the value that the user provided. In order to initialize the edit control on the dialog, and to use the value that the user entered, the edit box control needs to be connected to a member variable of COptionsDialog. ClassWizard handles this very nicely. Here's what to do:

1. Click on the Member Variables tab.
2. Choose COptionsDialog from the Class name drop-down list box.
3. Choose IDC_OPTIONS_STRING (the resource ID that you gave the edit box) from the list box.
4. Click Add Variable to bring up the Add Member Variable dialog.
5. Fill in a name that starts m_, such as m_string.
6. The rest of the dialog is fine; Class Wizard knows the ways that people are most likely to use each control. Figure 17.14 shows the completed Add Member Variable dialog.

FIG. 17.14

The Add Member Variable dialog connects dialog controls to members of the dialog class.

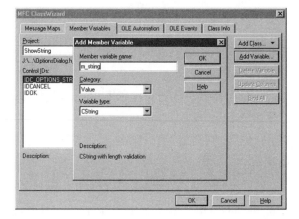

7. Click OK to close this dialog and then click OK to close ClassWizard.

You're ready to write OnToolsOptions(), shown in Listing 17.9.

Listing 17.9   ShowStringDoc.cpp—OnToolsOptions()

```cpp
void CShowStringDoc::OnToolsOptions()
{
    COptionsDialog dlg;
    dlg.m_string = string;
    if (dlg.DoModal() == IDOK)
    {
        string = dlg.m_string;
```

```
        SetModifiedFlag();
        UpdateAllViews(NULL);
    }

}
```

This code fills the member variable of the dialog with the member variable of the document (ClassWizard added m_string as a public member variable of COptionsDialog, so the document can change it) and then puts up the dialog by calling DoModal(). If the user clicks OK, the member variable of the document is changed, the modified flag is set (so that the user will be prompted to save the document on exit), and the view is asked to redraw itself with a call to UpdateAllViews(). In order for this to compile, of course, the compiler must know what a COptionsDialog is, so add this line at the beginning of ShowStringDoc.cpp:

```
#include "OptionsDialog.h"
```

At this point, you can build the application and run it. Choose Tools, Options and change the string. Click OK and you'll see the new string in the view. Exit the application, and you'll be asked whether to save the file. Save it, restart the application, and open the file again. The default "Hello world" document remains open, and the changed document is open with a different string. The application works, as you can see in Figure 17.15 (the windows are resized to let them both fit in the figure.)

FIG. 17.15

ShowString can change the string, save it to a file, and reload it.

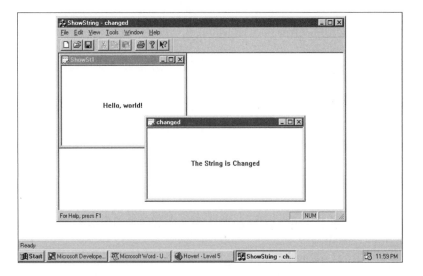

Adding Appearance Options to the Options Dialog

ShowString doesn't have much to do, just demonstrate menus and dialogs. But the only dialog control that ShowString uses is an edit box. In this section, you add a set of radio buttons and check boxes to change the way the string is drawn in the view.

Part
III

Ch
17

Changing the Options Dialog

It is quite simple to incorporate a full-fledged Font dialog into an application, but the example in this section is going to do something much simpler. A group of radio buttons will let the user choose among several colors. One check box will allow the user to specify that the text should be centered horizontally, and another will allow that the text be centered vertically. Because these are check boxes, the text can be either, neither, or both.

Open the IDD_OPTIONS dialog by double-clicking on it in the ResourceView window and then add the radio buttons by following these steps:

1. Stretch the dialog taller to make room for the new controls.
2. Click the radio button in the Controls floating toolbar and then click on the Options dialog to drop the control.
3. Choose Edit, Properties and then pin the properties box in place.
4. Change the resource ID of the first radio button to IDC_OPTIONS_BLACK and change the caption to &Black.
5. Check the Group box to indicate that this is the first of a group of radio buttons.
6. Add another radio button with resource ID IDC_OPTIONS_RED and, as caption, &Red. Do not check the Group box since the Red radio button does not start a new group but is part of the group that started with the Black radio button.
7. Add a third radio button with resource ID IDC_OPTIONS_GREEN and, as caption, &Green. Again, do not check Group.
8. Drag the three radio buttons into a horizontal arrangement, and select all three.
9. Choose Layout, Align Controls, Bottom (to even them up).
10. Choose Layout, Space Evenly, Across to space the controls across the dialog.

Next, add the check boxes by follwing these steps:

1. Click on the check box in the Controls floating toolbar and then click the Options dialog, dropping a check box onto it.
2. Change the resource ID of this check box to IDC_OPTIONS_HORIZCENTER and the caption to Center &Horizontally.
3. Check the Group box to indicate the start of a new group after the radio buttons.
4. Drop another check box onto the dialog as in Step 1 and give it the resource ID IDC_OPTIONS_VERTCENTER and the caption Center &Vertically.
5. Arrange the check boxes under the radio buttons.
6. Click the Group box on the Controls floating toolbar and then click and drag a group box around the radio buttons. Change the caption to Text Color.
7. Move the OK and Cancel buttons down to the bottom of the dialog.
8. Select each horizontal group of controls and use Layout, Center in Dialog Horizontally to neaten things up.

9. Choose <u>E</u>dit, Select A<u>l</u>l and then drag all the controls up toward the top of the dialog. Shrink the dialog to fit around the new controls. It should now resemble Figure 17.16.

FIG. 17.16

The options dialog for ShowString has been expanded.

 T I P If you don't recognize the icons on the Controls toolbar, use the *tooltips*. If you hold the cursor over any of the toolbar buttons, a tip will pop up after a few seconds, telling you what control the button represents.

Finally, set the tab order by choosing <u>L</u>ayout, <u>T</u>ab Order and clicking on the controls, in this order:

1. `IDC_OPTIONS_STRING`
2. `IDC_OPTIONS_BLACK`
3. `IDC_OPTIONS_RED`
4. `IDC_OPTIONS_GREEN`
5. `IDC_OPTIONS_HORIZCENTER`
6. `IDC_OPTIONS_VERTCENTER`
7. `IDOK`
8. `IDCANCEL`

Then click away from the dialog to leave the two static text controls as positions 9 and 10.

Adding Member Variables to the Dialog Class

Having added controls to the dialog, you need to add corresponding member variables to the class, COptionsDialog. Bring up ClassWizard and add member variables for each control. Figure 17.17 shows the summary of the member variables created. The check boxes are connected to BOOL variables; these member variables will be TRUE if the box is checked and FALSE if it is not. The radio buttons are handled differently. Only the first—the one with the Group box checked in its properties box—is connected to a member variable. That integer is a zero-based index that indicates which button is selected. In other words, when the Black button is selected, m_color will be 0; when Red is selected, m_color will be 1; and when Green is selected, m_color will be 2.

Part

III

Ch

17

FIG. 17.17

Member variables in
the dialog class are
connected to individual
controls or the group of
radio buttons.

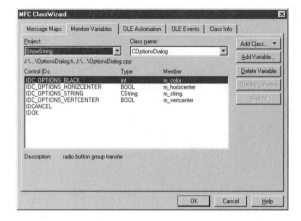

Adding Member Variables to the Document

The variables to be added to the document are the same ones that were added to the
dialog. They need to be added to the CShowStringDoc class definition in the header file, to
OnNewDocument(), and to Serialize(). The top few lines of the class definition should now
look like Listing 17.10.

Listing 17.10   ShowStringDoc.h—CShowStringDoc Member Variables

```
private:
    CString string;
    int     color;
    BOOL horizcenter;
    BOOL vertcenter;
public:
    CString GetString() {return string;}
    int     GetColor() {return color;}
    BOOL GetHorizcenter() {return horizcenter;}
    BOOL GetVertcenter() {return vertcenter;}
```

As with string, these are private variables with public get functions but no set functions.
All these options should be serialized; the new Serialize() is shown in Listing 17.11.

Listing 17.11   ShowStringDoc.cpp—Serialize()

```
void CShowStringDoc::Serialize(CArchive& ar)
{
    if (ar.IsStoring())
    {
        ar << string;
```

```
        ar << color;
        ar << horizcenter;
        ar << vertcenter;
    }
    else
    {
        ar >> string;
        ar >> color;
        ar >> horizcenter;
        ar >> vertcenter;
    }
}
```

What are good defaults for these new member variables? Black text, centered in both directions, was the old behavior, and it makes sense to use it as the default. The new OnNewDocument() is shown in Listing 17.12.

Listing 17.12 ShowStringDoc.cpp—OnNewDocument()

```
BOOL CShowStringDoc::OnNewDocument()
{
    if (!CDocument::OnNewDocument())
        return FALSE;

    string = "Hello, world!";
    color = 0;        //black
    horizcenter = TRUE;
    vertcenter = TRUE;

    return TRUE;
}
```

Of course, at the moment, these member variables are never changed from these defaults. To allow the user to change the variables, you will have to change the function that handles the dialog box.

Changing *OnToolsOptions()*

The OnToolsOptions() function sets the values of the dialog member variables from the document member variables and then displays the dialog. If the user clicked OK, the document member variables are set from the dialog member variables and the view is redrawn. Having just added three member variables to the dialog and the document, you have three lines to add before the dialog is displayed and then three more to add in the block that's called after OK is clicked. The new OnToolsOptions() is shown in Listing 17.13.

Listing 17.13   ShowStringDoc.cpp—OnToolsOptions()

```
void CShowStringDoc::OnToolsOptions()
{
    COptionsDialog dlg;
    dlg.m_string = string;
    dlg.m_color = color;
    dlg.m_horizcenter = horizcenter;
    dlg.m_vertcenter = vertcenter;

    if (dlg.DoModal() == IDOK)
    {
        string = dlg.m_string;
        color = dlg.m_color;
        horizcenter = dlg.m_horizcenter;
        vertcenter = dlg.m_vertcenter;
        SetModifiedFlag();
        UpdateAllViews(NULL);
    }

}
```

So what happens when the user brings up the dialog box and changes the value of a control, say, by unselecting Center Horizontally? The framework—through Dialog Data Exchange (DDX), as set up by ClassWizard—changes the value of COptionsDialog::m_horizcenter to FALSE. This code in OnToolsOptions() changes the value of CShowStringDoc::horizcenter to FALSE. When the user saves the document, Serialize() will save horizcenter. This is all good, but none of this code actually changes the way the view is drawn. That involves OnDraw().

Changing *OnDraw()*

The single call to DrawText() in OnDraw() gets a little more complex now. The document member variables are used to set the appearance of the view.

The color is set with CDC::SetTextColor() before the call to DrawText(). It's a good idea to save the old text color and restore it when you are finished. The parameter to SetTextColor() is a COLORREF, and you can directly specify combinations of red, green, and blue as hex numbers in the form 0x00bbggrr, so that, for example, 0x000000FF is bright red. Most people prefer to use the RGB macro, which takes hex numbers from 0x0 to 0xFF, specifying the amount of each color; bright red is RGB(FF,0,0). Add the lines shown in Listing 17.14 lines before the call to DrawText() to set up everything.

Listing 17.14 ShowStringDoc.cpp—OnDraw () Additions Before DrawText() Call

```
COLORREF oldcolor;
switch (pDoc->GetColor())
{
case 0:
    oldcolor = pDC->SetTextColor(RGB(0,0,0)); //black
    break;
case 1:
    oldcolor = pDC->SetTextColor(RGB(0xFF,0,0)); //red
    break;
case 2:
    oldcolor = pDC->SetTextColor(RGB(0,0xFF,0)); //green
    break;
}
```

Part

III

Ch

17

Add this line after the call to DrawText():

```
pDC->SetTextColor(oldcolor);
```

There are two approaches to setting the centering flags. The brute-force way is to list the four possibilities (neither, horizontal, vertical, and both) and have a different DrawText() statement for each. If you were to add other settings, this would quickly become unworkable. It's better to set up an integer to hold the DrawText() flags and "or in" each flag, if appropriate. Add the lines shown in Listing 17.15 before the call to DrawText().

Listing 17.15 ShowStringDoc.cpp—OnDraw () Additions After DrawText() Call

```
int DTflags = 0;
if (pDoc->GetHorizcenter())
{
    DTflags |= DT_CENTER;
}
if (pDoc->GetVertcenter())
{
    DTflags |= (DT_VCENTER|DT_SINGLELINE);
}
```

The call to DrawText() now uses the DTflags variable:

```
pDC->DrawText(pDoc->GetString(), &rect, DTflags);
```

Now the settings from the dialog box have made their way to the dialog class, to the document, and finally to the view, to actually affect the appearance of the text string. Build and execute ShowString and then try it out. Any surprises?

From Here...

This is not the last you will see of ShowString; it will reappear in Chapter 21, "Help," and throughout Part IV, "ActiveX Applications and ActiveX Controls." But there's a lot of other material to cover between here and there. The rest of this part of the book presents sample applications and how-to instructions for everyday tasks all developers face:

- Implementing property sheets is covered in Chapter 9, "Property Pages and Sheets and Wizards."
- Adding buttons to toolbars and implementing status bars are covered in Chapter 18, "Interface Issues."
- Printing is covered in Chapter 19, "Printing and Print Preview."
- You can learn about debugging in Chapter 20, "Debugging."

CHAPTER 18

Interface Issues

Building a good user interface is half the battle of programming a Windows application. Luckily, Visual C++ and its AppWizard supply an amazing amount of help in creating an application that supports all the expected user-interface elements, including menus, dialog boxes, toolbars, and status bars. The subjects of menus and dialog boxes are covered elsewhere in this book. In this chapter, however, you get a lesson in how to get the most out of toolbars and status bars, as well as get a look at the Windows 95 Registry. ■

How to add or delete toolbar buttons

The buttons on a toolbar must reflect your application's specific command set.

How to specify tool tips and descriptions for your toolbar buttons

When a user places the mouse pointer over a button, your application can display useful information about that particular command.

How to respond to toolbar buttons

Just like menu commands, toolbar buttons must be associated with message-response functions.

How to add panes to a status bar

You're not stuck with MFC's default status bar. Your application's status bar can display whatever information you'd like it to display.

How to store information in the Registry

Don't run screaming from the room. In an MFC program, the Registry is easier to handle than you might believe.

Working with Toolbars

Although you can add a toolbar to your application with AppWizard, you still need to use a little programming polish to get things just right. This is because every application is different and AppWizard can create only the most generally useful toolbar for most applications. When you create your own toolbars, you'll probably want to add or delete buttons to support your application's unique command set.

For example, when you create a standard AppWizard application with a toolbar, AppWizard creates the toolbar shown in Figure 18.1. This toolbar provides buttons for the commonly used commands in the File and Edit menus, as well as a button for displaying the About dialog box. But what if your application doesn't support these commands? It's up to you to modify the default toolbar to fit your application.

FIG. 18.1

The default toolbar provides buttons for commonly used commands.

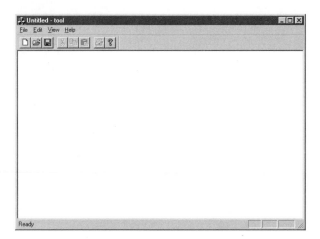

Deleting Toolbar Buttons

The first step in modifying the toolbar is to delete buttons you no longer need. To do this, first select the ResourceView tab to display your application's resources. Then, select the IDR_MAINFRAME toolbar resource, as shown in Figure 18.2. When you do, the toolbar editor appears, also shown in Figure 18.2.

After you have the toolbar editor on the screen, deleting buttons is as easy as dragging the unwanted buttons from the toolbar. Just place your mouse pointer on the button, hold down the left mouse button, and drag the button away from the toolbar. When you release the mouse button, the toolbar button disappears. Figure 18.3 shows the edited toolbar with only the Help button remaining. The single, blank button template is only a starting point for the next button you may want to create. If you leave it blank, it doesn't appear in the final toolbar.

FIG. 18.2

The toolbar editor enables you to customize your application's toolbar.

ResourceView window

Toolbar editor

Resource View tab

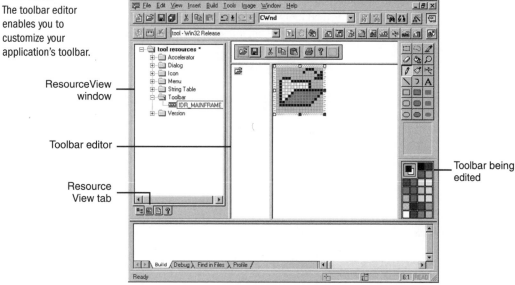

Toolbar being edited

FIG. 18.3

This edited toolbar has only a single button left (not counting the blank button template).

Template for next button to add

Single remaining button

Adding Buttons to a Toolbar

Adding buttons to a toolbar is a bit more complicated because you not only have to draw the button's icon, but you must also match the button with the command that it selects. To draw the new button, first click the blank button template in the toolbar. The blank button appears, enlarged, in the edit window, as shown in Figure 18.4.

FIG. 18.4

Click the button template to bring it up in the button editor.

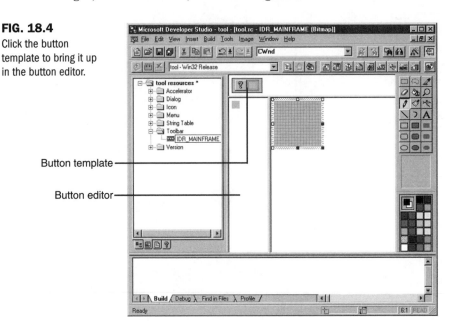

Button template

Button editor

Suppose you want to create a toolbar button that draws a circle in the application's window. You draw a circle on the blank button, which takes care of creating the button's icon, but now you need a way to associate the button with the program command. First, double-click the button in the toolbar to display its Toolbar Button Properties property sheet. Then, give the button an appropriate ID, which, in this case, might be something like ID_CIRCLE.

Now you need to define the button's tool tip and description. The tool tip appears whenever the user leaves his mouse pointer over the button for a second or two and acts as a reminder of the button's purpose. A tool tip of "Draw a circle" would be appropriate for the circle button. The description appears in the application's status bar. In this case, a description of "Draws a red circle in the window" might be good. You type these two text strings into the Prompt box. The description comes first, followed by the newline character (\n) and the tool tip, as shown in Figure 18.5.

FIG. 18.5

After drawing the button, you specify its properties.

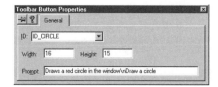

You've now defined a command ID for your new toolbar button. You need to associate that ID with a message-handler function, which MFC will automatically call when the user clicks the button. To do this, make sure the button for which you want to create a message handler is selected in the custom toolbar, and then click the ClassWizard button. The MFC ClassWizard property sheet appears, with the button's ID already selected (see fig. 18.6). To add the message-response function, select, in the Class Name box, the class to which you want to add the function. Then, double-click the COMMAND selection in the Messages box. Accept the function name that MFC suggests in the next message box, and you're all set. Click the OK button to finalize your changes.

> **N O T E** If you haven't defined a message-response function for a toolbar button, MFC disables the button when you run the application. This is also true for menu commands that have not yet been associated with a message-response function. In fact, for all intents and purposes, toolbar buttons *are* menu commands. ■

FIG. 18.6

You can use ClassWizard to create message-response functions for your toolbar buttons.

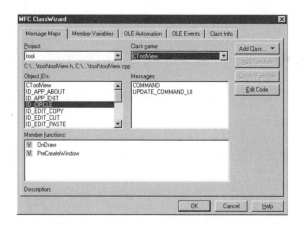

> **N O T E** Ordinarily, toolbar buttons duplicate menu commands, providing a quicker way for the user to select commonly used commands in the menus. In this case, the menu item and the toolbar button both represent the exact same command and you give both the same ID. Then, the same message-response function gets called whether the user selects the command from the menu bar or from the toolbar. ■

If you compile and run the application now, you'll see the window shown in Figure 18.7. In the figure, you can see the new toolbar button, as well as its tool tip and description line. The toolbar looks a little sparse in this example, but you can add as many buttons as you like.

FIG. 18.7

The new toolbar button shows its tool tip and description.

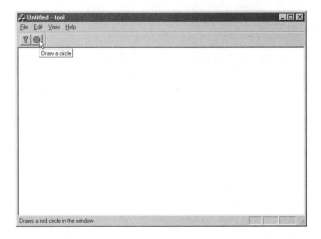

You can create as many buttons as you need, just follow the above procedures for each. After you have the buttons created, you're through with the toolbar resources and are ready to write the code that responds to the buttons. For example, in the previous example, a circle button was added to the toolbar and a message-response function, called OnCircle(), was added to the program. MFC will call that message-response function whenever the user clicks the associated button. However, right now, that function doesn't do anything, as shown in Listing 18.1.

Listing 18.1   LST18_1.TXT—An Empty Message-Response Function

```
void CToolView::OnCircle()
{
    // TODO: Add your command handler code here

}
```

Although the circle button is supposed to draw a circle in the window, you can see that the OnCircle() function is going to need a little help accomplishing that task. But, by adding the lines shown in Listing 18.2 to the function, the circle button will actually do what it's supposed to do, as shown in Figure 18.8.

Listing 18.2   LST18_2.TXT—Drawing a Circle

```
CClientDC clientDC(this);
CBrush newBrush(RGB(255,0,0));
CBrush* oldBrush = clientDC.SelectObject(&newBrush);
clientDC.Ellipse(20, 20, 200, 200);
clientDC.SelectObject(oldBrush);
```

FIG. 18.8
After adding the appropriate code to *OnCircle()*, the new toolbar button actually does something.

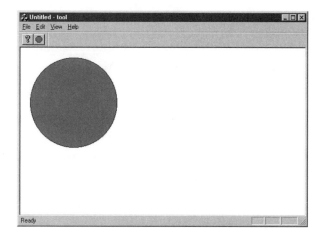

N O T E You can find the circle-drawing application in the CHAP18\TOOL directory of this book's CD-ROM. ▪

The *CToolBar* Class's Member Functions

In most cases, after you have created your toolbar resource and associated its buttons with the appropriate command IDs, you don't need to bother any more with the toolbar. The code generated by AppWizard creates the toolbar for you, and MFC takes care of calling the buttons' response functions for you. However, there may be times when you want to change the toolbar's default behavior or appearance in some way. In those cases, you can call upon the CToolBar class's member functions, which are listed in Table 18.1 along with their descriptions. Please refer to your Visual C++ online documentation for more details.

Table 18.1   Member Functions of the *CToolBar* Class

Function	Description
CommandToIndex()	Gets the index of a button given its ID
Create()	Creates the toolbar
GetButtonInfo()	Gets information about a button
GetButtonStyle()	Gets a button's style
GetButtonText()	Gets a button's text label
GetItemID()	Gets the ID of a button given its index
GetItemRect()	Gets an item's display rectangle given its index
GetToolBarCtrl()	Gets a reference to the CToolBarCtrl object represented by the CToolBar object

continues

Table 18.1   Continued

Function	Description
LoadBitmap()	Loads the toolbar's button images
LoadToolBar()	Loads a toolbar resource
SetBitmap()	Sets a new toolbar button bitmap
SetButtonInfo()	Sets a button's ID, style, and image number
SetButtons()	Sets the IDs for the toolbar buttons
SetButtonStyle()	Sets a button's style
SetButtonText()	Sets a button's text label
SetHeight()	Sets the toolbar's height
SetSizes()	Sets the buttons' sizes

Normally, you don't need to call the toolbar's methods, but you can get some unusual results when you do, such as the extra high toolbar shown in Figure 18.9. (The buttons are the same size, but the toolbar window is bigger.) This toolbar resulted from a call to the toolbar object's SetHeight() member function. Truthfully, it's not suggested that you monkey with the size of the toolbar, but you can use other member functions to modify the toolbar's buttons in response to a user's command. For example, there may be times when you need to display different buttons at different times. The CToolBar class's member functions enable you to perform this sort of toolbar trickery.

FIG. 18.9
You can use a toolbar object's member functions to change how the toolbar looks and acts.

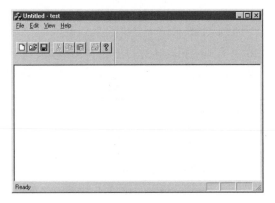

Working with Status Bars

Status bars are mostly benign objects that sit at the bottom of your application's window, doing whatever MFC instructs them to do. This consists of displaying command descriptions and the status of various keys on the keyboard, including the Caps Lock and Scroll Lock keys. In fact, status bars are so mundane from the programmer's point of view (at least, they are in an AppWizard application) that they aren't even represented by a resource that you can edit like a toolbar. When you tell AppWizard to incorporate a status bar into your application, there's not much left for you to do.

Or is there? A status bar, just like a toolbar, must reflect the interface needs of your specific application. For that reason, the CStatusBar class features a set of methods with which you can customize the status bar's appearance and operation. Table 18.2 lists the methods along with brief descriptions.

Table 18.2   Methods of the *CStatusBar* Class

Method	Description
CommandToIndex()	Gets an indicator's index given its ID
Create()	Creates the status bar
GetItemID()	Gets an indicator's ID given its index
GetItemRect()	Gets an item's display rectangle given its index
GetPaneInfo()	Gets information about an indicator
GetPaneStyle()	Gets an indicator's style
GetPaneText()	Gets an indicator's text
GetStatusBarCtrl()	Gets a reference to the CStatusBarCtrl object represented by the CStatusBar object
SetIndicators()	Sets the indicators' IDs
SetPaneInfo()	Sets the indicators' IDs, widths, and styles
SetPaneStyle()	Sets an indicator's style
SetPaneText()	Sets an indicator's text

Part
III

Ch
18

When you create a status bar as part of an AppWizard application, you get a window similar to that shown in Figure 18.10. The status bar has several parts, called *panes*, that display certain information about the status of the application and the system. These panes, which are marked in Figure 18.10, include indicators for the Caps Lock, Num Lock, and Scroll Lock keys, as well as a message area for showing status text and command descriptions. To see a command description, place your mouse pointer over a button on the toolbar (see fig. 18.11).

The most common way you can customize a status bar is to add new panes. This process can be a little tricky, though. To add a pane to a status bar, you must complete these steps:

1. Create a command ID for the new pane.
2. Create a default string for the pane.

3. Add the pane's command ID to the status bar's indicators array.

4. Create a command-update handler for the pane.

The following sections cover these steps in detail.

FIG. 18.10

The default MFC status bar contains a number of informative panes.

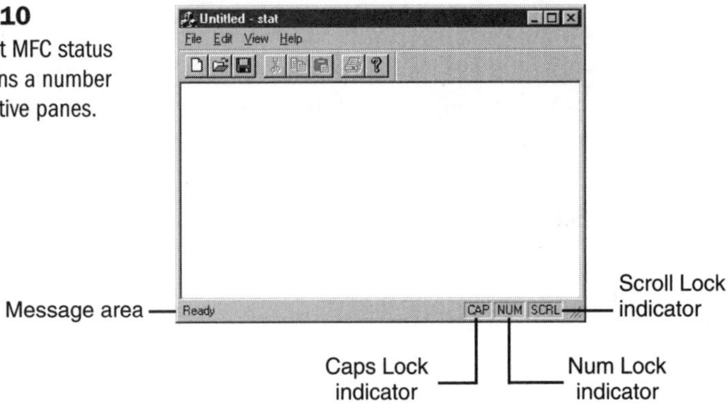

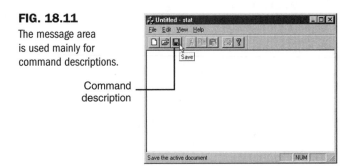

Message area ——

Scroll Lock indicator

Caps Lock indicator

Num Lock indicator

FIG. 18.11

The message area is used mainly for command descriptions.

Command description

Creating a New Command ID

This step is easy, thanks to Visual C++'s symbol browser. To add the command ID, first choose the View, Resource Symbols command on Visual C++'s menu bar. When you do, you see the Resource Symbols dialog box (see fig. 18.12), which displays the currently defined symbols for your application's resources. Click the New button, and the New Symbol dialog box appears. Type the new ID into the Name box, and the ID's value into the Value box (see fig. 18.13). Usually, you can just accept the value that MFC suggests for the ID.

Click the OK and Close buttons to finalize your selections, and your new command ID is defined.

FIG. 18.12

Use the Resource Symbols dialog box to add new command IDs to your application.

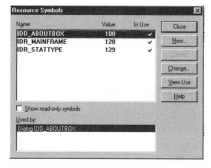

FIG. 18.13

Type the new ID's name and value into the New Symbol dialog box.

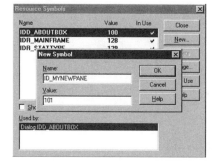

Creating the Default String

The Visual C++ compiler insists that every status bar pane has a default string defined for it. To define the string, first go to the ResourceView window (by clicking the ResourceView tab) and open the String Table resource into the string table editor, as shown in Figure 18.14. (To open the string table editor, double-click the String Table resource.)

FIG. 18.14

You define the new pane's default string in the application's string table resource.

ResourceView window

Double-click here to open the string table editor

Resource View tab

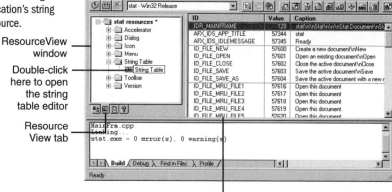

String table editor

Now, select the Insert, New String command from the menu bar, which brings up the String Properties dialog box. Type the new pane's command ID into the ID box and the default string into the Caption box (see fig. 18.15). (Instead of typing the command ID, you can select it from the drop-down list.)

FIG. 18.15

Use the String Properties dialog box to define the new pane's default string.

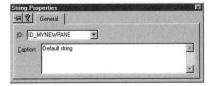

Adding the ID to the Indicators Array

When MFC constructs your status bar, it uses an array of IDs to determine which panes to display and where to display them. This array of IDs is passed as an argument to the status bar's SetIndicators() member function, which is called in the CMainFrame class's OnCreate() function. You find this array of IDs, shown in Listing 18.3, near the top of the MAINFRM.CPP file.

Listing 18.3   LST18.3.TXT—The Indicator Array

```
static UINT indicators[] =
{
    ID_SEPARATOR,            // status line indicator
    ID_INDICATOR_CAPS,
    ID_INDICATOR_NUM,
    ID_INDICATOR_SCRL,
};
```

To add your new pane to the array, type the pane's ID into the array at the position in which you want it to appear in the status bar, followed by a comma. (The first pane, ID_SEPARATOR, should always remain in the first position.) Listing 18.4 shows the indicator array with the new pane added.

Listing 18.4   LST18_4.TXT—Adding the New Pane's ID

```
static UINT indicators[] =
{
    ID_SEPARATOR,            // status line indicator
    ID_MYNEWPANE,
    ID_INDICATOR_CAPS,
    ID_INDICATOR_NUM,
    ID_INDICATOR_SCRL,
};
```

Creating the Pane's Command-Update Handler

MFC does not automatically enable new panes when it creates the status bar. Instead, you must create a command-update handler for the new pane, and enable the pane yourself. (You first learned about command-update handlers in Chapter 5, "Messages and Commands.") You must also add whatever code is needed to display information in the pane, assuming that the default string you defined in an earlier step is only a placeholder.

First, you must declare the new command-update handler in the MAINFRM.H header file. Unfortunately, although you can use ClassWizard to add command-update handlers for menu commands, you have to create status bar handlers by hand. The prototype to add to the header file looks like this:

```
afx_msg void OnMyNewPane(CCmdUI *pCmdUI);
```

Of course, the actual name of the handler varies from pane to pane, but the rest of the line should look exactly as it does here.

Next, you have to add the handler to the class's message map, which is what associates the command ID with the handler. Because the handler was not added by ClassWizard, be sure that you place the table entry outside of the AFX_MSG_MAP comments, as shown in Listing 18.5. You can find the message map defined near the top of the MAINFRM.CPP file (or near the top of the implementation file for the class to which you're adding the command-update handler).

On the CD

Listing 18.5 LST18_5.TXT—Adding the Handler to the Message Map

```
BEGIN_MESSAGE_MAP(CMainFrame, CFrameWnd)
    //{{AFX_MSG_MAP(CMainFrame)
        // NOTE - the ClassWizard will add and remove mapping macros here.
        //    DO NOT EDIT what you see in these blocks of generated code !
    ON_WM_CREATE()
    //}}AFX_MSG_MAP

    ON_UPDATE_COMMAND_UI(ID_MYNEWPANE, OnMyNewPane)
END_MESSAGE_MAP()
```

As you learned in Chapter 5, "Messages and Commands," you use the ON_UPDATE_COMMAND_UI macro to associate command IDs with their UI handers. The macro's two arguments are the command ID and the name of the command-update handler.

Now you're ready to write the new command-update handler. In the handler, you have to enable the new pane, as well as set the pane's contents. Listing 18.6 shows the command-update handler for the new pane. The command-update handler should be placed in the class implementation file that contains the message map entries for the status bar. In this example, that class is CMainFrame.

Listing 18.6   LST18_6.TXT—The Pane's Command-Update Handler

```
void CMainFrame::OnMyNewPane(CCmdUI *pCmdUI)
{
    pCmdUI->Enable();
    pCmdUI->SetText(m_paneString);
}
```

If you don't understand how a command-update handler works, please refer to Chapter 5, "Messages and Commands," where these important functions that control a command item's appearance are discussed in detail. (A status bar pane is not a command item, but it uses the same mechanism for updating.) In the previous code example, m_paneString is the text that you want displayed in the pane. You can replace m_paneString with a string literal or with a variable that contains the string you want to appear in the status bar.

Setting the Status Bar's Appearance

If you want to see the status bar tricks described in the previous sections in action, check out the CHAP18\STAT folder of this book's CD-ROM. When you run the program there, called Status Bar Demo, you see the window shown in Figure 18.16. As you can see, the status bar contains an extra panel displaying the text "Default string." If you select the File, Change String command or click the Change String toolbar button, a dialog box appears into which you can type a new string for the panel. When you exit the dialog box via the OK button, not only does the text appear in the new panel, but the panel also resizes itself to accommodate the new string (see fig. 18.17). In this section, you see how the new panel works.

FIG. 18.16

The Status Bar Demo application shows how to add and manage a status bar panel.

In Listing 18.6, m_paneString is a CString object that holds the text to display in the pane. At the beginning of the program, this string, which is a data member of the CMainFrame class, is initialized to "Default string," which is the string that appears in the new pane when the Status Bar Demo program starts up. As you already know, the panel is enabled, and its contents set, in the OnMyNewPanel() command-update handler.

How does the panel resize itself? This happens when the user changes the panel's text with the Change String command. When the user selects this command, MFC calls the OnChangestring() message-response function, which is shown in Listing 18.7.

FIG. 18.17

The new panel resizes itself to fit the selected string.

Listing 18.7   LST18_7.TXT—Changing the Panel's Text and Size

```
void CMainFrame::OnChangestring()
{
    // TODO: Add your command handler code here

    CPaneDlg dialog(this);
    dialog.m_paneString = m_paneString;

    int result = dialog.DoModal();

    if (result == IDOK)
    {
        m_paneString = dialog.m_paneString;
        CClientDC dc(this);
        SIZE size = dc.GetTextExtent(m_paneString);
        int index = m_wndStatusBar.CommandToIndex(ID_MYNEWPANE);
        m_wndStatusBar.SetPaneInfo(index,
            ID_MYNEWPANE, SBPS_POPOUT, size.cx);
    }
}
```

In OnChangestring(), the program displays the dialog box, and, if the user exits the dialog box by clicking the OK button, the program changes the text string and resets the size of the pane. It does this by first calling the GetTextExtent() function, which returns the size of the string. To get the index of the pane, the program calls the status bar's CommandToIndex() member function, which returns the index given the pane's ID. Then the program uses the string size and index in the call to the status bar's SetPaneInfo() member function. This function's arguments are the pane index, the pane's new ID (in this case, you're not changing the ID), the pane's style, and the pane's width. The SBPS_POPOUT style creates a pane that seems to stick out from the status bar, rather than being indented.

The Registry

The days of huge WIN.INI files or myriad private INI files are now gone. When an application wants to store information about itself, it does so using a centralized system registry. And,

Part III

Ch 18

although the Registry makes sharing information between processes easier, it admittedly makes things more confusing for the programmer. This is, of course, the price programmers always pay for greater user satisfaction. In this section, you uncover some of the mysteries of the Registry, as well as learn how to manage it in your applications.

How the Registry Is Set Up

Unlike INI files, which are plain text files that can be edited with any text editor, the Registry contains binary and ASCII information that can be edited only using the Registry Editor or using special API function calls specially created for managing the Registry. If you've ever used the Registry Editor to browse your system's Registry, you know that it contains a huge amount of information that's organized into a tree structure. Figure 18.18 shows how the Registry appears when you first run the Registry Editor. (You can find the Registry Editor, called REGEDIT.EXE, in your main Windows folder, or you can run it with the Start menu's Run command by selecting the Run command and then typing **regedit**.)

FIG. 18.18

The Registry Editor displays the Registry.

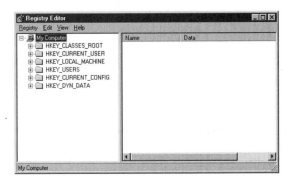

The stuff listed in the left-hand window is the Registry's predefined keys. The plus marks next to the keys in the tree indicate that you can "open" the keys and view more detailed information associated with the key. In short, keys can have subkeys lower in the hierarchy. Subkeys can themselves have subkeys. And, any key may or may not have a value associated with it. If you explore a key deep enough in the hierarchy, you see a list of values appear in the right-hand window. In Figure 18.19, you can see the current user's screen appearance. To get there, you have to browse from HKEY_CURRENT_USER to Control Panel to Appearance. You can go one level deeper to Schemes, and view the various desktop schemes that are installed on the system.

The Predefined Keys

In order to know where things are stored in the Registry, you need to know about the predefined keys and what they mean. From Figure 18.18, you can see that the six predefined keys are HKEY_CLASSES_ROOT, HKEY_CURRENT_USER, HKEY_LOCAL_MACHINE, HKEY_USERS, HKEY_CURRENT_CONFIG, and HKEY_DYN_DATA.

FIG. 18.19

The Registry is structured as a tree containing a huge amount of information.

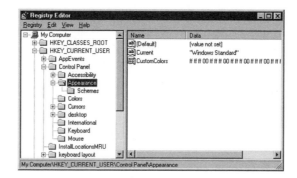

The HKEY_CLASSES_ROOT key holds document types and properties, as well as class information about the various applications installed on the machine. For example, if you explore this key on your system, you'd probably find an entry for the .DOC file extension, under which you'd find entries for the applications that can handle this type of document (see fig. 18.20).

FIG. 18.20

The HKEY_CLASSES_ROOT key holds document information.

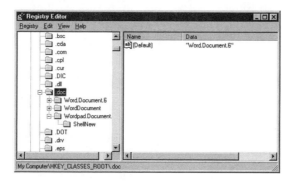

The HKEY_CURRENT_USER key contains all the system settings the current user has established, including color schemes, printers, and program groups. The HKEY_LOCAL_MACHINE key, on the other hand, contains status information about the computer, and the HKEY_USERS key organizes information about each user of the system, as well as the default configuration. Finally, the HKEY_CURRENT_CONFIG key holds information about the hardware configuration, and the HKEY_DYN_DATA key contains information about dynamic registry data, which is data that changes frequently.

Using the Registry in an MFC Application

Now that you know a little about the Registry, let me say that it would take an entire book to explain how to fully access and use the Registry. As you may imagine, the Win32 API features many functions for manipulating the Registry. And, if you're going to use those functions, you sure better know what you're doing! However, you can easily use the Registry with your MFC applications to store information that the application needs from one session to

Part
III

Ch
18

another. To make this task as easy as possible, MFC provides the `CWinApp` class with the `SetRegistryKey()` member function, which creates (or opens) a key entry in the Registry for your application. All you have to do is supply a key name (usually a company name) for the function to use, like this:

```
SetRegistryKey("MyCoolCompany");
```

You should call `SetRegistryKey()` in the application class's `InitInstance()` member function, which is called once at program startup.

After you've called `SetRegistryKey()`, your application can create the subkeys and values it needs the old-fashioned way, by calling one of two functions. The `WriteProfileString()` function adds string values to the Registry, and the `WriteProfileInt()` function adds integer values to the Registry. To get values from the Registry, you can use the `GetProfileString()` and `GetProfileInt()` functions. (You can also use `RegSetValueEx()` and `RegQueryValueEx()` to set and retrieve Registry values.)

N O T E Normally, the `WriteProfileString()`, `WriteProfileInt()`, `GetProfileString()`, and `GetProfileInt()` functions transfer information to and from an INI file. But when you call `SetRegistryKey()`, MFC reroutes these profile functions to the Registry, making adding keys to the Registry an almost painless process. ▪

The Status Bar Demo Application Revisited

In this chapter, you might have noticed that the Status Bar Demo application has a <u>R</u>estore String command on its <u>F</u>ile menu. You can use this command to restore the string that was in the status bar's new pane when you last quit the application. Status Bar Demo stored this string in the Registry and reads it from the Registry when requested to do so.

Status Bar Demo calls `SetRegistryKey("MyCoolCompany")` in the `CStatApp` class's `InitInstance()` function, which creates the MyCoolCompany key if it doesn't exist or opens the key if it does. The first time you quit the application, the `CMainFrame` class calls `WriteProfileString()`, like this:

```
CWinApp* pApp = AfxGetApp();
pApp->WriteProfileString("StatusBarDemo",
    "PaneText", m_paneString);
```

The first line gets a pointer to the application object, which is the class in which the `WriteProfileString()` function is defined. The second line calls `WriteProfileString()` to store the string in the Registry. The function's three arguments are the section key, the item key, and the value for the item key. After this function call, which, in Status Bar Demo, is made in the `CMainFrame` class's `OnDestroy()` function, you have the keys shown in Figure 18.21 in your Registry.

If you select the <u>F</u>ile, <u>R</u>estore String command, the program reads the string from the Registry like this:

```
CWinApp* pApp = AfxGetApp();
m_paneString = pApp->GetProfileString("StatusBarDemo",
    "PaneText", "Default string");
```

FIG. 18.21

The Status Bar Demo application adds several keys to the Registry.

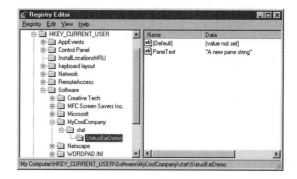

`GetProfileString()`'s three arguments are the section key, the item key, and the item value to return if the key doesn't yet exist.

From Here...

Part III Ch 18

Users of Windows applications expect to find certain user-interface elements in place when they run a new application. Two of the most visible of these interface elements are the toolbar and the status bar, which have become standard parts of just about every Windows application. The toolbar provides the user with shortcut buttons for selecting menu commands, whereas the status bar keeps the user apprised of the application's state, as well as displays messages such as command descriptions.

Although not a visible component of an application, the Registry is the place where you should store data that your application needs from session to session. Using the Registry can be tricky when relying solely on the Win32 Registry functions. However, MFC makes dealing with the Registry as easy as writing values to the old-fashioned INI files. For more information on related topics, please refer to the following chapters:

- Chapter 3, "AppWizard and ClassWizard," brings you up to speed with Visual C++'s excellent automated project and code generators, which create a document class containing the `Serialize()` function.

- Chapter 5, "Messages and Commands," describes MFC's message-mapping system, which enables you to respond to menu commands, as well as enable and disable those commands.

- Chapter 7, "Dialog and Controls," explains how to use dialog boxes in your applications.

- Chapter 12, "Persistence and File I/O," describes another way to store application data, by creating persistent objects.

- Chapter 17, "Building Menus and Dialogs," provides the information you need to build menus, dialog boxes, and other user interface elements.

CHAPTER 19

Printing and Print Preview

If you brought together 10 Windows programmers and asked them what part of creating Windows applications they thought was the hardest, probably at least half of them would choose printing documents. Although Windows' device-independent nature makes it easier for the user to get his peripherals working properly, the programmer must take up some of the slack, by programming all devices in a general way. In the original Windows system, printing was a nightmare that only the most experienced programmers could handle. Now, however, thanks to application frameworks like MFC, the job of printing documents from a Windows application is much simpler to complete. ■

How to create an application with basic printing capabilities

MFC does almost all the work required to get document printing and print preview incorporated into your AppWizard-generated application.

How to use graphics mapping modes to scale printer output

The different Windows mapping modes use different units of measure when interpreting output coordinates.

How to print a multiple-page document

Although MFC can handle basic printing tasks almost automatically, it needs a little help when it comes to multiple-page documents.

How MFC class member functions control the printing process

Knowing which member functions to override is the key to controlling the printing and print preview process in your applications.

Understanding Basic Printing and Print Preview with MFC

MFC handles so much of the printing task for you that, when it comes to simple, one-page documents, there's little you have to do on your own. To see what I mean, follow these steps to create a basic MFC application that supports printing and print preview:

1. Start a new AppWizard project workspace called Print1, as shown in Figure 19.1.

FIG. 19.1

Start an AppWizard project workspace called Print1.

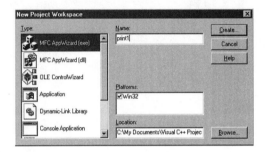

2. Give the new project the following settings in the AppWizard dialog boxes. The New Project Information dialog box should then look like Figure 19.2.

    Step 1: Single document

    Step 2: Default settings

    Step 3: Default settings

    Step 4: Printing and Print preview

    Step 5: Default settings

    Step 6: Default settings

3. Load the CPrint1View.cpp file, and add the following line to the OnDraw() function, right after the TODO: add draw code for native data here comment:

```
pDC->Rectangle(20, 20, 220, 220);
```

FIG. 19.2

The New Project
Information dialog box.

Believe it or not, you've just created a fully print-capable application that can display its data
(a rectangle) not only in its main window, but also in a print preview window and on the printer.
To run the Print1 application, first compile and link the source code by selecting the Build,
Build command or by pressing F7 on your keyboard. Then, select the Build, Execute command
to run the program. When you do, you see the window shown in Figure 19.3. This window
contains the application's output data, which is simply a rectangle. If you select the application's
File, Print Preview command, you see the print preview window shown in Figure 19.4. This
window displays the document as it will appear if you print it. Go ahead and print the document
(select the File, Print command).

FIG. 19.3

This is the Print1
application when you
first run it.

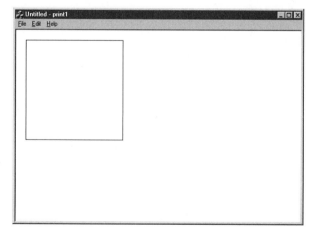

Part
III

Ch
19

FIG. 19.4

This is the Print1 application's print preview window.

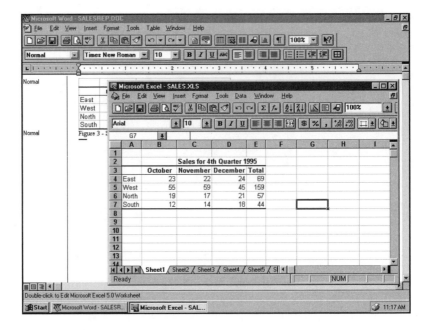

Scaling

One thing you may notice about the printed document and the one displayed on the screen is that, although the screen version of the rectangle takes up a fairly large portion of the application's window, the printed version is pretty tiny. That's because the pixels on your screen and the dots on your printer are different sizes. Although the rectangle is 200 dots square in both cases, the smaller printer dots yield a rectangle that appears smaller. This is how Windows' MM_TEXT graphics mapping mode, which is the default, works. If you want to scale the printed image to a specific size, you might want to choose a different mapping mode. Table 19.1 lists the mapping modes from which you can choose.

Table 19.1   Mapping Modes

Mode	Unit	X	Y
MM_HIENGLISH	0.001 inch	Increases right	Increases up
MM_HIMETRIC	0.01 millimeter	Increases right	Increases up
MM_ISOTROPIC	arbitrary	User defined	User defined
MM_LOENGLISH	0.01 inch	Increases right	Increases up

Mode	Unit	X	Y
MM_LOMETRIC	0.1 millimeter	Increases right	Increases up
MM_TEXT	Device pixel	Increases right	Increases down
MM_TWIPS	1/1440 inch	Increases right	Increases up

A good mapping mode for working with graphics is MM_LOENGLISH, which uses a hundredth of an inch, rather than a dot or pixel, as a unit of measure. To change the Print1 application so that it can accommodate the MM_LOENGLISH mapping mode, replace the line you added to the OnDraw() function with the following two lines:

```
pDC->SetMapMode(MM_LOENGLISH);
pDC->Rectangle(20, -20, 220, -220);
```

The first line sets the mapping mode for the device context. The second line draws the rectangle using the new coordinate system. Why the negative values? If you look at MM_LOENGLISH in Table 19.1, you see that although X coordinates increase to the right as you expect, Y coordinates increase upwards rather than downwards. Moreover, the default coordinates for the window are located in the lower right quadrant of the Cartesian coordinate system, as shown in Figure 19.5. Figure 19.6 shows the print preview window when the application uses the MM_LOENGLISH mapping mode. When you print the document, the rectangle is exactly two inches square. This is because a unit is now 1/100 of an inch and the rectangle is 200 units square.

FIG. 19.5
The MM_LOENGLISH mapping mode's default coordinates are derived from the Cartesian coordinate system.

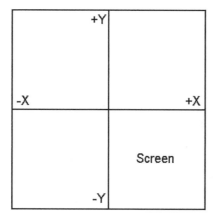

FIG. 19.6

The print preview window now shows a larger rectangle.

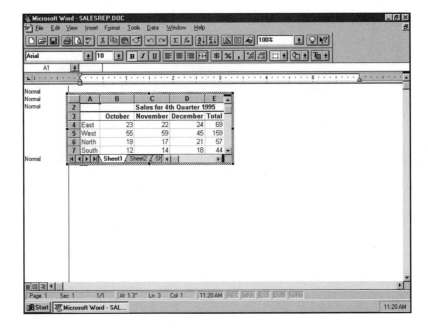

Printing Multiple Pages

When your application's document is as simple as Print1's, adding printing and print previewing capabilities to the application is virtually automatic. This is because the document is only a single page and requires no pagination. No matter what you draw in the document's window (except bitmaps), MFC handles all the printing tasks for you. Things get more complex, however, when you have larger documents that require pagination or some other special handling, like the printing of headers and footers.

To get an idea of the problems with which you're faced with a more complex document, modify the Print1 application as shown in the following steps:

1. Load the Print1View.h file and add the following lines to the end of the declaration's Attributes section:

   ```
   protected:
   int m_numRects;
   ```

   The m_numRects member variable holds the number of rectangles to display.

2. Load the Print1View.cpp file, and add the following line to the class's constructor:

   ```
   m_numRects = 5;
   ```

   This line initializes the number of rectangles to display to five.

3. Use ClassWizard to add the OnLButtonDown() function to the view class, as shown in Figure 19.7.

FIG. 19.7

Use ClassWizard to add the *OnLButtonDown()* function.

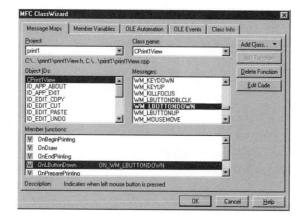

4. Click the <u>E</u>dit Code button, and add the following lines to the new `OnLButtonDown()` function, after the `TODO: Add your message handler code here and/or call default` comment:

```
++m_numRects;
Invalidate();
```

These lines increase the number of rectangles to display.

5. Use ClassWizard to add the `OnRButtonDown()` function to the view class, as shown in Figure 19.8.

FIG. 19.8

Use ClassWizard to add the *OnRButtonDown()* function.

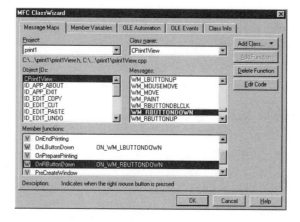

Part
III

Ch
19

6. Click the <u>E</u>dit Code button, and add the lines shown in Listing 19.1 to the new `OnRButtonDown()` function, after the `TODO: Add your message handler code here and/or call default` comment.

Listing 19.1 LST19_01.TXT—Lines for the *OnRButtonDown()* Function

```
if (m_numRects > 0)
{
    —m_numRects;
    Invalidate();
}
```

These lines decrease the number of rectangles to display.

7. Replace the code you added to the Print1 application's OnDraw() function with the lines shown in Listing 19.2.

Listing 19.2 LST19_02.TXT—New Lines for *OnDraw()*

```
pDC->SetMapMode(MM_LOENGLISH);

char s[10];
wsprintf(s, "%d", m_numRects);
pDC->TextOut(300, -100, s);

for (int x=0; x<m_numRects; ++x)
{
    pDC->Rectangle(20, -(20+x*200),
        200, -(200+x*200));
}
```

These lines draw the selected number of rectangles one below the other, which may or may not cause the document to span multiple pages. The preceding code also displays the number of rectangles that have been added to the document.

When you run the application now, you see the window shown in Figure 19.9. The window not only displays the rectangles, but also displays the rectangle count so you can see how many rectangles you've requested. When you choose the File, Print Preview command you see the print preview window. Click the Two Page button, and you see the window shown in Figure 19.10. The five rectangles are displayed properly on the first page, with the second page blank.

Now, go back to the application's main window and click inside the window twice to add two more rectangles. (The rectangle count displayed in the window should be seven.) After you add the additional rectangles, go back to the two-page print preview window. Figure 19.11 shows what you see. The program hasn't a clue as to how to print or preview the additional page. The sixth rectangle runs off the bottom of the first page, but nothing appears on the second page.

FIG. 19.9
The Print1 application now enables you to select the number of rectangles to display.

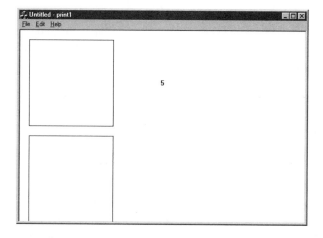

FIG. 19.10
Five rectangles are displayed properly on a single page.

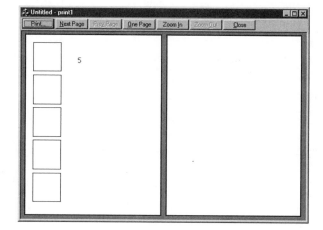

FIG. 19.11
Seven rectangles do not yet appear correctly on multiple pages.

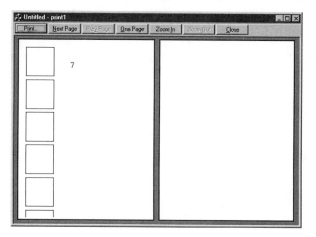

Part
III

Ch
19

The first problem with the program is that you have to tell MFC how many pages to print (or preview). You do this by calling the SetMaxPage() function in the view class's OnBeginPrinting() function. In the unmodified AppWizard application, OnBeginPrinting() looks like Listing 19.3.

Listing 19.3 LST19_03.TXT—The Default *OnBeginPrinting()*

```
void CPrint1View::OnBeginPrinting(CDC* /*pDC*/, CPrintInfo* /*pInfo*/)
{
    // TODO: add extra initialization before printing
}
```

The OnBeginPrinting() function receives two parameters, which are pointers to the printer device context and to a CPrintInfo object. Because the default version of OnBeginPrinting() doesn't refer to these two pointers, the parameter names are commented out to avoid compilation warnings. However, to set the page count, you need to access both the CDC and CPrintInfo objects, so your first task is to uncomment the function's parameters.

Now, you need to get some information about the device context (which, in this case, is a printer device context). Specifically, you need to know the height of a page (in single dots) and the number of dots per inch. You obtain the height of a page like this:

```
int pageHeight = pDC->GetDeviceCaps(VERTRES);
```

The GetDeviceCaps() member function of the CDC class returns specific information about the device context. What information it returns depends upon the constant you use as the function call's single argument. In this case, VERTRES requests the vertical resolution of the device, which, for a printer, is the number of printable dots from the top of the page to the bottom. If you want to get the horizontal resolution, just call GetDeviceCaps(HORZRES).

You may recall that you're currently using the MM_LOENGLISH mapping mode for the device context, which means that the printer output uses units of 1/1000 of an inch. To know how many rectangles are going to fit on a page, you have to know the height of a rectangle in dots. Currently, though, you only know that each rectangle is two inches high with 20/100 of an inch of space between each rectangle. The total distance between one rectangle and the next, then, is 2.2 inches. To figure out how many dots of resolution a rectangle consumes, you have to know the number of dots per inch. You can get this information with another call to GetDeviceCaps():

```
int logPixelsY = pDC->GetDeviceCaps(LOGPIXELSY);
```

The LOGPIXELSY gets the number of vertical dots per inch. If you need to, you can get the number of horizontal dots per inch by calling GetDeviceCaps(LOGPIXELSX).

Now that you know the number of dots per inch, you can calculate the height of a rectangle by multiplying 2.2 times the dots per inch:

```
int rectHeight = (int)(2.2 * logPixelsY);
```

You now have all the information to calculate the number of pages needed to fit the requested number of rectangles. That calculation looks like this:

```
int numPages = m_numRects * rectHeight / pageHeight + 1;
```

Finally, you can tell MFC how many pages you want to print, by calling the `SetMaxPage()` function, which is a member of the `CPrintInfo` class:

```
pInfo->SetMaxPage(numPages);
```

Listing 19.4 shows the completed `OnBeginPrinting()` function. Replace your current `OnBeginPrinting()` with the new version to enable multiple-page printing and print preview.

On the CD

Listing 19.4 LST19_04.TXT—The New *OnBeginPrinting()*

```
void CPrint1View::OnBeginPrinting(CDC* pDC, CPrintInfo* pInfo)
{
    // TODO: add extra initialization before printing

    int pageHeight = pDC->GetDeviceCaps(VERTRES);
    int logPixelsY = pDC->GetDeviceCaps(LOGPIXELSY);
    int rectHeight = (int)(2.2 * logPixelsY);
    int numPages = m_numRects * rectHeight / pageHeight + 1;
    pInfo->SetMaxPage(numPages);
}
```

When you run the new version of the program, add two rectangles by clicking twice in the main window. The displayed rectangle count should then be seven. Now, take a look at the two-page print preview window (see fig. 19.12). Whoops! You've obviously still got a serious problem somewhere. Although the application is previewing two pages, as it should with seven rectangles, it's printing exactly the same thing on both pages. Obviously, page two should take up where page one left off, rather than redisplay the same data from the beginning. Looks like you still have some work to do.

Part

III

Ch

19

FIG. 19.12

The Print1 application still doesn't display multiple pages correctly.

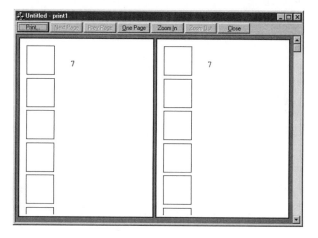

Setting the Origin

To get subsequent pages to print properly, you have to change where MFC believes the top of the page to be. Currently, MFC just draws the pages exactly as told to do in the OnDraw() function, which displays all seven rectangles from the top of the page to the bottom. To tell MFC where the new top of the page should be, you first need to override the view class's OnPrepareDC() function. You can do this easily using ClassWizard, as shown in Figure 19.13. After overriding the OnPrepareDC() function, add to the function the lines shown in Listing 19.5. Add the lines right after the line CView::OnPrepareDC(pDC, pInfo), which calls the base class's version of OnPrepareDC()to perform default processing.

FIG. 19.13

You can use ClassWizard to override the *OnPrepareDC()* function.

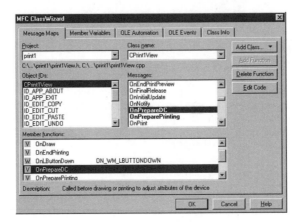

On the CD

Listing 19.5   LST19_05.TXT—Lines for the *OnPrepareDC()* Function

```
if (pDC->IsPrinting())
{
    int pageHeight = pDC->GetDeviceCaps(VERTRES);
    int originY = pageHeight * (pInfo->m_nCurPage - 1);
    pDC->SetViewportOrg(0, -originY);
}
```

The MFC framework calls OnPrepareDC() right before it displays data on the screen or before it prints the data to the printer. If the application is about to display data on the screen, you (probably) don't want to change the default processing performed by OnPrepareDC(). So, you must check whether or not the application is printing data. If it is, the device-context object's IsPrinting() function returns TRUE. Calling this function as part of an if statement prevents your custom code from executing when the application is updating the screen:

```
if (pDC->IsPrinting())
```

If the application is printing, you want to determine which part of the entire data to display on the page that's currently being printed. To do this, you first need to get the height in dots of a printed page:

```
int pageHeight = pDC->GetDeviceCaps(VERTRES);
```

Next, you must determine a new viewport origin (the position of the coordinates 0,0) for the display. Changing the origin tells MFC where to begin displaying data. You already know the size of one page, so the new origin should be the size of a page times the current page minus one. You can determine the page that's about to be printed by accessing the CPrintInfo object's m_nCurPage data member. The entire calculation, then, looks like this:

```
int originY = pageHeight * (pInfo->m_nCurPage - 1);
```

For example, my printer has a page height of 3175. When m_nCurPage is 1, the following calculation gets the page origin:

$$3175 * (1 - 1)$$

This evaluates to 0, which is the first line of the display. Obviously, because the program is printing the first page, it will want to begin on the first line. When the program is ready to print the second page, this calculation gets the new origin:

$$3175 * (2 - 1)$$

This evaluates to 3175, which is the starting line of the second page of data. Succeeding page origins are calculated similarly.

After you calculate the new origin, you need only give it to the program, which you do by calling the display-context object's SetViewportOrg() function, like this:

```
pDC->SetViewportOrg(0, -originY);
```

To see all this in action, compile and run your new version of Print1. When the program's main window appears, click twice in the window to add two additional rectangles to the display. (The displayed rectangle count should be seven.) Then, take a look at the two-page print preview window (see fig. 19.14). Now the program previews the document correctly. If you print the document, it will look the same in hard copy as it does in the preview.

Part

III

Ch

19

FIG. 19.14

The new version of Print1 finally previews and prints properly.

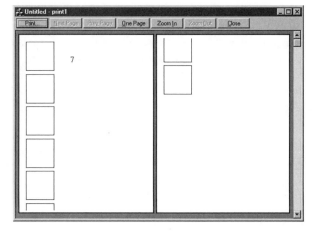

MFC and Printing

Now you've had a chance to see MFC's printing and print preview support in action. As you added more functionality to the Print1 application, you modified several member functions that were overridden in the class, including `OnDraw()`, `OnBeginPrinting()`, and `OnPrepareDC()`. These functions are important to the printing and print preview process. However, there are also other functions that enable you to add even more printing power to your applications. The functions important to the printing process are listed in Table 19.2 along with their descriptions.

Table 19.2 Printing Functions

Function	Description
`OnBeginPrinting()`	Override this function to create resources, such as fonts, that you need for printing the document. You can also set the maximum page count here.
`OnDraw()`	This function serves triple duty, displaying data in a frame window, a print preview window, or on the printer, depending on the device context sent as the function's parameter.
`OnEndPrinting()`	Override this function to release resources created in `OnBeginPrinting()`.
`OnPrepareDC()`	Override this function to modify the device context that is used to display or print the document. You can, for example, handle pagination here.
`OnPreparePrinting()`	Override this function to provide a maximum page count for the document. If you don't set the page count here, you should set it in `OnBeginPrinting()`.
`OnPrint()`	Override this function to provide additional printing services, such as printing headers and footers, not provided in `OnDraw()`.

To complete the printing task, MFC calls the functions listed in Table 19.2 in a specific order. The first function called is `OnPreparePrinting()`, which in turn calls a function called `DoPreparePrinting()`. `DoPreparePrinting()` is responsible for displaying the Print dialog box and creating the printer DC. When you create your application with AppWizard, your view class automatically overrides `OnPreparePrinting()`, embedding the call to `DoPreparePrinting()` in the body of the function, as shown in Listing 19.6.

On the CD

Listing 19.6 LST19_06.TXT—The Default Version of *OnPreparePrinting()*

```
BOOL CPrint1View::OnPreparePrinting(CPrintInfo* pInfo)
{
    // default preparation
    return DoPreparePrinting(pInfo);
}
```

As you can see, OnPreparePrinting() receives as a parameter a pointer to a CPrintInfo object. Using this object, you can obtain information about the print job, as well as initialize attributes such as the maximum page number. Table 19.3 lists the most useful data and function members of the CPrintInfo class, along with their descriptions.

Table 19.3 Members of the *CPrintInfo* Class

Member	Description
GetFromPage()	Gets the number of the first page that the user selected for printing.
GetMaxPage()	Gets the document's maximum page number.
GetMinPage()	Gets the document's minimum page number.
GetToPage()	Gets the number of the last page the user selected for printing.
m_bContinuePrinting	Controls the printing process. Setting the flag to FALSE ends the print job.
m_bDirect	Indicates whether the document is being directly printed.
m_bPreview	Indicates whether the document is in print preview.
m_nCurPage	Holds the current number of the page being printed.
m_nNumPreviewPages	Holds the number of pages (1 or 2) that are being displayed in print preview.
m_pPD	Holds a pointer to the print job's CPrintDialog object.
m_rectDraw	Holds a rectangle that defines the usable area for the current page.
m_strPageDesc	Holds a page-number format string.
SetMaxPage()	Sets the document's maximum page number.
SetMinPage()	Sets the document's minimum page number.

Part
III

Ch
19

When the DoPreparePrinting() function displays the Print dialog box, the user can set the value of many of the data members of the CPrintInfo class. Your program can, in turn, extract or set any of these values, as required for the specific print job. Usually, you'll at least want to call SetMaxPage(), which sets the document's maximum page number, which is then displayed in the Print dialog box. If you know ahead of time how many pages the document will be, you should call SetMaxPage() from OnPreparePrinting(). If you need to calculate a page length based on the selected printer, however, you have to wait until OnBeginPrinting(), when you have a printer DC for the printer.

After OnPreparePrinting(), MFC calls OnBeginPrinting(), which is not only another place to set the maximum page count, but also the place to create resources, such as fonts, that you need to complete the print job. OnPreparePrinting() receives as parameters a pointer to the printer DC and a pointer to the associated CPrintInfo object.

Next, MFC calls OnPrepareDC() for the first page in the document. This is the beginning of the print loop that is executed once for each page in the document. OnPrepareDC() is the place to control what part of the whole document will be printed on the current page. As you saw previously, you can handle this task by setting the document's viewport origin.

After OnPrepareDC(), MFC calls OnPrint() to print the actual page. Normally, OnPrint() calls OnDraw() with the printer DC, which automatically directs OnDraw()'s output to the printer rather than the screen. You can override OnPrint() to control how the document is printed. You can print headers and footers in OnPrint(), and then call the base class's version (which in turn calls OnDraw()) to print the body of the document, as demonstrated in Listing 19.7. Or, you can remove OnDraw() from the print loop entirely by doing your own printing in OnPrint() and not calling OnDraw() at all (see Listing 19.8).

Listing 19.7   LST19_07.TXT—Printing Headers and Footers in *OnPrint()*

```
void CPrint1View::OnPrint(CDC* pDC, CPrintInfo* pInfo)
{
    // TODO: Add your specialized code here and/or call the base class

    // Call local functions to print a header and footer.
    PrintHeader();
    PrintFooter();

    CView::OnPrint(pDC, pInfo);
}
```

Listing 19.8   LST19_08.TXT—Controlling the Entire Printing Process in *OnPrint()*

```
void CPrint1View::OnPrint(CDC* pDC, CPrintInfo* pInfo)
{
    // TODO: Add your specialized code here and/or call the base class

    // Call local functions to print a header and footer.
    PrintHeader();
    PrintFooter();

    // Call a local function to print the body of the document.
    PrintDocument();
}
```

As long as there are more pages to print, MFC continues to call `OnPrepareDC()` and `OnPrint()` for each page in the document. After the last page is printed, MFC calls `OnEndPrinting()`, where you can destroy any resources you created in `OnBeginPrinting()`. The entire printing process is summarized in Figure 19.15.

FIG. 19.15
MFC calls various member functions during the printing process.

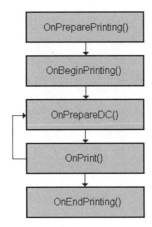

From Here...

Under MFC, printing and print preview can be as simple or complex as you want or need it to be. For example, MFC can print simple one-page documents almost automatically. All you have to do is supply code for the `OnDraw()` function, which is responsible for displaying data both in a window and on the printer. If you need to, however, you can override other member functions of the view class to gain more control over the printing process. You have to do this, for example, when printing multiple-page documents or when you want to separate the display duties of `OnDraw()` from the printing and print preview process.

Please refer to the following for more information on the topics covered in this chapter:

- Chapter 3, "AppWizard and ClassWizard," brings you up to speed with Visual C++'s excellent automated project and code generators.
- Chapter 6, "The Document/View Paradigm," explains how to coordinate your document and view classes in an MFC application.
- Chapter 11, "Drawing on the Screen," describes how to display graphics and text in a window.

Part
III

Ch
19

CHAPTER 20

Debugging

Debugging is still an art form. There seems to be less optimizing going on these days, but C++ developers can find more complex ways to add bugs into their programs than ever, albeit unintentionally. Why optimize when your user community can purchase faster PCs more cheaply than a development team can deliver a product, let alone optimize the 20 percent of code causing the bottleneck? C++ developers know that the C++ programming language allows language-smiths to write some pretty esoteric, hard-to-follow-for-the-average-person code.

Being able to write our own individual memory management schemes, or define how operators work with a myriad of types, can at best be a little intimidating and at worst extremely challenging to detect stray pointers, bad memory, or faulty logic.

This chapter shows you how to use the Developer Studio's debugging features, apply powerful techniques like assertions and code tracing, and demonstrate those MFC classes Microsoft has provided to assist you in finding a large variety of bugs.

Debugging is a proactive process that should occur during development. The worst way to debug is to postpone debugging until some magical time when a monolithic debugging process is supposed to occur. Where, when, and how you add debugging code is probably as important as the code that solves the original problem. You don't have to believe me. Ask Dave Thielen, the author of *No*

Using the Developer Studio basic debugging features

The basic debugging features have taken a long leap from the yesteryear of adding debug print statements. This section shows you how to find and use the debugging mechanisms in the Developer Studio.

Employing *ASSERT* and *TRACE*

Assertions and code tracing are more advanced techniques but they have been implemented for you. Learn how to use these powerful bug-crushing macros in this section.

MFC debugging classes

Microsoft has provided classes in the MFC library that aid in debugging. You'll find out about those here.

Advanced debugging tips

In addition to tried and true favorites like ASSERT, TRACE, and MFC debugging classes, this section has some additional tips that will assist you in orchestrating a complete bug eradication effort.

Bugs! Ask Microsoft why they incorporate ASSERTs and TRACEs into auto-generated code. (You can reach Microsoft Technical Support at (206) 635-7007 in the U.S.) ■

Using the Developer Studio Basic Debugging Features

The Integrated Development Environment (IDE) is the programmer's best friend. It is the context-sensitive, cross-referenced help, online tutorials, menus, hotkeys, and, more recently, speed buttons that provide developers with fingertip access to a wealth of information. To program well in C++, you need to know the language inside and out. Exercising the Developer Studio to its intended capacity helps you develop applications faster and more robustly. The easiest chunk of knowledge to acquire is that someone else probably experienced the problem. Knowing this suggests following in the footsteps of others. Except for the most trivial of problems, consult the online help and use the features provided in the IDE to get information about the state of your program and its objects.

To do this, you need to know all the crevices into which Microsoft has stuffed tips and tidbits to provide you with answers to the mysteries of programs. The days of writing print statements to get information about the state of a program have dwindled and passed for most of us. The developer studio has a wealth of options; read the next section to see where and what they are.

Debugging Menus, Hotkeys, and Toolbars

Hotkeys, menus, and toolbars are generally GUI synonyms for each other. Use menu options to get started because they are more verbose and easily found. Supplanting tedious menu options with hotkeys and speed buttons will ultimately make your development experience more expedient, but, so far, not using them will not be an impediment.

Table 20.1 describes most of the menu options by menu name and menu item name, followed by a description of the purpose of each.

Table 20.1 Menu Options That Promote Integrated Debugging

Menu	Hotkey	Description
File,		Find in FilesNone. Fill out the dialog box (refer to fig. 20.1) with a token, path, and file mask(s); it returns all references to the token.
Edit, Go To	Ctrl+G	Goes to line numbers, bookmarks, or addresses in compiled code. This menu item acts as a good central navigation spot (see fig. 20.2).
Edit, Bookmark	Alt+F2	Accepts an existing bookmark location (as demonstrated in fig. 20.3), enabling you to easily return to that spot with this menu item.

Menu	Hotkey	Description
Edit, Breakpoints	Alt+F9	This feature enables you to set simple, iterative, or conditional breakpoints in your code (see fig. 20.4).
View, Project Workspace	Alt+0	Activates the Project Workspace window.
View, InfoViewer	Alt+1	Activates the InfoViewer Topic window.
View, Output	Alt+2	Activates the output window.
View, Watch	Alt+3	Activates the watch window. (The remaining View options are enabled only during program execution.)
View, Variables	Alt+4	Displays variables in scope window.
View, Registers	Alt+5	Displays the microprocessor's registers in a window.
View, Memory	Alt+6	Enables you to display a snapshot of the state of memory at an address. (Figure 20.5 shows the key state BIOS address with the Caps Lock key on.)
View, Call Stack	Alt+7	Displays the function call stack. You can see an ordered list of the most recent to least recent function calls.
View, Disassembly	Alt+8	Shows the underlying assembly language produced from the compiled C++ source.
Build, Compile	Ctrl+F7	Compiles the active source file. (The Build menu is replaced by a Debug menu during debugging.)
Build, Build	F7	Builds the entire project.
Build, Rebuild All		Rebuilds all files regardless of dependencies
Build, Batch Build		Builds multiple projects in batch mode.
Build, Stop Build	Ctrl+Esc	Terminates the build in progress.
Build, Update All Dependencies		Updates dependencies for selected projects.
Build, Debug, Go	F5	Starts or continues the program.
Build, Debug, Step Into	F11	Steps into a function, as opposed to stepping over a function.

Part
III

Ch
20

continues

Table 20.1   Continued

Menu	Hotkey	Description
Build, Debug	Ctrl+F10	Executes the program up to the cursor location.
Build, Execute	Ctrl+F5	Executes the program.
Build, Settings	Alt+F7	Enables editing of build and debug settings.
Tools, Remote Connection		Enables remote serial, local or Network (TCP/IP) debugging (refer to fig. 20.6.)
Tools, Record Keystrokes	Ctrl+Q	Records keystrokes for playback.
Tools, Playback	Ctrl+Shift+Q	Plays back previously recorded keystrokes.
Recording Window Split		Splits the current window. This enables asynchronous code viewing and editing of the same window.
Window, Hide	Shift+Esc	Hides the active window.
Help, Contents		Displays Help Table of Contents.
Help, Search		Searches for help on a specific topic that includes articles on C++ printed in popular trade journals.
Help, Keyboard		Shows the keyboard help table, shown in Figure 20.7
Help, Tip of the Day		Shows a Tip of the Day.
Help, Technical Support		Displays a complete list of national and international technical suport information.

The File, Find in Files dialog box option, shown in Figure 20.1, enables you to search multiple files for text matching the input text. This dialog box presents a simple interface to options that are reminiscent of Grep, which was originally developed for UNIX systems.

FIG. 20.1

Shows the Find in Files item useful for finding text fragments in multiple source files.

In this section you will see those features showcased that will assist you when debugging applications using the Microsoft Developer Studio. The Edit, Go To (see fig. 20.2) option is a neat spin on an old favorite. This option not only enables you to move the cursor to specific lines of text or addresses of compiled programs, but to bookmarks and references too.

FIG. 20.2

The enhanced Go To dialog box can be used as a central IDE navigation facility.

Figure 20.3 clearly demonstrates the usage of this feature. Place a bookmark on some relevant line of code by selecting Edit, Bookmark enabling you to return to the bookmark quickly. You may also select bookmarks in other projects, which will have the effect of opening that project's workspace.

FIG. 20.3

Create a digital bookmark to relevant locations in your programs, making returning more easy.

The Edit, Breakpoint feature displays a tabbed dialog box (see fig. 20.4) that enables you to set very simple or complex breakpoints. The original breakpoint is the interrupt 3 function provided by the operating system. Setting a breakpoint puts a program on *soft-ice*, enabling you to restart the program. Setting a breakpoint may entail breaking anytime the line of code is executed or after a break condition occurs.

A problematic code fragment may be attacked by breaking when a Windows message occurs or after some number of iterations of code or a specific condition exists. Sometimes errors manifest themseleves only after a number of iterations over the error inducing code, or perhaps you may even have to view the memory (refer to fig. 20.5) used by an object to determine if its state is in error.

In addition to menu items, Table 20.1 contains the hotkeys that are associated with debugging activities. Many of these have menu equivalents; the table notes where this condition exists. Using the hotkeys to navigate the Developer Studio may feel more natural for many veteran programmers because the first text-based GUIs, like WordStar, employed this kind of feature.

Part
III

Ch
20

FIG. 20.4
Shows the Breakpoints dialog box; the simplest use is to break at a line of code.

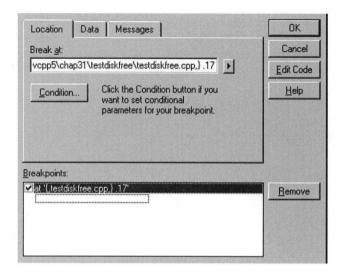

FIG. 20.5
View, Memory enables you to get a snapshot of just about anywhere in memory. (This shot shows the keyboard BIOS state at 0x00000417.)

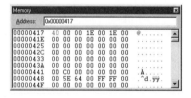

FIG. 20.6
The Tools, Remote Connection dialog box (mentioned in Table 20.1) can be used to connect to and debug remote machines over serial communications lines or using a TCP/IP network connection.

TIP Table 20.1 does not represent an exhaustive list. It does present those readily available as perceived by looking at the menus. The Help, Keyboard menu displays a dialog box that contains all of the keyboard commands by category.

The speed buttons on the menu bar provide an expedient way to perform common tasks. They are listed here for completeness, but today's IDEs provide ToolTips, which give the user a short hint as to the item's activity.

Figure 20.7 shows how the Microsoft Developer Studio Help Keyboard option displays a comprehensive table of Keyboard hotkeys, and Figure 20.8 shows the menu settings as activated by pressing Alt+F7.

FIG. 20.7

The Microsoft Developer Studio Help, Keyboard option displays a comprehensive table of keyboard hotkeys as shown.

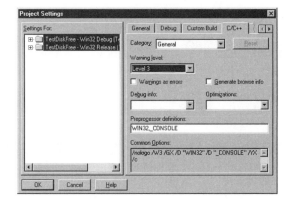

FIG. 20.8

Shows the menu settings activated by pressing Alt+F7.

The entire toolbar suite is shown in Figure 20.9. Those items critical to debugging are along the bottom-most row of buttons. Beginning with the left-most button, which looks like a stack of papers, we have the Compile speed button, followed by Build, Stop Build, a combobox which toggles between debug time and distribution build settings, the Go speed button, Insert/Remove Breakpoint, and the Remove All breakpoints button.

Part

III

Ch

20

Stepping Through a Project in the Developer Studio

A useful skill to develop early on is how to use the debugging features in concert to enable you to maximize debugging and testing within the Microsoft Developer Studio. This section walks you through debugging a *scaffolded* console application which tests the QuickSort algorithm presented in Chapter 32, "Additional Advanced Topics."

N O T E To follow along in this hands-on exercise, load the QuickSortScaffold Project Workspace from the CD-ROM included with this book. ■

FIG. 20.9
Displays the speed
buttons, including those
along the bottom
pertinent to debugging.

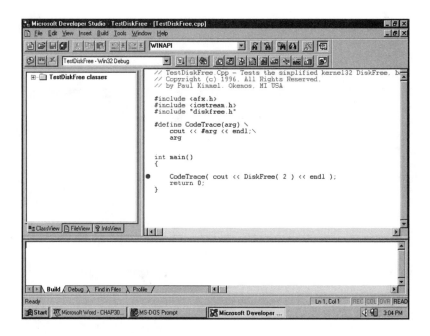

The code is listed first in Listing 20.1 for convenience. The areas of interest are referred to by line number in the listing.

Listing 20.1   SORTS.CPP—Demonstration of Developer Studio Debugging

```
1:    // SORTS.CPP - Contains the definitions and some test scaffolds
2:    // Copyright©  1995. All Rights Reserved.
3:    // By Paul Kimmel.
4:
5:    #include "sorts.h"
6:
7:    // Partitioning function for the RecursiveQuickSort.
8:    template <class T>
9:    unsigned long Partition( T data[], unsigned long left, unsigned long
      ➥right )
10:   {
11:          unsigned long j, k;
12:          T v = data[right];
13:
14:          j = left - 1;
15:          k = right;
16:
17:          for(;;)
18:          {
19:                  while( data[++j] < v )  ;
20:                  while( data[--k] > v )  ;
21:                  if( j >= k ) break;
22:                  Swap(data[j], data[k]);
23:          };
```

```
24:                Swap(data[j], data[right] );
25:                return j;
26:    }
27:
28:    // The QuickSort Function.
29:    template <class T>
30:    void RecursiveQuickSort( T data[], unsigned long left, unsigned long
       ➥right)
31:    {
32:            unsigned long j;
33:            if( right > left )
34:            {
35:                    j = Partition(data, left, right );
36:                    RecursiveQuickSort(data, left, j-1);
37:                    RecursiveQuickSort(data, j+1, right );
38:            }
39:    }
40:
41:    #ifdef SORTS_SCAFFOLD
42:    /* The scaffold is used only for testing the RecursiveQuickSort
43:     * template function. By defining SORTS_SCAFFOLD project-wide we
44:     * can easily remove the define, leaving the scaffold in place for
45:     * another time. For instance, we may want to optimize the quicksort,
46:     * or add additional functionality to this module.
47:     * An added benefit is that the scaffold code also demonstrates
48:     * to other users how to use the quicksort.
49:     */
50:
51:    #include <iostream.h>    // Contains cout object
52:    #include <stdlib.h>              // Contains srand() and rand() functions
53:    #include <time.h>                // Definition of time()
54:
55:    int main()
56:    {
57:            srand((unsigned long)time(NULL)); // Seed the random number
                ➥generator
58:            unsigned long elems[10];
59:            const unsigned long MAX = SIZEOF( elems );
60:            // Fill the elems with random numbers.
61:            for( unsigned long i = 0; i < MAX; i++ )
62:                    elems[i] = rand();
63:            // Sort the elements, specifying the template type implicitly
64:            unsigned long l = 0, r = MAX - 1;
65:            RecursiveQuickSort(elems, l, r );
66:            for( i = 0; i < MAX; i++ )
67:                    cout << i << ".=\t" << elems[i] << endl;
68:            return 0;
69:    }
70:    #endif
```

Part

III

Ch

20

 TIP Scaffolding discrete programs in stand-alone, simple programs is a much easier way to divide and conquer bugs. You are focusing on one very small part of code, and load times and compile times are much quicker than when testing them in a big application. Read Chapter 32, "Additional Advanced Topics," for more information on scaffolding.

The algorithm is a template recursive QuickSort. A QuickSort is used to sort unordered data. It has an order-of-magnitude—a term used to describe its performance—of $O(\log_2 N)$, which grows very slowly for a large number of elements, N. The sort works by dividing partitions of data in half successively until the partitions are very small. Then sorting each partition becomes very fast. The sort performs extremely well for randomly ordered data of very large sets.

In the small world of scaffolding we know the minimum and maximum element sizes, and because the RecursiveQuickSort function is called many times the first thing we can do is place a breakpoint in the Partition function. We might want to watch the first array access—the right index. The Partition function is critical to the success of this implementation of QuickSort, and accessing an array out of bounds is fatal.

To set a breakpoint on line 12, place the cursor on line 12 and press F9; or, place the cursor on line 12, click the right mouse button, and select Insert/Remove Breakpoint. In addition, two other areas in the Partition function where we need to ensure reliability are lines 19 and 20. The Partition function is called with a left and right bound for the relevant partition of array data. In addition to ensuring we don't go out of bounds on the entire array, we must also ensure that the index j is never incremented beyond the value of right and k is never less than 0 or less than left.

To set conditional breakpoints, we'll first set the breakpoints with F9 on lines 19 and 20. Then click the Condition button and enter the conditions for each breakpoint: for line 19, the condition is j<right, and for line 20, the conditions are k >= 0, k >= left. (Use Figure 20.10 as a visual guide.)

TIP   The paragraph on conditional breakpoints actually suggests a more maintainable solution, and one that is more visible. The use of assertions is applied the same way—write testable expressions that throw a flag when violated. For more details, read the section entitled "Employing *ASSERT* and *TRACE*" later in this chapter.

After you have selected good candidate watch zones, you can run the code lickety-split with F5 or step into it with F11. After you begin to step through the application, the Build menu is replaced by an extended Debug menu, as depicted in Table 20.3, and an added plus of this developer centric IDE is the fly-by hints displayed for objects and variables. In addition the View, Watch window is displayed. You may Hide this or any window by giving it the focus and pressing Shift+Esc or using the right mouse menu item, Hide. To View this or other debug windows after hiding them, select the View menu and the window name menu item.

TIP   The fly-by hints are available in debug mode for variables. Place the mouse cursor over an object or variable name for a fly-by quick watch hint.

Table 20.3   Added Menu Items and Hotkeys During Runtime Debugging

Menu	Hotkey	Description
Debug, Go	F5	Executes or restarts the current program
Debug, Restart	Ctrl+Shift+F5	Restarts the currently executing program
Debug, Stop Debugging	Shift+F5	Stops debugging the program
Debug, Break		Stops program execution while debugging
Debug, Step Into	F11	Traces into a line of code
Debug, Step Over	F10	Steps over the next statement
Debug, Step Out	Shift+F11	Exits the current function
Debug, Run to Cursor	Ctrl+F10	Executes until reaching the cursor location
Debug, Step Into Function		Steps through a specific Specific function
Debug, Exceptions		Edits debug actions taken when an exception occurs
Debug, Threads		Sets debug thread attributes
Debug, Settings	Alt+F7	Edits projects build and debug settings
Debug, QuickWatch	Shift+F9	Immediately evaluates variables and expressions

Now that we have our initial breakpoints and break conditions set we can run the scaffold, waiting for the debug engine to notify us if something is wrong.

There are several aspects to debugging during the micro-phase of development. Following is a debugging checklist:

- Set breakpoints for critical values like array indices.
- Step through the program ensuring that critical paths are all tested. (For example, if you have an `if` condition, make sure the `if` and `else` paths are both tested.)
- Step through the program performing quick watches initially, and after some arbitrarily high number of iterations, check the state of the sub-program at the extremities.

There are a few ways to perform the tasks in the preceding checklist. The old fashioned way, which still works, is code tracing: place output statements at key locations providing an ongoing retrospective of activity. The simplest form of this is to print statements to the console.

Part
III

Ch
20

A better way is write to a file, creating a persistent log. With the advent of IDEs, we can now set breakpoints with conditional tests based on the number of iterations or some logical test. The most maintainable way of all may be to use code.

What is referred to is macros like ASSERT, which you will read about in the upcoming section "Employing *ASSERT* and *TRACE*." These functions provide a sustained legacy of the activity that was employed to test key values and critical paths. Using assertions and traces is referred to as the most maintainable way because the codified assertions are self-commenting as to what can go wrong, and they are easily turned on or off by compiler directives, as opposed to a back- and-forth interaction with the IDE.

As an exercise, use the breakpoints we added and the F11 key, stepping through the program to see if you can determine what strengths or weaknesses the QuickSort implementation has. (Hint: The indices are wrapping at the extremities and in some circumstances are throwing Access Violations.)

Development vs. Delivery Constraints

Development constraints are those IDE settings and preprocessor definitions which enable you to quickly find books. Compared to in-development constraints, which would be perceived as obnoxious to users, delivery constrainment is more relaxed. Delivery constrainment includes the (preprocessor) removal of assertions, code tracing, and other debug code added by the IDE, or you, the developer. The constraints placed on a program during development should be at their highest. This includes having TRACE and ASSERT macros in place and active, and in the Microsoft Developer Studio, you may want to set the Warning level to its highest setting. The default setting is Level 3; the highest setting is Level 4 as shown in Figure 20.10.

FIG. 20.10

Set the debug warnings to the highest level, Level 4, during development.

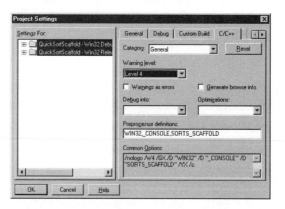

After you have developed your application with all of the debugging constraints—like assertions and code tracing—in place, the objective is not necessarily to remove them, but rather to disable them. Leaving this code in place acts as a road map to what was done to remove bugs and how it was done. It's a kind of a self-commenting history of debugging activity.

Any code that was added can be toggled with conditional compiler directives. Unfortunately, it is not as easy to do with Developer Studio settings. You have to make these changes within the Developer Studio to some extent. Reemphasizing my earlier suggestion that it was easier in some regard to use code to eke out bugs, an especially useful aspect of the Developer Studio is that you can save configurations and toggle any settings all at once. So, while you still have to make each set of configuration settings, you can quickly toggle between an entire configuration—between debug and release constraints—all at once.

To configure development versus delivery constraints for warning Level 4:

1. Click Build, Settings, which opens the Project Settings dialog box, as shown in Figure 20.11.

2. You can then expand the items in the Settings For list. By default, one item is for debug-time, and the other is for the release version.

3. Click the Win32 Debug version and set the C/C++ Warning level to Level 4, as shown in Figure 20.11. The default is Level 3, which we will use for the release version.

FIG. 20.11

The Project Settings dialog box enables you to set configuration items for different phases of development.

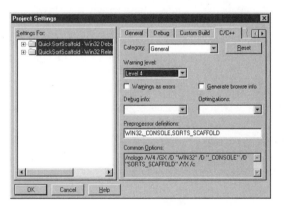

A great convenience is that in addition to being able to set group configuration settings, you can also set individual file settings by expanding the list and modifying configuration items for individual files. To toggle all settings, simply choose between default project configurations from the combobox on the toolbar depicted in Figure 20.9.

Part
III

Ch
20

Employing *ASSERT* and *TRACE*

The notion of asserting something and tracing code has been around awhile. The power and value they add to the software development process is weighty to say the least. Microsoft inserts them in its generated code. One of its best operating systems produced the book *No Bugs!* by Dave Thielen (also from Microsoft), published by Addison-Wesley, and littered with assertions and code tracing. It is shocking that the more subjective issues of quality software design are not taught nor emphasized in college curriculums (based on limited observation, at least). Equally shocking is that many mainstream languages do not directly support good debugging techniques, like assertions and tracing.

Understanding *ASSERT* and *TRACE*

Some of you may not even know what ASSERT and TRACE are. A synonym for assert is declare. When you are asserting, in essence, you are declaring that certain assumptions were made and to transgress these assumptions is a logical violation of the expected state of the program at the point of the assertion. The easiest way to declare an assumption about the state of a program at any point is with code. However, assertions are more powerful than runtime tests but not a replacement for runtime tests. While runtime tests are important, because assertions are for design-time only, assertions are used to throw a big, red, ugly flag up when something that you have declared to be true is not.

T I P   ASSERT and TRACE are debug or design-time only techniques. You never leave assertions or any debug code active in the delivered product. Neither though do you actively cut and paste assertions; rather, you leave them in and let the preprocessor strip them out based on whether _DEBUG is defined or not.

The #define _DEBUG is defined by debug in a Debugging build and undefined in a Release build.

The following short code listing demonstrates a simple assertion. It is not especially useful but demonstrates the technique, what happens (in this case in a console mode application, but a windows assertion produces the same information) when an assertion fails (see fig. 20.12). And, in addition, Figure 20.13 shows the View, Call Stack which shows the _assert function underlying the macro.

FIG. 20.12

The assertion in Assumption.Cpp failed. In a console application the assertion informa- tion is dumped to a CRT window; in a Windows application it is dumped to a message box; the information is the same though.

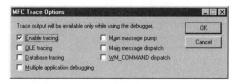

FIG. 20.13

The View, Call Stack shows the _assert function called when the assert macro line of code was reached.

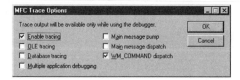

Listing 20.2 (Assumption.Cpp)—A Simple Use of *assert:* My Assumption Was Integers Are Initialized to 0 by Default; They Are Not

```
// Assumptiom.Cpp - Simpe demonstration of assert.
// Copyright  1996. All Rights Reserved.
// by Paul Kimmel. Okemos, MI USA
#include <assert.h>
void main()
{
      const int zero = 0;
      int initializesTo;
      // My assumption is that integers initialize to 0
      // Is the assumption True or False?
      assert( initializesTo == zero );
}
```

For example, suppose you declare an array of 10 elements. It would be an error to ever access the array outside of the range of 0 to 9. You should certainly test for this with conditional statements, and, better yet, use a smart class to bind the testing process to the array. But an assertion is used to tell the developer that her assertion/declaration/assumption is being violated. Using a bad index will cause bad things to happen, especially in Windows programs, so why go on? The assert macro is for the developer. It throws a red flag, so the problem can be addressed before it ever leaves the production line.

N O T E When referring to the assertion macro you may notice several case usages, ASSERT or assert, for example. This is not unintentional carelessness; rather, it was done intentionally because there are variations of the assertion macro—older C uses lowercase assert and MFC uses uppercase ASSERT among others—which all perform roughly the same activity and are used identically. The biggest difference between the variations of assert is the environments in which each is used.

A simple assertion can be implemented with a Boolean argument and some kind of code locator, like a file name and line number. If the Boolean argument evaluates to False then it is determined that the assumption is in error. You can then fix the code or fix the assumption before anyone is the wiser.

The concept behind tracing is that, instead of actively watching your program's activity, you can employ an agent to display the code progress to a second source. Examples of agents have historically been code that writes to a second monochrome monitor's debug windows within one screen, files, and printers. Actively steeping through a program and constantly turning on watch values is a pain in the neck. Using trace and assert macros makes the activity more passive, and you can get volumes of information at execution speeds.

The old standby DOS-based CRT assert macro exists written to the DOS-mode CRT. In a 32-bit, graphical user interface, switching to the text view and the windows view might be disruptive at a minimum. Therefore, Microsoft has created high-powered spinoffs that work within GUI environments—a normal and necessary transition.

What is the big hullabaloo? Well, using macros is flexible because you locate the code when the preprocessor pastes the macro inline. Better still, and much more important, is that asserts and traces become enforcers. With macros like assert, which immediately causes developers to become aware of misapplied logic; and trace, which provides a wealth of information, software developers can create styles of software development. One style is contractual programming. A contractual style of programming is where you document an expectation—like a hypothetical function that processes a pointed-to object, where the caller must ensure that the pointer points to a valid object—and you enforce it with an assertion. A pseudo-code example follows:

```
// Contract: User must ensure pointer is valid
void ProcessObject( Foo * fooObject )
{
        assert( fooObject != 0 );
        // process object
}
```

The developer clearly comments that the user must ensure the validity of the pointer. The assertion macro ensures that the contract is abided by. Contract programming without a town marshal is like lending money without a collection strategy: You may go bankrupt. The obligation in contract programming is that you have relegated responsibility, and if something goes wrong it's not your fault if the contract is broken. More importantly, as with written contracts, you are making it eminently clear what is expected of your programmer-user community.

TIP   Contract programming is useful if all developers are using some common practices. One such practice is that, except for the most trivial of applications, you should build debug versions of your applications before release version.

If a developer avoids abiding by the contract by never enabling debugging, then the curative is to get rid of the programmer.

The notion of tracing is equally important. How can you be reasonably sure your code is bug-free if you have not tested all code paths? And, how can you be sure when you are testing specific code paths? Code-tracing is the solution. If the cliché "information is power" is true then the way to gather information is to apply code tracing and asserting proactively.

Using ASSERT Constructively

There are several specific assert macros. They all work relatively the same way and perform the same action; that is, they send a message to the user of the asserted code and halt all activity, thus enabling the problem to be addressed at its earliest possible opportunity.

Using ASSERT constructively is not that hard. First, you have to determine which assert to use. Simple enough: Use lowercase assert by including <assert.h> and turning it off with #define NDEBUG when building console applications or scaffolding, and use uppercase ASSERT when building everything else. The assert macro can get the __LINE__ and __FILE__ values because they are maintained by the compiler, and the preprocessor pastes code in the macro at the location of the assert. Hence, when the assertion fails, a message indicating an assertion failure, the line number, and file name are readily available. You never have to remove the assertion code either. By toggling `#define NDEBUG` to disable all assertions and `#undef NDEBUG` to enable all assertions, you can write the assertion code as you go and leave the assertions in place for maintenance and future debugging.

The following are rules for using assert:

- Add assertions as you code, avoiding monolithic debug phases. You have the greatest knowledge about what might go wrong at the point which you are first implementing an algorithm.
- Assert all critical code paths.
- Always leave assertions in place, demonstrating that the code has been tested and is testable, and providing clues as to what should be tested for revisions and maintenance.
- Never replace runtime checking with assertions; use both together. Remember, assertions disappear from your code when NDEBUG is defined because the preprocessor strips them out.
- Debug code should always be read-only, never altering the flow of control.
- Use assertions to enforce contractual programming.
- Never distribute applications with assertions enabled. (You will get some really nasty e-mail.)

Some examples of assertions might appear in different code fragments like the following:

```
// #define NDEBUG        // Uncomment to disable assertions
#include <assert.h>
void ApplyRadiation( unsigned long rads )
{
        assert( rads < makesUmGlow );   // never make them glow
        if( rads >= makesUmGlow )       // normal runtime checking
                // perform shutdown
}
```

The preceding code demonstrates an assertion that enforces the notion that it is always a bad practice to irradiate something or someone too much. The test `if( rads >= makesUmGlow )` will shut down the system but the assert will alert us that perhaps we need to find out why bad values are being sent and what code-agent is sending the bad values. Assertions are not only to keep bad things from happening in our code, they are to alert us that they are happening so we can address them.

When you use the wizard to generate MFC applications, you may get a different flavor of assertion, but underneath it is and does pretty much the same thing.

```
////////////////////////////////////////////////////////////////////////
// CMainFrame diagnostics

#ifdef _DEBUG
void CMainFrame::AssertValid() const
{
        CFrameWnd::AssertValid();
}
```

Part
III

Ch
20

Assertions come up in an increasing variety. In the previous example, the idea behind a method like AssertValid() is to apply assertions to an object's state. The function can be used to assert the integrity of an entire object. Regardless of the specific orchestration, the goal behind assertions is to provide an early warning system as to when something goes far astray from its intended course, early and clearly.

Applying Code Tracing Techniques

Microsoft, having easily a user community in the 100+ million range and competing in a global market, is in a position to feel a reeling shockwave if it distributes applications with grave bugs. It is no wonder that its wizards produce code littered with assertions and traces.

These macros eke out things that could make even Microsoft's multi-billion dollar bank book squishy. If you are using MFC code, you don't have a lot of choice whether or not to use them, but Microsoft is using them to combat real economic disaster. If you are not using these techniques, you may want to consider becoming proactive. Learn to employ them by emulating the code produced by the wizards and existing code.

There are actually several TRACE macros. There is TRACE, TRACE0, TRACE1, TRACE2, and TRACE3. The number-suffix indicates the number of parametric arguments beyond a simple string, working much like printf. The different versions were implemented to save data segment space. All of the macros except TRACE place the code in the code segment saving DGROUP space.

The TRACE macros only work when compiled with the debug MFC classes and are stripped out when compiling the release version of an application.

The following code shows you an example of where and how the MFC wizards may add traces to your code.

```
1: if (!m_wndToolBar.Create(this) ||
2:      !m_wndToolBar.LoadToolBar(IDR_MAINFRAME))
3: {
4:      TRACE0("Failed to create toolbar\n");
5:      return -1;       // fail to create
6: }
```

The TRACE macros write to afxDump, which can be defined as a debug window, a debug CRT, or stderr in Console applications. The number-suffix indicates the parametric argument count, and you use the parametric values within the string to indicate the passed data type. For example, to pass an integer:

```
TRACE1("Error Number: %d\n", -1 );
```

Or, to pass two arguments, maybe a string and an integer:

```
TRACE2("File Error %s, error number: %d\n", __FILE__, -1 );
```

The most difficult part of tracing is making it a habit. As with assertions, trace critical code paths to ensure they are actually tested. TRACE problem areas because it is faster to plot the course of code passively as opposed to stepping through it, and employ traces while coding, not in one monolithic effort to squeeze out all bugs at once.

Exploring MFC Debugging Features and Classes

Microsoft's approach to help documentation is to provide you access to articles as well as more traditional explanations and uses of functions. Because of this topic/article approach, there are literally more pages of information in the help system regarding help and diagnostics than were allotted for this entire chapter. Therefore, the approach chosen is to generalize what many of the primary features of the MFC diagnostic support are, tell you what articles and documentation you may find most useful, and finally demonstrate those techniques that support some of these ideas.

The following are general MFC debugging features:

- Debug classes have a virtual Dump constant member function which can be used to perform an object dump. Refer to the help articles entitled "Diagnostics: Dumping Object Contents" and "Diagnostics: Dumping All Objects" for more information, including example programs.

- The TRACE macros enable you to trace program execution. Refer to the help topic "Diagnostics: The TRACE Macro" for information and examples.

- Assertions come in a couple of different forms, all providing roughly the same end result. Refer to the previous section, entitled "Using ASSERT Constructively," of this chapter, and search the help documentation using the keywords assert, ASSERT, ASSERTE, NDEBUG, and AssertValid. The last one is a member function that provides for asserting the component parts of an object in one place. Also, refer to the article "Diagnostics: Checking Object Validity" in the Developer Studio help documentation.

- Memory diagnostics that enable you to check comparative states of memory. Check out "Diagnostics: Detecting Memory Leaks."

- The MFC Tracer utility. The article "TN007: Debugging Trace Options" covers this subject in detail, while the later subsection "Using MFC Tracer" provides a summarized overview.

- An important technique is to employ the DEBUG_NEW macro, which adds file name and line number location information for the debug build, but otherwise works just like new.

Part
III

Ch
20

In addition, it may ease your mind to note that there are only three other details you need to address to enable debugging.

Enabling and disabling debugging is as easy as 1-2-3; just follow these steps:

1. Define _DEBUG in your application, which causes the compiler to link in the MFC debug libraries. To do this, simply set the project configuration combobox to debug build or compile with the command-line option /D_DEBUG.

2. Wrap debug-only code in conditional compiler directives, allowing the preprocessor to strip them out during the release build. The preprocessor wrap takes this form:

```
#ifdef _DEBUG
        // debug code here!!!
#endif
```

3. Use the stand-alone Tracer utility to set the debug level.

In the remainder of this section, you will see examples demonstrating how to perform each of these three steps.

Using MFC Tracer

The MFC Tracer utility is a stand-alone application with an integrated menu item in the Developer Studio. You may run it from the Developer Studio in any way you run any other Windows application. The good news is that application tracing is enabled by default. I'll explain in a second. The bad news is that we need to discuss what that means, so you will know when it is off or on and how to modulate it.

To enable tracing you must define _DEBUG, and the value of `afxTraceFlags`, which modifies an AFX.INI file. It is enabled by default because the default build is a debug build, which defines _DEBUG. And if you look in the Tracer utility (shown in fig. 20.12) you will see that the enable tracing checkbox is also selected by default.

The easiest way to disable tracing is to simply rebuild the entire application with the release configuration selected, which undefines _DEBUG. You can modify the `afxTraceFlags` with code by assigning it flag values defined in `afxwin.h`. Listing 20.3 displays the values of each flag. Use Tracer to set the `afxTraceFlags` value.

Listing 20.3   afxwin.h—Possible Values for *afxTraceFlags*

```
extern AFX_DATA UINT afxTraceFlags;
enum AfxTraceFlags
{
        traceMultiApp = 1,      // multi-app debugging
        traceAppMsg = 2,        // main message pump trace (includes DDE)
        traceWinMsg = 4,        // Windows message tracing
        traceCmdRouting = 8,    // Windows command routing trace (set 4+8 for
                                 ➥control notifications)
        traceOle = 16,          // special OLE callback trace
        traceDatabase = 32      // special database trace
};
```

The code for the Tracer utility is included with Microsoft Visual C++, enabling you to customize it. A good way to experiment with the output provided by different Tracer values is to experiment with this application. As an exercise, load the Project Workspace \MSDev\Samples\ Mfc\Utiltiy\Tracer\Tracer.Mdp. Figure 20.13 shows the Debug output window with Enable tracing and WM_COMMAND dispatch checked in the MFC Trace utility. The highlighted line in the debug window shows the Tracer logging the Cancel button click.

Defining a *Dump* Member Function

The class `CObject` defines the member `Dump`. It is defined as:

```
virtual void Dump(CDumpContext& dc ) const;
```

In English, it is a virtual const member function. The virtual specifier suggests you should override the method in your derived classes, and the const specifier indicates that Dump works with both constant and non-constant objects, but you cannot modify the object state while Dumping.

The Dump member is used with debug compilations only. Therefore, you should wrap the declaration in the *interface* file, otherwise known as a header file, and also wrap the definition in a conditional compiler directive in the *implementation* file, usually referred to as the module or .CPP file.

In the header file, the declaration, including the preprocessor directive, appears like the following:

```
// CNewClass.H - Contains new class definition
// Copyright  1996. All Rights Reserved.
// By Joe CodeWriter
class CNewClass : public CObject
{
public:
        // other class stuff
        #ifdef _DEBUG
        virtual void Dump( CDumpContext& dc) const
        #endif
        // ...
};
```

And in the implementation file, the definition, which includes a code body, might look like this:

```
// CNewClass.CPP - Contains new class member definitions.
// Copyright  1996. All Rights Reserved.
// By Joe CodeWriter
#include "cnewclass.h"

#ifdef _DEBUG
void CNewClass::Dump( CDumpContext& dc ) const
{
        CObject::Dump( dc );     // Dump parent;
        // perhaps dump individual members, works like cout
        dc << "member: " << /* member here */ endl;
}
#endif
```

Using the *CDumpContext* Class   The MFC class CDumpContext is used by the Dump method to direct dump output to the debug window if the afxDump object is used. The object afxDump is instantiated as a CDumpContext when you are debugging. Typically this is the object you pass to Dump methods. The CDumpContext has an overloaded ostream<< operator, which you can use to write the contents of your object to either the output-debug window for Windows applications or the stderr (usually the Console) for Console applications.

If you want to use another CDumpContext object, the constructor is defined to take a pointer to a CFile object. Therefore, you have to initialize a CFile object first. The code listing in the next section demonstrates defining a Dump method, using the afxDump object and defining a CFile and CDumpContext object.

Part
III

Ch
20

A Demo Using *CDumpContext*, *CFile*, and *axfDump*   The demo in this section provides a codified example of using the MFC debugging class CDumpContext, another MFC class CFile, which is an argument type of CDumpContext's constructor, and the global axfDump object. The debug window output from this demo and the output CFile code are in Listing 20.4.

Listing 20.4   DumpContextDemo.Cpp—Demonstrates the MFC Debugging Class *CDumpContext* and *CFile*

```
1:   // DumpContextDemo.Cpp - Demonstrates using Dump, CDumpContext, afxDump,
         ➥and CFile
2:   // Copyright  1996. All Rights Reserved.
3:   // by Paul Kimmel. Okemos, MI USA
4:   #include <afx.h>
5:   // _DEBUG defined for debug build
6:   class CPeople : public CObject
7:   {
8:   public:
9:           // constructor
10:          CPeople( const char * name );
11:          // destructor
12:          virtual ~CPeople();
13:          #ifdef _DEBUG
14:                  virtual void Dump(CDumpContext& dc) const;
15:          #endif
16:  private:
17:          CString * person;
18:  };
19:  // constructor
20:  CPeople::CPeople( const char * name) : person( new CString(name)) {};
21:  // destructor
22:  CPeople::~CPeople(){ delete person; }
23:  #ifdef _DEBUG
24:  void CPeople::Dump( CDumpContext& dc ) const
25:  {
26:          CObject::Dump(dc);
27:          dc << person->GetBuffer( person->GetLength() + 1);
28:  }
29:  #endif
30:  int main()
31:  {
32:          CPeople person1("Nicholas Benavides");
33:          CPeople person2("Jim Kimmel");
34:          CPeople person3("Alex Kimmel");
35:          // Use existing afxDump with virtual dump member function
36:          person1.Dump( afxDump );
37:          // Instantiate a CFile object
38:          CFile dumpFile("discardme.txt", CFile::modeCreate ¦
39:                  CFile::modeWrite);
40:          if( !dumpFile )
41:          {
42:                  afxDump << "File open failed.";
43:          }
44:          else
45:          {
```

```
46:                    // Dump with other CDumpContext
47:                    CDumpContext context(&dumpFile);
48:                    person2.Dump(context);
49:          }
50:          return 0;
51: }
```

At line 4, the `<afx.h>` header file is included, which contains the `CObject` class definition and provides access to `afxDump`. The comment on line 5 was placed there to indicate that either the `/D_DEBUG` switch or definition of _DEBUG is defined when you compile the Debug version in the Developer Studio.

Lines 6 through 18 define a class `CPeople` derived from `CObject`. The purpose of the class was to demonstrate the placement of the redefined virtual `Dump` method and the conditional compiler wrap. When you are done testing a program using `Dump`, you will actually need to wrap all uses of `Dump` in conditional compiler directives.

Lines 23 through 29 show the `Dump` member definition. Use it to display the contexts of the object to a `CDumpContext` like the output-debug window (see fig. 20.14) or a text file (see Listing 20.5).

FIG. 20.14

Shows the debug-output window where the *afxDump* object writes its output.

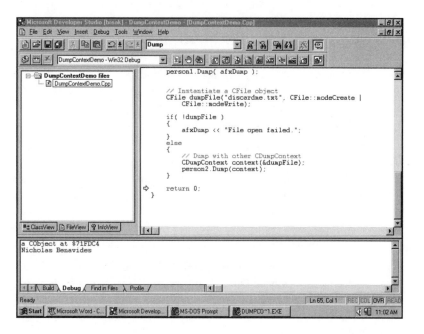

In the test main on line 16 the DumpContext `afxDump` which writes the output to the debug window, is used. Lines 38 to 48 demonstrate how you can create an alternate `CDumpContext`. Specifically, line 38 creates a `CFile` object. Line 47 shows you how to create and use a `CFile` object to create an alternate `CDumpContext`, passing the address because the `CDumpContext` constructor takes a pointer to a `CFile`. And finally, on line 48, the `CDumpContext` object can also be passed to the CPeople Dump method. The uses are similar whether you are writing Windows GUI applications or are actually targeting a Console program.

The debug-output window is shown in Figure 20.14. Refer to it during the description of the Dump function's output. The text file output, demonstrating the role of the CFile object is as follows:

Listing 20.5   discardme.txt—Output File from *DumpContextDemo.Exe*

```
a CObject at $71FDE4
Jim Kimmel
```

If you have learned the C++ language, then using any class requires relatively the same kinds of processes. You might ask, where was the CObject base class instantiated? Remember that if a child class does not call a constructor expressly, then the default base constructor is called. If you step through the demo program you see that that is exactly what happens.

There are additional measures that can be employed with MFC debugging classes. Among the lot is the CMemoryState class and the DEBUG_NEW macro. These are described in the last section of the chapter "Techniques for Sealing Memory Leaks."

MFC Run-Time Type Identification

MFC does not use the ANSI C++ specification for Runtime Type Identification (RTTI). Instead, MFC associates a class named CRunTimeClass with CObject, offering runtime type checking. One article you may find informative is CObject Class: Accessing Run-Time Class Information. The following section summarizes the idea of runtime checking using this class, and offers a short code example.

Before we embark, let me offer a few things for you to rattle about in your head. RTTI is a more recent introduction into the ANSI C++ specification. And so too is the introduction of non-RTTI classes like CRuntimeClass. The reason for this is because originally it was intended that you use virtual methods and enable polymorphism to determine or perform the precise, type-specific behavior. You may come across some rare circumstances where you feel you absolutely need to know the type of an object, but rampant use of type checking is probably indicative of a suffering design. With that in mind, let's take a look at what MFC has to offer.

There are several pieces of the puzzle to be assembled before you can use the MFC type-checking mechanisms. One is that the base class CObject has a method called IsKindOf. To use IsKindOf you need to use three macros in your code, the first, which detects compatibility, is IMPLEMENT_DYNAMIC(CChildClass, CParentClass). Another is

```
DECLARE_DYNAMIC( CChildClass )
```

in the class definition. And, add

```
RUNTIME_CLASS( CChildClass )
```

to the implementation (also referred to as the .CPP) file. Listing 20.6 lists the RunTimeDemo.Cpp source, which demonstrates the locality of the assembled pieces.

Listing 20.6 RunTimeDemo.Cpp—Demonstrates the MFC *CRuntimeClass*

```
1:      // RunTimeDemo.Cpp - Demonstrates using the CRuntimeClass.
2:      // Copyright  1996. All Rights Reserved.
3:      // by Paul Kimmel. Okemos, MI USA
4:      #include <afx.h>
5:      class CTypeCheck : public CObject
6:      {
7:              // Preprocesor generates runtime type declarations
8:              DECLARE_DYNAMIC( CTypeCheck );
9:      public:
10:             CTypeCheck(){};
11:     };
12:     // Preprocessor generates runtime type definitions.
13:     IMPLEMENT_DYNAMIC( CTypeCheck, CObject );
14:     int main()
15:     {
16:             CObject * newObject  = new CTypeCheck();
17:             if( newObject->IsKindOf( RUNTIME_CLASS( CTypeCheck) ))
18:                     afxDump << "newObject Is CTypeCheck\n";
19:             else
20:                     afxDump << "type mismatch\n";
21:             delete newObject;
22:             return 0;
23:     }
```

The example in Listing 20.6 is contrived for the sole purpose of demonstrating the relative placement of each of the pieces and the use of the member functions. The class CTypeCheck is derived from a public CObject. CObjects have a relationship to the struct CRuntimeClass via the method IsKindOf, the macros mentioned previously, and the _GetBaseClass member, which returns a pointer to a CRuntimeClass. (That's why you don't see CRuntimeClass explicitly in the preceding code.)

In the class (refer to line 8 of Listing 20.6), you need to call the macro DECLARE_DYNAMIC(CTypeCheck)—with whatever class name it is—to generate the class code necessary to use MFC runtime checking. If you examine the macro defined in afx.h, you will see why a macro is used. The macro definition is shown in Listing 20.7.

Part
III

Ch
20

Listing 20.7 afx.h—Short Listing Head

```
1:      // Shows the non-DLL version of DECLARE_DYNAMIC
2:      #define DECLARE_DYNAMIC(class_name) \
3:      public: \
4:              static AFX_DATA CRuntimeClass class##class_name; \
5:              virtual CRuntimeClass* GetRuntimeClass() const; \
6:      #endif
```

The macro adds two public declarations to your class (lines 4 and 5). Line 4 explains why you have to use macros: the ## is referred to as string-izing; in essence, the preprocessor generates code by concatenating a specific name—the one you passed to the macro—to the word class. Using our demo program, the resultant additional class definition looks like this for the CTypeCheck class:

```
public:
        static AFX_DATA CRuntimeClass classCTypeCheck;
        virtual CRuntimeClass * GetRuntimeClass() const;
```

If you generate a map file, it is easy to find the names in the produced symbol table. Fortunately, we only need to use the macros. Of course, if there are declarations in the class, then we need the definitions in the CPP file too. That's what the macro IMPLEMENT_DYNAMIC does on line 12. DECLARE_DYNAMIC makes the class entries and IMPLEMENT_DYNAMIC completes the definitions. It, too, is a macro because of the string-izing code generation performed by the preprocessor.

The definition of the RUNTIME_CLASS macro plays the same kind of role. It enables you to get the correct name when you are ready to use type checking. The definition

```
#define RUNTIME_CLASS(class_name) (&class_name::class##class_name)
```

of the macro produces a reference to the static class member. The code generated by the macro and preprocessor will be

```
(&CTypeCheck::classCTypeCheck)
```

and macros, again, were used for their ability to string-ize/generate code.

In line 16 of Listing 20.6 we use polymorphism to create a dynamic (heap-allocated) child type, pointed to by a CObject pointer. Then, in line 17, we use our rather contrived example to illustrate the use of the IsKindOf member and the RUNTIME_CLASS macro.

This type of runtime checking uses macro-trickery and contrivances. It will be ultimately better when RTTI is directly supported by the implementation. As a last word, before you resort to runtime checking, consider your design and see if virtual functions can provide the desired effect.

Advanced Data Watching Tips

In this section we take a look at those data watching features that make debugging easier and more enjoyable. My favorite is probably Data Tips. Data Tips are those hint-like messages that are displayed when you place the mouse over an object or variable. Besides Data Tips, we look at how the QuickWatch dialog box, the tabbed Watch dialog box, and AutoExpand and AutoDowncast make your job considerably easier.

What Are AutoExpand and AutoDowncast?

AutoDowncast was a feature in Visual C++ 2.0. It has been extended in this version to be a feature of QuickWatch windows (see fig. 20.16) as well as Watch windows (see fig. 20.17).

AutoDowncasting is what the compiler does to enable you to access the members of a child class when what you have is a pointer to a parent class. What AutoDowncast does is add an extra pointer to a parent, so if you have a pointer object like CObject (refer to Listing 20.4), but it really points to a child class such as CPeople, you can see (in a watch window) the entire object. This feature makes it easier to debug when you are employing polymorphism.

AutoExpand is useful too. When debugging, AutoExpand shows you the important aspects of a watched object. If you look at Figure 20.18, you may notice that the internal CString object person (from the demo in Listing 20.4) shows the value we might be interested in as regards to a CString object. A CString contains many things, including a char * (which is an address and a length value), but what we are most interested in is AutoExpanded. You can certainly access the rest of the members, but this approach provides what is arguably the most useful data, conserving "screen real estate."

Using Data Tips, Watch Windows, and QuickWatch

The Data Tips feature (see fig. 20.15) is my favorite. Simply pass the mouse over the object or variable name in the text window, and, as long as the object is in scope, a fly-by hint pops up showing you the AutoExpand value. The developers were even considerate enough to avoid evaluating objects or values that might throw exceptions.

FIG. 20.15

Shows a Data Tip displayed while an application is being run.

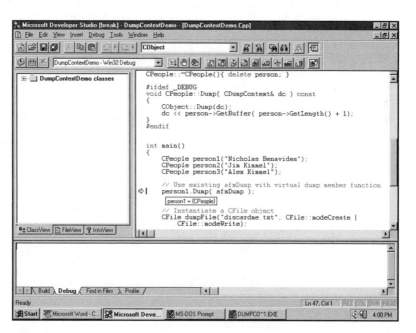

The QuickWatch window (see fig. 20.16) is easily accessed by placing the cursor on the object or variable in scope to be watched, clicking the right mouse button, and selecting QuickWatch. The QuickWatch window can be navigated by clicking plus symbols to expand nodes and minus symbols to collapse nodes. Note that in Figure 20.16—referring to the person member object—that the QuickWatch takes nice advantage of AutoExpand. With a QuickWatch view you can click the Add Watch button to add the current variable to one of the watch windows. Additionally, you can modify and Recalculate values in the QuickWatch window.

FIG. 20.16

The QuickWatch window.

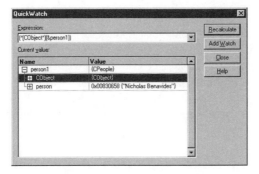

The Watch window stays open permanently, as opposed to the QuickWatch, which is a modal dialog box. The Watch window has four tabs, as illustrated in Figure 20.17. You can group items on the watch window by regions, scope, file, or however it makes sense to solve the problem at hand. You can use the View, Watch menu command to display the watch, the right mouse speed menu to Hide the Watch, and add objects from the QuickWatch dialog box to open the watch. Select the Watch tab you want an object to be displayed on prior to adding the object from QuickWatch. An intuitive tool is one that does things you might suppose, and you can cut from the edit window and paste to a watch window too, bypassing the QuickWatch phase.

FIG. 20.17

Add elements to the tabbed Watch window from the QuickWatch dialog box.

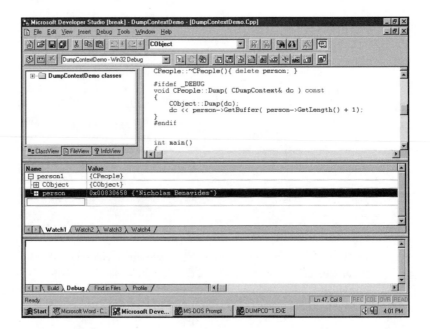

Techniques for Sealing Memory Leaks

A memory leak can be the most pernicious of errors. Memory leaks can take on many guises. You can introduce memory leaks in simple ways like forgetting to delete a heap-allocated object. You might accidentally delete a single element having allocated an array. Reassigning a pointer to a new heap without deallocating what was already pointed to leaves a hole of unrecoverable memory. Returning a reference to a chunk of memory from a function invites an opportunity for losing a block of memory.

The following fragments demonstrate the form of some very common errors that may not manifest themselves but cause memory leaks like those mentioned in the preceding paragraph.

```
// simple pointer leaving scope
{
  int * one = new int;
  *one = 1;
} // left scope no delete

// mismatched new and delete: new uses delete and new[] uses delete[]
{
float * f = new float[10];
// use array
delete f; // Oops! Deleted f[0] correct version is delete [] f;
}

// pointer of new memory goes out of scope before delete
{
    const char * DeleteP = "Don't forget P";
    char * p;
    strcpy( p = new char[strlen(DeleteP) + 1], DeleteP );
} // scope ended (e.g. a function or arbitrary scope)
  // before p delete[]

// returning heap allocated memory froma function
int * ReturnAnArrayOfIntegers()
{
    return new int[100];
}
```

The code fragments all represent ways in which memory can be allocated and the references lost before deallocation. Once the reference—in simple terms a pointer—goes out of scope you cannot reclaim the memory and no one else can use it, either. The last sample is not an error, but it can be because it requires the user of the function to remember to be responsible for deleting the memory. (There is at least one standard library function, strdup, that employs this exact technique, however.)

There is an entire class of memory management problems that can introduce serious memory leaks. User defined memory management is challenging. Exceptions occurring in functions can bypass the call to delete when the stack unwinds. Sometimes programs seem to run perfectly for short periods, all the while dropping little chunks of memory. However, that same program seizes up after running for an extended period of time. Thus, the problem is twofold: one is to know an error exists, and the other is to find the source of the problem.

In this section are three methods that will assist you in discovering a leak, the well-spring from whence it came, and a technique introduced in the *standard template library* (STL)—a template class called auto_ptr—which even bottles up leaks occurring during an exception. Some of the memory sealing techniques covered in this section are:

- DEBUG_NEW, introduced in an earlier section
- The MFC CMemoryState class
- Implementing an auto_ptr template class

You may certainly be able to disclose other tips for sealing memory leaks, but after having read this section, combining it with the rest of the chapter, you should be well armed in the war on bugs.

Here are some additional resource materials in the Help system you may find helpful:

- Diagnostics: Dumping All Objects explains how to perform and interpret a diagnostic dump.
- Diagnostics: Tracking Memory Allocations describes DEBUG_NEW.
- The topic CrtMemDumpAllObjectsSince has an eight-page code listing related to heap usage.
- The topic CrtDumpMemoryLeaks has an additional four-page code listing.
- Diagnostics: Detecting Memory Leaks discusses techniques MFC provides related to finding and removing memory leaks.

Using the MFC *CMemoryState* Class

You will find the CMemoryState class useful. It is easy to use and to the point. If you have a leak, it tells you (more or less) what, where, and how much. In keeping with the spirit of the user-friendliness of the MFC class CMemoryState, Listing 20.7 is an easy-to-follow, to the point program that demonstrates the kind of output you will get.

First, let me offer a few reminders. One is that this is a debug class, so you need to use conditional compiler directives to isolate the debug code. If you can localize that code, it makes the rest of your program more readable. When building a debug project, also remember that you will be linking the debug MFC libraries in by default. As a final note, if you get a linker LNK2001, then try rebuilding with the multi-threaded Debug libraries.

The code in Listing 20.7 simply allocates an array of characters that are not deallocated, causing a memory leak.

Listing 20.7 MemoryStateDemo.Cpp—Demonstrates the *CmemoryState* Class

```
 1:    // MemoryStateDemo.Cpp - Demonstrates using the MFC CMemoryState class
 2:    // Copyright  1996. All Rights Reserved.
 3:    // by Paul Kimmel
 4:    #include <afx.h>
 5:    #include <string.h>
 6:    // Using a macro cleans up the code where it is used.
 7:    #ifdef _DEBUG
 8:            CMemoryState start, stop, diff;
 9:            #define SnapShotStart() start.Checkpoint()
10:            #define SnapShotStop()  \
11:                    stop.Checkpoint();      \
12:                    if( diff.Difference( start, stop ))   \
13:                    {       TRACE( "Memory Leaked\n" );              \
14:                            diff.DumpStatistics();               \
15:                    }
16:    #else
17:            #define SnapShotStart()
18:            #define SnapShotStop()
19:    #endif
20:
21:    int main()
22:    {
23:            const char * WELCOME = "Welcome to Valhalla Tower material
                ➥Defender!\n";
24:            SnapShotStart();
25:            // Wow! Looks like it could have some errors.
26:            char * welcome;
27:            strcpy( welcome = new char[strlen(WELCOME) + 1], WELCOME );
28:            SnapShotStop();
29:            return 0;
30:    }
```

To use CMemoryState, you need to define three CMemoryState objects: one, which is used to take a snapshot of the heap for your starting point, another for an ending point, and a third to record the difference between the two. You can instantiate the three objects any time before you use them (refer to line 8). The snapshot is taken when you call the Checkpoint method (as in line 9). Passing the two relative points to the Difference method returns 0 if the images are identical, and returns non-zero otherwise.

Lines 7 through 19 can be written once, inserted into a header file, thus cleaning up your program and making it very easy to use this technique anywhere. The macro works simply: If the _DEBUG is defined, then the three objects and two other macros are defined. The macros (on lines 9 and 10 and 17 and 18 for non-debug versions) simply enable the preprocessor to paste the code automatically wherever they are used.

The code on lines 9 through 15 call start.Checkpoint(), stop.Checkpoint(), and the diff.Checkpoint(), spitting out the Difference (see Listing 20.8) if the two heap states differ. The addition of the TRACE macro (line 13) helps make it evident that what you are seeing is a memory leak condition. However, if you check Listing 20.8 you may notice that the CMemoryState object also did that on line 9.

If _DEBUG is undefined, as is the case with the Release build, then the macros are stripped out by the preprocessor. Note that the use of the CMemoryState object becomes very clean (lines 24 and 28).

The sample code on lines 20 to 21 allocate a dynamic character array with that bit of esoteric code on line 27, purposely forgetting to return the memory to the heap. Line 27 is a necessary reminder to add 1 to any string length, for the null character. As an exercise, remove that and see if the CMemoryState objects catch you.

Listing 20.8   Output from *MemoryStateDemo.Exe*

```
 1:    Memory Leaked
 2:    0 bytes in 0 Free Blocks.
 3:    46 bytes in 1 Normal Blocks.
 4:    0 bytes in 0 CRT Blocks.
 5:    0 bytes in 0 Ignore Blocks.
 6:    0 bytes in 0 Client Blocks.
 7:    Largest number used: 46 bytes.
 8:    Total allocations: 46 bytes.
 9:    Detected memory leaks!
10:    Dumping objects ->
11:    {18} normal block at 0x00830658, 46 bytes long.
12:     Data: <Welcome to Valha> 57 65 6C 63 6F 6D 65 20 74 6F 20 56 61 6C 68 61
13:    Object dump complete.
14:    The program MemoryStateDemo.exe has exited with code 0 (0x0).
```

As you can see from Listing 20.8, the CMemoryState.Difference() method provides quite a bit of detail. Here is a brief explanation. Line 1 is the output from TRACE. Line 3 indicates our error: that there were 46 bytes in one block leaked. And line 9 sums it all up nicely; there were errors. A complete explanation is found in the online help in the article Diagnostics: Detecting Memory Leaks. In essence, each line tells you the kind of memory leaked.

Using *DEBUG_NEW*

The last example provided us with a lot of information. Fortunately for us, though, the program was contrived, because, as is, it is easy to figure out what went wrong. In a real program, it may not be so easy. A straightforward modification to the way we do business, at no extra Release build cost, and MFC gives us the added information that makes it a trivial matter to track down the culprit.

The DEBUG_NEW macro works just like new when you build the release version. More importantly is what it does when you are debugging. When you are building the Debugging version of your application the DEBUG_NEW macro enables the preprocessor to include an overloaded new operator which tags a file name and line number to every allocation. The CMemoryState object can use this information when you DumpStatistics, for example.

NOTE As a reminder new and delete are operators, though they may appear to be more appropriately labeled as functions. And, almost all operators are overloadable, which includes new and delete. The file name and line number are already maintained by the compiler in __LINE__ and __FILE__, using a macro enables the overloaded new an oppotunity to use these maintained macros. ▪

If we had used DEBUG_NEW, line 11 of Listing 20.8 goes from

```
11: {18} normal block at 0x00830658, 46 bytes long.
```

to the more explicit

```
11. MemoryStateDemo.Cpp(36) : {18} normal block at 0x00830658, 46 bytes long
```

Notice that the file and the line number are added to the Dump. The (36) right after the file name is the line number. (White space is removed in the text listing. That is why the listing line numbers in 20.6 and the output do not jive.)

Using DEBUG_NEW is easy too. To use it define a macro for the regular new

```
#define new DEBUG_NEW
```

This macro enables you to use new as before and the preprocessor plugs in the DEBUG_NEW call, which by the way, is the debug version during the debug build and regular for the Release build. The document Diagnostics: Tracking memory Allocations will also inform you that if you use the macros IMPLEMENT_DYNCREATE and/or IMPLEMENT_SERIAL then define the macro (#define new DEBUG_NEW) after the last use of these macros. That's all there is to it.

Blocking Memory Leaks During an Exception

What is an auto_ptr class and why should you consider using it? To clearly understand how an auto_ptr class is contrived and why it works, let's consider some related, general background information, before we dive into an implementation.

When a program is executing within a particular scope, like a function, all variables allocated in that function are generally allocated in the stack space. The stack, like an accordion, shrinks and grows. It does so because it is a temporary storage space. The stack is used to store the current execution address prior to a function call, the arguments passed to the function, and the local function objects and variables. When the function returns, the *stack pointer* is reset to that location where the prior execution point was stored. (You have little control over this process.)

Effectively, by restoring the stack pointer to its position prior to the function call, the program has made the space available to whatever else needs it, which means those elements allocated on the stack in the function are gone. This process is referred to as *stack unwinding*.

NOTE Objects or variables defined with the keyword static are not allocated on the stack. ▪

Stack unwinding is also what happens when an unhandled exception occurs. To reliably restore the program to its state before an exception occurred in the function, the stack is unwound. Stack-wise variables are gone and the destructors for stack-wise objects are called and are also gone. Unfortunately, the same is *not* true for dynamic objects. The handles (for example, pointers) are unwound but delete is never called. The result is the *slicing problem*.

N O T E   The slicing problem refers to memory leaks caused by pointers that lose the address of heap allocated memory before delete is called. ▪

It may be easy enough to handle this problem by putting exception handlers everywhere you use new and delete, placing the new in a try block and delete in a catch block, but then you would have messy exception handlers everywhere.

The smart pointer class implemented in the standard template library solves the problem. Basically, the clever designers implemented a template class. (Listing 20.9 demonstrates some of the key members required to make the class work.)

Listing 20.9   A Scaled Down Version of the *auto_ptr* Class

```
1:      // This class is not complete. Use the complete definition in the
           ➥Standard Template Library.
2:      template <class T>
3:      class auto_ptr
4:      {
5:      public:
6:              auto_ptr( T *p = 0) : rep(p) {} // store pointer in the class
7:              ~auto_ptr(){ delete rep; }               // delete internal rep
8:              // include pointer conversion members
9:              inline T* operator->() const { return rep; }
10:             inline T& operator*() const { return *rep; }
11:     private:
12:             T * rep;
13:     };
```

The class encapsulates the pointer, providing access through operator functions. Instantiating an object, given some class C, with the auto_ptr might look something like this:

```
auto_ptr<C> dialog_ptr(new C());
```

Now we can access members of C via the auto_ptr, like this:

```
dialog_ptr->Method();    // pseudo-code
```

We do not have to explicitly delete this object, even in the event of an exception, because the auto_ptr is a stack-wise object. When a stack-wise object goes out of scope, its destructor is called and, in this case, it calls delete on the contained object C.

There are many aspects of C++ you have to master before creating and using classes like this. You must understand the template idiom, operator and function overloading, and you must learn to use the classes in the STL.

The preceding stripped down class is intentionally incomplete; there are many issues left that must be addressed for a complete definition of the class.

From Here...

In this chapter, you were introduced to existing concepts as they are implemented in Visual C++ and MFC and new concepts that will help you eke the bugs out of all of your code. No one technique is sufficiently more important to mitigate the necessity for learning the others, but if you have to choose a particular tactic to master first, then choose `assert`. Assert everything. If you do not know what testable values and assumptions are for the code you are writing, reconsider using that algorithm at all.

Some techniques, like the way MFC implements runtime checking, are unique to Microsoft's implementation of C++. Expect to see the ANSI C++ standard adopted in the near future. There are many topics you can learn to master writing bug-free code. Many of those topics, like codetracing, assertions, using the IDE, and implementing smart pointers, were discussed in this chapter.

There are many interesting discussions, articles, and books on writing bug-free code. Since maintenance and testing encompass the greatest cost, it makes good dollar sense to spend at least as much time and resource dollars on using the bug hunting techniques described in this chapter as you spend on every other aspect of programming, if not more.

To learn about other techniques and tools, see these chapters:

- Chapter 2, "Developer Studio Commands," describes how to use the entire developer studio, which includes buttons, menus, and hotkeys.
- Chapter 32, "Additional Advanced Topics," covers topics related to scaffolding, and discrete subprograms.

Part
III

Ch
20

CHAPTER 21

Help

Too many programmers neglect Help entirely. Even those who add Help to an application tend to leave it to the end of a project, and when the inevitable time squeeze comes, guess what? There's no time to write the Help text or make the software adjustments that arrange for that text to be displayed when the user requests Help. One of the reasons people do this is because they believe implementing Help is really hard. But with Visual C++, it's a lot easier than it could be. Visual C++ even writes some of your Help text for you! This chapter is going to add Help after the fact to the ShowString application built into Chapter 17, "Building Menus and Dialogs." ▪

Types of Help

There are a number of kinds of help and a number of ways of breaking Help into categories.

The file types making up Help

AppWizard and Help compiler generate files related to Help.

What AppWizard provides

Code and files are added to your project when you ask for context-sensitive Help.

Designing your Help

Good Help is designed before it is implemented. Many tasks are involved in the implementation, and there's a risk of getting lost.

Hooking in command Help

Dealing with Windows messages is quite simple.

Hooking in context Help

Dealing with Windows messages requesting context-sensitive Help is more difficult.

Composing Help text in Word

Using Word to compose Help files means learning all about footnote types, hidden text, and more.

Help table of Contents

Making sure the user can reach your new topics from the Help Contents list is vital.

Different Kinds of Help

There are a variety of ways of characterizing Help. This section presents four different questions you might ask about Help:

- How does the user invoke it?
- How does it look on the screen?
- What sort of answers does the user want?
- How does the developer implement it in code?

None of these questions has a single answer. There are at least nine different ways for a user to invoke Help, three standard Help appearances, and three different programming tasks you must implement in order to display Help. These different ways of looking at Help can help you understand why the implementation has a number of different techniques, which can be confusing at first.

Getting Help

The first way of characterizing Help is to ask, "How does the user bring it up?" There are a number of ways to bring up Help:

- Choosing an item from the Help menu, such as Help Topics. (Choosing What's This? or About does not bring up Help immediately.)
- Pressing F1.
- Clicking the Help button on a dialog box.
- Clicking a What's This? button on a toolbar, then clicking something else.
- Clicking a Question button on a dialog box, then clicking part of the dialog box.
- Right-clicking something and choosing What's This? from the Shortcut menu.
- Choosing What's This? from the Help menu (the System menu for dialog box-based apps) and then clicking something.
- In some older applications, by pressing Shift+F1 and then clicking something.
- Outside the application completely, by double-clicking the .HLP file.

For the first three actions in this list, the user does one thing (chooses a menu item, presses F1, or clicks a button) and Help appears immediately. For the next five actions there are two steps: typically one click to get into "Help mode" (more formally called "What's This?" mode) and another to indicate what Help is required. Users generally divide Help into single-step Help and two-step Help, accordingly.

N O T E You will get confused if you try to use Developer Studio itself to understand Help in general. Much of the information is presented by InfoViewer, though there are some circumstances under which more traditional Help appears. Use simple utilities and accessories that come with your operating system, or use your operating system itself, to follow along. If you have old versions of software like Word or Excel, they probably don't follow the Windows 95 guidelines for Help either, because these are quite different than the old Help guidelines. ▪

Presenting Help

The second way of characterizing Help is to ask, "How does it look?" There are a number of different-looking ways of showing Help:

■ *Help Topics dialog box*—As shown in Figure 21.1, this dialog box allows users to scroll through an index, look at a table of contents, or find a word within the Help text.

■ *Ordinary Help window*—As shown in Figure 21.2, this window has buttons like Help Topics, Back, and Options. It can be resized, minimized, maximized, or closed, and in many cases is always on top, like the system clock and other popular utilities.

■ Pop-up windows—As shown in Figure 21.3, pop-up windows are relatively small and do not have buttons or menus. They disappear when you click outside them, cannot be resized or moved, and are perfect for a definition or quick explanation.

FIG. 21.1
The Help Topics dialog box allows users to go through the contents or index, or search the Help text with Find.

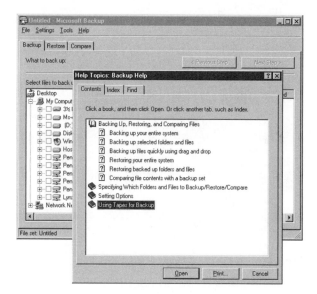

Using Help

A third way of characterizing Help, is according to the user's reasons for invoking it. Microsoft categorizes Help in this way and lists these kinds of Help:

■ Task-oriented—explains how to accomplish a certain task such as printing a document (it often contains numbered steps).

■ Reference—looking up function parameters or font names or other material that expert users need to refer to from time to time.

Part
III

Ch
21

These describe the content of the material presented to the user. While these content descriptions are important to a Help designer and writer, they are not very useful from a programming point of view.

FIG. 21.2
An ordinary Help window has buttons and may have menus. It can be treated like any other window.

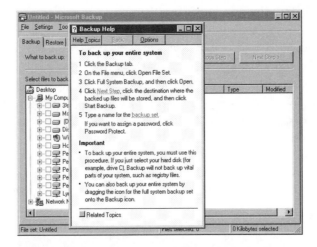

FIG. 21.3
A pop-up Help topic window gives the user far less control, and should only be used for short explanations.

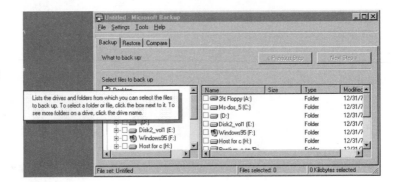

Programming Help

The final way of characterizing Help, and perhaps the most important to a developer, is by examining the code behind the scenes. There are three Windows messages that are sent when the user invokes Help in any of these ways:

- WM_COMMAND
- WM_HELP
- WM_CONTEXTMENU

When the user chooses a Help item from a menu, or clicks the Help button on a dialog box, the system sends a WM_COMMAND message as always. To display the associated Help, you catch these messages and call the WinHelp system.

When the user right-clicks an element of your application, a WM_CONTEXTMENU message is sent. You catch the message and build a shortcut menu on the spot. Because in most cases you will want a shortcut menu with only one item on it, What's This? you can use a prebuilt menu with just that item, and delegate the display of that menu to the Help system. More on this later, in the "Programming for Context Help" section.

When the user brings up Help in any other way, the framework handles most of it. You do not catch the message that puts the application into What's This? mode, you do not change the cursor, and you do not deal with clicks while in that mode. You catch a WM_HELP message that identifies the control, dialog box, or menu for which Help is required, and you provide that Help. Whether the user pressed F1 or went into What's This? mode and clicked the item does not matter, and in fact you cannot tell from within your application.

The WM_HELP and WM_CONTEXTMENU messages are handled almost identically, so from the point of view of the developer, there are two kinds of help. We'll call these *command help* and *context help*. Each is discussed later in this chapter, in the "Programming for Command Help" and "Programming for Context Help" sections, but keep in mind that there is no relationship between this split (between command and context help) and the split between one-step and two-step Help that users think of.

Components of the Help System

As you might expect, a large number of files interact to make online Help work. The final product, which you deliver to your user, is the Help file, with the .hlp extension. It is built from component files. In the list that follows, appname refers to the name of your application's .exe file. If no name appears, there may be more than one file with a variety of names. The component files produced by AppWizard are as follows:

- .h—These Header files define resource IDs and Help topic IDs for use within your C++ code.
- .hm—These Help Mapping files define Help topic IDs. appname.hm is generated every time you build your application—do not change it yourself.
- .rtf—These Rich Text Format files contain the Help text for each Help topic.
- appname.hpj—This Help ProJect file pulls together .hm and .rtf files to produce, when compiled, a .hlp file.

While being used, the Help system generates other files. When you uninstall your application be sure to look for and remove the following files, in addition to the .hlp file:

- appname.cnt is a table of contents file you use to create the Contents tab of the Help Topics dialog box. (You should distribute this contents file with your application in addition to the Help file.)
- appname.gid is a configuration file, typically hidden.

■ appname.fts is a full text search file, generated when your user does a Find through your Help text.

■ appname.ftg is a full text search group list, also generated when your user does a Find.

Help Topic IDs are the connection between your Help text and the Help system. Your program eventually directs the Help system to display a Help topic, using a name like HID_FILE_OPEN, and the system looks for this Help topic ID in the Help file, compiled from the .rtf files, including the .rtf file that contains your Help text for that Help topic ID. (This process is illustrated in Figure 21.4.) These topic IDs have to be defined twice—once for use by the Help system and once for use by your program. When the Help system is displaying a topic or the Help Topics dialog box, it takes over displaying other Help topics as the user requests them, with no work on your part.

FIG. 21.4
Your program, the Help system, and your Help files all work together to display a topic.

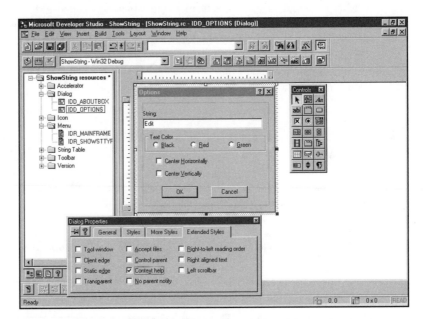

Help Support from AppWizard

When you build an MDI application (no database or OLE support) with AppWizard, and choose the Context Sensitive Help option, here's what you get:

1. Message map entries are added to catch the commands ID_HELP_FINDER, ID_HELP, ID_CONTEXT_HELP, and ID_DEFAULT_HELP. No code is added to handle these; they are passed to CMDIFrameWnd member functions.

2. A What's This? button is added to the toolbar.

3. A Help Topics item is added to the Help menu for both menus provided by AppWizard: the one used when a file is open and the smaller one used when no files are open.

4. Accelerators for F1 (ID_HELP) and Shift+F1 (ID_CONTEXT_HELP) are added.

5. The default message in the status bar is changed from Ready to For Help, press F1.

6. A status bar prompt is added, to be displayed while in What's This? mode: Select an object on which to get Help.

7. Status bar prompts are added for the Help menu and its items.

8. afxcore.rtf, a help text file for standard menu items like File, Open, is copied into the project.

9. afxprint.rtf, a help text file for printing and print previewing, is copied into the project. (These files are added separately because not all projects include printing and print previewing. If this project has database or OLE related features, more help is provided.)

10. Twenty two .bmp files, included as illustrations in the Help for topics like File Open, are copied into the project.

With this solid foundation, the task of implementing Help for this application breaks down into three steps:

- First, you must plan your Help. Do you intend to provide reference material only, task-oriented instructions only, or both? To what extent will you supplement these with context pop-ups?

- Second, you must provide the programming "hooks" that will result in the display of the Help topics you have designed. This is done differently for command and context Help, as you will see in the sections that follow.

- Third, you must build the .rtf files with the Help topic IDs and text to explain your application. If you have designed the Help system well, and truly understand your application, this should be simple, though time-consuming.

N O T E On large projects, the Help text is often written by a technical writer rather than a programmer. This will require careful coordination; for example, you will have to provide Topic IDs to the Help writer, and may have to explain some functions so that they can be described in Help. You will have to work closely throughout the project and respect each other's area of expertise. ▪

Planning Your Help Approach

Developing Help is like developing your software. You shouldn't do it without a plan. And, strictly speaking, you shouldn't do it last. A famous experiment decades ago split a programming class into two groups. One group was required to hand in a completed user manual for a program before writing the program, the other to finish the program before writing the manual. The group that wrote the manual first produced better programs: it noticed design errors early, before they were carved in code, and it found the program much easier to write, as well.

If your application is of any size, the work involved in developing a Help system for it would fill a book. If you need further information on how to do this, consider the book *Designing Windows 95 Help: A Guide to Creating Online Documents*, by Mary Deaton and Cheryl Lockett Zubak, published by Que. In this section, there is only room for a few basic guidelines.

The result of this planning process is a list of Help topics and the primary way they will be reached. The topics you plan are likely to include:

- A page or so of Help on each menu item, reached by getting into What's This? mode and clicking the item.
- A page, reachable from the Contents, that lists all the menus and their menu items, with links to the pages for those items.
- A page, reachable from the Contents, for each major task that a user might perform with the application. This includes examples or tutorials.
- Context help for the controls on all dialog boxes.

While that may seem like a lot of work, remember that all the boilerplate resources have been documented already in the material provided by AppWizard. That includes menu items, common dialog boxes, and more.

After you have a complete list of material and the primary way each page is reached, think about links between pages (for example, the AppWizard-supplied help for File, Open mentions using File, New, and vice versa) and pop-up definitions for jargon and keywords.

In this section you will plan Help for ShowString, the application introduced in Chapter 17, "Building Menus and Dialogs." This simple application displays a string that the user can set. The string may be centered vertically or horizontally, and can be black, green, or red. There is a new menu (Tools,) with one item (Options) that brings up a dialog box on which the user can set all these options at once. The Help tasks you need to tackle include:

- Changing AppWizard's placeholder strings to ShowString or other strings specific to this application
- Adding a topic about the Tools menu and the Options item
- Adding a topic about each control on the Options dialog box
- Adding a Question button to the Options dialog box
- Changing the text supplied by AppWizard and displayed when the user requests context Help about the view
- Adding an Understanding Centering topic to the Help menu and writing it
- Adjusting the Contents to point to the new pages

The remainder of this chapter tackles this list of tasks.

Programming for Command Help

Command help is actually quite simple from a developer's point of view. (Of course, you probably still have to write the explanations, so don't get too relaxed.) As you've seen, AppWizard added the Help Topics menu item and the message map entries to catch it, and the MFC class CMDIChildFrame has the member function that will process it, so you have no work to do for that. But if you choose to add another menu item to your Help menu, you do so just like any other menu, using the Resource View. Then have your application class, CShowStringApp, catch the message. Say, for example, that ShowString deserves an item on the Help menu called Understanding Centering. Add this item to both menus, and let Developer Studio assign it the resource ID ID_HELP_UNDERSTANDINGCENTERING. Actually, this is one occasion where a slightly shorter resource ID wouldn't hurt, but this chapter will present it with the longer ID.

Use Class Wizard to arrange for CShowStringApp to catch this message, as discussed in Chapter 17, "Building Menus and Dialogs." (You may want to open the Help version of this project now and follow along, or make a copy of the ShowString you built in Chapter 17 and make these changes as you read.) The new function looks like this:

```
void CShowStringApp::OnHelpUnderstandingcentering()
{
    WinHelp(HID_CENTERING);
}
```

This single line of code fires up the Help system, passing it the Help topic ID HID_CENTERING. For this to compile, that Help topic ID has to be known to the compiler, so in showstring.h, add this line:

```
#define HID_CENTERING 0x01
```

The help topic IDs in the range 0x0000 to 0xFFFF are reserved for user-defined Help topics, so 0x01 is a fine choice. Now the C++ compiler is happy, but when this runs, the call to WinHelp() is not going to find the topic that explains centering. You need to add a *help mapping entry*. This should be done in a new file, named showstringx.hm (the x is for extra.) Choose File, New, Text File, and type in this line:

```
HID_CENTERING    0x01
```

Save the file as showstringx.hm in the hlp folder of the ShowString project. Next you need to edit the Help project file, Showstring.hpj. If you double-click this from a folder such as Windows 95 Explorer, it will be opened with the Help Compiler. In this case you actually want to edit it as text, so you should open it with Developer Studio. In Developer Studio's Project Workspace Window, click the FileView tab, then open Showstring.hpj by double-clicking it in the File View (and you wondered what the File View was good for) and add this line at the very bottom:

```
#include <ShowStringX.hm>
```

Now both the Help system and the compiler know about this new Help topic ID. When you write the Help text, don't forget to add a section that explains centering, and connect it to this Help topic ID.

Part
III

Ch
21

N O T E Microsoft is now recommending that all context numbers have identifiers that start with the letters IDH; in the past the convention had been HIDD for dialogs, HIDR for resources, and so on. Unfortunately, the MAKEHELP.BAT generated by AppWizard still creates context numbers using the old convention, so you'll have to choose between using the old convention or changing MAKEHELP.BAT. For clarity, the sample code presented in this chapter all uses the old convention; MAKEHELP.BAT has not been changed. ▆

The other common use of command help is to add a Help button to a dialog box that gives an overview of the dialog box. This used to be standard behavior but is now recommended only for large dialog boxes, especially those with complex interactions between the various controls. Simply use the steps you followed to add the menu item Help, Understanding Centering, but add a button rather than a menu item. Do not create a new .hm file; add the button's Help topic ID to ShowStringX.hm, which will continue to grow in the next section.

Programming for Context Help

Your first task in arranging for context help is to get a Question button onto the Options dialog box, since AppWizard already added one to the toolbar. Open the Options dialog box by double-clicking it in the Resource View, then choose Edit, Properties. Click the Extended Styles tab, then check the Context Help checkbox, as shown in Figure 21.5.

FIG. 21.5

The Context Help checkbox on the Extended Styles tab of the Dialog Properties dialog box arranges for the Question box on the Options dialog box of ShowString.

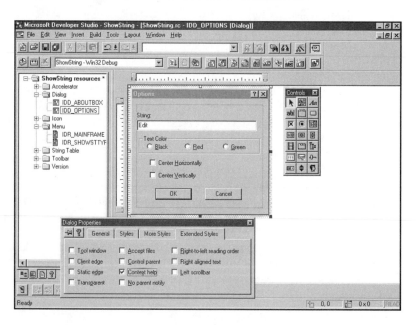

As mentioned earlier, there are two messages sent in context help: WM_HELP when a user clicks something while in What's This? mode, and WM_CONTEXTMENU when a user right-clicks something. You need to arrange for your dialog class, COptionsDialog, to catch these messages.

You do so by adding entries outside the special ClassWizard comments. The message map in OptionsDialog.h should look like this:

```
// Generated message map functions
//{{AFX_MSG(COptionsDialog)
    // NOTE: the ClassWizard will add member functions here
//}}AFX_MSG
afx_msg BOOL OnHelpInfo(HELPINFO* lpHelpInfo);
afx_msg void OnContextMenu(CWnd* pWnd, CPoint point);
    DECLARE_MESSAGE_MAP()
```

The message map in OptionsDialog.cpp should look like this:

```
BEGIN_MESSAGE_MAP(COptionsDialog, CDialog)
    //{{AFX_MSG_MAP(COptionsDialog)
        // NOTE: the ClassWizard will add message map macros here
    //}}AFX_MSG_MAP
    ON_WM_HELPINFO()
    ON_WM_CONTEXTMENU()
END_MESSAGE_MAP()
```

These macros arrange for WM_HELP to be caught by OnHelpInfo(), and for WM_CONTEXTMENU to be caught by OnContextMenu(). The next step is to write those functions. They both need to use a table to connect resource IDs to Help topic IDs. Add these lines at the beginning of OptionsDialog.cpp:

```
static DWORD aHelpIDs[] =
{
    IDC_OPTIONS_STRING, HIDD_OPTIONS_STRING,
    IDC_OPTIONS_BLACK, HIDD_OPTIONS_BLACK,
    IDC_OPTIONS_RED, HIDD_OPTIONS_RED,
    IDC_OPTIONS_GREEN, HIDD_OPTIONS_GREEN,
    IDC_OPTIONS_HORIZCENTER, HIDD_OPTIONS_HORIZCENTER,
    IDC_OPTIONS_VERTCENTER, HIDD_OPTIONS_VERTCENTER,
    IDOK, HIDD_OPTIONS_OK,
    IDCANCEL, HIDD_OPTIONS_CANCEL,
    0, 0
};
```

The Help system uses this array (you pass the address to the WinHelp() function) to connect resource IDs and Help topic IDs. The compiler, however, has never heard of HIDD_OPTIONS_STRING, so add these lines to OptionsDialog.h:

```
#define HIDD_OPTIONS_STRING 2
#define HIDD_OPTIONS_BLACK 3
#define HIDD_OPTIONS_RED 4
#define HIDD_OPTIONS_GREEN 5
#define HIDD_OPTIONS_HORIZCENTER 6
#define HIDD_OPTIONS_VERTCENTER 7
#define HIDD_OPTIONS_OK 8
#define HIDD_OPTIONS_CANCEL 9
```

The numbers are chosen arbitrarily. Now, as before, the compiler is happy, since all these constants are defined, but the Help system doesn't know what's going on, because these topics are not in the help mapping file yet. So, add these lines to ShowStringX.hm:

```
HIDD_OPTIONS_STRING       0x02
HIDD_OPTIONS_BLACK        0x03
HIDD_OPTIONS_RED        0x04
HIDD_OPTIONS_GREEN        0x05
HIDD_OPTIONS_HORIZCENTER      0x06
HIDD_OPTIONS_VERTCENTER      0x07
HIDD_OPTIONS_OK      0x08
HIDD_OPTIONS_CANCEL        0x09
```

Be sure to use the same numbers as in the #define statements in OptionsDialog.h. The stage is set; all that remains is to write the functions. Here's what OnHelpInfo() looks like:

```
BOOL COptionsDialog::OnHelpInfo(HELPINFO *lpHelpInfo)
{
    if (lpHelpInfo->iContextType == HELPINFO_WINDOW) // must be for a control
    {
        // have to call SDK WinHelp not CWinApp::WinHelp
        // because CWinApp::WinHelp doesn't take a
        // handle as a parameter.
        ::WinHelp((HWND)lpHelpInfo->hItemHandle,
            AfxGetApp()->m_pszHelpFilePath,
            HELP_WM_HELP, (DWORD)aHelpIDs);
    }
    return TRUE;
}
```

This function just calls the SDK WinHelp function and passes the handle to the control, the path to the Help file, the command HELP_WM_HELP to request a context-sensitive pop-up Help topic, and the table of resource IDs and Help topic IDs built earlier. There's no other work for your function to do after kicking WinHelp() into action.

TIP If you've never seen the :: scope resolution operator used without a class name before it, it means call the function that is not in any class, and in Windows programming that means the SDK function.

N O T E The third parameter of this call to WinHelp directs the Help system to put up a certain style of Help window. HELP_WM_HELP gets you a pop-up menu, as does HELP_WM_CONTEXTMENU. HELP_CONTEXT gets an ordinary Help window, which can be resized and moved, and allows Help navigation. HELP_FINDER brings up the Help Topics dialog box. HELP_CONTENTS and HELP_INDEX are obsolete and should be replaced with HELP_FINDER if you maintain code that uses them. ▨

OnContextMenu() is even simpler:

```
void COptionsDialog::OnContextMenu(CWnd *pWnd, CPoint /*point*/)
{
        ::WinHelp((HWND)*pWnd, AfxGetApp()->m_pszHelpFilePath,
                HELP_CONTEXTMENU, (DWORD)aHelpIDs);
}
```

This function doesn't need to check that the right-click is on a control as OnHelpInfo() did, so it just calls the SDK WinHelp. WinHelp() takes care of displaying the shortcut menu with only a What's This item, and then displays Help when that item is chosen.

To check your typing, build the project by choosing Build, Build, then compile the Help file by giving focus to showstring.hpj and choosing Build, Compile. (You can also right-click on Showstring.hpj in the File View of the Project Workspace Window and choose Compile from the shortcut menu.) There's not much point in testing it though; the AppWizard stuff is sure to work, and without Help content connected to those topics, none of the code you just added will succeed in displaying content.

Writing Help Text

You write Help text in an RTF file, using special formatting codes, which mean something rather different than they usually do. The traditional way to do this was in Word, but a large crop of Help authoring tools have sprung up that are far easier to use than Word. Rather than teach you yet another tool, this section presents instructions for writing Help text in Word. However, do keep in mind that there are easier ways, and on a project of a decent size you easily save the time and money you invested in choosing a Help authoring tool. There is an entire chapter in *Designing Windows 95 Help* on choosing an authoring tool.

Figure 21.6 shows afxcore.rtf open in Word. Choose View, Footnotes to display the footnotes across the bottom of the screen—they are vital. This is how the text connects to the Help topic IDs. Choose Tools, Options, select the View tab, and make sure the hidden text checkbox is selected. This is how links between topics are entered. The topics are separated by page breaks.

FIG. 21.6

Help text, like this boilerplate provided by AppWizard, can be edited in Word for Windows.

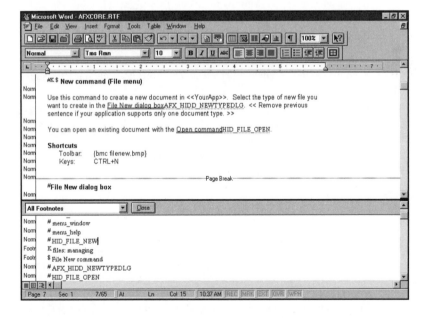

Part

III

Ch

21

There are eight kinds of footnotes and each has a different meaning. Only the first three foot-note types in the following list are in general use:

- #, the Help topic ID—The SDK WinHelp function looks for this topic ID when displaying Help.
- $, the topic title—This title is displayed in search results.
- K, keywords—These appear in the Index tab of the Help Topics dialog box.
- A, A-keyword—These keywords can be jumped to but do not appear in the Index tab of the Help Topics dialog box.
- +, browse code—This marks the topic's place in a sequence of topics.
- !, macro entry—Makes this topic a macro to be run when the user requests the topic.
- *, build tag—Used to include certain tags only in certain builds of the Help file.
- >, window type—Overrides the type of window for this topic.

The double-underlined text, followed by hidden text, identifies a jump to another Help topic. If a user clicks to follow the link, this Help topic leaves the screen. If the text before the hidden text was single-underlined, following the link brings up a pop-up over this Help topic, perfect for definitions and notes. (You may also see Help text files in which strikethrough text is used; this is exactly the same as double-underlined, a jump to another topic.) In all three cases, the hidden text is the topic ID of the material to be jumped to or popped up.

Figure 21.7 shows how the File New Help material appears from within ShowString. To display it yourself, run Showstring by choosing Build, Execute from within Developer Studio, then choose Help, Help topics in ShowString. Open the menus book, double-click the File menu topic, and click New.

With the programming out of the way, it's time to tackle the list of Help To Dos for ShowString from earlier in this chapter. These instructions assume you are using Word.

FIG. 21.7
ShowString displays
the boilerplate help
generated by
AppWizard.

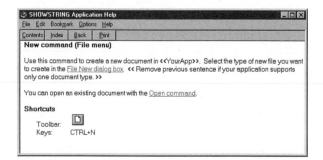

Changing Placeholder Strings

To change the placeholder strings left behind by AppWizard in the boilerplate help files, open afxcore.rtf in Word. (It's in the hlp folder of the ShowString project folder.) Then follow these steps:

1. Position the cursor at the very beginning of the document and choose <u>E</u>dit, <u>R</u>eplace.

2. Enter **<<YourApp>>** in the Find What box and **ShowString** in the Replace With box

3. Click Replace All.

Open `afxprint.rtf` and repeat these steps.

Switch back to `afxcore.rtf`, and look through the text for << characters (use <u>E</u>dit, <u>F</u>ind if you wish, and remember that `Shift+F4` is the shortcut to repeat your previous Find.) These identify places where you must make a change or a decision. For ShowString, the changes in `afxcore.rtf` are:

- The first section in the file is the ShowString Help Index.Remove the How To section and the reminder to add some How To topics. In a real application, you would add topics here.

- The next section, after the page break, is a table describing the items on the <u>F</u>ile menu. Since there is no Send item on ShowString's <u>F</u>ile menu, remove the Send row of the File menu table.

- The third section is a table listing the items on the Edit menu. Remove the Paste Link, Insert New Object, and Links rows.

- The fourth section is for the View menu, and does not need any changes. The fifth section is for the Window menu. Remove the Split row from the Window menu table.

- The sixth section is for the Help menu, and does not need any changes. The seventh section is for the New command (File menu). Remove the sentence about choosing a file type, and the reminder to remove it.

- Delete the eighth section, the File New dialog box topic, entirely, including the page break before or after it.

- The next topic is for the File Open command and does not need any changes. Moving on to the File Open dialog box topic, mention that the List Files of Type list box contains only `All Files`.

- Continue down the file until you find the File Send topic, and remove it entirely including the page break before or after it.

- In the File Save As topic, remove the suggestion to describe other options, since there are none.

- When you reach the Edit Undo topic, you start to see why programs written after their manuals are better programs. As ShowString was written in Chapter 17, "Building Menus and Dialogs," the Undo item will never be enabled, nor will Cut, Copy, or Paste. You could remove the Help topics about these unsupported menu items, but it's probably better to plan to add support for the menu items to a later version of ShowString. Add some text to all these topics explaining that they are not implemented in this version of the product. Leave the shortcuts sections there so that users can find out why `Ctrl+Z` does nothing.

Part

III

Ch

21

- Continue down through the file to the Toolbar topic, where you will find this reminder: << Add or remove toolbar buttons from the list below according to which ones your application offers. >> Remove the reminder and delete the references to the Undo, First Record, Previous Record, Next Record, and Last Record buttons.

- About halfway down the file is a topic for `#Split Command (Window menu)`. Remove the entire topic.

- Move down to the `#Index` command (Help menu) topic and remove it. Also remove the Using Help command (Help menu) and `#About` command (Help menu) topics.

- In the Title Bar topic, remove the directive to insert a graphic. If you would rather follow the directive, create a bitmap in a `.bmp` file of the title bar with screen shot software, cropping the shot down to just the title bar, and insert the graphic with the bmc directive, just as the `bullet.bmp` graphic is inserted a few lines lower in the file.

- Because the ShowString view does not inherit from `CScrollView`, it doesn't scroll. Remove the Scrollbars Help topic and its page break.

- In the File Close topic, the shortcut for `Alt+F4` should be described like this: `closes ShowString`.

- Remove the Ruler, Choose Font, Choose Color, Edit Find, Find Dialog, Edit Replace, Replace dialog box, Edit Repeat, Edit Clear, Edit Clear All, Next Pane, and Previous Pane topics.

- Skip the How To Modify Text topic for now and leave it unchanged.

- Remove the final directive about tailoring the No Help Available messages to each message box.

That completes the extensive changes required to the boilerplate `afxcore.rtf` file generated by AppWizard. In the other boilerplate file, `afxprint.rtf`, simply scroll to the bottom and remove the Page Setup topic.

Would you like to test all this work? Save `afxcore.rtf` and `afxprint.rtf` within Word. Switch to Developer Studio and choose Build, Build to bring the project up to date. Then open `showstring.hpj` and choose Build, Compile. This pulls all the `.rtf` files together into `showstring.hlp`. Choose Build, Execute to run Showstring, and choose Help, Help Topics from the ShowString menus. As you can see in Figure 21.8, the Window menu topic is now substantially shorter. You can check that your other changes have been made as well.

FIG. 21.8

After saving the *.rtf* files and compiling the Help project, you can test to see that your changes have been made successfully.

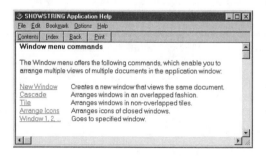

Adding Topics

When you are adding new topics, you don't add new topics to the boilerplate files that were provided. Those files should stay untouched unless you want to change the description of File, Open or other boilerplate topics. Instead, create a new file by choosing File New in Word and saving it in the `hlp` folder of the ShowString project folder as `ShowString.rtf`. (Make sure to change the Save File As Type list box selection to Rich Text Format.) If this was a large project, you could divide it up into several `.rtf` files, but one will suffice for ShowString. In Developer Studio, open `showstring.hpj` by double-clicking it in the FileView tab, and find the section headed `[FILES]`. Add this line at the end of that section:

`showstring.rtf`

The Tools Menu Back in Word, switch to `afxcore.rtf` and copy the topic for the File menu into the Clipboard, then switch back to `showstring.rtf` and paste it in. (Don't forget to include the page break after the topic in the selection when you copy.) Choose View, Footnotes to display the footnotes and Tools, Options, View tab, Hidden Text to display the hidden text. Now you are going to edit the copied File topic to make it the Tools topic. Change the footnotes first. They are as follows:

- The # footnote is the topic ID—The Help system uses this to find this topic from the Contents page. Change it to `menu_tools`.

- The K footnote is the keyword entry—While the Options dialog box probably deserves several keywords, this menu doesn't, so remove that footnote by selecting the letter K in the Help topic and pressing Delete. You must select the letter; it is not enough to click just before it. The footnote is deleted at the same time.

- The $ footnote is the topic title—Change it to `Tools menu commands`.

In the topic, change `File` to `Tools` on the first two lines, and delete all the rows of the table but one. Change the underlined text of that row to Options, the hidden text immediately following to `HID_TOOLS_OPTIONS`, and the right column of that row to `Changes string, color, and centering`. Figure 21.9 shows the way Showstring.rtf looks in Word after these changes.

FIG. 21.9
Change the Showstring.rtf file to explain the new menu item.

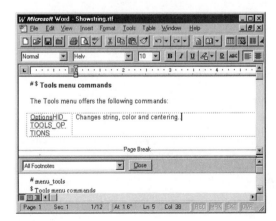

T I P If you can't remember the Help topic IDs your project is using, check your .hm files. The ones added by Developer Studio, such as HID_TOOLS_OPTIONS for the menu item with resource ID ID_TOOLS_OPTIONS, are in Showstring.hm, while ShowStringx.hm contains the Help topic IDs added by hand for context help.

The Tools, Options Menu Item   Switch back to afxcore, copy the File New topic, and paste it into showstring.rtf as before. The topic and its footnotes are copied together. Watch carefully to be sure you are working with the footnotes for the Tools Options topic and not the ones for the Tools menu. Follow these steps:

1. Change the # footnote to HID_TOOLS_OPTIONS.

2. Change the K keyword. You need several keywords to lead here, and each needs to be separated from the next by a semicolon (;). Some need to be two-level keywords with the levels separated by commas. A good first start is string, changing;color, changing;centering, changing;appearance, controlling.

3. Change the $ keyword to Tools Options command.

4. Change the first line of the topic to Options command (Tools menu).

5. Delete the rest of the topic and replace it with a short description of this menu item. The following text is OK:

```
Use this command to change the appearance of the ShowString
display with the Options dialog. The string being displayed,
color of the text, and vertical and horizontal centering are
all controlled from this dialog.
```

If you want to test this, too, save the files in Word, compile the Help project, run ShowString, and choose Tools. Highlight the Options item by moving the highlight with the cursor keys, but do not click Options to select it; press F1 instead. Figure 21.10 shows the Help window that is displayed.

FIG. 21.10

The new Tools Options Help is reached by pressing F1 while the item is highlighted on the menu.

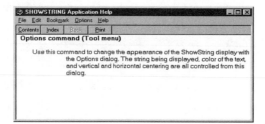

Each Control on the Options Dialog   Copy the File New topic into showstring.rtf again and cut it down drastically. To do this, follow these steps:

1. Remove the K and $ footnotes.

2. Change the # footnote to HIDD_OPTIONS.

3. Change the first line to (Options dialog).

4. Delete the other text in the topic.

Copy this block into the Clipboard and paste it in seven more times, so that you have a skeleton for each control on the dialog box. Remember to copy the page break, too. Then edit each skeleton to document the following topic IDs:

- HIDD_OPTIONS_STRING
- HIDD_OPTIONS_BLACK
- HIDD_OPTIONS_RED
- HIDD_OPTIONS_GREEN
- HIDD_OPTIONS_HORIZCENTER
- HIDD_OPTIONS_VERTCENTER
- HIDD_OPTIONS_OK
- HIDD_OPTIONS_CANCEL

Change the topic ID and add a sentence or two of text. Be consistent. The samples included with this chapter are all a single sentence that starts with an imperative verb like Click or Select and ends with a period(.). If you would rather choose a different style for your pop-up boxes, use the same style for all of them. It confuses the user if pop-up boxes are inconsistent, and tends to make them believe your coding is sloppy too.

Understanding Centering   In showstring.rtf, paste in another copy of the File New topic. Make the following changes:

1. Change the # footnote to HID_CENTERING (the topic ID you added to showstringx.hm and called in CShowStringApp::OnHelpUnderstandingcentering()).

2. Change the K footnote to centering.

3. Change the $ footnote to Understanding Centering.

4. Change the title on the first line to Understanding Centering.

5. Replace the text with a short explanation of centering, like this:

```
Showstring can center the displayed string within the view. The two
options, "center horizontally" and "center vertically", can be set
independently on the Options dialog, reached by choosing the Options
item on the Tools menu.  Text that is not centered horizontally is
displayed at the left edge of the window. Text that is not centered
vertically is displayed at the top of the window.
```

6. Add links from the word Tools to the menu_tools topic and from the word Options to HID_TOOLS_OPTIONS, as before. Remember to watch for extra spaces.

Test this change in the usual way, and when you choose Help Understanding Centering from the ShowString menus, you should see something like Figure 21.11. Try following the links; you can use the Back button to return to the centering topic.

Part
III

Ch

21

Changing the "How to Modify Text" Topic

AppWizard already provided a How To Modify Text topic at the bottom of `afxcore.rtf` that needs to be edited to explain how ShowString works. It is displayed when the user selects the view area for context help. Replace the text with a much shorter explanation that tells the user to choose Tools, Options. To add a link to that topic (short though it is), type **HID_TOOLS_OPTIONS** immediately after the word Options in the Help topic. While you're at it, type **menu_tools** immediately after the word Tools. Select the word Options and press CTRL+SHIFT+D to double-underline it, then do the same for Tools. Select HID_TOOLS_OPTIONS and press CTRL+SHIFT+H to hide it, then do the same for menu_tools.

FIG. 21.11

Display a teaching Help topic by choosing it from the Help menu.

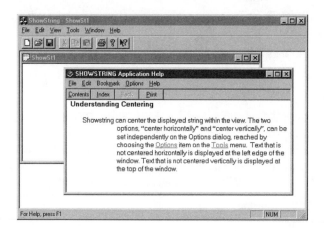

TIP There cannot be any spaces between the double-underlined text and the hidden text, or at the end of the hidden text. Word can give you some trouble about this, because the smart cut and paste feature that works so nicely with words can insert extra spaces where you didn't want them, or make it impossible to select only half a word. You can turn the feature off in Word by choosing Tools Options, the Edit tab, and by unselecting the Automatic Word Selection and Use Smart Cut and Paste boxes.

Ready to test again? Save the files in Word, compile the Help project file, execute ShowString, choose Tools, Options, click the Question button, and then click a control. Figure 21.12 shows the context help for the String edit box.

Adjustments to the Contents

This tiny little application is almost entirely documented now. You need to add the Tools menu and Understanding Centering to the Contents, and check the index. The easiest way to tackle the Contents is with Help Workshop. Close all the Help-related files that are open in Developer Studio and Word, and bring up Help Workshop (it's in the Developer Studio folder). Open showstring.cnt by choosing File Open and working your way through the Open dialog box. This is the Contents file for ShowString.

FIG. 21.12

Display Help for a dialog control by clicking the Question button in the upper-right and then clicking a control.

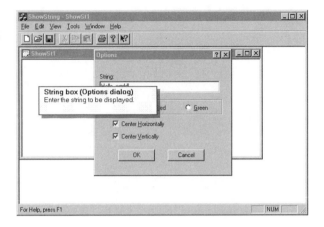

In the first open book, click the View item and then click the Add Below button. (Alternatively, click the Window item and then the Add Above button.) The Edit Contents Tab Entry dialog box, shown in Figure 21.13, appears. Fill it in as shown; by leaving the last two entries blank, the default Help File and Window Type are used. Click OK.

FIG. 21.13

Add entries to the Contents tab with Help Workshop's Edit Contents Tab Entry dialog box.

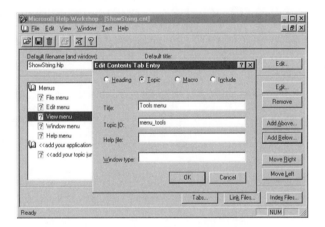

Click the placeholder book, and click Add Above again. When the Edit Contents Tab Entry dialog box appears, select the Heading radio button from the list across the top. As shown in Figure 21.14, only the title can be changed here. Do not use Understanding Centering, since that is the title of the only topic under this heading. Click OK.

Add a topic below the new heading for Understanding Centering, whose ID is HID_CENTERING, and remove the placeholder heading and topic. Save your changes, close Help Workshop, compile showstring.hpj in Developer Studio again, and test your Help. Choose Help Help Topics and you should see something like Figure 21.15.

Part
III

Ch

21

FIG. 21.14

Add headings to the Contents tab with Help Workshop's Edit Contents Tab Entry dialog box by selecting the Heading radio button.

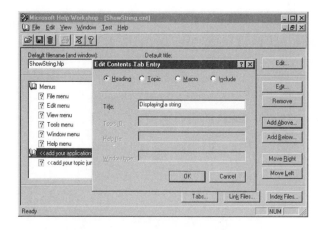

FIG. 21.15

After saving the *.cnt* file and compiling the *.hpj* file, display the new table of contents by choosing Help Help Topics.

While you have the Help Topics dialog box open, click the Index tab. Figure 21.16 shows how the K footnotes you entered throughout this section have all been added to the index. If it looks a little sparse, you can always go to the .rtf files and add more keywords, remembering to separate them with semicolons.

FIG. 21.16
The index has been built from the K footnotes in the *.rtf* files.

From Here...

This chapter has only scratched the surface of building a Help system. Although you have seen all of the types of Help, the different ways the user invokes it, and the behind-the-scenes code that brings it up on the screen, there is much more to cover. If you have a large system to document, you need a book just on Help, to give you a good perspective on designing and writing your Help content. Other parts of this book that might interest you include:

- Chapter 5, "Messages and Commands," gives more details on catching the messages generated when a user chooses a menu item or clicks a button.
- For information on Windows, see Chapter 8, "Win95 Common Controls"
- Chapter 17, "Building Menus and Dialogs," introduced ShowString.
- Part IV, "ActiveX Applications and ActiveX Custom Controls," continues to expand ShowString by adding various kinds of ActiveX functionality.

Part
III

Ch
21

ActiveX Applications and ActiveX Custom Controls

22   ActiveX Concepts   495

23   Building an ActiveX Container Application   507

24   Building an ActiveX Server Application   545

25   ActiveX Automation   575

26   Building an ActiveX Control   595

CHAPTER 22

ActiveX Concepts

This chapter covers the theory and concepts of ActiveX, which until recently was called OLE. Most new programmers have found OLE intimidating, and the new name is unlikely to lessen that. However, if you think of ActiveX technology as a way to use code already written and tested by someone else, and to save yourself the trouble of re-inventing the wheel, you'll see why it's worth learning. And Developer Studio and MFC make ActiveX much easier to understand and implement by doing much of the ground work for you. There are five chapters in Part IV, ActiveX Applications and ActiveX Controls, and together they demonstrate what ActiveX has become. ■

What ActiveX is for

An impressive way for applications to communicate with each other and for users to save time and work.

Object linking

Linking enables building a document from parts that were created with a variety of applications.

Object embedding

Each portion of a compound document is accessed with its own application.

Containers, servers, and why you would write one

ActiveX containers can contain embedded objects. ActiveX servers handle the editing of an object that is linked or embedded.

Drag and drop

Adding this feature to your application will increase its usability.

What ActiveX is built on

The Component Object Model is what makes ActiveX work.

ActiveX automation

Do your users need to write scripts or macros for your application?

ActiveX controls

Controls can liven up your application, improve your user interface, and save you coding effort.

The Purpose of ActiveX

Windows has always been a way to have several applications running at once, and right from the beginning programmers wanted to have a way for those applications to exchange information while running. The Clipboard was a marvelous innovation, though, of course, the user had to do a lot of the work. DDE, Dynamic Data Exchange, allowed applications to "talk" to each other but had some major limitations. Then came OLE 1, Object Linking and Embedding. Later there was OLE 2, and then Microsoft just called it OLE, until it moved so far beyond its original roots that it was renamed ActiveX.

ActiveX lets users and applications be document-centered, and this is probably the most important thing about it. If a user wants to create an annual report by choosing ActiveX-enabled applications, the user stays focused on that annual report. Perhaps parts of it are being done with Word and parts with Excel, but, to the user, these applications are not really the point. This shift in focus is happening on many fronts, and corresponds to a more object-oriented way of thinking among many programmers. It seems more natural now to share work among several different applications and arrange for them to communicate than to write one huge application that can do everything.

Here's a simple test to see whether you are document-centered or application-centered: How is your hard drive organized?

The directory structure in Figure 22.1 is application-centered: the directories are named for the applications that were used to create the documents they hold. All Word documents are together, even though they may be for very different clients or projects.

FIG. 22.1

An application-centered directory structure arranges documents by type.

```
Microsoft Office
   Word
      Building Internet Apps
      Using Visual C++
      Acme Corp
         Training
         Web Pages
   Excel
      Journal
      Sales estimates
      Invoices
   ABC Inc
      Payroll System
      Inventory System
Microsoft Developer Studio
   ABC Inc Payroll System
   ABC Inc Inventory System
```

The directory structure in Figure 22.2 is document-centered: the directories are named for the client or project involved. All the sales files are together, even though they can be accessed with a variety of different applications.

FIG. 22.2

An document-centered directory structure arranges documents by meaning or content.

```
Clients
    Acme Corp
        Training
        Web Pages
        Invoices
    ABC Inc
        Payroll System
        Inventory System
        Invoices
Books
    Building Internet Apps
    Using Visual C++
        ...
Overhead
    Accounting
    Sales
```

If you've been using desktop computers long enough, you remember when using a program involved a program disk and a data disk. Perhaps you remember installing software that demanded to know the data directory where you would keep all the files created with that product. That was application-centered thinking, and it's fast being supplanted by document-centered thinking.

Why? What's wrong with application-centered thinking? Well, where do you put the documents that are used with two applications equally often? There was a time when each product could read its own file formats and no others. But these days, the lines between applications are blurring; a document created in one word processor can easily be read into another, a spreadsheet file can be used as a database, and so on. If a client sends you a WordPerfect document, and you don't have WordPerfect, do you make a \WORDPERFECT\DOCS directory to put it in, or add it to your \MSOFFICE\WORD\DOCS directory, or what? If you have your hard drive arranged in a more document-centered manner, you can just put it in the directory for that client.

The Windows 95 interface, now incorporated into Windows NT as well, encourages document-centered thinking by having users double-click documents to automatically launch the applications that created them. This isn't new; File Manager has had that capability for years, but it feels very different to double-click an icon that's just sitting on the desktop than it does to start an application and then double-click an entry in a list box. More and more it doesn't matter just what application or applications were involved in creating this document; you just want to see and change your data, and you want to do that quickly and simply.

After you start being document-centered, you start to see the appeal of compound documents, files created with more than one application. If your report needs an illustration, you create it in some graphic program and then stick it in with your text when it's done. If your annual report needs a table, and you already have the numbers in a spreadsheet, you don't retype them into the table feature of your word processor, or even import them, you incorporate them as a spreadsheet excerpt, right in the middle of your text. This isn't earth-shatteringly new, of course. Early desktop publishing programs, like Ventura, pulled together text and graphics from a variety of sources into one complex compound document. What's new is being able to do it simply, intuitively, and with so many different applications.

Object Linking

Figure 22.3 shows a Word document with an Excel spreadsheet linked into it.

FIG. 22.3

A Microsoft Word document can contain a link to an Excel file.

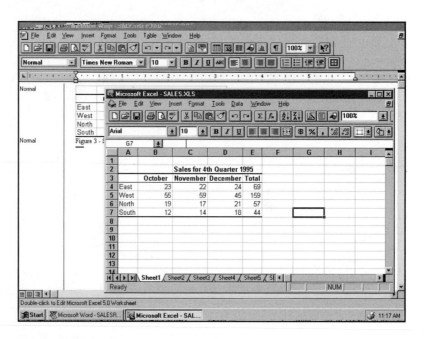

Follow these steps to create a similar document yourself:

1. Start Word and enter your text.

2. Click where you want the table to go.

3. Choose Insert, Object.

4. Select the Create From File tab.

5. Enter or select the file name as though this were a File Open dialog box.

6. Be sure to check the Link to File box.

7. Click OK.

The entire file appears in your document. If you make a change in the file on disk, the change is reflected in your document. You can edit the file in its own application by double-clicking it within Word. The other application is launched to edit it, as shown in Figure 22.4. If you delete the file from disk, your Word document still displays what the file last looked like, but you are not able to edit it.

FIG. 22.4

Double-clicking a linked object launches the application that created it.

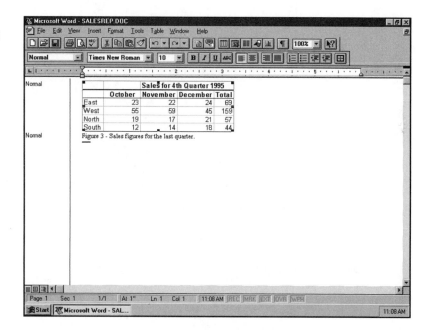

You link files into your documents if you plan to use the same file in many documents and contexts, because your changes are automatically reflected everywhere that you have linked the file. Linking doesn't increase the size of your document files dramatically, since only the location of the file and a little bit of presentation information needs to be kept in your document.

Object Embedding

Embedding is similar to linking, but a copy of the object is made and placed into your document. If you change the original, the changes are not reflected in your document. You can't tell by looking whether the Excel chart you see in your Word document is linked or embedded. Figure 22.5 shows a spreadsheet embedded within a Word document.

FIG. 22.5

A file embedded within another file looks just like a linked file.

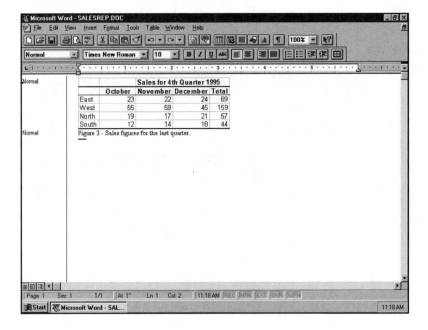

Follow these steps to create a similar document yourself:

1. Start Word and enter your text.

2. Click where you want the table to go.

3. Choose Insert, Object.

4. Select the Create From File tab.

5. Enter or select the file name as though this were a File Open dialog box.

6. Do not check the Link to File box.

7. Click OK.

What's the difference? You'll see when you double-click the object to edit it. The menus and toolbars of Word disappear and are replaced with their Excel equivalents, as shown in Figure 22.6. Changes you make here are not made in the file you originally embedded. They are made in the copy of that file that has become part of your Word document.

You embed files into your documents if you plan to build a compound document and then use it as a self-contained whole, without using the individual parts again. Any changes you make do not affect any other files on your disk, not even the one you copied from in the first place. Embedding makes your document much larger than it was, but you can delete the original if space is a problem.

FIG. 22.6
Editing in place is
the magic of OLE
embedding.

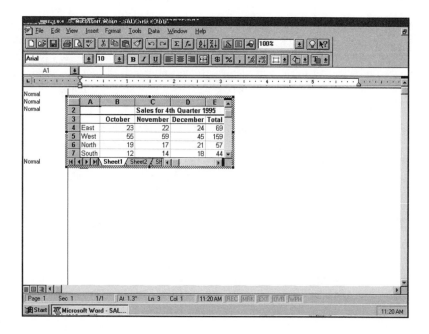

Containers and Servers

To embed or link one object into another, you need a *container* and a *server*. The container is
the application into which the object is linked or embedded—Word in these examples. The
server is the application that made them, and that can be launched (perhaps in place) when the
object is double-clicked—Excel in these examples.

Why would you develop a container application? To save yourself work. Imagine you have a
product already developed and in the hands of your users. It does a specific task like gets a
sales team organized, or schedules games in a league sport, or calculates life insurance rates.
Then your users tell you that they wish it had a spreadsheet capability, so they could do small
calculations on-the-fly. How long will it take you to add that functionality? Do you really have
time to learn how spreadsheet programs parse the functions that users type?

If your application is a container app, it doesn't take any time at all. Tell them to link or embed
in an Excel sheet, and let Excel do the work. If they don't own a copy of Excel, they need some
spreadsheet application that can be an ActiveX server. You get to piggyback on the effort of
other developers.

It's not just spreadsheets, either. What if users want a scratch pad, a place to scribble a few
notes? Let them embed a Word document. And for bitmaps and other illustrations? Microsoft
Paint, or a more powerful graphics package if they have one and it can act as an ActiveX server.
You don't have to concern yourself with adding functionality like this to your programs because
you can just make your application a container and your users can embed whatever they want
without any more work on your part.

Why would you develop a server application, then? Look back over the reasons for writing a container application. A lot of users are going to contact developers asking for a feature to be added, and be told they can have that feature immediately—they just need an application that does spreadsheets, text, pictures, or whatever, and can act as an ActiveX server. If your application is an ActiveX server, people will buy it so that they can add its functionality to their container apps.

Together, container and server apps allow users to build the documents they want. They represent a move toward building block software and a document-centered approach to work. And if you want your application to carry the Windows 95 logo, it must be a server, a container, or both. But there is much more to ActiveX than just linking and embedding. Read on!

Toward a More Intuitive User Interface

What if the object you want to embed is not in a file, but is part of a document you have open at the moment? You may have already discovered that you can use the Clipboard to transfer ActiveX objects. For example, to embed part of a Word document into an Excel spreadsheet, you can follow these steps:

1. Open Excel.
2. Open Word.
3. In Excel, select the portion you want to copy.
4. Choose Edit, Copy to copy the block onto the Clipboard.
5. Switch to Word and choose Edit, Paste Special.
6. Select the Paste radio button.
7. Select Microsoft Excel 6.0 Document from the list box.
8. Make sure that Display as Icon is not checked.
9. The dialog box should look like Figure 22.7. Click OK.

FIG. 22.7

The Paste Special dialog box is used to link or embed selected portions of a document.

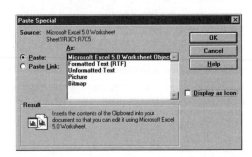

A copy of the block is now embedded into the spreadsheet. If you choose Paste Link, changes in the spreadsheet are reflected immediately in the Word document, not just when you save them. (You may have to click the selection in Word to get it updated.) This is true even if the spreadsheet document has no name and has never been saved. Try it yourself! This is certainly better than saving dummy files just to embed them into compound documents, then deleting them, isn't it?

Another way to embed part of a document into another is drag and drop. This is a user-interface paradigm that works in a variety of contexts. You click on something (an icon, a high-lighted block of text, a selection in a list box) and hold the mouse button down while moving it. The thing you clicked moves with the mouse, and when you let go of the mouse button, it is dropped to the new location. That's very intuitive for things like moving or resizing windows, but now you can use it to do much, much more. For example, here's how that Excel-in-Word example would be done with drag and drop:

1. Open Word and size it to less than full screen.
2. Open Excel and size it to less than full screen. If you can arrange the Word and Excel windows so they don't overlap, that's great.
3. In Excel, select the portion you want to copy by highlighting it with the mouse or cursor keys.
4. Click the border of the selected area (the thick black line) and hold.
5. Drag the block into the Word window and let go.

The selected block is embedded into the Word document. If you double-click it, you are editing in place with Excel. Dragging and dropping also works within a document to move or copy a selection.

 TIP The block is moved by default, which means it is deleted from the Excel sheet. If you want a copy, hold down the Ctrl key while dragging, and release the mouse button before the Ctrl key.

You can also use drag and drop with icons. On your desktop, if you drag a file to a folder, it is moved there. (Hold down Ctrl while dragging to copy it.) If you drag it to a program icon, it is opened with that program. This is very useful when you have a document you use with two applications. For example, pages on the World Wide Web are HTML documents, often created with an HTML editor, but viewed with a World Wide Web browser like Netscape Navigator. If you double-click an HTML document icon, your browser is launched to view it. If you drag that icon onto the icon for your HTML editor, the editor is launched and opens the file you dragged. After you realize you can do this, you will find your work speeds up dramatically.

All of this is ActiveX, and all of this requires a little bit of work from programmers to make it happen. So what's going on?

The Component Object Model

The heart of modern ActiveX is the Component Object Model. This is an incredibly complex topic that deserves a book of its own. Luckily, the Microsoft Foundation Classes and the Visual

C++ AppWizard do much of the behind-the-scenes work for you, and so the discussion in these chapters is just what you need to know to use OLE as a developer.

The Component Object Model (COM) is a binary standard for Windows objects. That means that the executable code (in a .DLL or .EXE) that describes an object can be executed by other objects. Even if two objects were written in different languages, they are able to interact using the COM standard.

How do they interact? Through an *interface*. An ActiveX interface is a collection of functions, or really just function names. It's a C++ class with no data, only pure virtual functions. Your objects inherit from this class and provide code for the functions. Other programs get to your code by calling these functions. All ActiveX objects must have an interface called IUnknown (and usually have many more, all with names that start with I, the prefix for interfaces).

N O T E   If you look at the MFC source code, you see that interfaces are actually declared like this:

```
interface IUnknown
```

Snoop around a little further and you find this line:

```
#define interface struct
```

So, in fact, an interface isn't exactly a class, it's a struct. There's very little difference. Members are private by default in a class and public by default in a struct. That's it, in C++. You can even have functions in a C++ struct, though you can't in C. And yes, a class can inherit from a struct. Microsoft made an interface a struct, because much of The ActiveX frameworkcode is written to work in both C and C++, with #ifdef __cplusplus tests scattered throughout the code. By making it a struct in both C and C++, The Microsoft developers get away with a few less #ifdefs. In C, by the way, they use pointers to functions, and implement the virtual function stuff in a way you probably don't want to learn about.

The IUnknown interface has only one purpose: finding other interfaces. It has a function called QueryInterface() that takes an interface ID and returns a pointer to that interface for this object. All the other interfaces have a QueryInterface(), too, since they inherit from IUnknown, and you have to write them, or you would if there was no MFC. MFC implements a number of macros that simplify the job of writing OLE interfaces and their functions, as you will shortly see.

ActiveX Automation

An ActiveX Automation application lets other applications tell it what to do. It *exposes* functions and data, called *methods* and *properties*. For example, Microsoft Excel is an ActiveX Automation object, and programs written in Visual C++ or Visual Basic can call Excel functions and set properties like column widths. That means you don't need to write a scripting language for your application any more. If you expose all the functions and properties of your application, any programming language that can use an ActiveX Automation application can be a scripting language for your application. Your users, your customers, may already know your scripting language. They essentially will have no learning curve for writing macros to automate your application (though they will need to learn the names of the methods and properties you expose).

The important thing to know about interacting with ActiveX Automation is that one program is always in control, calling the methods or changing the properties of the other running application. The application that is in control is called an ActiveX Automation controller. The application that exposes methods and functions is called an ActiveX Automation server. Excel, Word, and other members of the Microsoft Office suite are ActiveX Automation servers, and your programs can use the functions of these applications to really save you coding time.

For example, imagine being able to use the function called by the Word menu item Format, Change Case to convert the blocks of text your application uses to all uppercase, all lowercase, sentence case (the first letter of the first word in each sentence is uppercase, the rest are not), or title case (the first letter of every word is uppercase, the rest are not).

The description of how ActiveX Automation really works is far longer and more complex than the interface summary of the previous section. It involves a special interface called IDispatch, a simplified interface that works from a number of different languages.

ActiveX Controls

ActiveX controls are tiny little ActiveX Automation servers that load *in place*. That means they are remarkably fast. They were originally called OLE Custom Controls and were designed to replace VBX controls, 16-bit controls written for use in Visual Basic and Visual C++. (There are a number of good technical reasons why the VBX technology could not be extended to the 32-bit world.) Since OLE Custom Controls were traditionally kept in files with the extension .OCX, many people referred to an OLE Custom Control as an OCX or an OCX control. Although the technology has been renamed, ActiveX controls produced by Visual C++ 4.2 are still kept in files with the .OCX extension.

The original purpose of VBX controls was to allow programmers to provide unusual interface controls to their users. Controls that looked like gas gauges or volume knobs became easy to develop. But almost immediately, VBX programmers moved beyond simple controls to modules that involved significant amounts of calculation and processing. In the same way, many ActiveX controls are far more than just controls; they are *components* that can be used to build powerful applications quickly and easily.

N O T E If you have built an OCX in earlier versions of Visual C++, you might think it is a difficult thing to do. The Control Developer Kit, integrated into Visual C++ as of version 4.0, takes care of the ActiveX (OLE) aspects of the job and allows you to concentrate on the calculations, display, or whatever else it is that makes your control worth using. The OLE Control Wizard makes getting started with an empty ActiveX control simple. (The wizard will presumably be renamed soon.) ■

Because controls are actually little ActiveX Automation servers, they need to be used by an ActiveX Automation controller, but the terminology is too confusing if there are controls and controllers, so we say that ActiveX controls are used by *container* applications. Visual C++ and Visual Basic are both container applications, as are many members of the Office suite as well as non-Microsoft products.

In addition to properties and methods, OLE Controls have *events*. To be specific, a control is said to *fire* an event, and it does so when there is something that the container needs to be aware of. For example, when the user clicks a portion of the control, the control deals with it, perhaps changing its appearance or making a calculation, but it may also need to pass on word of that click to the container application so that a file can be opened or some other container action can be performed.

From Here...

This chapter has given you a brief tour through the concepts and terminology used in ActiveX technology, and a glimpse of the power you can add to your applications by incorporating ActiveX into them. The remainder of the chapters in this part work you through the creation of ActiveX applications using MFC and the wizards in Visual C++. Check out the following:

- Chapter 23, "Building an ActiveX Container Application," demonstrates a simple ActiveX container, a program that can contain embedded or linked objects.
- Chapter 24, "Building an ActiveX Server Application," demonstrates a simple ActiveX server. This application can create objects that can be embedded or linked into ActiveX container applications.
- Chapter 25, "ActiveX Automation," builds an ActiveX Automation object that can use Visual Basic as its scripting language.
- Chapter 26, "Building an ActiveX Control," builds an ActiveX control that can be embedded into a Visual C++ or Visual Basic program.

CHAPTER 23

Building an ActiveX Container Application

You can get a rudimentary ActiveX container by asking AppWizard to make you one, but it will have a lot of shortcomings. A far harder task is to understand how an ActiveX container works, and what you have to do to really use it. In this chapter, by turning the ShowString application of earlier chapters into an ActiveX container and then making it a truly functional container, you get a backstage view of ActiveX in action. Adding drag-and-drop support brings your application into the modern age of intuitive, document-centered user interface design. ∎

Transforming ShowString into a container

An ActiveX container can contain its documents created in another application. This section shows you how to build one, and how they work.

Moving, resizing, and tracking the contained object

The container code generated for you does not handle some of the user interface tasks well. This section shows you how to handle those tasks yourself.

Handling multiple objects and object selection

Improving your container so that it can contain more than one object, and letting the user click on an object to select it, is another enhancement to your user interface.

Implementing drag and drop

Users love drag and drop. This section shows you how to implement drag and drop in your ActiveX container.

Deleting a contained object

A final improvement to your user interface is enabling the user to delete an object that has been embedded or linked into the container.

Changing ShowString

ShowString was built originally in Chapter 17, "Building Menus and Dialogs," and has no ActiveX support. You could make the changes by hand to implement ActiveX container support, but there would be over 30 changes. It's quicker to build a new ShowString application, this time asking for ActiveX container support, and then make changes to that code to get the ShowString functionality again.

AppWizard Generated ActiveX Container Code

Build the new ShowString in a different directory, making almost exactly the same AppWizard choices as before: call it ShowString, choose an MDI application, no database support, OLE container, a docking toolbar, status bar, printing and print preview, context-sensitive Help, and 3D controls. Finally, select source file comments and a shared DLL.

N O T E Even though the technology is now called ActiveX, the AppWizard dialogs still refer to OLE. Many of the class names that are used throughout this chapter have Ole in their names, and comments refer to OLE. While Microsoft has changed the name of the technology, it has not propagated that change throughout Visual C++ yet. You will have to live with these contradictions until the next release of Visual C++. ▨

There are a lot of differences between the application you have just built and a do-nothing application without ActiveX container support. The remainder of this section describes and explains these differences and their effects.

Menus There's another entire menu, called IDR_SHOWSTTYPE_CNTR_IP, shown in Figure 23.1. The name refers to a container whose *contained* object is being edited *in place*. During in-place editing, the menu bar is built from the container's in-place menu and the server's in-place menu. The pair of vertical bars in the middle of IDR_SHOWSTTYPE_CNTR_IP are separators; the server menu items will be put between them. This is discussed in more detail in Chapter 24, "Building an ActiveX Server Application."

The Edit menu, as shown in Figure 23.2, has four new items:

- ▨ Paste Special—The user chooses this item to insert an item into the container from the Clipboard.

- ▨ Insert New Object—Choosing this item brings up the Insert Object dialog box, shown in Figures 23.3 and 23.4, so the user can insert an item into the container.

- ▨ Links—When an object has been linked into the container, choosing this item brings up the Links dialog box, shown in Figure 23.5, to allow control of the way that the copy of the object is updated after a change is saved to the file.

- ▨ <<OLE VERBS GO HERE>>—Each kind of item has different verbs associated with it, like Edit, Open, or Play. When a contained item has focus, this spot on the menu is replaced by an object type like those in the Insert Object dialog box, with a menu cascading from it that lists the verbs for this type, like the one shown in Figure 23.6.

FIG. 23.1
AppWizard adds another menu for editing in place.

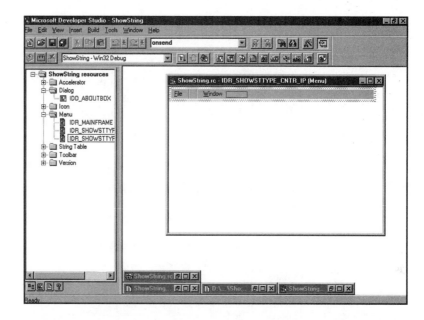

FIG. 23.2
AppWizard adds items to the Edit menu of the IDR_SHOWSTTYPE resource.

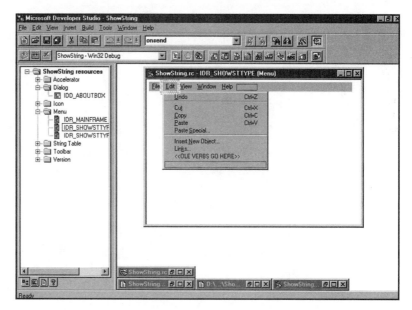

FIG. 23.3
The Insert Object dialog box can be used to embed new objects.

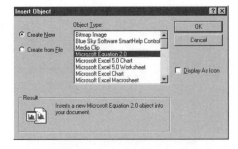

FIG. 23.4
The Insert Object dialog box can be used to embed or link objects that are in a file.

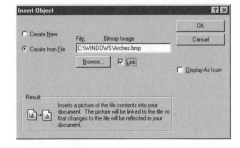

FIG. 23.5
The Links dialog box controls the way linked objects are updated.

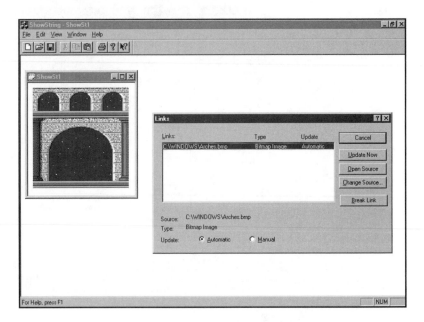

CShowStringApp CShowStringApp::InitInstance() has several changes from the InitInstance() method provided by AppWizard for applications that are not ActiveX containers. The lines in Listing 23.1 initialize the ActiveX (OLE) libraries.

FIG. 23.6
Each object type adds a cascading menu item to the Edit menu when it has focus.

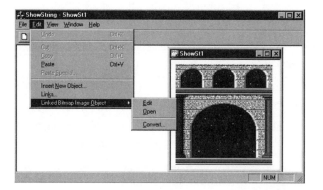

Listing 23.1 Excerpt from ShowString.cpp—Library Initialization

```
// Initialize OLE libraries
if (!AfxOleInit())
{
    AfxMessageBox(IDP_OLE_INIT_FAILED);
    return FALSE;
}
```

Still in `CShowStringApp::InitInstance()`, after the `MultiDocTemplate` is initialized, but before the call to `AddDocTemplate()`, this line is added to register the menu used for in-place editing:

`pDocTemplate->SetContainerInfo(IDR_SHOWSTTYPE_CNTR_IP);`

CShowStringDoc   The document class, `CShowStringDoc`, now inherits from `COleDocument` rather than `CDocument`. As well, this line is added at the top of ShowStringDoc.cpp:

`#include "CntrItem.h"`

CntrItem.h describes the container item class, `CShowStringCntrItem`, discussed later. Still in ShowStringDoc.cpp, the macros in Listing 23.2 have been added to the message map.

Listing 23.2 Excerpt from ShowString.cpp—Message Map Additions

```
ON_UPDATE_COMMAND_UI(ID_EDIT_PASTE,
➥COleDocument::OnUpdatePasteMenu)
ON_UPDATE_COMMAND_UI(ID_EDIT_PASTE_LINK,
➥COleDocument::OnUpdatePasteLinkMenu)
ON_UPDATE_COMMAND_UI(ID_OLE_EDIT_CONVERT,
➥COleDocument::OnUpdateObjectVerbMenu)
ON_COMMAND(ID_OLE_EDIT_CONVERT,
➥COleDocument::OnEditConvert)
ON_UPDATE_COMMAND_UI(ID_OLE_EDIT_LINKS,
➥COleDocument::OnUpdateEditLinksMenu)
ON_COMMAND(ID_OLE_EDIT_LINKS,
➥COleDocument::OnEditLinks)
ON_UPDATE_COMMAND_UI(ID_OLE_VERB_FIRST,
➥COleDocument::OnUpdateObjectVerbMenu)
```

Part
IV

Ch
23

These enable and disable the following menu items:

- Edit, Paste
- Edit, Paste Link
- Edit, Links
- The OLE verbs section including the Convert verb

The new macros also handle Convert and Edit Links. Notice that the messages are handled by functions of COleDocument and don't have to be written by you.

The constructor, CShowStringDoc::CShowStringDoc(), has a line added:

```
EnableCompoundFile();
```

This turns on the use of compound files. CShowStringDoc::Serialize() has a line added as well:

```
COleDocument::Serialize(ar);
```

This call to the base class Serialize() takes care of serializing all the contained objects, with no further work for you.

CShowStringView   The view class, CShowStringView, includes CntrItem.h just as the document does. The view class has these new entries in the message map:

```
ON_WM_SETFOCUS()
ON_WM_SIZE()
ON_COMMAND(ID_OLE_INSERT_NEW, OnInsertObject)
ON_COMMAND(ID_CANCEL_EDIT_CNTR, OnCancelEditCntr)
```

These are in addition to the messages caught by the view before it was a container. These catch WM_SETFOCUS, WM_SIZE, the menu item Edit, Insert New Object, and the cancellation of editing in place. An accelerator has already been added to connect this message to Esc.

In ShowStringView.h, a new member variable has been added, as shown in Listing 23.3.

Listing 23.3   Excerpt from ShowStringView.h—m_pSelection

```
// m_pSelection holds the selection to the current
// CShowStringCntrItem. For many applications, such
// a member variable isn't adequate to represent a
// selection, such as a multiple selection or a selection
// of objects that are not CShowStringCntrItem objects.
// This selection mechanism is provided just to help you
// get started.

// TODO: replace this selection mechanism with one appropriate to your app.
   CShowStringCntrItem* m_pSelection;
```

This new member variable shows up again in the view constructor, Listing 23.4, and the revised OnDraw(), Listing 23.5.

Listing 23.4 ShowStringView.cpp—Constructor

```
CShowStringView::CShowStringView()
{
    m_pSelection = NULL;
    // TODO: add construction code here
}
```

Listing 23.5 ShowStringView.cpp— CShowStringView::OnDraw()

```
void CShowStringView::OnDraw(CDC* pDC)
{
    CShowStringDoc* pDoc = GetDocument();
    ASSERT_VALID(pDoc);

    // TODO: add draw code for native data here
    // TODO: also draw all OLE items in the document

    // Draw the selection at an arbitrary position.  This code should be
    //   removed once your real drawing code is implemented.  This position
    //   corresponds exactly to the rectangle returned by CShowStringCntrItem,
    //   to give the effect of in-place editing.

    // TODO: remove this code when final draw code is complete.

    if (m_pSelection == NULL)
    {
        POSITION pos = pDoc->GetStartPosition();
        m_pSelection = (CShowStringCntrItem*)pDoc->GetNextClientItem(pos);
    }
    if (m_pSelection != NULL)
        m_pSelection->Draw(pDC, CRect(10, 10, 210, 210));
}
```

The code supplied for OnDraw() draws only a single contained item. It doesn't draw any native data, in other words, elements of ShowString that are not contained items. At the moment there is no native data, but after the string is added to the application, OnDraw() is going to have to draw it. What's more, this code only draws one contained item, and it does so in an arbitrary rectangle. OnDraw() is going to see a lot of changes as you work through this chapter.

The view class has gained a lot of new functions. They are as follows:

- OnInitialUpdate()
- IsSelected()
- OnInsertObject()
- OnSetFocus()
- OnSize()
- OnCancelEditCntr()

Each of these new functions is discussed in the subsections that follow.

OnInitialUpdate()   OnInitialUpdate() is called the very first time the view is to be displayed. The boilerplate code (Listing 23.6) is pretty dull:

Listing 23.6   ShowStringView.cpp—CShowStringView::OnInitialUpdate()

```
void CShowStringView::OnInitialUpdate()
{
    CView::OnInitialUpdate();

    // TODO: remove this code when final selection
    // model code is written
    m_pSelection = NULL;    // initialize selection

}
```

The base class OnInitialUpdate() calls the base class OnUpdate(), which calls Invalidate(), requiring a full repaint of the client area.

IsSelected()   IsSelected() can't really work right now, because the selection mechanism is so rudimentary. Listing 23.7 shows what you get, and it works, sort of:

Listing 23.7   ShowStringView.cpp—CShowStringView::IsSelected()

```
BOOL CShowStringView::IsSelected(const CObject* pDocItem) const
{
    // The implementation below is adequate if your selection consists of
    //   only CShowStringCntrItem objects.  To handle different selection
    //   mechanisms, the implementation here should be replaced.

    // TODO: implement this function that tests for a selected OLE client item

    return pDocItem == m_pSelection;
}
```

This function is passed a pointer to a container item. If that is the same as the current selection, it returns TRUE.

OnInsertObject()   OnInsertObject() is called when the user chooses Edit, Insert New Object. It's quite a long function, so it is presented in parts. The overall structure is presented in Listing 23.8.

Listing 23.8   ShowStringView.cpp—CShowStringView::OnInsertObject()

```
void CShowStringView::OnInsertObject()
{
    //display the Insert Object dialog box
```

```
        CShowStringCntrItem* pItem = NULL;
        TRY
        {
            // Create new item connected to this document.
            // Initialize the item
            // set selection and update all views
        }
        CATCH(CException, e)
        {
            // handle failed create
        }
        END_CATCH

        // tidy up
}
```

Each comment here is replaced with a small block of code, discussed in the remainder of this section. The TRY and CATCH statements, by the way, refer to exception handling, discussed in Chapter 30, "Power-User C++ Features."

First, this function displays the Insert Object dialog box, as shown in Listing 23.9.

Listing 23.9 ShowStringView.cpp—Display the Insert Object Dialog Box

```
// Invoke the standard Insert Object dialog box to obtain information
//   for new CShowStringCntrItem object.
COleInsertDialog dlg;
if (dlg.DoModal() != IDOK)
    return;
BeginWaitCursor();
```

If the user clicks Cancel, this function returns and nothing is inserted. If the user clicks OK, the cursor is set to an hourglass while the rest of the processing occurs.

To create a new item, the code in Listing 23.10 is inserted.

Listing 23.10 ShowStringView.cpp—Create a New Item

```
// Create new item connected to this document.
CShowStringDoc* pDoc = GetDocument();
ASSERT_VALID(pDoc);
pItem = new CShowStringCntrItem(pDoc);
ASSERT_VALID(pItem);
```

This code makes sure there is a document, even though the menu item is only enabled if there is, and then creates a new container item, passing it the pointer to the document. As you see later, container items hold a pointer to the document that contains them.

The code in Listing 23.11 initializes that item.

Listing 23.11 ShowStringView.cpp—Initializing the Inserted Item

```
// Initialize the item from the dialog data.
if (!dlg.CreateItem(pItem))
    AfxThrowMemoryException();  // any exception will do
ASSERT_VALID(pItem);
// If item created from class list (not from file) then launch
//   the server to edit the item.
if (dlg.GetSelectionType() == COleInsertDialog::createNewItem)
    pItem->DoVerb(OLEIVERB_SHOW, this);

ASSERT_VALID(pItem);
```

The code in Listing 23.11 calls the CreateItem() function of the dialog class, ColeInsertDialog. That may seem a strange place to keep such a function, but the function needs to know all the answers that were given on the dialog box, so if it was a member of another class, it would have to interrogate the dialog for the type, file name, was it link or embedded, and so on. It calls member functions of the container item like CreateLinkFromFile(), CreateFromFile(), CreateNewItem(), and so on. So it's not that the code to actually fill the object from the file is in the dialog box, but rather that the work is partitioned between the objects, instead of passing information back and forth between them.

Then, one question is asked of the dialog box: was this a new item? If so, the server is called to edit it. Objects created from a file can just be displayed.

Finally, the selection is updated and so are the views, as shown in Listing 23.12.

Listing 23.12 ShowStringView.cpp—Update Selection and Views

```
// As an arbitrary user interface design, this sets the selection
//   to the last item inserted.

// TODO: reimplement selection as appropriate for your application

m_pSelection = pItem;   // set selection to last inserted item
pDoc->UpdateAllViews(NULL);
```

If the creation of the object failed, execution ends up in the CATCH block, shown in Listing 23.13.

Listing 23.13 ShowStringView.cpp—CATCH Block

```
CATCH(CException, e)
{
    if (pItem != NULL)
    {
    ASSERT_VALID(pItem);
    pItem->Delete();
    }
    AfxMessageBox(IDP_FAILED_TO_CREATE);
```

```
}
END_CATCH
```

This deletes the item that was created and gives the user a message box.

Finally, that hourglass cursor can go away:

```
EndWaitCursor();
```

OnSetFocus()   OnSetFocus(), shown in Listing 23.14, is called whenever this view sets focus.

Listing 23.14   ShowStringView.cpp—CShowStringView::OnSetFocus()

```
void CShowStringView::OnSetFocus(CWnd* pOldWnd)
{
    COleClientItem* pActiveItem = GetDocument()->GetInPlaceActiveItem(this);
    if (pActiveItem != NULL &&
        pActiveItem->GetItemState() == COleClientItem::activeUIState)
    {
        // need to set focus to this item if it is in the same view
        CWnd* pWnd = pActiveItem->GetInPlaceWindow();
        if (pWnd != NULL)
        {
            pWnd->SetFocus();    // don't call the base class
            return;
        }
    }

    CView::OnSetFocus(pOldWnd);
}
```

If there is an active item and its server is loaded, then that active item sets focus. If not, focus remains with the old window, and, to the user, it appears that the click was ignored.

OnSize()   OnSize(), shown in Listing 23.15, is called when the application is resized.

Listing 23.15   ShowStringView.cpp—CShowStringView::OnSize()

```
void CShowStringView::OnSize(UINT nType, int cx, int cy)
{
    CView::OnSize(nType, cx, cy);
    COleClientItem* pActiveItem = GetDocument()->GetInPlaceActiveItem(this);
    if (pActiveItem != NULL)
        pActiveItem->SetItemRects();
}
```

This resizes the view using the base class function, and then, if there is an active item, onsize () tells it to adjust to the resized view.

OnCancelEditCntr() OnCancelEditCntr() is called when a user who has been editing in place presses Esc. The server must be closed and the object stops being active. The code is shown in Listing 23.16.

Listing 23.16   ShowStringView.cpp—CShowStringView::OnCancelEditCntr()

```
void CShowStringView::OnCancelEditCntr()
{
    // Close any in-place active item on this view.
    COleClientItem* pActiveItem =
        GetDocument()->GetInPlaceActiveItem(this);
    if (pActiveItem != NULL)
    {
        pActiveItem->Close();
    }
    ASSERT(GetDocument()->GetInPlaceActiveItem(this) == NULL);
}
```

CShowStringCntrItem The container item class is a completely new addition to ShowString. It describes an item that is contained in the document. As you've already seen, the document and the view use this object quite a lot, primarily through the m_pSelection member variable of CShowStringView. It has no member variables other than those inherited from the base class, COleClientItem. It has overrides for a lot of functions though. They are as follows:

- A constructor
- A destructor
- GetDocument()
- GetActiveView()
- OnChange()
- OnActivate()
- OnGetItemPosition()
- OnDeactivateUI()
- OnChangeItemPosition()
- AssertValid()
- Dump()
- Serialize()

The constructor simply passes the document pointer along to the base class. The destructor does nothing. GetDocument() and GetActiveView() are inline functions that return member variables inherited from the base class by calling the base class function with the same name and casting the result.

OnChange() is the first of these functions that has more than one line of code. It's in Listing 23.17.

Listing 23.17 CntrItem.cpp—CShowStringCntrItem::OnChange()

```
void CShowStringCntrItem::OnChange(OLE_NOTIFICATION nCode,
    DWORD dwParam)
{
    ASSERT_VALID(this);

    COleClientItem::OnChange(nCode, dwParam);

    // When an item is being edited (either in-place or fully open)
    // it sends OnChange notifications for changes in the state of the
    // item or visual appearance of its content.

    // TODO: invalidate the item by calling UpdateAllViews
    // (with hints appropriate to your application)

    GetDocument()->UpdateAllViews(NULL);
        // for now just update ALL views/no hints
}
```

Okay, so it has three lines of code. The comments are actually more useful than the code. When the user changes the contained item, the server notifies the container. Calling UpdateAllViews() is a rather drastic way of refreshing the screen, but it gets the job done.

OnActivate() (Listing 23.18) is called when a user double-clicks an item to activate it and edit it in place. ActiveX objects are usually outside-in, which means that a single-click of the item selects it but does not activate it. Activating an outside-in object requires a double-click, or a single-click followed by choosing the appropriate OLE verb from the Edit menu.

Listing 23.18 CntrItem.cpp—CShowStringCntrItem::OnActivate()

```
void CShowStringCntrItem::OnActivate()
{
    // Allow only one inplace activate item per frame
    CShowStringView* pView = GetActiveView();
    ASSERT_VALID(pView);
    COleClientItem* pItem = GetDocument()->GetInPlaceActiveItem(pView);
    if (pItem != NULL && pItem != this)
        pItem->Close();

    COleClientItem::OnActivate();
}
```

This code makes sure that the current view is valid, closes the active item, if any, and then activates this item.

OnGetItemPosition() (Listing 23.19) is called as part of the in-place activation process.

Listing 23.19   Cntrltem.cpp—CShowStringCntrltem:: OnGetltemPosition()

```
void CShowStringCntrItem::OnGetItemPosition(CRect& rPosition)
{
    ASSERT_VALID(this);

    // During in-place activation,
    // CShowStringCntrItem::OnGetItemPosition
    // will be called to determine the location of this item.
    // The default implementation created from AppWizard simply
    // returns a hard-coded rectangle.  Usually, this rectangle
    // would reflect the current position of the item relative
    // to the view used for activation. You can obtain the view
    // by calling CShowStringCntrItem::GetActiveView.

    // TODO: return correct rectangle (in pixels) in rPosition

    rPosition.SetRect(10, 10, 210, 210);
}
```

Like OnChange(), the comments are more useful than the actual code. At the moment, the View's OnDraw() function draws the contained object in a hard-coded rectangle, so this function returns that same rectangle. You are instructed to write code that asks the active view where the object is.

OnDeactivateUI() (Listing 23.20) is called when the object goes from being active to inactive.

Listing 23.20   Cntrltem.cpp—CShowStringCntrltem:: OnDeactivateUI()

```
void CShowStringCntrItem::OnDeactivateUI(BOOL bUndoable)
{
    COleClientItem::OnDeactivateUI(bUndoable);

    // Hide the object if it is not an outside-in object
    DWORD dwMisc = 0;
    m_lpObject->GetMiscStatus(GetDrawAspect(), &dwMisc);
    if (dwMisc & OLEMISC_INSIDEOUT)
        DoVerb(OLEIVERB_HIDE, NULL);
}
```

While the default behavior for contained objects is outside-in, as discussed earlier, you can write inside-out objects. These are activated simply by moving the mouse pointer over them; clicking in the object has the same effect that clicking in that region has while editing the object. For example, if the contained item is a spreadsheet, clicking might select the cell that was clicked. This can be really nice for the user, who can completely ignore the borders between the container and the contained item, but it is harder to write.

OnChangeItemPosition() is called when the item is moved during in-place editing. It, too, contains mostly comments, as shown in Listing 23.21.

Listing 23.21 Cntrltem.cpp—CShowStringCntrItem:: OnChangeItemPosition()

```
BOOL CShowStringCntrItem::OnChangeItemPosition(const CRect& rectPos)
{
    ASSERT_VALID(this);

    // During in-place activation
    // CShowStringCntrItem::OnChangeItemPosition
    // is called by the server to change the position
    // of the in-place window.  Usually, this is a result
    // of the data in the server document changing such that
    // the extent has changed or as a result of in-place resizing.
    //
    // The default here is to call the base class, which will call
    //   COleClientItem::SetItemRects to move the item
    //   to the new position.

    if (!COleClientItem::OnChangeItemPosition(rectPos))
        return FALSE;

    // TODO: update any cache you may have of the item's rectangle/extent

    return TRUE;
}
```

This code is supposed to handle moving the object, but it doesn't really. That's because OnDraw() always draws the contained item in the same place. You'll fix that later.

AssertValid() and Dump() are debug functions that simply call the base class functions. The last function in CShowStringCntrItem is Serialize(), which is called by COleDocument:: Serialize(), which in turn is called by the document's Serialize(), as you've already seen. It is shown in Listing 23.22.

Listing 23.22 Cntrltem.cpp—CShowStringCntrItem:: Serialize()

```
void CShowStringCntrItem::Serialize(CArchive& ar)
{
    ASSERT_VALID(this);

    // Call base class first to read in COleClientItem data.
    // Since this sets up the m_pDocument pointer returned from
    //   CShowStringCntrItem::GetDocument, it is a good idea to call
    //   the base class Serialize first.
    COleClientItem::Serialize(ar);

    // now store/retrieve data specific to CShowStringCntrItem
    if (ar.IsStoring())
    {
        // TODO: add storing code here
    }
```

continues

Listing 23.22 Continued

```
    else
    {
        // TODO: add loading code here
    }
}
```

All this does at the moment is call the base class function. `COleDocument:: Serialize()` stores or loads a number of counters and numbers to keep track of several different contained items, then calls helper functions called `WriteItem()` or `ReadItem()` to actually deal with the item. These functions and the helper functions they call are a bit too "behind-the-scenes" for most people, but if you'd like to take a look at them, they are in the MFC source folder (C:\MSDEV\MFC\SRC on many installations) in the file olecli1.cpp. They do their job, which is to serialize the contained item for you.

Shortcomings of This Container This container application isn't ShowString yet, of course, but it has more important things wrong with it. It isn't a very good container, and that's a direct result of all those TODO tasks that haven't been done. Still, the fact that it is a functioning container is a good measure of the power of the MFC classes `COleDocument` and `COleClientItem`. So why not build the application now and run it? After it's running, choose Edit, Insert New Object and insert a Bitmap image. Now that you've seen the code, it shouldn't be a surprise that Paint is immediately launched to edit the item in place, as you see in Figure 23.7.

FIG. 23.7

The boilerplate container can contain items and activate them for in-place editing, like this bitmap image being edited in Paint.

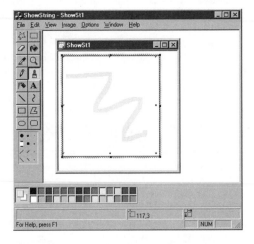

Click outside the bitmap to unselect the item and return control to the container, and nothing happens. Click outside the document and again nothing happens. Are you even still in ShowString? Choose File, New, and you see that you are. The Paint menus and toolbars go away, and a new ShowString document is created. Click the bitmap item again, and you are still editing it in Paint. How can you insert another object into the first document, when the menus are those of Paint? Press Esc to cancel in-place editing, and the menus are ShowString menus again. Insert an Excel chart into the container, and the bitmap disappears as the new Excel chart is inserted, as shown in Figure 23.8. Obviously, this container leaves a lot to be desired.

FIG. 23.8

Inserting an Excel chart gets you a default chart, but it completely covers the old bitmap.

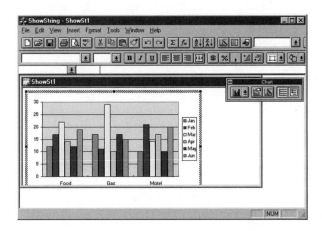

Press Esc to cancel the in-place editing and notice that the view changes a little, as shown in Figure 23.9. That's because `CShowStringView::OnDraw()` draws the contained item in a 200×200 pixel rectangle, so the chart has to be squeezed a little to fit into that space. It is the server, Excel, in this case, that decides how to fit the item into the space given to it by the container.

FIG. 23.9

Items can look quite different when they are not active.

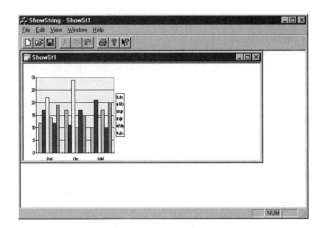

As you can see, there's a lot to be done to make this feel like a real container. But first, you have to turn it back into ShowString.

Returning the ShowString Functionality

This section is a quick summary of the steps in Chapter 17, "Building Menus and Dialogs." Open the files from the old ShowString as you go so that you can copy code and resources wherever possible. Follow these steps:

1. In ShowStringDoc.h, add the private member variables and public `Get` functions to the class.

2. In `CShowStringDoc::Serialize()` paste in the code that saves or restores these member variables. Leave the call to `COleDocument::Serialize()` in place.

3. In `CShowStringDoc::OnNewDocument()` paste in the code that initializes the member variables.

4. In `CShowStringView::OnDraw()` add the code that draws the string before the code that handles the contained items. Remove the `TODO` about drawing native data.

5. Copy the entire Tools menu from the old ShowString to the new container ShowString: Choose File, Open to open the old ShowString.rc, open the IDR_SHOWSTTYPE menu, click the Tools menu, and choose Edit, Copy. Open the new ShowString's IDR_SHOWSTTYPE menu, click the Window menu, and choose Edit, Paste. Do not paste it into the IDR_SHOWSTTYPE_CNTR_IP menu.

6. Add the accelerator Ctrl+T for ID_TOOLS_OPTIONS as described in Chapter 17, "Building Menus and Dialogs." Add it to the IDR_MAINFRAME accelerator only.

7. Delete the IDD_ABOUTBOX dialog box from the new ShowString. Copy IDD_ABOUTBOX and IDD_OPTIONS from the old ShowString to the new.

8. While IDD_OPTIONS has focus, choose View, Class Wizard. Create the `COptionsDialog` class as in the original ShowString. Remember not to add it to the Component Gallery.

9. Use Class Wizard to arrange for `CShowStringDoc` to catch the ID_TOOLS_OPTIONS command.

10. In ShowStringDoc.cpp, replace the Class Wizard version of `CShowStringDoc::OnToolsOptions()` with the `OnToolsOptions()` from the old ShowString, that puts up the dialog box.

11. In ShowStringDoc.cpp, add **`#include "OptionsDialog.h"`** after the #include statements already present.

12. Use Class Wizard to connect the dialog controls to `COptionsDialog` member variables, as described in Chapter 17.

Build the application, fix any typos or other simple errors, then execute it. It should run as before, saying `Hello, world!` in the center of the view. Convince yourself that the Options dialog box still works and that you have restored all the old functionality. Then resize the application and the view as large as possible, so that when you insert an object it does not land on the string. Insert an Excel chart as before, and press Esc to stop editing in place. There you have it: a version of ShowString that is also an ActiveX container. Now it's time to get to work making it a *good* container.

Moving, Resizing, and Tracking

The first thing you want to do, even when there is only one item contained in ShowString, is to allow the user to move and resize that item. It makes life simpler for the user if you also provide a tracker rectangle, a hashed line around the contained item. This is easy to do with the MFC class CRectTracker.

The first step is to add a member variable to the container item (CShowStringCntrItem) definition in CntrItem.h, to hold the rectangle occupied by this container item. Use the MFC class CRect, like this:

```
public:
    CRect m_rect;
```

Why public? Doesn't that break encapsulation? Yes, but implementing both Set and Get functions, or making other classes friends, does too. This makes the code easier to type and read, without any real loss of information hiding.

This needs to be initialized in a function that is called when the container item is first used and then never again. While view classes have OnInitialUpdate() and document classes have OnNewDocument(), container item classes have no such called-only-once function except the constructor. So, initialize the rectangle in the constructor, as shown in Listing 23.23.

Listing 23.23   CntrItem.cpp—Constructor

```
CShowStringCntrItem::CShowStringCntrItem(CShowStringDoc* pContainer)
    : COleClientItem(pContainer)
{
    m_rect = CRect(10,10,210,210);
}
```

The numerical values used here are those in the boilerplate OnDraw() provided by AppWizard. Now, you need to start using the m rect member variable, and setting it. The functions affected are presented in the same order as in the earlier section on CShowStringView.

First, CShowStringView::OnDraw(). Find this line:

```
m_pSelection->Draw(pDC, CRect(10, 10, 210, 210));
```

Replace it with this:

```
m_pSelection->Draw(pDC, m_pSelection->m_rect);
```

Next, you will change CShowStringCntrItem::OnGetItemPosition(), which needs to return this rectangle. Take away all the comments and the old hardcoded rectangle (leave the ASSERT_VALID macro call), and add this line:

```
rPosition = m_rect;
```

The partner function, CShowStringCntrItem::OnChangeItemPosition(), is called when the user moves the item. Here is where m_rect gets changed from the initial value. Remove the comments and add code immediately after the the call to the base class function, COleClientItem::OnChangeItemPosition(). The code to add is:

```
m_rect = rectPos;
    GetDocument()->SetModifiedFlag();
    GetDocument()->UpdateAllViews(NULL);
```

Finally, the new member variable needs to be incorporated into
`CShowStringCntrItem::Serialize()`. Remove the comments and add lines in
the storing and saving blocks so that the function looks like Listing 23.24.

Listing 23.24   CntrItem.cpp—CShowStringCntrItem::Serialize()

```
void CShowStringCntrItem::Serialize(CArchive& ar)
{
    ASSERT_VALID(this);

    // Call base class first to read in COleClientItem data.
    // Since this sets up the m_pDocument pointer returned from
    //   CShowStringCntrItem::GetDocument, it is a good idea to call
    //   the base class Serialize first.
    COleClientItem::Serialize(ar);

    // now store/retrieve data specific to CShowStringCntrItem
    if (ar.IsStoring())
    {
        ar << m_rect;
    }
    else
    {
        ar >> m_rect;
    }
}
```

Build and execute the application, insert a bitmap, and scribble something in it. Press Esc to
cancel editing in place, and your scribble shows up in the top-right corner as well. Choose Edit,
Bitmap Image Object and then Edit. (Choosing Open allows you to edit it in a different window.) Use the resizing handles that appear to drag the image over to the left, then press Esc to
cancel editing in place. The image is drawn at the new position, as expected.

Now for the tracker rectangle. The Microsoft tutorials recommend writing a helper function,
`SetupTracker()`, to handle this. Add these lines to `CShowStringView::OnDraw()`, just after the
call to `m_pSelection->Draw()`:

```
CRectTracker trackrect;
SetupTracker(m_pSelection,&trackrect);
trackrect.Draw(pDC);
```

(The one-line statement after the `if` was not in brace brackets before; don't forget to add
them.)

Add the following public function to ShowStringView.h (inside the class definition):

```
void SetupTracker(CShowStringCntrItem* item,
CRectTracker* track);
```

Add the code in Listing 23.25 to ShowStringView.cpp immediately after the destructor.

Listing 23.25 ShowStringView.cpp—CShowStringView::SetupTracker()

```cpp
void CShowStringView::SetupTracker(CShowStringCntrItem* item,
    CRectTracker* track)
{
    track->m_rect = item->m_rect;

    if (item == m_pSelection)
    {
        track->m_nStyle |= CRectTracker::resizeInside;
    }

    if (item->GetType() == OT_LINK)
    {
        track->m_nStyle |= CRectTracker::dottedLine;
    }
    else
    {
        track->m_nStyle |= CRectTracker::solidLine;
    }
    if (item->GetItemState() == COleClientItem::openState ||
        item->GetItemState() == COleClientItem::activeUIState)
    {
        track->m_nStyle |= CRectTracker::hatchInside;
    }
}
```

This code first sets the tracker rectangle to the container item rectangle. Then it adds styles to the tracker. The styles available are as follows:

- solidLine—Used for an embedded item
- dottedLine—Used for a linked item
- hatchedBorder—Used for an in-place active item
- resizeInside—Used for a selected item
- resizeOutside—Used for a selected item
- hatchInside—Used for an item whose server is open

This code first compares the pointers to this item and the current selection. If they are the same, this item is selected and it gets resize handles. It's up to you whether they go on the inside or the outside. Then it asks the item whether it is linked (dotted line) or not (solid line). Finally, it adds hatching to active items.

Build and execute the application, and try it out. You still cannot edit the contained item by double-clicking it: choose Edit from the cascading menu added at the bottom of the Edit menu. You can't move and resize an inactive object, but if you activate it you can resize it while active, and when you press Esc, it is drawn at its new position.

Handling Multiple Objects and Object Selection

The next step is to catch mouse clicks and double-clicks so that the item can be resized, moved, and activated more easily. This involves testing to see if a click is over a contained item or not.

Hit Testing

You need to write a helper function that returns a pointer to the contained item that the user clicked, or NULL if the user clicked in an area of the view that has no contained item. This function runs through all the items contained in the document. Add the code in Listing 23.26 to ShowStringView.cpp immediately after the destructor.

Listing 23.26   ShowStringView.cpp—CShowStringView::SetupTracker()

```
CShowStringCntrItem* CShowStringView::HitTest(CPoint point)
{
    CShowStringDoc* pDoc = GetDocument();
    CShowStringCntrItem* pHitItem = NULL;

    POSITION pos = pDoc->GetStartPosition();
    while (pos)
    {
        CShowStringCntrItem* pCurrentItem =
            (CShowStringCntrItem*) pDoc->GetNextClientItem(pos);
        if ( pCurrentItem->m_rect.PtInRect(point) )
        {
            pHitItem = pCurrentItem;
        }
    }

    return pHitItem;
}
```

 TIP Don't forget to add the declaration of this public function to the header file.

This function is given a CPoint that describes the point on the screen where the user clicked. Each container item has a rectangle, m_rect, as you've seen earlier, and the CRect class has a member function called PtInRect() that takes a CPoint and returns TRUE if the point is in the rectangle, FALSE if it is not. This code simply loops through the items in this document, using the OLE document member function GetNextClientItem(), and calls PtInRect() for each.

What happens if there are several items in the container, and the user clicks at a point where two or more overlap? The one on top is selected. That's because GetStartPosition() returns a pointer to the bottom item, and GetNextClientItem() works its way up through the items. If two items cover the spot where the user clicked, pHitItem is set to the lower one first, and then, on a later iteration of the while loop, it is set to the higher one. It is the pointer to the higher item that is returned.

Drawing Multiple Items

While that code to loop through all the items is still fresh in your mind, why not fix
`CShowStringView::OnDraw()` so it draws all the items? Leave all the code that draws the string,
and replace the code in Listing 23.27 with that in Listing 23.28.

Part

IV

Ch

23

Listing 23.27   ShowStringView.cpp—Lines in OnDraw() to Replace

```
// Draw the selection at an arbitrary position.  This code should
// be removed once your real drawing code is implemented.  This
// position corresponds exactly to the rectangle returned by
// CShowStringCntrItem, to give the effect of in-place editing.

// TODO: remove this code when final draw code is complete.

if (m_pSelection == NULL)
{
    POSITION pos = pDoc->GetStartPosition();
    m_pSelection = (CShowStringCntrItem*)pDoc->GetNextClientItem(pos);
}
if (m_pSelection != NULL)
{
    m_pSelection->Draw(pDC, m_pSelection->m_rect);
    CRectTracker trackrect;
    SetupTracker(m_pSelection,&trackrect);
    trackrect.Draw(pDC);
}
```

Listing 23.28   ShowStringView.cpp—New Lines in OnDraw()

```
POSITION pos = pDoc->GetStartPosition();
while (pos)
{
    CShowStringCntrItem* pCurrentItem =
        (CShowStringCntrItem*) pDoc->GetNextClientItem(pos);
    pCurrentItem->Draw(pDC, pCurrentItem->m_rect);

    if (pCurrentItem == m_pSelection )
    {
        CRectTracker trackrect;
        SetupTracker(pCurrentItem,&trackrect);
        trackrect.Draw(pDC);
    }
}
```

Now each item is drawn, starting from the bottom and working up, and if it is selected it gets a
tracker rectangle.

Handling Single Clicks

When the user clicks in the client area of the application, a WM_LBUTTONDOWN message is sent. This message should be caught by the view. Because you are editing the view source now, use the WizardBar to add a handler for this message. Click the Messages box in the WizardBar and scroll down until you find WM_LBUTTONDOWN, then select it. A message box appears like the one in Figure 23.10, asking if you want to add a function to handle this message. Click Yes, and a function is added to the class for you and the file scrolls to the skeleton implementation.

FIG. 23.10
Using the WizardBar makes adding a function as simple as selecting a message that is not yet handled.

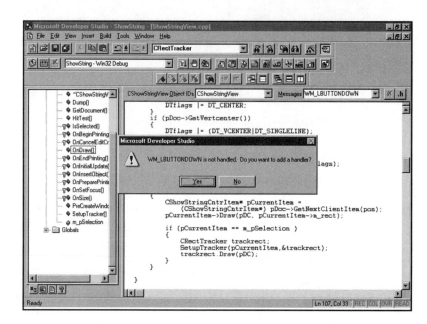

Add the code in Listing 23.29 to the empty OnLButtonDown() that the Wizard bar generated.

Listing 23.29   ShowStringView.cpp—CShowStringView::OnLButtonDown()

```cpp
void CShowStringView::OnLButtonDown(UINT nFlags, CPoint point)
{
    CShowStringCntrItem* pHitItem = HitTest(point);
    SetSelection(pHitItem);
    if (pHitItem)
    {
        CRectTracker track;
        SetupTracker(pHitItem, &track);
        UpdateWindow();
        if (track.Track(this,point))
        {
            Invalidate();
            pHitItem->m_rect = track.m_rect;
            GetDocument()->SetModifiedFlag();
        }
```

```
        }

        CView::OnLButtonDown(nFlags, point);
    }
```

This determines which item has been selected and sets it. (`SetSelection()` isn't written yet.) Then, if something has been selected, it draws a tracker rectangle around it and calls `CRectTracker::Track()`, which allows the user to resize the rectangle. After the resizing, the item is sized to match the tracker rectangle and is redrawn.

`SetSelection()` is pretty straightforward. Add the definition of this public member function to the header file, ShowStringView.h, and the code in Listing 23.30 to ShowStringView.cpp.

> **Part**
> **IV**
>
> **Ch**
> **23**

Listing 23.30   ShowStringView.cpp—CShowStringView:: SetSelection()

```
void CShowStringView::SetSelection(CShowStringCntrItem* item)
{
    // if an item is being edited in place, close it
    if ( item == NULL ¦¦ item != m_pSelection)
    {
        COleClientItem* pActive =
            GetDocument()->GetInPlaceActiveItem(this);
        if (pActive != NULL && pActive != item)
        {
            pActive->Close();
        }
    }
    Invalidate();
    m_pSelection = item;
}
```

This closes the item being edited in place if a different item, or no item, has been selected. Then it calls for a redraw, and sets `m_pSelection`. Build and execute ShowString, insert an object, move it away, insert another—you should see something like Figure 23.11. Notice the resizing handles around the bitmap, indicating that it is selected.

You may have noticed that the cursor doesn't change as you move or resize. That's because you didn't tell it to. Luckily, it's easy to tell it to: `CRectTracker` has a `SetCursor()` member function, and all you need to do is call it when a WM_SETCURSOR message is sent. Again, it should be the view that catches this message, and, again, Wizard Bar is the quickest way to catch it. Choose WM_SETCURSOR from the Messages box on the Wizard Bar (scroll to the very bottom), and say Yes when asked if you want a new function. Add the code in Listing 23.31 to the empty function that was generated for you.

FIG. 23.11

ShowString can now hold multiple items, and the user can move and resize them intuitively.

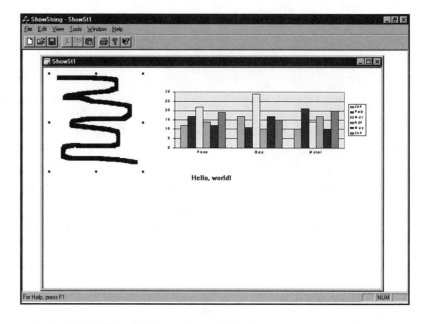

Listing 23.31 ShowStringView.cpp—CShowStringView:: OnSetCursor()

```cpp
BOOL CShowStringView::OnSetCursor(CWnd* pWnd, UINT nHitTest,
    UINT message)
{
    if (pWnd == this && m_pSelection != NULL)
    {
        CRectTracker track;
        SetupTracker(m_pSelection, &track);
        if (track.SetCursor(this, nHitTest))
        {
            return TRUE;
        }
    }

    return CView::OnSetCursor(pWnd, nHitTest, message);
}
```

This code does nothing unless the cursor change involves this view and there is a selection. It gives SetCursor() a chance to change the cursor, since the tracking object knows where the rectangle is and whether the cursor is over a boundary or sizing handle, and, if SetCursor() didn't deal with it, it lets the base class handle it. Build and execute ShowString and you should see cursors that give you feedback as you move and resize.

Handling Double-Clicks

When a user double-clicks a contained item, the *primary verb* should be called. For most objects, the primary verb is to edit in place, but for some, such as sound files, it is Play.

Use Wizard Bar to catch the WM_LBUTTONDBLCLK message, and add the code in Listing 23.32 to the new function:

Listing 23.32   ShowStringView.cpp—CShowStringView:: OnLButtonDblClk()

```
void CShowStringView::OnLButtonDblClk(UINT nFlags, CPoint point)
{
    OnLButtonDown(nFlags, point);

    if( m_pSelection)
    {
        if (GetKeyState(VK_CONTROL) < 0)
        {
            m_pSelection->DoVerb(OLEIVERB_OPEN, this);
        }
        else
        {
            m_pSelection->DoVerb(OLEIVERB_PRIMARY, this);
        }
    }

    CView::OnLButtonDblClk(nFlags, point);
}
```

First, this function handles the fact that this item has been clicked; calling OnLbuttonDown() draws the tracker rectangle, sets m_pSelection, and so on. Then, if the user holds down Ctrl while double-clicking, the item is opened, otherwise the primary verb is called. Finally, the base class function is called. Build and execute ShowString and try double-clicking. Insert an object, press Esc to stop editing it, move it, resize it, and double-click it to edit in place.

Implementing Drag and Drop

The last step to make ShowString a completely up-to-date ActiveX container application is to implement drag and drop. The user should be able to grab a contained item and drag it out of the container, or hold down Ctrl while dragging to drag out a copy and leave the original behind. The user should also be able to drag items from elsewhere and drop them into this container just as though they had been inserted through the Clipboard. In other words, the container should operate as a *drag source* and a *drop target*.

Implementing a Drag Source

Because CShowStringCntrItem inherits from COleClientItem, implementing a drag source is really easy. When a user clicks a contained object, he may start to drag it away. Add these lines at the end of CShowStringView::OnLButtonDown() just before the call to the base class function:

```
if (m_pSelection)
{
```

```
        CPoint newpoint = point - m_pSelection->m_rect.TopLeft();
        if (m_pSelection->DoDragDrop(m_pSelection->m_rect,
            newpoint) == DROPEFFECT_MOVE)
        {
            Invalidate();
            delete m_pSelection;
            m_pSelection = NULL;
        }
    }
}
```

This code just calls the DoDragDrop() member function of CShowStringCntrItem, inherited from COleClientItem and not overridden. It returns DROPEFFECT_MOVE if the item was moved out of the container and needs to be deleted. Build and execute ShowString, insert a new object, press Esc to stop editing in place, then drag the inactive object to an ActiveX container application such as Microsoft Excel.

Implementing a Drop Target

It is harder to make ShowString a drop target (it could hardly be easier). If you dragged a contained item out of ShowString and dropped it into another container, try dragging that item back into ShowString. The cursor changes to a circle with a slash through it, meaning "you can't drop that here." In this section, you make the necessary code changes that allow you to drop it there after all.

You need to register your view as a place that things can be dropped. Next, you need to handle the following four events that can occur:

- An item might be dragged across the boundaries of your view. This will require a cursor change or other indication you will take the item.
- In the view, the item will be dragged around within your boundaries, and you should give the user feedback about that process.
- That item might then be dragged out of the window again, having just passed over your view on the way to its final destination.
- Finally, the user may drop the item in your view.

Registering the View as a Drop Target

To register the view as a drop target, add a COleDropTarget member variable to the view. In showstringview.h, add this line to the class definition:

```
COleDropTarget m_droptarget;
```

To handle registration, override OnCreate() for the view, called when the view is created. Use ClassWizard or the Wizard bar to catch the WM_CREATE message. Add the code in Listing 23.33 to the empty function generated for you.

Listing 23.33 ShowStringView.cpp—CShowStringView::OnCreate()

```
int CShowStringView::OnCreate(LPCREATESTRUCT lpCreateStruct)
{
    if (CView::OnCreate(lpCreateStruct) == -1)
        return -1;

    if (m_droptarget.Register(this))
    {
        return 0;
    }
    else
    {
        return -1;
    }
}
```

OnCreate() returns 0 if everything is going well, and -1 if the window should be destroyed. This code calls the base class function, then uses COleDropTarget::Register() to register this view as a place to drop things.

Setting Up Function Skeletons and Adding Member Variables

The four events that happen in your view correspond to four virtual functions you must override: OnDragEnter(), OnDragOver(), OnDragLeave(), and OnDrop(). Use the Wizard bar to add overrides of these functions. The function names appear before the actual messages in the Messages drop-down input box.

OnDragEnter() sets up a *focus rectangle* that shows the user where the item would go if it were dropped here. This is maintained and drawn by OnDragOver(). But first, a number of member variables related to the focus rectangle must be added to CShowStringView. Add these lines to ShowStringView.h:

```
CPoint m_dragpoint;
CSize m_dragsize;
CSize m_dragoffset;
```

A data object contains a great deal of information about itself, in various formats. There is, of course, the actual data, as text, device independent bitmap (DIB), or whatever other format is appropriate. But there is also information about the object itself. If you request data in the "Object Descriptor" format, you can find out the size of the item and where on the item the user originally clicked, and the offset from the mouse to the upper-left corner of the item. These formats are generally referred to as Clipboard formats because they were originally used for cut and paste through the Clipboard.

To ask for this information, you call the data object's GetGlobalData() member function, passing it a parameter that means "Object Descriptor, please." Rather than building this parameter from a string every time, you build it once and store it in a static member of the class. When a class has a static member variable, every instance of the class looks at the same memory location to see that variable. It is initialized (and memory is allocated for it) once, outside the class.

Add this line to showstringview.h:

```
static CLIPFORMAT m_cfObjectDescriptorFormat;
```

In showstringview.cpp, just before the first function, add these lines:

```
CLIPFORMAT CShowStringView::m_cfObjectDescriptorFormat =
    (CLIPFORMAT) ::RegisterClipboardFormat("Object Descriptor");
```

This makes a CLIPFORMAT from the string "Object Descriptor" and saves it in the static member variable for all instances of this class to use. Using a static member variable speeds up dragging over your view.

Your view does not accept any and all items that get dropped on it. Add a BOOL member variable to the view that indicates whether it accepts the item that is now being dragged over it:

```
BOOL m_OKtodrop;
```

There is one last member variable to add to CShowStringView. As the item is dragged across the view, a focus rectangle is repeatedly drawn and erased. Add another BOOL member variable that tracks the status of the focus rectangle:

```
BOOL m_FocusRectangleDrawn;
```

Initialize this, in the view constructor, to FALSE:

```
CShowStringView::CShowStringView()
{
    m_pSelection = NULL;
    m_FocusRectangleDrawn = FALSE;
}
```

OnDragEnter

OnDragEnter() is called when the user first drags an item over the boundary of the view. It sets up the focus rectangle and then hands over to OnDragOver(). As the item continues to move, OnDragOver() is called repeatedly until the user drags the item out of the view or drops it in the view. The overall structure of OnDragEnter() is shown in Listing 23.34.

Listing 23.34 ShowStringView.cpp—CShowStringView::OnDragEnter()

```
DROPEFFECT CShowStringView::OnDragEnter(COleDataObject* pDataObject,
DWORD dwKeyState, CPoint point)
{
    ASSERT(!m_FocusRectangleDrawn);

    // check that the data object can be dropped in this view
    // set dragsize and dragoffset with call to GetGlobalData
    // convert sizes with a scratch dc
    // hand off to OnDragOver
    return OnDragOver(pDataObject, dwKeyState, point);
}
```

First, you check that whatever `pDataObject` carries is something you can make a `COleClientItem` (and therefore a `CShowsStringCntrItem`) from. If not, the object cannot be dropped here, and you return `DROPEFFECT_NONE`, as shown in Listing 23.35.

Listing 23.35   ShowStringView.cpp—Can Object Be Dropped?

```
// check that the data object can be dropped in this view
m_OKtodrop = FALSE;
if (!COleClientItem::CanCreateFromData(pDataObject))
    return DROPEFFECT_NONE;

m_OKtodrop = TRUE;
```

Now the weird stuff starts. The `GetGlobalData()` member function of the data item that is being dragged into this view is called to get the object descriptor information mentioned earlier. It returns a handle of a global memory block. Then the SDK function `GlobalLock()` is called to convert the handle into a pointer to the first byte of the block and prevent any other object from allocating the block. This is cast to a pointer to an object descriptor structure (the undyingly curious can check about 2,000 lines into oleidl.h, in the C:\MSDEV\include folder for most installations, to see the members of this structure) so that the `sizel` and `pointl` elements can be used to fill the `m_dragsize` and `m_dragoffset` member variables.

 There is not a number 1 at the end of those structure elements, but a lowercase letter L. And the elements of the `sizel` structure are `cx` and `cy`, but the elements of the `pointl` structure are `x` and `y`. Don't get carried away cutting and pasting.

Finally `GlobalUnlock()` reverses the effects of `GlobalLock()`, making the block accessible to others, and `GlobalFree()` frees the memory. It ends up looking like Listing 23.36.

Listing 23.36   ShowStringView.cpp—Set dragsize and dragoffset

```
// set dragsize and dragoffset with call to GetGlobalData
HGLOBAL hObjectDescriptor = pDataObject->GetGlobalData(
    m_cfObjectDescriptorFormat);
if (hObjectDescriptor)
{
    LPOBJECTDESCRIPTOR pObjectDescriptor =
        (LPOBJECTDESCRIPTOR) GlobalLock(hObjectDescriptor);
    ASSERT(pObjectDescriptor);
    m_dragsize.cx = (int) pObjectDescriptor->sizel.cx;
    m_dragsize.cy = (int) pObjectDescriptor->sizel.cy;
    m_dragoffset.cx = (int) pObjectDescriptor->pointl.x;
    m_dragoffset.cy = (int) pObjectDescriptor->pointl.y;
    GlobalUnlock(hObjectDescriptor);
    GlobalFree(hObjectDescriptor);
}
```

continues

Listing 23.36   Continued

```
else
{
    m_dragsize = CSize(0,0);
    m_dragoffset = CSize(0,0);
}
```

N O T E   Global memory, also called shared application memory, is allocated from a different place than the memory available from your process space. It is the memory to use when two different processes need to read and write the same memory, and so it comes into play when using ActiveX.

For some ActiveX operations, global memory is too small—imagine trying to transfer a 40MB file through global memory. There is a more general function than `GetGlobalData`, called (not surprisingly) `GetData`, which can transfer the data through a variety of storage medium choices. Since the object descriptors are small, asking for them in global memory is a sensible approach. ■

If the call to `GetGlobalData()` didn't work, set both member variables to zero by zero rectangles. Next, convert those rectangles from OLE coordinates (which are device-independent) to pixels:

```
// convert sizes with a scratch dc
CClientDC dc(NULL);
dc.HIMETRICtoDP(&m_dragsize);
dc.HIMETRICtoDP(&m_dragoffset);
```

`HIMETRICtoDP()` is a very useful function that happens to be a member of `CClientDC`, which inherits from the familiar `CDC` of Chapter 11, "Drawing on the Screen." You create an instance of `CClientDC` just so you can call the function.

`OnDragEnter()` closes with a call to `OnDragOver()`, so that's the next function to write.

OnDragOver

This function returns a `DROPEFFECT`. As you saw earlier in the drag source section, if you return `DROPEFFECT_MOVE` the source deletes the item from itself. Returning `DROPEFFECT_NONE` rejects the copy. It is `OnDragOver()` that deals with preparing to accept or reject a drop. The overall structure of the function looks like this:

```
DROPEFFECT CShowStringView::OnDragOver(COleDataObject* pDataObject,
DWORD dwKeyState, CPoint point)
{
    // return if dropping is already rejected
    // determine drop effect according to keys depressed
    // adjust focus rectangle
}
```

First, check to see if `OnDragEnter()` or an earlier call to `OnDragOver()` already rejected this possible drop:

```
// return if dropping is already rejected
if (!m_OKtodrop)
{
    return DROPEFFECT_NONE;
}
```

Next, look at the keys that the user is holding down now, available in the parameter passed to this function, dwKeyState. The code you need to add (Listing 23.37) is pretty straightforward.

Listing 23.37   ShowStringView.cpp—Determine Drop Effect

```
// determine drop effect according to keys depressed
DROPEFFECT dropeffect = DROPEFFECT_NONE;

if ((dwKeyState & (MK_CONTROL¦MK_SHIFT) )
    == (MK_CONTROL¦MK_SHIFT))
{
    // Ctrl+Shift force a link
    dropeffect = DROPEFFECT_LINK;
}

else if ((dwKeyState & MK_CONTROL)      == MK_CONTROL)
{
    // Ctrl forces a copy
    dropeffect = DROPEFFECT_COPY;
}
else if ((dwKeyState & MK_ALT) == MK_ALT)
{
    // Alt forces a move
    dropeffect = DROPEFFECT_MOVE;
}
else
{
    // default is to move
    dropeffect = DROPEFFECT_MOVE;
}
```

N O T E   This code has to be a lot more complex if the document might be smaller than the view, as can happen when you are editing a bitmap in Paint, and especially if the view can scroll. The OLE container sample included on the CD handles these contingencies. Look in the CD folder MSDVEV\SAMPLES\MFC\OLE\DRAWCLI for the file drawvw.cpp and compare that code for OnDragOver to this code. ▪

If the item has moved since the last time OnDragOver() was called, the focus rectangle has to be erased and redrawn at the new location. Because the focus rectangle is a simple XOR of the colors, drawing it a second time in the same place removes it. The code to adjust the focus rectangle is in Listing 23.38.

Listing 23.38 ShowStringView.cpp—Adjust the Focus Rectangle

```
// adjust focus rectangle

point -= m_dragoffset;
if (point == m_dragpoint)
{
    return dropeffect;
}

CClientDC dc(this);

if (m_FocusRectangleDrawn)
{
    dc.DrawFocusRect(CRect(m_dragpoint, m_dragsize));
    m_FocusRectangleDrawn = FALSE;
}

if (dropeffect != DROPEFFECT_NONE)
{
    dc.DrawFocusRect(CRect(point, m_dragsize));
    m_dragpoint = point;
    m_FocusRectangleDrawn = TRUE;
}
```

The first time OnDragOver() is called, m_dragpoint is uninitialized. That doesn't matter, because m_FocusRectangleDrawn is FALSE, and an ASSERT in OnDragEnter() guarantees it. When m_FocusRectangleDrawn is set to TRUE, m_dragpoint gets a value at the same time.

Finally, replace the return statement that was generated for you with one that returns the calculated DROPEFFECT:

```
return dropeffect;
```

OnDragLeave

Sometimes a user drags an item right over your view and out the other side. OnDragLeave() just tidies up a little by removing the focus rectangle, as shown in Listing 23.39.

Listing 23.39 ShowStringView.cpp—ShowStringView::OnDragLeave()

```
void CShowStringView::OnDragLeave()
{
    CClientDC dc(this);
    if (m_FocusRectangleDrawn)
    {
        dc.DrawFocusRect(CRect(m_dragpoint, m_dragsize));
        m_FocusRectangleDrawn = FALSE;
    }
}
```

OnDragDrop

If the user lets go of an item that is being dragged over ShowString, the item lands in the container and OnDragDrop() is called. The overall structure is in Listing 23.40.

Listing 23.40 ShowStringView.cpp—Structure of OnDrop()

```
BOOL CShowStringView::OnDrop(COleDataObject* pDataObject, DROPEFFECT dropEffect,
CPoint point)
{
    ASSERT_VALID(this);
    // remove focus rectangle
    // paste in the data object
    // adjust the item dimensions, and make it the current selection
    // update views and set modified flag
    return TRUE;
}
```

Removing the focus rectangle is simple, as shown in Listing 23.41.

Listing 23.41 ShowStringView.cpp—Removing the Focus Rectangle

```
// remove focus rectangle
CClientDC dc(this);
if (m_FocusRectangleDrawn)
{
    dc.DrawFocusRect(CRect(m_dragpoint, m_dragsize));
    m_FocusRectangleDrawn = FALSE;
}
```

Next, create a new item to hold the data object, as shown in Listing 23.42.

Listing 23.42 ShowStringView.cpp—Paste in the Data Object

```
// paste in the data object
CShowStringDoc* pDoc = GetDocument();
CShowStringCntrItem* pNewItem = new CShowStringCntrItem(pDoc);
ASSERT_VALID(pNewItem);
if (dropEffect & DROPEFFECT_LINK)
{
    pNewItem->CreateLinkFromData(pDataObject);
}
else
{
    pNewItem->CreateFromData(pDataObject);
}
ASSERT_VALID(pNewItem);
```

Part
IV

Ch
23

The size of the container item needs to be set, as shown in Listing 23.43.

Listing 23.43   ShowStringView.cpp—Adjust Item Dimensions

```
// adjust the item dimensions, and make it the current selection
CSize size;
pNewItem->GetExtent(&size, pNewItem->GetDrawAspect());
dc.HIMETRICtoDP(&size);
point -= m_dragoffset;
pNewItem->m_rect = CRect(point,size);
m_pSelection = pNewItem;
```

Notice that this code adjusts the place where the user drops the item (point) by m_dragoffset, the coordinates into the item where the user clicked originally.

Finally, make sure the document gets saved on exit, since pasting in a new container item changes it, and redraw the view:

```
// update views and set modified flag
pDoc->SetModifiedFlag();
pDoc->UpdateAllViews(NULL);
return TRUE;
```

This function always returns TRUE since there is no error checking at the moment that might require a return of FALSE. Notice, however, that most problems have been prevented—for example, if the data object cannot be used to create a container item, then the DROPEFFECT would have been set to DROPEFFECT_NONE in OnDragEnter() and this code would never have been called. You can be confident this code works.

Testing the Drag Target

All the confidence in the world is no substitute for testing. Build and execute ShowString, and try dragging something into it. To test both the drag source and drop target aspects at once, drag something out and then drag it back in. Now this is starting to become a really useful container. There's only one thing left to do.

Deleting an Object

You can remove an object from your container by dragging it away somewhere, but it makes sense to implement deleting in a more obvious and direct way. The menu item generally used for this is Edit Delete, so you start by adding this item to the IDR_SHOWSTTYPE menu before the Insert New Object item. Don't let Developer Studio set the ID to ID_EDIT_DELETE; instead, change it to ID_EDIT_CLEAR, the traditional resource ID for the command that deletes a contained object. Move to another menu item and then return to Edit, Delete, and you see that the prompt has been filled in for you as Erase the selection\nErase automatically.

It is the view that needs to handle this command, so use the Wizard bar in Showstringview.cpp to catch it. Choose ID_EDIT_CLEAR from the Object IDs drop-down box, and COMMAND from the Messages box, agree to add a function, and then choose UPDATE_COMMAND_UI from the Messages box and add another function. The code for these two handlers is very simple. Since the update handler is simpler, add it first:

```
void CShowStringView::OnUpdateEditClear(CCmdUI* pCmdUI)
{
    pCmdUI->Enable(m_pSelection != NULL);
}
```

If there is a current selection, it can be deleted. If there is not a current selection, the menu item is disabled (grayed). The code to handle the command isn't much longer: it's in Listing 23.44.

> **Listing 23.44 ShowStringView.cpp—CShowStringView::OnEditClear()**
>
> ```
> void CShowStringView::OnEditClear()
> {
>     if (m_pSelection)
>     {
>         m_pSelection->Delete();
>         m_pSelection = NULL;
>         GetDocument()->SetModifiedFlag();
>         GetDocument()->UpdateAllViews(NULL);
>     }
> }
> ```

This code checks that there is a selection (even though the menu item is grayed when there is no selection), and then deletes it, sets it to NULL so there is no longer a selection, makes sure the document is marked as modified so the user is prompted to save it when exiting, and gets the view redrawn without the deleted object.

Build and execute ShowString, insert something, and delete it. Now it's an intuitive container that does what you expect a container to do.

From Here...

This chapter developed a powerful container. The boilerplate code generated by AppWizard produced a container that has a number of shortcomings, but the steps presented in this chapter corrected them and built an inuitive interface for the ActiveX container version of ShowString. To learn more about some related topics, check these chapters:

- Chapter 22, "ActiveX Concepts," is a roadmap to Part IV of this book and defines many of the concepts used in this and related chapters.
- Chapter 24, "Building an ActiveX Server Application," builds the third version of ShowString, which acts as an ActiveX server.

Part

IV

Ch

23

■ Chapter 25, "ActiveX Automation," builds the fourth version of ShowString, an ActiveX Automation server that can be controlled from Visual Basic.

■ Chapter 26, "Building on ActiveX Control," leaves ShowString behind and builds a control you can include in any Visual C++ or Visual Basic program.

CHAPTER 24

Building an ActiveX Server Application

Just as AppWizard builds ActiveX containers, it also builds ActiveX servers. However, unlike containers the AppWizard code is complete, so there isn't much work to be done to improve the AppWizard code. This chapter builds a version of ShowString that is only a server, and discusses how to build another version that is both container and server. You also learn about ActiveX documents and how they can be used in other applications. ■

How to incorporate your viewing preferences into Excel's display settings

Windows 95 supports most five-disk compression schemes, Double-Space, DriveSpace, Stacker, SuperStor, and AddStor.

Transforming ShowString into a server

An ActiveX server can supply its documents to ActiveX container applications like the one in the previous chapter. This section shows you how to build one, and how they work.

Container and Server Applications

An application can be both a container and a server at the same time. This section discusses the implications of nested objects.

ActiveX documents

ActiveX document objects take being an ActiveX server one step further. This section explains what an ActiveX doc object is, how to make one, and gives you a peek into what Windows will become.

Adding Server Capabilities to ShowString

Like Chapter 23, "Building an ActiveX Container Application," this chapter starts by building an ordinary server application with AppWizard and then adds the functionality that makes it ShowString. This is far quicker, because ShowString doesn't do very much and can be written quickly.

AppWizard's Server Boilerplate

Build the new ShowString in a different directory, making almost exactly the same AppWizard choices as when you built versions of ShowString in Chapters 17 and 23: call it ShowString, and choose an MDI application with no database support. In AppWizard's Step 3, select an OLE full server. This enables the checkbox for ActiveX document support. Leave this unchecked for now. Later in this chapter you see the consequences of selecting this option. Continue the AppWizard process selecting a docking toolbar, status bar, printing and print preview, context sensitive Help, and 3D controls. Finally, select source file comments and a shared DLL.

> **N O T E** Even though the technology is now called ActiveX, the AppWizard dialogs still refer to OLE. Many of the class names that are used throughout this chapter have `Ole` in their names. While Microsoft has changed the name of the technology, it has not propagated that change throughout Visual C++ yet. You will have to live with these contradictions until the next release of Visual C++. ▩

There are a lot of differences between the application you have just generated and a do-nothing application without ActiveX server support. These differences are explained in the next few sections.

Menus There are two new menus in an ActiveX server application. The first, called IDR_SHOWSTTYPE_SRVR_IP, is shown in Figure 24.1. When an item is being edited in place, the container in-place menu (called IDR_SHOWSTTYPE_CNTR_IP in the container version of ShowString) is combined with the server in-place menu, IDR_SHOWSTTYPE_SRVR_IP, to build the in-place menu as shown in Figure 24.2. The double separators in each partial menu show where the menus are joined.

The second new menu is IDR_SHOWSTTYPE_SRVR_EMB, used when an embedded item is being edited in a separate window. Figure 24.3 shows this new menu next to the more familiar IDR_SHOWSTTYPE menu, used when ShowString is acting not as a server but as an ordinary application. The File menus have different items: IDR_SHOWSTTYPE_SRVR_EMB has Update in place of Save, and Save Copy As in place of Save As. This is because the item the user is working on in the separate window is not a document of its own, but is embedded in another document. File, Update updates the embedded item; File, Save As does not save the whole document, but just a copy of this embedded portion.

FIG. 24.1
AppWizard adds another menu for editing in place.

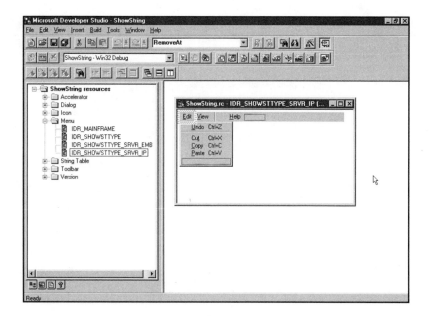

FIG. 24.2
The container and server in-place menus are interlaced during editing in place.

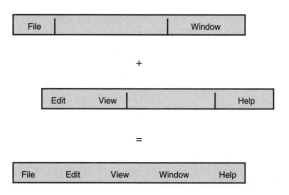

CShowStringApp Another member variable has been added to this class. It is declared in showstring.h as:

```
COleTemplateServer m_server;
```

`COleTemplateServer` handles most of the work of connecting documents to code, as you will see.

The following line is added at the top of showstring.cpp:

```
#include "IpFrame.h"
```

This sets up the class `CInPlaceFrame`, discussed later in this chapter. Just before `InitInstance()`, the lines shown in Listing 24.1 are added:

FIG. 24.3

The embedded menu has different items under File than the usual menu.

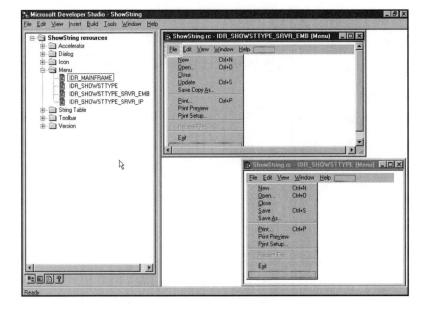

Listing 24.1 Excerpt from ShowString.cpp—CLSID

```
// This identifier was generated to be statistically unique for
// your app. You may change it if you prefer to choose a specific
// identifier.

// {0B1DEE40-C373-11CF-870C-00201801DDD6}
static const CLSID clsid =
{ 0xb1dee40, 0xc373, 0x11cf,
    { 0x87, 0xc, 0x0, 0x20, 0x18, 0x1, 0xdd, 0xd6 } };
```

The numbers will be different in your code. This Class ID identifies your server application and document type. Applications that support several kinds of documents (for example, text and graphics) use a different CLSID for each type of document.

As it did for the OLE container version of ShowString, CShowStringApp::InitInstance() has several changes from the non-ActiveX ShowString you developed in Chapter 17. The code in Listing 24.2 initializes the ActiveX (OLE) libraries:

Listing 24.2 Excerpt from ShowString.cpp—Initializing Libraries

```
// Initialize OLE libraries
if (!AfxOleInit())
{
    AfxMessageBox(IDP_OLE_INIT_FAILED);
    return FALSE;
}
```

Still in `CShowStringApp::InitInstance()`, after the `MultiDocTemplate` is initialized, but before the call to `AddDocTemplate()`, the following line is added to register the menu used for in-place editing and for separate-window editing:

```
pDocTemplate->SetServerInfo(
    IDR_SHOWSTTYPE_SRVR_EMB, IDR_SHOWSTTYPE_SRVR_IP,
    RUNTIME_CLASS(CInPlaceFrame));
```

A change that was not in the container version is connecting the template for the document to the class ID, like this:

```
// Connect the COleTemplateServer to the document template.
//  The COleTemplateServer creates new documents on behalf
//  of requesting OLE containers by using information
//  specified in the document template.
m_server.ConnectTemplate(clsid, pDocTemplate, FALSE);
```

Now when a user chooses Create New when inserting an object, the document used for that creation will be available.

When a server application is launched to edit an item in place or in a separate window, the system DLLs add /Embedded to the invoking command line, as mentioned in Chapter 16, "Choosing an Application Type and Building an Empty Shell." But if the application is already running, and it is an MDI application, a new copy is not launched. Instead, a new MDI window is opened in that application. That particular piece of magic is accomplished with one function call, as shown in Listing 24.3.

Part

IV

Ch

24

Listing 24.3   Excerpt from ShowString.cpp—Registering Running MDI Apps

```
// Register all OLE server factories as running.  This enables the
//  OLE libraries to create objects from other applications.
COleTemplateServer::RegisterAll();
// Note: MDI applications register all server objects without regard
//  to the /Embedding or /Automation on the command line.
```

After parsing the command line, the AppWizard boilerplate code checks to see if this application is being launched as an embedded (or automation) application. If it is, there is no need to continue with the initialization, so this function returns, as shown in Listing 24.4.

Listing 24.4   Excerpt from ShowString.cpp—Checking How the App Was Launched

```
 // Check to see if launched as OLE server
if (cmdInfo.m_bRunEmbedded ¦¦ cmdInfo.m_bRunAutomated)
{
    // Application was run with /Embedding or /Automation.  Don't show the
    //  main window in this case.
    return TRUE;
}
```

If the application is being run stand-alone, execution continues with a registration update:

```
// When a server application is launched stand-alone, it is a good idea
//  to update the system registry in case it has been damaged.
m_server.UpdateRegistry(OAT_INPLACE_SERVER);
```

ActiveX information is stored in the Registry. When a user chooses Insert, Object or Edit, Insert Object, the Registry provides the list of object types that can be inserted. So, before ShowString can appear in such a list, it must be registered. Many developers add code to their install programs to register their server applications, and MFC takes this one step further, registering the application every time it is run. If the application files are moved or changed, the registration is automatically updated the next time the application is run stand-alone.

CShowStringDoc   The document class, CShowStringDoc, now inherits from COleDocument rather than CDocument. As well, the following line is added at the top of showstringdoc.cpp:

```
#include "SrvrItem.h"
```

This header file describes the server item class, CShowStringSrvrItem, discussed in the CShowStringSrvrItem subsection of this section. The constructor, CShowStringDoc::CShowStringDoc(), has the following line added:

```
EnableCompoundFile();
```

This turns on the use of compound files.

There is a new public function, inlined in the header file, so that other functions can access the server item:

```
CShowStringSrvrItem* GetEmbeddedItem()
    { return (CShowStringSrvrItem*)COleServerDoc::GetEmbeddedItem(); }
```

This calls the base class GetEmbeddedItem(), which in turn calls the virtual function OnGetEmbedded Item(). That function must be overridden in the showstring document class as shown in Listing 24.5.

Listing 24.5   ShowStringDoc.cpp—CShowStringDoc::OnGetEmbeddedItem()

```
COleServerItem* CShowStringDoc::OnGetEmbeddedItem()
{
    // OnGetEmbeddedItem is called by the framework to get the COleServerItem
    //  that is associated with the document.  It is only called when necessary.

    CShowStringSrvrItem* pItem = new CShowStringSrvrItem(this);
    ASSERT_VALID(pItem);
    return pItem;
}
```

This makes a new server item from this document and returns a pointer to it.

CShowStringView   The view class has a new entry in the message map:

```
ON_COMMAND(ID_CANCEL_EDIT_SRVR, OnCancelEditSrvr)
```

This catches ID_CANCEL_EDIT_SRVR, the cancellation of editing in place. An accelerator has already been added to connect this message to Esc. The function that catches it looks like this:

```
void CShowStringView::OnCancelEditSrvr()
{
    GetDocument()->OnDeactivateUI(FALSE);
}
```

This function simply deactivates the item. There are no other view changes—server views are so much simpler than container views.

CShowStringSrvrItem The server item class is a completely new addition to ShowString. It provides an interface between the container application that has caused ShowString to be launched, and a ShowString document. It describes an entire ShowString document that is embedded into another document, or a portion of a ShowString document that is linked to part of a container document. It has no member variables other than those inherited from the base class, COleServerItem. It has overrides for eight functions. They are as follows:

Part

IV

Ch

24

- A constructor
- A destructor
- GetDocument()
- AssertValid()
- Dump()
- Serialize()
- OnDraw()
- OnGetExtent()

The constructor simply passes the document pointer along to the base class. The destructor does nothing. GetDocument() is an inline function that calls the base class function with the same name and casts the result. AssertValid() and Dump() are debug functions that simply call the base class functions. Serialize() actually does some work, as shown in Listing 24.6.

Listing 24.6   SrvrItem.cpp—CShowStringSrvrItem::Serialize()

```
void CShowStringSrvrItem::Serialize(CArchive& ar)
{
    // CShowStringSrvrItem::Serialize will be called by the framework if
    //  the item is copied to the clipboard.  This can happen automatically
    //  through the OLE callback OnGetClipboardData.  A good default for
    //  the embedded item is simply to delegate to the document's Serialize
    //  function.  If you support links, then you will want to serialize
    //  just a portion of the document.

    if (!IsLinkedItem())
    {
        CShowStringDoc* pDoc = GetDocument();
        ASSERT_VALID(pDoc);
        pDoc->Serialize(ar);
    }
```

There is no need to duplicate effort here. If the item is embedded, then it is an entire document and that document has a perfectly good Serialize() that can handle the work. AppWizard doesn't provide boilerplate to handle serializing a linked item because it is application specific. You would save just enough information to describe what part of the document has been linked in, for example, cells A3 to D27 in a spreadsheet. This doesn't make sense for ShowString, so don't add any code to Serialize().

You may feel that OnDraw() is out of place here. It is normally thought of as a view function. But this OnDraw() draws a depiction of the server item when it is inactive. It should look very much like the view when it is active, and it makes sense to share the work between CShowStringView::OnDraw() and CShowStringSrvrItem::OnDraw(). The boilerplate that AppWizard provides is in Listing 24.7.

Listing 24.7 SrvrItem.cpp—CShowStringSrvrItem::OnDraw()

```
BOOL CShowStringSrvrItem::OnDraw(CDC* pDC, CSize& rSize)
{
    CShowStringDoc* pDoc = GetDocument();
    ASSERT_VALID(pDoc);

    // TODO: set mapping mode and extent
    //  (The extent is usually the same as the size returned from OnGetExtent)
    pDC->SetMapMode(MM_ANISOTROPIC);
    pDC->SetWindowOrg(0,0);
    pDC->SetWindowExt(3000, 3000);
    // TODO: add drawing code here.  Optionally, fill in the HIMETRIC extent.
    //  All drawing takes place in the metafile device context (pDC).

    return TRUE;
```

This will change a great deal, but it's worth noting now that, unlike CShowStringView::OnDraw(), this function takes two parameters. The second is the size in which the inactive depiction is to be drawn. The extent, as mentioned in the boilerplate comments, typically comes from OnGetExtent(), which is shown in Listing 24.8.

Listing 24.8 SrvrItem.cpp—CShowStringSrvrItem:: OnGetExtent()

```
BOOL CShowStringSrvrItem::OnGetExtent(DVASPECT dwDrawAspect, CSize& rSize)
{
    // Most applications, like this one, only handle drawing the content
    //  aspect of the item.  If you wish to support other aspects, such
    //  as DVASPECT_THUMBNAIL (by overriding OnDrawEx), then this
    //  implementation of OnGetExtent should be modified to handle the
    //  additional aspect(s).

    if (dwDrawAspect != DVASPECT_CONTENT)
        return COleServerItem::OnGetExtent(dwDrawAspect, rSize);

    // CShowStringSrvrItem::OnGetExtent is called to get the extent in
    //  HIMETRIC units of the entire item.  The default implementation
```

```
    //   here simply returns a hard-coded number of units.
    CShowStringDoc* pDoc = GetDocument();
    ASSERT_VALID(pDoc);

    // TODO: replace this arbitrary size

    rSize = CSize(3000, 3000);    // 3000 x 3000 HIMETRIC units
    return TRUE;
}
```

You will replace this with real code very shortly.

CInPlaceFrame   The in-place frame class, which inherits from COleIPFrameWnd, handles the frame around the server item and the toolbars, status bars, and dialog bars, collectively known as *control bars*, that it displays. It has the following three protected member variables:

```
CToolBar     m_wndToolBar;
COleResizeBar    m_wndResizeBar;
COleDropTarget m_dropTarget;
```

The CToolBar class is discussed in Chapter 18, "Interface Issues." COleDropTarget is discussed in the drag and drop section of Chapter 23, "Building an ActiveX Container Application." COleResizeBar looks just like a CRectTracker, which was used extensively in Chapter 23, but allows the resizing of a server item rather than a container item.

The following are the seven member functions of CInPlaceFrame:

- A constructor
- A destructor
- AssertValid()
- Dump()
- OnCreate()
- OnCreateControlBars()
- PreCreateWindow()

The constructor and destructor do nothing. AssertValid() and Dump() are debug functions that simply call the base class functions. OnCreate() actually has code, shown in Listing 24.9

Listing 24.9   IPFrame.cpp—CInPlaceFrame::OnCreate()

```
int CInPlaceFrame::OnCreate(LPCREATESTRUCT lpCreateStruct)
{
    if (COleIPFrameWnd::OnCreate(lpCreateStruct) == -1)
    return -1;

    // CResizeBar implements in-place resizing.
    if (!m_wndResizeBar.Create(this))
    {
        TRACE0("Failed to create resize bar\n");
        return -1;        // fail to create
```

continues

Listing 24.9   Continued

```
    }
    // By default, it is a good idea to register a drop-target that does
    //   nothing with your frame window.  This prevents drops from
    //   "falling through" to a container that supports drag-drop.
    m_dropTarget.Register(this);
    return 0;
}
```

This function catches the WM_CREATE message that is sent when an in-place frame is to be created and drawn on the screen. It calls the base class function, then creates the resize bar. Finally, it registers a drop target, so that if anything is dropped over this in-place frame, it is dropped on this server rather than the underlying container.

When a server document is activated in place, COleServerDoc::ActivateInPlace() calls CInPlaceFrame::OnCreateControlBars(), which is shown in Listing 24.10.

Listing 24.10   IPFrame.cpp—CInPlaceFrame::OnCreateControlBars()

```
BOOL CInPlaceFrame::OnCreateControlBars(CFrameWnd* pWndFrame, CFrameWnd*
pWndDoc)
{
    // Set owner to this window, so messages are delivered to correct app
    m_wndToolBar.SetOwner(this);

    // Create toolbar on client's frame window
    if (!m_wndToolBar.Create(pWndFrame) ¦¦
        !m_wndToolBar.LoadToolBar(IDR_SHOWSTTYPE_SRVR_IP))
    {
        TRACE0("Failed to create toolbar\n");
        return FALSE;
    }

    // TODO: Remove this if you don't want tool tips or a resizeable toolbar
    m_wndToolBar.SetBarStyle(m_wndToolBar.GetBarStyle() ¦
        CBRS_TOOLTIPS ¦ CBRS_FLYBY ¦ CBRS_SIZE_DYNAMIC);

    // TODO: Delete these three lines if you don't want the toolbar to
    //   be dockable
    m_wndToolBar.EnableDocking(CBRS_ALIGN_ANY);
    pWndFrame->EnableDocking(CBRS_ALIGN_ANY);
    pWndFrame->DockControlBar(&m_wndToolBar);

    return TRUE;
}
```

This function creates a docking, resizable toolbar with tool tips, docked against the edge of the main frame window for the application.

TIP If you are developing an MDI application and prefer the toolbar against the document frame, use pWndDoc instead of PWndFrame, but be sure to check that it is not NULL.

The last function in CInPlaceFrame is PreCreateWindow(). At the moment, it just calls the base class, as shown in Listing 24.11.

Listing 24.11 IPFrame.cpp—CInPlaceFrame::PreCreateWindow()

```
BOOL CInPlaceFrame::PreCreateWindow(CREATESTRUCT& cs)
{
    // TODO: Modify the Window class or styles here by modifying
    //   the CREATESTRUCT cs

    return COleIPFrameWnd::PreCreateWindow(cs);
}
```

This function is called before OnCreate() and sets up the styles for the frame window through a CREATESTRUCT.

Part
IV

Ch
24

CAUTION

Modifying these styles is not for the faint of heart. The Microsoft documentation recommends reading the source code for all the classes in the hierarchy of your CInPlaceFrame (Cwnd, CFrameWnd, COleIPFrameWnd) to see what CREATESTRUCT elements are already set before making any changes. For this sample application, don't change the CREATESTRUCT.

Shortcomings of This Server Apart from the fact that the starter application from AppWizard doesn't show a string, what's missing from this server? The OnDraw() and GetExtent() TODOs are the only significant tasks left for you by AppWizard. Try building ShowString, then run it once stand-alone just to register it.

Figure 24.4 shows the Object dialog box in Microsoft Excel, reached by choosing Insert, Object. ShowString appears in this list as ShowSt Document, not surprising considering the menu name was IDR_SHOWSTTYPE—Developer Studio calls this document a ShowSt document. This setting could have been overriden in AppWizard by choosing the Advanced button in Step 4 of AppWizard. Figure 24.5 shows this dialog box and the long and short OLE names of the file type.

So, the ActiveX (OLE) names have been set incorrectly for this project. The next few pages take you on a tour of the way ActiveX names are stored, and show how difficult they are to change.

The file type name has been stored in the string table. It is the caption of the IDR_SHOWSTTYPE resource, and AppWizard has set it to:

\nShowSt\nShowSt\n\n\nShowString.Document\nShowSt Document

FIG. 24.4
The ShowString document type, called ShowSt document, now appears in the Insert Object dialog box when inserting a new object into an Excel worksheet.

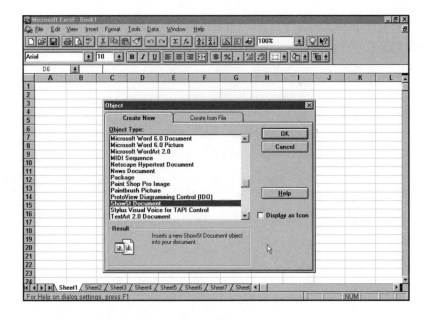

FIG. 24.5
The Advanced options dialog box of Step 4 of AppWizard provides an opportunity to change the name of the file type.

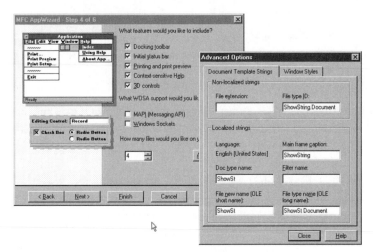

To look at this string, choose String Table from the Resource View, open the only string table there, click IDR_SHOWSTTYPE once to highlight it, and choose Edit, Properties. This string is saved in the document template when a new one is constructed in CShowStringApp::InitInstance(), as shown in Listing 24.12.

Listing 24.12 ShowString.cpp—Excerpt from *ShowStringApp::InitInstance()*

```
pDocTemplate = new CMultiDocTemplate(
    IDR_SHOWSTTYPE,
```

```
RUNTIME_CLASS(CShowStringDoc),
RUNTIME_CLASS(CChildFrame), // custom MDI child frame
RUNTIME_CLASS(CShowStringView));
```

The caption of the menu resource holds seven strings and each is used by a different part of the framework. They are separated by the newline character, \n. The seven strings, their purposes, and the values provided by AppWizard for ShowString are as follows:

- Window Title—Used by SDI apps in the title bar. For ShowString: not provided.
- Document Name—Used as the root for default document names. For ShowString: ShowSt, so that new documents will be ShowSt1, ShowSt2, and so on.
- File New Name—Prompt in the File New dialog box for file type. (For example, in Developer Studio there are eight file types, including Text File and Project Workspace.) For ShowString: ShowSt.
- Filter Name—An entry for the drop-down box List File of Type in the File Open dialog box. For ShowString: not provided.
- Filter Extension—The extension that matches the filter name. For ShowString: not provided.
- Registry File Type ID—A short string to be stored in the Registry. For ShowString: ShowString.Document.
- Registry File Type Name—A longer string to be shown in dialog boxes involving the Registry. For Showstring: ShowSt Document.

(Look again at fig. 24.5 and you can see where these values came from.) Try changing the last entry. In the properties box, change the caption so that the last element of the string is ShowString Document. Build the project. Run it once and exit. In the output section of Developer Studio you see these messages:

```
Warning: Leaving value 'ShowSt Document' for key 'ShowString.Document'
 in registry
 intended value was 'ShowString Document'.
Warning: Leaving value 'ShowSt Document' for key
 'CLSID\{0B1DEE40-C373-11CF-870C-00201801DDD6}' in registry
 intended value was 'ShowString Document'.
```

This means that the call to UpdateRegistry() did not change these two keys. There is a way to provide parameters to UpdateRegistry to insist that the keys be updated, but it's even more complicated than the route you will follow. Because no code has been changed from that provided by AppWizard, it's much quicker just to delete the ShowString directory and create it again, this time setting the long file type to ShowString Document.

CAUTION

Always test AppWizard-generated code before you add changes of your own. Until you are familiar with every default you are accepting, it is worth a few moments to see what you have before moving on. Rerunning AppWizard is easy, but if you've made several hours worth of changes and then decide to rerun it, it's not such a simple thing.

Delete the ShowString folder entirely and generate a new application with AppWizard as before. This time, in Step 4, click the Advanced button and change the OLE names as shown in Figure 24.6. After you click Finish, AppWizard asks whether you wish to reuse the existing CLSID, as shown in Figure 24.7. Click Yes and then OK to create the project. This makes a new showstring.reg file for you with the correct Registry values.

FIG. 24.6

The Advanced options dialog box of Step 4 of AppWizard is the place to improve the OLE object names.

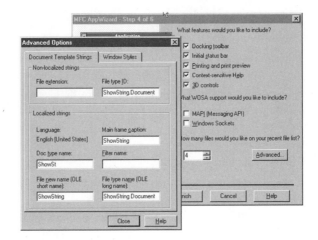

FIG. 24.7

AppWizard makes sure that you don't accidentally reuse a CLSID.

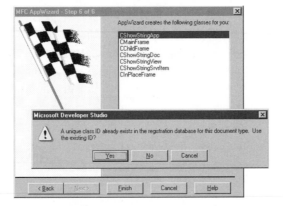

This changes the string table as well as the showstring.reg file, so you might be tempted to build and run the application to make this fix complete. And it's true, when you run the application, it will update the Registry for you using the values from the new string table. Alas, the registration update will fail yet again. If you were to try it, these messages would appear in the output window:

```
Warning: Leaving value 'ShowSt Document' for key
  'ShowString.Document' in registry
  intended value was 'ShowString Document'.
Warning: Leaving value 'ShowSt Document' for key
  'CLSID\{0B1DEE40-C373-11CF-870C-00201801DDD6}' in registry
```

```
intended value was 'ShowString Document'.
Warning: Leaving value 'ShowSt' for key
'CLSID\{0B1DEE40-C373-11CF-870C-00201801DDD6}\AuxUserType\2'
in registry
intended value was 'ShowString'.
```

So, how do you get out of this mess? You have to edit the Registry. If that sounds intimidating, it should be. Messing with the Registry can leave your system unusable. But you are not going to go in by hand and change keys; instead you are going to use the registry file that AppWizard generated for you. Here's what to do:

1. Choose Start Run.

2. Type **regedit** and press Enter.

3. Choose Registry Import Registry File from the Registry Editor menu.

4. Using the Import Registry File, move through your folders until you reach the one where the replacement ShowString server was just generated by AppWizard, as shown in Figure 24.8. Click Open.

5. A success message is shown. Click OK.

6. Close the Registry Editor.

Now if you run the application again, those error messages do not appear. Run Excel again, and choose Insert Object. The Object dialog box now has a more meaningful ShowString entry, as shown in Figure 24.9.

Part

IV

Ch

24

FIG. 24.8

Registry files generated by AppWizard have the extension .reg.

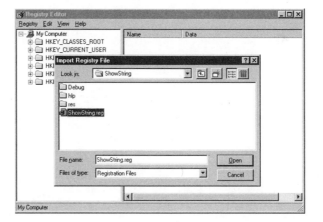

N O T E There are three morals to this side-trip. The first is that you should think really carefully before clicking Finish on the AppWizard dialog box. The second is that you cannot ignore the Registry if you are an OLE programmer. The third is that anything can be changed if you have the nerve for it. ■

Click OK on the Object dialog box to insert a ShowString object into the Excel sheet. You can immediately edit it in place, as shown in Figure 24.10. You can see that the combined server and container in-place menus are being used. There's not much you can do at this point, because the ShowString code that actually shows a string has not been added. Press Esc to finish editing in place and the menus return to the usual Excel menus, as shown in Figure 24.11.

FIG. 24.9

The updated long OLE name appears in the Insert Object dialog box of other applications.

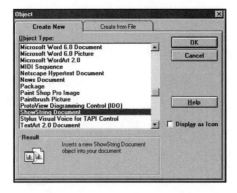

FIG. 24.10

While editing in place, the in-place menus replace the Excel menus.

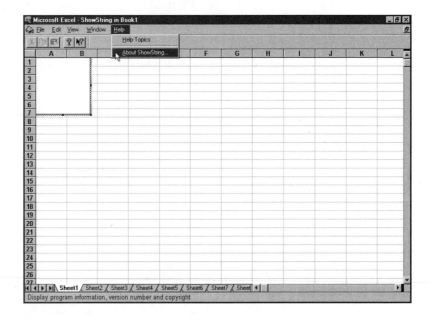

Although this server doesn't do anything, it is a perfectly good server. You can resize and move the embedded item while it is active or inactive, and everything operates exactly as you expect. All that remains is to restore the ShowString functionality.

Showing a String Again

As you did in Chapter 23, "Building an ActiveX Container Application," it is time to add the ShowString functionality to this version of the program. If you went through this process before, it will be even quicker this time. Remember to open the ShowString files from Chapter 17,

"Building Menus and Dialogs," so that you can copy code and resources from the functional ShowString to the do-nothing OLE server you have just created and explored. Here's what to do:

1. In ShowStringDoc.h, add the private member variables and public `Get` functions to the class.

2. In `CShowStringDoc::Serialize()`, paste in the code that saves or restores these member variables.

3. In `CShowStringDoc::OnNewDocument()`, paste in the code that initializes the member variables.

4. Copy the entire Tools menu from the old ShowString to the new server ShowString: choose File, Open to open the old ShowString.rc, open the `IDR_SHOWSTTYPE` menu, click the Tools menu, and choose Edit, Copy. Open the new ShowString's `IDR_SHOWSTTYPE` menu, click the Window menu, and choose Edit, Paste.

5. Paste the Tools menu into the `IDR_SHOWSTTYPE_SRVR_IP` and `IDR_SHOWSTTYPE _SRVR_EMB` menus in the same way.

6. Add the accelerator Ctrl+T for ID_TOOLS_OPTIONS as described in Chapter 17, "Building Menus and Dialogs." Add it to all three accelerators.

7. Delete the IDD_ABOUTBOX dialog box from the new ShowString. Copy IDD_ABOUTBOX and IDD_OPTIONS from the old ShowString to the new.

8. While IDD_OPTIONS has focus, choose View, Class Wizard. Create the `COptionsDialog` class as in the original ShowString. Remember not to add it to the Component Gallery.

9. Use Class Wizard to arrange for `CShowStringDoc` to catch the `ID_TOOLS_OPTIONS` command.

10. In ShowStringDoc.cpp, replace the Class Wizard version of `CShowStringDoc :: OnToolsOptions()` with the one that puts up the dialog box.

11. In ShowStringDoc.cpp, add `#include "OptionsDialog.h"` after the `#include` statements already present.

12. Use Class Wizard to connect the dialog controls to `COptionsDialog` member variables as before.

You haven't restored `CShowStringView::OnDraw()` yet, because there are actually going to be two `OnDraw()` functions. The first is in the view class, shown in Listing 24.13. It draws the string when ShowString is running stand-alone and when the user is editing in place, and it's the same as in the old version of ShowString. Just copy it into the new one. Figure 24.11 shows how Excel reminds the user of the object type when the object is inactive.

FIG. 24.11

When the object is inactive, Excel reminds the user of the object type.

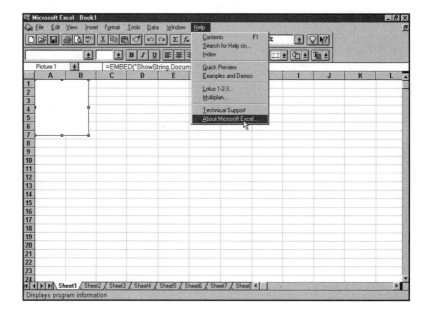

Listing 24.13 ShowStringView.cpp—CShowStringView::OnDraw()

```cpp
void CShowStringView::OnDraw(CDC* pDC)
{
    CShowStringDoc* pDoc = GetDocument();
    ASSERT_VALID(pDoc);

    COLORREF oldcolor;
    switch (pDoc->GetColor())
    {
    case 0:
        oldcolor = pDC->SetTextColor(RGB(0,0,0)); //black
        break;
    case 1:
        oldcolor = pDC->SetTextColor(RGB(0xFF,0,0)); //red
        break;
    case 2:
        oldcolor = pDC->SetTextColor(RGB(0,0xFF,0)); //green
        break;
    }

    int DTflags = 0;
    if (pDoc->GetHorizcenter())
    {
        DTflags |= DT_CENTER;
    }
    if (pDoc->GetVertcenter())
    {
        DTflags |= (DT_VCENTER|DT_SINGLELINE);
    }
```

```
      CRect rect;
      GetClientRect(&rect);
      pDC->DrawText(pDoc->GetString(), &rect, DTflags);
      pDC->SetTextColor(oldcolor);
}
```

When the embedded ShowString item is inactive, `CShowStringSrvrItem::OnDraw()` draws it. The code in here should be very like the view's `OnDraw`, but because it is a member of `CShowStringSrvrItem` rather than `CShowStringView`, it doesn't have access to the same member variables. So although there is still a `GetDocument()` function you can call, `GetClientRect` doesn't work. It's a member of the view class but not of the server item class. You use a few CDC member functions instead. It's a nice touch to draw the item slightly differently, to help remind the user that it is not active, as shown in Listing 24.14.

Listing 24.14   Srvrltem.cpp—CShowStringSrvrltem::OnDraw()

```
BOOL CShowStringSrvrItem::OnDraw(CDC* pDC, CSize& rSize)
{
      CShowStringDoc* pDoc = GetDocument();
      ASSERT_VALID(pDoc);

      // TODO: set mapping mode and extent
      //   (The extent is usually the same as the size returned from OnGetExtent)
      pDC->SetMapMode(MM_ANISOTROPIC);
      pDC->SetWindowOrg(0,0);
      pDC->SetWindowExt(3000, 3000);

      COLORREF oldcolor;
      switch (pDoc->GetColor())
      {
      case 0:
            oldcolor = pDC->SetTextColor(RGB(0x80,0x80,0x80)); //gray
            break;
      case 1:
            oldcolor = pDC->SetTextColor(RGB(0xB0,0,0)); // dull red
            break;
      case 2:
            oldcolor = pDC->SetTextColor(RGB(0,0xB0,0)); // dull green
            break;
      }

      int DTflags = 0;
      if (pDoc->GetHorizcenter())
      {
            DTflags |= DT_CENTER;
      }
      if (pDoc->GetVertcenter())
      {
            DTflags |= (DT_VCENTER|DT_SINGLELINE);
      }
```

continues

Listing 24.14 Continued

```
    CRect rect;
    rect.TopLeft() = pDC->GetWindowOrg();
    rect.BottomRight() = rect.TopLeft() + pDC->GetWindowExt();
    pDC->DrawText(pDoc->GetString(), &rect, DTflags);
    pDC->SetTextColor(oldcolor);

    return TRUE;
}
```

The function starts with the boilerplate from AppWizard. With an application that doesn't just draw itself in whatever space is provided, you would want to add code to determine the extent rather than just using (3000,300). (You'd want to add the code to OnGetExtent(), too.) But hardcoding the numbers works for this simple example. Next, paste in the drawing code from the view's OnDraw(), but change the colors slightly to give the user a reminder.

Build the application, fix any typos or other simple errors, and then start Excel and insert a ShowString document into your worksheet. ShowString should run as before, saying Hello, world! in the center of the view. Convince yourself that the Options dialog box still works and that you have restored all the old functionality. Be sure to change at least one thing: the string, the color, or the centering. Then, press Esc to finish editing in place. Oops! It still draws the old Hello, world! in gray in the center of the server area. Why?

Remember that in CShowStringDoc::OnToolsOptions(), after the user clicks OK, you tell the document that it has been changed and arrange to have the view redrawn:

```
SetModifiedFlag();
UpdateAllViews(NULL);
```

You need to add another line there to make sure that any containers that hold this document are also notified:

```
NotifyChanged();
```

Now, build it again, and insert a different ShowString object into a different Excel worksheet. This time the changes are reflected in the inactive server display as well. Figure 24.12 shows a ShowString item being edited in place, and Figure 24.13 shows the same item inactive.

> **N O T E** There is one oddity you may notice as you edit. If you choose to have the string centered
> horizontally, when it is inactive, the first character of the string is centered, but when it is
> active the entire string is centered. Because the code is identical for these cases, this behavior has to
> be blamed on MFC. ▓

Good old ShowString has been through a lot. It's time for one more transformation.

FIG. 24.12
This ShowString item is
being edited in place.

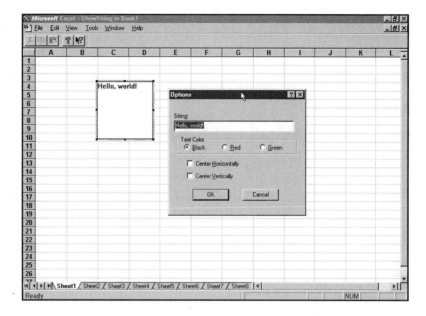

Part
IV
Ch
24

FIG. 24.13
This ShowString item is
inactive.

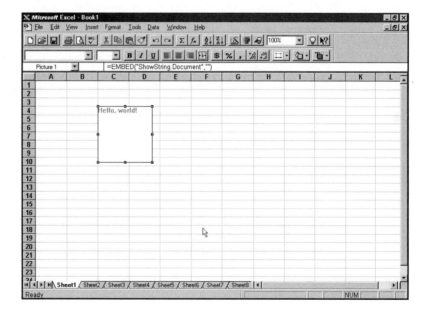

Applications That Are Both Container and Server

As you might expect, adding container features to this version of ShowString is as difficult as adding them to the ordinary ShowString of the previous chapter. If you add these features, you gain an application that can tap the full power of OLE to bring extraordinary power to your work and your documents.

Building Another Version of ShowString

The way to get a ShowString that is both a container and a server is to follow these steps:

1. Build a new ShowString with AppWizard that is a container and a full server. Run AppWizard as usual, but in a different directory than the one where you created the server-only ShowString. Be sure to select the Both Container And Server radio button in Step 3. In Step 4, be sure to click the Advanced button and change the OLE strings as you did earlier in this chapter. And finally, when asked whether you want to use the same CLSID, say No. This is a different application.

2. Make the container changes from the previous chapter. When adding the Tools Options menu item and accelerator, add it to the main menu, the server in-place menu, and the server-embedded menu.

3. Make the server changes from this chapter.

4. Add the ShowString functionality.

This section does not present the process of building a container and server application in detail; it is covered in the "Adding Server Capabilities to ShowString" section of this chapter and all of the previous chapter. Rather, the focus is on the consequences of building such an application.

Nesting and Recursion Issues

After an application is both a server, which can be embedded in other applications, and a container, it is possible to create nested documents. For example, an Excel spreadsheet might contain a Word document, which, in turn, contains a bitmap, as shown in Figure 24.14.

Within Excel, you can double-click the Word document to edit it in place, as shown in Figure 24.15, but you cannot go on to double-click the bitmap and edit it in place, too. You can edit it in a window of its own, as shown in Figure 24.16. It is a limitation of ActiveX that you cannot nest in-place editing sessions indefinitely.

FIG. 24.14
This Excel spreadsheet contains a Word document that contains a bitmap.

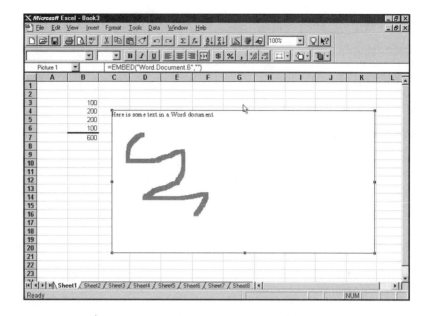

FIG. 24.15
This Word document is being edited in place.

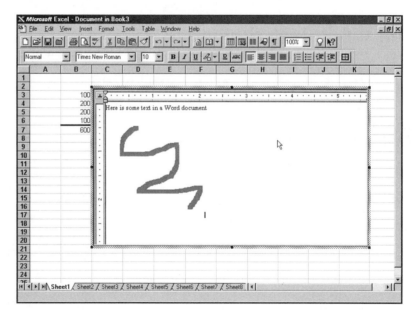

FIG. 24.16

This bitmap is nested within a Word document within an Excel spreadsheet, and so cannot be edited in place. Instead, it is edited in a separate window.

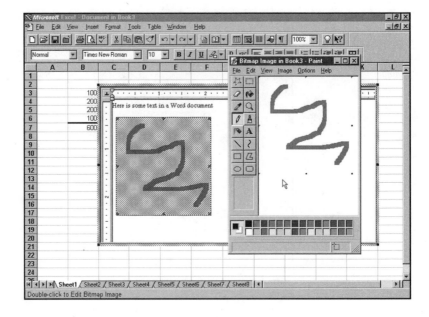

ActiveX Documents

The final important recent addition to ActiveX is ActiveX documents, also known as ActiveX Document Objects. An ordinary ActiveX server takes over the menus and interface of a container application when the document is being edited in place, but does so in cooperation with the container application. An ActiveX Document server takes over far more dramatically.

What ActiveX Documents Do

The first application to demonstrate the use of ActiveX Documents is the Microsoft Office Binder, shown in Figure 24.17. To the user, it appears that this application can open any Office document. In reality, the documents are opened with their own server applications while the frame around them and the list of other documents remain intact. Microsoft Internet Explorer 3.0 is also an ActiveX Document container—Figure 24.18 shows a Word document open in Explorer. Notice the menus are Word menus, but the Explorer toolbar can still be used. For example, clicking the Back button closes this Word document and opens the document that was loaded previously.

What this means to users is a complete transition to a document-centered approach. No matter what application the user is working with, any kind of document can be opened and edited, using the code written to work with that document.

FIG. 24.17
The Microsoft Office Binder makes it simple to pull Office documents together.

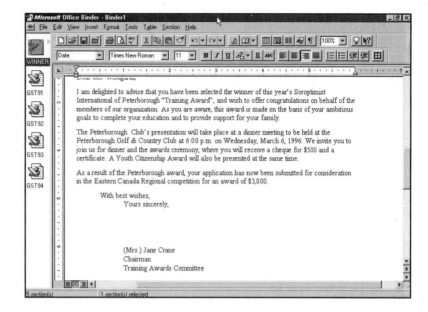

FIG. 24.18
Microsoft Internet Explorer is also a container for ActiveX documents.

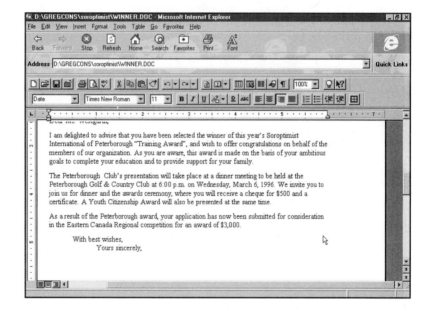

Making ShowString an ActiveX Document Server

Making yet another version of ShowString, this one as an ActiveX document server, is pretty simple. Follow the instructions from the "AppWizard's Server Boilerplate" subsection at the beginning of this chapter, with two exceptions: in AppWizard's Step 3, select ActiveX document support, and in AppWizard's Step 4, click the Advanced button. Fix the OLE names, and fill in the file extension as sst, as shown in Figure 24.19. This helps ActiveX document containers to determine what application to launch when you open a ShowString file.

FIG. 24.19

The Advanced Options dialog box of App Wizard's Step 4 is where you specify the extension for ShowString files.

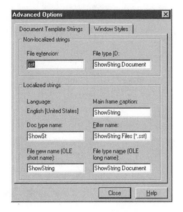

Document Extension Boilerplate   Any one of the versions of ShowString built up to this point could have had a document extension specified. AppWizard adds these lines to `CShowStringApp::InitInstance()` when you specify a document extension for an ActiveX document server application:

```
// Enable drag/drop open
m_pMainWnd->DragAcceptFiles();

// Enable DDE Execute open
EnableShellOpen();
RegisterShellFileTypes(TRUE);
```

It is the call to `RegisterShellFileTypes` that matters here, though the drag and drop is a nice touch. You're able to drag files from your desktop or a folder onto the ShowString icon or an open copy of ShowString, and the file opens in ShowString.

ActiveX Document Server Boilerplate   Selecting ActiveX document support makes remarkably little difference to code generated by AppWizard. In `CShowStringApp:: InitInstance ()`, the versions of ShowString that were not ActiveX document servers had this call to update the Registry:

```
m_server.UpdateRegistry(OAT_INPLACE_SERVER);
```

The ActiveX document version of Showstring has this line:

```
m_server.UpdateRegistry(OAT_DOC_OBJECT_SERVER);
```

In both cases, m_server is a CShowStringSrvrItem, but now the ActiveX document server version has a server item that inherits from CDocObjectServerItem. This causes a number of little changes throughout the source and includes files for CShowStringSrvrItem, where base class functions are called. Similarly, the in-place frame object, CInPlaceFrame, now inherits from COleDocIPFrameWnd.

Showing Off the Newest ShowString   Restore the ShowString functionality once again as described in the section "Showing a String Again," earlier in this chapter. Build the application, run it once to register it, and then run the Microsoft Binder (if you have Office installed). Choose Section Add to bring up the Add Section dialog box shown in Figure 24.20. Highlight ShowString Document and click OK.

FIG. 24.20

Not many applications on the market are ActiveX document servers, but you can write one in minutes.

Part
IV
Ch
24

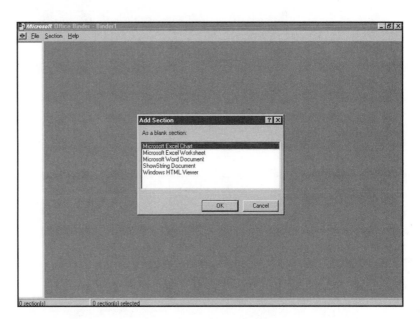

The menus include ShowString's Tools menu, as before. Choose Tools Options and change something—for example, in Figure 24.21, the string has been changed to "Hello from the Binder" and the vertical centering has been turned off. You have access to all of ShowString's functionality although it doesn't look as though you are running ShowString.

Now run ShowString alone and save the document by choosing File, Save. You do not need to enter an extension: the extension sst is used automatically. Open Internet Explorer 3.0 and choose File, Open. On the Open dialog box, shown in Figure 24.22, click Browse and explore until you reach the file you saved, then click Open.

Your ShowString document opens in Explorer, as you can see in Figure 24.23. The toolbar is clearly the Explorer toolbar, but the menu has the Tools item, and you can change the string, centering, and color as before. If you use the Back button on the Explorer toolbar, you reload the previous document you had open. If you change the ShowString document before clicking

Back, you're even prompted to save your changes! Microsoft plans to integrate the desktop in the next generation of Windows with the Internet Explorer interface. What you see here is a sneak preview of how that will work.

FIG. 24.21

All of ShowString's functionality is available from within the Binder.

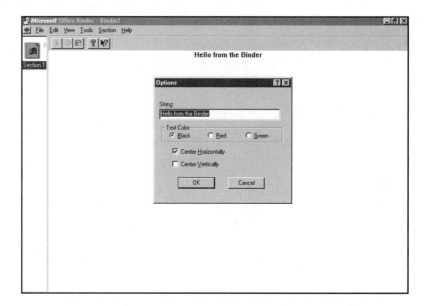

FIG. 24.22

The Internet Explorer Open dialog box is used to open files on your hard drive or the Internet.

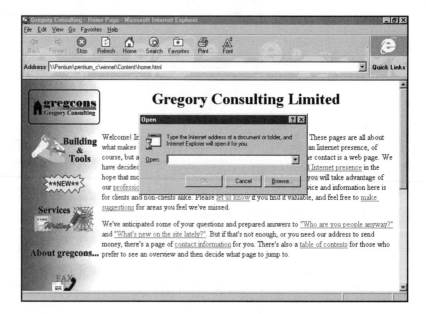

FIG. 24.23
Internet Explorer
appears to be able
to read and write
ShowString files now.

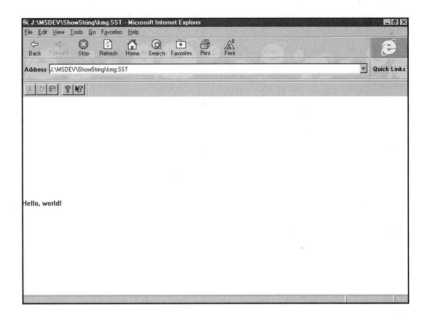

From Here...

This chapter built a third version of ShowString that can act as an ActiveX server.
The AppWizard boilerplate did not need to be modified much, and now you can embed a
ShowString document in any ActiveX container. You also saw how to construct a ShowString
that is both a server and a container. Your glimpse into the future of Windows came with the
ActiveX document objects, the Microsoft Office Binder, and the idea of opening a Word document in another application like Microsoft Internet Explorer. Eventually Windows will look
very much like Internet Explorer, and it's ActiveX doc objects that will make that possible.

To explore some related material, try these chapters:

- Chapter 17, "Building Menus and Dialogs," introduced the ShowString application.
- Chapter 22, "ActiveX Concepts," is a roadmap to Part IV of this book and defines many of
  the concepts used in this and related chapters.
- Chapter 23, "Building an ActiveX Container Application," built the second version of
  ShowString, which acts as an ActiveX container.
- Chapter 25, "ActiveX Automation," builds a fourth version of ShowString; this time it's an
  ActiveX Automation server that can be controlled from Visual Basic.
- Chapter 26, "Building an ActiveX Control," leaves ShowString behind and builds a
  control you can include in any Visual C++ or Visual Basic program.

ActiveX Automation

ActiveX Automation is about writing code that other programs can call. Other programs call your code, not in the insulated manner of a DLL, but directly. The jargon is that your code exposes both methods (functions) and properties (variables) to other applications. The good part is that you don't have to create a macro language for your application; you only have to make hooks for a more universal macro language, Visual Basic for Applications, to grab onto. ■

ShowString as an *ActiveX* Automation Server

An ActiveX Automation Server is straightforward to build, as you'll see in this section.

DispTest as an *ActiveX* Automation Controller

Once built, your Automation server must be tested. DispTest is an application included with Visual C++ that you can use to test ActiveX Automation Servers.

ActiveX Type Libraries

For those who want to know what's going on behind the scenes, this chapter introduces you to the ODL file and what it means.

Designing ShowString Again

If you've been building the sample applications throughout this book, you can probably design ShowString in your sleep by now, but it's time to do it once again. This time, ShowString is not going to have a Tools, Options menu—instead, other programs will directly set the string and other display options. The member variables in the document will be the same, and the code in OnDraw() will be the same as in all the other implementations of ShowString.

AppWizard's Automation Boilerplate

To build the version of ShowString that is an ActiveX Automation server, first use AppWizard to create an empty shell. Run AppWizard as usual, but in a different directory from your other versions of ShowString. Make almost exactly the same AppWizard choices as before: call it ShowString and then choose an MDI application and no database support. In AppWizard's Step 4, choose no support for OLE *compound documents* (the radio buttons at the top of the dialog box) but turn on support for OLE Automation. Continue through the AppWizard process, selecting a docking toolbar, status bar, printing and print preview, and 3-D controls. Finally, select source file comments and a shared DLL.

N O T E Even though the technology is now called ActiveX, the AppWizard dialogs still refer to OLE. Many of the class names that are used throughout this chapter have Ole in their names, and comments refer to OLE. While Microsoft has changed the name of the technology, it has not propagated that change throughout Visual C++ yet. You will have to live with these contradictions until the next release of Visual C++. ▮

There are just a few differences in this application from the do-nothing application without ActiveX Automation support, primarily in the application object and the document.

CShowStringApp   The application object, CShowStringApp, has a number of changes. In the source file, just before InitInstance(), the code shown in Listing 25.1 has been added:

Listing 25.1 ShowString.cpp—CLSID

```
// This identifier was generated to be statistically unique for your app.
// You may change it if you prefer to choose a specific identifier.

// {4E28FA6A-E3C0-11CF-B5C2-0080C81A397C}
static const CLSID clsid =
{ 0x4e28fa6a, 0xe3c0, 0x11cf, { 0xb5, 0xc2, 0y0, 0x80, 0xc8,
    0x1a, 0x39, 0x7c } };
```

The numbers will be different in your code. This class ID identifies your ActiveX Automation application.

CShowStringApp::InitInstance() has several changes. The lines of code in Listing 25.2 initialize the ActiveX (OLE) libraries.

Listing 25.2   ShowString.cpp—Initializing Libraries

```
// Initialize OLE libraries
if (!AfxOleInit())
{
    AfxMessageBox(IDP_OLE_INIT_FAILED);
    return FALSE;
}
```

As with the server application, `InitInstance()` goes on to connect the document template to the `COleTemplateServer`, after the document template has been initialized:

`m_server.ConnectTemplate(clsid, pDocTemplate, FALSE);`

Then `InitInstance()` checks to see if the server is being launched to edit an embedded object or as an automation server; if so, there is no need to display the main window, so the function returns early, as shown in Listing 25.3.

Listing 25.3   ShowString.cpp—How the app Was Launched

```
// Check to see if launched as OLE server
if (cmdInfo.m_bRunEmbedded || cmdInfo.m_bRunAutomated)
{
    // Application was run with /Embedding or /Automation.  Don't show the
    //   main window in this case.
    return TRUE;
}

// When a server application is launched stand-alone, it is a good idea
//   to update the system registry in case it has been damaged.
m_server.UpdateRegistry(OAT_DISPATCH_OBJECT);
COleObjectFactory::UpdateRegistryAll();
```

If ShowString is being run as a stand-alone application, the code in Listing 25.3 updates the Registry as discussed in Chapter 24, "Building an ActiveX Server Application."

CShowStringDoc   The document class, `CShowStringDoc`, still inherits from `CDocument` rather than from any OLE document class, but that's where the similarities to the old non-OLE `CShowStringDoc` end. The first block of new code in ShowStringDoc.cpp is right after the message map and is shown in Listing 25.4

Listing 25.4   ShowStringDoc.cpp—Dispatch Map

```
BEGIN_DISPATCH_MAP(CShowStringDoc, CDocument)
    //{{AFX_DISPATCH_MAP(CShowStringDoc)
        // NOTE - the ClassWizard will add and remove mapping macros here.
        //     DO NOT EDIT what you see in these blocks of generated code!
    //}}AFX_DISPATCH_MAP
END_DISPATCH_MAP()
```

This is an empty *dispatch map*. A dispatch map is like a message map, in that it maps events in the real world into function calls within this C++ class. When you expose methods and properties of this document with ClassWizard, the dispatch map will be updated.

After the dispatch map is another unique identifier, the IID (interface identifier). As Listing 25.5 shows, the IID is added as a static member, like the CLSID.

Listing 25.5 ShowStringDoc.cpp—IID

```
// Note: we add support for IID_IShowSt to support typesafe binding
//    from VBA.  This IID must match the GUID that is attached to the
//    dispinterface in the .ODL file.

// {4E28FA6C-E3C0-11CF-B5C2-0080C81A397C}
static const IID IID_IShowSt =                                      \
{ 0x4e28fa6c, 0xe3c0, 0x11cf, { 0xb5, 0xc2, 0x0, 0x80,
    0xc8, 0x1a, 0x39, 0x7c } };
```

Then the *interface map* looks like this:

```
BEGIN_INTERFACE_MAP(CShowStringDoc, CDocument)
    INTERFACE_PART(CShowStringDoc, IID_IShowSt, Dispatch)
END_INTERFACE_MAP()
```

An interface map hides ActiveX functions like QueryInterface() from you, the programmer, and, like a message map, allows you to think at a more abstract level. ShowString will not have multiple entries in the interface map, but many applications do. Entries in the interface map are managed for you by ClassWizard.

The document constructor has some setting up to do. The AppWizard code is in Listing 25.6.

Listing 25.6 ShowStringDoc.cpp—Constructor

```
CShowStringDoc::CShowStringDoc()
{
    // TODO: add one-time construction code here
    EnableAutomation();
    AfxOleLockApp();
}
```

EnableAutomation() does just what its name suggests: it enables ActiveX Automation for this document. AfxOleLockApp() is used to ensure that an application is not closed while one of its documents is still in use elsewhere. Imagine that a user has two applications open that use ShowString objects. When the first application is closed, ShowString should not be closed because it is needed by the other application. ActiveX technology implements this by keeping a count, within the framework, of the number of active objects. AfxOleLockApp() increases this count. If it is nonzero when the user tries to close an application, the application is hidden but not actually closed.

It shouldn't be surprising, then, to see the destructor for ShowString's document:

```
CShowStringDoc::~CShowStringDoc()
{
    AfxOleUnlockApp();
}
```

`AfxOleUnlockApp()` decreases the count of active objects so that eventually the application can be closed.

Properties to Expose

At this point, you have an ActiveX Automation server that does not expose any methods or properties. Also, the four member variables of the document that have been in all the previous versions of ShowString have not been added to this version. These member variables are the following:

- `string` The string to be shown
- `color` 0 for black, 1 for red, and 2 for green
- `horizcenter` TRUE if the string should be centered horizontally
- `vertcenter` TRUE if the string should be centered vertically

These variables will be added as ActiveX Automation properties, so you will not type their names into the class definition for `CShowStringDoc`. Bring up ClassWizard by clicking on its toolbar button or choosing View, ClassWizard. Click on the OLE Automation tab, shown in Figure 25.1, to add properties and methods.

Part

IV

Ch

25

FIG. 25.1

ClassWizard's OLE Automation tab handles most of the work of building an Automation server.

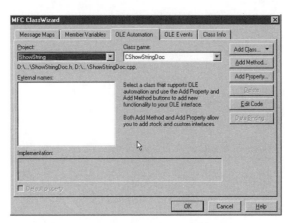

The first step in restoring the old ShowString functionality is to add member variables to the document class that will be exposed as properties of the ActiveX Automation server. There are two ways to expose properties: as a variable and with functions. Exposing a property as a variable is rather like declaring a public member variable of a C++ class: other applications can look at the value of the property and change it directly. A notification function within your server is called when the variable is changed from the outside. Exposing with Get and Set functions is like implementing a private member variable with public access functions. Other applications appear to access the variable directly, but the framework arranges for a call to your functions to Get and Set the property. Your Get may make sure that the object is in a valid state (for example, that a sorted list is currently sorted or that a total has been calculated) before returning the property value. Your Set function may do error checking (validation) or may calculate other variables that depend on the property that the outside application is changing. To make a property read-only, you add it as a Get/Set function property and then do not implement a Set function.

For the purposes of this chapter, you will add the two centering flags to the CShowStringDoc class with Get and Set functions, and the string and color properties as direct-access properties. To do so, follow these steps:

1. Make sure that CShowStringDoc is the selected class, then click the Add Property button to bring up the Add Property dialog box.

2. Type **String** in the External name box, and ClassWizard types along with you, filling in the Variable name and Notification function boxes for you.

3. Choose CString from the drop-down list box for Type, and then the dialog box should resemble Figure 25.2.

FIG. 25.2

Add *String* as a direct-access property.

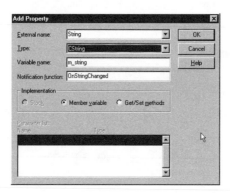

4. Click OK, click Add Property again, and then add Color as a direct-access property, as shown in Figure 25.3. Use short as the data type.

FIG. 25.3

Add *Color* as a direct-access property.

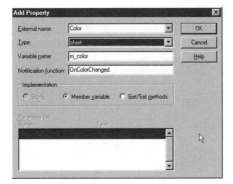

5. Click OK, click Add Property again, and then add HorizCenter.

6. Choose BOOL for the type and then select the Get/Set methods radio button. The Variable name and Notification function boxes are replaced by Get function and Set function, already filled in, as shown in Figure 25.4. (If the type changes from BOOL, choose BOOL again.) Click OK.

7. Add VertCenter in the same way that you added HorizCenter.

FIG. 25.4

Add *HorizCenter* as a Get/Set method property.

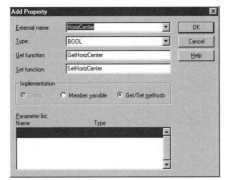

> **CAUTION**
>
> Once you have clicked OK to add a property, you cannot change the type, external name or other properties of the property. You will have to delete it and then add one that has the new type or external name or whatever. Always look over the Add Property Dialog before clicking OK.

Figure 25.5 shows the ClassWizard summary of exposed properties and methods. The details of each property are shown in the Implementation box below the list of properties. In Figure 25.5, VertCenter is highlighted, and the Implementation box reminds you that VertCenter has a Get function and a Set function, showing their declarations.

FIG. 25.5
ClassWizard provides a summary of the properties you have added.

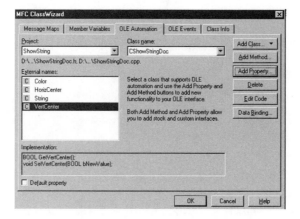

It should come as no surprise that as a result of these additions, ClassWizard has made changes to the header and source files for CShowStringDoc. The new dispatch map in the header file is in Listing 25.7.

Listing 25.7 ShowStringDoc.cpp—Dispatch Map

```
/{{AFX_DISPATCH(CShowStringDoc)
CString m_string;
afx_msg void OnStringChanged();
short m_color;
afx_msg void OnColorChanged();
afx_msg BOOL GetHorizCenter();
afx_msg void SetHorizCenter(BOOL bNewValue);
afx_msg BOOL GetVertCenter();
afx_msg void SetVertCenter(BOOL bNewValue);
//}}AFX_DISPATCH
DECLARE_DISPATCH_MAP()
```

Two new member variables have been added: m_string and m_color.

N O T E It's natural to wonder if these are actually public member variables; they are not. Just above this dispatch map is this line:

```
DECLARE_MESSAGE_MAP()
```

And that macro, when it expands, declares a number of protected variables. Since these declarations are immediately afterward, they are protected member variables and protected functions. They are accessed in just the same way that protected message-catching functions are: they are called by a member function hidden in the class that directs traffic using these maps. ■

A block of code has been added in the source file, but it's pretty boring, as you can see by looking at Listing 25.8.

Listing 25.8 ShowStringDoc.cpp—Notification, Get, and Set Functions

```
//////////////////////////////////////////////////////////////
// CShowStringDoc commands


void CShowStringDoc::OnColorChanged()
{
    // TODO: Add notification handler code

}

void CShowStringDoc::OnStringChanged()
{
    // TODO: Add notification handler code

}

BOOL CShowStringDoc::GetHorizCenter()
{
    // TODO: Add your property handler here

    return TRUE;
}

void CShowStringDoc::SetHorizCenter(BOOL bNewValue)
{
    // TODO: Add your property handler here

}

BOOL CShowStringDoc::GetVertCenter()
{
    // TODO: Add your property handler here

    return TRUE;
}

void CShowStringDoc::SetVertCenter(BOOL bNewValue)
{
    // TODO: Add your property handler here

}
```

Part
IV

Ch
25

The class still does not have member variables for the centering flags. Add them by hand to the header file, as private member variables:

```
// Attributes
private:
    BOOL m_horizcenter;
    BOOL m_vertcenter;
```

Now you can write their Get and Set functions; Listing 25.9 shows the code.

> **Listing 25.9   ShowStringDoc.cpp—Get and Set Functions for the Centering Flags**

```
BOOL CShowStringDoc::GetHorizCenter()
{
    return m_horizcenter;
}

void CShowStringDoc::SetHorizCenter(BOOL bNewValue)
{
    m_horizcenter = bNewValue;
}

BOOL CShowStringDoc::GetVertCenter()
{
    return m_vertcenter;
}

void CShowStringDoc::SetVertCenter(BOOL bNewValue)
{
    m_vertcenter = bNewValue;
}
```

The *OnDraw()* Function

Restoring the member variables takes you halfway to the old functionality of ShowString. Changing the view's OnDraw() function will take you most of the rest of the way.

To write a version of OnDraw() that shows a string properly, open an old version of ShowString—either from your own work in Chapter 17, "Building Menus and Dialogs," or from the CD that comes with this book—and then paste in the following bits of code. (If any of this code is unfamiliar to you, Chapter 17 explains it fully.) First, CShowStringDoc::OnNewDocument() (Listing 25.10) should initialize the member variables.

> **Listing 25.10   ShowStringDoc.cpp—Get and Set Functions for the Centering Flags**

```
BOOL CShowStringDoc::OnNewDocument()
{
    if (!CDocument::OnNewDocument())
        return FALSE;

    m_string = "Hello, world!";
    m_color = 0;      //black
    m_horizcenter = TRUE;
    m_vertcenter = TRUE;

    return TRUE;
}
```

Don't forget to change the member variable names; in this version of ShowString, you should use Microsoft's Hungarian notation, with m_ indicating that these are member variables, so as to be compatible with the code generated by ClassWizard. Next, copy in the document's Serialize function, shown in Listing 25.11.

Listing 25.11 ShowStringDoc.cpp— CShowStringDoc::Serialize()

```
void CShowStringDoc::Serialize(CArchive& ar)
{
    if (ar.IsStoring())
    {
        ar << m_string;
        ar << m_color;
        ar << m_horizcenter;
        ar << m_vertcenter;
    }
    else
    {
        ar >> m_string;
        ar >> m_color;
        ar >> m_horizcenter;
        ar >> m_vertcenter;
    }
}
```

Finally, the view's OnDraw() function (Listing 25.12) actually shows the string.

Listing 25.12 ShowStringDoc.cpp— CShowStringView::OnDraw()

```
void CShowStringView::OnDraw(CDC* pDC)
{

    CShowStringDoc* pDoc = GetDocument();
    ASSERT_VALID(pDoc);

    COLORREF oldcolor;
    switch (pDoc->GetColor())
    {
    case 0:
        oldcolor = pDC->SetTextColor(RGB(0,0,0)); //black
        break;
    case 1:
        oldcolor = pDC->SetTextColor(RGB(0xFF,0,0)); //red
        break;
    case 2:
        oldcolor = pDC->SetTextColor(RGB(0,0xFF,0)); //green
        break;
    }

    int DTflags = 0;
    if (pDoc->GetHorizcenter())
    {
```

Part IV

Ch

25

continues

Listing 25.12   Continued

```
        DTflags |= DT_CENTER;
    }
    if (pDoc->GetVertcenter())
    {
        DTflags |= (DT_VCENTER|DT_SINGLELINE);
    }

    CRect rect;
    GetClientRect(&rect);
    pDC->DrawText(pDoc->GetString(), &rect, DTflags);
    pDC->SetTextColor(oldcolor);

}
```

In order for this code to work, you need to add public functions to the document class to get the private member variables m_string, m_color, m_horizcenter, and m_vertcenter. The best names are already taken and are protected functions. You could either make the view a friend to the document so that it can access the member variables directly, or you could settle for not-so-good names for the access functions. You can add the functions inline to the header file, pasting from the old ShowString.

```
public:
    CString GetDocString() {return m_string;}
    int     GetDocColor() {return m_color;}
    BOOL GetHorizcenter() {return m_horizcenter;}
    BOOL GetVertcenter() {return m_vertcenter;}
```

In CShowStringView::OnDraw(), change the call to GetColor() to a call to GetDocColor(), and change the call to GetString() to a call to GetDocString(). Build the project to check for any typing mistakes or forgotten changes. While it may be tempting to run ShowString now, it's not going to do what you expect until you make a few more changes.

Showing the Window

By default, ActiveX Automation servers do not have a main window. Remember the little snippet from CShowStringApp::InitInstance() in Listing 25.13.

Listing 25.13   ShowString.cpp— How the app Was Launched

```
// Check to see if launched as OLE server
if (cmdInfo.m_bRunEmbedded || cmdInfo.m_bRunAutomated)
{
    // Application was run with /Embedding or /Automation.  Don't show the
    //   main window in this case.
        return TRUE;
}
```

This code returns before showing the main window. While you could remove this test so that ShowString always shows its window, it's more common to add a ShowWindow() method for the controller application to call. You'll also need to add a RefreshWindow() method that updates the view after a variable is changed; ClassWizard makes it simple to do this. Bring up ClassWizard, click the OLE Automation tab, and then click Add Method. Fill in the external name as ShowWindow(). ClassWizard fills in the internal name for you, and there's no need to change it. Choose void from the Return type drop-down list box. Figure 25.6 shows the dialog box after it's been filled in.

FIG. 25.6

ClassWizard makes it simple to add a ShowWindow() method.

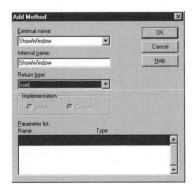

Click OK on the dialog box, and ShowWindow() appears in the middle of the list of properties, which turns out to be a list of properties and methods in alphabetical order. The *C* next to the properties reminds you that these properties are custom properties (other types of properties are discussed in the "Displaying the Current Value" section of the next chapter, "Building an ActiveX Control"). The *M* next to the methods reminds you that these are methods. With ShowWindow() highlighted, click Edit Code and then type in the function, as shown in Listing 25.14.

Part
IV
Ch
25

Listing 25.14 ShowStringDoc.cpp—CShowStringDoc::ShowWindow()

```cpp
void CShowStringDoc::ShowWindow()
{
    POSITION pos = GetFirstViewPosition();
    CView* pView = GetNextView(pos);
    if (pView)
    {
        CFrameWnd* pFrameWnd = pView->GetParentFrame();
        pFrameWnd->ActivateFrame(SW_SHOW);
    }

}
```

This code activates the view and asks for it to be shown. Bring up ClassWizard again, click Add Method, and add RefreshWindow(), returning void. Click OK and then Edit Code. The code for RefreshWindow(), shown in Listing 25.15, is even simpler.

Listing 25.15   ShowStringDoc.cpp—CShowStringDoc::RefreshWindow()

```
void CShowStringDoc::RefreshWindow()
{
    UpdateAllViews(NULL);
    SetModifiedFlag();
}
```

This arranges for the view (now that it's active) to be redrawn. And, because a change to the document is almost certainly the reason for the redraw, this is a handy place to put the call to SetModifiedFlag(), though if you prefer, you can put it in each Set function and the notification functions for the direct-access properties. You will add a call to RefreshWindow() to each of those functions now. For example, SetHorizCenter() is shown in Listing 25.16.

Listing 25.16   ShowStringDoc.cpp—CShowStringDoc::SetHorizCenter()

```
void CShowStringDoc::SetHorizCenter(BOOL bNewValue)
{
    m_horizcenter = bNewValue;
    RefreshWindow();
}
And OnColorChanged() looks like this:
void CShowStringDoc::OnColorChanged()
{
    RefreshWindow();
}
```

Add the same RefreshWindow() call to SetVertCenter() and OnStringChanged(). Now you are ready to build and test. Build the project and correct any typing errors. Run ShowString as a stand-alone application, both to register it and to test your drawing code. You cannot change the string, color, or centering as you could with older versions of ShowString, because this version does not implement the Tools, Options menu item and its dialog box. The controller application is going to do that for this version.

DispTest

This chapter has mentioned a controller application several times, and you may have wondered where it's going to come from. You are going to put it together in DispTest, a watered-down version of Visual Basic that comes with Visual C++. It's not added to the Start menu, but you can run DISPTEST.EXE from the C:\MSDEV\BIN folder or from your Visual C++ CD-ROM's \MSDEV\BIN folder. Figure 25.7 shows the DispTest interface.

FIG. 25.7
At first glance, DispTest looks just like Visual Basic.

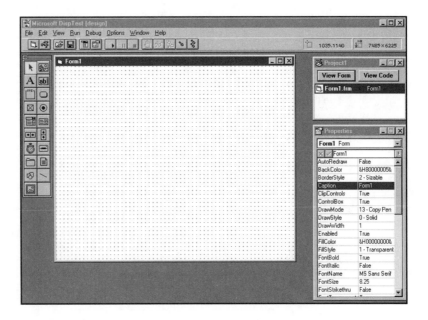

T I P   If you have Visual Basic, you may choose to use it instead of DispTest. For testing OLE Automation servers, it doesn't matter which you choose. If you've written VBA macros in Excel and have a copy of Excel, you can use that, too.

To build a controller application for the ShowString Automation server, start by running DispTest. In the window at the upper-right labeled Project1, click the View Code button. Choose Form from the right-hand drop-down list box in the new window that appears, and the Form_Load() subroutine is displayed. Enter the code in Listing 25.17 into that subroutine.

Listing 25.17   Form1.frm—DispTest code

```
Sub Form_Load ()
    Set ShowTest = CreateObject("ShowString.Document")
    ShowTest.ShowWindow
    ShowTest.HorizCenter = False
    ShowTest.Color = 1
    ShowTest.String = "Hello from DispTest"
    Set ShowTest = Nothing
End Sub
```

Choose (general) from the left-hand drop-down list box and then enter this line of code:

```
Dim ShowTest As Object
```

For those of you who don't read Visual Basic, this code makes more sense if you go through it a line at a time. Choose Debug Single Step to execute the first line of code. Then repeatedly press F8 to move through the routine. (Wait after each press until the cursor is back to normal.) The line in the general code sets up an object called ShowTest. When the form is loaded (which is whenever you run this little program), an instance of the ShowString object is created. The next line calls the ShowWindow method to display the main window on the screen. Whenever the debugger pauses, the dashed box is around the line of code that will run next. You should see something like Figure 25.8 with the default ShowString behavior.

FIG. 25.8

The *ShowWindow* method displays the main ShowString window.

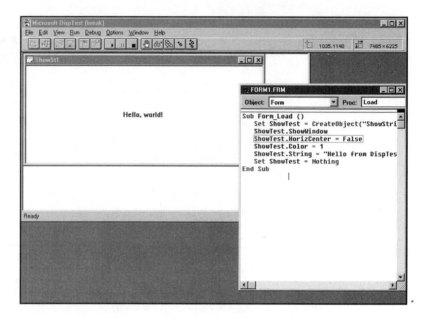

Press F8 again to run the line that turns off horizontal centering. Notice that you do not call the function SetHorizCenter. You exposed HorizCenter as a property of the OLE Automation server, and from Visual Basic, you access it as a property. The difference is that the C++ framework code calls SetHorizCenter to make the change, rather than just making the change and then calling a notification function to tell you that it was changed. After this line has executed, your screen will resemble Figure 25.9, because the SetHorizCenter method calls RefreshWindow() to immediately redraw the screen.

FIG. 25.9

The Visual Basic program has turned off centering.

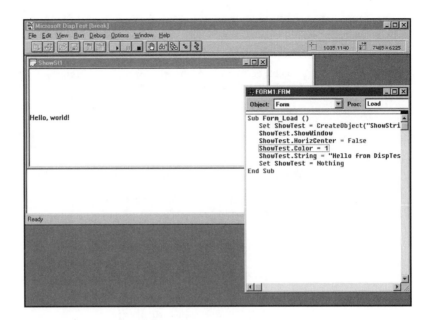

As you continue through this program, pressing F8 to move a step at a time, the string will turn red and then change to `Hello from DispTest`. Notice that the change to these directly exposed properties looks no different than the change to the Get/Set method property, `HorizCenter`. When the program finishes, the window goes away. You have successfully controlled your ActiveX Automation server from DispTest.

Type Libraries and ActiveX Internals

Many programmers are intimidated by ActiveX, and the last thing they want is to know what's happening under the hood. There's nothing wrong with that attitude at all. It's quite object-oriented, really, to trust the already-written ActiveX framework to handle the black magic of translating `ShowTest.HorizCenter = False` into a call to `CShowStringDoc::SetHorizCenter()`. But if you want to know how that "magic" happens, or what to do if it doesn't, you need to add one more piece to the puzzle. You have already seen the dispatch map for ShowString, but you haven't seen the *type library*. It is not meant for humans to read, but it's for ActiveX and the Registry. It is generated for you as part of a normal build from your Object Definition Language (ODL) file. This file was generated by AppWizard and is maintained by ClassWizard. `ShowString.odl` looks like Listing 25.18, which follows.

Listing 25.18   ShowString.odl—ShowString Type Library

```
// ShowString.odl : type library source for ShowString.exe

// This file will be processed by the Make Type Library (mktyplib) tool to
// produce the type library (ShowString.tlb).

[ uuid(4E28FA6B-E3C0-11CF-B5C2-0080C81A397C), version(1.0) ]
library ShowString
{
    importlib("stdole32.tlb");

    //  Primary dispatch interface for CShowStringDoc

    [ uuid(4E28FA6C-E3C0-11CF-B5C2-0080C81A397C) ]
    dispinterface IShowSt
    {
        properties:
            // NOTE - ClassWizard will maintain property information here.
            //     Use extreme caution when editing this section.
            //{{AFX_ODL_PROP(CShowStringDoc)
            [id(1)] BSTR String;
            [id(2)] short Color;
            [id(3)] boolean HorizCenter;
            [id(4)] boolean VertCenter;
            //}}AFX_ODL_PROP

        methods:
            // NOTE - ClassWizard will maintain method information here.
            //     Use extreme caution when editing this section.
            //{{AFX_ODL_METHOD(CShowStringDoc)
            [id(5)] void ShowWindow();
            [id(6)] void RefreshWindow();
            //}}AFX_ODL_METHOD
    };

    //  Class information for CShowStringDoc

    [ uuid(4E28FA6A-E3C0-11CF-B5C2-0080C81A397C) ]
    coclass Document
    {
        [default] dispinterface IShowSt;
    };

    //{{AFX_APPEND_ODL}}
};
```

This explains why Visual Basic just thought of all four properties as properties: that's how they
are listed in this ODL file. The two methods are here, too, in the methods section. The reason
you passed "ShowString.Document" to CreateObject() is that there is a coclass Document
section here. It points to a dispatch interface (dispinterface) called IShowSt. Here's the interface map from ShowStringDoc.cpp:

```
BEGIN_INTERFACE_MAP(CShowStringDoc, CDocument)
    INTERFACE_PART(CShowStringDoc, IID_IShowSt, Dispatch)
END_INTERFACE_MAP()
```

So a call to `CreateObject("ShowString.Document")` leads to the coclass section, which points to `IShowSt`. The interface map points from `IShowSt` to `CShowStringDoc`, which has a dispatch map that connects the properties and methods in the outside world to C++ code. You can see that editing any of these sections by hand could have disastrous results. Trust the wizards to do this for you.

From Here...

In this chapter, you built an ActiveX Automation server and controlled it from DispTest. ActiveX Automation servers are far more powerful than older ways of application interaction, but your server doesn't have any user interaction. If the Visual Basic program wanted to allow the user to choose the color, that would have to be built into the Visual Basic program. The next logical step is to allow the little embedded object to react to user events like clicks and drags, and to report to the controller program what has happened. That's what ActiveX controls do, as you'll see in the next chapter. Some chapters you may want to read include:

- Chapter 17, "Building Menus and Dialogs," introduced the ShowString application.
- Chapter 22, "ActiveX Concepts," is a roadmap to Part IV of this book and defines many of the concepts used in this and related chapters.
- Chapter 23, "Building an ActiveX Container Application," built the second version of ShowString, which acts as an ActiveX container.
- Chapter 24, "Building an ActiveX Server Application," built the third version of ShowString, which acts as an ActiveX server.
- Chapter 26, "Building an ActiveX Control," leaves ShowString behind and builds a control you can include in any Visual C++ or Visual Basic program.

Part

IV

Ch

25

Building an ActiveX Control

ActiveX controls replace OLE controls, though it's a change more in name than in anything else. (Much of the Microsoft documentation still refers to OLE controls.) The exciting behavior of these controls is powered by ActiveX, formerly known as OLE. This chapter draws, in part, on the ActiveX work of the earlier chapters. An ActiveX control is similar to an ActiveX Automation server, but it also exposes *events*, and these enable the control to direct the behavior of the container.

ActiveX controls take the place that VBX controls held in 16-bit Windows programming, allowing programmers to extend the control set provided by the compiler. The original purpose of VBX controls was to allow programmers to provide unusual interface controls to their users. Controls that looked like gas gauges or volume knobs became easy to develop. But almost immediately, VBX programmers moved beyond simple controls to modules that involved significant amounts of calculation and processing. In the same way, many ActiveX controls are far more than just controls; they are *components* that can be used to build powerful applications quickly and easily. ■

Designing a Die-Roll Control

The sample application for this chapter rolls a die. This section describes the control and starts the building process.

Displaying the Die

Adding a property to a control and drawing a control are explained in this section.

Reacting to Clicks: Rolling the Die

ActiveX controls notify their containers of user activities with events. This section explains events and works you through the process of getting your control to roll a new number when the user clicks on the control.

Improving the User Interface

Adding more properties gives the user more flexibility. This section shows you how.

Implementing Property Sheets

Adding property sheets to a control is quite simple, with much of the work already done for you. This section demonstrates the process.

A Rolling-Die Control

The sample application for this chapter is to be a *die,* one of a pair of dice. Imagine a picture of a cubic die with the familiar pattern of dots indicating the current value, between 1 and 6. When the user clicks the picture, a new number, chosen randomly, is shown. You might implement one or more dice into any game program.

Building the Control Shell

The process of building this die control starts, as always, with AppWizard. Start Developer Studio and then choose File, New. From the list that appears, choose Project Workspace and click OK, or double-click Project Workspace. Click OLE Control Wizard in the list at the left of the dialog box and fill in a project name at the top, choose an appropriate folder for the project files, and then click Create. Figure 26.1 shows the completed dialog box, with the project name Dieroll.

N O T E Even though the technology is now called ActiveX, the AppWizard dialogs still refer to OLE. Many of the class names that are used throughout this chapter have Ole in their names, and comments refer to OLE. While Microsoft has changed the name of the technology, it has not propagated that change throughout Visual C++ yet. You will have to live with these contradictions until the next release of Visual C++. ■

FIG. 26.1

AppWizard makes creating an ActiveX control simple.

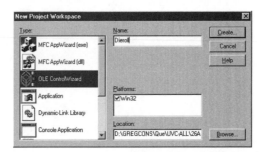

There are two steps in the ActiveX control wizard. Fill out the first dialog box as shown in Figure 26.2. You want one control, no runtime licensing, source-file comments, and no help files. After you have completed the dialog box, click Next.

Runtime Licensing

Many developers produce controls as a product that they sell. Other programmers buy the rights to use the control in their program. Imagine that a developer, Alice, produces a fantastic die control and sells it to Bob, who incorporates it into the best backgammon game ever. Carol buys the backgammon game and loves the die control, and she decides that it would be perfect for a children's board game she is planning. Since the file DIEROLL.OCX is in the backgammon package, there is nothing (other than ethics) to stop her from doing this.

Runtime licensing is simple: There is a second file, DIEROLL.LIC, that contains the licensing information. Without that file, a control cannot be embedded into a form or program, though a program into which the control is already embedded will work perfectly. Alice ships both DIEROLL.OCX and DIEROLL.LIC to Bob, but their licensing agreement states that only DIEROLL.OCX goes out with the backgammon game. Now Carol can admire DIEROLL.OCX, and it will work perfectly in the backgammon game, but if she wants to include it in the game she builds, she'll have to buy a license from Alice.

You arrange for runtime licensing with AppWizard when you first build the control. If you decide after the control is already built that you should have asked for runtime licensing after all, build a new control with licensing and copy your changes into that control.

FIG. 26.2
AppWizard's first step sets the basic parameters of your control.

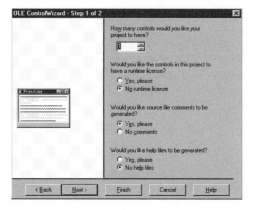

Part
IV

Ch
26

The second and final AppWizard step allows you to set the features of the new control. Make sure that Activates When Visible, Available in "Insert Object" Dialog, and Has an "About Box" are selected, as shown in Figure 26.3, and then click Finish. AppWizard summarizes your settings in a final dialog box. Click OK, and AppWizard creates 18 files for you and adds them to a project to make them easy to work with. These files are ready to compile, but they don't do anything at the moment. You have an empty shell, and it is up to you to fill it.

FIG. 26.3

AppWizard's second step governs the appearance and behavior of your control.

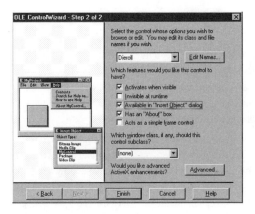

AppWizard's Code

Eighteen files sounds like a lot, but it isn't. There are only three classes: CDierollApp, CDierollCtrl, and CDierollPropPage. They take up six files; the other 12 are the project file, make file, resource file, ClassWizard database, ODL file, and so on.

CDierollApp CDierollApp is a very small class. It inherits from COleControlModule and provides overrides of InitInstance() and ExitInstance() that do nothing but call the base-class versions of these functions. This is where you find _tlid, the external globally unique ID for your control, and some version numbers that make delivering upgrades of your control simpler. The lines in Dieroll.cpp that set up these identifiers are the following:

```
const GUID CDECL BASED_CODE _tlid =
        { 0x46646b40, 0xea16, 0x11cf, { 0x87, 0xc, 0, 0x20, 0x18, 0x1, 0xdd,
        ➥0xd6 } };
const WORD _wVerMajor = 1;
const WORD _wVerMinor = 0;
```

CDierollCtrl The CDierollCtrl class inherits from COleControl, and it overrides the constructor and destructor, plus these four functions:

- ◾ OnDraw() draws the control.
- ◾ DoPropExchange() implements persistence and initialization.
- ◾ OnResetState() causes the control to be reinitialized.
- ◾ AboutBox() displays the About box for the control.

None of the code for these functions is particularly interesting. However, some of the maps that have been added to this class are interesting. There is an empty message map, ready to accept new entries, and an empty dispatch map, ready for the properties and methods that you choose to expose.

 Message maps were explained in the "Message Maps" section of Chapter 5, "Messages and Commands." Dispatch maps are discussed in the "AppWizard's Automation Boilerplate" section in Chapter 25, "ActiveX Automation."

Below the empty message and dispatch maps comes a new map, the *event map*. The event map in the header file is shown in Listing 26.1 and the source file event map is shown in Listing 26.2.

Listing 26.1   Excerpt from DierollCtl.h—Event Map

```
// Event maps
    //{{AFX_EVENT(CDierollCtrl)
        // NOTE - ClassWizard will add and remove member functions here.
        //    DO NOT EDIT what you see in these blocks of generated code !
    //}}AFX_EVENT
    DECLARE_EVENT_MAP()
```

Listing 26.2   Excerpt from DierollCtl.cpp—Event Map

```
BEGIN_EVENT_MAP(CDierollCtrl, COleControl)
    //{{AFX_EVENT_MAP(CDierollCtrl)
    // NOTE - ClassWizard will add and remove event map entries
    //    DO NOT EDIT what you see in these blocks of generated code !
    //}}AFX_EVENT_MAP
END_EVENT_MAP()
```

Event maps, like *message maps* and *dispatch maps,* link real-world happenings to your code. Message maps catch things the user does, like choosing a menu item or clicking a button. They also catch messages sent from one part of an application to another. Dispatch maps direct requests to access properties or invoke methods of an OLE Automation server or ActiveX control. Event maps direct notifications from an ActiveX control to the application that contains them (and are discussed in more detail later in this chapter).

There's one more piece of code worth noting in DierollCtl.cpp, shown in Listing 26.3.

Listing 26.3   Excerpt from DierollCtl.cpp—Property Pages

```
/////////////////////////////////////////////////////////////////////////////
// Property pages

// TODO: Add more property pages as needed.  Remember to increase the count!
BEGIN_PROPPAGEIDS(CDierollCtrl, 1)
    PROPPAGEID(CDierollPropPage::guid)
END_PROPPAGEIDS(CDierollCtrl)
```

The code in Listing 26.3 is part of the mechanism that implements powerful and intuitive property pages in your controls. That mechanism is discussed later in this chapter.

CDierollPropPage   The entire `CDierollPropPage` class is the property of ClassWizard. Like any class with a dialog box in it, it has significant data-exchange components. The constructor will initialize the dialog-box fields using code added by ClassWizard, shown in Listing 26.4.

Part
IV

Ch
26

Listing 26.4 DierollPropPage.cpp—CDierollPropPage::CDierollPropPage()

```
CDierollPropPage::CDierollPropPage() :
    COlePropertyPage(IDD, IDS_DIEROLL_PPG_CAPTION)
{
    //{{AFX_DATA_INIT(CDierollPropPage)
    // NOTE: ClassWizard will add member initialization here
    //    DO NOT EDIT what you see in these blocks of generated code !
    //}}AFX_DATA_INIT
}
```

The DoDataExchange() function moderates the exchange of data between CDierollPropPage, which represents the dialog box that is the property page, and the actual boxes on the user's screen. It, too, is written by ClassWizard—see Listing 26.5.

Listing 26.5 DierollPropPage.cpp—CDierollPropPage::DoDataExchange()

```
void CDierollPropPage::DoDataExchange(CDataExchange* pDX)
{
    //{{AFX_DATA_MAP(CDierollPropPage)
    // NOTE: ClassWizard will add DDP, DDX, and DDV calls here
    //    DO NOT EDIT what you see in these blocks of generated code !
    //}}AFX_DATA_MAP
    DDP_PostProcessing(pDX);
}
```

There is, not surprisingly, a message map for CDierollPropPage, and some registration code, shown in Listing 26.6, that will enable the OLE framework to call this code when a user edits the properties of the control.

Listing 26.6 DierollPropPage.cpp—CDierollPropPage::DoDataExchange()

```
/////////////////////////////////////////////////////////////////////////////
// Initialize class factory and guid

IMPLEMENT_OLECREATE_EX(CDierollPropPage, "DIEROLL.DierollPropPage.1",
    0x46646b44, 0xea16, 0x11cf, 0x87, 0xc, 0, 0x20, 0x18, 0x1, 0xdd, 0xd6)


/////////////////////////////////////////////////////////////////////////////
// CDierollPropPage::CDierollPropPageFactory::UpdateRegistry -
// Adds or removes system registry entries for CDierollPropPage

BOOL CDierollPropPage::CDierollPropPageFactory::UpdateRegistry(BOOL bRegister)
{
    if (bRegister)
        return AfxOleRegisterPropertyPageClass(AfxGetInstanceHandle(),
            m_clsid, IDS_DIEROLL_PPG);
    else
        return AfxOleUnregisterClass(m_clsid, NULL);
}
```

Designing the Control

Typically, a control has *internal data* (properties) and shows them in some way to the user. The control takes input from the user that changes its internal data and perhaps the way the control looks. Some controls present data to the user from other sources, such as databases or remote files. The only internal data that makes sense for the die-roll control, other than some appearance settings that we'll cover later, is a single integer between 1 and 6 representing the current number showing in the die. Eventually, the control will show a dot pattern like a real-world die, but the first implementation of OnDraw() will simply display the digit. Another simplification is to hard-code the digit to a single value while coding the basic structure and then add the code to roll the die later, while dealing with input from the user.

Displaying the Current Value

Before you can display the value, the control must have a value to display. That involves adding a property to the control and then writing the drawing code.

Adding a Property

OCX controls have four types of properties:

- Stock: These are standard properties supplied to every control, such as font or color. The developer must activate stock properties, but there is little or no coding involved.

- Ambient: These are properties of the environment that surrounds the control—of the container into which it has been placed. These cannot be changed, but the control can use them to adjust its own properties. For example, it can set the control's background color to match the container's background color.

- Extended: These are properties that will be handled by the container, typically involving size and placement on the screen.

- Custom: These are properties added by the control developer.

To add the value to the die-roll control, use ClassWizard to add a custom property called Number. Follow these steps:

1. Choose View, ClassWizard and then click the OLE Automation tab.

2. Make sure that the drop-down list box at the upper-left of the dialog box is set to Dieroll (unless you chose a different name when building the control with AppWizard) and that the right-hand box has the class name CDieRollCtrl.

3. Click the Add Property button and fill in the dialog box as shown in Figure 26.4.

4. Type **Number** into the External Name combo box and notice how ClassWizard fills in suggested values for the Variable name and Notification function boxes.

5. Select short for the type.

6. Click OK to close the Add Property dialog box and OK to close ClassWizard.

FIG. 26.4

ClassWizard simplifies the process of adding a custom property to your die-rolling control.

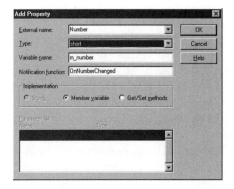

Before you can write code to display the value of the Number property, it needs to have a value. OCX properties are initialized in DoPropExchange(). This method actually implements *persistence*; that is, it allows the control to be saved as part of a document and read back in when the document is opened. Whenever a new control is created, the properties cannot be read from a file, so they are set to the default values provided in this method. Controls do not have a Serialize() method.

AppWizard generated a skeleton DoPropExchange() method whose code is in Listing 26.7.

Listing 26.7   DierollCtl.cpp—CDierollCtrl::DoPropExchange()

```
void CDierollCtrl::DoPropExchange(CPropExchange* pPX)
{
    ExchangeVersion(pPX, MAKELONG(_wVerMinor, _wVerMajor));
    COleControl::DoPropExchange(pPX);

    // TODO: Call PX_ functions for each persistent custom property.

}
```

Notice the use of the version numbers to be sure that a file holding the values was saved by the same version of the control. Take away the TODO comment that AppWizard left for you, and add this line:

```
PX_Short( pPX, "Number",  m_number, (short)3 );
```

PX_Short() is one of many property-exchange functions that you can call—one for each property type that is supported. The parameters you supply are as follows:

- The pointer that was passed to DoPropExchange().
- The external name of the property as you typed it on the ClassWizard Add Property dialog box.
- The member variable name of the property as you typed it on the ClassWizard Add Property dialog box.

- The default value for the property (later, you can replace this hard-coded 3 with a random value).

The following are the PX_ functions:

PX_Blob() (for binary large object [BLOB] types)

PX_Bool()

PX_Color()

PX_Currency()

PX_Double()

PX_Font()

PX_Float()

PX_IUnknown() (for LPUNKNOWN types)

PX_Long()

PX_Picture()

PX_Short()

PX_String()

PX_ULong()

PX_UShort()

Filling in the property's default value is simple for some properties, but not so simple for others. For example, set colors with the RGB() macro, which takes values for red, green, and blue from 0 to 255 and returns a COLORREF. Say that you had a property with the external name EdgeColor and the internal name m_edgecolor, and you wanted the property to default to gray. You would code that like the following:

```
PX_Short( pPX, " EdgeColor ", m_edgecolor, RGB(128,128,128) );
```

Controls with font properties should, by default, set the font to whatever the container is using. To get this font, call the COLEControl method AmbientFont().

Writing the Drawing Code

The code to display the number belongs in the OnDraw() method of the control class, CDierollCtrl. (Controls do not have documents or views.) This function is called automatically whenever Windows needs to repaint the part of the screen that includes the control. AppWizard generated a skeleton of this method too, shown in Listing 26.8.

Part

IV

Ch

26

Listing 26.8 DierollCtl.cpp—CDierollCtrl::OnDraw()

```
void CDierollCtrl::OnDraw(CDC* pdc, const CRect& rcBounds,
        const CRect& rcInvalid)
{
    // TODO: Replace the following code with your own drawing code.
    pdc->FillRect(rcBounds,
        CBrush::FromHandle((HBRUSH)GetStockObject(WHITE_BRUSH)));
    pdc->Ellipse(rcBounds);
}
```

As discussed in the "Scrolling windows" section of Chapter 11, "Drawing on the Screen," the framework passes the function a device context to draw in, a CRect describing the space occupied by your control, and another CRect describing the space that has been invalidated. The code in Listing 26.8 draws a white rectangle throughout rcBounds and then draws an ellipse inside that rectangle, using the default foreground color. Although you can keep the white rectangle for now, rather than draw an ellipse on it, draw a character that corresponds to the value in Number. To do that, replace the last line in the skeletal OnDraw() with these lines:

```
CString val; //character representation of the short value
val.Format("%i",m_number);
pdc->ExtTextOut( 0, 0, ETO_OPAQUE, rcBounds, val, NULL );
```

These lines of code convert the short value in m_number (which you associated with the Number property on the Add Property dialog box) to a CString variable called val, using the new CString::Format() function (which eliminates one of the last uses of sprintf() in C++ programming). The function ExtTextOut() draws a piece of text—the character in val—within the rcBounds rectangle. As the die-roll control is written now, that number will always be 3.

You can build and test the control right now if you would like to see how little it takes to make a control that does something. Unlike the other OLE applications, a control is not run as a stand-alone application in order to register it. Build the project and fix any typing mistakes that you may have made. Choose Tools, OLE Control Test Container to bring up the control test container, shown in Figure 26.5.

FIG. 26.5

The OLE Control Test Container is the ideal place to test your control.

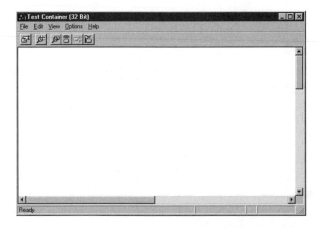

N O T E If the Tools menu in Developer Studio does not include an OLE Control Test Container item, you can add it to the menu by following these steps:

1. Choose Tools, Customize.

2. Click the Tools tab.

3. Look over the list of tools and make sure that OLE Control Test Container isn't there.

4. Click Add.

5. On the Add Tools dialog box that appears, click Browse.

6. Browse to your CD, or to the hard drive on which you installed Visual C++, and to the \MSDEV\BIN folder. Highlight tstcon32.exe and click OK to finish browsing.

7. Click OK on the Add Tools dialog box.

8. There should be no need to adjust the fields on the Tools tab for the test container entry. Click Close.

After you have installed the test container once, you will not need to do so again. By bringing up the test container from within Developer Studio like this, you make it simpler to load your die-roll control into the test container. ■

Within the test container, choose Edit, Insert OLE Control and then choose Dieroll Control from the list that is displayed. As Figure 26.6 shows, the control appears as a white rectangle displaying a small number 3. You can move and resize this control within the container, but that little 3 stays doggedly in the upper-left corner. The next step is to make that number change when a user clicks the die.

FIG. 26.6
By adding one property and changing two functions, you have transformed the empty shell into a control that displays a 3.

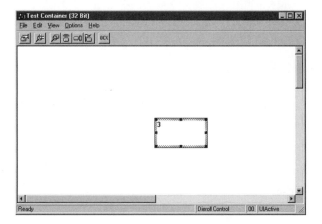

Reacting to a Mouse Click and Rolling the Die

There are actually two things that you want your control to do when the user clicks the mouse on the control: to inform the container that the control has been clicked and to roll the die and display the new internal value.

Notifying the Container

Let's tackle using an *event* to notify a container first. Events are how controls notify the container of a user action. Just as there are stock properties, there are stock events. These events are already coded for you:

- Click is coded to indicate to the container that the user clicked.
- DblClick is coded to indicate to the container that the user double-clicked.
- Error is coded to indicate an error that can't be handled any other way.
- KeyDown is coded to indicate to the container that a key has gone down.
- KeyPress is coded to indicate to the container that a complete keypress (down and then up again) has occurred.
- KeyUp is coded to indicate to the container that a key has gone up.
- MouseDown is coded to indicate to the container that the mouse button has gone down.
- MouseMove is coded to indicate to the container that the mouse has moved over the control.
- MouseUp is coded to indicate to the container that the mouse button has gone up.

The best way to tell the container that the user has clicked over the control is to fire a Click stock event. The first thing to do is to add it to the control with ClassWizard. Follow these steps:

1. Bring up ClassWizard by choosing View, ClassWizard and click the OLE Events tab.
2. Click the Add Event button and fill in the Add Event dialog box, as shown in Figure 26.7.

FIG. 26.7

ClassWizard helps you add events to your control.

3. The external name is Click; choose it from the drop-down list box and notice how the internal name is filled in as FireClick.
4. Click OK to add the event, and your work is done.

Now when the user clicks the control, the container class will be notified. So, if you are writing a backgammon game, for example, the container can respond to the click by using the new value on the die to evaluate possible moves or do some other backgammon-specific task.

The second part of reacting to clicks involves actually rolling the die and redisplaying it. Not surprisingly, ClassWizard helps implement this. When the user clicks over your control, you catch it with a message map entry, just as with an ordinary application. ClassWizard should still be up, but if not, bring it up, and follow these steps:

1. Select the Message Maps tab this time and make sure that your control class, CDierollCtrl, is selected in the Class Name combo box.

2. Scroll through the Messages list box until you find the WM_LBUTTONDOWN message, which is generated by Windows whenever the left mouse button is clicked over your control.

3. Click Add Function to add a function that will be called automatically whenever this message is generated—in other words, whenever the user clicks your control. This function must be named OnLButtonDown(), so there is no dialog box asking you to confirm the name.

4. ClassWizard has made a stub for you; click the Edit Code button to close ClassWizard and look at the new OnLButtonDown() code. Here's the stub:

```
void CDierollCtrl::OnLButtonDown(UINT nFlags, CPoint point)
{
    // TODO: Add your message handler code here and/or call default

    COleControl::OnLButtonDown(nFlags, point);
}
```

5. Replace the TODO comment with a call to a new function, Roll(), (this function will return a random number between 1 and 6) that you will write in the next section:

```
m_number = Roll();
```

6. To force a redraw, next add this line:

```
InvalidateControl();
```

7. Leave the call to COleControl::OnLButtonDown() at the end of the function; it takes care of the rest of the work of processing the mouse click.

Part
IV

Ch
26

Rolling the Die

To add Roll() to CDierollCtrl, right-click on CDierollCtrl in the ClassView pane and then choose Add Function from the shortcut menu that appears. As shown in Figure 26.8, Roll() should be a public function that takes no parameters and returns a short.

What should Roll() do? It should calculate a random value between 1 and 6. The C++ function that returns a random number is rand(), which returns an integer between 0 and RAND_MAX. Dividing by RAND_MAX + 1 gives a positive number that will always be less than 1, and multiplying by 6 gives a positive number that is less than 6. The integer part of the number will be between 0 and 5, in other words. Adding 1 produces the result that you want: a number between 1 and 6. The code is shown in Listing 26.9.

FIG. 26.8
Use the Add Member
Function dialog box to
speed routine tasks.

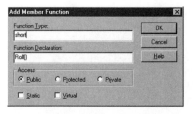

Listing 26.9   DierollCtl.cpp—CDierollCtrl::Roll()

```
short CDierollCtrl::Roll(void)
{
    double number = rand();
    number /= RAND_MAX + 1;
    number *= 6;
    return (short)number + 1;
}
```

N O T E If RAND_MAX + 1 isn't a multiple of 6, this code will roll low numbers slightly more often
than high ones. A typical value for RAND_MAX is 32,767, which means that 1 and 2 will on
the average come up 5,462 times in 32,767 rolls, but 3 through 6 will on the average come up 5,461
times. You're neglecting this inaccuracy.

Some die-rolling programs use the modulo function instead of this approach, but it is far less accurate.
The lowest digits in the random number are least likely to be accurate. The algorithm used here
produces a much more random die roll. ■

The random number generator must be seeded before it is used, and it's traditional (and practical) to use the current time as a seed value. In DoPropExchange(), add the following line before
the call to PX_Short():

```
srand( (unsigned)time( NULL ) );
```

Instead of hard-coding the start value to three, call Roll() to determine a random value.
Change the call to PX_Short() so that it reads as follows:

```
PX_Short( pPX, "Number", m_number, Roll());
```

Build and test the control again in the test container. As you click on the control, the number
that is displayed should change with each click. Play around with it a little: Do you ever see a
number less than 1 or more than 6? Any surprises at all?

A Better User Interface

Now that the basic functionality of the die-roll control is in place, it's time to neaten it a little.
It needs an icon, and it needs to display dots instead of a single digit.

A Bitmap Icon

Because some users of the die-roll control might want to add it to the Control Palette in Visual Basic, you should have an icon to represent it. Actually, AppWizard created one for you already, but it is just an MFC logo that doesn't represent your control in particular. You can create a better one with Developer Studio. Click the ResourceView tab of the Project Workspace window, click the + next to Bitmap, and double-click IDB_DIEROLL. You can now edit the bitmap one pixel at a time. Figure 26.9 shows an icon appropriate for a die. From now on, when you load the die-roll control into the test container, you will see your icon on the toolbar.

FIG. 26.9

The ResourceView of Visual C++ allows you to build your own icon to be added to the Control Palette in Visual Basic.

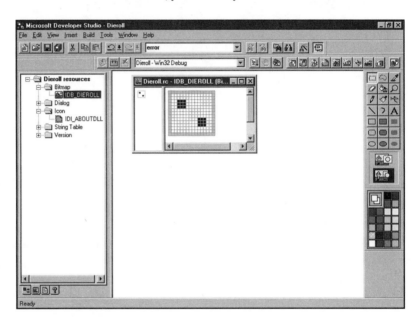

Part
IV

Ch

26

Displaying Dots

The next step in building this die-roll control is to make the control look like a die. A nice, three-dimensional effect with parts of some of the other sides showing is beyond the reach of an illustrative chapter like this one, but you can at least display a dot pattern.

The first step is to set up a switch statement in OnDraw(). Comment out the three drawing lines and then add the switch statement so that OnDraw() looks like Listing 26.10.

Listing 26.10 DierollCtl.cpp—CDierollCtrl::OnDraw()

```
void CDierollCtrl::OnDraw(
            CDC* pdc, const CRect& rcBounds, const CRect& rcInvalid)
{
    pdc->FillRect(rcBounds,
        CBrush::FromHandle((HBRUSH)GetStockObject(WHITE_BRUSH)));
```

continues

Listing 26.10 Continued

```
//    CString val; //character representation of the short value
//    val.Format("%i",m_number);
//    pdc->ExtTextOut( 0, 0, ETO_OPAQUE, rcBounds, val, NULL );

      switch(m_number)
      {
      case 1:
          break;
      case 2:
          break;
      case 3:
          break;
      case 4:
          break;
      case 5:
          break;
      case 6:
          break;
      }
}
```

Now all that remains is to add code to the case 1: block that draws one dot, to the case 2: block that draws two dots, and so on. If you happen to have a real die available, take a close look at it. The width of each dot is about one quarter of the width of the whole die's face. Dots near the edge are about one-sixteenth of the die's width from the edge. All the other rolls except 6 are contained within the layout for 5, anyway; for example, the single dot for 1 is in the same place as the central dot for 5.

The second parameter of OnDraw(), rcBounds, is a CRect that describes the rectangle occupied by the control. It has member variables and functions that return the upper-left coordinates, width, and height of the control. The default code that AppWizard generated called CDC::Ellipse()to draw an ellipse within that rectangle. Your code will call Ellipse() too, passing a small rectangle within the larger rectangle of the control. Your code will be easier to read—and will execute slightly faster—if you work in units that are one-sixteenth of the total width or height. Each dot will be four units wide or high. Add the following code before the switch statement:

```
int Xunit = rcBounds.Width()/16;
int Yunit = rcBounds.Height()/16;

int Top = rcBounds.top;
int Left = rcBounds.left;
```

Before drawing a shape by calling Ellipse(), you need to select a tool to draw with. Because your circles should be filled in, they should be drawn with a brush. This code creates a brush, and tells the device context pdc to use it, while saving a pointer to the old brush so that it can be restored later:

```
CBrush Black;
```

```
Black.CreateSolidBrush(RGB(0x00,0x00,0x00)); //solid black brush
CBrush* savebrush = pdc->SelectObject(&Black);
```

After the switch statement, add this line to restore the old brush:

```
pdc->SelectObject(savebrush);
```

Now you're ready to add lines to those case blocks to draw some dots. For example, rolls of 2, 3, 4, 5, or 6 all need a dot in the upper-left corner. This dot will be in a rectangular box that starts one unit to the right and down from the upper-left corner and extends to five units right and down. The call to Ellipse looks like this:

```
pdc->Ellipse(Left+Xunit, Top+Yunit,
                  Left+5*Xunit, Top + 5*Yunit);
```

The coordinates for the other dots are determined similarly. The switch statement ends up as shown in Listing 26.11.

Listing 26.11   DierollCtl.cpp—CDierollCtrl::OnDraw()

```
switch(m_number)
    {
    case 1:
        pdc->Ellipse(Left+6*Xunit, Top+6*Yunit,
                        Left+10*Xunit, Top + 10*Yunit); //center
        break;
    case 2:
        pdc->Ellipse(Left+Xunit, Top+Yunit,
                        Left+5*Xunit, Top + 5*Yunit);    //upper left
        pdc->Ellipse(Left+11*Xunit, Top+11*Yunit,
                        Left+15*Xunit, Top + 15*Yunit); //lower right
        break;
    case 3:
        pdc->Ellipse(Left+Xunit, Top+Yunit,
                        Left+5*Xunit, Top + 5*Yunit);    //upper left
        pdc->Ellipse(Left+6*Xunit, Top+6*Yunit,
                        Left+10*Xunit, Top + 10*Yunit); //center
        pdc->Ellipse(Left+11*Xunit, Top+11*Yunit,
                        Left+15*Xunit, Top + 15*Yunit); //lower right
        break;
    case 4:
        pdc->Ellipse(Left+Xunit, Top+Yunit,
                        Left+5*Xunit, Top + 5*Yunit);    //upper left
        pdc->Ellipse(Left+11*Xunit, Top+Yunit,
                        Left+15*Xunit, Top + 5*Yunit);   //upper right
        pdc->Ellipse(Left+Xunit, Top+11*Yunit,
                        Left+5*Xunit, Top + 15*Yunit);   //lower left
        pdc->Ellipse(Left+11*Xunit, Top+11*Yunit,
                        Left+15*Xunit, Top + 15*Yunit); //lower right
        break;
    case 5:
        pdc->Ellipse(Left+Xunit, Top+Yunit,
                        Left+5*Xunit, Top + 5*Yunit);    //upper left
        pdc->Ellipse(Left+11*Xunit, Top+Yunit,
```

Part
IV

Ch
26

continues

Listing 26.11 Continued

```
                        Left+15*Xunit, Top + 5*Yunit);   //upper right
        pdc->Ellipse(Left+6*Xunit, Top+6*Yunit,
                        Left+10*Xunit, Top + 10*Yunit); //center
        pdc->Ellipse(Left+Xunit, Top+11*Yunit,
                        Left+5*Xunit, Top + 15*Yunit);   //lower left
        pdc->Ellipse(Left+11*Xunit, Top+11*Yunit,
                        Left+15*Xunit, Top + 15*Yunit); //lower right
        break;
    case 6:
            pdc->Ellipse(Left+Xunit, Top+Yunit,
             Left+5*Xunit, Top + 5*Yunit);    //upper left
            pdc->Ellipse(Left+11*Xunit, Top+Yunit,
             Left+15*Xunit, Top + 5*Yunit); //upper right
            pdc->Ellipse(Left+Xunit, Top+6*Yunit,
             Left+5*Xunit, Top + 10*Yunit); //center left
            pdc->Ellipse(Left+11*Xunit, Top+6*Yunit,
                Left+15*Xunit, Top + 10*Yunit); //center right
            pdc->Ellipse(Left+Xunit, Top+11*Yunit,
             Left+5*Xunit, Top + 15*Yunit);  //lower left
            pdc->Ellipse(Left+11*Xunit, Top+11*Yunit,
             Left+15*Xunit, Top + 15*Yunit); //lower right
            break;
    }
```

Build the OCX again and try it out in the test container. You should see something like Figure 26.10, which actually looks like a die!

FIG. 26.10

Your rolling-die control now looks like a die.

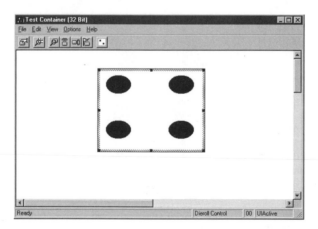

If you're sharp-eyed or if you stretch the die very large, you might notice that the pattern of dots is just slightly off center. That's because the height and width of the control are not always an exact multiple of 16. For example, if Width() returned 31, Xunit would be 1, and all the dots would be arranged between positions 0 and 16—leaving a wide blank band at the far right of the control. Luckily, the width is typically far more than 31 pixels, and so the asymmetry is less noticeable. If it bothers you, declare XUnit and YUnit as `double` variables rather than `int` and then cast to `int` only after multiplying (by 6, 11, or 15) within the switch. Your code will be a little less readable with 76 casts, but your die will look more balanced.

Property Sheets

ActiveX controls have property sheets that enable the user to set properties without any change to the container application. You set these up as dialog boxes, taking advantage of prewritten pages for font, color, and other common properties. For this control, the obvious properties to add are the following:

■ A flag to indicate whether the value should be displayed as a digit or a dot pattern

■ Foreground color

■ Background color

N O T E It's easy to get confused about what, exactly, a property page is. Is each one of the tabs on a dialog box a separate page? Or is the whole collection of tabs a page? Each tab is called a *page* and the collection of tabs is called a *sheet*. You set up each page as a dialog box and use ClassWizard to connect the values on that dialog box to member variables. ■

Digits versus Dots

It's a simple enough matter to allow the user to choose whether to display the current value as a digit or a dot pattern. Simply add a property that indicates this preference and then use the property in `OnDraw()`. The user can set the property using the property page.

First, add the property using ClassWizard. Here's how: Bring up ClassWizard and then select the OLE Automation tab. Make sure that the CDierollCtl class is selected and then click Add Property. On the Add Property dialog box, provide the external name Dots and the internal name m_dots. The type should be BOOL, because Dots can be either TRUE or FALSE. Implement this new property as a member variable (direct-access) property. Click OK to complete the Add Property dialog box and click OK to close ClassWizard. The member variable is added to the class, the dispatch map is updated, and a stub is added for the notification function, OnDotsChanged().

To initialize Dots and arrange for it to be saved with a document, add the following line to DoPropExchange() after the call to PX_Short():

```
PX_Bool( pPX, "Dots", m_dots, TRUE);
```

Initializing the Dots property to TRUE ensures that the default behavior of the control is to display the dot pattern.

In `OnDraw()`, uncomment those lines that displayed the digit. Wrap an `if` around them so the digit is displayed if m_dots is FALSE, and dots are displayed if it is TRUE. The code looks like Listing 26.12.

Part
IV

Ch

26

Listing 26.12   DierollCtl.cpp—CDierollCtrl::OnDraw()

```
void CDierollCtrl::OnDraw(
            CDC* pdc, const CRect& rcBounds, const CRect& rcInvalid)
{
    pdc->FillRect(rcBounds,
        CBrush::FromHandle((HBRUSH)GetStockObject(WHITE_BRUSH)));

    if (!m_dots)
    {
        CString val; //character representation of the short value
        val.Format("%i",m_number);
        pdc->ExtTextOut( 0, 0, ETO_OPAQUE, rcBounds, val, NULL );
    }
    else
    {
        //dots are 4 units wide and high, one unit from the edge
        int Xunit = rcBounds.Width()/16;
        int Yunit = rcBounds.Height()/16;

        int Top = rcBounds.top;
        int Left = rcBounds.left;

        CBrush Black;
        Black.CreateSolidBrush(RGB(0x00,0x00,0x00)); //solid black brush

        CBrush* savebrush = pdc->SelectObject(&Black);

        switch(m_number)
        {
        case 1:
                ...
        }
        pdc->SelectObject(savebrush);
    }
}
```

To give the user a way to set Dots, you build a property page by following these steps:

1. Click the ResourceView tab in the Project Workspace window and then click the + next to Dialog.

2. The OCX has two dialog boxes: one for the About box and one for the property page. Double-click IDD_PROPPAGE_DIEROLL to open it. The boilerplate property page generated by AppWizard is shown in Figure 26.11.

3. Remove the static control with the TODO reminder by highlighting it and pressing Delete.

4. Drag a check box from the Control Palette onto the dialog box; choose Edit, Properties; and then pin the Property dialog box in place.

5. Change the caption to Display Dot Pattern and change the resource ID to IDC_DOTS, as shown in Figure 26.12.

FIG. 26.11
AppWizard generates an empty property page.

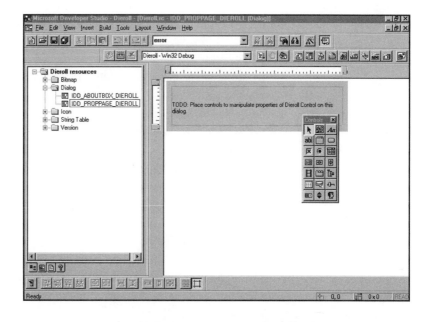

FIG. 26.12
You build the property page for the die-roll control like any other dialog box.

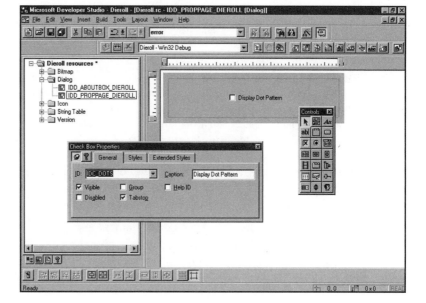

When the user brings up the property page and clicks to set or unset the check box, that does not directly affect the value of m_dots or the Dots property. To connect the dialog box to member variables, use ClassWizard and follow these steps:

1. Bring up Class Wizard while the dialog box is still open and on top and then select the Member Variables tab.

2. Make sure that CDierollPropPage is the selected class and that the IDC_DOTS resource ID is highlighted, and then click the Add Variable button.

3. Fill in m_dots as the name and BOOL as the type, and fill in the Optional OLE Property Name combo box with Dots, as shown in Figure 26.13.

4. Click OK, and ClassWizard generates code to connect the property page with the member variables in CDierollPropPage::DoDataExchange().

FIG. 26.13

You connect the property page to the properties of the control with ClassWizard.

The path that data follows can be a little twisty. When the user brings up the property sheet, the value of TRUE or FALSE is in a temporary variable. Clicking the check box toggles the value of that temporary variable. When the user clicks OK, that value goes into CDierollPropPage::m_dots and also to the OLE Automation property Dots. That property has already been connected to CDierollCtrl:: m_dots, so the dispatch map in CDierollCtrl will make sure that the other m_dots gets changed. Since the OnDraw() function uses CDierollCtrl:: m_dots, the appearance of the control changes in response to the change made by the user on the property page. Having the same name for the two member variables makes things more confusing to first-time control builders, but less confusing in the long run.

This works now. Build the control and insert it into the test container. To change the properties, choose Edit, Dieroll Control Object Properties; your own property page appears, as shown in Figure 26.14. Prove to yourself that the control displays dots or a digit, depending on the setting on this page, by changing the setting, clicking OK, and then watching the control redraw.

When the control is displaying the value as a number, you might want to display that number in a font that's more in proportion with the current width and height of the control and centered within the control. That's a relatively simple modification to OnDraw(), which we leave for you to investigate.

FIG. 26.14

Your own property page is displayed by the control test container.

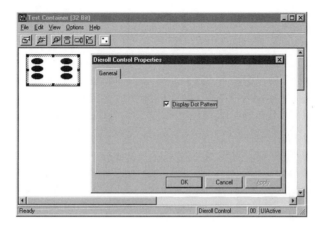

User-Selected Colors

The die you've created up to this point will always have black dots on a white background, but giving the user control to change this is remarkably simple. You will need a property for the foreground color and another for the background color. These have already been implemented as stock properties: `BackColor` and `ForeColor`.

Stock Properties   Here is the complete list of stock properties available to a control that you write:

- `Appearance`, which specifies the control's general look.
- `BackColor`, which specifies the control's background color.
- `BorderStyle`, which specifies the standard border or no border.
- `Caption`, which specifies the control's caption or text.
- `Enabled`, which specifies whether the control can be used.
- `Font`, which specifies the control's default font.
- `ForeColor`, which specifies the control's foreground color.
- `Text`, which also specifies the control's caption or text.
- `hWnd`, which specifies the control's window handle.

Ambient Properties   Controls can also access *ambient properties,* which are properties of the environment that surrounds the control—that is, properties of the *container* into which you place the control. You cannot change ambient properties, but the control can use them to adjust its own properties; for example, the control can set its background color to match that of the container.

The container provides all support for ambient properties. Any of your code that uses an ambient property should be prepared to use a default value if the container does not support that property. Here's how to use an ambient property called `UserMode`:

```
BOOL bUserMode;
    if( !GetAmbientProperty( DISPID_AMBIENT_USERMODE,
```

Part
IV

Ch

26

```
        VT_BOOL, &bUserMode ) )
    {
        bUserMode = TRUE;
    }
```

This code calls GetAmbientProperty() with the display ID (dispid) and variable type (vartype) required. It also provides a pointer to a variable into which to put the value. This variable's type must match the vartype. If GetAmbientProperty() returns FALSE, bUserMode is set to a default value.

olectl.h lists the following dispids:

DISPID_AMBIENT_BACKCOLOR

DISPID_AMBIENT_DISPLAYNAME

DISPID_AMBIENT_FONT

DISPID_AMBIENT_FORECOLOR

DISPID_AMBIENT_LOCALEID

DISPID_AMBIENT_MESSAGEREFLECT

DISPID_AMBIENT_SCALEUNITS

DISPID_AMBIENT_TEXTALIGN

DISPID_AMBIENT_USERMODE

DISPID_AMBIENT_UIDEAD

DISPID_AMBIENT_SHOWGRABHANDLES

DISPID_AMBIENT_SHOWHATCHING

DISPID_AMBIENT_DISPLAYASDEFAULT

DISPID_AMBIENT_SUPPORTSMNEMONICS

DISPID_AMBIENT_AUTOCLIP

DISPID_AMBIENT_APPEARANCE

Remember that not all containers support all these properties; some might not support any, and others might support properties not included in the preceding list.

The vartypes include those shown in Table 26.1.

Table 26.1   Variable Types for Ambient Properties

Vartype	Description
VT_BOOL	BOOL
VT_BSTR	CString
VT_I2	short
VT_I4	long

Vartype	Description
VT_R4	float
VT_R8	double
VT_CY	CY
VT_COLOR	OLE_COLOR
VT_DISPATCH	LPDISPATCH
VT_FONT	LPFONTDISP

Remembering which `vartype` goes with which `dispid` and checking the return from `GetAmbientProperty()` is a bothersome process, so the framework provides member functions of `COLEControl`, to get the most popular ambient properties:

- `OLE_COLOR AmbientBackColor()`
- `CString AmbientDisplayName()`
- `LPFONTDISP AmbientFont()` (Don't forget to release the font by using `Release()`.)
- `OLE_COLOR AmbientForeColor()`
- `LCID AmbientLocaleID()`
- `CString AmbientScaleUnits()`
- `short AmbientTextAlign()` (0 means general—numbers right, text left—1 means left-justify, 2 means center, and 3 means right-justify.)
- `BOOL AmbientUserMode()` (`TRUE` means user mode; `FALSE` means design mode.)
- `BOOL AmbientUIDead()`
- `BOOL AmbientShowHatching()`
- `BOOL AmbientShowGrabHandles()`

All these functions assign reasonable defaults if the container does not support the requested property.

Implementing *BackColor* and *ForeColor*   To add `BackColor` and `ForeColor` to the control, follow these steps:

1. Bring up ClassWizard, and select the OLE Automation tab.
2. Make sure that `CDierollCtrl` is the selected class, and click Add Property.
3. Choose `BackColor` from the top combo box, and the rest of the dialog box is filled out for you, grayed to remind you that you cannot set any of these fields for a stock property. Figure 26.15 shows the values that are provided for you.
4. Click OK and then add `ForeColor` in the same way. After you click OK, the OLE Automation tab of ClassWizard should resemble Figure 26.16. The S next to these new properties reminds you that they are stock properties.
5. Click OK to close Class Wizard.

Part
IV

Ch
26

FIG. 26.15

Stock properties are described for you by Class Wizard.

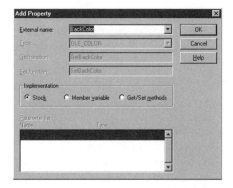

FIG. 26.16

Stock properties are highlighted with an *S* in the OLE Automation list of properties and methods.

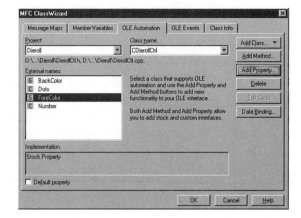

Setting up the property pages for these colors is almost as simple, because there is a prewritten page that you can use. Look through DierollCtl.cpp for a block of code like Listing 26.13.

Listing 26.13   DierollCtl.cpp—Property Pages

```
//////////////////////////////////////////////////////////
// Property pages

// TODO: Add more property pages as needed.
// Remember to increase the count!
BEGIN_PROPPAGEIDS(CDierollCtrl, 1)
    PROPPAGEID(CDierollPropPage::guid)
END_PROPPAGEIDS(CDierollCtrl)
```

Remove the TODO reminder, change the count to 2, and add another PROPPAGEID, so that the block looks like Listing 26.14.

Listing 26.14 DierollCtl.cpp—Property Pages

```
/////////////////////////////////////////////////////////////////////////
// Property pages

BEGIN_PROPPAGEIDS(CDierollCtrl, 2)
    PROPPAGEID(CDierollPropPage::guid)
    PROPPAGEID(CLSID_CColorPropPage)
END_PROPPAGEIDS(CDierollCtrl)
```

CLSID_CColorPropPage is a class ID for a property page that is used to set colors. Now when the user brings up the property sheet, there will be two property pages: One to set colors and the general page that you already created. Both ForeColor and BackColor will be available on this page, so all that remains to be done is to use the values that the user sets. You'll get a chance to see that very soon, but first, your code needs to use these colors.

Changes to *OnDraw()* In OnDraw(), your code can access the background color with GetBackColor(). This function was added by ClassWizard when you added the stock property, though you can't see it. The dispatch map for CDierollCtrl now looks like this:

Listing 26.15 DierollCtl.cpp—Dispatch map

```
BEGIN_DISPATCH_MAP(CDierollCtrl, COleControl)
    //{{AFX_DISPATCH_MAP(CDierollCtrl)
    DISP_PROPERTY_NOTIFY(CDierollCtrl, "Number", m_number, OnNumberChanged,
➥VT_I2)
    DISP_PROPERTY_NOTIFY(CDierollCtrl, "Dots", m_dots, OnDotsChanged, VT_BOOL)
    DISP_STOCKPROP_BACKCOLOR()
    DISP_STOCKPROP_FORECOLOR()
    //}}AFX_DISPATCH_MAP
    DISP_FUNCTION_ID(CDierollCtrl, "AboutBox", DISPID_ABOUTBOX, AboutBox,
➥VT_EMPTY, VTS_NONE)
END_DISPATCH_MAP()
```

The macro DISP_STOCKPROP_BACKCOLOR() expands to these lines:

```
#define DISP_STOCKPROP_BACKCOLOR() \
    DISP_PROPERTY_STOCK(COleControl, "BackColor", \
    DISPID_BACKCOLOR,        COleControl::GetBackColor, \
    COleControl::SetBackColor, VT_COLOR)
```

This code is calling another macro, DISP_PROPERTY_STOCK, which ends up declaring the GetBackColor() function as a member of CDierollCtrl, which inherits from COleControl. So although you can't see it, this function is available to you. It returns an OLE_COLOR, which you translate to a COLORREF with TranslateColor(). You can pass this COLORREF to CreateSolidBrush() and use that brush to paint the background. Access the foreground color with GetForeColor() and give it the same treatment. (Use SetTextColor() in the digit part of the code.) Here's how OnDraw ends up (with most of the switch statement cropped out):

Listing 26.16   DierollCtl.cpp—CDierollCtrl::OnDraw()

```
void CDierollCtrl::OnDraw(CDC* pdc, const CRect& rcBounds,
                          const CRect& rcInvalid)
{
    COLORREF back = TranslateColor(GetBackColor());
    CBrush backbrush;
    backbrush.CreateSolidBrush(back);
    pdc->FillRect(rcBounds, &backbrush);

    if (!m_dots)
    {
        CString val; //character representation of the short value
        val.Format("%i",m_number);
        pdc->SetTextColor(TranslateColor(GetForeColor()));
        pdc->ExtTextOut( 0, 0, ETO_OPAQUE, rcBounds, val, NULL );
    }
    else
    {
        //dots are 4 units wide and high, one unit from the edge
        int Xunit = rcBounds.Width()/16;
        int Yunit = rcBounds.Height()/16;

        int Top = rcBounds.top;
        int Left = rcBounds.left;

        COLORREF fore = TranslateColor(GetForeColor());
        CBrush forebrush;
        forebrush.CreateSolidBrush(fore);

        CBrush* savebrush = pdc->SelectObject(&forebrush);

        switch(m_number)
            . . .
    }
}
```

Build the control once again, insert it into the test container, and again bring up the property sheet by choosing Edit, Dieroll Control Object Properties. As Figure 26.17 shows, the new property page is just fine for setting colors. Change the foreground and background colors a few times and experiment with both dots and digit display to exercise all your new code.

FIG. 26.17
Stock property pages make short work of letting the user set colors.

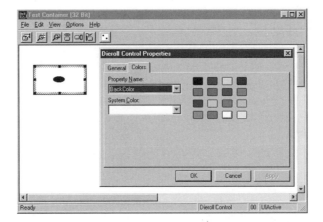

Future Improvements

The die-rolling control may seem complete, but it could be made even better.

Enable and Disable Rolling

In many dice games, you can roll the die only when it is your turn. At the moment, this control rolls whenever it is clicked, no matter what. Buy adding a custom property called RollAllowed, you can allow the container to control the rolling. When RollAllowed is FALSE, CDieCtrl::OnLButtonDown should just return without rolling and redrawing. Perhaps OnDraw should draw a slightly different die (gray dots?) when RollAllowed is FALSE. You decide; it's your control. The container would set this property like any OLE Automation property, according to the rules of the game in which the control is embedded.

Part
IV

Ch
26

Dice with Unusual Numbers of Sides

And why restrict yourself to six-sided dice? There are dice that have 4, 8, 12, 20, and even 30 sides; wouldn't they make an interesting addition to a dice game? You'll need to get one of these odd dice so that you can see what it looks like and change the drawing code in CDierollCtrl::OnDraw(). You'll then need to change the hard-coded 6 in Roll() to a custom property: An integer with the external name Sides and a member variable m_sides. Don't forget to change the property page to allow the user to set Sides, and add a line to CDieCtrl::DoPropExchange() to make Sides persistent and initialize it to 6.

T I P There is such a thing as a two-sided die; it's commonly called a *coin*.

Arrays of Dice

If you were writing a backgammon game, you would need two dice. One approach would be to embed two individual die controls. But how would you synchronize them so that they both rolled at once with a single click? Why not expand the control to be an *array* of dice? The number of dice would be another custom property, and the control would roll the dice all at once. The RollAllowed flag would apply to all of the dice, as would Sides, so that you could have two six-sided dice or three 12-sided dice, but not two four-sided dice and a 20-sider. Number would become an array.

From Here...

The die-roll control presented in this chapter is not significantly different from the OLE controls of earlier versions of Visual C++. Even the documentation can't seem to decide whether to call them OLE controls or ActiveX controls. Still, you will want to incorporate ActiveX controls into your programming repertoire so that you can build a user interface that is just what you want. To learn more about some related topics, check these chapters:

- Chapter 9, "Property Pages and Sheets and Wizards," explains how to add property pages to applications that are not ActiveX controls. You might want to compare that process to the one presented in this chapter.

- Chapter 22, "ActiveX Concepts," is a roadmap to Part IV of this book and defines many of the concepts used in this and related chapters.

- Chapter 23, "Building an ActiveX Container Application," built the second version of ShowString, which acts as an ActiveX container.

- Chapter 24, "Building an ActiveX Server Application," built the third version of ShowString, which acts as an ActiveX server.

- Chapter 25, "ActiveX Automation," built a fourth version of ShowString; an ActiveX Automation server that can be controlled from Visual Basic.

- Chapter 28, "Building an Internet ActiveX Control" discusses small efficient controls designed to run quickly and smoothly in an Internet Web page and makes some eye-opening changes to your die-roll control.

Advanced Topics

27 Internet Programming with the WinInet Classes 627

28 Building an Internet ActiveX Control 649

29 Power-User Features in Developer Studio 671

30 Power-User C++ Features 685

31 Multitasking with Windows Threads 715

32 Additional Advanced Topics 739

Internet Programming with the WinInet Classes

Chapter 13, "Sockets, MAPI, and the Internet," introduced the WinInet classes that you can use to build Internet client applications at a fairly high level. This chapter develops an Internet application that demonstrates a number of these classes. The application also serves a useful function: You can use it to learn more about the Internet presence of a company or organization. You don't need to learn about sockets or handle the details of Internet protocols to do this. ■

An Internet Query Program

The sample application investigates Internet domain names to see what services are offered.

Query Program Interface

A dialog-based application is a good choice for this application. See how to build one with AppWizard, and how to design and build the dialog box.

World Wide Web Queries

It's simple to write a function that reaches out to a Web site in the domain you are investigating.

FTP Queries

FTP queries are slightly more complex than Web queries, and this section shows how to write them.

Gopher Queries

Gopher is a text-based protocol much like the World Wide Web but older, and with links that are established by system administrators.

Finger Queries

Finger is an old protocol not directly supported by the WinInet classes.

Whois Queries

The Whois database includes contact names and phone numbers for every domain on the Internet.

Designing the Internet Query Application

Imagine that you have someone's e-mail address (**kate@gregcons.com**, for example) and you'd like to know more about the domain (**gregcons.com** in this example). Or perhaps you have a great idea for a domain name and want to know if it's taken already. This application, Query, will try connecting to **gregcons.com** (or **greatidea.org**, or any other domain name that you specify) in a variety of different ways and will report the result of those attempts to you.

This application will have a simple user interface. The only piece of information that the user will supply is the domain name that is being queried, and there is no need to keep this information in a document. You might want a menu item called Query that brings up a dialog box in which to specify the name of the site, but a better approach is to use a dialog-based application and incorporate a Query button into the dialog box.

Dialog-based applications, as discussed in the "A Dialog-Based Application" section of Chapter 16, "Choosing an Application Type and Building an Empty Shell," have no document and no menu. The application displays a dialog box at all times; closing the dialog box closes the application. You build the dialog box for this application like any other, with Developer Studio.

To build the shell of this application, choose File, New from within Developer Studio and then choose Project Workspace from the list to bring up AppWizard. Name the application Query, and in Step 1 choose a dialog-based application, as shown in Figure 27.1. Click Next to move to Step 2 of AppWizard.

FIG. 27.1
Choose a dialog-based application for Query.

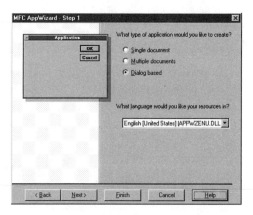

In Step 2 of AppWizard, request an About box, no context-sensitive help, 3-D controls, no OLE support, and no sockets support. (This application won't be calling socket functions directly.) Give the application a sensible title for the dialog box, and the AppWizard choices should be as summarized in Figure 27.2. Click Next to move to Step 3 of AppWizard.

The rest of the AppWizard process should be familiar by now: You want comments, want to link to the MFC libraries as a shared DLL, and don't need to change any of the class names suggested by AppWizard. When the AppWizard process is complete, you are ready to build the heart of the Query application.

FIG. 27.2
This application does not need help, OLE, or sockets.

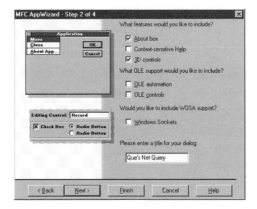

Building the Query Dialog Box

AppWizard produces an empty dialog box for you to start with, as shown in Figure 27.3. The following steps will transform this dialog box into the interface for the Query application.

FIG. 27.3
AppWizard generates an empty dialog box for you.

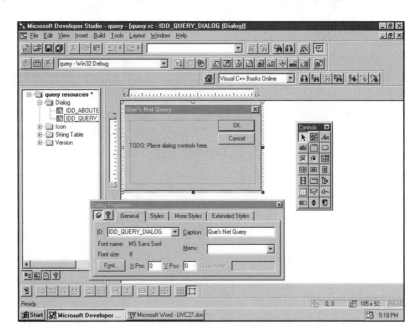

 TIP If working with dialog boxes is still new to you, be sure to read Chapter 17, "Building Menus and Dialogs," especially the "Building the ShowString Dialogs" and "Making the Dialog Work" sections.

Part
V

Ch
27

1. Change the caption on the OK button to `Query`.

2. Change the caption on the Cancel button to `Close`.

3. Delete the `TODO` static text.

4. Grab a sizing handle on the right edge of the dialog box and stretch it so that the dialog box is 300 pixels wide, or more.

5. Move the buttons to the right.

6. At the top of the dialog box, add an edit box with the resource ID `IDC_HOST`. Stretch the edit box as wide as possible.

7. Add a static label next to the dialog box. Set the text to `Site name`.

8. Grab a sizing handle along the bottom of the dialog box and stretch it longer, so that the dialog box is 150 pixels high, or more.

9. Add another edit box and resize it to fill as much as possible of the bottom part of the dialog box.

10. Give this edit box the resource ID `IDC_OUT`.

11. Click the Styles tab on the Properties box and select the Multi-line, Horizontal scroll, Vertical scroll, Border, and Read-only check boxes.

The finished dialog box, and the Style properties of the large edit box, should resemble Figure 27.4.

FIG. 27.4

Build the Query user interface as a single dialog box.

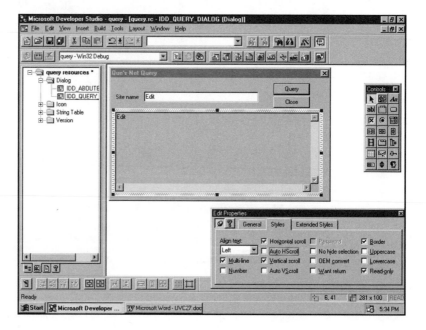

When the user clicks the Query button, this application should somehow query the site. The last step in the building of the interface is to connect the Query button to code with ClassWizard. Follow these steps:

1. Choose <u>V</u>iew, Class <u>W</u>izard to bring up ClassWizard.

2. There are three possible classes that could catch the command generated by the button click, but CQueryDlg is the logical choice, because the host name will be known by that class. Make sure that CQueryDlg is the class selected in the Class name drop-down list box.

3. Highlight ID_OK (you did not change the resource ID of the OK button when you changed the caption) in the left list box and BN_CLICKED in the right list box.

4. Click Add Function to add a function that will be called when the Query button is clicked.

5. ClassWizard suggests the name OnOK; change it to OnQuery, as shown in Figure 27.5, and then click OK.

FIG. 27.5

Add a function to handle a click on the Query button, whose ID is still *IDOK*.

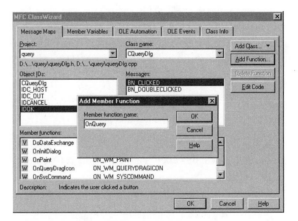

6. Click the Member Variables tab to connect the edit controls on the dialog box to member variables of the dialog class.

7. Highlight IDC_HOST and click <u>A</u>dd Variable. As shown in Figure 27.6, you will connect this control to a CString member variable of the dialog class called m_host.

8. Connect IDC_OUT to m_out, also a CString.

Now all that remains is to write CQueryDlg::OnQuery(), which will use the value in m_host to produce lines of output for m_out.

FIG. 27.6

Connect *IDC_HOST* to *CQueryDlg::m_host*.

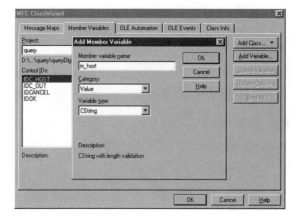

Querying HTTP Sites

The first kind of connection to try is HTTP, because so many sites have Web pages. The simplest way to make a connection using HTTP is to use the WinInet class CInternetSession and call its OpenURL() function. This will return a file, and you can display the first few lines of the file in m_out. First, add this line at the beginning of QueryDlg.cpp:

```
#include "afxinet.h"
```

Because this application will try a number of URLs, add a function to CQueryDlg called TryURL(). It takes a CString parameter called URL and returns void. Right-click on CQueryDlg in the ClassView and choose Add Function to add TryURL() as a protected member function.

The new function, TryURL(), will be called from CQueryDlg::OnQuery() as shown in Listing 27.1.

Listing 27.1 QueryDlg.cpp—CQueryDlg::OnQuery()

```cpp
void CQueryDlg::OnQuery()
{
        const CString http = "http://";

        UpdateData(TRUE);
        m_out = "";
        UpdateData(FALSE);

        TryURL(http + m_host);

        TryURL(http + "www." + m_host);
}
```

The call to UpdateData(TRUE) fills m_host with the value that the user typed. The call to UpdateData(FALSE) fills the IDC_OUT read-only edit box with the newly cleared m_out.

Then come two calls to TryURL(). If, for example, the user typed **microsoft.com**, the first call would try **http://microsoft.com** and the second would try **http://www.microsoft.com**.

TryURL() is shown in Listing 27.2.

Listing 27.2   QueryDlg.cpp—CQueryDlg::TryURL()

```cpp
void CQueryDlg::TryURL(CString URL)
{
        CInternetSession session;

        m_out += "Trying " + URL + "\r\n";
        UpdateData(FALSE);

        CInternetFile* file = NULL;
        try
        {
                //We know for sure this is an Internet file,
                //so the cast is safe
                file = (CInternetFile*) session.OpenURL(URL);
        }
        catch (CInternetException* pEx)
        {
                //if anything went wrong, just set file to NULL
                file = NULL;
                pEx->Delete();
        }
        if (file)
        {
                m_out += "Connection established. \r\n";
                CString line;

                file->SetReadBufferSize(4096);
                for (int i=0; i < 20 && file->ReadString(line); i++)
                {
                        m_out += line + "\r\n";
                }
                file->Close();
                delete file;
        }
        else
        {
                m_out += "No server found there. \r\n";
        }

        m_out += "-------------------------\r\n";
        UpdateData(FALSE);
}
```

The remainder of this section presents this code again, a few lines at a time. First, establish an Internet session by constructing an instance of CInternetSession. There are a number of parameters to this constructor, but they all have default values that will be fine for this application. The parameters are the following:

- **LPCTSTR pstrAgent** The name of your application. If NULL, it's filled in for you using the name that you gave to AppWizard.

- **DWORD dwContext** The context identifier for the operation. For synchronous sessions, this is not an important parameter.

- **DWORD dwAccessType** The access type, one of INTERNET_OPEN_TYPE_PRECONFIG (default), INTERNET_OPEN_TYPE_DIRECT, or INTERNET_OPEN_TYPE_PROXY.

- **LPCTSTR pstrProxyName** The name of your proxy, if access is INTERNET_OPEN_TYPE_PROXY.

- **LPCTSTR pstrProxyBypass** A list of addresses to be connected directly rather than through the proxy server, if access is INTERNET_OPEN_TYPE_PROXY.

- **DWORD dwFlags** Options that can be OR'ed together. The available options are INTERNET_FLAG_DONT_CACHE, INTERNET_FLAG_ASYNC, and INTERNET_FLAG_OFFLINE.

dwAccessType defaults to using the value in the Registry. Obviously, an application that insists on direct Internet access or proxy Internet access is less useful than one that allows users to configure that information. But making users set their Internet access type outside this program may be confusing. To set your default Internet access, double-click the My Computer icon on your desktop, then the Control Panel, and then the Internet tool in the Control Panel. Choose the Connection tab, shown in Figure 27.7, and complete the dialog box as appropriate for your setup:

FIG. 27.7

Set your Internet connection settings once, and all applications can retrieve them from the Registry.

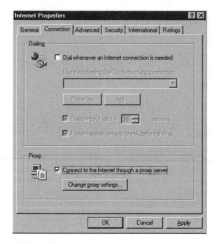

- If you dial up to the Internet, select the Dial check box and fill in the parameters in the top half of the page.

- If you connect to the Internet through a proxy server, select the Proxy check box and click the Change Proxy Settings button to identify your proxy addresses and ports.

- If you are connected directly to the Internet, leave both check boxes unselected.

If you want to set up an *asynchronous* (non-blocking) session, for the reasons discussed in the "Using Windows Sockets" section of Chapter 13, "Sockets, MAPI, and the Internet," your options in dwFlags must include INTERNET_FLAG_ASYNC. In addition, you must call the member function EnableStatusCallback() to set up the callback function. When a request is made through the session—such as the call to OpenURL() that occurs later in TryURL()—and the response will not be immediate, a non-blocking session returns a pseudo error code, ERROR_IO_PENDING. When the response is ready, these sessions automatically invoke the callback function.

For this simple application, there is no need to allow the user to do other work or interact with the user interface while waiting for the session to respond, so the session is constructed as a blocking session and all the other default parameters are also used:

```
CInternetSession session;
```

Having constructed the session, TryURL() goes on to add a line to m_out that echoes the URL passed in as a parameter. The "\r\n" characters are return and newline, and they separate the lines added to m_out. UpdateData(FALSE) gets that onto the screen:

```
m_out += "Trying " + URL + "\r\n";
UpdateData(FALSE);
```

Next is a call to the session's OpenURL() member function. This function returns a pointer to one of several different file types, since the URL might have been to one of four protocols:

- file:// opens a file. The function constructs a CStdioFile and returns a pointer to it.
- ftp:// goes to an FTP site and returns a pointer to a CInternetFile object.
- gopher:// goes to a Gopher site and returns a pointer to a CGopherFile object.
- http:// goes to a World Wide Web site and returns a pointer to a CHttpFile object.

Because CGopherFile and CHttpFile both inherit from CInternetFile, and because you can be sure that TryURL() will not be passed a file:// URL, it is safe to cast the returned pointer to a CInternetFile.

TIP There is some confusion in Microsoft's online documentation whenever example URLs are shown. A backslash (\) character will never appear in a URL. In any Microsoft example that includes backslashes, use forward slashes (/) instead.

Part
V

Ch
27

If the URL would not open, file will be NULL or OpenURL()_ will throw an exception. (For background on exceptions, see Chapter 30, "Power-User C++ Features.") While in a normal application it would be a serious error if a URL didn't open, in this application you are making up URLs to see if they work or not, and it's to be expected that some of them won't. As a result, you should catch these exceptions yourself and do something fairly mild, just enough to prevent runtime errors. In this case, it's enough to make sure that file is NULL when an exception is thrown. To delete the exception and prevent memory leaks, call CException::Delete(), which is not mentioned in the online documentation but does exist and safely deletes the exception. The block of code containing the call to OpenURL() is in Listing 27.3.

Listing 27.3 QueryDlg.cpp—CQueryDlg::TryURL()

```
CInternetFile* file = NULL;
try
{
        //We know for sure this is an Internet file,
        //so the cast is safe
        file = (CInternetFile*) session.OpenURL(URL);
}
catch (CInternetException* pEx)
{
        //if anything went wrong, just set file to NULL
        file = NULL;
        pEx->Delete();
}
```

If file is not NULL, this routine echoes another line to m_out, and then in a for loop, the routine calls CInternetFile::ReadString() to fill the CString line with the characters in file up to the first \r\n, which are stripped off. This code simply tacks line (and another \r\n) onto m_out. If you would like to see more or less than the first 20 lines of the page, adjust the number in this for loop. When the first few lines have been read, TryURL() closes and deletes the file. That block of code is shown in Listing 27.4.

Listing 27.4 QueryDlg.cpp—CQueryDlg::TryURL()

```
if (file)
{
        m_out += "Connection established. \r\n";
        CString line;

        file->SetReadBufferSize(4096); //for those without the 4.2a patch
        for (int i=0; i < 20 && file->ReadString(line); i++)
        {
                m_out += line + "\r\n";
        }
        file->Close();
        delete file;
}
```

N O T E The call to SetReadBufferSize() is a workaround for a flaw in ReadString(). It's explained in a comment in the source for TryURL() on the CD. If you have installed the 4.2a patch (available free from http://www.microsoft.com) so that your version of Visual C++ is now 4.2a or higher, you do not need this workaround. ■

If the file could not be opened, a message to that effect is echoed onto m_out:

```
else
{
        m_out += "No server found there. \r\n";
}
```

Then whether the file existed or not, a line of dashes is tacked onto m_out to indicate the end of this attempt, and one last call to UpdateData(FALSE) gets the new m_out onto the screen:

```
        m_out += "------------------------\r\n";
        UpdateData(FALSE);
}
```

You can now build and run this application. If you enter **microsoft.com** in the text box and click Query, you will discover that there are Web pages at both **http://microsoft.com** and **http://www.microsoft.com**. Figure 27.8 shows the result of that query.

FIG. 27.8
Query can find
Microsoft's Web sites.

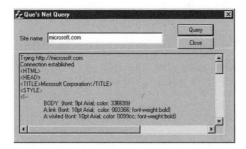

If Query doesn't find Web pages at either the domain name you provided or **www.** plus the domain name, it doesn't mean that the domain doesn't exist or even that the organization that owns the domain name doesn't have a Web page. It does make it less likely, however, that the organization both exists and has a Web page. If you see a stream of HTML, you may be able to read it yourself, but, even if you cannot, you can now connect to the site with a Web browser such as Microsoft's Internet Explorer.

Querying FTP Sites

As part of an investigation of a site name, you should check to see if there is an FTP site, too. Most FTP sites have names like **ftp.company.com**, though some older sites do not have names of that form. Checking for these sites is not as simple as just calling TryURL() again, because TryURL() assumes that the URL leads to a file, and URLs like **ftp.greatidea.org** lead to a list of files that cannot simply be opened and read. Rather than making TryURL() even more complicated, add a function to the class called TryFTPSite(CString host). (Right-click on CQueryDlg in the ClassView and choose Add Function to add the function. It can return void.)

TryFTPSite() has to establish a connection within the session, and if the connection is established, it has to get some information that can be added to m_out to show the user that the connection has been made. Getting a list of files is reasonably complex, so since this is just an illustrative application, the simpler task of getting the name of the default FTP directory is the way to go. The code is in Listing 27.5.

Part
V
Ch
27

Listing 27.5 QueryDlg.cpp—CQueryDlg::TryFTPSite()

```
void CQueryDlg::TryFTPSite(CString host)
{
        CInternetSession session;

        m_out += "Trying FTP site " + host + "\r\n";
        UpdateData(FALSE);

        CFtpConnection* connection = NULL;
        try
        {
                connection = session.GetFtpConnection(host);
        }
        catch (CInternetException* pEx)
        {
                //if anything went wrong, just set connection to NULL
                connection = NULL;
                pEx->Delete();
        }
        if (connection)
        {
                m_out += "Connection established. \r\n";
                CString line;

                connection->GetCurrentDirectory(line);
                m_out += "default directory is " + line + "\r\n";

                connection->Close();
                delete connection;
        }
        else
        {
                m_out += "No server found there. \r\n";
        }

        m_out += "------------------------\r\n";
        UpdateData(FALSE);
}
```

This code is very much like TryURL(), except that instead of opening a file with
session.OpenURL(), it opens an FTP connection with session.GetFtpConnection().
Again, exceptions are caught and essentially ignored, with the routine just making sure
that the connection pointer won't be used. The call to GetCurrentDirectory() returns the
directory on the remote site that sessions start in. The rest of the routine is just like TryURL().

Add two lines at the end of OnQuery() to call this new function:

```
TryFTPSite(m_host);
TryFTPSite("ftp." + m_host);
```

Build the application and try it: Figure 27.9 shows Query reporting no FTP site at
microsoft.com and finding one at **ftp.microsoft.com**.

FIG. 27.9

Query finds one
Microsoft FTP site.

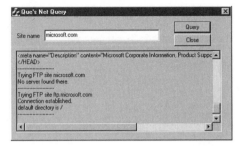

If Query hasn't found Web pages or FTP sites, it is getting less likely that this domain exists at all, or has any Internet services other than e-mail, but there are a few more investigative tricks available.

Querying Gopher Sites

As was the case with FTP, TryURL() won't work for querying a Gopher site like **gopher. company.com,** because this returns a list of file names rather than a single file. The solution is to write a function called TryGopherSite() that is almost identical to TryFTPSite(), except that it opens a CGopherConnection, and instead of a single line describing the default directory, it echoes a single line describing the Gopher locator associated with the site. Add TryGopherSite to CQueryDlg by right-clicking on the class name in ClassView and choosing Add Function, as you did for TryFTPSite(). The code for TryGopherSite() is in Listing 27.6.

Listing 27.6   QueryDlg.cpp—CQueryDlg::TryGopherSite()

```
void CQueryDlg::TryGopherSite(CString host)
{
        CInternetSession session;

        m_out += "Trying Gopher site " + host + "\r\n";
        UpdateData(FALSE);

        CGopherConnection* connection = NULL;
        try
        {
                connection = session.GetGopherConnection(host);
        }
        catch (CInternetException* pEx)
        {
                //if anything went wrong, just set connection to NULL
                connection = NULL;
                pEx->Delete();
        }
        if (connection)
        {
                m_out += "Connection established. \r\n";
                CString line;
```

Part

V

Ch

27

continues

Listing 27.6   Continued

```
            CGopherLocator locator = connection->CreateLocator(NULL, NULL,
            ➥GOPHER_TYPE_DIRECTORY);
            line = locator;
            m_out += "first locator is " + line + "\r\n";

            connection->Close();
            delete connection;
    }
    else
    {
            m_out += "No server found there. \r\n";
    }

    m_out += "------------------------\r\n";
    UpdateData(FALSE);
}
```

The call to CreateLocator() takes three parameters. The first is the file name, which may include wild cards. NULL means any file. The second parameter is a selector that can be NULL. The third is one of the following types:

```
GOPHER_TYPE_TEXT_FILE

GOPHER_TYPE_DIRECTORY

GOPHER_TYPE_CSO

GOPHER_TYPE_ERROR

GOPHER_TYPE_MAC_BINHEX

GOPHER_TYPE_DOS_ARCHIVE

GOPHER_TYPE_UNIX_UUENCODED

GOPHER_TYPE_INDEX_SERVER

GOPHER_TYPE_TELNET

GOPHER_TYPE_BINARY

GOPHER_TYPE_REDUNDANT

GOPHER_TYPE_TN3270

GOPHER_TYPE_GIF

GOPHER_TYPE_IMAGE

GOPHER_TYPE_BITMAP

GOPHER_TYPE_MOVIE

GOPHER_TYPE_SOUND

GOPHER_TYPE_HTML

GOPHER_TYPE_PDF

GOPHER_TYPE_CALENDAR
```

```
GOPHER_TYPE_INLINE

GOPHER_TYPE_UNKNOWN

GOPHER_TYPE_ASK

GOPHER_TYPE_GOPHER_PLUS
```

Normally, you don't build locators for files or directories, but instead you ask the server for them. The locator that will be returned from this call to `CreateLocator()` describes the locator associated with the site you are investigating.

Add a pair of lines at the end of `OnQuery()` that call this new `TryGopherSite()` function:

```
TryGopherSite(m_host);
TryGopherSite("gopher." + m_host);
```

Build and run the program again. You may find the delay until results start to appear a little disconcerting. You could correct this by using asynchronous sockets, or *threading,* but for a simple demonstration application like this, just wait patiently until the results appear. Figure 27.10 shows that Query has found two Gopher sites for **harvard.edu**. In both cases, the locator describes the site itself. This is enough to prove that there is a Gopher site at **harvard.edu**, which is all that Query is supposed to do.

FIG. 27.10

Query finds two Harvard Gopher sites.

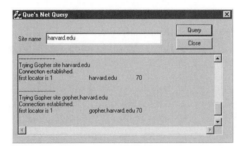

 Gopher is an older protocol that has been almost entirely supplemented by the World Wide Web. As a general rule, if a site has a Gopher presence, it's been on the Internet since before the World Wide Web existed (1989) or at least before the huge upsurge in popularity began (1992). What's more, the site was probably large enough in the early 1990s to have an administrator who would set up the Gopher menus and text.

Part
V

Ch
27

Using Gopher to Send a Finger Query

There is another protocol that can give you information about a site. It's one of the oldest protocols on the Internet, and it's called Finger. You can Finger a single user or an entire site, and, though many sites have disabled Finger, many more will provide you with useful information in response to a Finger request.

There is no MFC class or API function with the word *finger* in its name, but that doesn't mean you can't use the classes already presented. This section relies on a trick—and on knowledge of the Finger and Gopher protocols. While the WinInet classes are a boon to new Internet programmers who don't quite know how the Internet works, they also have a lot to offer to old-timers who know what's going on under the hood.

As discussed in the "Using Windows Sockets" section of Chapter 13, "Sockets, MAPI, and the Internet," all Internet transactions involve both a host and a port. Well-known services use standard port numbers. For example, when you call `CInternetSession::OpenURL()` with a URL that starts **http://**, the code behind the scenes connects to port 80 on the remote host. When you call `GetFtpConnection()`, the connection is made to port 21 on the remote host. Gopher uses port 70. If you look at Figure 27.10, you will see that the locator that describes the **gopher.harvard.edu** site includes a mention of port 70.

The Gopher documentation makes this clear: If you build a locator with a host name, port 70, Gopher type 0 (`GOPHER_TYPE_TEXT_FILE` is defined to be 0), and a string with a file name, any Gopher client simply sends the string, whether it's a file name or not, to port 70. The Gopher server listening on that port responds by sending the file.

Now, Finger is a simple protocol, too. If you send a string to port 79 on a remote host, the Finger server that is listening there will react to the string by sending a Finger reply. If the string is only `\r\n`, the usual reply is a list of all the users on the host and some other information about them, such as their real names. (Many sites consider this an invasion of privacy or a security risk, and they disable Finger. But many other sites deliberately make this same information available on their Web pages.)

Putting this all together, if you build a Gopher locator using port 79—rather than the default 70—and an empty file name, you can do a Finger query using the MFC WinInet classes. First, add another function to `CQueryDlg` called `TryFinger()`, which takes a `CString host` and returns `void`. The code for this function is very much like `TryGopherSite()`, except that the connection is made to port 79:

```
connection = session.GetGopherConnection(host,NULL,NULL,79);
```

Once the connection is made, a text file locator is created:

```
CGopherLocator locator = connection->CreateLocator(NULL, NULL,
➥GOPHER_TYPE_TEXT_FILE);
```

This time, rather than simply casting the locator into a `CString`, use it to open a file:

```
CGopherFile* file = connection->OpenFile(locator);
```

Then echo the first 20 lines of this file, just as `TryURL()` echoed the first 20 lines of the file returned by a Web server. The code to do this is in Listing 27.7.

Listing 27.7   QueryDlg.cpp—CQueryDlg::TryFinger() Excerpt

```
if (file)
{
        CString line;

        file->SetReadBufferSize(4096);
        for (int i=0; i < 20 && file->ReadString(line); i++)
        {
                m_out += line + "\r\n";
        }
        file->Close();
        delete file;
}
```

Putting it all together, TryFinger() is shown in Listing 27.8.

Listing 27.8   QueryDlg.cpp—CQueryDlg::TryFinger()

```
void CQueryDlg::TryFinger(CString host)
{
        CInternetSession session;

        m_out += "Trying to Finger " + host + "\r\n";
        UpdateData(FALSE);

        CGopherConnection* connection = NULL;

        try
        {
                connection = session.GetGopherConnection(host,NULL,NULL,79);
        }
        catch (CInternetException* pEx)
        {
                //if anything went wrong, just set connection to NULL
                connection = NULL;
                pEx->Delete();
        }
        if (connection)
        {
                m_out += "Connection established. \r\n";

                CGopherLocator locator = connection->CreateLocator(NULL, NULL,
                ➥GOPHER_TYPE_TEXT_FILE);

                CGopherFile* file = connection->OpenFile(locator);
                if (file)
                {
                        CString line;

                        file->SetReadBufferSize(4096);
                        for (int i=0; i < 20 && file->ReadString(line); i++)
                        {
```

Part
V

Ch

27

continues

Listing 27.8 Continued

```
                        m_out += line + "\r\n";
                }
                file->Close();
                delete file;
        }

        connection->Close();
        delete connection;
    }
    else
    {
        m_out += "No server found there. \r\n";
    }

    m_out += "------------------------\r\n";
    UpdateData(FALSE);

}
```

Add a line at the end of `OnQuery()` that calls this new function:

```
TryFinger(m_host);
```

Now build and run the application. Figure 27.11 shows the result of a query on the site **whitehouse.gov**, scrolled down to the Finger section.

FIG. 27.11

Query gets e-mail addresses from the White House Finger server.

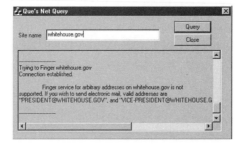

Using Gopher to Send a Whois Query

One last protocol provides information about sites. It, too, is an old protocol not supported directly by the WinInet classes. It is called Whois, and it's a service offered by only a few servers on the whole Internet. The servers that offer this service are maintained by the organizations that register domain names. For example, domain names that end in **.com** are registered through an organization called InterNIC, which runs a Whois server called **rs.internic.net** (the *rs* stands for Registration Services). Like Finger, Whois responds to a string sent on its own port; the Whois port is 43. Unlike Finger, you don't send an empty string in the locator; you send the name of the host that you want to look up. You connect to **rs.internic.net** every time. (Dedicated Whois servers offer users a chance to change this, but, in practice, no one ever does.)

So add a function called TryWhois(); as usual, it takes a CString host and returns void. The code is in Listing 27.9.

Listing 27.9 QueryDlg.cpp—CQueryDlg::TryWhois()

```
void CQueryDlg::TryWhois(CString host)
{
        CInternetSession session;

        m_out += "Trying Whois for " + host + "\r\n";
        UpdateData(FALSE);

        CGopherConnection* connection = NULL;
        try
        {
                connection = session.GetGopherConnection("rs.internic.net",
                ➥NULL,NULL,43);
        }
        catch (CInternetException* pEx)
        {
                //if anything went wrong, just set connection to NULL
                connection = NULL;
                pEx->Delete();
        }
        if (connection)
        {
                m_out += "Connection established. \r\n";
                CGopherLocator locator = connection->CreateLocator(NULL, host,
                ➥GOPHER_TYPE_TEXT_FILE);
                CGopherFile* file = connection->OpenFile(locator);
                if (file)
                {
                        CString line;
                        file->SetReadBufferSize(4096);
                        for (int i=0; i < 20 && file->ReadString(line); i++)
                        {
                                m_out += line + "\r\n";
                        }
                        file->Close();
                        delete file;
                }
                connection->Close();
                delete connection;
        }
        else
        {
                m_out += "No server found there. \r\n";
        }
        m_out += "-----------------------\r\n";
        UpdateData(FALSE);
}
```

Part
V

Ch
27

Add a line at the end of OnQuery() to call it:

TryWhois(m_host);

Build and run the application one last time. Figure 27.12 shows the Whois part of the report for **mcp.com**—this is the domain for Macmillan Computer Publishing, Que's parent company.

FIG. 27.12

Query gets real-life addresses and names from the InterNIC Whois server.

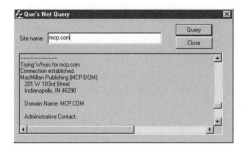

Future Work

The Query application built in this chapter does a lot, but it could do so much more. There are e-mail and news protocols that could be reached by stretching the WinInet classes a little more and using them to connect to the standard ports for these other services. You could also connect to some well-known Web search engines and submit queries by forming URLs according to the pattern used by those engines. In this way, you can automate the sort of poking around on the Internet that most of us do when we're curious about a domain name or an organization.

If you'd like to learn more about Internet protocols, port numbers, and what's happening when a client connects to a server, you can find out a lot by reading Que's *Building Internet Applications with Visual C++*. The book was written for Visual C++ 2.0, and though all the applications in the book compile and run under later versions of MFC, they would be much shorter and easier to write now. Still, the insight into the way the protocols work is valuable.

And the WinInet classes can do much more than you've seen here, too. Query doesn't use them to retrieve real files over the Internet. There are two WinInet sample applications included with Visual C++ 4.2 that do a fine job of showing how to retrieve files:

- FTPTREE builds a tree list of the files and directories on an FTP site.
- TEAR brings back a page of HTML from a Web site.

There are lots more Microsoft announcements coming over the next few months, as well. Keep an eye on its Web site, **www.microsoft.com**, for libraries and software development kits that will make Internet software development even easier and faster.

From Here...

This chapter introduced you to the WinInet classes as one way to write Internet programs. Some related chapters that may interest you include:

- Chapter 13, "Sockets, MAPI, and the Internet" introduces you to the concepts involved in Internet programming.

- Chapter 16, "Choosing an Application Type and Building an Empty Shell," compares dialog-based applications to the MDI or SDI applications that AppWizard can also generate for you.

- Chapter 28, "Building an Internet ActiveX Control," discusses small, efficient controls designed to run quickly and smoothly in an Internet Web page.

Part

V

Ch

27

Building an Internet ActiveX Control

In Chapter 26, "Building an ActiveX Control," you learned how to build your own controls and include them in forms-based applications written in Visual Basic, Visual C++, and the VBA macro language. There's one other place those controls can go: on a Web page. But the ActiveX controls generated by older versions of Visual C++ were too big and slow to put on a Web page. This chapter shows how to get these controls onto your Web pages, and how to write faster, sleeker controls that will make your pages a pleasure to use. ■

How Microsoft Explorer loads ActiveX controls

When you see a Web page with an ActiveX control in it, your jaw will drop!

How Netscape Navigator loads ActiveX controls

Netscape Navigator can display an ActiveX control. This section points you to the plug-in your users will need.

ActiveX controls versus Java applets

There's more than one way to allow a user to interact with a Web page. We compare ActiveX controls to Java applets.

AppWizard's Advanced Control options

AppWizard's OLE ControlWizard, despite the obsolete name, can add some nice optimizations to your controls.

Asynchronous properties

The last thing you want your control to do is slow down your Web page. The second last thing you want is for your control to be boring.

Using the Base Control class and the ActiveX Template Library

Brave souls can try other approaches to building controls for the Web.

Embedding an ActiveX Control into a Microsoft Explorer Web Page

It's a remarkably simple matter to put an ActiveX control onto a Web page that you know will be loaded by Microsoft Explorer 3.0. You use the <OBJECT> tag, a relatively new addition to HTML that describes a wide variety of, well, objects that you might want to insert into a Web page: a moving video clip, a sound, a Java applet, an ActiveX control, and many more kinds of information and ways of interacting with a user. Listing 28.1 shows the HTML source for a page that displays the dieroll control from Chapter 26.

Listing 28.1   fatdie.html—Using <OBJECT>

```
<HTML>
<HEAD>
<TITLE>A Web page with a rolling die</TITLE>
<BODY>
 <OBJECT
CLASSID="clsid:46646B43-EA16-11CF-870C-00201801DDD6"
CODEBASE="http://www.gregcons.com/test/dieroll.ocx"
ID=die1
WIDTH=200
HEIGHT=200
ALIGN=center
HSPACE=0
VSPACE=0
>
If you see this text, your browser does not support the OBJECT tag. </BR>
</OBJECT>

Here is some text after the die

</BODY>
</HTML>
```

The only ugly thing here is the CLSID, and the easiest way to get that, since you're a software developer, is to cut and paste it from dieroll.odl, the Object Description Library. Use FileView to open dieroll.odl quickly. Here's the section in dieroll.odl that includes the CLSID:

```
//  Class information for CDierollCtrl

[ uuid(46646B43-EA16-11CF-870C-00201801DDD6),
  helpstring("Dieroll Control"), control ]
```

This section is at the end of dieroll.odl—the earlier CLSIDs do not refer to the whole control, only to portions of it. Copy the uuid from inside the brackets into your HTML source.

 TIP Microsoft has a product called the Control Pad that gets CLSIDs from the Registry for you and makes life easier for Web page builders who are initimidated by instructions like "open the ODL file" or who don't have the ODL file, since it's not shipped with the control. Since you're building this control, and know how to open files in Developer Studio, this chapter will not describe the Control Pad tool. If you're curious, Microsoft's Control Pad Web page at **http://www.microsoft.com/workshop/author/cpad/** has more details.

The CODEBASE attribute of the <OBJECT> tag specifies where the OCX file is kept, so that if the user does not have a copy of the ActiveX control, one will be downloaded automatically. The use of the CLSID means that if this user has already installed this ActiveX control, there is no download time, the control is simply used right away.

T I P If you don't have access to a Web server where you can put controls while you're developing them, use a `file://` URL in the CODEBASE attribute that points to the location of the control on your hard drive.

The remainder of the attributes of the <OBJECT> tag should be fairly intuitive if you've built a Web page before: ID is used by other tags on the page to refer to this control, WIDTH and HEIGHT specify the size, in pixels, that the control should appear, and HSPACE and VSPACE are horizontal and vertical blank space, in pixels, around the entire control.

Everything after the <OBJECT ...> tag and before the </OBJECT> tag is ignored by browsers that understand the <OBJECT> tag. (The <OBJECT...> tag is usually many lines long and contains all the information to describe the object.) Browsers that do not understand the <OBJECT> tag ignore the <OBJECT ...> tag and the </OBJECT> tag and display the HTML between them, in this case a line of text pointing out that this browser does not support the tag. This is part of the specification for a Web browser: it should ignore tags it doesn't understand.

Figure 28.1 shows this page displayed in Microsoft Explorer 3.0. Clicking on the die rolls it, and everything works beautifully. Things certainly look simple and amazing. But two flaws appear immediately:

- Not all browsers support the OBJECT tag
- It can take a long time to download the control

Figure 28.2 shows the same page displayed in Netscape Navigator 2.0. It doesn't support the <OBJECT> tag, so it doesn't show the die. And Netscape Navigator is used by over 80% of the people who browse the web! Does that mean it's not worth writing ActiveX controls for web pages? Not at all. As you'll see in the very next section, there's a way that Navigator users can use the same controls you make available to Explorer users.

The size issue is a bigger worry. The release version of the Dieroll control, as built for Chapter 26, is 26 KB. Many designers put a 50K limit per Web page for graphics and other material to be downloaded, and this simple control uses half that limit. A more powerful control would easily exceed it. The majority of this chapter deals with ways to reduce that size or otherwise minimize the download time for ActiveX controls, so that Web page designers will be able to tap their full power without worrying that users will label their pages as "slow," one of the worst knocks against any Web site.

Part
V

Ch
28

FIG. 28.1
Microsoft Internet
Explorer can show
ActiveX controls.

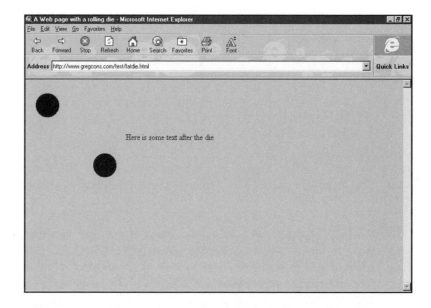

FIG. 28.2
Netscape Navigator
cannot show ActiveX
controls.

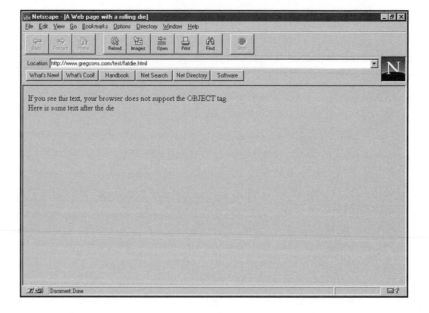

There's a third flaw that you won't notice, since you have Visual C++ installed on your computer. The control requires the MFC DLL. The user must download it and install it before the controls can run. The mechanism that automatically downloads and installs controls does not automatically download and install this DLL. Microsoft doesn't mention this problem very often, and doesn't offer much advice about getting the MFC DLL to your user or getting it installed. (They do claim, rather optimistically, that the DLL, roughly 1 MB, should download in about 10 minutes.) This is essentially the same issue, though, as developing an application using the MFC DLLs dynamically rather than statically linking them into the application.

N O T E It might occur to you to try linking the MFC library statically into your control. It seems easy enough to do: choose Build Settings, and on the General tab there is a drop down box inviting you to choose just that. If you do that and build, you'll get hundreds of linker errors: the COleControl and CPropPage functions are not in the DLL that is linked statically. (That's because Microsoft felt it would be foolish to link the MFC functions statically into a control.) Setting up another library to link in those functions is beyond the scope of this chapter, especially since all this work would lead to an enormous (over 1 MB) control that would take far too long to download the first time. ■

Embedding an ActiveX Control into a Netscape Navigator Web Page

NCompass Labs have produced a Netscape plug-in, called ControlActive, that allows you to embed an ActiveX control into a page that will be read with Netscape. As the control developer, you need to prepare an ODS (object data stream) file for your control to be used in this way. Full details are on the NCompass ControlActive page, **http://www.ncompasslabs.com/documents/authoring.htm#_Toc353797310** and elsewhere on the NCompass site.

Once your ODS file is prepared, change your HTML to activate the plug-in. Netscape plug-ins are added to a Web page with the EMBED tag. Including this tag between <OBJECT ...> and </OBJECT>, as shown in Listing 28.2, means that browsers that don't know the <OBJECT> tag get another chance to show the control, this time with EMBED and the plug-in.

Listing 28.2 fatdie2.html—Using <OBJECT> and <EMBED>

```
<HTML>
<HEAD>
<TITLE>A Web page with a rolling die</TITLE>
</HEAD>
<BODY>
 <OBJECT
CLASSID="clsid:46646B43-EA16-11CF-870C-00201801DDD6"
CODEBASE="dieroll.ocx"
ID=die1
WIDTH=200
HEIGHT=200
ALIGN=center
HSPACE=0
VSPACE=0
>
<PARAM NAME="Image" VALUE="http://www.gregcons.com/test/beans.bmp">
If you see this text, your browser does not support the OBJECT tag -- the
EMBED tag is being used instead. </BR>
```

Part
V

Ch

28

continues

Listing 28.2   Continued

```
<!-- NCompass plugin for Netscape -->
    <EMBED
    SRC="dieroll.ODS"
    CODEBASE="dieroll.OCX"
    WIDTH=200
    HEIGHT=200
    PARAM_Image="http://www.gregcons.com/test/beans.bmp">
</OBJECT>

Here is some text after the die

</BODY>
</HTML>
```

You will probably want to include a link on your page to the NCompass page to help your readers get and learn about the plug-in.

Microsoft is committed to establishing ActiveX controls as a cross-platform, multi-browser solution that will, in the words of its slogan, "Activate the Internet." The ActiveX control specification is no longer a proprietary document, but has been released to a committee that will maintain the standard. So don't pay any attention to people who suggest you should only build these controls if your readers use Internet Explorer!

Choosing between ActiveX and Java

Java is an application development language as well as an applet development language, which means you can develop ActiveX controls in Java if you choose to, using a tool like Microsoft's Visual J++ integrated into Developer Studio. But when most people frame a showdown like "ActiveX versus Java" they mean ActiveX versus Java *applets*, little tightly contained applications that run on a Web page and cannot run stand-alone.

Many people are concerned about the security of running an application they did not code, when they do not know the person or organization supplying the application. The Java approach attempts to restrict the actions that applets can perform, so that even malicious applets cannot do any real damage. But regular announcements of flaws in the restriction approach are damaging the credibility of Java. Some influential netters have gone so far as to say that a Java applet can never be guaranteed to be safe.

The approach taken by Microsoft with ActiveX, which is extendable to Java and any other code that can run, is the trusted supplier approach. Code is digitally signed so that you are sure who provided it, and that it has not been changed since it was signed. This won't prevent bad things from happening if you run the code, but will guarantee that you know who to go to afterward for compensation for those bad things. This is just the same as buying shrink-wrapped software from the shelf in the computer store. For more details, look at **http://www.microsoft.com/ie/most/howto/trusted.htm** and follow some of the links from that page.

Probably the biggest difference between the ActiveX approach and the Java applet approach is downloading. Java code is downloaded every time you load the page that contains it. ActiveX code is downloaded once, unless you already have the control installed some other way (perhaps a CD was sent to you in a magazine, for example) and then never again. A copy is stored on the user's machine and entered into the Registry. The Java code that is downloaded is small, because most of the code that's involved is in the Java Virtual Machine installed on your computer, probably as part of your browser. The ActiveX code that's downloaded can be much larger, though the optimizations discussed later in this chapter can reduce the size significantly by relying on DLLs and other code already on the user's computer. If the user will come to this page once and never again, they may be annoyed to find ActiveX controls cluttering up their disk and Registry. On the other hand, if they come to the same page repeatedly, they will be pleased to find that there is no download time: the control simply activates and runs.

Using AppWizard to Create Faster ActiveX Controls

Microsoft did not develop OCX controls to be placed into Web pages, and changing their name to ActiveX controls didn't magically make them smaller, or faster to load. So the AppWizard that comes with Visual C++ has a number of options available to achieve those ends. This chapter will change these options in the dieroll control that was already created just to show how it's done. Since Dieroll is a fairly lean control already, and loads quickly, these simple changes don't make much difference. It's worth learning the techniques, though, for your own controls, which will surely be fatter than Dieroll.

The first few options to reduce your control have always been available, on Step 2 of the OLE Control Wizard:

- Activates when visible
- Invisible at runtime
- Available in Insert Object dialog box
- Has an About box
- Acts as a simple frame control

If you are developing your control entirely for the Web, many of these settings don't matter any more. Whether your control has an About box or not, users won't be able to bring it up when they are viewing the control in a Web page, for example.

The `activates when visible` option is very important. Activating a control takes a lot of overhead, and should be postponed as long as possible. To unselect this option in the existing Dieroll code, open the Dieroll project in Developer Studio, and open DierollCtl.cpp with FileView. Look for a block of code like the one in Listing 28.3.

Listing 28.3   Excerpt from DierollCtl.cpp—Setting Activates when Visible

```
/////////////////////////////////////////////////////////////////////////
// Control type information

static const DWORD BASED_CODE _dwDierollOleMisc =
    OLEMISC_ACTIVATEWHENVISIBLE |
    OLEMISC_SETCLIENTSITEFIRST |
    OLEMISC_INSIDEOUT |
    OLEMISC_CANTLINKINSIDE |
    OLEMISC_RECOMPOSEONRESIZE;

IMPLEMENT_OLECTLTYPE(CDierollCtrl, IDS_DIEROLL, _dwDierollOleMisc)
```

Delete the OLEMISC_ACTIVATEWHENVISIBLE line. Build a release version of the application. Though the size of the Dieroll OCX file is unchanged, Web pages with this control should load more quickly, since the window is not created until the user first clicks the die. If you reload the Web page with the die in it, you'll see the first value immediately, even though the control is inactive. The window is created to catch mouse clicks, not to display the die roll.

There are more optimizations available: Figure 28.3 shows the list of advanced options for OLE Control Wizard, reached by clicking the Advanced button on Step 2. Each of these options can be chosen when you first build the application, through Control Wizard. They can also be changed in an existing application, saving you the trouble of redoing AppWizard and adding your own functionality again. The options are:

- Windowless activation
- Unclipped device context
- Flicker-free activation
- Mouse pointer notifications when inactive
- Optimized drawing code
- Loads properties asynchronously

FIG. 28.3

The Advanced button on Step 2 of the OLE Control Wizard leads to a choice of optimizations.

Windowless activation is going to be very popular. If you want a transparent control or one that is not a rectangle, you must use windowless activation. But because it reduces code size and speeds execution, every control should consider using this option. Modern containers will provide the functionality for the control: in older containers the control will create the window anyway, denying you the savings but ensuring the control still works.

To implement this in Dieroll, override `CDierollCtrl::GetControlFlags()` like this:

```
DWORD CDierollCtrl::GetControlFlags()
{
    return COleControl::GetControlFlags()¦ windowlessActivate;
}
```

Add the function quickly by right-clicking on `CDierollCtrl` in Class View and choosing Add Function. If you do this to Dieroll, build it, and reload the Web page that uses it, you will notice no apparent effect, because Dieroll is such a lean control. You will at least notice that it still functions perfectly, and doesn't mind not having a window.

The next two options, unclipped device context and flicker-free activation are not available to windowless controls. In a control with a window, choosing unclipped device context means that you are completely sure that you never draw outside the client rectangle of the control. Skipping the checks that make sure you don't makes your controls run faster, though it could mean trouble if you have an error in your draw code. If you were to do this in Dieroll, the override of `GetControlFlags()` would look like this:

```
DWORD CDierollCtrl::GetControlFlags()
{
    return COleControl::GetControlFlags()& ~clipPaintDC;
}
```

Don't try to combine this with windowless activation: it doesn't do anything.

Flicker-free activation is useful for controls which draw their inactive and active views identically. (Think back to Chapter 24, "Building an ActiveX Server Application," in which the server object was drawn in dimmed colors when the objects were inactive.) If there is no need to redraw, because the drawing code is the same, you can select this option and skip the second draw. Your users won't see an annoying flicker as the control activates, and activation will be a tiny bit quicker. If you were to do this in Dieroll, the `GetControlFlags()` override would be:

```
DWORD CDierollCtrl::GetControlFlags()
{
    return COleControl::GetControlFlags()¦ noFlickerActivate;
}
```

Like unclipped device context, don't try to combine this with windowless activation: it doesn't do anything.

Mouse pointer notifications, when inactive, enable more controls to turn off the activate when visible option. If the only reason to be active is to have a window to process mouse interactions, this option will divert those interactions to the container through an `IPointerInactive` interface. To enable this option in an application that is already built, you override `GetControlFlags()` again:

```
 DWORD CDierollCtrl::GetControlFlags()
{
    return COleControl::GetControlFlags()¦ pointerInactive;
}
```

Now your code will receive WM_SETCURSOR and WM_MOUSEMOVE messages through message map entries, even though you have no window. The container, whose window your control is using, will send these messages to you through the IPointerInactive interface.

The other circumstance under which you might want to process window messages while still inactive, and so without a window, is if the user drags something over your control and drops it. The control needs to activate at that moment, so that it has a window to be a drop target. You can arrange that with an override to GetActivationPolicy():

```
DWORD CDierollCtrl::GetActivationPolicy()
{
    return POINTERINACTIVE_ACTIVATEONDRAG;
}
```

Don't bother doing this if your control isn't a drop target, of course.

The problem with relying on the container to pass on your messages through the IPointerInactive interface is that the container may have no idea such an interface exists, and have no plans to pass your messages on with it. If you think your control might end up in such a container, then don't remove the OLEMISC_ACTIVATEWHENVISIBLE flag from the block of code like the one in Listing 28.4

Listing 28.4   Excerpt from DierollCtl.cpp—Fine-tuning Activates when Visible

```
//////////////////////////////////////////////////////////////////////////
// Control type information

static const DWORD BASED_CODE _dwDierollOleMisc =
    OLEMISC_ACTIVATEWHENVISIBLE |
    OLEMISC_SETCLIENTSITEFIRST |
    OLEMISC_INSIDEOUT |
    OLEMISC_CANTLINKINSIDE |
    OLEMISC_RECOMPOSEONRESIZE;

IMPLEMENT_OLECTLTYPE(CDierollCtrl, IDS_DIEROLL, _dwDierollOleMisc)
```

Instead, OR in another flag, OLEMISC_IGNOREACTIVATEWHENVISIBLE. This oddly named flag is meaningful to containers that understand IPointerInactive, and means, in effect "I take it back, don't activate when visible after all." Containers that don't understand IPointerInactive don't understand this flag either, and your control will activate when visible, and thus be around to catch mouse messages in these containers.

Optimized drawing code is only useful to controls that will be sharing the container with a number of other drawing controls. As you may recall from Chapter 11, "Drawing on the Screen," the typical pattern for drawing a view of any kind is to set the brush, pen, or other GDI object to a new value, saving the old, then use the GDI object, then restore it to the saved value. If there are a number of controls doing this in turn, all those restore steps could be skipped in favor of one restore at the end of all the drawing. The container saves all the GDI object values before instructing the controls to redraw, and restores them all afterwards.

If you would like your control to take advantage of this, there are two changes to be made. First, if a pen or other GDI object is to remain connected between draw calls, it must not go out of scope. That means any local pens, brushes, and fonts should be converted to member variables so that they stay in scope between function calls. Second, the code to restore the old objects should be surrounded by an if statement that calls COleControl::IsOptimizedDraw()to see if the restoration is necessary. A typical draw routine would set up the colors, then proceed like this:

```
...
if(!m_pen.m_hObject)
{
    m_pen.CreatePen(PS_SOLID, 0, forecolor);
}
if(!m_pen.m_hObject)
{
    m_brush.CreateSolidBrush(backcolor);
}

CPen* savepen = pdc->SelectObject(&m_pen);
CBrush* savebrush = pdc->SelectObject(&m_brush);

...
// use device context
...
if(!IsOptimizedDraw())
{
    pdc->SelectObject(savepen);
    pdc->SelectObject(savebrush);
}
...
```

The device context has the addresses of the member variables, so when it lets go of them at the direction of the container, their m_hObject member becomes NULL. As long as it is not NULL there is no need to reset the device context, and if this container supports optimized drawing code there is no need to restore it either.

If you select this optimized drawing code option with AppWizard, the if statement with the call to IsOptimizedDraw() is added to your draw code, with some comments to remind you what to do.

The last of the optimization options, loads properties asynchronously, is covered in the next section.

Speeding Control Loads with Asynchronous Properties

Asynchronous refers to spreading out activities over time, and not insisting that one activity be complete before another can begin. In the context of the Web, it's worth harking back to the features that made Netscape Navigator better than Mosaic, way back when it was first released. The number one benefit cited by people who were on the Web then was that the Netscape browser, unlike Mosaic, could display text while pictures were still loading. This is classic asynchronous behavior. You don't have to wait until the huge image files have transferred to see what the words on the page are and whether the images are worth waiting for.

Faster Internet connections and more compact image formats have lessened some of the concerns about waiting for images. Still, being asynchronous is a good thing. For one thing, waiting for video clips, sound clips, and executable code has made many Web users long for the good old days when they only had to wait 30 seconds for pages to find all their images.

Properties

The die that comes up in your Web page is the default die appearance. There's no way for the user to access the properties of the control. The Web page developer can, using the <PARAM> tag inside the <OBJECT> tag. (Browsers that ignore OBJECT also ignore PARAM.) Here's the HTML to include a die with a number rather than dots:

```
<HTML>
<HEAD>
<TITLE>A Web page with a rolling numbered die</TITLE>
<BODY>
 <OBJECT
CLASSID="clsid:46646B43-EA16-11CF-870C-00201801DDD6"
CODEBASE="http://www.gregcons.com/test/dieroll.ocx"
ID=die2
WIDTH=200
HEIGHT=200
ALIGN=center
HSPACE=0
VSPACE=0
>
<PARAM NAME="Dots" value="0">
If you see this text, your browser does not support the OBJECT tag. </BR>
</OBJECT>

Here is some text after the die

</BODY>
</HTML>
```

The <PARAM> tag has two attributes: NAME provides a name that matches the external OLE name (Dots in this case) and value provides the value (0, or FALSE, in this case.) The die displays with a number.

In order to demonstrate the value of asynchronous properties, Dieroll needs to have some big properties. So, since this is a demonstration application, the next step is to add a big property. A natural choice is to give the user more control over the appearance of the die. The user (which means the Web page designer if the control is being used in a Web page) can specify an image file and use that as the background for the die. Before you see how to make that happen, imagine what the Web page reader will have to wait for when loading a page that uses Dieroll:

- The HTML has to be loaded from the server
- The browser lays out the text and non-text elements and starts to display text
- The browser searches the Registry for the CLSID of the control
- If necessary, the control is downloaded, using the CODEBASE parameter
- The control properties are initialized using the <PARAM> tags
- The control runs and draws itself

When Dieroll gains another property, an image file that might be quite large, there will be another delay while the image file is retrieved from wherever it is kept. If nothing happens in the meantime, the Web page reader will eventually tire of staring at an empty square and go away to another page. Using asynchronous properties means that the control can draw itself roughly and start to be useful, even while the large image file is still being downloaded. For Dieroll, drawing the dots on a plain background using GetBackColor()will do until the image file is ready.

Using BLOBs

A BLOB is a Binary Large OBject. It's a generic name for things like the image file we are about to add to the Dieroll control. The way a control talks to a BLOB is through a moniker. That's not new, it's just that monikers have always been hidden away inside OLE. If you already understood them, you will have a great deal more to learn about them, because things are changing with the introduction of asynchronous monikers. If you've never heard of them be-fore, no problem. Eventually there will be all sorts of asynchronous monikers, but at the mo-ment only URL monikers have been implemented. These are a way for OLE to connect BLOB properties to URLs. If you're prepared to trust OLE to do this for you, you can achieve some amazing things. The remainder of this subsection explains how to work with URL monikers to load BLOB properties asynchronously.

Remember, the idea here is that the control will start drawing itself even before it has all of its properties. Your OnDraw() code will be structured like this:

```
// prepare to draw
if(AllPropertiesAreLoaded)
{
    // draw using the BLOB
}
else
{
    // draw without the BLOB
}
//cleanup after drawing
```

There are two problems to solve here. First, what will be the test to see if all the properties are loaded? And second, how can you arrange to have OnDraw called again when the properties are ready, if it's already been called, and has already drawn the control the "BLOBless" way?

The first problem has been solved by adding two new functions to COleControl. GetReadyState() returns one of these values:

Part
V

Ch
28

- READYSTATE_UNINITIALIZED means the control is completely uninitialized
- READYSTATE_LOADING means the control properties are loading
- READYSTATE_LOADED means the properties are all loaded
- READYSTATE_INTERACTIVE means the control can talk to the user but isn't fully loaded yet
- READYSTATE_COMPLETE means there is nothing more to wait for

The function InternalSetReadyState() sets the ready state to one of these values.

The second problem, getting a second call to OnDraw() after the control has already been drawn without the BLOB, has been solved by a new class called CDataPathProperty, and its derived class CCachedDataPathProperty. These classes have a member function called OnDataAvailable() which catches the Windows message generated when the property has been retrieved from the remote site. The OnDataAvailable() function invalidates the control, forcing a redraw.

Changing Dieroll

Make a copy of the Dieroll folder you created in Chapter 26, "Building an ActiveX Control," (or the Chapter 26 code from the CD) and change it to windowless activation as described earlier in this chapter. Now you're ready to begin. There is a lot to be done to implement asynchronous properties, but each step is quite straightforward.

> **CAUTION**
>
> Shortly after Visual C++ 4.2 was released, Microsoft prepared a patch called the 4.2a patch, available from **http://www.microsoft.com**. This patch updates some of the Internet-related code to reflect versions of Internet Explorer and the ActiveX SDK released after Visual C++ 4.2. What that means to you is this: if you have not installed the patch this control will not work for you. Get the patch and install it.

Add the *CDierollDataPathProperty* Class   Open ClassWizard, click the OLE Automation tab, and click the Add Class button. From the drop-down menu that appears under the button, choose New. This brings up the Create New Class dialog. Name the class CDierollDataPathProperty. Click the drop down box for Base class and choose CCachedDataPathProperty. Do not add this class to the Component Gallery. The dialog should resemble Figure 28.4.

The reason that the new class should inherit from CCachedDataProperty is that it will load the property information into a file, and that is an easier way to handle the bitmap. If the control has a property that was downloaded because it changed often (for example, current weather) then CDataPathProperty would be a better choice.

Add the Image Property to CDierollCtrl   With the new CDierollDataPathProperty class added to the Dieroll control, add the property to the original CDierollCtrl class that you copied. In ClassWizard, on the OLE Automation tab, make sure that CDierollCtrl is selected in the right most drop-down box. Click Add Property, and fill out the dialog as shown in

Figure 28.5. The external name you choose is the one that will appear in the HTML: `Image` is simple and doesn't require a lot of typing. The type should be `OLE_DATAPATH`—that choice won't be in the drop-down box for type until you change the Implementation to Get/Set method.

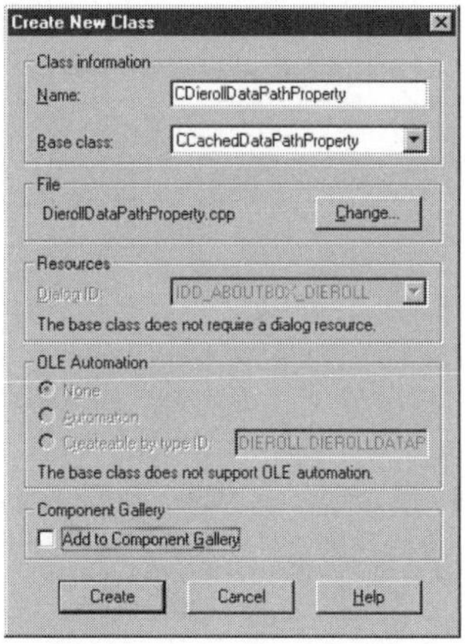

FIG. 28.4

Create a new class to handle asynchronous properties.

FIG. 28.5

The image file is added as an OLE_DATAPATH.

ClassWizard adds the Get and Set functions to your control class, but the TODO comments (see Listing 28.5) are a little longer than usual.

Listing 28.5   DierollCtl.cpp—Get and Set Functions

```
OLE_DATAPATH CDierollCtrl::GetImage()
{
    CString strResult;
    // TODO: Replace "VAR" with the name of a member variable
    //       whose type is derived from CDataPathProperty.

    // strResult = VAR.GetPath();

    return strResult.AllocSysString();
```

Part

V

Ch

28

continues

Listing 28.5   Continued

```
}

void CDierollCtrl::SetImage(LPCTSTR lpszNewValue)
{
    // TODO: Replace "VAR" with the name of a member variable
    //       whose type is derived from CDataPathProperty.

    // Load(lpszNewValue, VAR);

    SetModifiedFlag();
}
```

As with other Get and Set properties, you will have to add the member variable. It is an instance of the new CDierollDataPathProperty class. Right-click on CDierollCtrl in Class View and choose Add Variable. Figure 28.6 shows how to fill in the dialog to declare the member variable mdpp_image. (The dpp in the name is to remind you that this is a data path property.)

FIG. 28.6

The image file member variable is an instance of the new class.

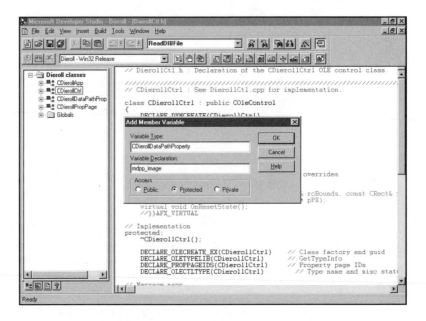

Now you can finish the Get and Set functions, as shown in Listing 28.6.

Listing 28.6   DierollCtl.cpp—Completed Get and Set Functions

```
OLE_DATAPATH CDierollCtrl::GetImage()
{
    CString strResult;
    strResult = mdpp_image.GetPath();
    return strResult.AllocSysString();
```

```
}

void CDierollCtrl::SetImage(LPCTSTR lpszNewValue)
{
    Load(lpszNewValue, mdpp_image);
    SetModifiedFlag();
}
```

At the top of the header file for CDierollCtrl, add this include statement:

```
#include "DierollDataPathProperty.h"
```

Now there are some bits and pieces to deal with because you are changing an existing control rather than turning on asynchronous properties when you first built Dieroll. First, in CDierollCtrl::DoPropExchange(), arrange persistence and initialization for mdpp_image by adding this line:

```
PX_DataPath( pPX, _T("Image"), mdpp_image);
```

Second, add a line to the stub of CDierollCtrl::OnResetState() that ClassWizard provided, to reset the data path property when the control is reset. The function is shown in Listing 28.7.

Listing 28.7   DierollCtl.cpp—CDierollCtrl::OnResetState()

```
/////////////////////////////////////////////////////////////////////////
// CDierollCtrl::OnResetState - Reset control to default state

void CDierollCtrl::OnResetState()
{
    COleControl::OnResetState();  // Resets defaults found in DoPropExchange

    mdpp_image.ResetData();
}
```

Add the ReadyStateChange Event and the ReadyState Property   Use ClassWizard to add the stock event ReadyStateChange. In ClassWizard, click the OLE events tab, then the Add Event button. Choose ReadyStateChange from the drop down box and click OK. Figure 28.7 shows the Add Event dialog for this event. Events, as discussed in Chapter 26, notify the container of the control that something has happened within the control. In this case, what has happened is that the rest of the control's data has arrived and the control's state of readiness has changed.

Use ClassWizard to add a property to CDierollCtrl for the ready state. In ClassWizard, click the OLE Automation tab, then the Add Property button. Choose ReadyState from the drop down box, and since this is a stock property, the rest of the dialog is filled in for you, as shown in Figure 28.8. ClassWizard doesn't add a stub function for GetReadyState() because CDierollCtrl will inherit this from COleControl.

FIG. 28.7
Add a stock event to notify the container of a change in the readiness of the control.

FIG. 28.8
Add a stock property to track the readiness of the control.

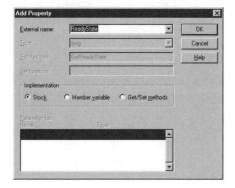

Add a line to the constructor to initialize the member variable in COleControl that is used in COleControl::GetReadyState() and set by COleControl::InternalSetReadyState(). Since the control can be used right away, the readiness state should start at READYSTATE_INTERACTIVE. Listing 28.8 shows the new constructor:

Listing 28.8 DierollCtl.cpp—CDierollCtrl::GetImage()

```
CDierollCtrl::CDierollCtrl()
{
    InitializeIIDs(&IID_DDieroll, &IID_DDierollEvents);

    m_lReadyState = READYSTATE_INTERACTIVE;
}
```

Implement CDierollDataPathProperty   There is some work to do in CDierollDataPathProperty before changing CDierollCtrl::OnDraw(). This class loads a bitmap, and this chapter is not going to explain most of what's involved in reading a .BMP file into a CBitmap object. The most important function is OnDataAvailable(), which is in Listing 28.9.

Listing 28.9   DierollDataPathProperty.cpp—OnDataAvailable()

```
void CDierollDataPathProperty::OnDataAvailable(DWORD dwSize, DWORD grfBSCF)
{
    CCachedDataPathProperty::OnDataAvailable(dwSize, grfBSCF);

    if(grfBSCF & BSCF_LASTDATANOTIFICATION)
    {
        m_Cache.SeekToBegin();
        if (ReadBitmap(m_Cache))
        {
            BitmapDataLoaded = TRUE;
            // safe because this control has only one property:
            GetControl()->InternalSetReadyState(READYSTATE_COMPLETE);
            GetControl()->Invalidate();
        }
    }
}
```

Every time a block of data is received from the remote site, this function is called. The first line of code uses the base class version of the function to deal with that block and set the flag called grfBSCF. If, after dealing with the latest block, the download is complete, the ReadBitmap() function is called to read the cached data into a bitmap object that can be displayed as the control background. The code for ReadBitmap() will not be presented or discussed here, though it is on the CD for those who would like to read it.

Once the bitmap has been read, the control's ready state is complete and the call to Invalidate() arranges for a redraw.

Revise CDierollCtrl::OnDraw()   The structure of CDierollCtrl::OnDraw() was laid out long ago. The background is filled in before the code that checks whether to draw dots or a number, in this block of code:

```
COLORREF back = TranslateColor(GetBackColor());
CBrush backbrush;
backbrush.CreateSolidBrush(back);
pdc->FillRect(rcBounds, &backbrush);
```

Replace that block with the one in Listing 28.10.

Listing 28.10   DierollDataPathProperty.cpp—New Code for *OnDraw()*

```
CBrush backbrush;
BOOL drawn = FALSE;
if(GetReadyState()== READYSTATE_COMPLETE)
{
    CBitmap* image = mdpp_image.GetBitmap(*pdc);
    if(image)
    {
        CDC memdc;
        memdc.CreateCompatibleDC(pdc);
        memdc.SelectObject(image);
```

Part

V

Ch

28

continues

Listing 28.10   Continued

```
            BITMAP bmp;                    //just for height and width
            image->GetBitmap(&bmp);
            pdc->StretchBlt(0,             //upper left
                            0,             //upper right
                            rcBounds.Width(), // target width
                            rcBounds.Height(), // target height
                            &memdc,        // the image
                            0,             //offset into image -x
                            0,             //offset into image -y
                            bmp.bmWidth, // width
                            bmp.bmHeight, // height
                            SRCCOPY);     //copy it over

            drawn = TRUE;
        }
    }
    if(!drawn)
    {
        COLORREF back = TranslateColor(GetBackColor());
        backbrush.CreateSolidBrush(back);
        pdc->FillRect(rcBounds, &backbrush);
    }
```

The BOOL variable drawn ensures that if the control is complete, but something goes wrong with the attempt to use the bitmap, the control will be drawn the old way. If the control is complete, the image is loaded into a CBitmap*, and then drawn into the device context. Bitmaps can only be selected into a memory device context, and then copied over to an ordinary device context. Using StretchBlt()will stretch the bitmap during the copy, though a sensible web page designer will have specified a bitmap that matches the HEIGHT and WIDTH attributes of the OBJECT tag. The old drawing code is still here, used if drawn remains FALSE.

Testing and Debugging Dieroll

Having made all those changes, build the control, which will register it. One way to test it would be to bring up that HTML page in Explorer again, but you may prefer to debug the control. It is possible to debug a control even though you cannot run it stand alone. Normally, a developer would arrange to debug the control in the Test Container, but you can use any application that can contain the control.

In Developer Studio, choose Build Settings. Click on the Debug tab, and make sure that all the lines in the left most list box are selected. Select General in the top drop-down box, and in the edit box labeled Executable for debug session, enter the full path to Microsoft Internet Explorer on your computer. (Figure 28.9 shows an example.) Now when you choose Build Debug Go, or click the Go toolbar button, Explorer will launch. Open a page of HTML that loads the control, and the control will run in the debugger. You can set breakpoints, step through code, and examine variables just as with any other application.

FIG. 28.9
Arrange to run Explorer when you debug the control.

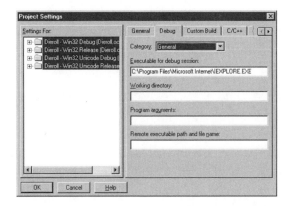

Here's the syntax for an OBJECT tag that sets the Image property:

```
<OBJECT
CLASSID="clsid:46646B43-EA16-11CF-870C-00201801DDD6"
CODEBASE="http://www.gregcons.com/test/dieroll.ocx"
ID=die1
WIDTH=200
HEIGHT=200
ALIGN=center
HSPACE=0
VSPACE=0
>
<PARAM NAME="Dots" VALUE="1">
<PARAM NAME="Image" VALUE="http://www.gregcons.com/test/beans.bmp">
If you see this text, your browser does not support the OBJECT tag. </BR>
</OBJECT>
```

 Remember, don't just copy these HTML samples to your own machine if you are building Dieroll yourself. You need to use your own CLSID, and a URL to the location of your copy of the OCX, and the image file you are using.

Figure 28.10 shows the control with a background image of jelly beans. It takes thirty seconds to a minute to load this 40K image through the Web, and while it is loading, the control is perfectly usable as a plain die with no background image. That's the whole point of asynchronous properties, and that's what all the effort of the previous sections achieves.

The Base Control Framework and the ActiveX Template Library (ATL)

There is a way to build an ActiveX control that does not need the MFC DLLs. Microsoft has provided a framework and some samples, collectively called the Base Control Framework, that you can build on to produce a control. Typically the OCX files produced are larger than those produced by the OLE Control Wizard, but far smaller than the MFC DLL. The work involved is considerable, though. Microsoft recommends that you choose this route only if you understand

Part
V

Ch
28

the fundamentals of OLE Automation and dual interfaces, are willing to edit .ODL files, and understand and are willing to work with OLE persistence interfaces. In addition, most of the instructions provided with the framework assume you are comfortable running a make tool from an MS-DOS prompt.

FIG. 28.10
Now the die displays on a field of jelly beans, or any other image you choose.

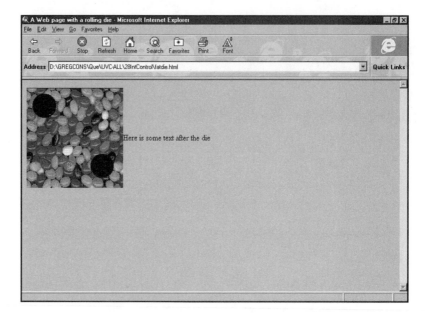

For those who are even braver, the ActiveX Template Library can also be used to build controls, though it would be a very dificult job to implement a significant user interface on such a control. The controls produced are certainly very small, but the work involved is not.

To learn more about BaseCtl and ATL, and to read Microsoft's disclaimers about "not for the faint-of-heart" and "not for the timid," point your Web browser at **http://www.microsoft.com/ intdev/controls/controls.htm** and scroll to the bottom of the page.

From Here...

ActiveX controls are changing fast. Watch for more announcements from Microsoft of development kits and other add-ons to make building Internet-ready controls faster and easier. Look also for upgrades to the not-quite-complete material that shipped with Visual C++ 4.2. If you'd like to learn more about programming for the Internet, try one of these chapters:

- Chapter 13, "Sockets, MAPI, and the Internet" introduces you to some of the ways you can write your own Internet programs rather than writing a control that is delivered over the Internet.

- Chapter 27, "Internet Programming with the WinInet Classes," introduces the latest MFC classes, and shows you how quickly you can build a truly useful (and unique) Internet application.

CHAPTER 29

Power-User Features in Developer Studio

Developer Studio is a terrifically complex application, enabling you to manage your programming products in almost any way imaginable. Some features of Developer Studio are easy to use, once you know what they do. Others require sophisticated knowledge of programming and of the various tools that Developer Studio puts at your disposal. In this chapter, you get an introduction to some of the more useful advanced features of Developer Studio, with which you may not yet have had experience. ■

How to Add Components to Component Gallery

Reusable components can be anything from a dialog box to an OLE control. Component Gallery organizes components so that you can add them to your projects with a couple of mouse clicks.

About Creating Custom AppWizards

Custom AppWizards enable you to set up automatic code generation for your own types of project workspaces. Although creating AppWizards is a complex topic, the brief introduction that you'll get in this chapter will help dispel some of the mystery.

How to Add Tools to Developer Studio

Although Developer Studio features its own set of tools, you can add your own to the Tools menu and then run those tools with a click of the mouse.

About Developer Studio's Editor Emulation

You can set Developer Studio's built-in editor to act like one of several different popular editors, including BRIEF and Epsilon.

About Code optimization

Do you want your programs to be fast, but larger? Or would you prefer compact—but slower?

Using Component Gallery

In these days of complex programs, reusability has become more than just a buzzword. It's become a survival technique for programmers who find themselves with the awesome task of creating hundreds of thousands of lines of working source code in a minimum amount of time. Component Gallery (Figure 29.1) is one way that Developer Studio helps support the concept of reusability. Component Gallery gives you instant access to everything from reusable classes and OLE controls to wizards. You can even create your own components and add them to Component Gallery. In fact, in its default installation, Developer Studio automatically adds a category to Component Gallery for new AppWizard applications that you create.

FIG. 29.1

Component Gallery organizes reusable components, including classes and OLE controls.

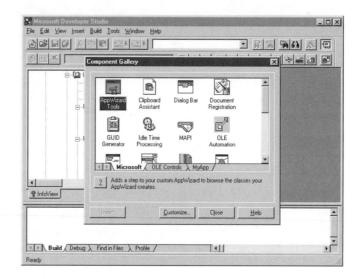

Suppose you have a dialog box that you use frequently in projects. You can create this dialog box just once, add it to Component Gallery, and then merge it into new projects whenever you need it. To see how this might work, follow these steps:

1. Start a new AppWizard project workspace called MyApp. (Just use all the default AppWizard settings.)

2. Create the dialog-box resource shown in Figure 29.2, giving the dialog box the IDD_NAMEDLG resource ID.

3. Use ClassWizard to associate the dialog-box object with a class called CNameDlg. Make sure that the Add to Component Gallery option in the Create New Class dialog box is checked, as shown in Figure 29.3. Developer Studio then adds the component to Component Gallery.

4. Start another AppWizard project workspace, this time called MyApp2.

5. Select the Insert, Component command from Developer Studio's menu bar. Component Gallery appears.

FIG. 29.2

This is the dialog box you'll add to Component Gallery.

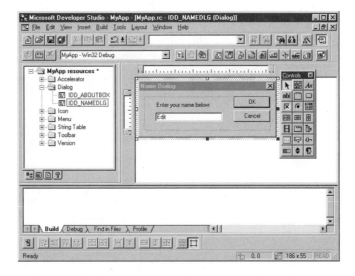

FIG. 29.3

Use ClassWizard to create a class for the dialog box.

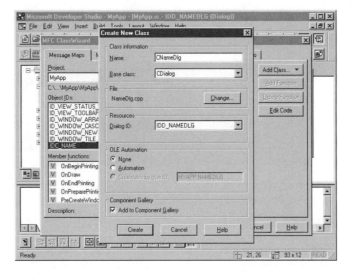

6. Select the MyApp tab. The components in the MyApp project appear (Figure 29.4).

7. Select the NameDlg component and then click the Insert button. Developer Studio asks whether you want to insert the component. Click the Yes button. Click the Close button to exit from Component Gallery.

8. Check the MyApp2 project's classes, and you'll see that Component Gallery has added the CNameDlg dialog box (Figure 29.5). You'll also find the class's .cpp and .h files added to the project's file list.

FIG. 29.4

You'll find the new dialog-box component on the MyApp page.

FIG. 29.5

The dialog-box component has now been added to the project.

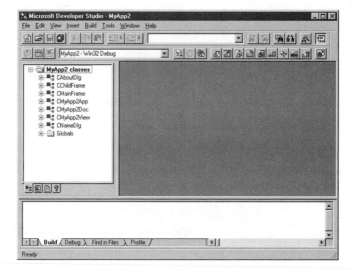

You can use Component Gallery to manage many other types of components, including those that you might get from a friend or buy from a third-party supplier. Component Gallery can add, delete, import, and edit components in a variety of ways, depending upon the type of component with which you're working. Take some time to experiment with Component Gallery, and you'll quickly see how easy it is to use. (Your Visual C++ online documentation contains more information on Component Gallery.)

Introducing Custom AppWizards

AppWizard is a sensational tool for getting projects started quickly and easily. However, because of its general nature, AppWizard makes many assumptions about the way you want a new project created. Sometimes, you may need a special type of AppWizard project that isn't supported by the default AppWizard. If this special project is a one-time deal, you'd probably just go ahead and create the project by hand. However, if you need to use this custom project type again and again, you might want to consider creating a custom AppWizard.

You can create a custom AppWizard in three ways: using the existing AppWizard steps as a starting point, using an existing project as a starting point, or starting completely from scratch. However, no matter what method you choose, creating a custom AppWizard can be a complicated task, requiring that you understand and be able to write script files using the macros and commands provided by Visual C++ for this purpose. The creation of these script files is beyond the scope of this book. However, the following procedures will give you a general idea of how to create a custom AppWizard.

1. Start a new AppWizard project workspace, choosing Custom AppWizard as the project type (Figure 29.6).

FIG. 29.6

First, start a custom AppWizard project workspace.

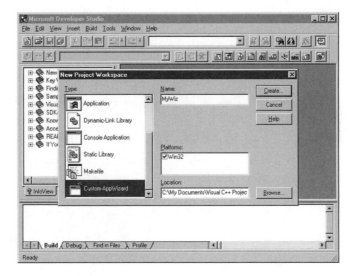

2. Click the Create button. The Step 1 of 2 dialog box appears.

3. Choose the type of custom AppWizard that you want to create. In this case, select Standard AppWizard Steps, and name the project type MyWizard, as shown in Figure 29.7.

FIG. 29.7

You use this dialog box to choose the type of AppWizard you want to create.

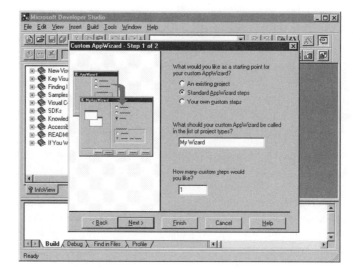

4. Set the number of custom steps (near the bottom of the dialog box) to 6.

5. Click the <u>N</u>ext button. The Step 2 of 2 dialog box appears.

6. Choose whether you want the AppWizard to create an executable file or a DLL. Also, select the languages that the AppWizard will support (Figure 29.8).

FIG. 29.8

In this dialog box, you select the program type, as well as choose language support.

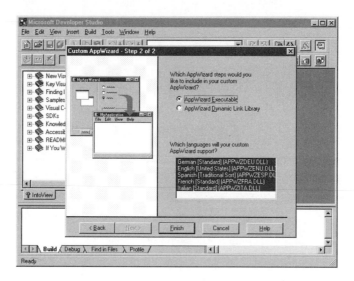

7. Click the Finish button. Your custom AppWizard's settings appear. Click the OK button to generate the project workspace.

After you've completed the preceding steps, your custom AppWizard project is ready for you to add the custom code needed to create the wizard. As you can see in Figure 29.9, the new project looks a lot like any other project you might create with Developer Studio, except that it contains some file types with which you may not yet be familiar.

FIG. 29.9

A custom AppWizard project workspace is much like other workspaces you've used.

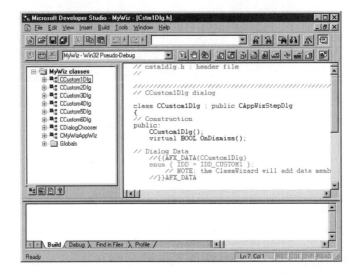

The classes that end with "Dlg" are the classes that represent the dialog boxes that'll appear for each step of the wizard. You need to use the resource editor to customize the dialog-box objects that are associated with each of the classes. As mentioned previously, there are also script files—CONFIRM.INF and NEWPROJ.INF—that you must customize to create the wizard's steps.

When you compile the custom AppWizard, Developer Studio creates the final files and stores them in your Msdev\Template directory. The next time you choose to start a new project workspace, your custom AppWizard will be listed in the project types (Figure 29.10). To remove the custom AppWizard, delete the wizard's .awx and .pdb files from your Msdev\Template directory.

FIG. 29.10

After you compile your custom AppWizard, it'll appear as a project type in the New Project Workspace dialog box.

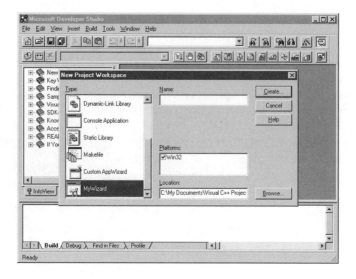

Integrating External Tools

When you first install Visual C++, it supplies a set of default tools that you can use to help manage and create your programs. These tools include Spy++, MFC Tracer, OLE Control Test Container, and others. Although these tools are handy, you'll undoubtedly run into other tools that you might like to add to your Visual C++ programming environment. Suppose, for example, that you want to install WordPad as an editor on your Tool menu. You'd just follow the procedure given here:

1. Select the Tools, Customize command from Developer Studio's menu bar. The Customize property sheet appears (Figure 29.11). Click on the Tools tab.

FIG. 29.11

You add tools from the Customize property sheet.

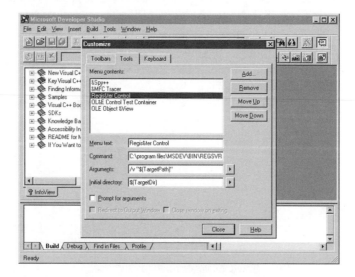

2. Click the <u>A</u>dd button. The Add Tool dialog box appears.

3. Use the <u>B</u>rowse button to locate the new tool on your hard drive. In this case, the new tool is WRITE.EXE, as shown in Figure 29.12. When you've located the tool, click OK.

Part

V

Ch

29

FIG. 29.12

Use the Browse button to locate the new tool.

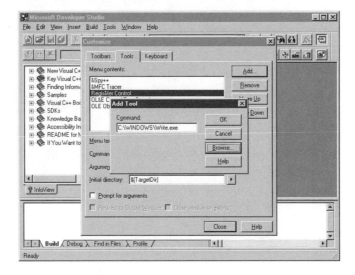

4. Type **WordPad** in the <u>M</u>enu Text box. This is the name of the tool as it will appear in the Tool menu.

5. In the Argum<u>e</u>nts box, type the arguments that you want sent to the tool when the tool is run (Figure 29.13). In this case, type **$(FileName)$(FileExt)**, which will cause the full name of the currently open source-code file to be sent as an argument to the tool. (You can select these arguments from a drop-down list if you click on the arrow button to the right of the text box.)

FIG. 29.13

You can have arguments passed to the tools by typing the arguments in the Arguments text box.

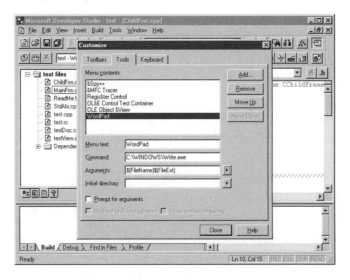

6. Click the Close button to finalize your selections. Developer Studio adds the new tool to the Tool menu (Figure 29.14), from which you can run the tool easily.

FIG. 29.14
The newly added tool appears on the Tool menu.

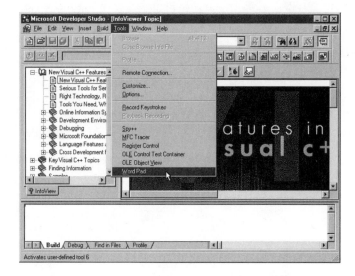

You can purchase many additional tools from software vendors, not the least of which includes Microsoft's Visual SourceSafe—a project version-control manager—and VisualTest—a program-test automator. Other tools you might like to add include sophisticated source-code editors and debugging utilities.

Using Editor Emulation

The type of text editor you like is often a product of your experience. That is, once you've learned one way of doing things, you tend to be resistant to change. Previously, you learned that you can add your text editor of choice to Developer Studio's Tools menu. In addition, Developer Studio's built-in editor is capable of emulating two text editors: BRIEF and Epsilon. The text editor can also act like the text editor that came with Visual C++ 2.0. If you want to use the built-in editor, you should experiment with these various emulations to find the one that best suits your working habits. To set editor options, including emulation, follow these steps:

1. Select the Tools, Options command from Developer Studio's menu bar. The Options property sheet appears.

2. On the Editor page (Figure 29.15), set the Window Settings and Save Options for the text editor.

3. On the Tabs page (Figure 29.16), set the way you want the text editor to handle tabbing.

FIG. 29.15

You use the Editor page to control general text-editor settings.

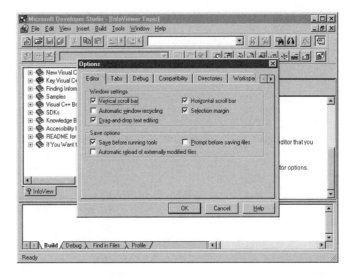

FIG. 29.16

You can also set how the text editor deals with tabs.

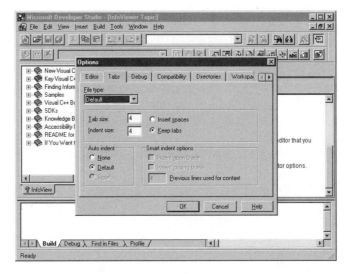

4. On the Compatibility page (Figure 29.17), set the editor type in the Recommended Options For text box.

5. Set the options in the Options box by checking those features that you want active.

6. On the Format page (Figure 29.18), set the formatting features that you want used in your text windows, including fonts and text colors.

FIG. 29.17

You set the actual emulation on the Compatibility page.

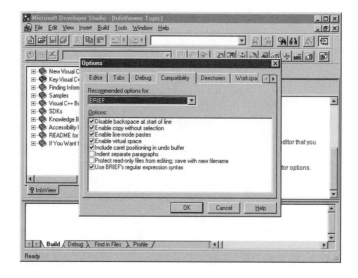

FIG. 29.18

The Format page enables you to set the appearance of text windows.

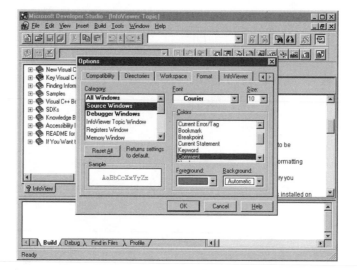

Using Optimization

As most programmers know, the size and speed of a program are inversely proportional. That is, making a program faster often also makes it larger. Conversely, making a program smaller often also makes it run slower. Just as you're presented with these types of choices as you're creating the source code for your application, so too is the compiler forced to decide between different ways of producing executable code. By setting different optimization options, you can tell the compiler whether you want fast or slow code.

To find the optimization options, select the Build, Settings command from Developer Studio's menu bar. (You must have a project open in order to enable the Settings command. The settings are specific to the current project.) When you do, the Project Settings property sheet appears. Go to the C/C++ page and select Optimizations in the Category box. As you can see by examining the Optimizations box, Developer Studio defaults to no optimization. To select a type of optimization, just choose from the drop-down list, as shown in Figure 29.19.

FIG. 29.19

Select from the list the type of optimization that you want.

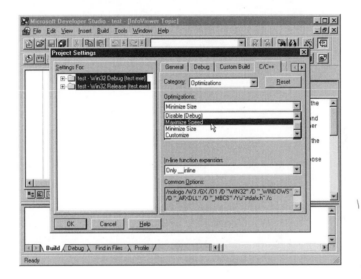

N O T E If you select the Customize option in the Optimizations box, you can select from the list of individual optimizations, including Assume No Aliasing, Global Optimizations, Favor Fast Code, Generate Intrinsic Functions, Frame-Pointer Omission, and more. However, as you can tell from the names of these optimizations, you really have to know what you're doing to set up a custom optimization scheme. ■

From Here...

This chapter only touched upon the many advanced features you can discover in Developer Studio. Your Visual C++ online documentation contains a wealth of information about the features covered in this chapter and about many other features not mentioned here. The more you become familiar with Developer Studio's many advanced features, the better you'll understand the program-creation process.

For more information on related topics, please refer to the following chapters:

- Chapter 2, "Developer Studio Commands," gives you an overview of the Developer Studio's menus and toolbar.

- Chapter 3, "AppWizard and ClassWizard," introduces you to the AppWizard code generator.

- Chapter 26, "Building an ActiveX Control," describes one type of component you can add to Component Gallery.

- Chapter 32, "Additional Advanced Topics," introduces you to many of the tools included with Visual C++.

CHAPTER 30

Power-User C++ Features

C++ is an evolving language, and, as such, it frequently undergoes review and improvement. New power features that have been added to C++ in the recent past are exceptions, templates, Run-Time Type Information (RTTI), and namespace support. These are programming issues that will become more and more important to Windows developers. For that reason, learning to implement these new features into your programming projects is a must-do task. ■

How to Catch, Throw, and Define Exception Objects

Exceptions are a better way of handling runtime errors in your programs than using old-fashioned error-handling techniques. If you're not currently using exceptions, you better get on the ball!

About Function Templates

Function templates enable you to create a general blueprint for a function. The compiler can then create the different versions of the function in order to accommodate your program.

How to Create and Use Class Templates

Class templates are similar to function templates, except that they act as a blueprint for classes rather than for functions.

About Run-Time Type Information

Run-Time Type Information (RTTI) adds to C++ the ability to safely downcast polymorphic-object pointers, as well as to get information about objects at runtime.

How to Define and Use Namespaces

Identifier scope can be a hassle when you have to include several external libraries into your project. Namespaces help you avoid identifier-name conflict.

Understanding Exceptions

When you write applications using Visual C++, sooner or later you're going to run into *exceptions*. An exception is a special type of error object that is created when something goes wrong in a program. After Visual C++ creates the exception object, it sends it to your program, an action called *throwing an exception*. It's up to your program to *catch* the exception. You do this by writing the exception-handling code. In this section, you get the inside info on these important error-handling objects.

Simple Exception Handling

The mechanism used by exception-handling code is really pretty simple. You place the source code that you want guarded against errors inside a `try` block. You then construct a `catch` program block that acts as the error handler. If the code in the `try` block (or any code called from the `try` block) generates an exception (called throwing an exception, remember), the `try` block immediately ceases execution and the program continues inside the `catch` block.

For example, memory allocation is one place in a program where you might expect to run into trouble. Listing 30.1 shows a nonsensical little program that allocates some memory and then immediately deletes it. Because memory allocation could fail, the code that allocates the memory is enclosed in a `try` program block. If the pointer returned from the memory allocation is NULL, the `try` block throws an exception. In this case, the exception object is a string.

Listing 30.1   EXCEPTION.CPP—Simple Exception Handling

```cpp
#include <iostream.h>

int main()
{
    int* buffer;
    char* msg[] = {"Memory allocation failed!"};

    try
    {
        buffer = new int[256];

        if (buffer == NULL)
            throw *msg;
        else
            delete buffer;
    }
    catch(char* exception)
    {
        cout << exception << endl;
    }

    return 0;
}
```

When the program throws the exception, program execution jumps to the first line of the catch program block. In the case of Listing 30.1, this line just prints out a message, after which the function's return line is executed and the program ends.

If the memory allocation is successful, the program executes the entire try block, deleting the buffer. Then program execution skips over the catch block completely, in this case going directly to the return statement.

Part
V

Ch
30

NOTE The catch program block does more than direct program execution. It actually catches the exception object thrown by the program. For example, in Listing 30.1, you can see the exception object being caught inside the parentheses following the catch keyword. This is very similar to a parameter being received by a method. In this case, the type of the "parameter" is char* and the name of the parameter is exception. ■

Exception Objects

The beauty of C++ exceptions is that the exception object thrown can be just about any kind of data structure you like. For example, you might want to create an exception class for certain kinds of exceptions that occur in your programs. Listing 30.2 shows a program that defines a general-purpose exception class called CException. In the case of a memory-allocation failure, the main program creates an object of the class and throws it. The catch block catches the CException object, calls the object's GetError() member function to get the object's error string, and then displays the string on the screen.

Listing 30.2 EXCEPTION2.CPP—Creating an Exception Class

```
#include <iostream.h>

class CException
{
protected:
    char* m_msg;

public:
    CException(char *msg)
    {
        m_msg = msg;
    };

    ~CException(){};

    char* GetError()
    {
        return m_msg;
    };
};

int main()
```

continues

Listing 30.2   Continued

```
{
    int* buffer;

    try
    {
        buffer = new int[256];

        if (buffer == NULL)
        {
            CException* exception =
                new CException("Memory allocation failed!");
            throw exception;
        }
        else
            delete buffer;
    }
    catch(CException* exception)
    {
        char* msg = exception->GetError();
        cout << msg << endl;
    }

    return 0;
}
```

An exception object can be as simple as an integer error code or as complex as a fully developed class. Whatever works best for your program is the way to go. You might, for example, want to derive specific types of exception classes from the general exception class developed in Listing 30.2.

Placing the *catch* Block

The catch program block doesn't have to be in the same function as the one in which the exception is thrown. When an exception is thrown, the system starts "unwinding the stack," looking for the nearest catch block. If the catch block is not found in the function that threw the exception, the system looks in the function that called the throwing function. This search continues on up the function-call stack. If the exception is never caught, the program halts.

Listing 30.3 is a short program that demonstrates this concept. The program throws the exception from the AllocateBuffer() function but catches the exception in main(), which is the function from which AllocateBuffer() is called.

Listing 30.3 EXCEPTION3.CPP—Catching Exceptions Outside of the Throwing Function

```cpp
#include <iostream.h>

class CException
{
protected:
    char* m_msg;

public:
    CException(char *msg)
    {
        m_msg = msg;
    };

    ~CException(){};

    char* GetError()
    {
        return m_msg;
    };
};

int* AllocateBuffer()
{
    int* buffer = new int[256];

    if (buffer == NULL)
    {
        CException* exception =
            new CException("Memory allocation failed!");
        throw exception;
    }

    return buffer;
}

int main()
{
    int* buffer;

    try
    {
        buffer = AllocateBuffer();
        delete buffer;
    }
    catch(CException* exception)
    {
        char* msg = exception->GetError();
        cout << msg << endl;
    }

    return 0;
}
```

Handling Multiple Types of Exceptions

Because it's often the case that a block of code generates more than one type of exception, you can use multiple catch blocks with a try block. You might, for example, need to be on the lookout for both CException and char* exceptions. Because a catch block must receive a specific type of exception object (except in a special case that you'll learn about soon), you need two different catch blocks to watch for both CException and char* exception objects.

The special case I referred to in the previous paragraph is a catch block that can receive any type of exception object. You define this type of catch block by placing ellipses in the parentheses, rather than a specific argument. The problem with this sort of multipurpose catch block is that you have no access to the exception object received and so must handle the exception in some general way.

Listing 30.4 is a program that generates three different types of exceptions based on a user's input. When you run the program, you're instructed to enter a value between 4 and 8, except for 6. If you enter a value less than 4, the program throws a CException exception; if you enter a value greater than 8, the program throws a char* exception; and, finally, if you happen to enter 6, the program throws the entered value as an exception.

Although the program throws the exceptions in the GetValue() function, the program catches them all in main(). The try block in main() is associated with three catch blocks. The first catches the CException object, the second catches the char* object, and the third catches any other exception that happens to come down the pike.

N O T E Just as with if-else statements, the order in which you place catch program blocks can have a profound effect on program execution. You should always place the most specific catch blocks first. For example, in Listing 30.4, if the catch(...) block was first, none of the other catch blocks would ever be called. This is because the catch(...) is as general as you can get, catching every single exception that the program throws. In this case (as in most cases), you want to use catch(...) to receive only the leftover exceptions. ■

Listing 30.4   EXCEPTION4.CPP—Using Multiple *catch* Blocks

```cpp
#include <iostream.h>

class CException
{
protected:
    char* m_msg;

public:
    CException(char *msg)
    {
        m_msg = msg;
    };

    ~CException(){};
```

```cpp
    char* GetError()
    {
        return m_msg;
    };
};

int GetValue()
{
    int value;

    cout << "Type a number from 4 to 8 (except 6):" << endl;
    cin >> value;

    if (value < 4)
    {
        CException* exception =
            new CException("Value less than 4!");
        throw exception;
    }
    else if (value > 8)
    {
        throw "Value greater than 8!";
    }
    else if (value == 6)
    {
        throw value;
    }
    return value;
}

int main()
{
    try
    {
        int value = GetValue();
        cout << "The value you entered is okay." << endl;
    }
    catch(CException* exception)
    {
        char* msg = exception->GetError();
        cout << msg << endl;
    }
    catch(char* msg)
    {
        cout << msg << endl;
    }
    catch(...)
    {
        cout << "Caught unknown exception!" << endl;
    }

    return 0;
}
```

N O T E   When your program catches an exception, it has several courses of action at its disposal. It can handle the exception, it can rethrow the exception for handling somewhere else in the program, or it can both handle the exception and rethrow it. To rethrow an exception, use the `throw` keyword with no argument. ■

Exploring Templates

It's my guess that, at one time or another, you wished you could develop a single function or class that could handle any kind of data. Sure, you can use function overloading to write several versions of a function, or you can use inheritance to derive several different classes from a base class. But, in these cases, you still end up writing many different functions or classes. If only there was a way to make functions and classes a little smarter, so that you could write just one that handled any kind of data you wanted to throw at it. Guess what? There is a way to accomplish this seemingly impossible task. You need to use something called *templates*, which are the focus of this section.

Introducing Templates

A template is a kind of blueprint for a function or class. You write the template in a general way, supplying placeholders, called *parameters*, for the data objects that the final function or class will manipulate. A template always begins with the keyword `template` followed by a list of parameters between angle brackets, like this:

```
template<class Type>
```

You can have as many parameters as you need, and you can name them whatever you like, but each must begin with the `class` keyword (in this case, `class` doesn't refer to a C++ class) and must be separated by commas, like this:

```
template<class Type1, class Type2, class Type3>
```

As you may have guessed from the previous discussion, there are two types of templates: function and class. The following sections describe how to create and use both types of templates.

Creating Function Templates

A function template starts with the `template` line you just learned about, followed by the function's declaration, as shown in Listing 30.5. The `template` line specifies the types of arguments that will be used when calling the function, whereas the function's declaration specifies how those arguments are to be received as parameters by the function. Every parameter specified in the `template` line must be used by the function declaration. Notice the `Type1` immediately before the function name. `Type1` is a placeholder for the function's return type, which will vary depending upon how the template is used.

Listing 30.5 LST30_05.TXT—The Basic Form of a Function Template

```
template<class Type1, class Type2>
Type1 MyFunction(Type1 data1, Type1 data2, Type2 data3)
{
    // Place the body of the function here.
}
```

An actual working example will help you understand how function templates become functions. A common example is a `Min()` function that can accept any type of arguments. Listing 30.6 is a short program that defines a template for a `Min()` function and then uses that function in `main()`. When you run the program, the program displays the smallest value of whatever data is sent as arguments to `Min()`. This works because the compiler takes the template and creates functions for each of the data types that are compared in the program.

Listing 30.6 TEMPLATE.CPP—Using a Typical Function Template

```
#include <iostream.h>

template<class Type>
Type Min(Type arg1, Type arg2)
{
    Type min;

    if (arg1 < arg2)
        min = arg1;
    else
        min = arg2;

    return min;
}

int main()
{
    cout << Min(15, 25) << endl;
    cout << Min(254.78, 12.983) << endl;
    cout << Min('A', 'Z') << endl;

    return 0;
}
```

N O T E Notice how, in Listing 30.6, the `Min()` template uses the data type `Type` not only in its parameter list and function argument list, but also in the body of the function, in order to declare a local variable. This illustrates how you can use the parameter types just as you would use any specific data type such as `int` or `char`. ▪

Part
V

Ch
30

Because function templates are so flexible, they can often lead to trouble. For example, in the `Min()` template, you have to be sure that the data types that you supply as parameters can be compared. If you tried to compare two classes, your program would not compile unless the classes overloaded the < and > operators.

Another way you can run into trouble is when the arguments you supply to the template are not used as you think. For example, what if you added the following line to `main()` in Listing 30.6?

```
cout << Min('APPLE', 'ORANGE') << endl;
```

If you don't think about what you're doing in the previous line, you may jump to the conclusion that the returned result will be APPLE. The truth is, however, that the preceding line may or may not give you the result you expect. Why? Because the "APPLE" and "ORANGE" string constants result in pointers to char. This means that the program will compile fine, with the compiler creating a version of `Min()` that compares char pointers. But there's a big difference between comparing two pointers and comparing the data to which the pointers point. If "ORANGE" happens to be stored at a lower address than "APPLE", the preceding call to `Min()` results in "ORANGE".

A way to avoid this problem is to provide a specific replacement function for `Min()` that defines exactly how you want the two string constants compared. When you provide a specific function, the compiler uses that function instead of creating one from the template. Listing 30.7 is a short program that demonstrates this important technique. When the program needs to compare the two strings, it doesn't call a function created from the template but instead uses the specific replacement function.

Listing 30.7   TEMPLATE2.CPP—Using a Specific Replacement Function

```
#include <iostream.h>
#include <string.h>

template<class Type>
Type Min(Type arg1, Type arg2)
{
    Type min;

    if (arg1 < arg2)
        min = arg1;
    else
        min = arg2;

    return min;
}

char* Min(char* arg1, char* arg2)
{
    char* min;

    int result = strcmp(arg1, arg2);
```

```
        if (result < 0)
            min = arg1;
        else
            min = arg2;

        return min;
    }

    int main()
    {
        cout << Min(15, 25) << endl;
        cout << Min(254.78, 12.983) << endl;
        cout << Min('A', 'Z') << endl;
        cout << Min("APPLE", "ORANGE") << endl;

        return 0;
    }
```

Part
V

Ch
30

Creating Class Templates

Just as you can create abstract functions with function templates, so too can you create abstract classes with class templates. A class template represents a class, which in turn represents an object. When you define a class template, the compiler takes the template and creates a class. You then instantiate objects of the class. As you can see, class templates add another layer of abstraction to the concept of classes.

You define a class template much as you define a function template, by supplying the `template` line followed by the class's declaration, as shown in Listing 30.8. Notice that, just as with a function template, you use the abstract data types given as parameters in the `template` line in the body of the class in order to define member variables, return types, and other data objects.

Listing 30.8   LST30_08.TX—Defining a Class Template

```
template<class Type>
class CMyClass
{
protected:
    Type arg;

public:
    CMyClass(Type arg)
    {
        CMyClass::arg = arg;
    }

    ~CMyClass() {};
};
```

When you're ready to instantiate objects from the template class, you must supply the data type that'll replace the template parameters. For example, to create an object of the CMyClass class, you might use a line like this:

```
CMyClass<int> myClass(15);
```

The previous line creates a CMyClass object that uses integers in place of the abstract data type. If you wanted the class to deal with floating-point values, you'd create an object of the class something like this:

```
CMyClass<float> myClass(15.75);
```

For a more complete example, suppose that you want to create a class that stores two values and that has member functions that compare those values. Listing 30.9 is a program that does just that. First, the listing defines a class template called CCompare. This class stores two values that are supplied to the constructor. The class also includes the usual constructor and destructor, as well as member functions for determining the larger or smaller of the values, or to determine whether the values are equal.

Listing 30.9   TEMPLATE3.CPP—Using a Class Template

```
#include <iostream.h>

template<class Type>
class CCompare
{
protected:
    Type arg1;
    Type arg2;

public:
    CCompare(Type arg1, Type arg2)
    {
        CCompare::arg1 = arg1;
        CCompare::arg2 = arg2;
    }

    ~CCompare() {}

    Type GetMin()
    {
        Type min;

        if (arg1 < arg2)
            min = arg1;
        else
            min = arg2;

        return min;
    }

    Type GetMax()
    {
```

```
        Type max;

        if (arg1 > arg2)
            max = arg1;
        else
            max = arg2;

        return max;
    }

    int Equal()
    {
        int equal;

        if (arg1 == arg2)
            equal = 1;
        else
            equal = 0;

        return equal;
    }
};

int main()
{
    CCompare<int> compare1(15, 25);
    CCompare<double> compare2(254.78, 12.983);
    CCompare<char> compare3('A', 'Z');

    cout << "THE COMPARE1 OBJECT" << endl;
    cout << "Lowest: " << compare1.GetMin() << endl;
    cout << "Highest: " << compare1.GetMax() << endl;
    cout << "Equal: " << compare1.Equal() << endl;
    cout << endl;

    cout << "THE COMPARE2 OBJECT" << endl;
    cout << "Lowest: " << compare2.GetMin() << endl;
    cout << "Highest: " << compare2.GetMax() << endl;
    cout << "Equal: " << compare2.Equal() << endl;
    cout << endl;

    cout << "THE COMPARE2 OBJECT" << endl;
    cout << "Lowest: " << compare3.GetMin() << endl;
    cout << "Highest: " << compare3.GetMax() << endl;
    cout << "Equal: " << compare3.Equal() << endl;
    cout << endl;

    return 0;
}
```

The main program instantiates three objects from the class template, one that deals with integers, one that uses floating-point values, and one that stores and compares character values. After creating the three CCompare objects, main() calls the objects' member functions in order to display information about the data stored in each object. Figure 30.1 shows the program's output.

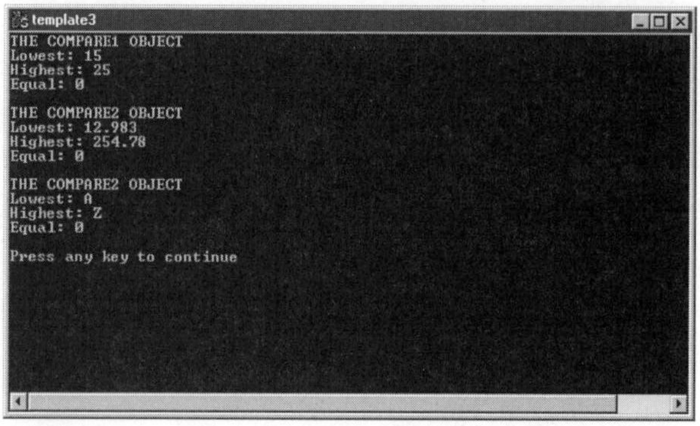

FIG. 30.1

The Template3 program creates three different objects from a class template.

You can, of course, pass as many parameters as you like to a class template, just as you can with a function template. Listing 30.10 shows a class template that uses two different types of data.

Listing 30.10 LST30_10.TXT—Using Multiple Parameters with a Class Template

```
template<class Type1, class Type2>
class CMyClass
{
protected:
    Type1 arg1;
    Type2 arg2;

public:
    CMyClass(Type1 arg1, Type2 arg2)
    {
        CMyClass::arg1 = arg1;
        CMyClass::arg2 = arg2;
    }

    ~CMyClass() {}
};
```

To instantiate an object of the CMyClass class, you might use a line like this:

```
CMyClass<int, char> myClass(15, 'A');
```

Finally, you can use specific data types, as well as the placeholder data types, as parameters in a class template. You just add the specific data type to the parameter list, just as you add any other parameter. Listing 30.11 is a short program that creates an object from a class template that uses two abstract parameters and one specific data type.

Listing 30.11 TEMPLATE4.CPP—Using Specific Data Types as Parameters in a Class Template

```
#include <iostream.h>

template<class Type1, class Type2, int num>
class CMyClass
{
protected:
    Type1 arg1;
    Type2 arg2;
    int num;

public:
    CMyClass(Type1 arg1, Type2 arg2, int num)
    {
        CMyClass::arg1 = arg1;
        CMyClass::arg2 = arg2;
        CMyClass::num = num;
    }

    ~CMyClass() {}
};

int main()
{
    CMyClass<int, char, 0> myClass(15, 'A', 10);

    return 0;
}
```

Using Run-Time Type Information

Run-Time Type Information (RTTI) was added to C++ so that programmers could obtain information about objects at runtime. This ability is especially useful when you're dealing with polymorphic objects, because it enables your program to determine at runtime what exact type of object it's currently working with. Later in this section, you'll see how important this type of information can be when you're working with class hierarchies. RTTI can also be used to safely downcast an object pointer. In this section, you'll discover how RTTI works and why you'd want to use it.

Introducing RTTI

The RTTI standard introduces three new elements to the C++ language. The dynamic_cast operator performs downcasting of polymorphic objects; the typeid operator retrieves information (in the form of a `type_info` object) about an object; and the `type_info` class stores information about an object, providing member functions that can be used to extract that information.

The public portion of the `type_info` class is defined in Visual C++ as shown in Listing 30.12.

Listing 30.12   LST30_12.TXT—The *type_info* Class

```
class type_info {
public:
     virtual ~type_info();
     int operator==(const type_info& rhs) const;
     int operator!=(const type_info& rhs) const;
     int before(const type_info& rhs) const;
     const char* name() const;
     const char* raw_name() const;
};
```

As you can see, the class provides member functions that can compare objects for equality, as well as return the object's name, both as a readable text string and as a raw decorated object name. The `before()` member function remains a bit mysterious and poorly documented. According to Microsoft, the Visual C++ implementation of `before()` is used "to determine the collating sequence of types." Microsoft further states that "there is no link between the collating order of types and inheritance relationships."

Performing Safe Downcasts

Once you start writing a lot of OOP programs, you'll run into times when you need to downcast one type of object to another. *Downcasting* is the act of converting a base-class pointer to a derived-class pointer (a *derived class* being a class that's derived from the base class). You use `dynamic_cast` to downcast an object, like this:

```
Type* ptr = dynamic_cast<Type*>(Pointer);
```

In the preceding example, `Type` is the type to which the object should be cast, and `Pointer` is a pointer to the object. If the pointer cannot be safely downcast, the `dynamic_cast` operator returns 0.

Suppose, for example, that you have a base class called `CBase` and a class derived from `CBase` called `CDerived`. Because you want to take advantage of polymorphism, you obtained a pointer to `CDerived`, like this:

```
CBase* derived = new CDerived;
```

Notice that, although you're creating a `CDerived` object, the pointer is of the base-class type, `CBase`. This is a typical scenario in programs that take advantage of OOP polymorphism.

Now suppose that you want to safely downcast the `CBase` pointer to a `CDerived` pointer. You might use `dynamic_cast`, as follows:

```
CDerived* ptr = dynamic_cast<CDerived*>(derived);
```

If `ptr` gets a value of 0, the downcast was not allowed.

Getting Object Information

As I mentioned previously, you can use the `typeid` operator to obtain information about an object. Although the `dynamic_cast` operator applies only to polymorphic objects, you can use `typeid` on any type of data object. For example, to get information about the `int` data object, you could use lines like these:

```
const type_info& ti = typeid(int);
cout << ti.name();
```

In the first line, you can see that the `typeid` operator returns a reference to a `type_info` object. You can then use the object's member functions to extract information about the data object. In the preceding example, the `cout` object will output the word `int`. The `typeid` operator's single argument is the name of the data object for which you want a `type_info` object.

Of course, a better use for `typeid` is to compare and get information about classes that you have defined in your program. Listing 30.13 is a short program that prints out information about the classes it defines.

Listing 30.13 RTTI.CPP—Using the *typeid* Operator

```
#include <iostream.h>
#include <typeinfo.h>

class CBase
{
public:
    CBase() {};
    ~CBase() {};
};

class CDerived : public CBase
{
public:
    CDerived() {};
    ~CDerived() {};
};

int main()
{
    CBase* base = new CBase;
    CBase* derived = new CDerived;

    const type_info& ti1 = typeid(CBase);
    const type_info& ti2 = typeid(CDerived);

    cout << "First object's name: " << ti1.name() << endl;
    cout << "First object's raw name: " << ti1.raw_name() << endl;
```

continues

Part

V

Ch

30

Listing 30.13   Continued

```
    cout << endl;

    cout << "Second object's name: " << ti2.name() << endl;
    cout << "Second object's raw name: " << ti2.raw_name() << endl;
    cout << endl;

    if (ti1 == ti2)
        cout << "The two objects are equal." << endl;
    else
        cout << "The two objects are not equal." << endl;

    cout << endl;

    delete base;
    delete derived;

    return 0;
}
```

Listing 30.13 first defines a base class called CBase. The program then derives a second class, called CDerived, from the base class. In main(), the program instantiates an object from each class, the objects being called base and derived. Then the program calls typeid to obtain type_info objects for each class. Finally, the program calls the type_info member functions to extract information about the classes, as well as to compare the classes for equality. Figure 30.2 shows the program's output. If you have trouble running the RTTI program shown in Listing 30.13, jump ahead to the next section, which tells you how to enable RTTI.

FIG. 30.2

This is Listing 30.13 in action.

Preparing to Use RTTI

If you got a strange error message or warning when you tried to compile the RTTI program, you probably don't yet have RTTI enabled. To enable RTTI, follow the procedure below:

1. Select the Build, Settings command from Developer Studio's menu bar. The Project Settings dialog box appears (Figure 30.3).

FIG. 30.3

The Project Settings dialog box.

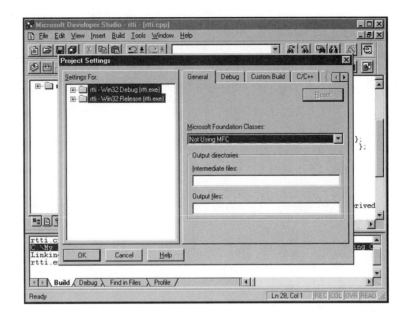

2. Click the C/C++ tab. The C/C++ setting-options page appears, as shown in Figure 30.4.

FIG. 30.4

The C/C++ options page.

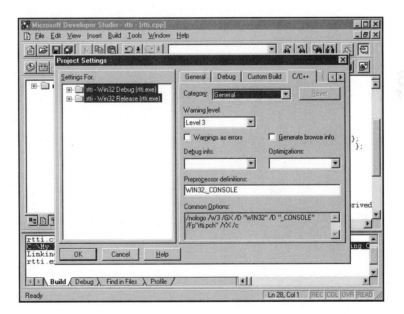

3. In the Category box, select the C++ Language item. The C++ language options appear (Figure 30.5).

FIG. 30.5

The C++ language options.

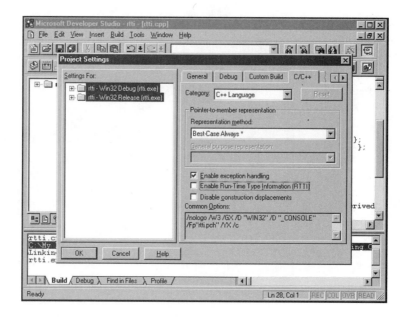

4. Select the Enable Run-Time Type Information (RTTI) option and then click OK to finalize your choices.

Also, be sure that you include the TYPEID.H header file in any source-code file that calls the `typeid` operator. If you fail to do this, your program will not compile.

A Common Use for RTTI

All of the previous discussion is okay from a nuts-and-bolts perspective, but why would you want to use RTTI in the first place? When you're writing programs that incorporate polymorphic objects, RTTI comes in handy. To see why, first take a look at Listing 30.14, which is a program that uses a simple case of polymorphism. The program defines two classes. The CBase class acts as the base class for the second class, CDerived. That is, CDerived is derived from CBase. In addition, CDerived overrides CBase's two virtual functions so that the functions perform as is appropriate for a Derived object.

Listing 30.14 RTTI2.CPP—A Typical Case of Class Derivation

```
#include <iostream.h>
#include <typeinfo.h>

class CBase
{
public:
    CBase() {};
    ~CBase() {};

    virtual char* Func1() { return "CBase Func1()";};
```

```
        virtual char* Func2() { return "CBase Func2()"; };
};

class CDerived : public CBase
{
public:
    CDerived() {};
    ~CDerived() {};

    char* Func1() { return "CDerived Func1()";};
    char* Func2() { return "CDerived Func2()"; };
};

int main()
{
    CBase* base = new CBase;
    CBase* derived = new CDerived;

    cout << base->Func1() << endl;
    cout << base->Func2() << endl;
    cout << endl;

    cout << derived->Func1() << endl;
    cout << derived->Func2() << endl;
    cout << endl;

    delete base;
    delete derived;

    return 0;
}
```

In main(), the program creates an object from each class. But notice how pointers to both objects are of the CBase type. This is how polymorphism works. Although both pointers are of the CBase type, when the pointers are used to call the polymorphic Func1() and Func2() functions, the correct versions of the functions are called for the object type. You can tell from the program output, shown in Figure 30.6, that this is true. You've just witnessed polymorphism in action. Although both pointers are of the base-class type, the program automatically knows which set of member functions to call.

Now suppose that the CBase class's Func2() member function was not virtual, but you still wanted to override the function in a derived class. As long as you're using pointers to the specific class types—that is, the derived class's pointer is of the derived class's type rather than of the base class's type—you won't have any problem overriding the function. But what if you're still using polymorphism in the program? Then, when you try to call the derived object's Func2() member function, the base class's Func2() gets called instead. That keyword virtual sure makes a big difference, eh?

The solution to this dilemma is to use RTTI casting when needed to downcast the class pointers when you need to be sure that the derived class's version of the function is called rather than the base class's. Listing 30.15 is a program that demonstrates how this works. As in

Listing 30.14, this program defines the CBase and CDerived classes. However, in this case, we've removed the virtual keyword from CBase's Func2() member function. In other words, Func2() is no longer a polymorphic function.

FIG. 30.6

Listing 30.14's output demonstrates polymorphism in action.

Listing 30.15 RTTI3.CPP—Using Casting

```cpp
#include <iostream.h>
#include <typeinfo.h>

class CBase
{
public:
    CBase() {};
    ~CBase() {};

    virtual char* Func1() { return "CBase Func1()";};
    char* Func2() { return "CBase Func2()"; };
};

class CDerived : public CBase
{
public:
    CDerived() {};
    ~CDerived() {};

    char* Func1() { return "CDerived Func1()";};
    char* Func2() { return "CDerived Func2()"; };
};

int main()
{
    CBase* base = new CBase;
    CBase* derived = new CDerived;

    cout << base->Func1() << endl;
    cout << base->Func2() << endl;
    cout << endl;
```

```
        cout << "BEFORE CAST:" << endl;
        cout << derived->Func1() << endl;
        cout << derived->Func2() << endl;
        cout << endl;

        CDerived* ptr = dynamic_cast<CDerived*>(derived);

        cout << "AFTER CAST: " << endl;
        cout << ptr->Func1() << endl;
        cout << ptr->Func2() << endl;
        cout << endl;

        delete base;
        delete derived;

        return 0;
    }
```

In `main()`, the program instantiates objects from both the CBase and CDerived classes, with the pointers to these objects both being of the CBase type. Figure 30.7 shows the program's output. When the program tries to call the `derived` object's `Func2()` through the CBase pointer, it gets CBase's `Func2()`. Because the base class's `Func2()` is no longer virtual, polymorphism fails to operate. (`Func1()` is still virtual, so it performs just fine, thank you.) However, after using the `dynamic_cast` operator on the `derived` object in order to cast the pointer to the CDerived type, the call to `Func2()` works properly.

FIG. 30.7

This version of the program must downcast a pointer to get the results you want.

Of course, in the case of Listing 30.15, you might as well just go ahead and ignore polymorphism completely, using the specific pointer types in the first place rather than downcasting a pointer later in the program. What happens, though, when you have an array of objects that you want to process in a loop? All of the pointers in the array have to be of the same type, but you need to know when to call the nonvirtual `Func2()` for the derived object.

You can do this by using dynamic_cast to downcast the pointer. If the downcast is successful, you have a CBase pointer that points to a CDerived object and must call that object's specific Func2(). If, however, the downcast fails, you have a CBase pointer that points to a CBase object.

Listing 30.16 is a program that demonstrates how this process works. The program creates an array of CBase pointers, one of which actually points to an object of the CDerived class. In the first for loop, the program processes the pointer array without concern for the object that each pointer represents. As you can see in the program's output (Figure 30.8), when it comes time to call the CDerived object's Func2(), the CBase class's Func2() gets called instead. However, in the second for loop, before calling Func2(), the program attempts to cast the pointer in the array to a pointer of the CDerived type. If the cast succeeds (ptr doesn't equal 0), the program must call Func2() through the new pointer in order to ensure that the correct version of the function is called. If the cast fails, the program calls Func2() through the original pointer.

Listing 30.16   RTTI4.CPP—A Final Example of RTTI Downcasting

```cpp
#include <iostream.h>

class CBase
{
public:
    CBase() {};
    ~CBase() {};

    virtual char* Func1() { return "CBase Func1()";};
    char* Func2() { return "CBase Func2()"; };
};

class CDerived : public CBase
{
public:
    CDerived() {};
    ~CDerived() {};

    char* Func1() { return "CDerived Func1()";};
    char* Func2() { return "CDerived Func2()"; };
};

int main()
{
    int x;
    CBase* ptrs[3];

    ptrs[0] = new CBase;
    ptrs[1] = new CBase;
    ptrs[2] = new CDerived;

    cout << "WITHOUT RTTI DOWNCASTING:" << endl;

    for (x=0; x<3; ++x)
    {
        cout << ptrs[x]->Func1() << endl;
```

```
            cout << ptrs[x]->Func2() << endl;
            cout << endl;
        }


    cout << "WITH RTTI DOWNCASTING:" << endl;

    for (x=0; x<3; ++x)
    {
        cout << ptrs[x]->Func1() << endl;

        CDerived* ptr = dynamic_cast<CDerived*>(ptrs[x]);

        if (ptr)
            cout << ptr->Func2() << endl;
        else
            cout << ptrs[x]->Func2() << endl;

        cout << endl;

        delete ptrs[x];
    }


    return 0;
}
```

FIG. 30.8
This is a run of Listing
30.16.

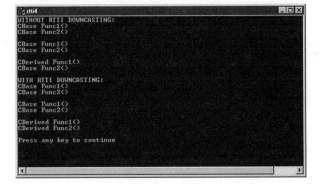

Namespaces

Every programmer is already familiar with the concept of *namespaces*. Basically, a namespace defines a scope in which duplicate identifiers cannot be used. For example, you already know that you can have a global variable named `value` and then also define a function with a local variable called `value`. Because the two variables are in different namespaces, your program knows that it should use the local `value` when inside the function and the global `value` everywhere else.

Namespaces, however, do not extend far enough to cover some very thorny problems. One example is duplicate names in external classes or libraries. This issue crops up when a programmer is using several external files within a single project. None of the external variables and functions can have the same name as other external variables or functions. To avoid this type of problem, third-party vendors frequently add prefixes or suffixes to variable and function names in order to reduce the likeliness of some other vendor's using the same name.

Obviously, the C++ gurus have come up with a solution to such scope-resolution problems. Otherwise, we wouldn't be having this discussion! The solution is user-defined namespaces, about which you'll study in this section.

Defining a Namespace

To accommodate user-defined namespaces, the keyword namespace was added to the C++ language. In its simplest form, a namespace is not unlike a structure or a class. You start the namespace definition with the namespace keyword, followed by the namespace's name and the declaration of the identifiers that'll be valid within the scope of that namespace.

Listing 30.17 shows a namespace definition. The namespace is called A and includes two identifiers, i, and j, and a function, Func(). Notice that the Func() function is completely defined within the namespace definition. You can also choose to define the function outside of the namespace definition, but in that case, you must prefix the function definition's name with the namespace's name, much as you would prefix a class's member-function definition with the class's name. Listing 30.18 shows this form of namespace function definition.

Listing 30.17   LST30_17.TXT—Defining a Namespace

```
namespace A
{
    int i;
    int j;

    int Func()
    {
        return 1;
    }
}
```

Listing 30.18   LST30_18.TXT—Defining a Function Outside of the Namespace Definition

```
namespace A
{
    int i;
    int j;

    int Func();
}
```

```
int A::Func()
{
    return 1;
}
```

N O T E Namespaces must be defined at the file level of scope or within another namespace
definition. They cannot be defined, for example, inside of a function. ■

Namespace Scope Resolution

Namespaces add a new layer of scope to your programs, but this means that you need some
way of identifying that scope. The identification is, of course, the namespace's name, which you
must use in your programs to resolve references to identifiers. For example, to refer to the
variable i in namespace A, you'd write something like this:

```
A::i = 0;
```

You can, if you like, nest one namespace definition within another, as shown in Listing 30.19. In
the case shown in the listing, however, you have to use more complicated scope resolutions in
order to differentiate between the i variable declared in A and B, like this:

```
A::i = 0;
A::B::i = 0;
```

Listing 30.19 LST30_19.TXT—Nesting Namespace Definitions

```
namespace A
{
    int i;
    int j;

    int Func()
    {
        return 1;
    }

    namespace B
    {
        int i;
    }
}
```

If you're going to frequently reference variables and functions within namespace A, you can
avoid using the A:: resolution by preceding the program statements with a using line, as
shown in Listing 30.20.

Listing 30.20   LDT30_20.TXT—Resolving Scope with the *using* Keyword

```
using namespace A;
i = 0;
j = 0;
int num1 = Func();
```

Unnamed Namespaces

Just to be sure that you're thoroughly confused, Visual C++ allows you to have unnamed namespaces. You define an unnamed namespace exactly as you would any other namespace, except you leave off the name. Listing 30.21 shows the definition of an unnamed namespace.

Listing 30.21   LST30_21.TXT—Defining an Unnamed Namespace

```
namespace
{
    int i;
    int j;

    int Func()
    {
        return 1;
    }
}
```

You refer to the identifiers in the unnamed namespace without any sort of extra scope resolution, like this:

```
i = 0;
j = 0;
int num1 = Func();
```

Namespace Aliases

There may be times when you run into namespaces that have long names. In these cases, having to use that long name over and over in your program in order to access the identifiers defined in the namespace can be a major chore. To solve this problem, Visual C++ enables you to create *namespace aliases*, which are just replacement names for a namespace. You create an alias like this:

```
namespace A = LongName;
```

In the previous line of code, LongName is the original name of the namespace, and A is the alias. After the preceding line executes, you can access the LongName namespace using either A or LongName. You can think of an alias as a nickname. If your name is Robert, you probably respond to Bob, too, right? Listing 30.22 is a short program that demonstrates namespace aliases.

Listing 30.22 NAMESPACE.CPP—Using a Namespace Alias

```
namespace ThisIsANamespaceName
{
    int i;
    int j;

    int Func()
    {
        return 2;
    }
}

int main()
{
    namespace ns = ThisIsANamespaceName;

    ns::i = 0;
    ns::j = 0;
    int num1 = ns::Func();

    return 0;
}
```

Part
V

Ch
30

From Here...

You've covered a lot of ground in this chapter, all of it dealing with advanced programming techniques. If you feel a little disoriented, read a comic book, and then come back for another pass at this chapter. The techniques covered here, although fairly new to C++ programming, are rapidly becoming must-know techniques for all C++ programmers. Exceptions and templates, especially, are things that you'll run into often when you examine other programmers' code—or, more importantly, when you apply for that programmer's job.

For more information on related topics, please refer to the following chapters:

■ Chapter 10, "Utility and Collection Classes," describes some MFC classes that are implemented through templates.

■ Chapter 20, "Debugging," helps you find those pesky errors that produce exceptions in your programs.

■ Chapter 29, "Power-User Features in Developer Studio," offers advanced tips for customizing your Developer Studio projects.

■ Chapter 31, "Multitasking with Windows Threads," describes even more advanced C++ Windows programming techniques.

Multitasking with Windows Threads

When using Windows 95 (and other modern operating systems), you know that you can run several programs simultaneously. This ability is called *multitasking*. What you may not know is that many of today's operating systems also allow *threads,* which are separate processes that are kind of a step down from a complete application. A thread is a lot like a subprogram. An application can create several threads—several different flows of execution—and run them concurrently. Threads give you the ability to have multitasking inside multitasking. The user knows that he or she can run several applications at a time. The programmer knows that each application can run several threads at a time. In this chapter, you'll learn how to create and manage threads in your applications. ▪

How to Create and Run Threads

Writing a thread and getting it started is easy under MFC. In fact, one function call is all it takes to get your thread running.

About Inter-Thread Communication

Although threads are like self-contained subprograms, they still need to communicate with other threads, including the main program. There are several ways of doing this; the best are Windows messages and event objects.

About Synchronizing Threads with Critical Sections

You often have to ensure that data can be accessed by only one thread at a time. Critical sections help you accomplish this type of data protection.

How to Use Mutexes to Synchronize Threads

Mutexes are a lot like critical sections in that they enable you to guard data against thread corruption.

About Using Semaphores to Manage Multiple Resource Accesses

Semaphores count the number of threads that are accessing a resource and limit accesses to a given maximum of threads.

Understanding Simple Threads

When you come right down to it, a thread is little more than a function that the system runs concurrently with the main program. That is, to create a thread using MFC, all you have to do is write a function that represents the thread and then call `AfxBeginThread()` to start the thread. The thread remains active as long as the thread's function is executing. When the thread function exits, the thread is destroyed. A simple call to `AfxBeginThread()` looks like this:

```
AfxBeginThread(ProcName, param, priority);
```

In the previous line, `ProcName` is the name of the thread's function, `param` is any 32-bit value you want to pass to the thread, and `priority` is the thread's priority, which is represented by a number of predefined constants. Those constants and their descriptions are shown in Table 31.1.

Table 31.1   Thread Priority Constants

Constant	Description
THREAD_PRIORITY_ABOVE_NORMAL	Sets a priority one point higher than normal.
THREAD_PRIORITY_BELOW_NORMAL	Sets a priority one point lower than normal.
THREAD_PRIORITY_HIGHEST	Sets a priority two points above normal.
THREAD_PRIORITY_IDLE	Sets a base priority of 1. For a REALTIME_PRIORITY_CLASS process, sets a priority of 16.
THREAD_PRIORITY_LOWEST	Sets a priority two points below normal.
THREAD_PRIORITY_NORMAL	Sets normal priority.
THREAD_PRIORITY_TIME_CRITICAL	Sets a base priority of 15. For a REALTIME_PRIORITY_CLASS process, sets a priority of 30.

N O T E   A thread's priority determines how often the thread takes control of the system relative to the other running threads. Generally, the higher the priority, the more running time the thread gets, which is why the value of THREAD_PRIORITY_TIME_CRITICAL is so high. ▣

In order to see a simple thread in action, build the Thread application as detailed in the following steps.

1. Start a new AppWizard project workspace called Thread, as shown in Figure 31.1.

FIG. 31.1

Start an AppWizard
project workspace
called Thread.

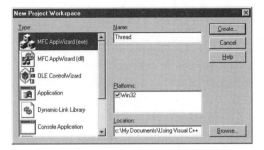

2. Give the new project the following settings in the AppWizard dialog boxes. The New
   Project Information dialog box should then look like Figure 31.2.

   Step 1: Single document

   Step 2: Default settings

   Step 3: Default settings

   Step 4: Turn off all options

   Step 5: Default settings

   Step 6: Default settings

FIG. 31.2

These are the
AppWizard settings for
the Thread project.

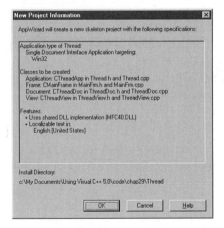

3. Use the resource editor to add a Thread menu to the application's menu bar. Give the
   menu one command called Start Thread with a command ID of ID_STARTTHREAD, as
   shown in Figure 31.3.

Part

V

Ch

31

FIG. 31.3
Add a Thread menu
with a Start Thread
command.

4. Use ClassWizard to associate the ID_STARTTHREAD command with the OnStartthread()
   message-response function, as shown in Figure 31.4. Make sure that you have
   CThreadView selected in the Class Name box before you add the function.

FIG. 31.4
Add the *OnStartthread()*
message-response
function to the view
class.

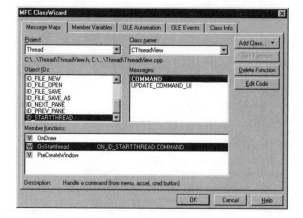

5. Click the Edit Code button and then add the following lines to the new OnStartthread()
   function, right after the TODO: Add your command handler code here comment:

```
HWND hWnd = GetSafeHwnd();
AfxBeginThread(ThreadProc, hWnd, THREAD_PRIORITY_NORMAL);
```

6. Add the function shown in Listing 31.1 to the program, being sure to place it right before
   the OnStartthread() function. Note that ThreadProc() is a global function and not a
   member function of the CThreadView class, even though it's placed in the view class's
   implementation file.

Listing 31.1   LST31_01.TXT—The *ThreadProc()* Function

```
UINT ThreadProc(LPVOID param)
{
    ::MessageBox((HWND)param, "Thread activated.", "Thread", MB_OK);

    return 0;
}
```

When you run the Thread program, the main window appears. Select the Thread, Start Thread command, and the system starts the thread represented by the `ThreadProc()` function and displays a message box, as shown in Figure 31.5.

FIG. 31.5

The simple secondary thread in the Thread program displays a message box and then ends.

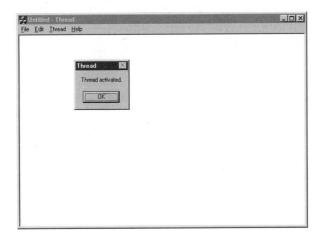

If you examine the Thread program's source code, you'll see that when you select the Thread, Start Thread command, MFC calls the `OnStartthread()` function, which starts the secondary thread with this line:

```
AfxBeginThread(ThreadProc, hWnd, THREAD_PRIORITY_NORMAL);
```

The function's first argument indicates that the thread is represented by the `ThreadProc()` function. That is, to start the thread, the system calls `ThreadProc()` and runs `ThreadProc()` concurrently with the program's main thread, almost as if `ThreadProc()` were a completely separate program. The second argument in the preceding call to `AfxBeginThread()` is the application's main window handle, and the third argument is the requested thread priority. Because the `ThreadProc()` thread has no critical processor time-sharing needs, the priority is set to a normal setting.

N O T E Any application always has at least one thread, which is the program's primary or main thread. You can start and stop as many additional threads as you need, but the main thread keeps running as long as the application is active. ■

Understanding Thread Communication

Usually, a secondary thread performs some sort of task for the main program, which implies that there needs to be a channel of communication between the program (which is also a thread) and its secondary threads. There are several ways to accomplish these communications tasks: using global variables, using event objects, and using messages. In this section, you'll explore these thread-communication techniques.

Communicating with Global Variables

Suppose you want your main program to be able to stop the thread. You need a way, then, to tell the thread when to stop. One way to do this would be to set up a global variable and then have the thread monitor the global variable for a value that signals the thread to end. To see how this technique works, perform the following steps to modify the Thread application.

1. Use the resource editor to add a Stop Thread command to the application's Thread menu. Give this new command the ID_STOPTHREAD ID, as shown in Figure 31.6.

FIG. 31.6
Add a Stop Thread command to the Thread menu.

2. Use ClassWizard to associate the ID_STOPTHREAD command with the OnStopthread() message-response function, as shown in Figure 31.7. Make sure that you have CThreadView selected in the Class Name box before you add the function.

FIG. 31.7
Add the *OnStopthread()* message-response function.

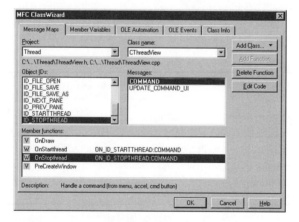

3. Add the following line to the OnStopthread() function, right after the TODO: Add your command handler code here comment:

   ```
   threadController = 0;
   ```

4. Add the following line to the top of the ThreadView.cpp file, right after the endif directive:

   ```
   volatile int threadController;
   ```

5. Add the following line to the OnStartthread() function, right after the TODO: Add your command handler code here comment:

   ```
   threadController = 1;
   ```

6. Replace the `ThreadProc()` function with the one shown in Listing 31.2.

Listing 31.2   LST31_2.TXT—The New *ThreadProc()* Function

```
UINT ThreadProc(LPVOID param)
{
    ::MessageBox((HWND)param, "Thread activated.", "Thread", MB_OK);

    while (threadController == 1);

    ::MessageBox((HWND)param, "Thread stopped.", "Thread", MB_OK);

    return 0;
}
```

Part

V

Ch

31

When you run the program, select the Thread, Start Thread command to start the secondary thread. When you do, a message box appears telling you that the new thread was started. To stop the thread, select the Thread, Stop Thread command. Again, a message box appears, this time telling you that the thread is stopping.

The main program communicates with the thread through the global variable `threadController`. Before starting the thread, the main program sets this variable to 1, which indicates to the thread that it should continue to run. After setting the variable, the main program starts the thread, which is represented by the `ThreadProc()` function.

In `ThreadProc()`, the thread first displays a message box, telling the user that the thread is starting. Then a `while` loop continues to poll the `threadController` global variable, waiting for its value to change to 0. Although this `while` loop is trivial, it is here that you would place the code that performs whatever task you want the thread to perform, being sure not to tie things up for too long before rechecking the value of `threadController`.

When the user selects the Thread, Stop Thread command, MFC calls the `OnStopthread()` function, where the main program sets `threadController` to 0. This action causes the thread function to exit its `while` loop, after which it displays the final message box and exits.

CAUTION

Using global variables to communicate between threads is, to say the least, an unsophisticated approach to thread communication and can be a dangerous technique if you're not sure how C++ handles variables from an assembly-language level. Other thread-communication techniques are safer and more elegant.

Communicating with User-Defined Messages

Now you have a simple, albeit unsophisticated, method for communicating information from your main program to your thread. How about the reverse? That is, how can your thread communicate with the main program? The easiest method to accomplish this communication is to incorporate user-defined Windows messages into the program.

The first step is to define a user message, which you can do easily, like this:

```
const WM_USERMSG = WM_USER + 100;
```

The WM_USER constant, defined by Windows, holds the first available user-message number. Because MFC may use some of the user messages for its own purposes, the preceding line sets WM_USERMSG to WM_USER+100.

After defining the message, you call ::PostMessage() from the thread in order to send the message to the main program whenever you need to. Such a code line might look like this:

```
::PostMessage((HWND)param, WM_USERMSG, 0, 0);
```

PostMessage()'s four arguments are the handle of the window to which the message should be sent, the message identifier, and the message's WPARAM and LPARAM parameters.

T I P The double colons in front of a function name indicate a call to a Windows API function, rather than an MFC class member function. You can use the colons to force the program to call an original Windows function rather than the one defined in an MFC class. For example, inside an MFC window class, you can call MessageBox("Hi, There!") to display "Hi, There!" to the user. This form of Message Box() is a member function of the MFC window classes. To call the original Windows version , you'd write something like ::MessageBox(0, "Hi, There!", "Message", MB_OK). Notice the colons in front of the function name (not to mention the additional function arguments).

Modify the Thread application according to the next steps in order to see how to implement posting user messages from a thread.

1. Add the following line to the top of the ThreadView.h header file, right before the beginning of the class declaration:

   ```
   const WM_THREADENDED = WM_USER + 100;
   ```

2. Still in the header file, add the following line to the class's Implementation section, right after the protected keyword:

   ```
   afx_msg LONG OnThreadended(WPARAM wParam, LPARAM lParam);
   ```

3. Load the ThreadView.cpp file and then add the following line to the class's message map, making sure to place it right *after* the }}AFX_MSG_MAP comment:

   ```
   ON_MESSAGE(WM_THREADENDED, OnThreadended)
   ```

4. Replace the ThreadProc() function with the one shown in Listing 31.3:

Listing 31.3   LST31_03.TXT—The New *ThreadProc()* Function

```
UINT ThreadProc(LPVOID param)
{
    ::MessageBox((HWND)param, "Thread activated.", "Thread", MB_OK);

    while (threadController == 1);
```

```
    ::PostMessage((HWND)param, WM_THREADENDED, 0, 0);

    return 0;
}
```

5. Add the function shown in Listing 31.4 to the end of the `ThreadView.cpp` file.

Listing 31.4 LST31_04.TXT—The *OnThreadended()* Function

```
LONG CThreadView::OnThreadended(WPARAM wParam, LPARAM lParam)
{
    MessageBox("Thread ended.");
    return 0;
}
```

When you run the new version of the Thread program, select the Thread, Start Thread command to start the thread. When you do, a message box appears telling you that the thread has started. To end the thread, select the Thread, Stop Thread command. Just as with the previous version of the program, a message box appears, telling you that the thread has ended.

Although this version of the Thread application seems to run identically to the previous version, there's a subtle difference. Now the program displays the message box that signals the end of the thread in the main program rather than from inside the thread. The program can do this because, when the user selects the Stop Thread command, the thread sends a WM_THREADENDED message to the main program. When the program receives that message, it displays the final message box.

Communicating with Event Objects

A slightly more sophisticated method of signaling between threads is to use *event objects,* which under MFC are represented by the CEvent class. An event object can be in one of two states: signaled and nonsignaled. Threads can watch for events to be signaled and so perform their operations at the appropriate time. Creating an event object is as easy as declaring a global variable, like this:

```
CEvent threadStart;
```

Although the CEvent constructor has a number of optional arguments, you can usually get away with creating the default object, as shown in the previous line of code. Upon creation, the event object is automatically in its nonsignaled state. To signal the event, you call the event object's SetEvent() member function, like this:

```
threadStart.SetEvent();
```

After the preceding line executes, the threadStart event object will be in its signaled state. Your thread should be watching for this signal, so that the thread knows it's okay to get to work. How does a thread watch for a signal? By calling the Windows API function, `WaitForSingleObject()`:

```
::WaitForSingleObject(threadStart.m_hObject, INFINITE);
```

This function's two arguments are the handle of the event for which to check and how long the function should wait for the event. (The event's handle is stored in the event object's `m_hObject` data member.) The predefined `INFINITE` constant tells `WaitForSingleObject()` not to return until the specified event is signaled. In other words, if you place the preceding line at the beginning of your thread, the system suspends the thread until the event is signaled. Even though you've started the thread execution, it's halted until whatever you need to have happen happens. When your program is ready for the thread to perform its duty, you call the `SetEvent()` function, as described a couple of paragraphs ago.

Once the thread is no longer suspended, it can go about its business. But if you want to signal the end of the thread from the main program, the thread must watch for this next event to be signaled. The thread can do this by polling for the event. To poll for the event, you again call `WaitForSingleObject()`, only this time you give the function a wait time of 0, like this:

```
::WaitForSingleObject(threadend.m_hObject, 0);
```

In this case, if `WaitForSingleObject()` returns `WAIT_OBJECT_0`, the event has been signaled. Otherwise, the event is still in its nonsignaled state.

To better see how event objects work, follow the steps given next to further modify the Thread application.

1. Add the following line to the top of the `ThreadView.cpp` file, right after the line `#include "ThreadView.h"`:

   ```
   #include "afxmt.h"
   ```

2. Add the following lines near the top of the `ThreadView.cpp` file, after the `volatile int threadController` line that you placed there previously:

   ```
   CEvent threadStart;
   CEvent threadEnd;
   ```

3. Delete the `volatile int threadController` line from the file.

4. Replace the `ThreadProc()` function with the one shown in Listing 31.5.

Listing 31.5 LST31_05.TXT—Yet Another New *ThreadProc()* Function

```
UINT ThreadProc(LPVOID param)
{
    ::WaitForSingleObject(threadStart.m_hObject, INFINITE);
    ::MessageBox((HWND)param, "Thread activated.",
        "Thread", MB_OK);

    BOOL keepRunning = TRUE;
    while (keepRunning)
    {
        int result =
```

```
            ::WaitForSingleObject(threadEnd.m_hObject, 0);
        if (result == WAIT_OBJECT_0)
            keepRunning = FALSE;
    }

    ::PostMessage((HWND)param, WM_THREADENDED, 0, 0);

    return 0;
}
```

5. Replace the code in the OnStartthread() function with the following line:

   threadStart.SetEvent();

6. Replace the code in the OnStopthread() function with the following line:

   threadEnd.SetEvent();

7. Use ClassWizard to add an OnCreate() function, as shown in Figure 31.8. Make sure that you have CThreadView selected in the Class Name box before you add the function.

Part

V

Ch

31

FIG. 31.8

Use ClassWizard to add the *OnCreate()* function.

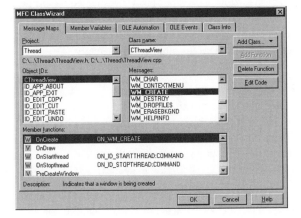

8. Add the following lines to the OnCreate() function, right after the TODO: Add your specialized creation code here comment:

```
HWND hWnd = GetSafeHwnd();
AfxBeginThread(ThreadProc, hWnd);
```

Again, this new version of the program seems to run the same as the previous version. However, the program is now using both event objects and user-defined Windows messages to communicate between the main program and the thread. No more messing with clunky global variables.

One big difference from previous versions of the program is that the secondary thread gets started in the OnCreate() function, which is called when the application first starts up.

However, because the first line of the thread function is the call to `WaitForSingleObject()`, the thread immediately suspends execution and waits for the `threadStart` event to be signaled.

When the `threadStart` event object becomes signaled, the thread is free to display the message box and then enter its `while` loop, where it polls the `threadEnd` event object. The `while` loop continues to execute until `threadEnd` becomes signaled, at which time the thread sends the `WM_THREADENDED` message to the main program and exits. Because the thread is started in `OnCreate()`, once the thread ends, it cannot be restarted.

Using Thread Synchronization

Using multiple threads can lead to some interesting problems. For example, how do you prevent two threads from accessing the same data at the same time? What if, for example, one thread is in the middle of trying to update a data set when another thread tries to read that data? The second thread will almost certainly read corrupted data, since only some of the data set will have been updated.

Trying to keep threads working together properly is called *thread synchronization*. Event objects, about which you just learned, are actually a form of thread synchronization. In this section, you'll learn about *critical sections, mutexes,* and *semaphores*—thread synchronization objects that make your thread programming even safer.

Using Critical Sections

Critical sections are an easy way to ensure that only one thread at a time can access a data set. When you use a critical section, you give your threads an object that they have to share between them. Whichever thread possesses the critical-section object has access to the guarded data. Other threads have to wait until the first thread releases the critical section, after which another thread can grab the critical section in order to access the data in turn.

Because the guarded data is represented by a single critical-section object, and because only one thread can own the critical section at any given time, the guarded data can never be accessed by more than a single thread at a time.

To create a critical-section object in an MFC program, you create an instance of the `CCriticalSection` class, like this:

```
CCriticalSection criticalSection;
```

Then, when program code is about to access the data that you want to protect, you call the critical-section object's `Lock()` member function, like this:

```
criticalSection.Lock();
```

If another thread doesn't already own the critical section, `Lock()` gives the object to the calling thread. That thread can then access the guarded data, after which it calls the critical-section object's `Unlock()` member function:

```
criticalSection.Unlock();
```

Unlock() releases the ownership of the critical-section object so that another thread can grab it and access the guarded data.

The best way to implement something like critical sections is to build the data you want to protect into a thread-safe class. When you do this, you no longer have to worry about thread synchronization in the main program; the class handles it all for you. As an example, look at Listing 31.6, which is the header file for a thread-safe array class.

Listing 31.6 COUNTARRAY.H—The *CCountArray* Class's Header File

```
#include "afxmt.h"

class CCountArray
{
private:
    int array[10];
    CCriticalSection criticalSection;

public:
    CCountArray() {};
    ~CCountArray() {};

    void SetArray(int value);
    void GetArray(int dstArray[10]);
};
```

Part

V

Ch

31

The header file starts off by including the MFC header file, afxmt.h, which gives the program access to the CCriticalSection class. Within the CCountArray class declaration, the file declares a ten-element integer array, which is the data that the critical section will guard, and declares the critical-section object, here called criticalSection. The CCountArray class's public member functions include the usual constructor and destructor, as well as functions for setting and reading the array. It's these latter two member functions that must deal with the critical-section object, because it's those functions that access the array.

Listing 31.7 is the CCountArray class's implementation file. Notice that, in each member function, the class takes care of locking and unlocking the critical-section object. This means that any thread can call these member functions without worrying about thread synchronization. For example, if thread one calls SetArray(), the first thing SetArray() does is call criticalSection.Lock(), which gives the critical-section object to thread one. The complete for loop then executes, without any fear of being interrupted by another thread. If thread two calls SetArray() or GetArray(), the call to criticalSection.Lock() suspends thread two until thread one releases the critical-section object, which it does when SetArray() finishes the for loop and executes the criticalSection.Unlock() line. Then the system wakes up thread two and gives it the critical-section object. In this way, all threads have to wait politely for their chance to access the guarded data.

Listing 31.7 COUNTARRAY.CPP—The *CCountArray* Class's Implementation File

```cpp
#include "stdafx.h"
#include "CountArray.h"

void CCountArray::SetArray(int value)
{
    criticalSection.Lock();

    for (int x=0; x<10; ++x)
        array[x] = value;

    criticalSection.Unlock();
}

void CCountArray::GetArray(int dstArray[10])
{
    criticalSection.Lock();

    for (int x=0; x<10; ++x)
        dstArray[x] = array[x];

    criticalSection.Unlock();
}
```

Now that you've had a chance to see what a thread-safe class looks like, it's time to put the class to work. Perform the following steps, which modify the Thread application to test the CCountArray class.

1. Place the CountArray.cpp and CountArray.h files in the Thread project's directory.

2. Select the Insert, Files into Project command and then add the CountArray.cpp file to the project, as shown in Figure 31.9.

FIG. 31.9

Adding CountArray
.cpp to the Thread
project.

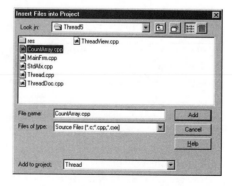

3. Load `ThreadView.cpp` and then add the following line near the top of the file, after the line #include "afxmt.h", which you placed there previously:

   ```
   #include "CountArray.h"
   ```

4. Add the following line near the top of the file, after the CEvent threadEnd line you placed there previously:

   ```
   CCountArray countArray;
   ```

5. Delete the CEvent threadStart and CEvent threadEnd lines from the file.

6. Delete the lines ON_MESSAGE(WM_THREADENDED, OnThreadended), ON_COMMAND(ID_STOPTHREAD, OnStopthread), and ON_WM_CREATE() from the message map.

7. Replace the ThreadProc() function with the thread functions shown in Listing 31.8.

Part

V

Ch

31

Listing 31.8   LST31_08.TXT—New Thread Functions

```cpp
UINT WriteThreadProc(LPVOID param)
{
    for(int x=0; x<10; ++x)
    {
        countArray.SetArray(x);
        ::Sleep(1000);
    }

    return 0;
}

UINT ReadThreadProc(LPVOID param)
{
    int array[10];

    for (int x=0; x<20; ++x)
    {
        countArray.GetArray(array);
        char str[50];
        str[0] = 0;
        for (int i=0; i<10; ++i)
        {
            int len = strlen(str);
            wsprintf(&str[len], "%d ", array[i]);
        }
        ::MessageBox((HWND)param, str, "Read Thread", MB_OK);
    }

    return 0;
}
```

8. Replace the code in the OnStartthread() function with the following lines:

   ```cpp
   HWND hWnd = GetSafeHwnd();
   AfxBeginThread(WriteThreadProc, hWnd);
   AfxBeginThread(ReadThreadProc, hWnd);
   ```

9. Delete the `OnStopthread()`, `OnThreadended`, and `OnCreate()` functions from the file.

10. Load the `ThreadView.h` file and then delete the line `const WM_THREADENDED = WM_USER + 100` from the listing.

11. Also in `ThreadView.h`, delete the line `afx_msg LONG OnThreadended(WPARAM wParam, LPARAM lParam)`.

12. In the message map functions, delete the lines `afx_msg void OnStopthread()` and `afx_msg int OnCreate(LPCREATESTRUCT lpCreateStruct)`.

13. Using the resource editor, remove the Stop Thread command from the Thread menu.

Now you can compile and run the new version of the Thread application. When you do, the main window appears. Select the Thread, Start Thread command to get things hopping. The first thing you'll then see is a message box (Figure 31.10) displaying the current values in the guarded array. Each time you dismiss the message box, it reappears with the new contents of the array. The message box will reappear 20 times. The values you see listed in the message box depend upon how often you dismiss the message box. The first thread is writing new values into the array once a second, even as you're viewing the array's contents in the second thread.

FIG. 31.10
This message box displays the current contents of the guarded array.

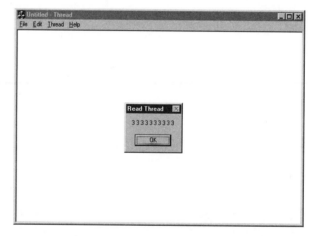

The important thing to notice is that at no time does the second thread interrupt when the first thread is changing the values in the array. You can tell that this is true because the array always contains ten identical values. If the first thread was interrupted as it modified the array, the ten values in the array would not be identical, as shown in Figure 31.11.

If you examine the source code carefully, you'll see that the first thread, named `WriteThreadProc()`, is calling the array class's `SetArray()` member function ten times within a `for` loop. Each time through the loop, `SetArray()` gives the thread the critical-section object, changes the array contents to the passed number, and then takes the critical-section object away again. Note the call to the Sleep() function, which suspends the thread for the number of milliseconds given as the function's single argument.

FIG. 31.11

Without thread synchronization, you might see something like this in the message box.

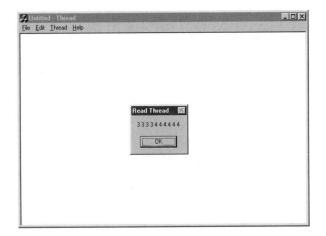

The second thread, named ReadThreadProc(), is also trying to access the same critical-section object in order to construct a display string of the values contained in the array. But if WriteThreadProc() is currently trying to fill the array with new values, ReadThreadProc() has to wait. The inverse is also true. That is, WriteThreadProc() can't access the guarded data until it can regain ownership of the critical section from ReadThreadProc().

If you really want to prove that the critical-section object is working, remove the criticalSection.Unlock() line from the end of the CCountArray class's SetArray() member function. Then compile and run the program. This time when you start the threads, no message box appears. Why? Because WriteThreadProc() takes the critical-section object and never lets it go, which forces the system to suspend ReadThreadProc() forever (or at least until you exit the program).

Using Mutexes

Mutexes are a lot like critical sections but are a little more complicated, because they enable safe sharing of resources not only between threads in the same application, but also between threads of different applications. Although synchronizing threads of different applications is beyond the scope of this chapter, you can get a little experience with mutexes by using them in place of critical sections.

Listing 31.9 is the CCountArray2 class's header file. Except for the new class name and the mutex object, this header file is identical to the original CountArray.h. Listing 31.10 is the modified class's implementation file. As you can see, the member functions look a lot different when they are using mutexes instead of critical sections, even though both objects provide essentially the same type of services.

Part
V

Ch
31

Listing 31.9 CCOUNTARRAY2.H—The *CCountArray2* Class's Header File

```
#include "afxmt.h"

class CCountArray2
{
private:
    int array[10];
    CMutex mutex;

public:
    CCountArray2() {};
    ~CCountArray2() {};

    void SetArray(int value);
    void GetArray(int dstArray[10]);
};
```

Listing 31.10 COUNTARRAY2.CPP—The *CCountArray2* Class's Implementation File

```
#include "stdafx.h"
#include "CountArray2.h"

void CCountArray2::SetArray(int value)
{
    CSingleLock singleLock(&mutex);
    singleLock.Lock();

    for (int x=0; x<10; ++x)
        array[x] = value;
}

void CCountArray2::GetArray(int dstArray[10])
{
    CSingleLock singleLock(&mutex);
    singleLock.Lock();

    for (int x=0; x<10; ++x)
        dstArray[x] = array[x];
}
```

In order to access a mutex object, you must create a `CSingleLock` or `CMultiLock` object, which performs the actual access control. The `CCountArray2` class uses `CSingleLock` objects, because this class is dealing with only a single mutex. When the code is about to manipulate guarded resources (in this case, the array), you create a `CSingleLock` object, like this:

```
CSingleLock singleLock(&mutex);
```

The constructor's argument is a pointer to the thread-synchronization object that you want to control. Then, to gain access to the mutex, you call the CSingleLock object's Lock() member function:

```
singleLock.Lock();
```

If the mutex is unowned, the calling thread becomes the owner. If another thread already owns the mutex, the system suspends the calling thread until the mutex is released, at which time the waiting thread is awakened and takes control of the mutex.

To release the mutex, you call the CSingleLock object's Unlock() member function. However, if you create your CSingleLock object on the stack (rather than on the heap, using the new operator) as shown in Listing 31.10, you don't have to call Unlock() at all. When the function exits, the object goes out of scope, which causes its destructor to execute. The destructor automatically unlocks the object for you.

To try out the new CCountArray2 class in the Thread application, place the CountArray2.h and CountArray.cpp files in the Thread project's folder and then delete the original CountArray.h and CountArray.cpp files. Finally, add the CountArray2.cpp file to the project and, in ThreadView.cpp, change all references to CCountArray to CCountArray2. Because all the thread synchronization is handled in the CCountArray2 class, no further changes are necessary in order to use mutexes rather than critical sections. Convenient, eh?

Part
V
Ch
31

Using Semaphores

Although semaphores are used like critical sections and mutexes in an MFC program, they serve a slightly different function. Rather than allowing only one thread to access a resource simultaneously, semaphores allow multiple threads to access a resource, but only to a point. That is, semaphores allow a maximum number of threads to access a resource simultaneously.

When you create the semaphore, you tell it how many threads should be allowed simultaneous access to the resource. Then, each time a thread grabs the resource, the semaphore decrements its internal counter. When the counter reaches 0, no further threads are allowed access to the guarded resource until another thread releases the resource, which increments the semaphore's counter.

You create a semaphore by supplying the initial count and the maximum count, like this:

```
CSemaphore Semaphore(2, 2);
```

Because, in this section, you'll be using a semaphore to create a thread-safe class, it's actually more convenient to declare a CSemaphore pointer as a data member of the class and then create the CSemaphore object dynamically in the class's constructor, like this:

```
semaphore = new CSemaphore(2, 2);
```

You should do this because you have to initialize a data member in the constructor rather than at the time you declare it. With the critical-section and mutex objects, you didn't have to supply arguments to the class's constructors, so you were able to create the object at the same time you declared it.

Once you have the semaphore object created, it's ready to start counting resource access. To implement the counting process, you first create a CSingleLock (or CMultiLock, if you're dealing with multiple thread-synchronization objects) object, giving it a pointer to the semaphore you want to use, like this:

```
CSingleLock singleLock(semaphore);
```

Then, to decrement the semaphore's count, you call the CSingleLock object's Lock() member function:

```
singleLock.Lock();
```

At this point, the semaphore object has decremented its internal counter. This new count remains in effect until the semaphore object is released, which you can do explicitly by calling the object's Unlock() member function:

```
singleLock.Unlock();
```

Alternatively, if you've created the CSingleLock object locally on the stack, you can just let the object go out of scope, which not only automatically deletes the object but also releases the hold on the semaphore. In other words, both calling Unlock() and deleting the CSingleLock object increments the semaphore's counter, enabling a waiting thread to access the guarded resource.

Listing 31.11 is the header file for a class called CSomeResource. CSomeResource is a mostly useless class whose only calling is to demonstrate the usage of semaphores. The class has a single data member, which is a pointer to a CSemaphore object. The class also has a constructor and destructor, as well as a member function called UseResource(), which is where the semaphore will be used.

Listing 31.11   SOMERESOURCE.H—The *CSomeResource* Class's Header File

```
#include "afxmt.h"

class CSomeResource
{
private:
    CSemaphore* semaphore;

public:
    CSomeResource();
    ~CSomeResource();

    void UseResource();
};
```

Listing 31.12 shows the CSomeResource class's implementation file. You can see that the CSemaphore object is constructed dynamically in the class's constructor and deleted in the destructor. The UseResource() member function simulates accessing a resource by attaining a count on the semaphore and then sleeping for five seconds, after which the hold on the semaphore is released when the function exits and the CSingleLock object goes out of scope.

Listing 31.12   SOMERESOURCE.CPP—The *CSomeResource* Class's Implmentation File

```
#include "stdafx.h"
#include "SomeResource.h"

CSomeResource::CSomeResource()
{
    semaphore = new CSemaphore(2, 2);
}

CSomeResource::~CSomeResource()
{
    delete semaphore;
}

void CSomeResource::UseResource()
{
    CSingleLock singleLock(semaphore);
    singleLock.Lock();

    Sleep(5000);
}
```

Part
V

Ch
31

Modifying the Thread application to use the CSomeResource object, you can actually watch semaphores at work. Follow the next steps to perform this program modification.

1. Delete the CountArray2.cpp file from the project, by highlighting the file in the FileView window and pressing your keyboard's Delete key.

2. Delete the CountArray2.h and CountArray.cpp files from the project's directory.

3. Place the SomeResource.h and SomeResource.cpp files into the project directory.

4. Add the SomeResource.cpp file to the project, as shown in Figure 31.12.

FIG. 31.12

Add the SomeResource.cpp file to the project.

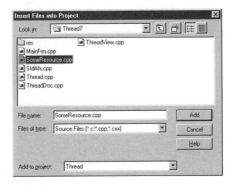

5. Load `ThreadView.cpp` and replace the line `#include "CountArray2.h"` with the following:

```
#include "SomeResource.h"
```

6. Replace the line `CCountArray2 countArray` with the following:

```
CSomeResource someResource;
```

7. Replace the `WriteThreadProc()` and `ReadThreadProc()` functions with the functions shown in Listing 31.13.

Listing 31.13   LST31_13.TXT—New Thread Functions

```
UINT ThreadProc1(LPVOID param)
{
    someResource.UseResource();

    ::MessageBox((HWND)param,
        "Thread 1 had access.", "Thread 1", MB_OK);

    return 0;
}

UINT ThreadProc2(LPVOID param)
{
    someResource.UseResource();

    ::MessageBox((HWND)param,
        "Thread 2 had access.", "Thread 2", MB_OK);

    return 0;
}

UINT ThreadProc3(LPVOID param)
{
    someResource.UseResource();

    ::MessageBox((HWND)param,
        "Thread 3 had access.", "Thread 3", MB_OK);

    return 0;
}
```

---

8. Replace the code in the `OnStartthread()` function with that shown in Listing 31.14.

Listing 31.14   LST31_14.TXT—New Code for the *OnStartthread()* Function

```
HWND hWnd = GetSafeHwnd();
AfxBeginThread(ThreadProc1, hWnd);
AfxBeginThread(ThreadProc2, hWnd);
AfxBeginThread(ThreadProc3, hWnd);
```

Now compile and run the new version of the Thread application. When the main window appears, select the Thread, Start Thread command. In about five seconds, two message boxes will appear informing you that Thread one and Thread two had access to the guarded resource. About five seconds after that, a third message box will appear, telling you that Thread three also had access to the resource. Thread three took five seconds longer because Thread one and Thread two grabbed control of the resource first. The semaphore is set to allow only two simultaneous resource accesses, so Thread three had to wait for Thread one or Thread two to release its hold on the semaphore.

N O T E Although the sample programs in this chapter have demonstrated using a single thread-synchronization object, you can have as many synchronization objects as you need in a single program. You can even use critical sections, mutexes, and semaphores all at once in order to protect different data sets and resources in different ways.

From Here...

For complex applications, threads offer the ability to keep data processing moving along fast and efficiently. You no longer have to wait for one part of the program to finish its task before moving on to something else. For example, a spreadsheet application could use one thread to update the calculations while the main thread continued accepting entries from the user. Using threads, however, leads to some interesting problems, not the least of which is the need to control access to shared resources. Writing a threaded application requires some thought and careful consideration of how the threads will be used and what resources they'll access.

For more information on related topics, please refer to the following chapters:

- Chapter 5, "Messages and Commands," can give you some review on how MFC applications process Windows messages with message maps.
- Chapter 29, "Power-User Features in Developer Studio," offers advanced tips for customizing your Developer Studio projects.
- Chapter 30, "Power-User C++ Features," describes additional advanced C++ Windows programming techniques.

CHAPTER 32

Additional Advanced Topics

There are a number of topics that have not been covered elsewhere in this book. The four topics gathered together in this chapter have little in common other than a reputation as advanced or intimidating. Typically you will not use these techniques on your first project, though they are not, in fact, as difficult as many people imagine. Once you are comfortable generating ordinary Windows applications with AppWizard, consider these techniques to move you beyond ordinary Windows programming. ■

Creating Console Applications

This section describes how to build Console applications with Visual C++ 4.2. There are important Console applications, like Telnet and FTP, and techniques like scaffolding, for which console applications are ideally suited.

32-bit Dlls

Follow the example program to see how easy writing and using 32-bit DLLs can be.

Sending Messages and Commands

An integral part of an event driven operating system like Windows is its Messaging capability. This section shows how to extend that capability with messages of your own devising.

International Issues and the Unicode Standard

Unicode is a 2-byte character set standard enabling programs to work with international languages whose alphabet requires more than 8-bits of storage. MFC makes support for Unicode easy, and this section shows how.

Creating Console Applications

Console applications are also referred to as DOS applications. Interestingly enough you can still create applications with MS-Visual C++ that run under DOS. More importantly they can still play a beneficial role in software development, even Windows 95 or Windows NT software development. That's right, you heard it here first. There are still a few great uses for DOS applications, including the ftp and telnet console applications that come with Windows 95 and NT. But an important use of Console apps for Windows developers is a technique called scaffolding, used to test objects before integrating them into a large application.

Creating a Console Executable

A Console (or DOS) application is still executed from the DOS command line or by choosing Start, Run and typing the full name of the application. Console applications are probably still among the easiest programs to create and this version of the compiler supports them directly.

You can also invoke a DOS box from the "programs" item in the Start Menu. BOB. Start button

Let's walk together through the few steps necessary to create a basic Console application and then we'll explore some beneficial uses of creating these kinds of applications. The first Console application we'll create is a spin on the classic "Hello, World!" Kernighan and Ritchie—the creators of C++'s ancestor C—created in the 1970s.

Open the Microsoft Developer Studio and follow these steps to create a Console application:

1. In the Microsoft Developer Studio, select File, New
2. From the New dialog, select Project Workspace. (This option displays the dialog in fig. 32.1.)

FIG. 32.1
Creating a new Console
Project Workspace
enables you to create
DOS executable
applications or scaffolds
for testing algorithms.

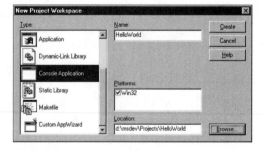

3. Using Figure 32.1 as a guide, select the Console Application type from the Type list, and Name the project HelloWorld.
4. Click Create.
5. Select File, New from the file menu and select Text File from the New dialog box.
6. Add the code to the text file in Listing 32.1.

7. Select Eile, Save As saving the file as HelloWorld.Cpp. (Remember, we can use more than eight characters in the filename in Windows 95. Select Insert, Files into Project, inserting the just saved HelloWorld.Cpp file into the HelloWorld WorkSpace.

8. To test the Console program click the Go button on the Project toolbar.

N O T E Although this application may be small, Visual C++ creates a lot of overhead files. One small application may produce 3 or 4 megabytes of intermediate files. Developers in general need plenty of disk space.

When compiled using a Debug Build, HelloWorld requires about 850K bytes on my system. ▪

If you followed the steps as described above precisely and did not make any prior modifications to the Microsoft Developer Studio, the code in Listing 32.1 should have compiled error-free and produced the output:

"Welcome to Valhalla Tower Material Defender."

from the cool game "Descent II" from Interplay.

Listing 32.1   (HelloWorld.Cpp) "Welcome to Valhalla Tower..."

```
// HelloWorld.Cpp - A new spin on an old classic<g>.
// Copyright (c) 1996. All Rights Reserved.
// by Paul Kimmel. Okemos, MI USA
#include <iostream.h>
int main()
{    const char * const GREETINGS =
         "Welcome to Valhalla Tower Material Defender.\n";
     cout << GREETINGS;
     return 0;
}
```

Building a trivial application is a place to start. There are still many software developers living in a DOS world, but better yet, there are still valid uses for DOS-based applications. One of these is prototyping, as we'll discuss in the next section.

Scaffolding Discrete Algorithms

The best argument for anyone to build a DOS application these days is to *scaffold* small code fragments. This refers to building a temporary framework around the code you want to test. The simplest possible framework is a console application like the one you just built.

Further, if such a scaffold cannot be built around your algorithm, then management and other computer scientists may have a valid argument for calling into question the completeness and robustness of the design.

By the time many single functions make it into your application, they themselves should have been tested in smaller programs a few times at least. While it is a subjective call how many lines of code require a scaffold, it is a simple enough process to scaffold at the function level. If we are reusing those functions, they will be incorporated in other functions that are scaffolded too.

One possible algorithm you might want to test is a sorting algorithm. This section will present a *template* quicksort algorithm.

To scaffold the quicksort or any subprogram, the technique involves:

- Creating a new Console App just for the scaffolding process.
- Adding a main function to the .CPP file to be scaffolded.
- Wrapping a conditional compiler directive around the main function and any other functionality which is part of the scaffold. I use the module name as a prefix to the word SCAFFOLD, like SORTS_SCAFFOLD, as an easy to way to contrive my compiler directive. In this way you can easily turn on or off a set of test code.
- Modify the Build, Settings Project Settings dialog (see fig. 32.2) C++ tab, adding the preprocessor definition SORTS_SCAFFOLD. This has the effect of making the scaffold a project-wide directive.

Having followed those steps, you can now test the quicksort code (Listings 32.2 and 32.3) thoroughly, focusing only on the performance characteristics and correctness of the quicksort. Scaffolding holds true to the canon of software development which states: "Design in the large and program in the small."

FIG. 32.2
Use the Project Settings dialog box shown to set project-wide compiler directives

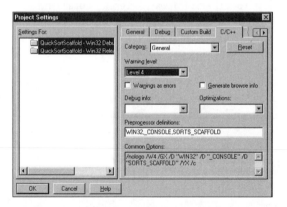

Listing 32.2   (SORTS.H) The Header File Contains the RecursiveQuicksort Function Declaration

```
// SORTS.H - Contains global sort function declarations.
// Copyright (c) 1996. All Rights Reserved.
// by Paul Kimmel. Okemos, MI USA
#ifndef __SORT_H
```

```
#define __SORTS_H
// A technique for 'measuring' the number of elements in an array.
#define SIZEOF( array ) sizeof(array) / sizeof( array[0] )
template <class T>
inline void Swap( T& a, T& b ){ T t = a; a = b; b = t; }
// The larger stack space of 32-bit platforms enables us to more
// reliably use recursive functions, being less likely to underflow the stack.
template <class T>
void RecursiveQuickSort( T data[], unsigned long left, unsigned long right );
#endif
```

Listing 32.3   (SORTS.CPP) The Quicksort and Parsing Function Definitions and Scaffold

```
// SORTS.CPP - Contains the definitions and some test scaffolds
// Copyright (c) 1995. All Rights Reserved.
// By Paul Kimmel.
#include "sorts.h"
// Partitioning function for the RecursiveQuickSort.
template <class T>
unsigned long Partition( T data[], unsigned long left, unsigned long right )
{
    unsigned long j, k;
    T v = data[right];
    j = left - 1;
    k = right;
    for(;;)
    {
        while( data[++j] < v )    ;
        while( data[--k] > v )    ;
        if( j >= k ) break;
        Swap(data[j], data[k]);
    };
    Swap(data[j], data[right] );
    return j;
}
// The QuickSort Function.
template <class T>
void RecursiveQuickSort( T data[], unsigned long left, unsigned long right)
{
    unsigned long j;
    if( right > left )
    {
        j = Partition(data, left, right );
        RecursiveQuickSort(data, left, j-1);
        RecursiveQuickSort(data, j+1, right );
    }
}
#ifdef SORTS_SCAFFOLD
/* The scaffold is used only for testing the RecursiveQuickSort
 * template function. By defining SORTS_SCAFFOLD project-wide we
 * can easily remove the define, leaving the scaffold in place for
```

Part

V

Ch

32

continues

Listing 32.3 Continued

```
 * another time. For instance, we may want to optimize the quicksort,
 * or add additional functionality to this module.
 * An added benefit is that the scaffold code also demonstrates
 * to other users how to use the quicksort.
 */
#include <iostream.h>      // Contains cout object
#include <stdlib.h>           // Contains srand() and rand() functions
#include <time.h>            // Definition of time()
int main()
{
    srand((unsigned long)time(NULL)); // Seed the random number generator

    unsigned long elems[10];
    const unsigned long MAX = SIZEOF( elems );
    // Fill the elems with random numbers.
    for( unsigned long i = 0; i < MAX; i++ )
        elems[i] = rand();
    // Sort the elements, specifying the template type implicitly
    unsigned long l = 0, r = MAX - 1;
    RecursiveQuickSort(elems, l, r );
    for( i = 0; i < MAX; i++ )
        cout << i << ".=\t" << elems[i] << endl;
    return 0;
}
#endif
```

 TIP

The sort code is a template, so that this code can be used to sort numbers, strings, or other kinds of objects. Templates are covered in the "Templates" section of Chapter 30, "Power-User C++ Features."

By applying a scaffold to any algorithm you are helping to ensure accuracy. Remember, there are additional benefits involved, too: by placing the scaffold code directly into the module you are clearly documenting that the code has been tested and how to use it. You make it available for further testing, debugging, or extending at a later date.

Creating and Using a 32-bit Dynamic Link Library

Dynamic Link Libraries (DLL) are still the backbone of the Windows 95 and Windows NT operating systems. Windows 95 uses Kernel32.Dll, User32.Dll, and Gdi32.Dll to perform the vast majority of its work, and you can use them as well. The Microsoft Visual C++ On-line Books are a good source of information for API functions found in these three DLLs.

Another tool for poking around in Windows applications is the DumpBin utility in \MSDEV\BIN. This utility is a command line program that will show you the imports and exports of executable files and dynamic link libraries. Listed on the following pages is an excerpted example of the output produced when using DumpBin to examine the executable file for Spy++, one of the utilities provided with Visual C++.

```
dumpbin -imports spyxx.exe
Microsoft (R) COFF Binary File Dumper Version 3.00.5270
Copyright (C) Microsoft Corp 1992-1995. All rights reserved.

Dump of file spyxx.exe

File Type: EXECUTABLE IMAGE

        Section contains the following Imports

            USER32.dll
                167    LoadCursorA
                135    GetWindowTextA
                1DF    SetDlgItemTextW
                153    IsChild
                 D7    GetClassLongA
                 D8    GetClassLongW
                 C5    FillRect
                165    LoadBitmapA
                16B    LoadIconA
                 E6    GetDC
                1F4    SetRectEmpty
                15B    IsRectEmpty
                1F3    SetRect
                141    InflateRect
                1FE    SetTimer
                162    KillTimer
                1CF    SetActiveWindow
                249    wsprintfA
                 80    DeleteMenu
                122    GetSystemMenu
                1A1    PeekMessageA
                100    GetLastActivePopup
                  2    AdjustWindowRectEx
                  4    AppendMenuA
                 51    CreatePopupMenu
                 C1    EnumWindows
                 B1    EnumChildWindows
                188    MessageBoxA
                206    SetWindowPlacement
                  A    BringWindowToTop
                197    OffsetRect
                132    GetWindowPlacement
                13A    GetWindowWord
                15E    IsWindowUnicode
                243    WinHelpA
                 DF    GetClipboardFormatNameA
                12F    GetWindowDC
                160    IsZoomed
                1B9    ReleaseDC
                 D0    GetCapture
                 33    ClientToScreen
                246    WindowFromPoint
                1D8    SetCursor
                237    UpdateWindow
```

Part V

Ch 32

```
12D    GetWindow
15F    IsWindowVisible
 E8    GetDesktopWindow
204    SetWindowLongA
1B8    ReleaseCapture
1D0    SetCapture
1A8    PtInRect
 F0    GetFocus
120    GetSysColor
 CB    FrameRect
 9B    DrawFocusRect
 F9    GetKeyState
187    MessageBeep
22C    TranslateMessage
 8C    DispatchMessageA
159    IsIconic
  1    AdjustWindowRect
133    GetWindowRect
1BF    ScreenToClient
 C2    EqualRect
148    InvalidateRect
 DC    GetClientRect
123    GetSystemMetrics
15C    IsWindow
 D9    GetClassNameA
130    GetWindowLongA
 D3    GetClassInfoA
1A3    PostMessageA
20E    SetWindowsHookExA
22E    UnhookWindowsHookEx
 7D    DefWindowProcA
139    GetWindowThreadProcessId
1AF    RegisterClipboardFormatA
 DB    GetClassWord
 86    DestroyWindow
1AB    RegisterClassA
 52    CreateWindowExA
 AB    EnableWindow
1C6    SendMessageA
115    GetParent
1E2    SetForegroundWindow
232    UnpackDDElParam
216    ShowWindow
```

Summary

```
10000  .data
 3000  .idata
 8000  .rdata
 8000  .reloc
 F000  .rsrc
36000  .text
```

As you can see, the utility program Spy++ uses the User32.Dll extensively.

A Dyanamic Link Library (DLL) contains compiled code that is maintained external to an executable program which might use it. DLLs by default are loaded into memory by Windows when a program referrring to a DLL function calls the DLL function. If Windows loads the DLL, then Windows will automatically unload when the last program using it is done or un-loaded. Alternatively, you can gain control over the loading and unloading of DLLs by using the API functions LoadLibrary and FreeLibrary.

Making a 32-bit DLL

16-bit Windows DLL development required the developer to write a LibMain and a *WEP* (Win-dows Exit Procedure) for the library to work correctly. There is only a single function used for 32-bit DLL development now and even this is not absolutely required.

The function is named DllMain and an empty shell version looks like the following:

```
BOOL WINAPI DllMain (HINSTANCE hinstDll, DWORD fdwReason, LPVOID lpvReserved )
{
    switch (fdwReason)
    {
    case DLL_PROCESS_ATTACH:
        // Called when the Dll is mapped into the processes address space.
        break;
    case DLL_THREAD_ATTACH:
        // Called when the a thread is being created.
        break;
    case DLL_THREAD_DETACH:
        // Called when a thread is exiting.
        break;
    case DLL_PROCESS_DETACH:
        // Called when a process is being unmapped.
        break;
    };
}
```

hinstDll is the handle of the calling process, lpvReserved is reserved for later use and should be NULL, and fdwReason is one of the four reasons in the switch statement: DLL_PROCESS_ATTACH, DLL_PROCESS_DETACH, DLL_THREAD_ATTACH, and DLL_THREAD_DETACH. The same function is called to attach a DLL to a process (start using it) or detach it (stop using it).

N O T E The macro definition WINAPI is used in place of FAR PASCAL, which was used for 16-bit DLLs. The keyword FAR instructs the compiler to use a 32-bit address. All addresses are 32-bit in Windows 95 and Windows NT; therefore, the directive would now be redundant.

The keyword PASCAL has to do with pushing the function arguments on the stack in-order as opposed to reverse-order. Reverse-order is the default for C and C++. Microsoft chose the PASCAL calling convention for Windows, perhaps because it may be more efficient or because it is the one Visual Basic uses. ▪

Part
V

Ch
32

You may not even need to write this function. For many DLLs the default `DllMain` Microsoft Visual C++ will add for you will be sufficient. You will need to create a DllMain if your DLL requires startup and cleanup code. Otherwise, writing a DLL is much like writing any other modules with functions and variables in them. In this section you'll use the default `DllMain` included by the compiler.

N O T E   Many developers believe that DLLs are easier to build than applications because DLLs are usually a set of autonomous functions that any application can use.

In many cases a DLL is often thought of as an application requiring individual testing prior to releasing it. This kind of thoroughness can and should be applied to all subprograms regardless of whether they will ultimately be used in a package like a DLL or part of a much larger program.

Importing and Exporting Functions   Your DLLs may need to both import and export functions. You will import those functions and variables from other DLLs which help your DLL function and will export those functions and variables that comprise the functionality of your DLL.

Microsoft has extended the syntax for exporting and importing functions and variables in DLLs. To designate a symbol as an exportable symbol, use the following syntax:

```
_ _declspec(dllexport) data_type int var_name; // for variables
```

or

```
_ _declspec(ddlexport) return_type func_name( [argument_list ] ); // for func-
tions
```

Importing functions is almost identical: simply replace the keyword tokens, _ _declspec(dllexport) with __declspec(dllimport). Using an actual function and variable to demonstrate the syntax this time:

```
_ _declspec(dllimport) int referenceCount;
_ _declspec(dllimport) void DiskFree( lpStr Drivepath );
```

 TIP   Two (2) underscores precede the keyword _ _declspec.

By convention, Microsoft uses a header file and a preprocessor macro to make the inclusion of DLL declarations much simpler. The technique simply requires that you make a preprocessor token using a unique token—the header file name works easily, and requires very little in the way of memorization—and define a macro which will (when the preprocessor runs) replace the token with the correct import or export statement. Thus, assuming a header file named DISKFREE.H, the preprocessor macro in the header file would be:

```
// DISKFREE.H - Contains a simpler function for returning the amount of free disk
  ➥space.
// Copyright (c) 1996. All Rights Reserved.
// By Paul Kimmel. Okemos, MI USA
```

```
#ifndef _ _DISKFREE_H
#define _ _DISKFREE_H

#ifndef _ _DISKFREE_ _
#define DISKFREELIB _ _declspec(dllimport)
#else
#define DISKFREELIB _ _declspec(dllexport)
#endif
// Use the macro to control an import or export declaration.
DISKFREELIB unsigned long DiskFree( unsigned int drive ); // (e.g. o = A:, 1 =
➥B:, 2 = C:
#endif
```

Simply by including the header file you can specify and define the token `_DISKFREE_`, which you only need to do in the actual DLL code, or if not, you can let the preprocessor do all of the work for you.

Creating the DiskFree DLL   The DiskFree utility was designed to demonstrate creating a DLL (and it also provides a simple way to determine the amount of free disk space for any given drive). The underlying functionality is the GetDiskFreeSpace function found in Kernel32.Dll. Listings 32.4 and 32.5 contain the complete source code listing for the dynamic link library, DiskFree.Dll.

Part

V

Ch

32

Listing 32.4   (DiskFree.h) Contains the Declarations and Reusable Import and Export Macros

```
// DiskFree.H - Contains a simpler DiskFree function, demonstrating 32-bit DLL
➥techniques
// Copyright (c) 1996. All Rights Reserved.
// By Paul Kimmel. Okemos, MI USA
// EDITOR: You might want to comment here a reference to the preprocessor
➥directives that you discuss above. BOB

#ifndef _ _DISKFREE_H
#define _ _DISKFREE_H
#ifndef _ _DISKFREE_ _
#define _ _DISKFREELIB_ _ _declspec(dllimport)
#else
#define _ _DISKFREELIB_ _ _declspec(dllexport)
#endif
// Returns the amount of free space on drive number (e.g. 0 = A:, 1= B:, 2 = c:)
_ _DISKFREELIB_ _ unsigned long WINAPI DiskFree( unsigned int drive );
#endif
```

Listing 32.5   (DiskFree.Cpp) Contains the Functionality. Winbase.H Causes the GetDiskFreeSpace kernel32 Function to be Imported

```
// DiskFree.Cpp - Contains the DLL code for diskfree
// Copyright (c) 1996. All Rights Reserved.
// by Paul Kimmel. Okemos, MI USA
```

continues

Listing 32.5 Continued

```
/* Intentionally compiled with the default libraries and
 *  configuration. It will be much smaller if you remove
 * unnecessary libraries and turn off debugging code.
 */
#include <afx.h>
#include <winbase.h>      // Contains the kernel32 GetDiskFreeSpace declaration.
#define _ _DISKFREE_ _     // Define the token before the inclusion of the
                               ➥library
#include "diskfree.h"
// Returns the amount of free space on drive number (e.g. 0 = A:, 1= B:, 2 = c:)
_ _DISKFREELIB_ _ unsigned long WINAPI DiskFree( unsigned int drive )
{
    unsigned long bytesPerSector, sectorsPerCluster,
        freeClusters, totalClusters;
    char DrivePath[4] = { char( drive + 65 ), ':', '\\', '\0' };
    if( GetDiskFreeSpace( DrivePath, &sectorsPerCluster,
        &bytesPerSector, &freeClusters, &totalClusters ))
    {
        return sectorsPerCluster * bytesPerSector * freeClusters;
    }
    else
    {
        return 0;
    }
}
```

In the next section we'll take a look at using 32-bit DLLs in general, including how Windows finds DLLs on your system.

The most common use of a DLL is to provide extended, reusable functionality and let Windows implicitly load the DLL. Topics that will not be discussed in this book, that you might want to explore for yourself, include:

- Dynamic versus static linking of MFC
- Implicit versus explicit DLL loading, which requires the use of LoadLibrary and FreeLibrary
- Multithreading DLLs
- Sharing data across DLL boundaries

In this section you are going to use a default compile of DiskFree, using an implicit DllMain (the compiler added one), and an implicit loading of the DLL, allowing Windows to manage loading and unloading the library.

N O T E A good example of a case in which you might want to explicitly load and unload a DLL is multilingual versions of resource DLLs where the DLL is loaded after the user indicates a language of choice. ▨

Using 32-bit DLLs

If, in preparation to use a DLL, you load the library with the Windows LoadLibrary function, then you may certainly specify the path to the DLL. However, many DLLs are loaded implicitly and their loading and unloading are managed by Windows. Libraries loaded in this fashion are searched for like executables: first the directory of the application loading the DLL is searched, followed by the current directory, the Windows\System directory, the Windows directory, and finally, each directory specified in the PATH.

It is a common practice to place a DLL in the Windows or Windows\System directories once the application is shipped, but in the meantime you may use the development directory of the executable for temporary storage. One thing to safeguard against is that you do not end up with multiple versions of the DLL in each of the Windows, Windows\System, or project directories.

Using a DLL   Implicitly loading and using a DLL is about as simple as using any other function. This is especially true if you created the header file as described in the above section. When you compile your DLL, Microsoft Visual C++ creates a coincidental .LIB file. (So, DISKFREE.DLL has a coincidental DISKFREE.LIB created by the compiler.) The library (.LIB) file is used to resolve the load address of the DLL and specify the full pathname of the dynamic link library, and the header file provides the declaration.

All you have to do is include the header in the file using the DLL functionality and add the .LIB name to the Build, Settings Project Settings dialog, on the Link tab (see fig. 32.3), in the Object/library modules edit field.

Part

V

Ch

32

FIG. 32.3

To use a DLL, add the LIB filename to the Project Settings, Link tab, in the Object/ library modules edit field.

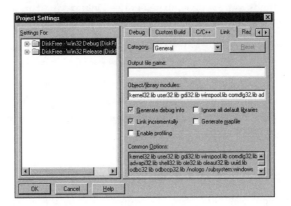

Listing 32.6 demonstrates a Console application that shows the simplest use of the DiskFree DLL.

Listing 32.6 (TestDiskFree.Cpp) A Console Application Which Tests the DiskFree.Dll

```
// TestDiskFree.Cpp - Tests the simplified kernel32 DiskFree, based on
GetDiskFreeSpace, function.
// Copyright (c) 1996. All Rights Reserved.
// by Paul Kimmel. Okemos, MI USA
#include <afx.h>
#include <iostream.h>
#include "diskfree.h"
#define CodeTrace(arg) \
    cout << #arg << endl;\
    arg
int main()
{
    CodeTrace( cout << DiskFree( 2 ) << endl );
    return 0;
}
```

Follow these steps to produce the Console application in Listing 32.6:

1. Create a File, New Workspace named TestDiskFree (using a Console target).

2. Copy the files DiskFree.H, DiskFree.Lib, and DiskFree.Dll to the directory TestDiskFree (created by the Microsft Developer Studio).

3. Add the DiskFree.Lib file to the Project Settings dialog on the Link tab. (Use fig. 32.3 as a visual guide.)

4. In Build, Settings, on the C++ tab select the Debug Multithreaded item in the Use run-time library combobox.

5. Add a new text file, TestDiskFree.Cpp to the current WorkSpace, save the file and press F5 to test it.

A Console application is the simplest way to demonstrate using a DLL because you do not have to surround the program with a lot of MFC code. Once you have tested the DLL, using it in any program requires the same number of steps. The biggest change will be the code that actually uses this housekeeping function.

Sending Messages and Commands

As discussed in Chapter 5, "Messages and Commands," messages are the heat of Windows. Everything that happens in a Windows application happens because a message showed up to make it happen. When you move your mouse and click a button, a huge number of messages are generated, including WM_MOUSEMOVE for each movement of the mouse, WM_LBUTTONDOWN when the button goes down, WM_LBUTTONCLICK when the button is released, and higher level, more abstract messages like the WM_COMMAND message with the button's resource ID as one of its parameters. You can ignore the lower-level messages if you wish and many programmers do.

What you may not know is that *you* can generate messages too. There are two functions that generate messages: `CWnd::SendMessage()` and `CWnd::PostMessage()`. Each of these gets a message to an object that inherits from `CWnd`. An object that wants to send a message to a window using one of these functions must have a pointer to the window, and the window must be prepared to catch the message. A very common approach to this situation is to have a member variable in the sending object that stores a pointer to the window that will receive the message and another that stores the message to be sent:

```
CWnd* m_messagewindow;
UINT m_message;
```

Messages are represented by unsigned integers. They appear to have names only because names like WM_MOUSEMOVE are connected to integers with `#define` statements.

The sending class has a member function to set these member variables, typically very short:

```
void Sender::SetReceiveTarget(CWnd *window, UINT message)
{
    m_messagewindow = window;
    m_message = message;
}
```

When the sending class needs to get a message to the window, it calls SendMessage:

```
m_messagewindow->SendMessage(m_message, wparam, lparam);
```

Or PostMessage:

```
m_messagewindow->PostMessage(m_message, wparam, lparam);
```

The difference between sending and posting a message is that `SendMessage()` does not return until the message has been handled by the window that received it, but `PostMessage()` just adds the message to the message queue and returns right away. If, for example, you build an object, pass that object's address as the `lparam`, and then delete the object, you should choose `SendMessage()`, since you can't delete the object until you are sure that the message-handling code has finished with it. If you are not passing pointers, you can probably use `PostMessage()` and move on as soon as the message has been added to the queue.

The meaning of the `wparam` and `lparam` values depends on the message you are sending. If it is a defined system message like WM_MOUSEMOVE, you can read the online documentation to learn what the parameters are. If, as is more likely, you are sending a message that you have invented, the meaning of the parameters is entirely up to you. You are the one who is inventing this message, and writing the code to handle it when it arrives at the other window.

To invent a message, add a defining statement to the header file of the class that will catch it:

```
#define WM_HELLO WM_USER + 300
```

WM_USER is an unsigned integer that marks the start of the range of message numbers available for user defined messages. In this release of MFC, its value is 0x4000, though you should not depend on that. User-defined messages have message numbers between WM_USER and 0x7FFF.

Then add a line to the message map, in both the header and source files, outside the ClassWizard comments. The source file message map might look like this:

```
BEGIN_MESSAGE_MAP(CMainFrame, CMDIFrameWnd)
        //{{AFX_MSG_MAP(CMainFrame)
                // NOTE - the ClassWizard will add and remove mapping macros
                ➡ here.
                //    DO NOT EDIT what you see in these blocks of generated code!
        //}}AFX_MSG_MAP
        ON_MESSAGE(WM_HELLO, OnHello)
END_MESSAGE_MAP()
```

The entry added outside the //AFX_MSG_MAP comments catches the WM_HELLO message and arranges for the OnHello() function to be called. The header file message map might look like this:

```
// Generated message map functions
protected:
        //{{AFX_MSG(CMainFrame)
        afx_msg int OnCreate(LPCREATESTRUCT lpCreateStruct);
                // NOTE - the ClassWizard will add and remove member functions
                ➡ here.
                //    DO NOT EDIT what you see in these blocks of generated code!
        //}}AFX_MSG
        afx_msg LRESULT OnHello(WPARAM wParam, LPARAM lParam);
        DECLARE_MESSAGE_MAP()
```

Then you add an implementation of OnHello() to the source file to complete the process.

Considering International Software Development Issues

International boundaries are shrinking at incredible rates. As access to wider serial communications widens and the preponderance of discrete resalable components continues, more and more demands for pieces built by vendors worldwide will grow. Even in-house software development will less-frequently be able to ignore international markets. This means your applications should be able to communicate with users in languages other than English and in character sets other than the typical Western character set.

Microcomputers were created in the United States which explains why we have 8-bit character-based operating systems. There are only 26 letters in our alphabet and ten digits, which leaves plenty of room (about 220 characters worth) for punctuation and other miscellaneous characters. But countries like Japan and China require a character set in the thousands.

Unicode is one way to tackle the character set problem. The Unicode standard was developed and is supported by a consortium of some of the biggest players in the international computing markets; among these are Adobe, Aldus, Apple, Borland, Digital, IBM, Lotus, Microsoft, Novell, and Xerox.

Unicode uses two bytes for each character, whereas ASCII uses only one. One byte, 8 bits, can represent 2^8 or 256 characters. Two bytes, 16 bits, can represent 65,536 characters. This is enough not just for one language, but for all the character sets in general use. For example, the Japanese character set, one of the largest, needs about 5,000 characters. Most require far less. The Unicode specification sets aside different ranges for different character sets and can cover almost every language on Earth in one universal code—a Unicode.

MFC has full Unicode support, with Unicode versions of almost every function. For example, consider the function CWnd::SetWindowText(). It takes a string and sets the title of the window, or the caption of a button, to that string. What kind of string it takes depends on whether you have Unicode support turned on in your application. In reality, there are two different functions to set the window text on, a Unicode version and a non-Unicode version, and in WINUSER.H, the block of code shown in Listing 32.7 changes the function name that you call to SetWindowTextA if you are not using Unicode, or SetWindowTextW if you are.

Listing 32.7 Microsoft's WINUSER.H Implementing Unicode Support

```
WINUSERAPI BOOL WINAPI SetWindowTextA(HWND hWnd, LPCSTR lpString);
WINUSERAPI BOOL WINAPI SetWindowTextW(HWND hWnd, LPCWSTR lpString);

#ifdef UNICODE
#define SetWindowText   SetWindowTextW
#else
#define SetWindowText   SetWindowTextA
#endif // !UNICODE
```

Part
V

Ch
32

The difference between these two functions is the type of the second parameter: LPCSTR for the A version and LPCWSTR for the W version—W stands for Wide.

If you are using Unicode, whenever you pass a literal string (like "Hello") to a function, wrap it in the _T macro, like this:

    pWnd->SetWindowText(_T("Hello"));

To turn on Unicode support, use the Default Project Configuration box on the Project toolbar. You can choose Unicode Debug or Unicode Release in addition to the familiar Debug and Release versions.

If you can deal with the annoyance of wrapping all text strings in _T macros, choose this option and just like that, your application is Unicode-aware. When you prepare your Greek or Japanese version of the application, life will be much simpler.

N O T E Windows 95 was built on old Windows, so it was not built using Unicode. This means that if you use Unicode in your Windows 95 programs, you are going to suffer performance penalties because the Windows 95 kernel will have to convert Unicode strings back to ordinary strings. Windows NT was designed at Microsoft from scratch, so it is completely compatible with Unicode.

If you are developing for several platforms with C++ and intend using Unicode, your Win95 version may seem sluggish in comparison to the Windows NT version. ■

From Here...

This chapter demonstrated the way to build a console application and a major use for console applications called scaffolding. Because scaffolding allows you to test small pieces of your application at a time, it is a way to speed your software development and reduce the number of bugs in your code. You also learned how to use a dynamic-link library (DLL), how to create your own DLL, and how to send custom messages to another part of your application. Finally you learned how to ready your applications for the international market with Unicode.

To learn about related topics see:

- Chapter 2, "Developer Studio Commands," for a review of the Developer Studio toolbars and the menu commands their buttons are connected to

- Chapter 3, "AppWizard and ClassWizard," for an introduction to AppWizard and the way it builds empty starter applications for you

- Chapter 5, "Messages and Commands" for an introduction to the importance of messages and how message maps work

- Chapter 30, "Power-User C++ Features" for more examples using templates to speed program development

Index

Symbols

:: , double colons (function names), 722

... , ellipsis (catch blocks), 690

3D controls option (AppWizard), 81

4.2a patch (ActiveX controls), 662

32-bit DLLs (Dynamic Link Libraries)
creating, 744-752
DiskFree utility, 749-750
DllMain function, 747-748
importing/exporting functions, 748-749
implicitly loading, 751-752

A

Abort( ) CFile member function, 289

About box (ShowString dialogs), 379-380

About command (Help menu), 153, 470

About Developer Studio command (Help menu), 70

accelerators, Resource View (Developer Studio), 13

Accept CASynchSocket member function, 298

access
databases, 110, 314

activating (ActiveX controls)
flicker-free activation, 657
windowless activation, 656

ActiveX, 496-498
automation, 576-588
AppWizard automation boilerplate, 576-579
Automation application, 504-505
exposing properties, 579-584
OnDraw( ) function, 584-586
showing windows, 586-588
Component Object Model, 503-504
containers, ShowString (changing), 501-502, 508-524
AppWizard container code, 508-523
deleting an object, 542-543
drag and drop, 533-542
enabling, 523-524
moving, resizing and tracking items, 524-527
multiple objects, 528-533
controls, 505-506
adding properties, 601-603
ambient properties, 617-619
asynchronous properties, 659-669
BLOBs (Binary Large OBjects), 661-662
compared to Java applets, 654-655

creating with ActiveX Template Library (ATL), 670
creating with Base Control Framework, 669-670
Dieroll sample application, 662-668
drawing code (writing), 603-605
embedding in Microsoft Explorer Web pages, 650-653
embedding in Netscape Navigator Web pages, 653-654
installing MFC DLL, 652-653
notifying containers of mouse clicks, 606-607
optimizing with AppWizard, 655-659
<PARAM> tag, 660-661
property sheets, 613
rolling-die controls, 596-601
size, 651
stock properties, 617
user interfaces, 608-613
DispTest, 588-591
intuitive user interfaces, 502-503
object embedding, 499-500
object linking, 498-499
servers (building), 546-564, 566
alternate ShowString versions, 566
AppWizard server boilerplate, 546-560

documents, 568-572
nesting and recursion, 566
reopening string files,
560-566

ActiveX Template Library
(creating ActiveX controls),
670

Add Class menu button, 216

Add Data Source dialog
box, 315

Add Event dialog box, 606

Add Member Function dialog
box, 326, 385

Add Member Variable dialog
box, 216, 321, 386

Add Node dialog box, 240

Add Property dialog box,
580, 601, 604, 613

Add Tools dialog box, 605

Add( ) function, 234

Add( ) array member
function, 230

Add( ) CImageList member
function, 184

AddDocTemplate( ) function,
148, 511, 549

AddHead( ) function, 240

AddHead( ) list class member
function, 237

Adding A Class dialog box,
216

AddNew( ) member
function, 329

AddString( ) member
function, 167

AddTail( ) function, 241

AddTail( ) list class member
function, 237

AddTail( ) member
function, 240

Advanced Options dialog box
(creating applications), 81

advanced text finding features
(finding files), 37

AFX_DATA ClassWizard
Comment Delimiter, 343

AFX_DATA_INIT ClassWizard
Comment Delimiter, 343

AFX_DATA_MAP ClassWizard
Comment Delimiter, 343

AFX_DISP ClassWizard
Comment Delimiter, 343

AFX_DISP_MAP ClassWizard
Comment Delimiter, 343

AFX_EVENT ClassWizard
Comment Delimiter, 343

AFX_EVENT_MAP
ClassWizard Comment
Delimiter, 343

AFX_FIELD ClassWizard
Comment Delimiter, 343

AFX_FIELD_INIT
ClassWizard Comment
Delimiter, 343

AFX_FIELD_MAP
ClassWizard Comment
Delimiter, 344

AFX_MSG ClassWizard
Comment Delimiter, 344

AFX_MSG_MAP ClassWizard
Comment Delimiter, 344

AFX_VIRTUAL ClassWizard
Comment Delimiter, 344

AfxAbort( ) exception
function, 348

AfxBeginThread( ) function,
342, 716

AfxCheckMemory( )
diagnostic function, 346

AfxDoForAllClasses( )
diagnostic function, 346

AfxDoForAllObjects( )
diagnostic function, 346

AfxDump( ) diagnostic
function, 346

AfxEnableMemoryTracking( )
diagnostic function, 346

AfxEndThread( ) function,
342

AfxFormatString1( )
function, 345

AfxFormatString2( )
function, 345

AfxGetApp( ) function, 342

AfxGetAppName( )
function, 342

AfxGetInstanceHandle( )
function, 342

AfxGetMainWnd( )
function, 342

AfxGetResourceHandle( )
function, 343

AfxGetThread function, 343

AfxIsMemoryBlock( )
diagnostic function, 346

afxMemDF global variable,
347

AfxMessageBox( ) function,
345

AfxOleLockApp( ) function,
578

AfxOleUnlockApp( )
function, 579

AfxRegisterClass( )
function, 343

AfxRegisterWndClass( )
function, 343

AfxSetAllocHook( ) diagnostic
function, 347

AfxSetResourceHandle( )
function, 343

AfxSocketInit( ) function, 343

AfxThrowArchiveException( )
exception function, 348

AfxThrowDAOException( )
exception function, 348

AfxThrowDBException( )
exception function, 348

AfxThrowFileException( )
exception function, 348

AfxThrowMemoryException( )
exception function, 348

AfxThrowNotSupportedException( )
exception function, 348

AfxThrowOleDispatchException( )
exception function, 348

AfxThrowOleException( )
exception function, 348

AfxThrowResourceException( )
exception function, 348

AfxThrowUserException( )
exception function, 348

afxTraceEnabled global
variable, 347

afxTraceFlags global variable, 347

algorithms (scaffolding with console applications), 741-744

aliases (for namespaces), 712-713

Ambient OCX property, 601

ambient properties, ActiveX controls, 617-619
variable types, 618-619

AmbientFont( ) function, 603

AND_CATCH exception macro, 348

AND_CATCH_ALL exception macro, 348

API functions, *see* **functions**

Appearance ActiveX control stock property, 617

appearance options (creating applications), 80-83

applets, Java (compared to ActiveX controls), 654-655

Application option (New Project Workspace dialog box), 89

applications
ActiveX Automation, 504-505
building, 85
console applications
creating, 89, 740-744
executing, 740-741
scaffolding functions, 741-744
testing DLLs, 751-752
Control1 (sample control app), 163-171
declaring a friend function, 164-165
initializing dialog box controls, 166-168
manipulating controls with classes, 165-166
responding to the OK Button, 168-170
creating, 76-85
database support, 78-79
file/class names, 84
interface appearance options, 80-83
OLE support, 79-80

statically linked compared to shared DLLs, 83-84
types of, 76-78
demo
Array Demo app, 231-236
List Demo app, 237-243
Map Demo app, 244-247
wizard demo app, 222-224
Dialog (sample dialog app), 153-162
CDlg1 class, 155
controls, 155
creating class objects, 159-162
displaying a simple dialog, 154-155
writing classes, 155-159
dialog boxes (coding with ClassWizard), 92-93
dialog-based
changing file/class names, 357-358
creating with AppWizard, 356-361
editing (with AppWizard), 90
executing, 85
File demo, 278-282
document classes, 279-280
source code, 280-283
File demo 2, 283-284
CMessages class, 284-288
File demo 3, 288, 290-293
CFile class, 289-290
MDI, multiple document interface (creating with AppWizard), 365-367
menus (coding with ClassWizard), 90-92
MFC (Registry), 411-412
naming, 81
optimizing, 682-683
Paint1 demo app, 257-269
brushes, 265-266
changing displays, 267-268
font usage, 261-264
painting basics, 259-261
pens, 264-265
sizing and positioning windows, 268-269
property sheet demo, 221-222
creating, 211-220
running the demo, 220
Query sample application
designing, 628
dialog box (creating), 629-631

Finger queries, 641-644
FTP sites (querying), 637-639
Gopher sites (querying), 639-641
HTTP sites (querying), 632-637
improvements to, 646
Whois queries, 644-646
Rectangles sample application
creating, 133-139
displaying document data, 142-143
editing document data, 143-144
executing, 139
initializing document data, 140-141
serializing document data, 141-142
storing document data, 140
SDI, single document interface (creating with AppWizard), 361-365
Status Bar Demo, 412-413
string (building), 372-375
creating empty shells with AppWizard, 372
displaying strings, 372-375
Thread application, 716-719

appname.cnt files (Help system components), 473

appname.ftg files (Help system components), 474

appname.fts files (Help system components), 474

appname.gid files (Help system components), 473

appname.hpj files (Help system components), 473

AppWizard, 85-90, 211, 270, 279, 302, 309, 314, 317-318, 349
ActiveX container code, 508-523
CShowStringApp class, 510-511
CShowStringDoc class, 511-512
CShowStringView class, 512-518
Application option (New Project Workspace dialog box), 89

applications
  creating, 76-85
  database support, 78-79
  editing, 90
  file/class names, 84
  interface appearance
    options, 80-83
  OLE support, 79-80
  statically linked compared
    to shared DLLs, 83-84
  types of, 76-78
automation boilerplate,
  576-579
  CShowStringApp
    application object,
    576-577
  CShowStringDoc class,
    577-579
code (rolling-die ActiveX
  controls), 598-600
console applications
  (creating), 89
creating empty shells (string
  apps), 372
custom AppWizards
  (creating), 89-90, 675-677
decisions, 367-369
dialog-based applications
  changing file/class names,
    357-358
  creating, 356-361
Help system support, 474-475
Makefile option (New Project
  Workspace dialog box), 89
MDI (multiple document
  interface) applications
  (creating), 365-367
MFC AppWizard (DLL), 86-87
OLE Control Wizard, 87-89
optimizing ActiveX controls,
  655-659
SDI applications (creating),
  361-365
server boilerplate, 546-560
static library (creating), 89

AppWizard dialog box, 559

array classes, 230-236
  Array Demo Application,
    231-232
    adding elements, 233-234
    declaring and initializing
      the array, 233
    removing elements,
      235-236
  member functions, 230

**ASSERT diagnostic macro,
347, 445-451**

**ASSERT_VALID diagnostic
macro, 347**

**AssertValid( ) function, 521,
551, 553**

**asynchronous monikers,
BLOBs (Binary Large
OBjects), 661-662**

asynchronous properties
  ActiveX controls, 659-669
    BLOBs (Binary Large
      OBjects), 661-662
    Dieroll sample application,
      662-668
    <PARAM> tag, 660-661

**AsyncSelect CASynchSocket
member function, 298**

**ATL (ActiveX Template
Library) (creating ActiveX
controls), 670**

**Attach CASynchSocket
member function, 298**

**Attach( ) CImageList member
function, 184**

**attributes, CODEBASE
(<OBJECT> tag), 651**

**AutoDowncast (debugging
features), 458-459**

**AutoExpand (debugging
features), 458-459**

**automation (ActiveX),
576-588**
  AppWizard automation
    boilerplate, 576-579
  exposing properties, 579-584
  OnDraw( ) function, 584-586
  show windows, 586-588

**Automation application
(ActiveX), 504-505**
  controls, 505-506

B

**BackColor ActiveX control
stock property, 617**

base classes (defined), 104

**Base Control Framework
(creating ActiveX controls),
669-670**

**Batch Build command (Build
menu), 55-56**

**BEGIN_MESSAGE_MAP
macro, 117**

**BEGIN_MESSAGE_MAP
message-map macro, 349**

**BeginDrag( ) CImageList
member function, 184**

**BeginPaint( ) Windows API
function, 260**

**Binary File option (New
dialog box), 31**

**Binary Large OBjects
(BLOBs), 661-662**

**Bind CASynchSocket member
function, 298**

**Bitmap File option (New
dialog box), 32**

**bitmap icons (ActiveX control
interfaces), 609**

**Bitmap Image Object
command (Edit menu), 526**

**BLOBs (Binary Large
OBjects), 661-662**

**Bookmark command (Edit
menu), 44-46, 437**

BOOL data type, 345

**BorderStyle ActiveX control
stock property, 617**

**Breakpoint command (Edit
menu), 437**

breakpoints (setting), 442

**Breakpoints command (Edit
menu), 46**

**Browse command (Tools
menu), 61**

**Browse Info tab (Project
Settings dialog box), 58**

**brushes (Paint1 demo app),
265-266**

BSTR data type, 345

bugs, *see* **debugging**

**Build button (Project
toolbar), 73**

**Build menu commands,
54-60**
  Batch Build, 55-56
  Build, 55-56, 85, 358, 481

Compile, 55-56, 481, 484
Configurations, 59-60
Execute, 56-58, 85, 358, 482, 484
Rebuild All, 55-56
Set Default Configuration, 59-60
Settings, 56-58, 445
Stop Build, 56
Subprojects, 59-60
Update All Dependencies, 56

building
ActiveX controls
adding properties, 601-603
drawing code (writing), 603-605
notifying containers of mouse clicks, 606-607
property sheets, 613
rolling-die controls, 596-601
user interfaces, 608-613
ActiveX servers, 546-564, 566
alternate ShowString versions, 566
AppWizard server boilerplate, 546-560
documents, 568-572
nesting and recursion, 566
reopening string files, 560-566
applications, 85
ShowString dialogs, 379-385
About box, 379-380
dialog classes, 382-384
Options dialog, 381
ShowString menus, 375-378
string applications, 372-375
creating empty shells with AppWizard, 372
displaying strings, 372-375

buttons
graying (command updates), 124-126
Project toolbar, 72-73
Standard toolbar, 72

BYTE data type, 345

C

C++ programming (overview), 104-105

C/C++ tab (Project Settings dialog box), 57

CAboutDlg class, 384

Call Stack command (View menu), 446

CancelBlockingCall CSocket method, 300

CanPaste( ) CRichEditCtrl member function, 203

CanUndo( ) CRichEditCtrl member function, 203

CanUpdate( ) method, 330

Caption ActiveX control stock property, 617

captions (menus), 15

CArchive class, 142
objects (creating your own), 293

Cascade command (Window menu), 64-66

casting, *see* **downcasting**

CASynchSocket class (member functions), 297-300

catch blocks (exception handling), 688-689
multiple catch blocks, 690-692

CATCH exception macro, 348

CATCH_ALL exception macro, 348

catching, commands (via ClassWizard), 126-127

CBIndex( ) DDX function, 158

CBString( ) DDX function, 158

CBStringExact( ) DDX function, 158

CButton control class, 162, 165

CByteArray array class, 230

CChildFrame class, 384

CCmdTarget class, 108

CCmdUI class, 125

CColorDialog class, 150

CComboBox control class, 162

CCountArray class, 727-728

CCriticalSection class, 726

CCtrlView class, 145

CDaoDatabase class, 338

CDaoRecordset class, 338

CDaoRecordView class, 145, 338

CDaoWorkspace class, 338

CDatabase class, 314

CDialog class, 150

CDierollApp class, 598

CDierollCtl class, 613

CDieRollCtrl class, 601

CDierollCtrl class, 598, 607

CDierollDataPathProperty class (asynchronous ActiveX control properties), 662, 666

CDierollPropPage class, 598, 600

CDlg1 class, 155

CDocument class, 130-131

CDumpContext class, 453-456

CDWordArray array class, 230

CEdit control class, 162, 165

CEditView class, 145

CEmployeeSet class, 323

CEmployeeView class, 331, 334

CEvent class (communicating with threads), 723-726

CException class, 687-688

CFile class, 289-290
file mode flags, 291-292
member functions, 289-290

CFileDialog class, 150

CFileFind class, 306

CFontDialog class, 150

CFormView class, 145

CFtpConnection class, 306

CFtpFileFind class, 306

CGopherConnection class, 306

CGopherFile class, 306

CGopherFileFind class, 306

CGopherLocator class, 306

Change Message dialog box, 290

Change String command (File menu), 408

character sets (Unicode), 754-755

Check box dialog control, 163

CHECK BOX fields (Control1 sample app), 163

Check( ) DDX function, 158

checkboxes (Context Help), 478

Choose menu commands (Tools, Options), 481

CHtmlStream class, 308

CHttpFile class, 306

CHttpFilter class, 308

CHttpFilterContext class, 308

CHttpServer class, 308

CHttpServerContext class, 308

CImageList class (member functions), 184-185

CImageList member function, 184-185

CInPlaceFrame class, 547, 553, 555
   member functions, 553

CInternetConnection class, 306

CInternetException class, 306

CInternetFile class, 306

CInternetSession class, 306, 632-633

class keyword (templates), 692

Class Name combo box, 607

class names (creating applications), 84

class templates (creating), 695-699

Class View (Developer Studio), 19-21

Class Wizard command (View menu), 524, 561

Class Wizard property sheet, 326

classes
   array, 230-236
      Array Demo application, 231-236
      member functions, 230
   CAboutDlg, 384
   CArchive, 142
      objects (creating your own), 293
   CASynchSocket (member functions), 297-300
   CChildFrame, 384
   CCmdTarget, 108
   CCmdUI, 125
   CColorDialog class, 150
   CCountArray, 727-728
   CCriticalSection, 726
   CCtrlView, 145
   CDaoDatabase, 338
   CDaoRecordset, 338
   CDaoRecordView, 145, 338
   CDaoWorkspace, 338
   CDatabase, 314
   CDialog class, 150
   CDierollApp, 598
   CDierollCtl, 613
   CDieRollCtrl, 598, 601, 607
   CDierollDataPathProperty (asynchronous ActiveX control properties), 662, 666
   CDierollPropPage, 598, 600
   CDlg1, 155
   CDocument, 130-131
   CEditView, 145
   CEmployeeSet, 323
   CEmployeeView, 331, 334
   CEvent (communicating with threads), 723-726
   CException, 687-688
   CFile, 289-290
      file mode flags, 291-292
      member functions, 289-290
   CFileDialog class, 150
   CFileFind, 306
   CFontDialog class, 150
   CFormView, 145
   CFtpConnection, 306
   CFtpFileFind, 306
   CGopherConnection, 306
   CGopherFile, 306
   CGopherFileFind, 306
   CGopherLocator, 306
   CHtmlStream, 308
   CHttpFile, 306

CHttpFilter, 308
CHttpFilterContext, 308
CHttpServer, 308
CHttpServerContext, 308
CImageList (member functions), 184-185
CInPlaceFrame, 547, 553, 555
   member functions, 553
CInternetConnection, 306
CInternetException, 306
CInternetFile, 306
CInternetSession, 306, 632-633
CListView, 145
CMainFrame, 384
CMessages, 284-288
CMultiDocTemplate, 148
CObject, 107
COleClientItem, 533
ColeInsertDialog, 516
COleIPFrameWnd, 553
COleResizeBar, 553
COleServerItem (function overrides), 551
COleTemplateServer, 547
collection, 110
   helper functions, 344
   templates, 253-254
commands (relationship to messages), 123-124
control, 109-110, 165-166
   CButton, 162
   CComboBox, 162
   CEdit, 162
   CListBox, 162
   CStatic, 162
COptionsDialog, 384, 478, 524
CPaintDC, 260
CPoint, 528
CPrintInfo, 425
   members, 429
CProgressCtrl, 175
   member functions, 176
CPropertyPage, 210
CPropertySheet, 210
CQueryDlg, 632
creating windows, 101-104
CRecordSet, 314, 324
CRecordView, 145, 314, 324, 327
CRect, 528
CRectTracker, 525-526, 531, 553
CRichEditCtrl (member functions), 203-205
CRichEditView, 145-146

CScrollView, 145
CShowStringApp, 118, 373, 384, 510
CShowStringCntrItem, 521, 525, 533
CShowStringDoc, 372, 384, 511, 524, 550, 561, 577-580
CShowStringSrvrItem, 550-551, 563
CShowStringView, 384, 512, 550, 563
CSingleDocTemplate, 148
CSingleLock, 732-733
CSliderCtrl, 177
    member functions, 178-179
CSocket, 297-300
    methods, 300
CSpinButtonCtrl (member functions), 182
CString, 248-249
    formatting and message box functions, 344-345
CTime, 249
    member functions, 249-250
CTimeSpan, 249
    member functions, 250
CToolBar, 553
CTreeCtrl, 195
CTreeView, 145
CView, 131-133, 145
CWnd, 108-109
    encapsulation, 105-107
DAO database, 337-339
database access, 110
defined, 104
dialog box, 109-110, 389
    writing, 155-159
document, 109, 279-280
document template, 147-148
drawing, 110
encapsulation, 105-107
    defined, 104
HttpConnection, 306
I/O (input/output) classes, 110
inheritance (defined), 104
Internet, 305-307
ISAPI, 308
list, 236-243
    List Demo application, 237-243
    member functions, 237
map, 244-247
    functions, 244
    Map Demo application, 244-247

MAPI, 110
message maps, 116-120
    ClassWizard, 120-121
messages
    prefixes, 121-123
    routing, 114
ODBC database, 314
OnInitialUpdate( ), 525
OnNewDocument( ), 525
persistent, 282-288
    File demo 2 app, 283-288
polymorphism
    message maps, 119
    RTTI, 704-709
sockets, 110
string, 248-249
    member functions, 248
thread-safe, 727
time, 249-253
    CTime objects, 250-252
    CTimeSpan objects, 252-253
type_info, 700
utility, 110
view, 109, 144-146
virtual functions, 119
windows, 100
    WNDCLASS structure, 100-101

ClassWizard
    commands (catching/updating), 126-127
    comment delimiters, 343-344
    dialog boxes (coding), 92-93
    menus (coding), 90-92
    message maps, 120-121
ClassWizard Add Property dialog box, 602
ClassWizard button, 216
    Standard toolbar, 72
ClassWizard command (View menu), 49, 579, 601, 606
ClassWizard property sheet, 321, 331
Clear( ) CRichEditCtrl member function, 203
ClearSel( ) CSliderCtrl member function, 178
ClearTics( ) CSliderCtrl member function, 178
clicks
    double (ActiveX ShowString), 532-533

single (ActiveX ShowString), 530
Clipboard, 496
CListBox control class, 162, 165
CListView class, 145
Close command (File menu), 32-33
Close All command (Window menu), 66
Close Browse Info File command (Tools menu), 61
Close CASynchSocket member function, 298
Close Workspace command (File menu), 33
Close( ) CFile member function, 289
Close( ) function, 293
CLSID (ActiveX controls), 650
CMainFrame class, 384
CMapPtrToPtr map class, 244
CMapPtrToWord map class, 244
CMapStringToPtr map class, 244
CMapStringToString map class, 244
CMapWordToOb map class, 244
CMapWordToPtr map class, 244
CMemoryState class, 462-464
CMessages class, 284-286, 286-288
CMultiDocTemplate class, 148
CNTLDLG.CPP Control1 source file, 164
CNTLDLG.H Control1 source file, 164
CObArray array class, 230
CObject class, 107
CObList list class, 236

code
AppWizard (rolling-die
ActiveX controls), 598-600
drawing, (adding ActiveX
controls), 603-605
editing (Developer Studio),
23-24
shortcut menu, 25-26
source file toolbar, 26
syntax coloring, 25
text blocks, 24-25

**code reusability (Component
Gallery), 672-674**

**CODEBASE attribute
(<OBJECT> tag), 651**

coding
dialog boxes (with
ClassWizard), 92-93
menus (with ClassWizard),
90-92
messages (Wizard bar), 93-94

COleClientItem class, 533

COLEControl method, 603

**COleDropTarget member
variable, 534**

ColeInsertDialog class, 516

COleIPFrameWnd class, 553

COleResizeBar class, 553

**COleServerItem class
(function overrides), 551**

**COleTemplateServer class,
547**

collection classes, 110
helper functions, 344
templates, 253-254

**coloring, syntax (editing code
with Developer Studio),
25-26**

COLORREF data type, 345

**colors, user-selected (ActiveX
controls), 617-622**

**columns, list view controls
(creating), 189-191**

**Combo box dialog control,
163**

**COMBO BOX field (Control1
sample app), 163**

**Command help
(programming), 477-478**

command IDs, 350

command routing, 123-124

command updating, 124-126

**command-update handlers
(status bars), 407-408**

commands
Build menu, 54-60
Batch Build, 55-56
Build, 55-56, 85, 358, 481
Compile, 55-56, 481, 484
Configurations, 59-60
Execute, 56-58, 85, 358,
482, 484
Rebuild All, 55-56
Set Default Configuration,
59-60
Settings, 56-58, 445
Stop Build, 56
Subprojects, 59-60
Update All Dependencies,
56
catching (via ClassWizard),
126-127
Choose menu (Tools,
Options), 481
Dialog menu (Test), 153
Edit menu, 39-48
Bitmap Image Object, 526
Bookmark, 44-46, 437
Breakpoints, 46, 437
Copy, 41, 561
Cut, 40-41
Delete, 41
Find, 41-42, 483
Go To, 42-44, 437
InfoViewer Bookmarks, 44
Insert New Object, 508,
514, 522
Insert Object, 550
Insert OLE Control, 605
Links, 508, 512
Paste, 41, 512, 561
Paste Link, 512
Paste Special, 508
Properties, 13, 46-48, 478,
556, 614
Redo, 40-41
Replace, 42, 483
Select All, 41
Undo, 40
File menu, 30-38
Change String, 408
Close, 32-33
Close Workspace, 33

Exit, 38
Find, 436
Find In Files, 34-37
New, 31, 76, 139, 476, 522,
596
Open, 32, 139, 475-476, 561
Open Workspace, 33
Page Setup, 37-38
Print, 38, 139
Print Preview, 139
Recent Files and
Workspaces, 38
Restore String, 412
Save, 33, 139, 571
Save All, 33
Save As, 33
Update, 546
Wizard, 222
Help menu, 67-70
About, 153, 470
About Developer Studio,
70
Contents, 67-68
Define Subset, 69-71
Help Topics, 470, 482, 484
Keyboard, 68, 438
Search, 67-68
Set Default Subsets, 69-71
Technical Support, 69-71
Tip of the Day, 69-71
Use Extension Help, 68-71
Web Favorites, 70-71
What's This?, 470
ID_TOOLS_OPTIONS, 524,
561
Insert menu, 52-54
Component, 54, 672
File, 53
Files into Project, 53-54
New String, 406
Object, 550, 555
Project, 54
Resource, 53
Resource Copy, 53-54
relationship to messages,
123-124
Tools menu, 60-63
Browse, 61
Close Browse Info File, 61
Customize, 61, 605, 678
OLE Control Test
Container, 604
Options, 10, 61-63, 485,
488, 576, 588
Playback Recording, 63

Profile, 61
Record Keystrokes, 63
Remote Connection, 61
updating (via ClassWizard),
126-127
View menu, 48-52
Call Stack, 446
ClassWizard, 49, 524, 561,
579, 601, 606
Footnotes, 481, 485
Full Screen, 50-51
InfoViewer History List,
51-52
InfoViewer Query Results,
51
InfoViewer Topic, 52
Output, 52
Project Workspace, 52
Resource Includes, 50-51
Resource Symbols, 50
Toolbars, 50-51
Watch, 460
Window menu, 63-66
Cascade, 64-66
Close All, 66
Hide, 64-66
New Window, 64-66
Split, 64-66
Tile Horizontally, 64-66
Tile Vertically, 65-66
Windows, 66

**CommandToIndex( )
function, 401**

**CommandToIndex( )
member function, 409**

**CommandToIndex( )
method, 403**

**comment delimiters
(ClassWizard), 343-344**

**Common Messaging Calls
(MAPI), 303**

**communication (with
threads), 719-726**
via event objects, 723-726
via global variables, 720-721
via user-defined messages,
721-723

**Compare( ) string class
member function, 248**

**CompareElements( )
collection class helper
function, 344**

**CompareNoCase( ) string
class member function, 248**

**Compatibility tab (Options
dialog box), 62**

**Compile button (Project
toolbar), 73**

**Compile command (Build
menu), 55-56, 481, 484**

compilers, *see* **Developer
Studio**

**Component command (Insert
menu), 54, 672**

**component files (Help
systems), 473-474**

Component Gallery, 672-674

**Component Gallery button
(Project toolbar), 73**

**Component Object Model
(ActiveX), 503-504**

**compound files (creating
applications), 80**

**Configurations command
(Build menu), 59-60**

**Connect CASynchSocket
member function, 298**

console applications
creating, 89, 740-744
executing, 740-741
scaffolding functions, 741-744
testing DLLs, 751-752

constants
thread priority, 716
WM_USER, 722

**ConstructElements( )
collection class helper
function, 344**

constructors
CWnd, 105
defined, 104
initializing, 360

**containers (ActiveX),
501-502**
notifying of mouse clicks
(ActiveX controls), 606-607
ShowString (changing),
508-524
AppWizard container code,
508-523
deleting an object, 542-543
drag and drop, 533-542

enabling, 523-524
moving, resizing, and
tracking items, 524-527
multiple objects, 528-533

**Contents command (Help
menu), 67-68**

**context help (programming),
478-481**

Context Help checkbox, 478

**context sensitive help option
(AppWizard), 81**

Control Developer Kit, 505

**Control Dialog dialog box,
164**

Control Pad, 650

**ControlActive plug-in,
653-654**

controls
ActiveX, 505-506
adding properties, 601-603
ambient properties,
617-619
asynchronous properties,
659-669
compared to Java applets,
654-655
creating with ActiveX
Template Library (ATL),
670
creating with Base Control
Framework, 669-670
drawing code (writing),
603-605
embedding in Microsoft
Explorer Web pages,
650-653
embedding in Netscape
Navigator Web pages,
653-654
installing MFC DLL,
652-653
notifying containers of
mouse clicks, 606-607
optimizing with
AppWizard, 655-659
property sheets, 613-622
rolling-die controls,
596-601
size, 651
stock properties, 617
testing/debugging,
668-669
user interfaces, 608-613

classes, 109-110, 165-166
    CButton, 162
    CComboBox, 162
    CEdit, 162
    CListBox, 162
    CStatic, 162
Control1 sample application,
    163-171
    declaring a friend function,
        164-165
    initializing dialog box
        controls, 166-168
    manipulating controls with
        classes, 165-166
    responding to the OK
        Button, 168-170
designing (rolling-die ActiveX
    controls), 601
dialog programming, 162-163
    Check box, 163
    Combo box, 163
    Edit box, 163
    Group box, 163
    List box, 163
    Pushbutton, 163
    Radio button, 163
    Scroll bar, 163
    Static text, 162
Dialog sample application, 155
    data types, 156
IDs (defining), 152
image list (Win95), 182-185
    creating, 183
    initializing, 184-185
list view (Win95), 185-195
    creating, 187-189
    creating columns, 189-191
    creating items, 191-193
    image list association, 189
    initializing, 189
    manipulating, 193-195
    styles, 188-189
LoadStdProfileSettings( ), 363
ParseCommandLine( ), 363
ProcessShellCommand( ),
    363
progress bar (Win95), 174
    creating, 174-175
    initializing, 176
    manipulating, 176-177
rich edit (Win95), 201-207
    creating, 202-203
    initializing, 203-205
    manipulating, 205-207
    styles, 202-203

shells (rolling-die ActiveX
    controls), 596-597
trackbar (Win95), 177-180
    creating, 177-178
    CSliderCtrl member
        functions, 178-179
    initializing, 178-180
    manipulating, 180
    styles, 178
tree view (Win95), 195-201
    creating, 196-197
    initializing, 197-200
    manipulating, 200-201
    styles, 197
up-down (Win95), 180-182
    creating, 181-182
    styles, 181
**COptionsDialog class, 384,
478, 524**
**Copy button (Standard
toolbar), 72**
**Copy command (Edit menu),
41, 561**
**Copy( ) CRichEditCtrl
member function, 203**
CPaintDC class, 260
CPoint class, 528
CPrintInfo class, 425
    members, 429
CProgressCtrl class, 175
    member functions, 176
CPropertyPage class, 210
CPropertySheet class, 210
CPtrArray array class, 230
CPtrList list class, 236
CQueryDlg class, 632
**Create CASynchSocket
member function, 298**
Create CSocket method, 300
**Create New Class dialog box,
92, 216, 332, 382**
Create( ) function, 401
**Create( ) CImageList member
function, 184**
**Create( ) CProgressCtrl
member function, 176**
**Create( ) CRichEditCtrl
member function, 203**

**Create( ) CSliderCtrl member
function, 178**
**Create( ) CSpinButtonCtrl
member function, 182**
Create( ) method, 403
**CreateFontIndirect( )
function, 263**
**CreateFromFile( ) function,
516**
CreateItem( ) function, 516
**CreateLinkFromFile( )
function, 516**
**CreateListView( ) local
member function, 183**
**CreateLocator( ) function,
640-641**
**CreateNewItem( ) function,
516**
CreateObject( ) function, 592
**CreateProgressBar( )
function, 176**
**CreateProgressBar( ) local
member function, 175**
**CREATESTRUCT structure,
269**
**CreateTrackbar( ) local
member function, 177**
**CreateTreeView( ) local
member function, 183**
**CreateUpDownCtrl( ) local
member function, 181**
**CreateWindow( ) API
function, 100, 103-104**
creating
    ActiveX controls
        ActiveX Template Library
            (ATL), 670
        Base Control Framework,
            669-670
    applications, 76-85
        database support, 78-79
        file/class names, 84
        interface appearance
            options, 80-83
        OLE support, 79-80
        statically linked compared
            to shared DLLs, 83-84
        types of, 76-78
    CArchive objects, 293

class templates, 695-699

console applications, 89, 740-744

custom AppWizards, 89-90, 675-677

dialog box (Query sample application), 629-631

dialog box resources, 151-153
defining dialog and control IDs, 152

DLLs (Dynamic Link Libraries), 89, 744-752
DiskFree utility, 749-750
DllMain function, 747-748
importing/exporting functions, 748-749
MFC AppWizard (DLL), 86-87

function templates, 692-695

image list controls, 183

list view controls, 187-189

OCXs (OLE Control Wizard), 87-89

ODBC database programs, 315-337
adding and deleting records, 324-328
creating the basic employee application, 317-320
database display (creating), 320-323
DoFilter( ) function, 336-337
OnMove( ) function, 329-330
OnRecordAdd( ) function, 328-329
OnRecordDelete( ) function, 330-331
OnSortDept( ) function, 335-336
registering the database, 315-316
sorting and filtering, 331-335

persistent classes, 282-288
File demo 2 app, 283-288

progress bar controls (Win95), 174-175

property sheet demo applications, 211-222
running the demo, 220

Rectangles sample application, 133-139

rich edit controls, 202-203

static library, 89

trackbar controls, 177-178

tree view control items, 197-200

tree view controls, 196-197

up-down controls, 181-182

windows, 101-104

wizard pages (wizard demo app), 224

CRecordSet class, 314, 324

CRecordView class, 145, 314, 324, 327

CRect class, 528

CRectTracker class, 525-526, 531, 553

CRichEditCtrl class, 203
member functions, 203-205

CRichEditCtrl member function, 203-204

CRichEditView class, 145-146

critical sections (thread synchronization), 726-731

CScrollView class, 145

CShowStringApp application object, 576-577

CShowStringApp class, 118, 373, 384, 510

CShowStringCntrItem class, 521, 525, 533

CShowStringCntrItem function, 518

CShowStringDoc class, 372, 384, 511, 524, 550, 561, 577-579, 580

CShowStringSrvrItem class, 550-551, 563

CShowStringView class, 384, 512, 550, 563

CSingleDocTemplate class, 148

CSingleLock class, 732-733

CSliderCtrl class (member functions), 177-179

CSocket class, 297-300
methods, 300

CSpinButtonCtrl class (member functions), 182

CStatic control class, 162

CStatusBar class (methods), 403

CStdioFile function, 307

CString class, 248-249

CString classes (formatting and message box functions), 344-345

CStringArray array class, 230

CStringList list class, 236

CTime class, 249
member functions, 249-250
objects, 250-252

CTimeSpan class, 249
member functions, 250
objects, 252-253

CToolBar class, 553
member functions, 401-404

CTreeCtrl class, 195

CTreeView class, 145

CUIntArray array class, 230

Cursor File option (New dialog box), 32

Custom AppWizards (creating), 89-90, 675-677

Custom OCX property, 601

Customize command (Tools menu), 61, 605, 678

Cut button (Standard toolbar), 72

Cut command (Edit menu), 40-41

Cut( ) CRichEditCtrl member function, 203

CView class, 131-133, 145

CWnd class, 108-109
encapsulation, 105-107

CWordArray array class, 230

D

DAO classes, 337-339

Data Source Name text box, 315

Data Sources dialog box, 315

Data Tips (debugging features), 459-460

data types, 345-346
  Dialog sample app controls, 156

database management system (DBMS), 312

Database Options dialog box, 318

database support (creating applications), 78-79

databases, 312-314
  accessing, 110, 314
  DAO classes, 337-339
  flat model, 312
  ODBC classes, 314
  ODBC program (creating), 315-337
    adding and deleting records, 324-328
    creating the basic employee application, 317-320
    database display (creating), 320-323
    DoFilter( ) function, 336-337
    OnMove( ) function, 329-330
    OnRecordAdd( ) function, 328-329
    OnRecordDelete( ) function, 330-331
    OnSortDept( ) function, 335-336
    registering the database, 315-316
    sorting and filtering, 331-335
  relational model, 312

DDV functions, 159

DDX functions, 158-159

Debug tab (Options dialog box), 62

DEBUG_NEW, 464-465

DEBUG_NEW diagnostic macro, 347

debugging
  ActiveX controls, 668-669
  features, 433-434
    ASSERT, 445-448, 451-452
    AutoDowncast, 458-459

AutoExpand, 458-459
CDumpContext class, 453-456
classes, 451-452
CMemoryState class, 462-464
CRunTimeClass, 456-458
Data Tips, 459-460
DEBUG_NEW, 464-465
development vs. delivery constraints, 444-445
Dump member functions (defining), 452-456
memory, 461-467
menus, hotkeys and toolbars, 434-439
QuickWatch, 459-460
TRACE, 445-448, 450-452
Tracer, 452
Watch Windows, 459-460
projects (QuickSortScaffold), 439-444
View menu items for, 52

decisions (AppWizard), 367-369

DECLARE_DYNAMIC run-time services macro, 350

DECLARE_DYNCREATE macro, 147

DECLARE_DYNCREATE run-time services macro, 350

DECLARE_MESSAGE_MAP macro, 117

DECLARE_MESSAGE_MAP message-map macro, 349

DECLARE_OLECREATE run-time services macro, 350

DECLARE_SERIAL run-time services macro, 350

DECLARE_SERIAL( ) macro, 284-285

Default Project Configuration dialog box, 59-60

Define Subset command (Help menu), 69-71

defining, see user-defined

Delete command (Edit menu), 41

DeleteContents( ) function, 141

DeleteImageList( ) CImageList member function, 184

deleting toolbar buttons, 396

delimiters (ClassWizard comment), 343-344

delivery vs. development constraints (debugging features), 444-445

demo applications
  Array, 231-233
    adding elements, 233-234
    removing elements, 235-236
  File, 278-282
    document classes, 279-280
    source code, 280-283
  File demo 2, 283-284
    CMessages class, 284-288
  File demo 3, 288, 290-293
    CFile class, 289-290
  List, 237-240
    adding nodes, 240-241
    deleting nodes, 241-242
  Map, 244-245
    creating and initializing the map, 245-246
    retrieving values, 246-247
  Paint1 Application, 257-269
    brushes, 265-266
    changing displays, 267-268
    font usage, 261-264
    painting basics, 259-261
    pens, 264-265
    sizing and positioning windows, 268-269

DeptStore.mdb file, 315

derived classes (defined), 104

Description text box, 315

DeselectObject( ) function, 264

designing
  controls (rolling-die ActiveX controls), 601
  Query sample application, 628

DestructElements( ) collection class helper function, 344

destructors (defined), 104

Detach CASynchSocket member function, 298

Detach( ) CImageList member function, 184

Developer Studio
Component Gallery, 672-674
custom AppWizards, 675-677
debugging features, *see* debugging features
editing code
shortcut menu, 25-26
source file toolbar, 26
syntax coloring, 25
text blocks, 24-25
typing/editing, 23-24
files
make, 10
project workspace, 10
hypertext links (changing colors), 10
InfoView (toolbar buttons), 12
integrated development environment, 8
optimization settings, 682-683
projects, 8
Resource View
accelerators, 13
dialog boxes, 13-14
icons, 14-15
menus, 15-16
string tables, 17
toolbars, 17
version information, 18
text editor emulation, 680-681
tools (installing), 678-680
views
choosing, 8-10
Class, 19-21
File, 22
Info, 10-12
Ouput, 23
Resource, 13-18
WizardBar, 26

Developer Studio dialog box editor, 151-153

device contexts, 256-257
Paint1 Application, 257-269
brushes, 265-266
changing displays, 267-268
font usage, 261-264
painting basics, 259-261
pens, 264-265
sizing and positioning windows, 268-269

scrolling windows, 269-274
initializing scroll bars, 271-272
Scroll demo application, 270
updating scrollbars, 272-274

device independent bitmap (DIB), 535

diagnostic function, 346

diagnostic macro, 347

diagnostic services, 346-347

dialog boxes, 150-151
About Developer Studio, 70
Add Data Source, 315
Add Event, 606
Add Member Function, 326, 385
Add Member Variable, 216, 321, 386
Add Node, 240
Add Property, 580, 601, 604, 613
Add Tools, 605
Adding a Class, 216
adding to MFC applications, 150
Advanced Options (creating applications), 81
AppWizard, 559
Bookmark, 44-46
Breakpoints, 46
Browse, 61
CColorDialog class, 150
CDialog class, 150
CFileDialog class, 150
CFontDialog class, 150
Change Message, 290
classes, 109-110
ClassWizard Add Property, 602
coding (with ClassWizard), 92-93
Configurations, 59-60
Control Dialog, 164
Create New Class, 92, 216, 332, 382
creating resources, 151-153
defining dialog and control IDs, 152
Customize, 61
Data Sources, 315
Database Options, 318

Default Project Configuration, 59-60
Define Subset, 69-71
Developer Studio editor, 151-153
Dialog sample application, 154-162
CDlg1 class, 155
controls, 155
creating class objects, 159-162
displaying a simple dialog, 154-155
writing classes, 155-159
Edit Contents Tab Entry, 489
editing, 14
File New, 483
Files, 436
Filter, 335
Find, 41-42
Find In Files, 34-37
Go To, 42-44
Guide Settings, 379
Help Keyboard, 68
help systems, 471
Help Topics, 471, 474, 482
IDD_ABOUTBOX, 213, 524, 561
IDD_EMPLOYEE_FORM, 320
InfoViewer Bookmarks, 44
Insert Object, 508
Insert Project, 54
Insert Resource, 53, 151
modal, 379
modeless, 379
New, 31, 76
New Project Information, 211, 319, 416
New Project Workspace, 76, 317
Application option, 89
Makefile option, 89
Object, 555, 559
ODBC Microsoft Access 7.0 Setup, 316
Open, 32
Open Workspace, 33
Options, 10, 61-63, 476, 524, 564
Page Setup, 37-38
Print, 38, 429
programming controls, 162
Project Settings, 56-58, 445

Properties, 14
Property, 614
Replace, 42, 484
Resource Includes, 50-51
Resource Symbols, 50
Resource View (Developer Studio), 13-14
Search, 67-68
Select Database Tables, 318
ShowString (building), 379-394
    About box, 379-380
    adding member variables to dialog classes, 389
    adding member variables to documents, 390-391
    changing Options dialog, 388-389
    dialog classes, 382-384
    OnDraw( ) function, 392-394
    OnToolsOption( ) function, 391-392
    Options, 381
    Step 1, 317
    Step 2, 318
    Step 4, 319, 372
    String Properties, 406
    Subproject, 59-60
    Toolbar, 50-51, 70
    Window Styles, 81

dialog classes, 358
    adding member variables, 389

Dialog menu commands, 153

Dialog Properties sheet, 214

dialog-based applications, 77
    creating (with AppWizard), 356-361
    files/classes (changing names), 357-358

Dieroll sample application (asynchronous ActiveX control properties), 662-668

DIEROLL.LIC file, 597

DIEROLL.OCX file, 597

diff.Checkpoint( ) function, 463

Directories tab (Options dialog box), 62

DiskFree utility, 749-750

DispatchMessage( ) API function, 115

DisplayFonts( ) function, 263

displaying document data (Rectangles sample application), 142-143

displays
    Paint1 demo app (changing), 267-268
    pattern values (digit vs. dots), 613-616

DispTest, 588-591

DLG1.H file (Dialog sample app), 154

DllMain function, 747-748

DLLs (Dynamic Link Libraries), 89
    creating, 89, 744-752
        DiskFree utility, 749-750
        DllMain function, 747-748
        importing/exporting functions, 748-749
    implicitly loading, 751-752
    MFC AppWizard (DLL), 86-87
    MFC DLL (installing for ActiveX controls), 652-653
    shared DLLs (vs. statically linked applications), 83-84

docking toolbar option (AppWizard), 80

document classes, 109, 130-131, 279-280
    Rectangles sample application (creating), 133-139

document data
    displaying (Rectangles sample application), 142-143
    editing (Rectangles sample application), 143-144
    initializing (Rectangles sample application), 140-141
    serializing (Rectangles sample application), 141-142
    storing (Rectangles sample application), 140

Document Extension Boilerplate, 570

Document Name ShowString value, 557

Document Template Strings tab (Advanced Options dialog box), 81

document templates, 147-148

documents
    ActiveX (building servers), 568-572
    adding member variables, 390-391

DoDataExchange( ) function, 383-384, 600

DoDragDrop( ) member function, 534

DoFilter( ) function, 334, 336-337

domain names (querying)
    creating dialog box, 629-631
    designing sample application, 628
    Finger queries, 641-644
    FTP sites, 637-639
    Gopher sites, 639-641
    HTTP sites, 632-637
    Whois queries, 644-646

DoModal( ) function, 361, 387

DoModal( ) member function, 150, 154, 221

DoPreparePrinting( ) function, 428

DoPropExchange( ) function, 602

DOS applications, *see* console applications

dottedLine SetupTracker( ) style, 527

double colons (::) (function names), 722

double-clicks (ActiveX ShowString), 532-533

DoUpdate( ) function (CCmdUI class), 125

downcasting objects (RTTI), 700-701, 708

drag and drop, ShowString (ActiveX), 533-542
    drag sources, 533-534
    drop targets, 534
    function skeletons, 535-536
    member variables (adding), 535-536
    OnDragDrop( ) function, 541-542
    OnDragEnter function, 536-538

OnDragLeave( ) function, 540
OnDragOver( ) function, 538-540
testing drag targets, 542
views as drop targets, 534-535

drag targets (testing), 542

DragEnter( ) CImageList member function, 184

DragLeave( ) CImageList member function, 184

DragShowNolock( ) CImageList member function, 184

Draw( ) CImageList member function, 184

drawing
classes, 110
code, adding (ActiveX controls), 603-605
optimizing for ActiveX controls, 658-659
multiple items (ActiveX ShowString), 529

DrawText( ) function, 374

Dump member functions (defining), 452-456

Dump( ) function, 521, 551, 553

DumpBin utility, 744-747

DumpElements( ) collection class helper function, 344

Duplicate( ) CFile member function, 289

DWORD data type, 345

dwStyle parameter (CreateWindow( ) API function), 103

Dynamic Link Libraries, see DLLs

dynamic_cast operator, 699-701, 708

E

Edit box dialog control, 163

Edit Contents Tab Entry dialog box, 489

EDIT CONTROL field (Control1 sample app), 163

Edit menu commands, 39-48
Bitmap Image Object, 526
Bookmark, 44-46, 437
Breakpoint, 46, 437
Copy, 41, 561
Cut, 40-41
Delete, 41
Find, 41-42, 483
Go To, 42-44, 437
InfoViewer Bookmarks, 44
Insert New Object, 508, 514, 522
Insert Object, 550
Insert OLE Control, 605
Links, 508, 512
Paste, 41, 512, 561
Paste Link, 512
Paste Special, 508
Properties, 13, 46-48, 478, 556, 614
Redo, 40-41
Replace, 42, 483
Select All, 41
Undo, 40

Edit Properties property sheet, 320

editing
applications (with AppWizard), 90
code (with Developer Studio), 23-26
dialog boxes, 14
document data (Rectangles sample application), 143-144

editor emulation, 680-681

Editor tab (Options dialog box), 62

editors (Developer Studio dialog box), 151-153

ElementAt( ) array member function, 230

Ellipse( ) function, 610

ellipsis (...) (catch blocks), 690

<EMBED> tag, 653-654

embedding
ActiveX controls
in Microsoft Explorer Web pages, 650-653
in Netscape Navigator Web pages, 653-654
objects (ActiveX), 499-500

Empty( ) string class member function, 248

EmptyUndoBuffer( ) CRichEditCtrl member function, 203

emulation, text editor, 680-681

Enable( ) function (CCmdUI class), 125

EnableAutomation( ) function, 578

EnableCompoundFile( ) function, 550

Enabled ActiveX control stock property, 617

enabling (RTTI), 702-704

encapsulation, 105-107
defined, 104

END_CATCH exception macro, 348

END_CATCH_ALL exception macro, 348

END_MESSAGE_MAP macro, 117

END_MESSAGE_MAP message-map macro, 349

EndDrag( ) CImageList member function, 184

EndPaint( ) function, 260

error exceptions, 686-692
catch block placement, 688-689
CException class, 687-688
handling, 686-687
multiple catch blocks, 690-692
throwing, 686

ES_AUTOHSCROLL rich edit style, 202

ES_AUTOVSCROLL rich edit style, 202

ES_CENTER rich edit style, 202

ES_LEFT rich edit style, 202

ES_LOWERCASE rich edit style, 202

ES_MULTILINE rich edit style, 202

ES_NOHIDESEL rich edit style, 202

ES_OEMCONVERT rich edit style, 202

ES_PASSWORD rich edit style, 202

ES_READONLY rich edit style, 203

ES_RIGHT rich edit style, 203

ES_UPPERCASE rich edit style, 203

ES_WANTRETURN rich edit style, 203

event objects (communicating with threads), 723-726

events
ReadyStateChange (asynchronous ActiveX control properties), 665

exception processing, 347-348
functions, 348-351

exceptions, 686-692
catch block placement, 688-689
CException class, 687-688
handling, 686-687
memory (blocking leaks), 465-467
multiple catch blocks, 690-692
throwing, 686

Execute command (Build menu), 56-58, 85, 358, 482, 484

executing
applications, 85
console applications, 740-741
Rectangles sample application, 139

Exit command (File menu), 38

ExitInstance( ) function, 598

exporting/importing (functions in DLLs), 748-749

Extended MAPI, 305

Extended OCX property, 601

Extension Wizard (ISAPI), 308

external tools (installing in Developer Studio), 678-680

ExtractIcon( ) CImageList member function, 184

ExtTextOut( ) function, 604

F

FAR keyword, 747

fields, LOGFONT (Paint1 demo app), 261

File command (Insert menu), 53

File demo application, 278-282
document classes, 279-280
source code, 280-283

File demo 2 application, 283-284
CMessages class, 284-288

File demo 3 application, 288, 290-293
CFile class (member functions), 289-290

file I/O (input/output) classes, 110

File menu commands, 30-38
Change String, 408
Close, 32-33
Close Workspace, 33
Exit, 38
Find, 436
Find In Files, 34-37
New, 31, 76, 139, 476, 522, 596
Open, 32, 139, 475-476, 561
Open Workspace, 33
Page Setup, 37-38
Print, 38, 139
Print Preview, 139
Recent Files and Workspaces, 38
Restore String, 412
Save, 33, 139, 571
Save All, 33
Save As, 33
Update, 546
Wizard, 222

file mode flags, 291-292

file names (creating applications), 84

File New dialog box, 483

File New Name ShowString value, 557

File View (Developer Studio), 22

files
DEBUG_NEW, 464-465
Help system components, 473-474
make (Developer Studio), 10
Print1View.cpp, 420
Print1View.h, 420
project workspace (Developer Studio), 10
reading and writing directly, 288-293
File demo 3 app, 288-293
README.TXT, 365
REGEDIT.EXE, 410
saving, 34
source (toolbars), 26
string, reopening (adding ShowString), 560-566

Files dialog box, 436

Files into Project command (Insert menu), 53-54

Filter dialog box, 335

Filter Extension ShowString value, 557

Filter Name ShowString value, 557

filtering (ODBC database program), 331-335

Find button (Standard toolbar), 72

Find command (Edit menu), 41-42, 483

Find command (File menu), 436

Find In Files button (Standard toolbar), 72

Find In Files command (File menu), 34-37

Find Previous button (Standard toolbar), 72

Find( ) list class member function, 237

Find( ) string class member function, 248

FindIndex( ) list class member function, 237

FindText( ) CRichEditCtrl member function, 203

Finger queries (Query sample application), 641-644

flags, file mode, 291-292

flat database model, 312

flicker-free activation (ActiveX controls), 657

Flush( ) CFile member function, 289

fly-by hints (toolbars), 73

Font ActiveX control stock property, 617

fonts (Paint1 demo app), 261-264
    LOGFONT fields, 261

footnotes (writing Help text), 482

Footnotes command (View menu), 481, 485

ForeColor ActiveX control stock property, 617

Format tab (Options dialog box), 62

Format( ) CTime member function, 249

Format( ) CTimeSpan member function, 250

Format( ) function, 251
    format codes, 251-252

FormatGmt( ) CTime member function, 249

FormatRange( ) CRichEditCtrl member function, 203

formatting, functions (CString class), 344-345

frames (creating applications), 81-83

FreeExtra( ) array member function, 230

FromHandle CASynchSocket member function, 298

FTP sites (Query sample application querying), 637-639

Full Screen command (View menu), 50-51

functions, 563
    Add( ), 234
    AddDocTemplate( ), 148, 511, 549

AddHead( ), 240

AddNew( ) member, 329

AddString( ) member, 167

AddTail( ), 241

AddTail( ) member, 240

AfxBeginThread( ), 342, 716

AfxEndThread( ), 342

AfxFormatString1( ), 345

AfxFormatString2( ), 345

AfxGetApp( ), 342

AfxGetAppName( ), 342

AfxGetInstanceHandle( ), 342

AfxGetMainWnd( ), 342

AfxGetResourceHandle( ), 343

AfxGetThread, 343

AfxMessageBox( ), 345

AfxOleLockApp( ), 578

AfxOleUnlockApp( ), 579

AfxRegisterClass( ), 343

AfxRegisterWndClass( ), 343

AfxSetResourceHandle( ), 343

AfxSocketInit( ), 343

AmbientFont( ), 603

array class member, 230

AssertValid( ), 521, 551, 553

BeginPaint( ) Windows API, 260

CASynchSocket class member, 298-299

CFile member, 289-290

CImageList member, 184-185

CInPlaceFrame member, 553

Close( ), 293

coding messages (Wizard bar), 93-94

CommandToIndex( ), 401, 409

CPrintInfo member, 429

CProgressCtrl member, 176

Create( ), 401

CreateFontIndirect( ), 263

CreateFromFile( ), 516

CreateItem( ), 516

CreateLinkFromFile( ), 516

CreateListView( ) local member, 183

CreateLocator( ), 640-641

CreateNewItem( ), 516

CreateObject( ), 592

CreateProgressBar( ), 176

CreateProgressBar( ) local member, 175

CreateTrackbar( ) local member, 177

CreateTreeView( ) local member, 183

CreateUpDownCtrl( ) local member, 181

CreateWindow( ) API function, 100, 103-104

CRichEditCtrl member, 203-205

CShowStringCntrItem, 518

CSliderCtrl member, 178-179

CSpinButtonCtrl member, 182

CStdioFile, 307

CString class (formatting and message-box display), 344-345

DDV, 159

DDX, 158-159

defined, 104

DeleteContents( ), 141

DeselectObject( ), 264

diff.Checkpoint( ), 463

DispatchMessage( ) API function, 115

DisplayFonts( ), 263

DllMain, 747-748

DoDataExchange( ), 150, 383-384, 600

DoDragDrop( ) member, 534

DoFilter( ), 334, 336-337

DoModal( ), 361, 387

DoModal( ) member, 150, 154, 221

DoPreparePrinting( ), 428

DoPropExchange( ), 602

DoUpdate( ) (CCmdUI class), 125

DrawText( ), 374

Dump (defining), 452-456

Dump( ), 521, 551, 553

Ellipse( ), 610

Enable( ) (CCmdUI class), 125

EnableAutomation( ), 578

EnableCompoundFile( ), 550

encapsulation, 105-107

EndPaint( ), 260

exception processing, 348-351

ExitInstance( ), 598

ExtTextOut( ), 604

Format( ), 251
    format codes, 251-252

GetAmbientProperty( ), 618-619

GetAt( ) member, 235

GetButtonInfo( ), 401

GetButtonStyle( ), 401
GetButtonText( ), 401
GetCheck( ), 226
GetClientRect( ), 274, 375
GetColor( ), 586
GetCurrentTime( ), 250
GetCurSel( ) member, 169
GetDeviceCaps( ), 424
GetDeviceCaps( ) member, 424
GetDlgItem( ), 165, 226
GetDocColor( ), 586
GetDocString( ), 586
GetEmbeddedItem( ), 550
GetExtent( ), 555
GetFilePath( ), 292, 293
GetFtpConnection( ), 307
GetGlobalData( ), 538
GetGlobalData( ) member, 535, 537
GetGopherConnection( ), 307
GetHeadPosition( ) member, 243
GetHttpConnection( ), 307
GetItemID( ), 401
GetItemRect( ), 401
GetLBText( ) member, 170
GetLength( ), 292-293
GetLocalTm( ), 252
GetMessage( ), 286
GetMessage( ) API function, 115
GetMinute( ), 252
GetMonth( ), 252
GetNext( ) member, 243
GetNextAssoc( ) member, 247
GetNextClientItem( ), 528
GetProfileInt( ), 412
GetProfileString( ), 412
GetStartPosition( ), 247, 528
GetStartPosition( ) member, 247
GetString( ), 586
GetTextExtent( ), 409
GetToolBarCtrl( ), 401
GetYear( ), 252
global, 342-343
GlobalLock( ), 537
GlobalUnlock( ), 537
helper (collection class), 344
importing/exporting in DLLs, 748-749
InitInstance( ), 121, 147, 360, 366, 412, 510, 598

InsertAt( ), 234
Invalidate( ), 234, 267
IsBOF( ), 330
IsEmpty( ) member, 243
IsEOF( ), 330
IsPrinting( ), 426
IsSelected( ), 514
LineTo( ), 265
list class member, 237
LoadBitmap( ), 402
LoadToolBar( ), 402
Lock( ), 726
Lookup( ) member, 247
map classes, 244
member, 19-21
    CToolBar class, 401-404
message maps (adding to), 121
MFC printing, 428-431
MoveLast( ), 330
MoveNext( ), 330
MoveTo( ), 265
NotifyChanged( ), 564
ON_WM_PAINT( ), 259
OnActivate( ), 519
OnAppAbout( ), 121, 364, 366
OnBeginPrinting( ), 424
OnCancel( ) member, 168
OnCancelEditCntr( ), 518
OnChange( ), 520
OnChangestring( ), 408
OnCircle( ), 400
OnContextMenu( ), 479-480
OnCreate( ), 175, 406, 535, 553
OnCreateControlBars( ), 553
OnDeactivateUI( ), 520
OnDestroy( ), 412
OnDialogTest( ) message-response, 170
OnDragDrop( ), 541
OnDragEnter( ), 535-536, 540
OnDragLeave( ), 535, 540
OnDragOver( ), 535-536, 538, 540
OnDraw( ), 143, 247, 372, 374, 392-394, 416, 426, 521, 555, 561, 584-586, 613
OnDraw( ) member, 279
OnEditChangemessage( ) member, 290
OnEndOfNetSession( ), 309
OnFileNew( ), 373
OnFileSave( ), 291
OnFilterDept( ), 334, 336

OnFilterID( ), 334, 336
OnFilterName( ), 334, 336
OnFilterRate( ), 334, 336
OnGetEmbedded Item( ), 550
OnGetExtent( ), 552, 564
OnHelpAbout( ), 154
OnHelpInfo( ), 479-480
OnInitDialog( ), 166
OnInitialUpdate( ), 514
OnInitialUpdate( ) member, 271
OnInsertObject( ), 514
OnLarge( ), 193
OnLButtonDown( ), 144, 234, 240, 273, 420, 421, 607
OnLbuttonDown( ), 533
OnLButtonDown( ) message-response, 267
OnList( ), 193
OnMove( ), 327, 329-330
OnMove( ) member, 327
OnNewDocument( ), 141, 372, 524, 561
OnNewDocument( ) member, 279
OnOK( ) member, 168, 170
OnPaint( ), 260
OnPrepareDC( ), 426
OnPreparePrinting( ), 428
OnPropsheet( ), 219
OnRButtonDown( ), 235, 273, 421
OnRecordAdd( ), 327-329
OnRecordDelete( ), 330-331
OnReport( ), 193
OnSetActive( ), 224
OnSetFocus( ), 517
OnSize( ), 517
OnSmall( ), 193
OnSortDept( ), 333, 335-336
OnSortID( ), 333
OnSortName( ), 334
OnSortRate( ), 334
OnStringChanged( ), 588
OnTimer( ), 177
OnToolsOption( ), 391-392
OnToolsOptions( ), 385-386, 524, 564
OnUpdate( ) member, 272
OnUpdateFileSendMail( ), 302
OnWizard( ) member, 226
OnWizardBack( ), 224
OnWizardFinish( ), 224
OnWizardNext( ), 224

OpenURL( ), 307
Partition, 442
PostMessage, 753
PreCreateWindow( ), 268, 553, 555
PtInRect( ), 528
PX_, 603
QueryInterface( ), 504
RecursiveQuickSort, 442
RefreshWindow( ), 587-588, 590
Register( ), 535
RegisterClass( ) API function, 100
RegQueryValueEx( ), 412
RegSetValueEx( ), 412
RemoveAll( ) member, 236
RemoveAt( ), 236
RemoveHead( ) member, 242
RemoveTail( ), 242
scaffolding with console applications, 741-744
SelectObject( ), 264
SelectObject( ) member, 266
sending messages, 753
SendMessage, 753
Serialize( ), 142, 281, 283-284, 293, 302, 372, 521, 551, 561
Serialize( ) member, 280
SetAt( ), 234
SetAtGrow( ), 234
SetBitmap( ), 402
SetButtonInfo( ), 402
SetButtons( ), 402
SetButtonStyle( ), 402
SetButtonText( ), 402
SetCheck( ) (CCmdUI class), 125
SetCheck( ) member, 167
SetCurSel( ), 167
SetCursor( ) member, 531
SetHeight( ), 402
SetHorizCenter( ), 588
SetIndicators( ), 406
SetMaxPage( ), 425
SetMessage( ), 286
SetModifiedFlag( ), 281
SetRadio( ) (CCmdUI class), 125
SetReadOnly( ) member, 329
SetRegistryKey( ), 412
SetScrollSizes( ), 272, 274
SetSelection( ), 531
SetSize( ), 233
SetSizes( ), 402

SetText( ) (CCmdUI class), 125
SetupTracker( ), 526
SetVertCenter( ), 588
SetViewportOrg( ), 427
SetWindowLong( ), 194
SetWizardMode( ) member, 226
ShowBrushes( ), 260, 266
ShowFonts( ), 260
ShowPens( ), 260, 264
skeletons (ActiveX ShowString), 535-536
specific replacement functions (template functions), 694-695
start.Checkpoint( ), 463
StepIt( ), 177
stop.Checkpoint( ), 463
string class member, 248
templates (creating), 692-695
TextOut( ) member, 263
ThreadProc( ), 718
threads, 716
TranslateMessage( ) API function, 115
Unlock( ), 726
Update( ) member, 330
UpdateAllViews( ), 142, 387
UpdateAllViews( ) member, 272
UpdateData( ), 329
UpdateData( ) member, 330
UpdateRegistry( ), 557
virtual functions, 119
WaitForSingleObject( ), 724
WindowProc( ), 200
WinHelp( ), 480
WinMain( ), 114-115
WndProc( ), 115-116
Write( ) member, 292
WriteProfileInt( ), 412
WriteProfileString( ), 412

G

General tab (Project Settings dialog box), 56
GetAccel( ) CSpinButtonCtrl member function, 182
GetAmbientProperty( ) function, 618-619
GetAt( ) member function, 235

GetAt( ) array member function, 230
GetAt( ) list class member function, 237
GetAt( ) string class member function, 248
GetBase( ) CSpinButtonCtrl member function, 182
GetBkColor( ) CImageList member function, 184
GetBuddy( ) CSpinButtonCtrl member function, 182
GetBuffer( ) string class member function, 248
GetButtonInfo( ) function, 401
GetButtonStyle( ) function, 401
GetButtonText( ) function, 401
GetChannelRect( ) CSliderCtrl member function, 178
GetCharPos( ) CRichEditCtrl member function, 203
GetCheck( ) function, 226
GetClientRect( ) function, 274, 375
GetColor( ) function, 586
GetCount( ) list class member function, 237
GetCount( ) map class function, 244
GetCurrentTime( ) function, 250
GetCurrentTime( ) CTime member function, 249
GetCurSel( ) member function, 169
GetDay( ) CTime member function, 249
GetDayOfWeek( ) CTime member function, 249
GetDays( ) CTimeSpan member function, 250
GetDefaultCharFormat( ) CRichEditCtrl member function, 203
GetDeviceCaps( ) function, 424

GetDeviceCaps( ) member function, 424

GetDlgItem( ) function, 165, 226

GetDocColor( ) function, 586

GetDocString( ) function, 586

GetDragImage( ) CImageList member function, 184

GetEmbeddedItem( ) unction, 550

GetEventMask( ) CRichEditCtrl member function, 203

GetExtent( ) function, 555

GetFileName( ) CFile member function, 289

GetFilePath( ) CFile member function, 289

GetFilePath( ) function, 292, 293

GetFileTitle( ) CFile member function, 289

GetFirstVisibleLine( ) CRichEditCtrl member function, 203

GetFromPage( ) CPrintInfo member function, 429

GetFtpConnection( ) function, 307

GetGlobalData( ) function, 538

GetGlobalData( ) member function, 535, 537

GetGmtTm( ) CTime member function, 249

GetGopherConnection( ) function, 307

GetHead( ) list class member function, 237

GetHeadPosition( ) list class member function, 237

GetHeadPosition( ) member function, 243

GetHour( ) CTime member function, 249

GetHours( ) CTimeSpan member function, 250

GetHttpConnection( ) function, 307

GetImageCount( ) CImageList member function, 184

GetImageInfo( ) CImageList member function, 184

GetIRichEditOle( ) CRichEditCtrl member function, 203

GetItemID( ) function, 401

GetItemID( ) method, 403

GetItemRect( ) function, 401

GetItemRect( ) method, 403

GetLastError CASynchSocket member function, 298

GetLBText( ) member function, 170

GetLength( ) CFile member function, 289

GetLength( ) function, 292-293

GetLength( ) string class member function, 248

GetLimitText( ) CRichEditCtrl member function, 203

GetLineSize( ) CSliderCtrl member function, 178

GetLocalTm( ) CTime member function, 250

GetLocalTm( ) function, 252

GetMaxPage( ) CPrintInfo member function, 429

GetMessage( ) API function, 115

GetMessage( ) function, 286

GetMinPage( ) CPrintInfo member function, 429

GetMinute( ) function, 252

GetMinute( ) CTime member function, 250

GetMinutes( ) CTimeSpan member function, 250

GetModify( ) CRichEditCtrl member function, 204

GetMonth( ) CTime member function, 250

GetMonth( ) function, 252

GetNext( ) member function, 243

GetNext( ) list class member function, 237

GetNextAssoc( ) map class function, 244

GetNextAssoc( ) member function, 247

GetNextClientItem( ) function, 528

GetNumTics( ) CSliderCtrl member function, 178

GetPageSize( ) CSliderCtrl member function, 178

GetPaneInfo( ) method, 403

GetPaneStyle( ) method, 403

GetPaneText( ) method, 403

GetPeerName CASynchSocket member function, 298

GetPos( ) CSliderCtrl member function, 179

GetPos( ) CSpinButtonCtrl member function, 182

GetPosition( ) CFile member function, 289

GetPrev( ) list class member function, 237

GetProfileInt( ) functions, 412

GetProfileString( ) functions, 412

GetRange( ) CSliderCtrl member function, 179

GetRange( ) CSpinButtonCtrl member function, 182

GetRangeMax( ) CSliderCtrl member function, 179

GetRangeMin( ) CSliderCtrl member function, 179

GetSafeHandle( ) CImageList member function, 184

GetSecond( ) CTime member function, 250

GetSeconds( ) CTimeSpan member function, 250

GetSelection( ) CSliderCtrl member function, 179

GetSelectionType( ) CRichEditCtrl member function, 204

GetSelText( ) CRichEditCtrl member function, 204

GetSize( ) array member function, 230

GetSockName CASynchSocket member function, 298

GetSockOpt CASynchSocket member function, 298

GetStartPosition( ) function, 247, 528

GetStartPosition( ) map class function, 244

GetStartPosition( ) member function, 247

GetStatus( ) CFile member function, 289

GetStatusBarCtrl( ) method, 403

GetString( ) function, 586

GetTail( ) list class member function, 237

GetTailPosition( ) list class member function, 237

GetTextExtent( ) function, 409

GetTextLength( ) CRichEditCtrl member function, 204

GetThumbRect( ) CSliderCtrl member function, 179

GetTic( ) CSliderCtrl member function, 179

GetTicArray( ) CSliderCtrl member function, 179

GetTicPos( ) CSliderCtrl member function, 179

GetTime( ) CTime member function, 250

GetToolBarCtrl( ) function, 401

GetToPage( ) CPrintInfo member function, 429

GetTotalHours( ) CTimeSpan member function, 250

GetTotalMinutes( ) CTimeSpan member function, 250

GetTotalSeconds( ) CTimeSpan member function, 250

GetUpperBound( ) array member function, 230

GetYear( ) function, 252

GetYear( ) CTime member function, 250

global functions, 342-343

global variables (communicating with threads), 720-721

GlobalLock( ) function, 537

GlobalUnlock( ) function, 537

Go button (Project toolbar), 73

Go To command (Edit menu), 42-44, 437

Gopher sites
Finger queries, 641-644
querying with Query sample application, 639-641
Whois queries, 644-646

graying menus/buttons (command updates), 124-126

grep utility (UNIX), 34

Group box dialog control, 163

Guide Settings dialog box, 379

H

.h files (Help system components), 473

handles, 103-104

handling exceptions, 686-687

HashKey( ) (collection class helper function), 344

hatchedBorder SetupTracker( ) style, 527

hatchInside SetupTracker( ) style, 527

Header files (Help systems), 473

Hello, World! console application (creating), 740-741

Help, 470-473, 475-476
AppWizard support, 474-475
dialog and window differences, 471
programming, 472-473
Command help, 477-478
context help, 478-481
WM_COMMAND message, 472-482
WM_CONTEXTMENU message, 473-482
WM_HELP message, 473-482
reference, 471
system component files, 473-474
task-oriented, 471
user activation, 470-471
writing text, 481-488
adding topics, 485-487
placeholder strings (changing), 482-484

Help command (Help menu), 482, 484

Help menu
adding items, 478
context sensitive help option (AppWizard), 81

Help menu commands, 67-70
About, 153, 470
About Developer Studio, 70
Contents, 67-68
Define Subset, 69-71
Help Topics, 470, 482, 484
Keyboard, 68, 438
Search, 67-68
Set Default Subsets, 69-71
Technical Support, 69-71
Tip of the Day, 69-71
Use Extension Help, 68-71
Web Favorites, 70-71
What's This?, 470

Help Topics command (Help menu), 470

Help Topics dialog box, 471, 474, 482

helper functions (collection class), 344

Hide command (Window menu), 64-66

HideSelection( ) CRichEditCtrl member function, 204

hInstance parameter (CreateWindow( ) API function), 103

hit testing (ActiveX ShowString), 528

.hm files (Help system components), 473

hMenu parameter (CreateWindow( ) API function), 103

hotkeys (debugging features), 434-439

HTML tags
<EMBED>, 653-654
<OBJECT>, 650-653
<PARAM>, 660-661

HTTP sites (Query sample application querying), 632-637

HttpConnection class, 306

Hungarian notation, 101-102

hWnd ActiveX control stock property, 617

hWndParent parameter (CreateWindow( ) API function), 103

hypertext links (changing colors), 10

I

I/O (input/output) classes, 110

Icon File option (New dialog box), 32

icons
bitmap (ActiveX control interfaces), 609
Resource View (Developer Studio), 14-15

ID_DEFAULT_HELP command, 474

ID_HELP, ID_CONTEXT_HELP command, 474

ID_HELP_FINDER command, 474

ID_TOOLS_OPTIONS command, 524, 561

IDD_ABOUTBOX dialog box, 213, 524, 561

IDD_EMPLOYEE_FORM dialog box, 320

IDispatch interface (ActiveX Automation application), 505

IDR_SHOWSTTYPE _SRVR_EMB menu, 561

IDR_SHOWSTTYPE_SRVR_EMB menu, 546

IDR_SHOWSTTYPE_SRVR_IP menu, 546, 561

IDs
command and window, 350
control (defining), 152
dialog (defining) 152

image list controls (Win95), 182-185
creating, 183
initializing, 184-185

IMPLEMENT_DYNAMIC run-time services macro, 350

IMPLEMENT_DYNCREATE macro, 147

IMPLEMENT_DYNCREATE run-time services macro, 350

IMPLEMENT_OLECREATE run-time services macro, 350

IMPLEMENT_SERIAL run-time services macro, 350

IMPLEMENT_SERIAL( ) macro, 285

implicitly loading DLLs (Dynamic Link Libraries), 751-752

importing/exporting (functions in DLLs), 748-749

InfoView (Developer Studio), 10-12
toolbar buttons, 12

InfoViewer Bookmarks command (Edit menu), 44

InfoViewer History List command (View menu), 51-52

InfoViewer Query Results command (View menu), 51

InfoViewer tab (Options dialog box), 62

InfoViewer Topic command (View menu), 52

inheritance (defined), 104

initial status bar option (AppWizard), 81

initializing
constructors, 360
document data (Rectangles sample application), 140-141

InitInstance( ) function, 121, 147, 360, 366, 510, 598

InitInstance( ) member function, 412

Insert menu commands, 52-54
Component, 54, 672
File, 53
Files into Project, 53-54
New String, 406
Object, 550, 555
Project, 54
Resource, 53
Resource Copy, 53-54

Insert New Object command (Edit menu), 508, 514, 522

Insert Object command (Edit menu), 550

Insert Object dialog box, 508

Insert OLE Control command (Edit menu), 605

Insert Resource dialog box, 151

Insert/Remove Breakpoint button (Project toolbar), 73

InsertAfter( ) list class member function, 237

InsertAt( ) function, 234

InsertAt( ) array member function, 230

InsertBefore( ) list class member function, 237

installing
MFC DLL for ActiveX
controls, 652-653
tools in Developer Studio,
678-680

**integrated development
environments, 8**

**interface appearance options
(creating applications),
80-83**

**interfaces, user (ActiveX
controls), 608-613**
bitmap icons, 609-613
displaying dots, 609-613
intuitive, 502-503

**international software
development issues,
754-755**

Internet classes, 305-307

Internet Server API, *see*
ISAPI

**Invalidate( ) function, 234,
267**

**IOCtl CASynchSocket
member function, 298**

ISAPI, 307-310
classes, 308
Extension Wizard, 308

**ISAPI (Internet Server API),
90**

ISAPI Extension Wizard, 90

**IsBlocking CSocket method,
300**

IsBOF( ) function, 330

**IsEmpty( ) list class member
function, 237**

**IsEmpty( ) map class
function, 244**

**IsEmpty( ) member
function, 243**

**IsEmpty( ) string class
member function, 248**

IsEOF( ) function, 330

IsPrinting( ) function, 426

IsSelected( ) function, 514

items
list view controls (creating),
191-193
multiple, drawing (ActiveX
ShowString), 529

J-K

**Java applets (compared to
ActiveX controls), 654-655**

**Keyboard command
(Help menu), 68, 438**

**keys (predefined Registry),
410-411**

keywords
class, 692
FAR, 747
namespace, 710
PASCAL, 747
template, 692
using, 712

L

**LBIndex( ) DDX function,
158**

**LBString( ) DDX function,
158**

**LBStringExact( ) DDX
function, 159**

**Left( ) string class member
function, 248**

**left-button clicks (message
handling), 138-139**

**lfCharSet LOGFONT field
(Paint1 demo app), 261**

**lfClipPrecision LOGFONT
field (Paint1 demo app),
261**

**lfEscapement LOGFONT field
(Paint1 demo app), 261**

**lfFaceName LOGFONT field
(Paint1 demo app), 261**

**lfHeight LOGFONT field
(Paint1 demo app), 261**

**lfItalic LOGFONT field
(Paint1 demo app), 261**

**lfOrientation LOGFONT field
(Paint1 demo app), 261**

**lfOutPrecision LOGFONT
field (Paint1 demo app),
261**

**lfPitchAndFamily LOGFONT
field (Paint1 demo app),
261**

**lfQuality LOGFONT field
(Paint1 demo app), 261**

**lfStrikeOut LOGFONT field
(Paint1 demo app), 261**

**lfUnderline LOGFONT field
(Paint1 demo app), 261**

**lfWeight LOGFONT field
(Paint1 demo app), 261**

**lfWidth LOGFONT field
(Paint1 demo app), 261**

**libraries, type (ActiveX),
591-593**

**LineFromChar( )
CRichEditCtrl member
function, 204**

**LineIndex( ) CRichEditCtrl
member function, 204**

**LineLength( ) CRichEditCtrl
member function, 204**

**LineScroll( ) CRichEditCtrl
member function, 204**

LineTo( ) function, 265

**Link tab (Project Settings
dialog box), 57**

**linking objects (ActiveX),
498-499**

**Links command (Edit menu),
512**

List box dialog control, 163

**LIST BOX field (Control1
sample app), 163**

**list class member function,
237**

list classes, 236-243
List Demo Application,
237-238, 239-240
adding nodes, 240-241
deleting nodes, 241-242
member functions, 237

**list view controls (Win95),
185-195**
creating, 187-189
creating columns, 189-191
creating items, 191-193
image list association, 189
initializing, 189

manipulating, 193-195
styles, 188-189

**Listen CASynchSocket
member function, 298**

listings
4.1 WNDCLASSA Structure
from WINUSER.H, 100
4.2 CWnd::CreateEx( ) from
WINCORE.CPP, 106
5.1 Typical WinMain( )
Routine, 114-115
5.2 Typical WndProc( )
Routine, 115-116
5.3 Message Map from
CHAP17\showstring.h,
116-117
5.4 Message Map from
CHAP17\showstring .cpp,
117
6.1 APP1DOC.H—The
Header File for the
CApp1Doc Class, 130-131
6.2 APP1VIEW.H—The
Header File for the
CApp1View Class, 131-132
6.3 LST6_3.TXT—Code for
Saving the Document's
Data, 137
6.4 LST6_4.TXT—Code for
Loading the Document's
Data, 137
6.5 LST6_5.TXT—Code for
Displaying the Application's
Data, 138
6.6 LST6_6.TXT—Code to
Handle Left-Button Clicks,
138-139
6.7 LST6_7.TXT—Declaring
the Rectangles Application's
Document Data, 140
6.8 LST6_8.TXT—The
Rectangles Application's
OnNewDocument( )
Function, 141
6.9 LST6_9.TXT—The
Rectangles Application's
Serialize( ) Function, 142
6.10 LST6_10.TXT—The
Rectangles Application's
OnDraw( ) Function, 143
6.11 LST6_11.TXT—The
Rectangles Application's
OnLButtonDown( )
Function, 144

6.12 LST6_12.TXT—
Initializing an Application's
Document, 147
7.1 LST7_1.TXT—Declaring
Data Members for the
Dialog Box's Controls., 155
7.2 LST7_2.TXT—Including
the Appropriate Header
Files,
156-157
7.3 LST7_3.TXT—
Constructing a CDlg1
Object, 157
7.4 LST7_4.TXT—Overriding
the DoDataExchange( )
function, 157-158
7.5 LST7_5.TXT—Declaring
Storage for Dialog-Box
Data, 160
7.6 LST7_6.TXT—Initializing
the Frame-Window's Data
Members, 160
7.7 LST7_7.TXT-Transferring
Data to the Dialog-Box
Object
7.8 LST7_8.TXT-Retrieving
Data from the Dialog Box
7.9 LST7_8.TXT—Declaring
Data Members for the
Dialog-Box Class, 166
7.10 LST7_10.TXT—
Initializing a List Box, 167
7.11 LST7_11.TXT—
Initializing a Combo Box,
168
7.12 LST7_12.TXT—Storing
the Status of the Radio
Buttons, 169
7.13 LST7_13.TXT—Storing
the Status of the Check
Boxes, 169
7.14 LST7_14.TXT—Copying
the Dialog Box's Data, 171
8.1 LST8_1.TXT—Declaring
the View Class's Controls,
175
8.2 LST8_2.TXT—Initializing
the Trackbar Control, 179
8.3 LST8_3.TXT—Responding
to a Trackbar Control, 180
8.4 LST8_4.TXT—Creating
the List View's Image Lists,
187-188
8.5 LST8_5.TXT—The
LV_COLUMN Structure,
190

8.6 ST8_6.TXT—Initializing
the LV_COLUMN
Structure, 190
8.7 LST8_7.TXT—Creating
the SubItem Columns, 191
8.8 LST8_8.TXT—The
LV_ITEM Structure, 191
8.9 LST8_9.TXT—Initializing
the LV_ITEM Structure, 192
8.10 LST8_10.TXT—Creating
a List View Item, 192
8.11 LST8_11.TXT—Creating
Additional Items and
SubItems, 193
8.12 LST8_12.TXT—Creating
the View Buttons, 193
8.13 LST8_13.TXT—
Changing to the List View,
194
8.14 LST8_14.TXT—Creating
the Tree View Control's
Image List, 196
8.15 LST8_15.TXT—The
TV_ITEM Structure, 198
8.16 LST8_16.TXT—The
TV_INSERTSTRUCT
Structure, 198-199
8.17 LST8_17.TXT—Creating
the Root Item, 199
8.18 LST8_18.TXT—Inserting
the Child Items into the
Tree View Control, 199-200
8.19 LST8_19.TXT—Handling
Tree-View Notifications, 200
8.20 LST8_20.TXT—Creating
Editing Control Buttons, 205
8.21 LST8_21.TXT:—The
CHARFORMAT Structure,
206
8.22 LST8_22.TXT—
Determining Whether to
Turn Underlining On or Off,
206
8.23 LST8_23.TXT—
Changing Paragraph
Formats, 207
9.1 LST9_1.TXT-Code for the
OnDraw( )Function
9.2 LST9_2.TXT—Code for
the OnPropSheet( )
Function, 219-220
9.3 LST9_3.TXT—Handling
the Property Sheet's Return
Value, 222

9.4 LST9_4.TXT—The OnSetActive( ) Member Function, 224

9.5 LST9_5.TXT—Responding to Wizard Buttons, 225-226

9.6 LST9_6.TXT—Displaying a Property Sheet as a Wizard, 359-360

10.1 LST10_1.TXT—The OnLButtonDown( ) Function, 234

10.2 LST10_2.TXT—Array Demo's OnDraw( ) Function, 235

10.3 LST10_3.TXT—The OnRButtonDown( ) Function, 235-236

10.4 LST10_4.TXT—The CNode Structure, 239

10.5 LST10_5.TXT—Creating the First Node, 240

10.6 LST10_6.TXT—List Demo's OnLButtonDown( ) Function, 240

10.7 LST10_7.TXT—The OnRButtonDown( ) Function, 241

10.8 LST10_8.TXT—The List Demo Application's OnDraw( ) Function, 242

10.9 LST10_9.TXT—Deleting the List's Objects, 243

10.10 LST10_10.TXT—Initializing the Map Object, 246

10.11 LST10_11.TXT—The Map Demo Application's OnLButtonDown( ) Function, 246

10.12 LST10_12.TXT—The Map Demo Application's OnDraw( ) Function, 247

10.13 LST10_13.TXT—The tm Structure, 252

10.14 LST10_14.TXT—Calculating a Time Span, 253

10.15 LST10_15.TXT—A Sample Structure, 253

11.1 LST11_1.TXT—The Application's Message Map, 259

11.2 LST11_2.TXT—Creating the Paint DC on the Stack, 261

11.3 LST11_3.TXT—Initializing a LOGFONT Structure, 262

11.4 LST11_4.TXT—Creating Brush Objects, 266

11.5 LST11_5.TXT—Changing the Value of m_display, 267

11.6 LST11_6.TXT—Overriding the PreCreateWindow( ) Member Function, 268

11.7 LST11_7.TXT—The CREATESTRUCT Structure, 269

11.8 LST11_8.TXT—The OnInitialUpdate( ) Function, 272

11.9 LST11_9.TXT—Initializing the Scroll Application's LOGFONT Structure, 272-273

11.10 LST11_10.TXT—Displaying the Lines of Text, 273

11.11 LST11_11.TXT—Changing the Line Count, 273-274

12.1 LST12_1.TXT—Initializing the Document's Data, 280

12.2 LST12_2.TXT—Displaying the Document's Data, 280

12.3 LST12_3.TXT—Changing the Document's Data, 281

12.4 LST12_4.TXT—The Document Class's Serialize( ) Function, 281-282

12.5 LST12_5.TXT—One Way to Save the New Class's String's, 282

12.6 MESSAGES.H—The CMessages Class's Header File, 284

12.7 MESSAGES.CPP—The CMessages Class's Implementation File, 285

12.8 LST12_8.TXT—Initializing the Data Object, 286

12.9 LST12_9.TXT—Editing the Data Strings, 287

12.10 LST12_10.LST—Serializing the Data Object, 287

12.11 LST12_11.TXT—Changing the Display String, 290

12.12 LST12_12.TXT—The Application's OnFileSave( ) Function, 291

12.13 LST12_13.TXT—Reading from the File, 292-293

13.1 (Excerpt from \MSDev\Include\XCMC.H) Command Definitions /* NAME TYPES */, 304-305

14.1 LST14_01.TXT:—Code for the OnRecordAdd( ) Function, 327

14.2 LST14_02.TXT:—Code for the OnMove( ) Function, 328

14.3 LST14_03.TXT:—Code for the OnRecordDelete( ) Function, 328

14.4 LST14_04.TXT:—Code for the OnSortDept( ) Function, 333

14.5 LST14_05.TXT:—Code for the OnSortID( ) Function, 333

14.6 LST14_06.TXT:—Code for the OnSortName( ) Function, 334

14.7 LST14_07.TXT:—Code for the OnSortRate( ) Function, 334

14.8 LST14_08.TXT:—The DoFilter( ) Function, 334-335

16.1 dialog16.h-Main Header File

16.2 CDialog16App::InitInstance( ), 360-361

16.3 Chap16sdi.h—Main Header File for the CHAP16SDI Application, 361-362

16.4 CChap16sdiApp::InitInstance( ), 362-363

16.5 Chap16mdi.h—Main Header File for the CHAP16MDI Application, 365-366

16.6 CChap16mdiApp::InitInstance ( ), 366-367

17.1 ShowStringDoc.cpp—CShowStringDoc::Serialize ( ), 373

17.2 ShowString.cpp—Message Map, 373-374

17.3 ShowStringDoc.cpp—CShowStringDoc::OnNewDocument ( ), 374

17.4 ShowStringView.cpp—CShowStringView::OnDraw ( ), 374

17.5 OptionsDialog.h—Header File for COptionsDialog, 383

17.6 OptionsDialog.cpp—Implementation File for COptionsDialog, 383-384

17.7 ShowStringDoc.h—Message Map for CShowStringDoc, 385

17.8 ShowStringDoc.cpp—Message Map for CShowStringDoc, 385

17.9 ShowStringDoc.cpp—OnToolsOptions ( ), 386-387

17.10 ShowStringDoc.h—CShowStringDoc Member Variables, 390

17.11 ShowStringDoc.cpp—Serialize ( ), 390-391

17.12 ShowStringDoc.cpp—OnNewDocument ( ), 391

17.13 ShowStringDoc.cpp—OnToolsOptions ( ), 392

17.14 ShowStringDoc.cpp—OnDraw ( ) Additions Before DrawText( ) Call, 393

17.15 ShowStringDoc.cpp—OnDraw ( ) Additions After DrawText( ) Call, 393

18.1 LST18_1.TXT—An Empty Message-Response Function, 400

18.2 LST18_2.TXT—Drawing a Circle, 400-401

18.3 LST18.3.TXT—The Indicator Array, 406

18.4 LST18_4.TXT—Adding the New Pane's ID, 406-407

18.5 LST18_5.TXT—Adding the Handler to the Message Map, 407

18.6 LST18_6.TXT—The Pane's Command-Update Handl, 408

18.7 LST18_7.TXT—Changing the Panel's Text and Size, 409

19.1 LST19_01.TXT—Lines for the OnRButtonDown ( ) Function, 422

19.2 LST19_02.TXT—New Lines for OnDraw ( ), 422

19.3 LST19_03.TXT—The Default OnBeginPrinting ( ), 424

19.4 LST19_04.TXT—The New OnBeginPrinting ( ), 425

19.5 LST19_05.TXT—Lines for the OnPrepareDC ( ) Function, 426

19.6 LST19_06.TXT—The Default Version of OnPreparePrinting ( ), 428

19.7 LST19_07.TXT—Printing Headers and Footers in OnPrint ( ), 430

19.8 LST19_08.TXT—Controlling the Entire Printing Process in OnPrint ( ), 430

20.1 SORTS.CPP—Demonstration of Developer Studio Debugging, 440-441

20.2 (Assumption.Cpp)—A Simple Use of assert: My Assumption Was Integers Are Initialized by Default; They Are Not, 447

20.3 afxwin.h—Possible Values for afxTraceFlags, 452

20.4 DumpContextDemo.Cpp—Demonstrates the MFC Debugging ClassCDump Context and CFile, 454-455

20.5 discardme.txt—Output File from DumpContextDemo.Exe, 456

20.6 RunTimeDemo.Cpp—Demonstrates the MFc CRuntimeClass, 457

20.7 MemoryStateDemo. Cpp—Demonstrates the CmemoryState Class, 463

20.8 Output from MemoryStateDemo.Exe, 464

20.9 A Scaled Down Version of the auto_ptrClass, 466

23.1 Excerpt from ShowString.cpp—Library Initialization, 511

23.2 Excerpt from ShowString.cpp—Message Map Additions, 511

23.3 Excerpt from ShowStringView.h—m_pSelection, 512

23.4 ShowStringView.cpp—Constructor, 513

23.5 ShowStringView.cpp—CShowStringView::OnDraw ( ), 513

23.6 ShowStringView.cpp—CShowStringView::OnInitialUpdate ( ), 514

23.7 ShowStringView.cpp—CShowStringView::IsSelected ( ), 514

23.8 ShowStringView.cpp—CShowStringView::OnInsertObject ( ), 514-515

23.9 ShowStringView.cpp—Display the Insert Object Dialog Box, 515

23.10 ShowStringView.cpp—Create a New Item, 515

23.11 ShowStringView.cpp—Initializing the Inserted Item, 516

23.12 ShowStringView.cpp—Update Selection and Views, 516

23.13 ShowStringView.cpp—CATCH Block, 516-517

23.14 ShowStringView.cpp—CShowStringView::OnSetFocus ( ), 517

23.15 ShowStringView.cpp—CShowStringView::OnSize ( ), 517

23.16 ShowStringView.cpp—CShowStringView::OnCancelEditCntrl ( ), 518

23.17 CntrItem.cpp—CShowStringCntrItem::OnChange ( ), 519

23.18 CntrItem.cpp—CShowStringCntrItem::OnActivate, 519

23.19 CntrItem.cpp—
CShowStringCntrItem::
OnGetItemPosition( ), 520

23.20 CntrItem.cpp—
CShowStringCntrItem ::
OnDeactivateUI( ), 520

23.21 CntrItem.cpp—
CShowStringCntrItem
::OnchangeItemPosition( ),
521

23.22 CntrItem.cpp—
CShowStringCntrItem
::Serialize( ), 521-522

23.23 CntrItem.cpp—
Constructor, 525

23.24 CntrItem.cpp—
CShowStringCntrItem
::Serialize( ), 526

23.25 ShowStringView.cpp—
CShowStringView
::SetupTracker( ), 527

23.26 ShowStringView.cpp—
CShowStringView::
SetupTracker( ), 528

23.27 ShowStringView.cpp—
Lines in OnDraw( ) to
Replace, 529

23.28 ShowStringView.cpp—
New Lines in OnDraw( ),
529

23.29 ShowStringView.cpp—
CShowStringView
::ONLButtonDown( ),
530-531

23.30 ShowStringView.cpp—
CShowStringView
::SetSelection( ), 531

23.31 ShowStringView.cpp—
CShowStringView
::OnSetCursor( ), 532

23.32 ShowStringView.cpp—
CShowStringView
::OnLButtonDblClk( ), 533

23.33 ShowStringView.cpp—
CShowStringView::OnCreate( ),
535

23.34 ShowStringView.cpp—
CShowStringView
::OnDragEnter( ), 536, 537

23.35 ShowStringView.cpp—
Can Object Be Dropped?,
537

23.36 ShowStringView.cpp—
Set dragsize and dragoffset,
537-538

23.37 ShowStringView.cpp—
Determine Drop Effect, 539

23.38 ShowStringView.cpp—
Adjust the Focus
Rectangles, 540

23.39 ShowStringView.cpp—
ShowStringView
::OnDragLeave( ), 540

23.40 ShowStringView.cpp—
Structure of OnDrop( ), 541

23.41 ShowStringView.cpp—
Removing the Focus
Rectangle, 541

23.42 ShowStringView.cpp—
Paste in the Data Object,
541

23.43 ShowStringView.cpp—
Adjust Item Dimensions,
542

23.44 ShowStringView.cpp—
CShowStringView
::OnEditClear( ), 543

24.1 Excerpt from
ShowString.cpp—CLSID,
548

24.2 Excerpt from
ShowString.cpp—Initializing
Libraries, 548

24.3 Excerpt from
ShowString.cpp—
Registering Running MDI
Apps, 549

24.4 Excerpt from
ShowString.cpp—Checking
How the App Was
Launched, 549

24.6 SrvrItem.cpp—
CShowStringSrvrItem
::Serialize( ), 551

24.7 SrvrItem.cpp—
CShowStringSrvrItem
::OnDraw( ), 552

24.8 SrvrItem.cpp—
CShowStringSrvrItem
::OnGetExtent( ), 552-553

24.9 IPFrame.cpp—
CInPlaceFrame::OnCreate( ),
553-554

24.10 IPFrame.cpp—
CInPlaceFrame::
OnCreateControlBars( ),
554

24.11 IPFrame.cpp—
CInPlaceFrame::
PreCreateWindow( ), 555

24.12 ShowString.cpp—
Excerpt from
ShowStringApp::InitInstance( ),
556-557

24.13 ShowStringView.cpp—
CShowStringView
::OnDraw( ), 562-563

24.14 SrvrItem.cpp—
CShowStringSrvrItem
::OnDraw( ), 563-564

25.1 ShowString.cpp—CLSID,
576

25.2 ShowString.cpp—
Initializing Libraries, 577

25.3 ShowString.cpp—How
the app Was Launched, 577

25.4 ShowStringDoc.cpp—
Dispatch Map, 577

25.5 ShowStringDoc.cpp—
IID, 578

25.6 ShowStringDoc.cpp—
Constructor, 578

25.7 ShowStringDoc.cpp—
Dispatch Map, 582

25.8 ShowStringDoc.cpp—
Notification, Get, and Set
Functions, 583

25.9 ShowStringDoc.cpp—
Get and Set Functions for
the Centering Flags, 584

25.10 ShowStringDoc.cpp—
Get and Set Functions, 584

25.11 ShowStringDoc.cpp—
CShowStringDoc
::Serialize( ), 585

25.12 ShowStringDoc.cpp—
CShowStringView
::OnDraw( ), 585-586

25.13 ShowString.cpp— How
the app Was Launched, 586

25.14 ShowStringDoc.cpp—
CShowStringDoc
::ShowWindow( ), 587

25.15 ShowStringDoc.cpp—
CShowStringDoc
::RefreshWindow( ), 588

25.16 ShowStringDoc.cpp—
CShowStringDoc
::SetHorizCenter( ), 588

25.17 Form1.frm—DispTest
code, 589

25.18 ShowString.odl—
ShowString Type Library,
592

26.1 Excerpt from DierollCtl.h—Event Map, 599

26.2 Excerpt from DierollCtl.cpp—Event Map, 599

26.3 Excerpt from DierollCtl.cpp—Property Pages, 599

26.4 DierollPropPage.cpp—CDierollPropPage::CDierollPropPage(), 600

26.5 DierollPropPage.cpp—CDierollPropPage::DoDataExchange(), 600

26.6 DierollPropPage.cpp—CDierollPropPage::DoDataExchange(), 600

26.7 DierollCtl.cpp—CDierollCtrl::DoPropExchange(), 602

26.8 DierollCtl.cpp—CDierollCtrl::OnDraw(), 604

26.9 DierollCtl.cpp—CDierollCtrl::Roll(), 608

26.10 DierollCtl.cpp—CDierollCtrl::OnDraw(), 609-610

26.11 DierollCtl.cpp—CDierollCtrl::OnDraw(), 611-612

26.12 DierollCtl.cpp—CDierollCtrl::OnDraw(), 614

26.13 DierollCtl.cpp—Property Pages, 620

26.14 DierollCtl.cpp—Property Pages, 621

26.15 DierollCtl.cpp—Dispatch map, 621

26.16 DierollCtl.cpp—CDierollCtrl::OnDraw(), 622

27.1 QueryDlg.cpp—CQueryDlg::OnQuery(), 632

27.2 QueryDlg.cpp—CQueryDlg::TryURL(), 633

27.3 QueryDlg.cpp—CQueryDlg::TryURL(), 636

27.4 QueryDlg.cpp—CQueryDlg::TryURL(), 636

27.5 QueryDlg.cpp—CQueryDlg::TryFTPSite(), 638

27.6 QueryDlg.cpp—CQueryDlg::TryGopherSite(), 639-640

27.7 QueryDlg.cpp—CQueryDlg::TryFinger() Excerpt, 643

27.8 QueryDlg.cpp—CQueryDlg::TryFinger(), 643-644

27.9 QueryDlg.cpp—CQueryDlg::TryWhois(), 645

28.1 fatdie.html—Using <OBJECT>, 650

28.2 fatdie2.html—Using <OBJECT> and <EMBED>, 653-654

28.3 Excerpt from DierollCtl.cpp—Setting Activates when Visible, 656

28.4 Excerpt from DierollCtl.cpp— Fine-tuning Activates when Visible, 658

28.5 DierollCtl.cpp—Get and Set Functions, 663-664

28.6 DierollCtl.cpp—Completed Get and Set Functions, 664-665

28.7 DierollCtl.cpp—CDierollCtrl::OnResetState(), 665

28.8 DierollCtl.cpp—CDierollCtrl::GetImage(), 666

28.9 DierollDataPathProperty.cpp—OnDataAvailable(), 667

28.10 DierollDataPathProperty.cpp—New Code for OnDraw(), 667-668

30.1 EXCEPTION.CPP—Simple Exception Handling, 686

30.2 EXCEPTION2.CPP—Creating an Exception Class, 687-688

30.3 EXCEPTION3.CPP—Catching Exceptions Outside of the Throwing Function, 689

30.4 EXCEPTION4.CPP—Using Multiple Catch Blocks, 690-691

30.5 LST30_05.TXT—The Basic Form of a Function Template, 693

30.6 TEMPLATE.CPP—Using a Typical Function Template, 693

30.7 TEMPLATE2.CPP—Using a Specific Replacement Function, 694-695

30.8 LST30_08.TX—Defining a Class Template, 695

30.9 TEMPLATE3.CPP—Using a Class Template, 696-697

30.10 LST30_10.TXT—Using Multiple Parameters with a Class Template, 698

30.11 TEMPLATE4.CPP—Using Specific Data Types as Parameters in a Class Template, 699

30.12 LST30_12.TXT—The type_info Class, 700

30.13 RTTI.CPP—Using the typeid Operator, 701-702

30.14 RTTI2.CPP—A Typical Case of Class Derivation, 704-705

30.15 RTTI3.CPP—Using Casting, 706-707

30.16 RTTI4.CPP—A Final Example of RTTI Downcasting, 708-709

30.17 LST30_17.TXT—Defining a Namespace, 710

30.18 LST30_18.TXT—Defining a Function Outside of the Namespace Definition, 710-711

30.19 LST30_19.TXT—Nesting Namespace Definitions, 711

30.20 LDT30_20.TXT—Resolving Scope with the using Keyword, 712

30.21 LST30_21.TXT—Defining an Unnamed Namespace, 712

30.22 NAMESPACE.CPP—Using a Namespace Alias, 713

31.1 LST31_01.TXT—The ThreadProc() Function, 718

31.2 LST31_2.TXT—The New ThreadProc( ) Function (global variables), 721

31.3 LST31_03.TXT—The New ThreadProc( ) Function (user-defined messages), 722-723

31.4 LST31_04.TXT—The OnThreadended( ) Function, 723

31.5 LST31_05.TXT—Yet Another New ThreadProc( ) Function (event objects), 724-725

31.6 COUNTARRAY.H—The CCountArray Class's Header File, 727

31.7 COUNTARRAY.CPP— The CCountArray Class's Implementation File, 728

31.8 LST31_08.TXT—New Thread Functions, 729

31.9 CCOUNTARRAY2.H— The CCountArray2 Class's Header File, 732

31.10 COUNTARRAY2.CPP— The CCountArray2 Class's Implementation File, 732

31.11 SOMERESOURCE.H— The CSomeResource Class's Header File, 734

31.12 SOMERESOURCE.CPP— The CSome Resource Class's Implementation File, 735

31.13 LST31_13.TXT—New Thread Functions, 736

31.14 LST31_14.TXT—New Code for the OnStartthread( ) Function, 736

32.1 (HelloWorld.Cpp) "Welcome to Valhalla Tower...", 741

32.2 (SORTS.H) The Header File Contains the RecursiveQuicksort Function Declaration, 742-743

32.3 (SORTS.CPP) The Quicksort and Parsing Function Definitions and Scaffold, 743-744

32.4 (DiskFree.h) Contains the Declarations and Reusable Import and Export Macros, 749

32.5 (DiskFree.Cpp) Winbase.H Causes the GetDiskFreeSpace Function to be Imported, 749-750

32.6 (TestDiskFree.Cpp) A Console Application Which Tests the DiskFree.Dll, 752

32.7 Microsoft's WINUSER.H Implementing Unicode Support, 755

LoadBitmap( ) function, 402

loading
DLLs implicitly, 751-752
document data, 137

LoadStdProfileSettings( ) controls, 363

LoadToolBar( ) function, 402

Lock( ) function, 726

LockRange( ) CFile member function, 289

LOGFONT fields (Paint1 demo app), 261

logo requirements, Windows 95 (MAPI), 302-303

LONG data type, 345

Lookup( ) map class function, 244

Lookup( ) member function, 247

LPARAM data type, 345

lpClassName parameter (CreateWindow( ) API function), 103

LPCRECT data type, 345

LPCSTR data type, 345

lpParam parameter (CreateWindow( ) API function), 103

LPSTR data type, 345

LPVOID data type, 345

lpWindowName parameter (CreateWindow( ) API function), 103

LRESULT data type, 345

LVS_ALIGNLEFT list view style, 188

LVS_ALIGNTOP list view style, 188

LVS_AUTOARRANGE list view style, 188

LVS_EDITLABELS list view style, 188

LVS_ICON list view style, 188

LVS_LIST list view style, 188

LVS_NOCOLUMNHEADER list view style, 188

LVS_NOITEMDATA list view style, 188

LVS_NOLABELWRAP list view style, 188

LVS_NOSCROLL list view style, 188

LVS_NOSORTHEADER list view style, 188

LVS_OWNERDRAWFIXED list view style, 188

LVS_REPORT list view style, 188

LVS_SHAREIMAGELISTS list view style, 188

LVS_SINGLESEL list view style, 189

LVS_SMALLICON list view style, 189

LVS_SORTASCENDING list view style, 189

LVS_SORTDESCENDING list view style, 189

M

m_bContinuePrinting CPrintInfo member function, 429

m_bDirect CPrintInfo member function, 429

m_bPreview CPrintInfo member function, 429

m_nCurPage CPrintInfo member function, 429

m_nNumPreviewPages CPrintInfo member function, 429

m_numRects member variable, 420

m_pPD CPrintInfo member function, 429

m_rectDraw CPrintInfo member function, 429

m_strPageDesc CPrintInfo member function, 429

macros
DECLARE_DYNCREATE, 147
IMPLEMENT_DYNCREATE, 147
message-map, 117-118, 348-349
run-time object services, 349-350
RUNTIME_CLASS, 147

MAINFRM.CPP file (Dialog sample app), 154

MAINFRM.CPP Control1 source file, 164

MAINFRM.H Control1 source file, 164

MAINFRM.H file (Dialog sample app), 154

make files (Developer Studio), 10

Makefile option (New Project Workspace dialog box), 89

MakeLower( ) string class member function, 248

MakeReverse( ) string class member function, 248

MakeUpper( ) string class member function, 248

map class function, 244

map classes, 244-247
functions, 244
Map Demo Application, 244-245
creating and initializing the map, 245-246
retrieving values, 246-247

MAPI, 110
advanced functions, 303-310
Common Messaging Calls (CMC), 303
Extended MAPI, 305
OLE Messaging, 305
Win95 logo requirements, 302-303

MAPI option (AppWizard), 81

mapping modes (scaling), 418-419

MaxChars( ) DDV function, 159

MDI (Multiple Document Interface) applications, 77

MDI (multiple document interface) applications, creating (with AppWizard), 365-367

member functions, 19-21
CommandToIndex( ), 409
CToolBar class, 401-404
Dump (defining), 452-456
InitInstance( ), 412
SetIndicators( ), 406
SetRegistryKey( ), 412

member functions, see functions

member variables, 19-21
ActiveX ShowString, 535-536
defined, 104
dialog box controls (connecting to), 92-93

Member Variables tab, 616

memory
blocking leaks during exceptions, 465-467
sealing leaks, 461-467

menus
Build, 54-60
coding (with ClassWizard), 90-92
debugging features, 434-439
Edit, 39-48
File, 30-38
graying (command updates), 124-126
Help, 67-70
adding items, 478
IDR_SHOWSTTYPE _SRVR_EMB, 561
IDR_SHOWSTTYPE_SRVR_EMB, 546
IDR_SHOWSTTYPE_SRVR_IP, 546, 561
Insert, 52-54
Resource View (Developer Studio), 15-16
shortcut
editing code (with Developer Studio), 25-26

ShowString (building), 375-378
System menu, 470
Tools, 60-63
unique mnemonics in, 56
View, 48-52
Window, 63-66

message loops, 114-116

message maps, 116-120
adding user-defined messages to, 754
ClassWizard, 120-121
coding menus, 91-92
functions (adding to), 121
macros, 117-118
polymorphism, 119

message-box display functions (CString class), 344-345

message-map macros, 348-349

messages, 109, 113
ActiveX controls, 657, 658
coding (Wizard bar), 93-94
left-button clicks (handling), 138-139
posting, 753
prefixes, 121-123
relationship to commands, 123-124
routing, 114
sending, 752-754
user-defined, 753-754
communicating with threads, 721-723
WM_COMMAND (programming Help systems), 472
WM_CONTEXTMENU programming Help systems, 473
WM_HELP (programming Help systems), 473
WM_LBUTTONDOWN, 607

Messaging API, see MAPI

methods
CanUpdate( ), 330
COLEControl, 603
CommandToIndex( ), 403
Create( ), 403
CSocket class, 300
GetItemID( ), 403
GetItemRect( ), 403
GetPaneInfo( ), 403

GetPaneStyle( ), 403
GetPaneText( ), 403
GetStatusBarCtrl( ), 403
of the CStatusBar class, 403
SetIndicators( ), 403
SetPaneInfo( ), 403
SetPaneStyle( ), 403
SetPaneText( ), 403
ShowWindow( ), 586
see also functions

MFC (Microsoft Foundation Classes), 99
printing functions, 428-431
see also classes

MFC applications (Registry), 411-412

MFC AppWizard (DLL), 86-87

MFC ClassWizard property sheet, 216

MFC DLL (installing for ActiveX controls), 652-653

MFC Tracer, *see* Tracer

Microsoft Explorer Web pages (embedding ActiveX controls), 650-653

Microsoft Foundation Classes (MFC), 99

Microsoft Office Binder, 568

Mid( ) string class member function, 248

MinMaxByte( ) DDV function, 159

MinMaxDouble( ) DDV function, 159

MinMaxDWord( ) DDV function, 159

MinMaxFloat( ) DDV function, 159

MinMaxInt( ) DDV function, 159

MinMaxLong( ) DDV function, 159

MinMaxUInt( ) DDV function, 159

MM_HIENGLISH mapping mode, 418

MM_HIMETRIC mapping mode, 418

MM_ISOTROPIC mapping mode, 418

MM_LOENGLISH mapping mode, 418

MM_LOMETRIC mapping mode, 419

MM_TEXT mapping mode, 419

MM_TWIPS mapping mode, 419

mnemonics (unique in menus), 56

modal dialog box, 379

modeCreate (CFile mode flag), 291

modeless dialog box, 379

models
Component Object Model (ActiveX), 503-504
database
flat, 312
relational, 312

modeNoInherit CFile mode flag, 291

modeNoTruncate CFile mode flag, 292

modeRead CFile mode flag, 292

modeReadWrite CFile mode flag, 292

modes, mapping (scaling), 418-419

modeWrite CFile mode flag, 292

monikers, BLOBs (Binary Large OBjects), 661-662

MoveLast( ) function, 330

MoveNext( ) function, 330

MoveTo( ) function, 265

moving items, ShowString (ActiveX), 524-527

multiple catch blocks (exception handling), 690-692

Multiple Document Interface (MDI) applications, 77

multiple items, drawing (ActiveX ShowString), 529

multiple objects (ActiveX ShowString), 528-533
hit testing, 528-529

multitasking (defined), 715

mutexes (thread synchronization), 731-733

N

Name text box, 155

namespaces, 709-713
aliases for, 712-713
scope resolution, 711-712
unnamed, 712
user-defined, 710-711

naming
applications, 81
files/classes (application creation), 84
variables (Hungarian notation), 101-102

nesting
dual-purpose ActiveX applications, 566
namespace definitions, 711

Netscape Navigator Web pages (embedding ActiveX controls), 653-654

New Accelerator button (Project toolbar), 73

New Bitmap button (Project toolbar), 73

New command (File menu), 31, 76, 139, 476, 522, 596

New Cursor button (Project toolbar), 73

New Dialog button (Project toolbar), 73

New Icon button (Project toolbar), 73

New Menu button (Project toolbar), 73

New Project Information dialog box, 211, 319, 416

New Project Workspace dialog box, 76, 317
Application option, 89
Makefile option, 89

New Source File button
(Standard toolbar), 72

New String command (Insert
menu), 406

New String Table button
(Project toolbar), 73

New Toolbar button (Project
toolbar), 73

New Version button (Project
toolbar), 73

New Window command
(Window menu), 64-66

nHeight parameter
(CreateWindow( ) API
function), 103

nodes (List Demo app)
adding, 240-241
deleting, 241-242

NotifyChanged( ) function,
564

Number OCX properties, 601

nWidth parameter
(CreateWindow( ) API
function), 103

O

Object command (Insert
menu), 550, 555

Object Definition Language
(ODL), 591

Object dialog box, 555, 559

Object Linking and
Embedding, *see* OLE

<OBJECT> tag, 650-653

objects
CArchive (creating your
own), 293
CShowStringApp, 576-577
CTime class, 250-252
CTimeSpan class, 252-253
defined, 104
deleting, ShowString
(ActiveX), 542-543
embedding (ActiveX), 499-500
linking (ActiveX), 498-499
multiple, ShowString
(ActiveX), 528-533
persistence, 278
File demo app, 278-282

run-time model services,
349-350
ShowTest, 590-591

OCXs, creating (OLE Control
Wizard), 87-89

ODBC database classes, 314

ODBC database program
(creating), 315-337
adding and deleting records,
324-328
creating the basic employee
application, 317-320
database display (creating),
320-323
DoFilter( ) function, 336-337
OnMove( ) function, 329-330
OnRecordAdd( ) function,
328-329
OnRecordDelete( ) function,
330-331
OnSortDept( ) function,
335-336
registering the database,
315-316
sorting and filtering, 331-335

ODBC Microsoft Access 7.0
Setup dialog box, 316

OffsetPos( ) CProgressCtrl
member function, 176

OLE (Object Linking and
Embedding), 79
Control Test Container
command (Tools menu),
604
Control Wizard, 87-89, 505
Messaging (MAPI), 305
support (creating
applications), 79-80
Types tab (Project Settings
dialog box), 58

ON_COMMAND macro, 117

ON_COMMAND message-
map macro, 349

ON_COMMAND_RANGE
macro, 117

ON_COMMAND_RANGE
message-map macro, 349

ON_COMMAND_UPDATE_UI_RANGE
macro, 118

ON_CONTROL macro, 117

ON_CONTROL message-map
macro, 349

ON_CONTROL_RANGE
macro, 117

ON_CONTROL_RANGE
message-map macro, 349

ON_MESSAGE macro, 118

ON_MESSAGE message-map
macro, 349

ON_NOTIFY macro, 118

ON_NOTIFY_EX macro, 118

ON_NOTIFY_EX_RANGE
macro, 118

ON_NOTIFY_RANGE
macro, 118

ON_REGISTERED_MESSAGE
macro, 118

ON_REGISTERED_MESSAGE
message-map macro, 349

ON_UPDATE_COMMAND_UI
macro, 118

ON_UPDATE_COMMAND_UI
message-map macro, 349

ON_UPDATE_COMMAND_UI_RANGE
message-map macro, 349

ON_WM_PAINT( ) function,
259

OnAccept CASynchSocket
member function, 298

OnActivate( ) function, 519

OnAppAbout( ) function, 121,
364, 366

OnBeginPrinting( )
function, 424

OnBeginPrinting( ) MFC
printing function, 428

OnCancel( ) member
function, 168

OnCancelEditCntr( )
function, 518

OnChange( ) function, 520

OnChangestring( ) function,
408

OnCircle( ) function, 400

OnClose CASynchSocket
member function, 299

OnConnect CASynchSocket
member function, 299

OnContextMenu( ) function,
479-480

OnCreate( ) function, 175, 406, 535, 553

OnCreateControlBars( ) function, 553

OnDeactivateUI( ) function, 520

OnDestroy( ) function, 412

OnDialogTest( ) message-response function, 170

OnDragDrop( ) function, 541

OnDragEnter( ) function, 535-536, 540

OnDragLeave( ) function, 535, 540

OnDragOver( ) function, 535-536, 538, 540

OnDraw( ) function, 143, 247, 372, 374, 392-394, 416, 426, 521, 555, 561, 584-586, 613

OnDraw( ) member function, 279

OnDraw( ) MFC printing function, 428

OnEditChangemessage( ) member function, 290

OnEndOfNetSession( ) function, 309

OnEndPrinting( ) MFC printing function, 428

OnFileNew( ) function, 373

OnFileSave( ) function, 291

OnFilterDept( ) function, 334, 336

OnFilterID( ) function, 334, 336

OnFilterName( ) function, 334, 336

OnFilterRate( ) function, 334, 336

OnGetEmbedded Item( ) function, 550

OnGetExtent( ) function, 552, 564

OnHelpAbout( ) function, 154

OnHelpInfo( ) function, 479, 480

OnInitDialog( ) function, 166

OnInitialUpdate( ) class, 525

OnInitialUpdate( ) function, 514

OnInitialUpdate( ) member function, 271

OnInsertObject( ) function, 514

OnLarge( ) function, 193

OnLButtonDown( ) function, 144, 234, 240, 273, 420, 421, 607

OnLbuttonDown( ) function, 533

OnLButtonDown( ) message-response function, 267

OnList( ) function, 193

OnMessagePending CSocket method, 300

OnMove( ) function, 327, 329-330

OnMove( ) member function, 327

OnNewDocument( ) class, 525

OnNewDocument( ) function, 141, 372, 524, 561

OnNewDocument( ) member function, 279

OnOK( ) member function, 168, 170

OnOutOfBandData CASynchSocket member function, 299

OnPaint( ) function, 260

OnPrepareDC( ) function, 426

OnPrepareDC( ) MFC printing function, 428

OnPreparePrinting( ) function, 428

OnPreparePrinting( ) MFC printing function, 428

OnPrint( ) MFC printing function, 428

OnPropsheet( ) function, 219

OnRButtonDown( ) function, 235, 273, 421

OnReceive CASynchSocket member function, 299

OnRecordAdd( ) function, 327-329

OnRecordDelete( ) function, 330-331

OnReport( ) function, 193

OnSend CASynchSocket member function, 299

OnSetActive( ) function, 224

OnSetFocus( ) function, 517

OnSize( ) function, 517

OnSmall( ) function, 193

OnSortDept( ) function, 333, 335-336

OnSortID( ) function, 333

OnSortName( ) function, 334

OnSortRate( ) function, 334

OnStringChanged( ) function, 588

OnTimer( ) function, 177

OnToolsOptions( ) function, 385-386, 391-392, 524, 564

OnUpdate( ) member function, 272

OnUpdateFileSendMail( ) function, 302

OnWizard( ) member function, 226

OnWizardBack( ) function, 224

OnWizardFinish( ) function, 224

OnWizardNext( ) function, 224

Open button (Standard toolbar), 72

Open command (File menu), 32, 139, 475-476, 561

Open Workspace command (File menu), 33

Open( ) CFile member function, 289

OpenURL( ) function, 307

operators
dynamic_cast, 699, 700-701, 708
typeid, 699, 701-702

optimizing ActiveX controls
applications, 682-683
with AppWizard, 655-659

Options command (Tools menu), 61-63, 485, 488, 576, 588

Options commands (Tools menu), 10

Options dialog box, 10, 476, 524, 564

Options dialog box (ShowString), 381

origins, setting (printing), 426-427

Output command (View menu), 52

Output View (Developer Studio), 23

P

Page Setup command (File menu), 37-38

Paint1 Application, 257-269
brushes, 265-266
changing displays, 267-268
font usage, 261-264
LOGFONT fields, 261
painting basics (WM_PAINT message), 259-261
pens, 264-265
styles, 265
sizing and positioning windows, 268-269

paradigm (defined), 109

<PARAM> tag, 660-661

parameters
CInternetSession class, 633-634
class templates, 696-699
CreateLocator( ) function, 640-641
CreateWindow( ) API function, 103
templates, 692

ParseCommandLine( ) control, 363

Partition function, 442

PASCAL keyword, 747

Paste button (Standard toolbar), 72

Paste command (Edit menu), 41, 508, 512, 561

Paste Link command (Edit menu), 512

Paste( ) CRichEditCtrl member function, 204

PasteSpecial( ) CRichEditCtrl member function, 204

patches, 4.2a patch (ActiveX controls), 662

pens (Paint1 demo app), 264-265
styles, 265

persistence
classes, 110
creating persistant classes, 282-288
File demo 2 app, 283-288
objects, 278
File demo app, 278-282

placeholder strings, changing (writing Help text), 482-484

Playback Recording command (Tools menu), 63

plug-ins (Netscape) (ControlActive), 653-654

pointers (downcasting), 700-701, 708

polymorphism
message maps, 119
RTTI, 704-709

port numbers, 642

POSITION data type, 346

posting (messages), 753

PostMessage function, 753

PreCreateWindow( ) function, 268, 553, 555

prefixes (for messages), 121-123

Print command (File menu), 38, 139

Print dialog box, 429

Print Preview command (File menu), 139

Print1View.cpp file, 420

Print1View.h file, 420

printing, 416-417
AppWizard, 81
CPrintInfo class members, 429
MFC functions, 428-431
multiple pages, 420-425
scaling, 418-419
mapping modes, 418-419
setting origins, 426-427

Printing and Print Preview you brought together 1, 415

priority (threads), 716

ProcessShellCommand( ) control, 363

Profile command (Tools menu), 61

programming
dialog controls, 162-163
Check box, 163
Combo box, 163
Edit box, 163
Group box, 163
List box, 163
Pushbutton, 163
Radio button, 163
Scroll bar, 163
Static text, 162
Help systems, 472-473
WM_COMMAND message, 472-482
WM_CONTEXTMENU message, 473-482
WM_HELP message, 473-482
help systems
Command help, 477-478
context help, 478-481

programs, *see* **applications**

progress bar control (Win95), 174-177
creating, 174-175
initializing, 176
manipulating, 176-177

Project command (Insert menu), 54

Project Settings dialog box, 56-58, 445

Project toolbar, 72-73

Project Workspace button (Standard toolbar), 72

Project Workspace command (View menu), 52

project workspace files (Developer Studio), 10

Project Workspace option (New dialog box), 31

projects, 8
QuickSortScaffold (debugging), 439-444

prompts (prompts), 15

properties
adding (ActiveX controls), 601-603
asynchronous (ActiveX controls), 659-669
exposing (ActiveX automation), 579-584

Properties command (Edit menu), 13, 46-48, 478, 556, 614

Properties dialog box, 14

properties, *see* member variables

Property dialog box, 614

property sheets, 46-48, 210
ActiveX controls, 613
digit vs. dot display pattern values, 613-616
user-selected colors, 617-622
changing to wizards, 222-227
creating wizard pages, 224
displaying wizards, 226-227
responding to wizard's buttons, 225-226
running wizard demo application, 222-224
setting wizard's button, 224-225
ClassWizard, 321, 326, 331
creating the demo application, 211-222
running the demo, 220
Edit Properties, 320
MFC ClassWizard, 216
Toolbar Button Properties, 325

protocols (port numbers), 642

PS_DASH pen style (Paint1 demo app), 265

PS_DASHDOT pen style (Paint1 demo app), 265

PS_DASHDOTDOT pen style (Paint1 demo app), 265

PS_DOT pen style (Paint1 demo app), 265

PS_INSIDEFRAME pen style (Paint1 demo app), 265

PS_NULL pen style (Paint1 demo app), 265

PS_SOLID pen style (Paint1 demo app), 265

PtInRect( ) function, 528

Pushbutton dialog control, 163

PX_ functions, 603

Q

Query sample application
designing, 628
dialog box, creating, 629-631
Finger queries, 641-644
FTP sites (querying), 637-639
Gopher sites (querying), 639-641
HTTP sites (querying), 632-637
improvements to, 646
Whois queries, 644-646

querying (Query sample application)
Finger queries, 641-644
FTP sites, 637-639
Gopher sites, 639-641
HTTP sites, 632-637
Whois queries, 644-646

QueryInterface( ) function, 504

QuickSorts, 442

QuickSortScaffold Project (debugging), 439-444

QuickWatch (debugging features), 459-460

R

Radio button dialog control, 163

RADIO BUTTON field (Control1 sample app), 163

Radio( ) DDX function, 159

Read( ) CFile member function, 289

Read( ) CImageList member function, 185

reading files, 288-293
File demo 3 app, 288-293

README.TXT file, 365

ReadyStateChange event (asynchronous ActiveX control properties), 665

Rebuild All command (Build menu), 55-56

Receive CASynchSocket member function, 299

ReceiveFrom CASynchSocket member function, 299

Recent Files and Workspaces command (File menu), 38

Record Keystrokes command (Tools menu), 63

Rectangles sample application
creating, 133-139
displaying document data, 142-143
editing document data, 143-144
executing, 139
initializing document data, 140-141
serializing document data, 141-142
storing document data, 140

recursion (dual-purpose ActiveX applications), 566

RecursiveQuickSort function, 442

Redo button (Standard toolbar), 72

Redo command (Edit menu), 40-41

reference Help, 471

RefreshWindow( ) function, 587-588, 590

REGEDIT.EXE file, 410

Register( ) function, 535

RegisterClass( ) API function, 100

Registry, 410
keys (predefined), 410-411
MFC applications, 411-412
Registry Editor, 410
setup, 410

Registry File Type ID ShowString value, 557

Registry File Type Name ShowString value, 557

RegQueryValueEx( ) function, 412

RegSetValueEx( ) function, 412

regular expressions (finding files), 35

relational database model, 312

Remote Connection command (Tools menu), 61

Remove All Breakpoints button Project toolbar, 73

Remove( ) CFile member function, 290

Remove( ) CImageList member function, 185

RemoveAll( ) member function, 236

RemoveAll( ) array member function, 230

RemoveAll( ) list class member function, 237

RemoveAt( ) function, 236

RemoveAt( ) array member function, 230

RemoveAt( ) list class member function, 237

RemoveHead( ) member function, 242

RemoveHead( ) list class member function, 237

RemoveTail( ) function, 242

Rename( ) CFile member function, 290

Replace command (Edit menu), 42, 483

Replace dialog box, 484

ReplaceSel( ) CRichEditCtrl member function, 204

RequestResize( ) CRichEditCtrl member function, 204

resizeInside SetupTracker( ) style, 527

resizeOutside SetupTracker( ) style, 527

resizing items, ShowString (ActiveX), 524-527

Resource command (Insert menu), 53

Resource Copy command (Insert menu), 53-54

resource IDs
ClassWizard (coding menus), 91-92
commands, 123
menus, 15

Resource Includes command (View menu), 50-51

Resource Script option (New dialog box), 31

Resource Symbols command (View menu), 50

Resource Template option (New dialog box), 31

Resource View (Developer Studio), 13-18
accelerators, 13
dialog boxes, 13-14
icons, 14-15
menus, 15-16
string tables, 17
toolbars, 17
version information, 18

RESOURCE.H dialog resource ID file, 152

resources, dialog box (creating), 151-153

Resources tab (Project Settings dialog box), 58

ResourceView tab, 212

Restore String command (File menu), 412

reusability of code (Component Gallery), 672-674

rich edit controls (Win95), 201-207
creating, 202-203
initializing, 203-205
manipulating, 205-207
styles, 202-203

Rich Text Format files, *see* **.rtf files**

Right( ) string class member function, 248

rolling-die controls (ActiveX), 596-601
AppWizard code, 598-600
control design, 601
control shells (building), 596-597

routines, *see* **functions**

routing
commands, 123-124
messages, 114

.rtf files (Help system components), 473

RTTI
downcasting objects, 700-701, 708
enabling, 702-704
overview, 699-700
polymorphism, 704-709
typeid operator, 701-702

RTTI (Run-Time Type Information), 456-458, 699-709

run-time object model services, 349-350

Run-Time Type Information, *see* **RTTI**

runtime licensing, 597

RUNTIME_CLASS macro, 147

RUNTIME_CLASS run-time services macro, 350

S

sample applications
Control1 (controls), 163-171
declaring a friend function\, 164-165
initializing dialog box controls, 166-168
manipulating controls with classes, 165-166

responding to the OK
Button, 168-170
Dialog (dialog boxes), 153-162
CDlg1 class, 155
controls, 155
creating class objects,
159-162
displaying a simple dialog,
154-155
writing classes, 155-159

**Save All button (Standard
toolbar), 72**

**Save All command (File
menu), 33**

**Save As command (File
menu), 33**

**Save button (Standard
toolbar), 72**

**Save command (File menu),
33, 139, 571**

saving
document data, 137
files, 34

**scaffolding functions (with
console applications),
741-744**

**scaling, printing (mapping
modes), 418-419**

**scope resolution
(namespaces), 711-712**

screen (drawing classes), 110

Scroll bar dialog control, 163

Scroll demo application, 270

Scroll( ) DDX function, 159

scrollbars
initializing (Scroll demo app),
271-272
updating (Scroll demo app),
272-274

scrolling windows, 269-274
initializing scroll bars, 271-272
Scroll demo application, 270
updating scrollbars, 272-274

**SDI (Single Document
Interface), 279**
applications, 77
creating (with AppWizard),
361-365

**Search button (Standard
toolbar), 72**

**Search command (Help
menu), 67-68**

**Seek( ) CFile member
function, 290**

**SeekToBegin( ) CFile member
function, 290**

**SeekToEnd( ) CFile member
function, 290**

**Select All command (Edit
menu), 41**

**Select Database Tables dialog
box, 318**

SelectObject( ) function, 264

**SelectObject( ) member
function, 266**

**semaphores (thread
synchronization), 733-737**

**Send CASynchSocket member
function, 299**

sending messages, 752-754

SendMessage function, 753

**SendTo CASynchSocket
member function, 299**

**Serialize( ) function, 142,
281, 283-284, 293, 302,
372, 521, 551, 561**

**Serialize( ) member function,
280**

**SerializeElements( ) collection
class helper function, 344**

**serializing document data
(Rectangles sample
application), 141-142**

**servers, ActiveX (building),
501-502, 546-564, 566**
alternate ShowString
versions, 566
AppWizard server boilerplate,
546-560
documents, 568-572
nesting and recursion, 566
reopening string files, 560-566

**Set Default Configuration
command (Build menu),
59-60**

**Set Default Project
Configuration button
(Project toolbar), 73**

**Set Default Subsets command
(Help menu), 69-71**

**SetAccel( ) CSpinButtonCtrl
member function, 182**

SetAt( ) function, 234

**SetAt( ) array member
function, 230**

**SetAt( ) list class member
function, 237**

**SetAt( ) map class function,
244**

**SetAtGrow( ) array member
function, 230**

SetAtGrow( ) function, 234

**SetBackgroundColor( )
CRichEditCtrl member
function, 204**

**SetBase( ) CSpinButtonCtrl
member function, 182**

SetBitmap( ) function, 402

**SetBkColor( ) CImageList
member function, 185**

**SetBuddy( ) CSpinButtonCtrl
member function, 182**

**SetButtonInfo( ) function,
402**

SetButtons( ) function, 402

**SetButtonStyle( ) function,
402**

**SetButtonText( ) function,
402**

**SetCheck( ) function
(CCmdUI class), 125**

**SetCheck( ) member function,
167**

SetCurSel( ) function, 167

**SetCursor( ) member
function, 531**

**SetDefaultCharFormat( )
CRichEditCtrl member
function, 204**

**SetDragCursorImage( )
CImageList member
function, 185**

**SetEventMask( )
CRichEditCtrl member
function, 204**

SetFilePath( ) CFile member function, 290

SetHeight( ) function, 402

SetHorizCenter( ) function, 588

SetIndicators( ) member function, 406

SetIndicators( ) method, 403

SetLength( ) CFile member function, 290

SetLineSize( ) CSliderCtrl member function, 179

SetMaxPage( ) function, 425

SetMaxPage( ) CPrintInfo member function, 429

SetMessage( ) function, 286

SetMinPage( ) CPrintInfo member function, 429

SetModifiedFlag( ) function, 281

SetModify( ) CRichEditCtrl member function, 204

SetOLECallback( ) CRichEditCtrl member function, 204

SetOptions( ) CRichEditCtrl member function, 204

SetOverlayImage( ) CImageList member function, 185

SetPageSize( ) CSliderCtrl member function, 179

SetPaneInfo( ) method, 403

SetPaneStyle( ) method, 403

SetPaneText( ) method, 403

SetParaFormat( ) CRichEditCtrl member function, 204

SetPos( ) CProgressCtrl member function, 176

SetPos( ) CSliderCtrl member function, 179

SetPos( ) CSpinButtonCtrl member function, 182

SetRadio( ) function (CCmdUI class), 125

SetRange( ) CProgressCtrl member function, 176

SetRange( ) CSliderCtrl member function, 179

SetRange( ) CSpinButtonCtrl member function, 182

SetRangeMax( ) CSliderCtrl member function, 179

SetRangeMin( ) CSliderCtrl member function, 179

SetReadOnly( ) CRichEditCtrl member function, 205

SetReadOnly( ) member function, 329

SetRect( ) CRichEditCtrl member function, 205

SetRegistryKey( ) function, 412

SetRegistryKey( ) member function, 412

SetScrollSizes( ) function, 272, 274

SetSel( ) CRichEditCtrl member function, 205

SetSelection( ) CSliderCtrl member function, 179

SetSelection( ) function, 531

SetSelectionCharFormat( ) CRichEditCtrl member function, 205

SetSize( ) array member function, 230

SetSize( ) function, 233

SetSizes( ) function, 402

SetSockOpt CASynchSocket member function, 299

SetStatus( ) CFile member function, 290

SetStep( ) CProgressCtrl member function, 176

SetTargetDevice( ) CRichEditCtrl member function, 205

SetText( ) function (CCmdUI class), 125

SetTic( ) CSliderCtrl member function, 179

SetTicFreq( ) CSliderCtrl member function, 179

Settings command (Build menu), 56-58, 445

SetupTracker( ) function, 526

SetVertCenter( ) function, 588

SetViewportOrg( ) function, 427

SetWindowLong( ) function, 194

SetWizardMode( ) member function, 226

SetWordCharFormat( ) CRichEditCtrl member function, 205

shareCompat (CFile mode flag), 292

shared DLLs (compared to statically linked applications), 83-84

shareDenyNone CFile mode flag, 292

shareDenyRead CFile mode flag, 292

shareDenyWrite CFile mode flag, 292

shareExclusive CFile mode flag, 292

shells, control (rolling-die ActiveX controls), 596-597

shortcut menus, editing code (with Developer Studio), 25-26

ShowBrushes( ) function, 260, 266

ShowFonts( ) function, 260

ShowPens( ) function, 260, 264

ShowString, 576-588
    adding server capabilities, 546-564, 566
        alternate versions, 566
        AppWizard server boilerplate, 546-560
        nesting and recursion, 566
        reopening string files, 560-566
    AppWizard's automation boilerplate, 576-579
        CShowStringApp application object, 576-577

CShowStringDoc class,
577-579
as an ActiveX Document
Server, 570-572
changing (ActiveX
containers), 508-524
AppWizard container code,
508-523
deleting an object, 542-543
drag and drop, 533-542
enabling, 523-524
moving, resizing, and
tracking items, 524-527
multiple objects, 528-533
exposing properties, 579-584
OnDraw( ) function, 584-586
show windows (ActiveX
automation), 586-588

ShowString dialogs, 386-387
building, 379-385
About box, 379-380
dialog classes, 382-384
Options dialog, 381

**ShowString menus (building),
375-378**

**ShowString Options dialog
box**
adding appearance options,
387-394
adding member variables
to dialog classes, 389
adding member variables
to documents, 390-391
changing Options dialog,
388-389
OnDraw( ) function,
392-394
OnToolsOption( )
function, 391-392

ShowTest, 590-591

ShowWindow( ) method, 586

**ShutDown CASynchSocket
member function, 299**

**single clicks (ActiveX
ShowString), 530-532**

**Single Document Interface
(SDI) applications, 77**

**single document interface
applications,** *see* **SDI
applications**

size (ActiveX controls), 651

**skeletons, function (ActiveX
ShowString), 535-536**

slicing problems, 466
sockets, 110
WinSock, 296-300
CAsyncSocket class,
297-300
CSocket class, 297-300

**sockets option (AppWizard),
81**

**software development
(international issues),
754-755**

**solidLine SetupTracker( )
style, 527**

**sorting (ODBC database
program), 331-335**

**source files, editing code
(with Developer Studio), 26**

**specific replacement
functions (template
functions), 694-695**

**Split command (Window
menu), 64-66**

**splitter windows (creating
applications), 81**

stack unwinding, 466

Standard toolbar, 72

**Stardust Labs Winsock
Resource Page Web site,
296**

**start.Checkpoint( ) function,
463**

static library (creating), 89

Static text dialog control, 162

**statically linked applications
(compared to shared DLLs),
83-84**

**Status Bar Demo application,
412-413**

status bars, 402-404
CStatusBar class (methods),
403
initial status bar option
(AppWizard), 81
panes (adding), 404-409
setting appearance, 408-409

Step 1 dialog box, 317

Step 2 dialog box, 318

Step 4 dialog box, 319, 372

**StepIt( ) CProgressCtrl
member function, 176**

StepIt( ) function, 177

Stock OCX property, 601

**stock properties (ActiveX
controls), 617**

**Stop Build button (Project
toolbar), 73**

**Stop Build command (Build
menu), 56**

**stop.Checkpoint( )
function, 463**

**storing, document data
(Rectangles sample
application), 140**

**StreamIn( ) CRichEditCtrl
member function, 205**

**StreamOut( ) CRichEditCtrl
member function, 205**

**string class member function,
248**

string classes, 248-249
member functions, 248

**string files (adding
ShowString), 560-566**

**String Properties dialog box,
406**

**string tables, Resource View
(Developer Studio), 17**

strings
applications (building),
372-375
creating empty shells with
AppWizard, 372
displaying strings, 372-375
displaying, 372-375
ShowString dialogs
(building), 379-387
About box, 379-380
dialog classes, 382-384
Options dialog, 381
ShowString menus (building),
375-378

structures
compared to objects, 104
WNDCLASS, 100-101

styles
list view controls, 188-189
pens (Paint1 demo app), 265
rich edit controls, 202-203
trackbar controls, 178
tree view controls, 197
up-down controls, 181

Subprojects command (Build menu), 59-60

synchronizing threads, 726-737
  via critical sections, 726-731
  via mutexes, 731-733
  via semaphores, 733-737

syntax coloring, editing code (with Developer Studio), 25-26

System menu, 470

System Menu check box, 214

T

tabs (ResourceView), 212

tags (HTML)
  <EMBED>, 653-654
  <OBJECT>, 650-653
  <PARAM>, 660-661

task-oriented Help, 471

TBS_AUTOTICKS Trackbar style, 178

TBS_BOTH Trackbar style, 178

TBS_BOTTOM Trackbar style, 178

TBS_ENABLESELRANGE Trackbar style, 178

TBS_HORZ Trackbar style, 178

TBS_LEFT Trackbar style, 178

TBS_NOTICKS Trackbar style, 178

TBS_RIGHT Trackbar style, 178

TBS_TOP Trackbar style, 178

TBS_VERT Trackbar style, 178

Technical Support command (Help menu), 69-71

templates, 692-699
  class templates (creating), 695-699
  collections class, 253-254
  function templates (creating), 692-695
  overview, 692

templates, document, 147-148

Test command (Dialog menu), 153

testing
  ActiveX controls, 668-669
  drag targets, 542

text, Help (writing), 481-488
  adding topics, 485-487
  placeholder strings (changing), 482-484

Text ActiveX control stock property, 617

text blocks, editing code (with Developer Studio), 24-26

text boxes
  Data Source Name, 315
  Description, 315
  Name, 155

text editor emulation, 680-681

Text File option (New dialog box), 31

Text( ) DDX function, 159

TextOut( ) member function, 263

Thread application, 716-719

thread-safe classes, 727

ThreadProc( ) function, 718

threads
  communication, 719-726
    with event objects, 723-726
    with global variables, 720-721
    with user-defined messages, 721-723
  defined, 715
  functions, 716
  overview, 716-719
  priority, 716
  synchronization, 726-737
    via critical sections, 726-731
    via mutexes, 731-733
    via semaphores, 733-737

THROW exception macro, 348

THROW_LAST exception macro, 348

throwing (exceptions), 686

Tile Horizontally command (Window menu), 64-66

Tile Vertically command (Window menu), 65-66

time classes, 249-253
  CTime
    member functions, 249-250
    objects, 250-252
  CTimeSpan
    member functions, 250
    objects, 252-253

Tip of the Day command (Help menu), 69-71

Toolbar Button Properties property sheet, 325

toolbars, 70-74
  buttons
    adding, 398-401
    deleting, 396
  CToolBar class (member functions), 401-404
  debugging features, 434-439
  Developer Studio (InfoView), 12
  docking toolbar option (AppWizard), 80
  Project toolbar, 72-73
  Resource View (Developer Studio), 17
  source files, 26
  Standard toolbar, 72

Toolbars command (View menu), 50-51

Toolbars dialog box, 70

tools (installing in Developer Studio), 678-680

Tools command (Choose menu), 481

Tools menu commands, 60-63
  Browse, 61
  Close Browse Info File, 61
  Customize, 61, 605, 678
  OLE Control Test Container, 604
  Options, 10, 61-63, 485, 488, 576, 588
  Playback Recording, 63
  Profile, 61
  Record Keystrokes, 63
  Remote Connection, 61

Tools Options command, 486

topics, adding (writing Help text), 485-487

TRACE, 445-452

TRACE diagnostic macro, 347

TRACE0 diagnostic macro, 347

TRACE3 diagnostic macro, 347

Tracer, 452

trackbar control (Win95), 177-180
  creating, 177-178
  CSliderCtrl member functions, 178-179
  initializing, 178-180
  manipulating, 180
  styles, 178

tracking items ShowString (ActiveX), 524-527

TranslateMessage( ) API function, 115

tree view controls (Win95), 195-201
  creating, 196-197
  initializing, 197-200
  manipulating, 200-201
  styles, 197

TrimLeft( ) string class member function, 248

TrimRight( ) string class member function, 248

try blocks (exception handling), 686

TRY exception macro, 348

TVS_DISABLEDRAGDROP tree view style, 197

TVS_EDITLABELS tree view style, 197

TVS_HASBUTTONS tree view style, 197

TVS_HASLINES tree view style, 197

TVS_LINESATROOT tree view style, 197

TVS_SHOWSELALWAYS tree view style, 197

type libraries (ActiveX), 591-593

type_info class, 700

typeBinary (CFile mode flag), 292

typeid operator, 699, 701-702

typeText (CFile mode flag), 292

U

UDS_ALIGNLEFT up-down control style, 181

UDS_ALIGNRIGHT up-down control style, 181

UDS_ARROWKEYS up-down control style, 181

UDS_AUTOBUDDY up-down control style, 181

UDS_HORZ up-down control style, 181

UDS_NOTHOUSANDS up-down control style, 181

UDS_SETBUDDYINT up-down control style, 181

UDS_WRAP up-down control style, 181

UINT data type, 346

unclipped device context (ActiveX controls), 657

Undo button (Standard toolbar), 72

Undo command (Edit menu), 40

Undo( ) CRichEditCtrl member function, 205

Unicode character set, 754-755

unique mnemonics in menus, 56

Unlock( ) function, 726

UnlockRange( ) CFile member function, 290

unnamed namespaces, 712

up-down controls (Win95), 180-182
  creating, 181-182
  styles, 181

Update All Dependencies command (Build menu), 56

Update command (File menu), 546

Update( ) member function, 330

UpdateAllViews( ) function, 142, 387

UpdateAllViews( ) member function, 272

UpdateData( ) function, 329

UpdateData( ) member function, 330

UpdateRegistry( ) function, 557

updating commands, 124-126
  via ClassWizard, 126-127

Use Extension Help command (Help menu), 68-71

user-defined messages, 753-754
  communicating with threads, 721-723

user-defined namespaces, 710-711

users
  activating help systems, 470-471
  interfaces, intuitive (ActiveX), 502-503
  interfaces (ActiveX controls), 608-613
    bitmap icons, 609
    displaying dots, 609-613

utilities
  DiskFree, 749-750
  DumpBin, 744-747
  grep utility (UNIX), 34
  Tracer, 452
  Windows Character Map (adding), 356

utility classes, 110

V

variables
  ambient property types, 618-619

COleDropTarget member, 534
global variables (communicating with threads), 720-721
Hungarian notation, 101-102
m_numRects member, 420
member, 19-21
   ActiveX ShowString, 535-536

variables, *see* member variables

VERIFY diagnostic macro, 347

VerifyPos( ) CSliderCtrl member function, 179

version information, Resource View (Developer Studio), 18

view classes, 109, 131-133, 144-146
Rectangles sample application (creating), 133-139

View menu commands, 48-52
Call Stack, 446
ClassWizard, 49, 524, 561, 579, 601, 606
Footnotes, 481, 485
Full Screen, 50-51
InfoViewer History List, 51-52
InfoViewer Query Results, 51
InfoViewer Topic, 52
Output, 52
Project Workspace, 52
Resource Includes, 50-51
Resource Symbols, 50
Toolbars, 50-51
Watch, 460

views (Developer Studio)
choosing, 8-10
Class View, 19-21
File View, 22
InfoView, 10-12
Output View, 23
Resource View, 13-18

virtual functions, 119

Visual C++ (4.2a patch), 662

W

WaitForSingleObject( ) function, 724

Watch command (View menu), 460

Watch Windows (debugging features), 459-460

Web Favorites command (Help menu), 70-71

Web pages
Microsoft Explorer (embedding ActiveX controls), 650-653
Netscape Navigator (embedding ActiveX controls), 653-654

What's This? command (Help menu), 470

Whois queries (Query sample application), 644-646

Win95
controls
   image list, 182-185
   list view, 185-195
   progress bar, 174-177
   rich edit, 201-207
   trackbar, 177-180
   tree view, 195-201
   up-down, 180-182

Win95 Controls App
image list controls, 182-185
   creating, 183
   initializing, 184-185
list view controls, 185-195
   creating, 187-189
   creating columns, 189-191
   creating items, 191-193
   image list association, 189
   initializing, 189
   manipulating, 193-195
   styles, 188-189
progress bar, 174-177
   creating, 174-175
   initializing, 176
   manipulating, 176-177
rich edit controls, 201-207
   creating, 202-203
   initializing, 203-205
   manipulating, 205-207
   styles, 202-203
trackbar control, 177-180
   creating, 177-178
   CSliderCtrl member functions, 178-179
   initializing, 178-180
   manipulating, 180
   styles, 178

tree view controls, 195-201
   creating, 196-197
   creating items, 197-200
   initializing, 197
   manipulating, 200-201
   styles, 197
up-down controls, 180-182
   creating, 181-182
   styles, 181

WinDiff, 367

Window menu commands, 63-66
Cascade, 64-66
Close All, 66
Hide, 64-66
New Window, 64-66
Split, 64-66
Tile Horizontally, 64-66
Tile Vertically, 65-66
Windows, 66

Window Styles dialog box, 81

Window Styles tab (Advanced Options dialog box), 81

Window Title ShowString value, 557

windowless activation (ActiveX controls), 656

WindowProc( ) function, 200

windows
classes, 100
   WNDCLASS structure, 100-101
creating, 101-104
Help systems, 471
IDs, 350
Paint1 demo app (sizing and positioning), 268-269
scrolling, 269-274
   initializing scroll bars, 271-272
   Scroll demo application, 270
   updating scrollbars, 272-274
showing (ActiveX automation), 586-588
WinSock, 296-300
   CAsyncSocket class, 297-300
   CSocket class, 297-300

Windows 95
logo requirements (MAPI), 302-303
Unicode support, 755

Windows Character Map (adding), 356

Windows command (Window menu), 66

Windows NT (Unicode support), 755

WinHelp( ) function, 480

WinInet classes (CInternetSession), 632, 633

WinMain( ) function, 114-115

WinSock, 296-300
    CAsyncSocket class, 297-300
    CSocket class, 297-300

WINSOCK.DLL, 296

WINUSER.H file, 100

Wizard bar, 93-94

Wizard command (File menu), 222

WizardBar, 26

wizards
    changing property sheets to wizards, 222-227
        creating wizard pages, 224
        displaying wizards, 226-227
        responding to wizard's buttons, 225-226
        running wizard demo application, 222-224
        setting wizard's button, 224-225
    Extension (ISAPI), 308

WM_COMMAND message (programming Help systems), 472-473

WM_CONTEXTMENU message (programming Help systems), 473

WM_HELP message (programming Help systems), 473

WM_LBUTTONDBLCLK message, 533

WM_LBUTTONDOWN message, 267, 607

WM_PAINT message, 267
    Paint1 demo app, 259-261

WM_USER constant, 722

WNDCLASS structure, 100-101

WNDPROC data type, 346

WndProc( ) function, 115-116

WORD data type, 346

Workspace tab (Options dialog box), 62

World Wide Web (ISAPI Extension Wizard), 90

WPARAM data type, 346

Write( ) CFile member function, 290

Write( ) CImageList member function, 185

Write( ) member function, 292

WriteProfileInt( ) function, 412

WriteProfileString( ) function, 412

writing
    dialog box classes, 155-159
    files, 288-293
        File demo 3 app, 288-293
    Help text, 481-488
        adding topics, 485-487
        placeholder strings (changing), 482-484

WSOCK32.DLL, 296

X-Y

x parameter (CreateWindow( ) API function), 103

y parameter (CreateWindow( ) API function), 103

QUE® has the right choice for every computer user

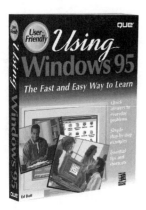

From the new computer user to the advanced programmer, we've got the right computer book for you. Our user-friendly *Using* series offers just the information you need to perform specific tasks quickly and move onto other things. And, for computer users ready to advance to new levels, QUE *Special Edition Using* books, the perfect all-in-one resource—and recognized authority on detailed reference information.

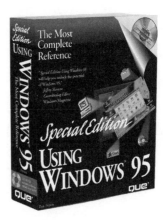

The *Using* series
for casual users

Who should use this book?

Everyday users who:

- Work with computers in the office or at home
- Are familiar with computers but not in love with technology
- Just want to "get the job done"
- Don't want to read a lot of material

The user-friendly reference

- The fastest access to the one best way to get things done
- Bite-sized information for quick and easy reference
- Nontechnical approach in plain English
- Real-world analogies to explain new concepts
- Troubleshooting tips to help solve problems
- Visual elements and screen pictures that reinforce topics
- Expert authors who are experienced in training and instruction

Special Edition Using
for accomplished users

Who should use this book?

Proficient computer users who:

- Have a more technical understanding of computers
- Are interested in technological trends
- Want in-depth reference information
- Prefer more detailed explanations and examples

The most complete reference

- Thorough explanations of various ways to perform tasks
- In-depth coverage of all topics
- Technical information cross-referenced for easy access
- Professional tips, tricks, and shortcuts for experienced users
- Advanced troubleshooting information with alternative approaches
- Visual elements and screen pictures that reinforce topics
- Technically qualified authors who are experts in their fields
- "Techniques from the Pros" sections with advice from well-known computer professionals

Check out Que® Books
on the World Wide Web
http://www.mcp.com/que

As the biggest software release in computer history, Windows 95 continues to redefine the computer industry. Click here for the latest info on our Windows 95 books

Make computing quick and easy with these products designed exclusively for new and casual users

Examine the latest releases in word processing, spreadsheets, operating systems, and suites

The Internet, The World Wide Web, CompuServe®, America Online®, Prodigy®—it's a world of ever-changing information. Don't get left behind!

Find out about new additions to our site, new bestsellers and hot topics

In-depth information on high-end topics: find the best reference books for databases, programming, networking, and client/server technologies

A recent addition to Que, Ziff-Davis Press publishes the highly-successful *How It Works* and *How to Use* series of books, as well as *PC Learning Labs Teaches* and *PC Magazine* series of book/disk packages

Stay on the cutting edge of Macintosh® technologies and visual communications

Find out which titles are making headlines

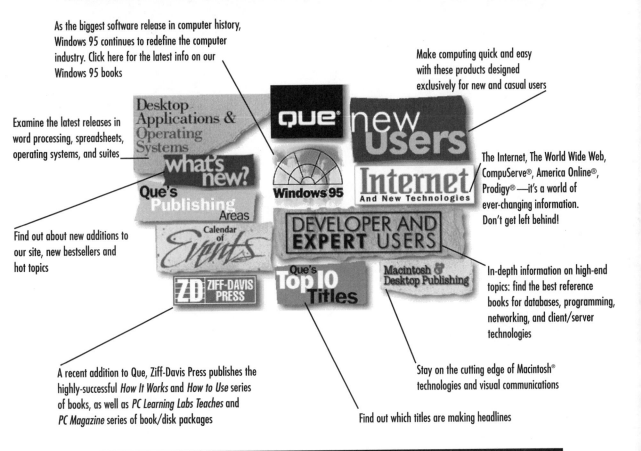

With 6 separate publishing groups, Que develops products for many specific market segments and areas of computer technology. Explore our Web Site and you'll find information on best-selling titles, newly published titles, upcoming products, authors, and much more.

- Stay informed on the latest industry trends and products available
- Visit our online bookstore for the latest information and editions
- Download software from Que's library of the best shareware and freeware

Complete and Return this Card
for a *FREE* Computer Book Catalog

Thank you for purchasing this book! You have purchased a superior computer book written expressly for your needs. To continue to provide the kind of up-to-date, pertinent coverage you've come to expect from us, we need to hear from you. Please take a minute to complete and return this self-addressed, postage-paid form. In return, we'll send you a free catalog of all our computer books on topics ranging from word processing to programming and the internet.

r. ☐   Mrs. ☐   Ms. ☐   Dr. ☐

ame (first) ☐☐☐☐☐☐☐☐☐ (M.I.) ☐ (last) ☐☐☐☐☐☐☐☐☐☐☐☐☐☐☐☐

ddress ☐☐☐☐☐☐☐☐☐☐☐☐☐☐☐☐☐☐☐☐☐☐☐☐☐☐☐☐

☐☐☐☐☐☐☐☐☐☐☐☐☐☐☐☐☐☐☐☐☐☐☐☐☐☐☐☐

ty ☐☐☐☐☐☐☐☐☐☐☐☐☐☐☐ State ☐☐ Zip ☐☐☐☐☐.☐☐☐☐

one ☐☐☐ ☐☐☐ ☐☐☐☐ Fax ☐☐☐ ☐☐☐ ☐☐☐☐

ompany Name ☐☐☐☐☐☐☐☐☐☐☐☐☐☐☐☐☐☐☐☐☐☐☐☐☐

-mail address ☐☐☐☐☐☐☐☐☐☐☐☐☐☐☐☐☐☐☐☐☐☐☐☐☐

Please check at least (3) influencing factors for purchasing this book.

ront or back cover information on book .... ☐
pecial approach to the content .... ☐
ompleteness of content .... ☐
uthor's reputation .... ☐
ublisher's reputation .... ☐
ook cover design or layout .... ☐
dex or table of contents of book .... ☐
rice of book .... ☐
pecial effects, graphics, illustrations .... ☐
ther (Please specify): _____ ☐

. How did you first learn about this book?

aw in Macmillan Computer Publishing catalog .... ☐
ecommended by store personnel .... ☐
aw the book on bookshelf at store .... ☐
ecommended by a friend .... ☐
eceived advertisement in the mail .... ☐
aw an advertisement in: _____ ☐
ead book review in: _____ ☐
)ther (Please specify): _____ ☐

. How many computer books have you purchased in the last six months?

his book only .... ☐   3 to 5 books .... ☐
books .... ☐   More than 5 .... ☐

4. Where did you purchase this book?

Bookstore .... ☐
Computer Store .... ☐
Consumer Electronics Store .... ☐
Department Store .... ☐
Office Club .... ☐
Warehouse Club .... ☐
Mail Order .... ☐
Direct from Publisher .... ☐
Internet site .... ☐
Other (Please specify): _____ ☐

5. How long have you been using a computer?

☐ Less than 6 months   ☐ 6 months to a year
☐ 1 to 3 years   ☐ More than 3 years

6. What is your level of experience with personal computers and with the subject of this book?

	With PCs	With subject of book
New	☐	☐
Casual	☐	☐
Accomplished	☐	☐
Expert	☐	☐

Source Code ISBN: 0-7897-0893-0

7. Which of the following best describes your job title?

Administrative Assistant .... ☐
Coordinator .... ☐
Manager/Supervisor .... ☐
Director .... ☐
Vice President .... ☐
President/CEO/COO .... ☐
Lawyer/Doctor/Medical Professional .... ☐
Teacher/Educator/Trainer .... ☐
Engineer/Technician .... ☐
Consultant .... ☐
Not employed/Student/Retired .... ☐
Other (Please specify): _____ ☐

8. Which of the following best describes the area of the company your job title falls under?

Accounting .... ☐
Engineering .... ☐
Manufacturing .... ☐
Operations .... ☐
Marketing .... ☐
Sales .... ☐
Other (Please specify): _____ ☐

9. What is your age?

Under 20 .... [
21-29 .... [
30-39 .... [
40-49 .... [
50-59 .... [
60-over .... [

10. Are you:

Male .... [
Female .... [

11. Which computer publications do you read regularly? (Please list)

_____
_____
_____
_____
_____
_____
_____
_____
_____
_____

Comments: _____
_____
_____

Fold here and scotch-tape to mail